About the Author

David Crabtree is the principal instructor of GMCS Ltd., a UK-wide manufacturing training company. Prior to his current position, he worked in production control and production management roles within a number of companies, including Henderson Engineering, Texaco and ICI (Zeneca). He was educated at The Manchester Grammar School and Brasenose College, Oxford, and is a Chartered Engineer, a Fellow of the British Computer Society and a Fellow of the Institute of Operations Management. David Crabtree lives in Lytham St Annes, Lancashire. He is married to Kathryn and has two grown-up children.

The Manufacturing Manager

A Comprehensive Guide for Professionals in Industry

David Crabtree

Oak Tree Press
19 Rutland Street,
Cork, Ireland.
www.oaktreepress.com

© 2001 David Crabtree

A catalogue record of this book is
available from the British Library.

ISBN 1-86076-202-6

All rights reserved. No part of this publication may be reproduced or transmitted in any form or by any means, including photocopying and recording, without written permission of the publisher. Such written permission must also be obtained before any part of this publication is stored in a retrieval system of any nature. Requests for permission should be directed to Oak Tree Press, 19 Rutland Street, Cork, Ireland.

Printed in Ireland by ePrint.

Contents

Acknowledgements .... *ix*

Preface .... *xi*

Chapter 1: The Manufacturing Company 1
   1.1 The Legal Framework of the Company 1
   1.2 The Directors and Managers of the Company 6
   1.3 Methods of Trading 9
   1.4 Company Tasks — An Overview in Relation to
       this Book 14

Chapter 2: Sales and Marketing 21
   2.1 Marketing 21
   2.2 Innovation 30
   2.3 Selling and Sales Management 35
   2.4 Sales Order Processing 40
   2.5 Sales Forecasting 44

Chapter 3: Product Innovation 51
   3.1 The Product Brief 51
   3.2 Product Design — The Principal Stages 53
   3.3 *"Design for"* Manufacture 62
   3.4 Failure and Reliability 74
   3.5 Bills of Materials Management 81

Chapter 4: Sales Forecasting 87
   4.1 Introduction to Short-term Forecasting 87
   4.2 Patterns of Data 89
   4.3 Sales Demand Data 101

    4.4 The Naïve Forecasting Family 108
    4.5 The Causal Forecasting Family 120
    4.6 Forecasting Management 130
    4.7 Dealing with Sporadic (Intermittent) Demand 133

Chapter 5: Safety Stock 139
    5.1 Justification for Safety Stock 139
    5.2 Factors Involved in Safety Stocks 141
    5.3 Customer Service Targets... 156
    5.4 Defining Customer Service in Theoretical Terms 157
    5.5 The Safety Stock System... 174

Chapter 6: Master Plan Formulation 179
    6.1 Definitions 179
    6.2 Overview of the MPS Process...................................... 184
    6.3 S&OP I: Business Review 189
    6.4 S&OP II: Resource Requirements Planning 193
    6.5 Detailed Master Scheduling I 199
    6.6 Detailed Master Scheduling II (Rough Cut) 208
    6.7 Commitment, Release, Commitment........................... 213

Chapter 7: Master Plan Management......................... 215
    7.1 Consuming the Forecast 216
    7.2 Available-to-Promise 228
    7.3 Master Scheduling New Products................................ 243

Chapter 8: Assemble-to-Order ("Quick Response") 247
    8.1 Introduction 247
    8.2 Redesign for Assemble-to-Order 249
    8.3 The Modular Bill and Option Choice 261
    8.4 The Super Bill 265
    8.5 The FAS and Master Scheduling................................. 267
    8.6 Forecasts and Option Overplan Amounts..................... 274
    8.7 Quick Response... 278

Chapter 9: Materials Planning 287
    9.1 Order Point... 288
    9.2 Planning and Manufacturing 290
    9.3 Levels in the Bill of Materials...................................... 293

Contents vii

    9.4 The Calculation of Material Requirements 298
    9.5 Gross Requirements to Plans 311
    9.6 Planning Rules 314

Chapter 10: Closed-Loop MRP 331
    10.1 Defining Closed-Loop MRP 331
    10.2 Plan Types in MRP 333
    10.3 The MRP Rescheduling Logic 340
    10.4 Total Regeneration and Net Change 349

Chapter 11: Shop Floor Control 353
    11.1 Work Scheduling 353
    11.2 The Release of Orders to the Shop 356
    11.3 Job Despatching Rules (Job Prioritising) 369
    11.4 Lead Time Management 378
    11.5 The Shop Floor Information System 383

Chapter 12: Advanced Planning Systems 401
    12.1 Introduction 401
    12.2 Discrete Job Systems 409
    12.3 Continuous Flow Systems 430
    12.4 Bottleneck APS Systems 447

Chapter 13: Total Quality Control 471
    13.1 The Imperative of Total Quality 471
    13.2 Total Quality in the Manufacturing Company 486
    13.3 ISO 9000:2000 503

Chapter 14: Statistical Quality Control (SQC) 513
    14.1 SPC — The Statistical Basis 514
    14.2 Using the Variable Control Chart 532
    14.3 The Attribute Control Charts 545
    14.4 Raw Material and Product Control 555

Chapter 15: Just-in-Time 581
    15.1 Two Definitions 581
    15.2 Establishing Production Rates 584
    15.3 SMED and Fast Changeovers 589
    15.4 Plant Organisation 598

15.5 Kanban 608
15.6 Equipment Maintenance 621
15.7 Workplace Management.. 632

Chapter 16: Purchasing 635
16.1 Suppliers 635
16.2 Order Placement 646
16.3 The Carriage and Receipt of Goods 660
16.4 Price and the Marketplace 670
16.5 Foreign Purchases 679

Chapter 17: Finance and Costing................................... 693
17.1 Financial Accounts 693
17.2 Assets 707
17.3 The Evaluation and Acquisition of Assets.................. 714
17.4 Cost Accounting 722

Chapter 18: The Stores and Stock Records 757
18.1 Stores Organisation 758
18.2 Stores Operations 770
18.3 Stock Records Accuracy... 775
18.4 Cycle Counting.. 784

Chapter 19: Human Resources 803
19.1 The Organisation 804
19.2 Reward Management 817
19.3 Working Relationships 840
19.4 Health and Safety 847

Chapter 20: Distribution 857
20.1 The Distribution Network 858
20.2 The Replenishment of the Network........................... 876
20.3 Network Transshipments 890
20.4 Transport of the Goods 900

Selected Bibliography... 905
Index.. 909

Acknowledgements

I wish to thank the following colleagues, friends and past attendees on my training courses for their advice and comments on various aspects of the subjects covered:

Mrs Katherine Arnold (GMCS Ltd., Lytham St Annes); Dr Ted Atherton (Wigan, and formerly of ICI Organics Division); Mr Graham Barton (formerly of ICI and AstraZeneca); Mrs Gill Brooks (Lloyd Instruments, Fareham); Miss Clare Gayton (Coutant Lambda, Ilfracombe); Mr Peter Currie (Bae Systems, Warton, Lancs); Mr Mike Ellarby (Lanner Group, Redditch, Worcs); Mr Mike Foot (Syngenta Ltd., Huddersfield); Mr George Harlock (Triangle Implementations, Milton Keynes); Mr Roland Henderson, CBE (MD, Henderson Engineering Ltd., Manchester); Mr Brian Langan (Senior Editor, Oak Tree Press, Dublin); Mr Paul McCherry (MD, Syscom Business Systems, Thornton-Cleveleys, Lancs); Miss Gemma Pockett (The University of Bristol); Mr Ron Rawstron (formerly of Whitehead and Howarth, Lytham St Annes); Mr Peris Roberts (Northwich, Cheshire); Mr Alan Shea (Lligwy, Anglesey); Mr Alex Simpson (The Change Works, Princes Risborough); and Mr Jeff Woodhams (formerly of Lanner Group).

My particular thanks are extended to: Mr Kevin Ellard, Librarian of the University of Central Lancashire, Preston, for the reading facilities made available at the University Library; and, for their advice and encouragement, to Mr John Harraway of CSG Ltd., Witney, Oxfordshire, and Mr Brian Matthews of Aurora Ltd., Kilmore, County Wexford, Republic of Ireland.

*This book is dedicated to
Kathryn Crabtree*

Preface

This is a book for managers, but it is not a management book. Because it is not a management book, the reader will not find here new theories of corporate organisation or exciting formulae for turning base metal into gold. Instead, the book contains solid facts and well-established ideas, set out in a plain, straightforward way. Two purposes were in mind in writing it.

The first was to create for study, consideration and reference a digest of the major topics in the considerable range of activities that constitute manufacturing, explanations to be in clear language and at a depth sufficient to allow the manager fully to comprehend their subject matter and the way in which they are interlinked. My hope was that the understanding thus gained would enable him to contribute to and influence debate within his own company when the occasions arose. One benefit of clarity is the laying bare of first principles. That can be no bad thing in an industrial society where, say, everyone has heard of ISO 9000 but no-one has heard of Walter Shewhart, and where every management consultant can describe the mechanics of activity-based costing but none can explain to his client just why product costing is undertaken in the first place. A glance through the list of contents will show how wide the range of topics must be besides quality and accountancy to encompass the interests of the modern company: the legal foundations of the company itself; sales and marketing; materials planning and scheduling; purchasing and contract law; JIT and APS; human resources; logistics . . .

As an aside, it is intended that as well as being of service to managers themselves, the book should also be so to management consultants within industry, to academic staff specialising in manufacturing and to manufacturing software experts, especially those involved in MRP, APS and ERP. Advisers such as these have their own problems, of course. Their tasks revolve round the identification of the need for change within companies and the provision of help in introducing the new systems and procedures concomitant with it. A hoped-for additional consequence of the book is therefore that for them it should provide readier, quicker access to the information they need, at sufficient depth, than has been available until now, so as to enable them to address the demands of their clients with deeper knowledge and understanding.

The second purpose in writing the book was also personal. This was that, throughout his career, it should become the constant companion and reference of the manager who owns it, free of the constrictions and tone of the conventional college textbook, yet having the same rigour of correctness and bearing the same authority. The purpose was personal because I remembered all those years ago, at the start of my own journey through industry, how difficult it was to obtain an appreciation of the landscape in which I was to spend my working life. My wish then had been to see a picture showing materials control and logistics, certainly, but, as well, all the commercial and technical-commercial functions carried on about me by my colleagues in other departments. In *The Manufacturing Manager*, categorising topics along these three lines of technical, commercial and technical-commercial, the split of chapters is about even between them, I believe fairly representing the diverse world that they describe.

David Crabtree
Lytham St Annes
May 2001

Chapter 1

The Manufacturing Company

1.1 THE LEGAL FRAMEWORK OF THE COMPANY

Before describing what a company *does* — what it sells, its methods of manufacture, how it controls operations from day to day — it is as well to spend a little time discussing what a company *is*. For example, what is it, apart from its likely scale, that distinguishes a *limited company* from a *partnership* or the business of the *sole trader*?

Two essential features mark out the limited company. The first is that it has a legal identity of its own, independent of the people who founded it, independent of its owners and independent of the directors who manage it. A shareholder can sue his own company in the courts. A company can claim damages from one of its own directors. The second feature is that the company's financial *liability* is *limited*. That is, the company's creditors, those to whom it owes money, have no redress for those debts beyond the company's assets.[1]

The notions of full juridic personality and limited liability were developed through successive laws variously enacted in Britain, France, the German states and the USA from 1809 to the end of the nineteenth century. In Britain, the principal authorising legislation

---

[1] The assets of the company include the original issued share capital provided by the shareholders, although this is most unlikely still to be in the form of cash. Issued share capital therefore represents the shareholders' maximum exposure to loss.

was introduced in 1862.[2] Because of the commercial power placed in a company's hands and in those of its directors, and because of a wish to protect *shareholders* who have invested in it but who have little or no say in its management, a succession of *companies acts* has been passed regulating what companies must do and cannot do and the information they are required to disclose. For example, when a company is formed, it is necessary for those founding it to file a *Memorandum of Association* and *Articles of Association* with the Registrar of Companies at Companies House in Cardiff. The Memorandum must show the origin of the company's capital and its trading objectives. The Articles are the internal company regulations as they affect its shareholders and directors. As the company trades, an annual report must be submitted to the Registrar, together with a copy of the *balance sheet* and the *profit and loss account* (see Figures 17.1 and 17.2). The information lodged at Companies House is available to anyone who enquires, and is widely circulated in summary form by a number of credit checking agencies and others. The Companies Act of 1985 consolidated all past relevant company regulations and restrictions, and superseded all previous acts. It is now the main reference point for company law.

Although they rarely receive a thought from the busy manufacturing manager, the owners of the company are the shareholders. It is the shareholders who, ultimately at least, have provided the capital on which the company has been founded — for the purchase of its machines and stock and for the payment of wages to its managers and other employees. If the company is a *public limited company* (with PLC after its name), the company has invited the public to subscribe to its shares. Once he has subscribed, the investor cannot cash in his share, but, subject to the rules and regulations of the Stock Exchange, may sell it to a third party. If the company is a *private limited company* (with Co. Ltd. after its name), shares have been subscribed to by private arrangement. These shares can also be transferred, provided the agreement of the

---

[2] Many of the earlier acts related only to private companies and limited partnerships. In her book *Shareholder Democracy: The Forgotten History* (2003, est. Harvard University Press), Colleen Dunlavy of the University of Wisconsin remarks on the scarcity of recorded history of these powerful institutions.

company is obtained. The persons who have bought the shares of a public or private company have no further obligations or responsibilities to it (although the company has so to the buyers). Instead, the shareholders appoint directors to manage the company on their behalf. The directors have statutory obligations and are paid fees (which are normal business expenses similar to wages).

The shares which comprise the company's capital (at the beginning, at any rate) are usually of two types, *preference* and *ordinary*.

Preference Shares

Preference shares entitle shareholders to a fixed percentage dividend each year. For example, *£1 7.0 per cent preference shares* means that the nominal, or par, value of each share is £1 and that the company will pay an annual dividend of 7 per cent (£0.07) to the shareholder. Preference shareholders are paid their dividends in full from the company's profits before any consideration is given to ordinary shareholders. (If the shares are *cumulative preference shares*, dividends which cannot be paid because of poor profits are held over and paid later when money is available.) Preference shareholders usually have no votes at shareholders' meetings. The price of the shares on the stock exchange fluctuates only in accordance with general economic indicators such as the prevailing rates of interest offered, say, by building societies or obtainable on local government bonds.

Ordinary Shares

Ordinary shareholders are the risk takers. In bad times, when the company has made no profit, they will receive nothing by way of dividend, and the market value of their shares will be low. In good times, they will be well paid and the value of each share is likely to be many times its mere nominal value. The shareholder's investment in ordinary shares is also called his *equity*. Ordinary shareholders are entitled to the balance of the profits, after all other claimants have taken their cuts — usually, therefore, after the preference shareholders. Or rather, ordinary shareholders receive that part of the balance recommended to be distributed to them by the directors. The directors will often wish to hold money back for reinvestment in the business. One ordinary share almost always carries one vote at shareholders' meetings. Note that the shareholders cannot by law vote to increase the dividend beyond what the directors recommend. While shareholders' votes can be used to dismiss or re-elect the directors, and in other motions of a very general nature, they cannot be used to regulate the company's operational management. The dividend per ordinary share of (say) £1 nominal value is expressed as a *sum per share*. If the dividend were 50p per £1, the market value of the share on the stock exchange would be far higher than £1, say £7, reflecting the rate of return on the shareholding (50p is 7.1 per cent of £7). It is well known that shares are often bought on the stock market not for investment but to sell later for a profit when the shares' value has risen (see Table 16.1).

Shares may be created by the company, other than at its foundation to obtain starting capital, by *rights issues* and by *capitalisation issues*.

Rights Issues

If a public company requires more money, perhaps to fund an expansion scheme, it may issue further shares with a *face value* equal to the shares' normal, nominal value. However, the shares so issued may be sold by the company, not at their nominal value, but at their market value. It is normal for the company, in fact, to offer such shares first to existing ordinary shareholders, at a price somewhat lower than the market value (i.e. at a *preferential discount*). If the shareholder does not want to take up his rights, the new shares are sold by the company at the full market price to the public and the shareholder is then entitled to the *premium* (i.e. the market price less the preferential price).

Debentures

Rights issues are not the only way the company can secure long-term working capital. As well, it may issue long-term loans bearing specified annual rates of interest and specified repayment dates. To make subscription to a loan attractive to investors, it might be issued at a nominal purchase discount, or with a bonus on final repayment. Debentures can be traded like shares. Debenture holders, however, are simply preferential creditors and have no shareholders' rights.

Capitalisation Issues

Profits retained in the business will be shown on the company's balance sheet as "revenue reserves". After a time, the company may decide that the profits so retained and held are of such an abiding nature that they should no longer be regarded as reserves, but are in effect permanent. To make this clear — and irreversible — the company may *capitalise* the amount concerned. This is done by the creation of further ordinary shares and their distribution to individual ordinary shareholders, free of cost and in proportion to their existing holdings. Although each shareholder will now have more shares than before, one notes that the value of the company — i.e. its assets less its liabilities — is unchanged. Consequently, the value of each ordinary share will be proportionately less than it was.

The Wealth of Nations

A most important measure of Britain's prosperity is the success and financial health of its trading and manufacturing companies — some say the triumph of the capitalist system and the affirmation of Adam Smith's conclusions.[3] The assets of very many of Britain's larger manufacturers exceed £1 billion.[4] In the financial pages of the daily press, the following indicators are often quoted when the country's firms are being publicly discussed.

Earnings per Share (ordinary shares)

The profit that could have been paid to ordinary shareholders (irrespective of the fact that part of it may have been retained in the business) *divided by* the ordinary share capital. Thus, for example:

---

[3] Adam Smith (1776), *Inquiry into the Nature and Causes of the Wealth of Nations*.
[4] The stock market valuation of pharmaceutical company Glaxo SmithKline amounted to some £107 billion at the time of its formation from Glaxo Wellcome and SmithKline Beecham in January of 2000.

$$\frac{£50,000 \ paid \ out + £40,000 \ retained}{200,000 \times £1} = 45p \ per \ share$$

PE Ratio (Price/Earnings Ratio)

The PE ratio is the share's market price divided by the earnings per share. For example:

$$\frac{£4.00 \ share \ price}{£0.40 \ earning \ per \ share} = 10.0$$

Gearing

Gearing is the ratio of all loan capital (i.e. debentures, and bank and other loans) and preference shares to the whole of the long-term capital (i.e. to ordinary shares and profits held in reserve). Gearing is an indication of the indebtedness of the firm, and hence its vulnerability to reversals of fortune. Twenty per cent might be considered acceptable but 40 per cent would not be.

1.2 THE DIRECTORS AND MANAGERS OF THE COMPANY

1.2.1 The Board of Directors

The directors of the company are appointed by the shareholders and have a legal or "official" status. The power and authority of the board of directors is appreciated when recalling from above that although the shareholders can vote directors out of office, they cannot interfere in the way they do their jobs. The appointment of the individuals themselves will specify the roles to which they are to be assigned — that is, the *managing director* (the MD — the boss), the *finance director*, the *sales and marketing director*, the *production* (or *operations*) director, etc. Although arrangements vary from company to company, depending on the particular challenges to the company and the views of the MD, in smaller companies only a few directors, such as financial, will be exclusively assigned to just one function. The remaining appointees are likely to have two or three functional areas in their charge, to ensure that each department manager at the next level in the organisational hierarchy has a board member to report to, able to protect his function's interests at board level. Although the board structure of

The Manufacturing Company

small to medium companies is relatively simple, as described, very large public companies have far more complex and sophisticated structures. There may be several "layers" of command in the directorate, and directors with such titles as "South East Asian business", "responsibility for technology X", etc.

Another feature of large companies not found in smaller ones is the existence, in their trading structure, of "divisions" and other operating entities which are run almost as if they were independent companies in their own right. (Many of the operating entities may, indeed, be limited companies wholly owned by the main company.) As a courtesy, the managers appointed to run divisions and subsidiaries are usually given the title of directors and are expected to manage the operations as "real" companies. The difference is that the managers respond to head office, not to shareholders. In the largest companies, "head office" may in reality be a complex control structure of committees.

The task of the directors is twofold. First, it is to manage the company from the viewpoint of its corporate (legal) and financial reality.[5] That is, the board is responsible for setting and achieving financial targets; for investment and loans; for profits; for recommending dividends; etc. Important and serious though they are, these responsibilities are unlikely to be unduly burdensome for competent people in smaller companies. In the UK's larger companies — the GECs and ICIs with assets exceeding many billions of pounds — this side of directors' jobs is onerous and complex, and is the reason why such companies will typically have several hundreds of people employed in their head offices to help carry it out. The second task of the directors concerns the functional operations of the company — that is, sales and marketing policy; preparation of accounts; purchase and use of new machine tools on the shop floor; and so on. Here, the role of individual functional directors is to plan and oversee that particular function. The instrument whereby the management part of this role is to be accomplished is, of course, the manager appointed to lead the functional department. The guidance

---

[5] An important figure in this regard is the company secretary, who answers to the Board and is responsible for corporate and legal administration and for giving legal advice. The company secretary is almost always a member of the Institute of Chartered Secretaries and in larger companies will be a qualified solicitor as well.

of the MD is crucial to this side of the job. After consultation and discussion at board level, it is the MD's responsibility to set clear goals and to ensure that his board is heading, as a team, in the right direction. The expression "singing to the same hymn sheet" has been used. No business can stand still. If it is to move forward and successfully meet the challenges of the future, strategies must be devised to enable it to do so — the development of new products or markets, the achievement of faster response to customer demand, the expansion of production, etc. The functional directors must show how strategy is to be translated into action while continuing to support the current sound operation of their individual departments.

1.2.2 Company Managers

The question of company organisation is discussed in sub-section 19.1.1. One may anticipate that discussion, however, by pointing out here that the overwhelming majority of companies are organised under traditional, hierarchical lines, with "departments" and, within departments, "sections". Whether the person in charge of a particular function or operation is to be a (senior) head of department or (junior) section head/leader will often depend on the nature of the company's business. For example, a company which makes products to order will not have a distribution department, since the element of distribution will be confined merely to the periodic transport of completed orders. Table 1.1 lists the titles of managers typically found in the manufacturing company and an indication whether the manager is likely to be a head of department (D) or section head (S). An attempt has been made to relate the table entries to the chapters of this book, though with some difficulty because so many activities are multidisciplinary. A number of them, such as master scheduling and quality control, might be better accommodated within a matrix structure than within a hierarchy.

Table 1.1: Principal Functional Departments and Sections

Manager	Level (Department or Section)	Chapter
Accounts	D	Chapter 17
Distribution	D or None	Chapter 20
Engineering	D	Chapter 3
Human Resources	D	Chapter 19
Marketing	D	Chapter 2
Master Scheduling	D or S	Chapters 6, 7 and 8
Production	D	Chapters 9 to 12 and 16
Production Control	S	Chapters 9 and 10
Purchasing	D	Chapter 16
Quality	D	Chapters 13 and 14
Sales	D or S	Chapter 2
Shop Floor Supervision	S	Chapters 11 and 12
Stores	S	Chapter 18

1.3 METHODS OF TRADING

1.3.1 Make-to-Stock

Make-to-stock means making sales goods in advance in the hope and expectation that customers will be forthcoming to buy the goods that have been made. Only in times of shortage and in the now defunct command economies would a company expect to be able automatically to *sell all that it can make*. Instead, in a market economy, the company *makes all that it can sell* — it is fully oriented to what the customer wants.[6] The critical importance of this stance is discussed in Chapter 2. For now, we can say that the company must start with market research and such other activities to discern what products to develop and put in its selling range, and the prices at which to offer them. A decision must also be

---

[6] A small number of companies, especially in assemble-to-order — certain car and computer mainframe manufacturers, for example — prepare a master plan for the year ahead based on their forecast of the market. This annual plan is then adhered to, within reason, even if actual demand proves to be rather greater or less than anticipated.

made as to how the goods are to be distributed — direct from our own factory, through wholesalers and merchants, through a network of depots, etc. Sales personnel must also advertise and promote the goods.

From the production viewpoint, assuming that a market for the goods exists and that the company is competent to manufacture them, the process begins with the formulation of a master schedule — this being a time-phased manufacturing plan to produce sales goods that takes into account demand forecasts, inventory holdings and the limits of manufacturing capacity. The master schedule is a planning blueprint. No company can succeed that manufactures its products in an *ad hoc*, disorganised fashion. If it attempts to do so, shortages and excesses will result, typically followed by loss of control, loss of quality, loss of business and ruin.

Following the issue of the master plan, it is necessary for production planning staff to draw up plans to manufacture supporting components and acquire raw materials. The calculations involved in this work and the subsequent task of formulating a detailed schedule of shop floor requirements are typically highly complex. Because of the inherent uncertainty of the predictions of sales demand on which the plan is partly based, the company which makes to stock must keep a close eye on the level of orders against the level expected, and must be prepared to rein back production if demand is below expectations. At the same time, the make-to-stock company must ensure that the service it offers its customers by way of product availability is "satisfactory" (i.e. as good as, if not better than, the service offered by competitors). It will usually be necessary, therefore, to hold safety stocks of products to guard against demand forecasts that prove to be too low.

The outlets through which the stock is sold are critically important to the selling effort. The least complex arrangement is simply the sale of goods direct from the company's factory to the ultimate user. A company making, say, ABS braking systems will sell to Ford or Vauxhall or Rover direct. Although there are exceptions, companies selling such consumer products as electric kettles or bottles of scotch will rarely choose to set up and operate a network of outlets accessible to the High Street shopper. A consumer nowadays would not consider the products of a single company as representing good choice.[7] Instead, the producer must attempt to sell his goods to wholesalers, merchants, supermarket chains and even individual retailers. These outlets constitute an efficient, cost effective and informal distribution network. The network, however, takes money to run, so that the price mark-up to the consumer over what was originally charged by the manufacturer is usually considerable. The distribution and merchandising skills of companies selling manufacturers' products direct to consumers are specialised and necessarily of an extremely high standard.

1.3.2 Make-to-Order

Like companies that make-to-stock, the company that makes to order offers a standard range of products and must similarly engage in market research and design to ensure its products are attractive to its market. However, the make-to-order company does not manufacture the products speculatively in the expectation of future business. Instead, it commences manufacture of a particular product on behalf of a specific customer, and only when that customer has confirmed that he wishes to buy. The customer, therefore, cannot take delivery of the goods at once, but must wait until the supplying company has completed the manufacture.

The length of time the customer must wait varies as widely as the range of goods which are sold on a make-to-order basis. A slot machine may be manufactured and "built" (assembled) for a pub in two weeks. The pre-sales technical discussion between manufacturer and customer in this case will be informal and uncomplicated. The variations of the brewery's order from a totally standard company product may similarly be superficial. By contrast, a large oil-fired electric generator will have a lead time of many months. The pre-sales technical, financial and design discussions in such a case are lengthy and complex.

There are other differences between make-to stock and make-to order besides customer waiting time, as described below.

---

[7] Despite these comments, a number of manufacturers do sell direct to the public via mail order and, increasingly, through e-commerce.

Demand Forecasts

Forecasts can be made of the demand for make-to-order products just as they can be of make-to-stock. However, for each product forecast, there are in reality two figures. First, there is the forecast of the orders related to when they are expected to be *received* from the customer. Secondly, there is the forecast of orders related to when the orders are expected to be *completed and despatched.* The demand forecasting system should be geared to the forecasting of order receipts. The master plan, however, must use forecasts in terms of order despatch. The difference in time, in this case, between order receipt and order despatch, is the standard order manufacture lead time (see sub-section 6.5.1).

The Order Book

Customers' orders which are under manufacture on their behalf are collectively known in the make-to-order company as the *order book*. A problem that can be seen at once is that the manufacturing company must finance it. That is, the manufacturer must pay for materials and expenses, and pay wages, but will receive no payment from its customers until the products are finished and delivered. (The make-to-stock company may argue that it must do the same thing, of course.) However, it is usual in contracts for longer lead time products for the manufacturer to require "stage payments" from customers to help finance its ongoing costs.

Late Deliveries

When an order is agreed, the agreement includes a promised date of completion and delivery. This promise date should be arrived at by the manufacturer taking into account the manufacturing capacity needed and available, other ongoing work and the rest. Notwithstanding their promises, however, a number of companies fail to deliver on time. The reasons for failure may be poor planning, poor control, unreasonable promise dates made only to secure the business in the first place, etc. Failure to meet delivery dates or the need to resort to firefighting and panic measures to achieve them is not acceptable in modern business. The customer buying from a company it suspects may not meet its promise date would do well to protect itself in the contract. A common means of doing so is through the insertion in it of *liquidated damages*. That is, a clause may be included whereby the supplier must make a specified payment to the customer in the event of non-fulfilment of the date (see sub-section 16.2.4).

1.3.3 Assemble-to-Order

A number of companies make a seemingly standard range of products, each of which has a basic form, but which then has incorporated within it a set of customer-specified options that make the product unique. For example, a *Ford Focus* can be considered as the car itself ("The Focus") and such options as manual/ automatic gears, sun roof / no sun roof, 1400cc/1600cc/1800cc/ 2000cc engine, colour (a choice of 10), etc. Although the options considered in isolation are standard and not so many in number, the number of alternative option *combinations* available to be ordered by customers is extremely large. Because of this, such products are treated in the following way:

1. Customers are offered the choice of options and must then wait a short time for their particular order to be assembled from the options selected. (The waiting time is days or weeks, not months.) The short final stage of manufacture is referred to as *final assembly scheduling* (FAS).

2. The manufacturer plans production in two distinct but closely interrelated stages: a master schedule of option types and common parts, planned and manufactured almost as if they were independent products, and an FAS stage, whereby final customer orders are to be configured.

1.3.4 Engineer-to-Order

The expression *engineer-to-order* denotes the provision of both a design and bespoke manufacturing service by the company. A homely example, literally, though not from manufacturing industry, is that of a firm of architects and builders specialising in domestic housing. The potential purchaser will describe his building plot, the number of bedrooms and his ideas, and little by little the house is designed. Following design comes construction of the new property. Companies that engineer-to-order are more usually termed *job shops*. Although the design side of such companies is unique to this method of trading, there are many resemblances on the production side to traditional make-to-order. In addition, many "one-off" designs often find their way onto the company's range of standard products, if the company offers both a make-to-order and an engineer-to-order service.

1.4 COMPANY TASKS — AN OVERVIEW IN RELATION TO THIS BOOK

1.4.1 Product Development and Sales

The company must discover what the market wishes to buy in relation to the skills and know-how it has to offer, so that its product range will be attractive. The customer is king. Tasks and activities involved in doing so include market research, price planning and so on. The department responsible for carrying them out is marketing. Indeed, because of the paramount importance of customer orientation ("the marketing concept"), the marketing department will have a considerable influence over other functional departments on matters that impinge on customer satisfaction — for example, on engineering design and distribution.

The responsibility of the design engineer is to take market requirements from the world of ideas and goals to final product. The three stages along the way are: the *specification* of the new product; the *conceptual* or broad design; and the *detailed* design. It is essential in this progression to involve others whose contributions are certain to have an impact on the final product and its acceptability to the customer, especially with regard to quality, cost and "manufacturability".

Finally, there is the requirement actually to sell the product on offer to customers. The majority of selling in industry is on a person-to-person basis, even though the placement of orders may be electronic or through the Internet. Salesmen are assigned to "territories" and are typically set targets in terms of sales volumes. See Chapters 2 and 3.

1.4.2 Output and Inventory Planning (Master Planning)

The planning of production output at the sales product level and the parallel planning of sales product inventory levels (make-to-stock) together are the heart of manufacturing operations. The subject is referred to as *master planning* or *master production scheduling,* and is comprised of two parts.

Part I of master planning is master plan formulation. This means the monthly creation of a manufacturing schedule for each sales product, taking into account the forecast of demand; the capacity of the plant to fulfil the manufacture; the implications of the plan in terms of inventory holding; and general business and economic prospects. It is at the master plan formulation stage that the inventory holding of make-to-stock companies is decided, since the option exists at this point of building up stock levels to meet anticipated surges in demand beyond the company's short-term capacity. When the master plan has finally been accepted and approved by all those who will be responsible for its fulfilment, commitment to it must be absolute. In order to play as a team, the company must have a plan. This is it.

Part II of master planning is master plan management. The company must first "explode" the master schedule to determine the corresponding requirements of components and raw materials needed to support it. However, the main thrust of MPS management is keeping an eye on the continuing validity, or appropriateness, of the plan in the light of events unfolding. "Events" are the receipt of actual customer orders and the completion of production. The master plan is a continual point of reference and an assurance of control. See Chapters 6, 7 and 8, and also Chapters 4 and 5.

1.4.3 Production Planning and External Supplies

When the master plan has been decided, it remains to find what plans to support it are needed for lower-level products including sub-assemblies, components and raw materials. The calculations required to do so are labyrinthine and lengthy, and are possible to complete efficiently only by computer. The data inputs to the calculation are formidable. They include the master plan itself; the bill of materials (i.e. data relating to the structure of the products);

current stocks of material; lead times of production; manufacturing lot sizes; and the demands of production in the various work centres. The output from the calculations is a time-phased set of plans for products at all levels in the bill from the top to raw materials.

When circumstances change — for one thing, due simply to the passage of time, but for another due to the completion of production or the occurrence of a problem — it is necessary to determine the repercussions of the change on the current plans. One system of production plan management is then to recalculate the plans and report to the production planner the differences between the previous and latest requirements. This technique is known as *closed loop MRP*. It has achieved considerable notoriety.

In all of the above, the requirement for raw materials is considered to be no different logically from the requirement for components and sub-assemblies. The expression has been coined *the outside shop*, meaning that the raw material supplier is to be regarded like any in-house manufacturing department, except for the fact of his being geographically remote. Consequently, there is a need to involve suppliers closely with the company from both the viewpoint of logistics and of quality. Other subjects of concern to the purchasing manager include vendor appraisal (the appraisal of potential suppliers in the supply marketplace); supplier performance analysis; commodity and foreign purchases; the drawing up of legal contracts; and trends in raw material prices and in their availability. See Chapters 9, 10 and 16.

1.4.4 Controlling Operations (Production)

The time-phased production plans described as being created above are usually insufficiently exact to allow actual physical manufacture to proceed without further painstaking refinement. The shop floor supervisor and production planner must turn the material requirements into a schedule of shop activity specifying particular machines, times of day, job run times and the rest. Until very recently, the task of creating a practical plan — a schedule of jobs tested to ensure that capacity is available to meet it — may have taken many days and resulted in a less-than-perfect result. Over the past few years, however, a new generation of *advanced planning systems* has appeared that offers the creation of superior schedules and interactive communication and simulation facilities

The Manufacturing Company

to explore alternative courses of action, all presented in attractive graphical forms on the VDU. These systems appear to be swiftly taking over the closed-loop functions of MRP.

There is more to running a factory floor than scheduling. Such issues must be dealt with as the release of orders to the shop in the first place; the assignment of priorities to jobs; the management of lead times and queues; and monitoring of the efficiency of individual work centres. In addition to these tasks, there may be the need in certain circumstances to install a manufacturing data reporting system.

The planning of production and the scheduling of jobs will come to nothing if the stock required for manufacture is not to hand. What is needed to assure the planner that the material he believes to be available will be there when it is wanted is not a mountain of contingency stock. Instead, a recording system must be in place, one maintaining stock quantities at, say, 98 per cent accuracy or better. The member of staff chiefly responsible for achieving this difficult target is the stores manager. The role of the stores also includes controlling the receipt of goods; the picking of stock; stock issue or order despatch; and maintaining materials handling equipment. See Chapters 11, 12 and 18.

1.4.5 Quality and Just-in-Time

As we regard the might and reputation of Japanese manufacturing, we may reflect with irony that the quality drive in Japan began with a lecture tour in 1950 by the American manufacturing and quality master, the late W. Edwards Deming, during the American occupation of that country following World War II. Deming's primary message concerned what is referred to as *statistical process control* (SPC). The essence of SPC is astonishingly simple. It is that when a manufacturing process is "under control" — that is, when it is working normally and producing 100 per cent conforming goods — the analysis of small samples of production taken every so often reveals a consistent, statistically familiar pattern. This pattern can continue to be tracked as verification that the process remains under control and that perfect quality continues to be maintained. When the pattern deviates — stop! — fix the problem!

Quality has been taken further than simply the quality of the physical output of production. The notion has been extended in the company to encompass all activities — design, administration, record keeping, accounting, planning, purchasing. This is referred to as *TQC — total quality control*. One approach to TQC is to recognise that the operation of a system of work achieves natural limits of performance, limits determined by *common causes* of variation. Any interference by management in the operation of the system by staff will cause a deterioration in its performance. To improve performance, management must address the underlying design and *modus operandi* of the system itself.

Closely associated with SPC, TQC and Japan is the famous Just-in-Time manufacturing system, begun in 1953 by the Toyota Motor Company. The original idea at Toyota was to eliminate waste — to clear away stock on the shop floor so that activity and potential problems could be seen more clearly. To achieve this, production was physically rearranged so that very small batches of products could be economically produced. The production and movement of material at Toyota is controlled by a simple system based on cards, now known throughout the world as "kanban". The idea of JIT has been extended to mean not merely the elimination of waste in the factory, but the development of a rapid response capability to changing external customer requirements. See Chapters 13, 14 and 15.

1.4.6 Finance

The need to maintain a system of accounts, periodically to prepare and review such vital documents as the balance sheet and to perform other tasks in the area of financial accountancy are understood everywhere. In the manufacturing company, there is especial emphasis also on the treatment of assets — in the valuation of stocks and the depreciation of plant, for example. One extensive and important topic unique to manufacturing and of great concern both to the accountant and the manufacturing manager is cost accountancy. Product costs and the data from which they are derived are needed for two purposes. First, they are needed to distinguish company expenditure considered from the accounting viewpoint, up to the point of sale, to be an investment, not an accounting expense. Secondly, they are needed to track and control production efficiency in financial terms, with regard to such matters as scrap and process yield. See Chapter 17.

1.4.7 Human Resources

Manpower planning, the policing of the company's organisational arrangements and the management of employee matters including industrial relations are the responsibility of the human resources department. Of particular concern here is the question of reward management, and the shaping of HR policy, through the institution of such schemes as broad banding and variable pay, to promote corporate objectives of enterprise and customer focus. Again of concern to HR and manufacturing is willing compliance with health and safety regulations. Two further subjects, affecting the process of manufacture itself, are teams and empowerment. Teams and empowerment are said to be essential at the FAS stage of assemble-to-order, but the evidence elsewhere in favour of this approach seems mixed. See Chapter 19.

1.4.8 Distribution

Goods which must be made available at short notice to a geographically extensive customer base, or which can be transported economically only as bulk loads, may have to be sold through a network of outlets throughout the UK and, perhaps, overseas. Normally, as stated earlier, the manufacturer will be content for specialist companies to undertake the distribution of its products. However, for reasons connected with cost or customer service, the manufacturing company may itself undertake distribution. If it does so, it must determine the structure of the network of outlets to be supported and the means by which the network's stock requirements are to be satisfied. Replenishment of network stocking points is likely to be determined through a central planning system such as DRP or "fair shares". An advantage of these systems is that they enable distribution demand and the provision of stock through the master schedule to be closely co-ordinated. See Chapter 20.

Chapter 2

Sales and Marketing

"It is the customer who determines what a business is. It is the customer alone whose willingness to pay for a good or service converts economic resources into wealth, things into goods. What the business thinks it produces is not of first importance — especially not to the future of the business and to its success. What the customer thinks he is buying, what he considers value, is decisive . . . The business enterprise has two — and only two — basic functions: marketing and innovation. The rest are costs." (Peter Drucker, *Management: Tasks, Responsibilities and Practices*).

2.1 MARKETING

2.1.1 The Marketing Concept

The central tenet of modern business is that its sole aim and justification are the satisfaction of customers' wants, and that all endeavour should be directed at determining what those wants are and then fulfilling them (while still making a reasonable profit). This principle is referred to as the *marketing concept*, and stands behind the definition of marketing compiled by the Chartered Institute of Marketing:

> "Marketing is the management process responsible for identifying, anticipating and satisfying customer requirements profitably."

Sales and Marketing departments are hardly alone in their embracing of the marketing concept. In its fullest sense it is, or should be, an article of faith of the whole company, including manufacturing, purchasing, distribution, design, etc. A criticism all too common, however, is that many managers have lost sight of this ideal as their companies have grown bigger and more complex. Long chains of communication between basic producers and ultimate consumers mean that the two sides never meet. The production expert becomes preoccupied by such targets as increased volumes of output, quality or cost efficiency. In answer to the question "what business are you in?", he replies in terms of what he produces, not in terms of what customers want.

Pursuit of the marketing concept is the only chance in a free society of long-term survival in business, for, without the support of its customers, the business will lose money and fail. The road is not an easy one. Competitors introduce products and services which differentiate them from the company's to their advantage or which they are able to produce at lower cost. Their products are offered with attractive new services. Social changes affect customers' aspirations. Technology may completely change the face of the market. The pace of marketing can be hot.

2.1.2 The Marketing Mix

The customer's satisfaction is not merely with the physical use of the entity he has bought. On examination we see that there are a whole range of "satisfactions" and benefits that the product might bring, stemming from attributes other than the product itself. Five elements of satisfaction are recognised in all — PPPP+S — each interacting one with every other. Their composite is known as the *marketing mix*. The individual components of the marketing mix are as follows:

- **Product** — The product must be wanted; it must have appeal. It must work properly and safely, and give satisfaction in use.

- **Price** — The product must be affordable. There must be a willingness by the customer to spend money on this and not on something else.

- **Place** — There is a limit to how far the customer is willing to go to obtain the product. (Such considerations as brand loyalty and price are important here.)

- **Promotion** — This includes packaging, "aura", style of promotion.

- **Service** — If after-sales service is necessary, what is its nature? (Might it be dispensed with?)

Within a particular company, operating within a particular market, an understanding of the marketing mix is clearly central to a pursuit of the marketing goal. But the importance to be attached to the various components of the mix is dictated by the ever-changing status of the product itself. The primary means of tracking the marketing status of a product is in relation to its *life cycle*.

The product life cycle is a well-established phenomenon — a progression of *launch – growth – maturity – market saturation – decline* illustrated in the graph of sales volume versus time in Figure 2.1. The initial acceptance and, ultimately, final rejection of the product arise because of changes in the market, not the product. Customers' fashions, their needs, habits, incomes, understanding and aspirations move onwards, leaving the old products behind.

Figure 2.1: The Product Life Cycle

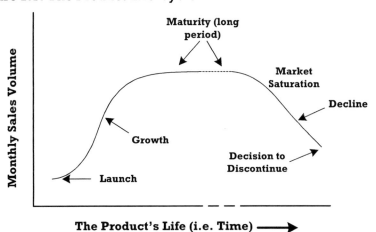

During the anxious *launch phase* of the life cycle, the focus of endeavour of the Marketing department is to establish product awareness and begin the long build-up of the customer base. Although product prices are high, so is marketing expenditure. And because overall sales volumes are still low, profits are negligible. Cash flow is negative.

In the *growth phase*, the focus switches to urgency of market penetration. Marketing expenditure is maintained at a high level to capture market share — for example, through extensive and intensive distribution. Although prices are likely to be somewhat softer as competitors also begin to emerge, rapidly increasing sales are likely to result in peak levels of profit.

Sales levels and profits begin to slow in the solid *maturity phase* as the Marketing department's strategic focus becomes one of consolidation and the defence of the company's market share, perhaps through the introduction of differentiated product variants (see below). The presence of increasing numbers of competitors results in price levels at their lowest in the whole life cycle. So although marketing expenditure declines, profits also decline.

In the final unsettled phases of the life cycle — *market saturation* and *decline* — strategy shifts once again, this time to the pursuit of high levels of productivity, selective distribution and a selling effort aimed at increasingly selective market sectors. Product ranges (see below) are likely to be rationalised. The number of competitors declines; product prices harden somewhat.

Table 2.1 summarises the salient points relating to the various life cycle phases, and is a very brief extract from a far more comprehensive table relating to product life cycle characteristics and responses containing 44 entries drawn up by Professor Peter Doyle of Warwick University.[1]

Table 2.1: Differing Responses in Marketing to Changes in Product Maturity

Phase	Development	Growth	Maturity	Market Saturation/ Decline
Sales	Low	Rapidly rising	Steady	Decline
Profits	(Loss)	High	Declining	Very low
Strategy	Expansion	Penetration	Defence	Productivity and selectivity
Price	High	Lower	Lowest	Rising

---

[1] Prof. Peter Doyle (1994), "Re-evaluating the Product Life Cycle", *Encyclopedia of Marketing* (ed. M. Baker), London: Routledge.

Sales and Marketing

Four ways in which the Marketing department may seek to protect the company's position as the phases progress through time are through:

1. **Market Penetration** — attempts are made through advertising and selling to increase sales of the company's current products in its current markets;
2. **Market Development** — current products are sold in new markets;
3. **Product Development** — product improvements and variations are devised to increase or defend sales in current markets;
4. **Product Diversification** — new product lines are developed, for launch in new markets.

Among the specific actions taken under these four headings are the development of product *ranges* so that the product variants within a range cover the whole market. For some products, this may be as simple as providing a wide range of pack sizes. Attempts may also be made to "differentiate" the product. These are made not necessarily through effecting physical product changes (recall the importance of the product mix). Thus, until the 1930s all beer bottles were of clear glass. An American manufacturer then switched to dark glass "to protect your product from the light". Again, the introduction of the circular tea bag in 1988 ("no corners for the leaves") temporarily increased Tetley's sales by 25 per cent, impressing Brooke Bond sufficiently for them to spend £25 million on advertising and merchandising[2] for the launch of their pyramidal tea bag nine years later. So although a few brands do seem to go on forever, we see the dangers of relying too heavily on too few products for too long. And, as each product has a limited life, then, depending where it is in the cycle, different management considerations will predominate and different elements within the marketing mix will be emphasised.

---

[2] "Merchandising" is the management of retail sales operations, and includes such subjects as the layout of the stores or shop, ensuring that the best mix of goods is available to buy, advertising displays, stock control and buying.

Although the life cycle is the principal context for considering the marketing mix (at least in the sense that it is inevitable and cannot be ignored) it is not the only one. The plans and preferences of individual companies also count. Nine alternative marketing strategies involving two elements of the marketing mix, price and quality, have been humorously suggested by marketing guru Professor Philip Kotler of the J.L. Kellogg School of Management, Northwestern University, Illinois.[3] They vary from the reprehensible upwards — see Table 2.2.

Table 2.2: Humorous View of Marketing Options

		Price		
		High	Medium	Low
Product Quality	High	Premium Strategy	Penetration Strategy	Superbargain Strategy
	Medium	Overpricing Strategy	Average Quality Strategy	Bargain Strategy
	Low	Hit-and-Run Strategy	Shoddy Goods Strategy	Cheap Goods Strategy

2.1.3 The Co-ordination Role of Marketing (Role 1 of 3)

If it is accepted that the marketing concept is the guiding principle of the whole company, not simply that of the Marketing department, then Marketing has the job of co-ordinating policy on such matters as quality, delivery standards, R&D and the production response to demand, in areas where these activities concern customer service and satisfaction.

Although the department may appear on the company's organisation chart as an *equal* to finance, production, purchasing and the rest, in fact it has a "dotted line" relationship with them so far as guidance on matters affecting marketing matters are concerned. That is, if the marketing concept is accepted, then it is accepted also that the Marketing department has at least an informal role in co-ordinating, conferring with and advising other functions, as illustrated in Figure 2.2.

---

[3] Philip Kotler (1999), *Marketing Management*, Prentice-Hall.

Figure 2.2: Links from Marketing Back to Other Functions

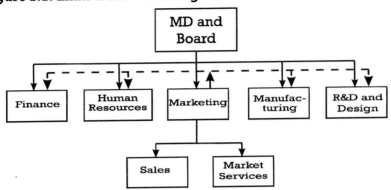

The relationship of marketing to the marketing concept interests of other departments is not unlike the relationship of the QA department to the quality interests of departments. As well, the exercise of Marketing's co-ordinating role threatens to conflict with the functions of Master Scheduling, as described in Chapters 6 and 7. Conflict may be avoided in two ways. First, the master scheduler might be a Marketing department appointee, even though his staff are technical personnel. Secondly, the company may very carefully delineate the master scheduler's role and marketing's, appointing a neutral company director as arbitrator if disputes should arise which cannot be otherwise resolved. The first solution is short-term, the second medium- to long-term.

2.1.4 The Planning Role of Marketing (Role 2 of 3)

At the early stages of the planning process at least, senior marketing managers are likely to share the drawing board with the MD and certain other directors. The tasks to be carried out include sales and profit planning; price planning; laying plans for major sales promotions; and the opening up of new areas of research and development.

One view of marketing planning is given again by Peter Drucker: *anticipating the future that has already happened.* Drucker suggests that economic, social and technical step changes or discontinuities occur for various reasons and often go unrecognised and unexploited for long periods. Major examples in the recent past are the rise in teenage purchasing power and the advent of computers. Perhaps more current examples are intensified international competition and greater price transparency brought about through the Internet. Whether the discontinuity is major or minor, the period of time between its occurring and its being acknowledged represents a marketing opportunity for the company. Companies that do not seize such opportunities are at risk — *tomorrow always arrives and it is always different.*

A second view is that marketing planning is *customer-focused, not customer-led.* An example of what this means was given by Ford UK executive John Gardener in relation to the design of the company's small saloon, the Ka. The reaction of customers to a prototype of the model was not especially favourable (*"too advanced"*), but from an in-depth analysis of the market and perceived trends in taste, Ford's designers persevered. The immense success of the Ka when launched two years later in production proved their original prediction to be correct.[4]

A study by management consultancy firm McKinsey in 1980 into companies that seemed best at seizing opportunities indicated that:

> "the excellent companies were, above all, brilliant on the basics. They insisted on top quality . . . fawned on their customers . . . allowed their innovative and product champions a long tether . . . quick action . . . experimentation."[5]

The process of marketing planning is illustrated in Figure 2.3. Comments on each stage follow.

Figure 2.3: The Processes of Marketing and Strategic Planning

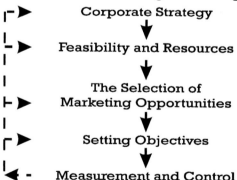

---

[4] *The Daily Telegraph*, 15 July 1998 (p. 35).
[5] Peters and Waterman (1982), *In Search of Excellence*.

- **Corporate Strategy:** This is the formulation of a plan, at an appropriately broad level of detail, which covers the whole future activity of the enterprise. The plan encompasses an evaluation of economic, technological and other trends; the company's areas of strengths and weaknesses; alternative quantified objectives; and assessments of what is needed to achieve them. The corporate plan may cover five years, perhaps with a year-by-year breakdown.

- **Feasibility and Resources:** The feasibility or otherwise of any corporate plan is determined by the infrastructure and resources available to the company. Infrastructure and resources include those relating to manufacturing; distribution; marketing; manpower, competence and know-how; and money. The belief that management energy will be able to make up for deficiencies in these areas too often leads companies to embark on plans that prove hopelessly beyond their capabilities.

- **The Selection of Marketing Opportunities:** The Marketing department must review current policy, forecasts and the findings of market research in order to uncover possible market opportunities and evaluate them to determine their likely profitability and the demands they will make on the company's resources. (There is no harm in coming up with a flash of brilliance in spotting marketing opportunities, provided it is supported by solid, *unbiased* facts and figures.)

- **Setting Objectives:** Because of the vital need for eventual measurement and control, goals must be set at this stage relating to sales volumes; profits; market size and market share; desirable product development features; and so on. Targets must be expressed quantitatively, though perhaps with upper and lower limits. Contingency plans might also be formulated in case of failure.

- **Measurement and Control:** As milestones are passed, actual achievement is compared with objectives, perhaps leading to corrective action. Important means of control here are the setting of budgets and subsequent budget surveillance. All too often, developments have run out of control, especially in R&D, because of a failure to set and strictly adhere to financial limits.

2.1.5 The Functional Role of Marketing (Role 3 of 3)

The term "functional role" means the role of management and administration of the activities performed within the department and described in this Chapter. Typically in industry, these activities are assigned to departmental sections. When so, sections typically include product planning; market research; advertising and promotion;[6] sales and sales management; and administration and personnel.

2.2 INNOVATION

2.2.1 The Development of New Products

The necessity for developing new products and product modifications has already been mentioned. The process of doing so, however, and launching them into the market is lengthy, difficult and costly. It can also on occasions be highly profitable.

The development of truly innovative products is rare and typically falls only to those companies making large expenditure on research and development over substantial time spans. More usually, "new" products are adaptations and refinements of existing ones — alternative designs, new component materials, new colours, additional technical features to expand the current products' functionality or (say) to enhance their durability.[7]

As those familiar with science and engineering know, discoveries and developments are very rarely made by chance. In the case of industrial R&D, it is essential that the company follow a highly

---

[6] As related in due course, this is unlikely to be a significantly large function in the industrial company, where the emphasis is usually on personal selling.

[7] Marketing must be willing to eliminate products that are consuming resources but contributing nothing to profits or prospects. *Get rid of the dogs*, as this analysis shows:

	Market Growth	
	Hi	Low
Market Share — Hi	Stars	Cash Cows
Market Share — Low	Problem Children	Dogs

Sales and Marketing

directed path that has a crystal clear objective set in terms of the new product development wanted and the appeal of such a development to the market. From the scientific point of view, the chance of successful development is not certain, and, from the marketing point of view, nor is the eventual appeal of the product. Uncertain as they may be, both must be present before work begins. Other factors (mentioned earlier) must be present as well, such as a commercial and technical infrastructure that will allow the company to carry its development through to a successful conclusion. A successful conclusion, then, is not simply a technical invention, but one that encompasses the invention's full-scale marketing, production and distribution, all within a reasonable timescale and within reasonable cost. The steps of the process are:

1. Finding gaps in the market;
2. Business and (tentative) cost analysis;
3. Product development;
4. Test marketing;
5. Launch and commercialisation.

Vital though the scientific contribution may be, we see then that it is only one step of the five. To repeat, the process is expensive, lengthy and uncertain. Failure is frequent and the further along the way it occurs, the more expensive it is. The strictest cost control is required, not least because of the common reluctance of enthusiastic managers to terminate developments in which they have invested much time and energy.[8]

---

[8] It has been said that a company must screen 50 serious new product ideas before it finds one worth carrying forward to development, and that of those that are developed, 50 per cent fail after the test marketing phase. A primary reason for failure in the later, more expensive stages, is the lack of a hard-headed assessment of the idea or development in question from such viewpoints as product attractiveness and product/company fit. Fit means infrastructure — marketing and production capability, finance, time, etc. Enthusiasm and "belief" in the new product obscure judgement.

2.2.2 Market Research

Market research is the gathering and analysis of facts relating to the sale of goods. It includes not only investigation into markets — their sizes, preferences, composition — but investigation into aspects of the marketing activity itself. In the field of consumer goods, this will include (say) the determination of the nature of the readership of magazines or of the patterns of TV viewing. In a large company, market research is carried out by a separate section within the Marketing department. The bulk of market research activity, however, is performed by specialist, independent agencies ranging from one-man bands to considerable international organisations.

Market research material available to any company includes the facts and conclusions obtainable from its own standard files, especially from analysis of those maintained through the sales order processing system. Published government statistics are also obtainable. Data derived from such sources as these are referred to as *secondary* market research data.

Primary market research data, by contrast, are data collected directly by an agency either by "experiment" or through a survey. The means by which data are obtained include test marketing; the in-depth interviewing of consumers; the analysis of completed magazine and mailshot questionnaires; and so on. Because collection is expensive and because (expensive) marketing actions may be taken based on the veracity of the results, the activity must be carried out with the clearest objectives in mind and with great attention to detail. It may be done on a semi-continuous basis or as and when required. Semi-continuous collection is useful for tracking trends. A well-known example is the government's monthly survey of prices to obtain the Retail Price Index. *Ad hoc* surveys will typically be undertaken by an agency on a company's behalf prior to the possible development of a new product. For example, in test marketing, a marketing area is investigated that it is believed is representative of the whole market in which the product is ultimately to be launched. Primary data are collected by the following means:

- **Retail Audit:** The best known agency undertaking retail audits is the international concern A.C. Nielsen Inc., founded in 1923

Sales and Marketing

and now a subsidiary company of the Dun and Bradstreet Corporation. Nielsen's shop auditors visit selected stores and shops every two months and determine the sales of brands and pack sizes. Companies subscribe to the published results.

- **Syndicated Research:** Surveys are conducted of aspects of consumer activities, such as driving or leisure, and into consumer preferences (say, in the purchase of footwear).

- **Qualitative Research:** In depth interviews of "typical" consumers are conducted to provide insight into motivation and beliefs.

- **Advertising Research:** Surveys are carried out to determine the effect on the public of advertising and, say, their TV commercial "recall".

- **Media Research:** JICARS is the Joint Industry Committee for National Reader Surveys, these breaking figures down by age, sex and occupational class. The classification scheme adopted since 2001 is shown in Table 2.3. It replaced a long-standing six-class system based on skills, the replacement being judged necessary because of the decline in numbers of blue-collar workers in heavy manufacturing industry and the rise of white collar workers, including women.

Table 2.3: Social Analysis of the UK Population

Class	Occupational Category	Example
1	Higher managerial and professional	director; accountant
2	Lower managerial and professional	supervisor; bank manager
3	Intermediate occupations	operator; police constable
4	Small employers and sole traders	self-employed builder; farmer
5	Lower supervisory and technical	plumber; bakery worker
6	Semi-routine occupations	security guard; postman
7	Routine occupations	construction worker; cleaner

2.2.3 Sampling

The backbone of market research is *sampling*. The basis of sampling is *statistical inference*, whereby the mean and variance of the "population" from which the sample is drawn are estimated from statistics relating to the mean and variance of the sample itself (see SQC and Chapter 14). In market research, however, statistics take second place to such challenges as finding a sample truly representative of the whole, accurately taking the opinions of the consumers sampled (at economic cost) and eliminating bias from the survey. One example of sample bias famous among those who work in this field relates to a write-in poll organised by an American magazine in 1936 as to presidential voting intentions that seemed to reveal that the Republican ($\equiv$ Conservative) candidate Landon had a substantial lead. The poll result was duly published, but the Democratic ($\equiv$ Labour) candidate Roosevelt won by the biggest landslide in American history. The composition of the magazine's readership had not been taken into account, nor the greater willingness of Republican voters to write in.

It is a counterintuitive and fortunate fact of statistics, an outcome proved through the famous *central limit theorem* (sub-section 14.1.1), that the size of a sample does not have to be proportionate to the size of the population from which it is taken to yield accurate results. That is, as the absolute size of the sample increases, a point is reached whereby the accuracy of the conclusions drawn from it is very high and beyond which further refinement is of no merit. A sample of 15,000 is quite sufficient to gauge the views of the UK with a population of 58.5 million. Indeed, a sample of 15,000 is rare. Nationwide samples of 2,000 to 5,000 consumers are usually considered quite large enough. In the opposite direction, however, a sample size that is too small is likely to give misleading results. This has a consequence if small groups of consumers are being analysed within an overall sample that is otherwise large. If the number of people falling into any one group is fewer than (say) 200, it may be necessary to obtain an additional sample of people in this small category to obtain an accurate analysis of it. An expert

Sales and Marketing

account of sampling and the perils of sampling is given by the eminent W. Edwards Deming[9] — see sub-section 13.1.4.

2.3 SELLING AND SALES MANAGEMENT

2.3.1 The Role of Selling

Selling and sales management are to do with the obtaining and processing of actual sales orders. The activity is one strand of the total marketing effort, and must be performed and managed in a way that fits in with the higher, overall marketing direction.

In industry, the predominant feature of selling is *personal* selling. It is the final link between supplier and buyer and an essential element of it, as we can see from the analysis of marketing communications in Table 2.4.

Table 2.4: How the Customer is Reached in Various Types of Market

	The Importance of Marketing Communication		
Activity	Industrial Goods	Consumer Durables	Consumer Non-Durables
Sales management and personal selling	Very high	High	High
Media advertising	Very low	Moderate	High
Special promotions	Low	Moderate	Moderate
Pack/Brand name	Low	Low	Moderate

For industrial goods, then, personal selling is the largest element of the sales effort and where the bulk of the selling budget is spent. If justification were needed, there are two reasons for this. First, assuming that market opportunities and customer requirements have been correctly identified, and assuming the appropriateness of the product, these facts must be communicated to the customer — the *information task* of the salesman. Secondly, despite the apparent justness (to the seller) of the seller's cause, prospective customers still have to be convinced that their needs will be

---

[9] W. Edwards Deming (1950), *Some Theory of Sampling* (see Barrie Dale (ed.) (1994), *Managing Quality,* Second edition, Prentice Hall Europe). Deming was at the centre of the sampling programme for the 1940 US census, the first ever use of sampling rather than a 100 per cent poll for a national census.

satisfied by *these* goods from *this* supplier. The tasks involved in selling have been summarised as a mnemonic, AIDAS which stands for:

- **Attention** — making contact with the customer;
- **Interest** — arousing his interest;
- **Desire** — creating a want for the goods, such as by showing the customer how they will satisfy his needs;
- **Action** — closing the sale, asking for and getting the order;
- **Satisfaction** — making sure the business is retained.

It has been shown, in conclusion, that AIDAS proceeds best and most effectively in industry when pursued through personal selling.

The Salesman

The obvious and most significant difference between selling and other aspects of the marketing effort is personal contact. What makes an effective *salesman* has defied objective analysis, although such words as *personality*, *psychology* and even *physical presence* have been mentioned. Salesmen cannot entirely rely on these mysteries to carry them through, however, and, depending on the company concerned, may be required to perform other tasks than the charming of customers. Examples are the provision of after-sales service; the progressing of orders and deliveries; the carrying out of stock checks; and so forth. The breakdown of a typical week might be as shown in Table 2.5.

Table 2.5: Breakdown of a Salesman's Time (in Manufacturing)

Pre-call preparation	10%
Driving and travelling	20%
Face-to-face selling	20%
Non-selling (see text)	20%
Administration and reports	10%
Meetings and phone	10%
Other	10%

Sales and Marketing 37

The Sales Manager

Although certain sales managers do allocate to themselves certain tasks that might be called selling, such as visiting key customers occasionally with salesmen in order to show how important those accounts are to the company, the job they hold must clearly be seen as comprising the *management* of the sales effort and the *management* of the sales *team*, not that of super salesman. The sales manager is there to get results through others, by encouraging salesmen, ensuring they adhere to company sales policy and generally bringing to bear people management and organisational skills. He is also responsible for carrying out tactical tasks, such as marketing analysis; for devising and evaluating the results of promotions; for assessing competitors' actions; and for planning the future of the sales force (e.g. recruitment). Finally, the sales manager has a strategic input to the company's marketing debate.

2.3.2 The Management of Sales

Sales Organisation and Territories

The principal way of organising the sales force in UK industry is by geographic region, such that all sales tasks within each specific region are the responsibility of a designated salesman. Advantages of doing so are the arrangement's subsequent straightforwardness of management and the easy ability it presents to compare and evaluate sales results. Notwithstanding these advantages, however, 50 per cent of UK companies choose a method of organisation other than by straight geography, as shown in Table 2.6.

Table 2.6: Preferences in Sub-dividing the Sales Market

UK Organisation	Percentage of Companies
Geographic region only	50%
Product only	4%
Market only	4%
Geography and Product	15%
Geography and Market	21%
Geography, Market and Product	6%

The reasons for organising by product or market, or by combination, rather than by straight geography, are technical complexity and specialisations, and so that individual salesmen can develop required expertise. Needless to say, careful thought must be given to the rules of deployment of salesmen when combinations are used such that two or more salesmen are likely then to be operating in the same physical region.

To facilitate effective sales force operations, to control selling expenses and to ensure that the market is comprehensively covered, salesmen are assigned exclusively to *territories*. If the organisation is simply geographic, then "territory" has the normal meaning of that word. If the organisation is not thus, then it has a more complex meaning — say, those customers in a region taking only certain products or those customers with factories of fewer than 100 staff.

It is possible for sales management to devise sales territories by the *breakdown* method, whereby the total market is divided into areas in such a way that the estimated mixture of the sales workload and the sales potential are roughly equalised. More thoroughly, the *build-up* method starts with a breakdown of the total area into a large number of small units, analysed and equalised by population or industry or other relevant measure. The sales potential and sales workload are then estimated for each unit, and finally the territories are built up from the units.

Both the organisation and number of assigned territories will be affected by the size of the sales force. This in turn will be determined by an estimate of the sales workload. An estimate may be obtained from the target number of sales calls to be made and their duration, taking account of the relative importance of potential customers.[10] (The ABC principle may be used to classify customers — see sub-section 18.4.1.)

Goals and Sales Evaluation

For performance evaluation purposes and as a means of providing incentives to salesmen individually, it is normal for sales management to set sales targets for each territory. Considerable thought

---

[10] *Selling: Principles, Practice and Management*, Simon Cooper (1997), Pitman Publishing.

Sales and Marketing

should be put into making these as fair as possible, especially when it is borne in mind that sales volume alone is not the only mark of the industrious and effective salesman. The salesman must undertake other tasks, as previously mentioned.

Consideration of sales targets will be made usually by reference to such factors as: the previous year's achieved sales volume; management judgement; and perceived market and economic indicators. Perhaps the most common targets are simply sales by volume and by sales value. Criticisms of these simple goals are that they discourage a balanced selling effort and that they can lead to an emphasis merely on selling more and more to the same customers rather than finding and winning new prospects. As a consequence, many managers have set such alternative measures as *sales targets for specific products, expenses-to-sales ratios, gross margins on orders* and *market share*.

Whatever the measure or measures chosen, purely quantitative targets have the weakness that they do not take into account the quality of back-up service provided by the salesman, the conscientiousness of his pursuit of potential new leads and — simply — the manner of his representation of the company's interests.

The Analysis of Sales Results

It is not sufficient merely to assess sales results in terms of the sales target set, although clearly this is important. The purposes of analysis include verification or otherwise of the achievement of marketing goals; assessment of the factors at work in the territories; further assessment, if possible, of the effectiveness of advertising; and confirmation of calculations, such as those relating to industrial activity present in each of the territories.

One approach to analysis is through the data collected in the sales order processing (SOP) system (but see sub-section 4.3.1). Figure 2.4 outlines a possible breakdown for a geographic territory. Such a report and many, many variants of it are straightforward to produce, always assuming that there has been a thorough classification of the data present on the sales order processing system history files.

Figure 2.4: Sales Analysis Prepared from SOP History

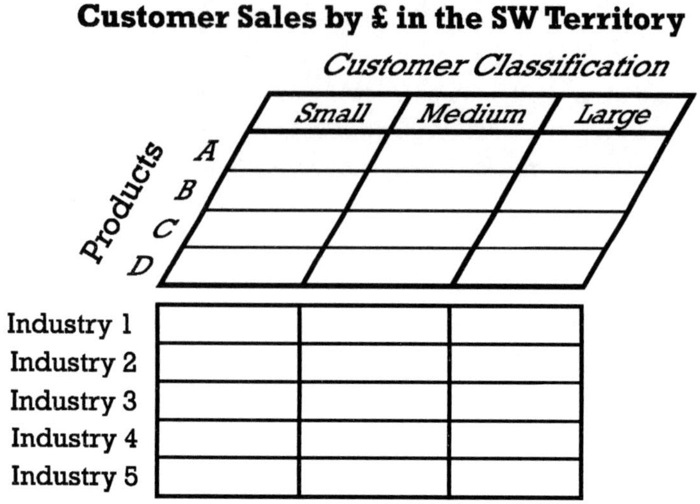

Customer Sales by £ in the SW Territory

Customer Classification

	Small	Medium	Large
Products A			
B			
C			
D			
Industry 1			
Industry 2			
Industry 3			
Industry 4			
Industry 5			

It should be borne in mind, however, that figures alone are not enough for the evaluation of results. Field reports and memos must be compiled and studied to discern the "soft" facts about the territories.

2.4 SALES ORDER PROCESSING

The receipt of a customer's order occasions much activity and involves a great many staff from different departments and functions within the firm. Sales clerks allocate stock to the order and make themselves generally responsible for the procedures that lead ultimately to the receipt of goods by the customer. Stores or warehouse staff retrieve goods and prepare them for despatch. Clerks within the accounting function generate and send the invoice. Distribution personnel transport the goods. The efficiency and good management of the SOP system contribute very markedly to the perception of service that its customers have of the company, although they are not, perhaps, as important contributors as freedom of the goods supplied from non-conformances or their availability from stock in the first place. Nevertheless, the SOP activities have their positions in any league table of customer service qualities. It is consequently desirable that the performance of each one should be monitored and tracked by Shewhart control charts,

Sales and Marketing

as described in sub-section 13.2.2 and illustrated in Figure 13.3. Individual SOP measures which might be subjected to monitoring are:

- The time to complete administration and produce documentation, from the point of order receipt (control limits from h_1 hours to h_2 hours);

- The delay between the despatch of goods and the issue of an invoice (range from ... to ...);

- The percentage of invoices that are error-free (range from $p_1\%$ to $p_2\%$);

- The percentage of despatches within the range of planned transport times (from ... to ...);

- The percentage of deliveries made within the planned time (range from ... to ...).

A characteristic of service valued by all customers as highly as quality and availability is dependability. Dependability — reliability and consistency of response to orders — comes about from the good management of an effective, stable system of procedures.

In the modern company employing a computerised, usually on-line, sales order processing system, access will have to be made to several important database files. These include free stock quantities on-hand, orders, accounts and others, and should include also direct access to the master schedule, for reasons explained in Section 7.2 in connection with "available-to-promise". A dataflow diagram of the complete SOP system is given in Figure 2.5, showing the database files typically involved.[11] The rounded rectangular blocks are *processes* or *activity steps*, and are commented on in the text below, roughly in the sequence top-to-bottom, left-to-right as the blocks are drawn. It need hardly be said that there will be considerable differences in detail from one company's system to another.

---

[11] *Structured Systems Analysis* by Chris Gane and Trish Sarson (1977), Improved System Technologies Inc. This book contains clear explanation of dataflow diagramming techniques and structured flowcharting.

42   *The Manufacturing Manager*

Figure 2.5: Dataflow Diagram of the Sales Order Processing System

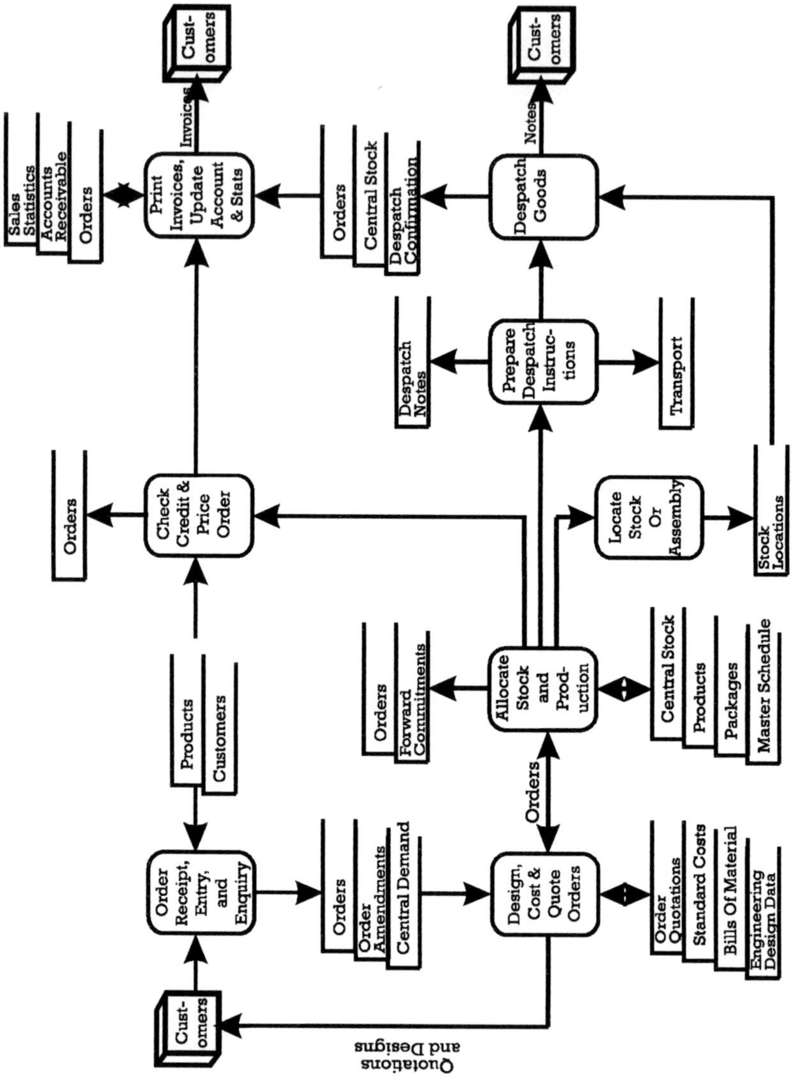

- **Order Receipt, Entry and Enquiry.** When an order is received, a unique company order number is assigned to it automatically by computer. From this point, the order number is the key to the availability of information throughout the system about the progress of the order and the key also to direct access to the order as more and more data are accrued and appended to the record.

- **Design, Cost and Quote Orders.** In companies that make to order, special data will need to be accessed prior to negotiation with the customer and the quotation of a price. In both orders direct from stock and orders to be specially made, "conditional" stock or production facilities will need to be held in a special *earmarked* category, to protect them for the time being against allocation by other data entry clerks, until negotiations are complete or until all orders in a multi-line order have been fully dealt with.

- **Allocate Stock and Production.** If there really is a prior stage of *Design, Cost and Quote*, this step is essentially the Available-to-Promise allocation explained in master schedule management (Section 7.2). If there is no such prior stage, then it follows that there is a direct link between *Order Receipt* and *Allocate Stock,* and receipt and allocation are asynchronous. That is, the actions are taken by a single order processing clerk in an unbroken succession of logically linked transactions — perhaps half a dozen transactions over about 60 seconds. The high efficiency achieved is typical of mail order companies and others in which the flow of work to the terminals can be manipulated by the seller; where stock allocation is simple; and in which there is no delay as the customer thinks over quotations.

- **Check Credit, Price Order.** The point in the system at which a customer's credit standing is to be checked varies widely from company to company.

- **Locate Stock or Assembly.** The required quantities of packaged products must be found within the stores or warehouse and moved to a preparation and despatch area.

- **Prepare Despatch Instructions.** Despatch instructions are produced for warehousemen, transport allocators, drivers and others, and shipping and export documentation if goods are to be shipped overseas. Firm arrangements are made at this stage for transportation itself, including the building up of trunk and container loads and the special handling of urgent or critical orders.

- **Despatch Goods.** Products are checked and sent. When stock is physically despatched, details are entered at a computer terminal to update the records on three database files:

  1. *The Despatch Confirmation*: a definitive description of what actually made up the load, used by accounting staff as a reference before the creation of the invoice;

  2. *The Central Stock File*: stock held at this point in the category of "allocated" is debited by the amount despatched;

  3. *The Database Orders File*: the order record is updated with the date and details of despatch.

- **Print Invoices, Update Accounts Receivable and Sales Statistics.** Despatch confirmation data from the "Despatch" process just described is matched with order details holding customer information, product quantities, prices, packages, tax and other financial and commercial data. Invoices are printed and sent to customers, and the company's Accounts Receivable file updated. Extracts of information are input to the Sales Statistics file. (When payment has been received, the order details will be transferred to a history file and the order record deleted from the main database file.)

2.5 Sales Forecasting

Although "sales forecasting" is a general term, in practice in the manufacturing concern it consists of, or ought to consist of, two distinct and separate activities, with separate objectives, performed by separate groups of staff: (1) medium- and long-term forecasting; and (2) short-term demand forecasting. Sales forecasts over medium- and long-term horizons are required for marketing, capi-

Sales and Marketing 45

tal and financial planning purposes and long-term consideration of the business. The forecasts are prepared by the Sales and Marketing department, and are worked on also by accountants, corporate planners and senior managers. Short-term demand forecasts are required as essential input to the master planning and distribution logistics processes. They are prepared largely by statistical means and most assuredly should not be in the hands of the Sales and Marketing department.

Because in many companies they *are* in fact in the hands of Sales and Marketing, a word of explanation is due. First, short-term forecasts, as the name says, range from the immediate month ahead up to the master plan horizon, and are projections based on current demand trends and patterns, obtained through objective statistical analysis. They are *not* medium-term prospects reflective of the hopes and aspirations of the Marketing department and the optimism and conviction of the sales force. It is inevitable that in the hands of Sales and Marketing staff, short-term forecasts that reflect what really is happening will be amended by them to reflect what they would like to see happening — i.e. to their own targets and quotas. Secondly, the short-term forecasting system itself must be run consistently and regularly to produce forecasts for every product, without fail, over the complete master plan horizon, taking into account such complex matters as seasonality, trend and random fluctuations in past demand, and stripping out the chatter of everyday sales. It is a dry numerical system, devoid of Marketing department razzmatazz.

Short-term forecasting is dealt with in Chapter 4, and, when they have read it, it is unlikely that many sales and marketing staff will wish to control the system involved. Even so, there is a requirement for them to contribute to it when they have specific evidence that a current pattern of product demand will soon undergo significant change not predictable statistically. Two circumstances under which sales must post information to the system are as described below.

New Products

As illustrated in Figure 2.1 and described in sub-section 2.1.2, the demand for a successful new product after the time of its launch goes through a period of rapid acceleration before levelling off to maturity. Statistical forecasting would extrapolate the initial growth far above the maturity level and if applied will produce misleading results. New products must therefore be flagged as exceptions and managed by sales staff within the system individually.

Promotions

The sudden change in demand created by a sales promotion clearly cannot be anticipated by statistics, and must be incorporated into the forecast in sufficient time for stocks to be built up by way of the master schedule. The potential effectiveness of the promotion may simply be guessed at from experience, or it may be gauged by first conducting trials in some small, defined local area. Although the outcome of the total promotion is usually very difficult to predict accurately before it starts, it is reported that once the effect on sales of the first week is available, the remaining sales in even quite a lengthy campaign are relatively easy to estimate.[12] Clearly, Sales and Marketing must feed back such revised figures to the master scheduler immediately. The change in demand pattern often obtained is illustrated in Figure 2.6. Point A in the Figure denotes the normal level of demand. At point B on the graph, the market holds back waiting for the offer to start. It reaches a first peak at C and, after declining, may achieve a second sharp peak at D as customers realise that the offer really is a good idea. Point E is the end of the promotion span, which rarely cuts off on the exact scheduled finish date. Depressed sales may well continue past point E because of previous stocking up by customers during the promotion itself.

Marketing must judge the shape, heights and timings of the uplifts and depressions from the first effects to the last. It is also necessary to predict the effect of extra demand for the promoted product on other items sold by the company.

Other requirements for Sales and Marketing's contribution to the short-term forecasting system occur when significant price changes are planned to important products and when product discontinuations are to be made. In conjunction with senior managers, estimates must also be made of the uplift in demand at, say,

---

[12] *Logistics Focus* (magazine of the Institute of Logistics, Corby) Vol. 5, No. 2 (March 1997), Anthony H. Lines.

Christmas and Easter for products with very heavy sales at those times.

Figure 2.6: Changes in Sales Volume during a Product Promotion

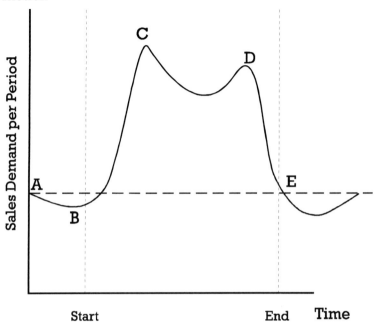

Intervention in short-term forecasting by sales and marketing staff is intended to add significantly to the forecast accuracy that would otherwise be achieved, not to provide a forum for analysing the latest sales leads. Consequently, individual forecast changes should be monitored and their effects, whether improvement or degradation, discussed by those responsible for the operation of the system. The topic is discussed further in Chapter 4.

We return now to medium and long-term forecasting, which truly are in the hands of the Sales and Marketing Department. Two techniques are described, the first commonly used to prepare annual forecasts and the second associated with forecasts over much longer terms.

1. The Consensus Method

This is a five-stage process illustrated in Figure 2.7. Comments are as follows:

- **Stage I:** Each salesman prepares a forecast by product, quarter by quarter, over (say) the next year for his territory.
- **Stage II:** The sales manager vets the figures and questions those that appear unusual or that are apparently inconsistent. Forecasts, in units, are converted to money terms.
- **Stage III:** The figures are adjusted by corporate planning or marketing staff to take account of known or believed new developments and trends and to correct obvious, gross misjudgements.
- **Stage IV:** Senior managers examine forecasts within the context of the corporate plan — implied levels of production, staff numbers, revenue, profit, etc. Sales forecasts may be revised in financial terms at the product group level.
- **Stage V:** Revised figures from Stage III are converted from money to units of product. They are issued and used in such detailed planning areas as mentioned earlier, i.e. marketing and financial planning, especially as they concern the setting of budgets and quotas and the formulation of the annual profit plan.

Figure 2.7: Procedures in Sales Forecasting by Consensus

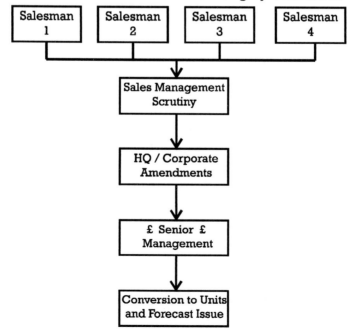

2. The Delphi Method

Despite a name that suggests at first that it might be more than a little esoteric, the Delphi Method has been found to be straightforward and to give good results. It is used when very long-term forecasts must be formulated — say, three or five years ahead, or still further. The steps are:

- **Step 1:** A group of experts is selected comprised of people who are believed to have a good knowledge of sales and the market — for example, senior salesmen, the sales manager, market research staff.

- **Step 2:** Each expert is sent a questionnaire by the exercise leader relating to sales in the period under question. The questions are open-ended or multiple choice. *Each questionnaire is to be completed in isolation by each expert receiving it.*

- **Step 3:** Returns are collected and analysed by the leader, and the averages and ranges of the (quantitative) replies worked out.

- **Step 4:** The averages and ranges worked out from all replies (Step 3) and a copy of his own replies to the original questionnaire are returned to each individual. Comments and corrections to his own original replies are elicited in the light of the group's opinions.

- **Step 5:** The returns from Step 4 are analysed. Secrecy and individualism are now abandoned, and, in a group, individual respondents who are persistent in their "extreme" views are asked to explain their reasons. The reasons, the discussion of them and the light they throw on the future are the most important outcomes of the Delphi process.

- **Step 6 and onwards:** Steps 4 and 5 are repeated until no further worthwhile change occurs.

Chapter 3

Product Innovation

3.1 THE PRODUCT BRIEF

The importance of product development to the very survival of the company, and the determination of the direction of that development, especially through market research, were dealt with at length in Chapter 2. There, the remark was made that the senior partner in decisions about new products and enhancements to existing ones is the Marketing Department. It is Marketing's job to establish what the customer wants. Very quickly, however, as customer preferences for a potential product are expanded on and the statements on goals relating to a product become firmer and more technical, the necessity for a team that includes design engineering expertise becomes apparent. Indeed, as matters proceed, the design engineer is likely to assume the team's leadership. Included on the team, for reasons that will be explained in due course, will be a representative of production engineering. Other members of it will include representatives from purchasing and cost accountancy. *The important point is that the team is multidisciplinary from the start, so that the expertise of its members can be contributed continuously to the successful achievement of the ultimate goal.*

The stage at which the product idea is formulated is referred to as the preparation of the *product brief*, or simply *the brief*. There are no rules for the degree of detail to be contained in the final document. Detail will, however, ultimately be needed. Senior management may be reluctant to sanction work and money on subsequent design stages if they regard the brief as superficial.

The following subjects are likely to be dealt with in the brief. The list is far from comprehensive, but gives a good idea of the background research and analysis needed.

- *Market Trends*: quarterly statistics on manufacturers' sales, business monitors, industrial surveys — see market research, sub-section 2.2.2;

- *Competitive and Analogous Products*: this data will include products sold abroad as well as in the UK, and are often obtainable from catalogues and other sales sources;

- *Parametric Analysis*: analyses of competitive products from the viewpoint of their physical characteristics, such as capacity, speed, power consumption, energy efficiency and so on. Parametric analysis may yield valuable pointers to gaps in the market;

- *Legislation and Patents*: examples here are data relating to noise levels, speed limits, the emission of fumes, age limits on machinery;

- *Reports and Proceedings*: it would not be unusual for a major brief to require the absorption by design engineers of several hundred papers from technical journals, including many in the area of pure research;

- *Official Bodies*: the BSI, trade associations and social pressure groups;

- *"Analysis of Features"*: the team may construct a matrix of successful competitive product models (on one axis) and product features (the second axis).

As said, the most important attribute of the product brief is that it should be a true and accurate statement of real customer wants (though perhaps with a dash of something extra — a little fizz besides). The system by which such a statement is compiled is referred to in design management as *Quality Function Deployment* (QFD). Quality function deployment is a procedure devised by

Yoji Akado in Japan, in 1966, and comprises three stages.[1] The *quality stage* entails identifying what it is the customer truly wants. The *function stage* is the identification of the product features or service functions needed to fulfil customers' wants. At the *deployment stage*, the means required to deliver function are analysed in terms of the resources at the company's disposal — research and design capability; manufacturing ability; marketing and selling organisation; the width and manner of distribution; and (say) any required ability to fulfil field service demands. Stage 1 of QFD is key, and is referred to by the highly apposite phrase *listening to the voice of the customer*. Quality function deployment is a procedure nowadays used heavily in design, and the point is made by practitioners that to hear what the customer is saying requires truly to discern real requirements, by positive investigation, and definitely not to guess or surmise what those wants may be. To summarise here in the product brief, the imperative is that the *voice of the customer* is heard above all others.

3.2 PRODUCT DESIGN — THE PRINCIPAL STAGES

The stages of design are shown in Figure 3.1, so that it may appear, at final completion at least, that everything proceeded in a straight line. In fact, the process is iterative, as indicated in the figure by the broken lines and backwards arrows. It may be found at Stage III that a physical infeasibility exists, leading to a review of Stage II or even of Stage I. There may be a product breakthrough — say, a realisation at Stage II that a different but greatly superior product is capable of being developed, with a specification different from Stage I. As said, the return to such prior stages is denoted by the backwards arrows. *The paramount point is that the right activities are carried out at the right stages. If they are not, confusion will result.* Engineering design must *not* be done at the specification stage. Specifications must *not* be altered at the design stage. If amendments to previous stages are needed, there must be a formal going back and a partial recommencement of the process.

---

[1] Yoki Akado (ed.) (1990), *Quality Function Deployment*, Productivity Press. This is the "original" book, but better for QFD, see R.G. Day (1993), *Quality Function Deployment: Linking a Company with its Customer*, ASQC Quality Press, Milwaukee, WI. See also Chapter 18 in Barrie Dale (1994), op. cit.

Figure 3.1: Links between the Principal Stages of Design

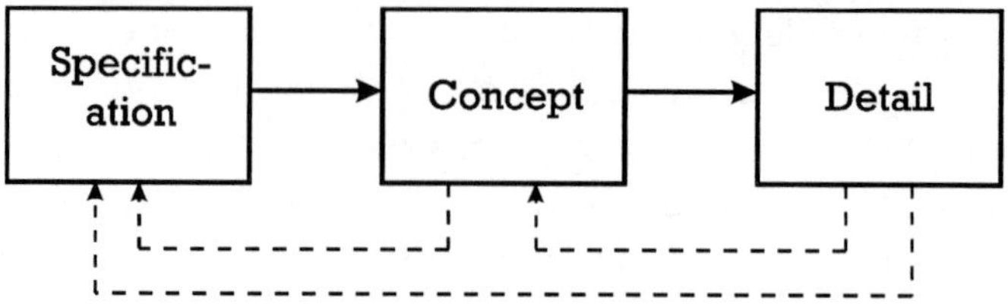

```
┌──────────┐      ┌──────────┐      ┌──────────┐
│ Specific-│      │          │      │          │
│   ation  │─────▶│ Concept  │─────▶│  Detail  │
│          │      │          │      │          │
└──────────┘      └──────────┘      └──────────┘
     ▲ ▲               ▲  ▲              ╷
     ╷ └───────────────┘  └──────────────┘
     └──────────────────────────────────────
```

3.2.1 The Product Design Specification

The *product design specification* (PDS) is a comprehensive and unambiguous statement of the features and characteristics that the new product is to have. A lengthy list of likely required features and characteristics to be covered is given in due course. While high technical expertise is needed to answer each point in any such list, it must be emphasised again that this is *specification*, not *design*; design solutions must not enter into the PDS process. If design ideas are generated during the process, they should simply be recorded for later consideration at the correct stage. Again, in later conceptual or even detailed design, a highly attractive idea may be formulated that might be at odds with the specification. Again, if it is to be pursued, there must be a formal going back to the PDS (or even back to the product brief stage).

The strict division between specification and design, while necessary, may often be difficult to maintain among enthusiastic young designers. Inevitably, the learning process of design itself in later stages will lead to new knowledge and create pressure to change the PDS, or will lead down exciting new avenues. The discipline of requiring a return to the PDS, before any deviation is explored from the engineering view, forces consideration to be taken of its repercussions in the cold light of the commercial reality on which the PDS and product brief were based. In short, the PDS may be a constantly evolving document, but as each step is taken, a check must be made with market requirements — constant attention to the voice of the customer.

A word should be said about the style of the PDS document. The important principle, again, is that it should contain what it is supposed to contain — specifications — and must not be an attempt to pre-empt design. That apart, it must be remembered by the design engineer that marketing and other non-technical staff must be able to comprehend it. Typically, the PDS will comprise tables, boxes, graphs and the like, rather than abstruse or over-detailed description. It must be recalled that at the end of the complete design activity, the form of the new product will be an image of the specification. A good PDS does not guarantee eventual success, but a poor one does guarantee failure.

Twenty-two major elements likely to be covered in a PDS are given in the list below. There should be no gaps in the specification. If gaps do exist, they are liable to be closed in time by *ad hoc* or informal solutions which may be excessively expensive to provide or may be contrary to what customers want. Attempts at the PDS stage to save time by skimping on detail will be paid for at later stages by disproportionate difficulties and delays.

Elements of the PDS

1. *Product Performance:*[2] speed limits, electrical tolerances etc., including the conditions under which performance is to be achieved (e.g. under water). Performance targets differentiate between maximum, general, limits, economic, etc.

2. *Environment*: the general conditions such as temperature and pressure ranges that the machine must withstand (dirt, dust, humidity, corrosive chemicals). *Environment* includes environment in manufacture, transport and storage, as well as in actual use. The degree of "misuse" to which the product is likely to be subjected should be considered. How will the machine be tested to gauge its performance in extreme conditions?

3. *Life in Service*: is this to be "long" or "short"? (And what is long or short?)

---

[2] The engineers setting specifications must beware a double trap: (1) setting limits of performance that are too narrow, making the product expensive to manufacture, and (2) over-specifying performance, especially with regard to functions that hardly matter. Over-specification is not uncommon with machines engineered to order, with the result that the client gets what he doesn't care about, and pays too much for it. See Taguchi, sub-section 3.3.5 below.

4. *Maintenance*: ease of access to parts required/not required; need for special tools, the need to provide spare parts (see, importantly, TPM — sub-section 15.6.2).

5. *Target Cost*: cost limits, target price and target profit. Running costs.

6. *Transportation and Delivery*: feasibility and costs of transporting to customers.

7. *Packing and Protection*.

8. *Quantity Expected to be Made*: from a "one-off" with little special tooling, to a major new range requiring complete retooling.

9. *Size and Weight*.

10. *Appearance*: shape, form, texture, general attractiveness. (Remember! the customer will see it before he uses it.)

11. *Materials*: what special materials are to be used, and which are to be avoided?

12. *Standards and/or Specifications*.

13. *Ergonomics*: "the study of the relationship between people and their working environment" (OED) — thus, the literal physical relationship between the machine and the person who will make it; and the physical relationship between the machine and the person who will eventually use it (the position of switches and other controls, operator comfort, accessibility for maintenance). A particularly powerful means of assessing potential ergonomic characteristics used increasingly widely in design is through virtual reality: links can be established between CAD files and relatively inexpensive VR emulation software.

14. *Customer*: preferences expressed through market research.

15. *Quality and Reliability* (see sub-section 3.4.2): Mean Time To Failure — MTTF.

16. *Shelf Life*.

17. *Processes of Manufacture*.

18. *Existing Company Products*: the relative performance and characteristics of other products on the company's range, and (i) the way this one fits in, and (ii) the possible displacement from the range of an existing product by this one.

19. *Legal*: product liability law and cases; likely repercussions in the event of the manufacture of non-conforming items.

20. *Installation*: power capability; holes for fixing supports.

21. *Documentation*: requirements here can vary from the need to provide only brief one-page instructions to the necessity for massive effort in compiling multi-volume manuals and instructional videos and CDs.

22. *Disposal*.

Design Reviews

Formal *design reviews* are an essential part of engineering design management and the proper framework for design improvements. The basis of the review process is the review of the PDS, because it is here where all design features have their origin. Design reviews should be carried out frequently, with comparisons made between progress and goals. The PDS must be formally updated after a review. The effect of a decision to change the product's design after it has entered manufacture must clearly be followed through in such areas as technical and sales literature, shop floor instructions, product routings and the bill of materials. Changes to the bill of materials are dealt with in Section 3.5. The PDS is a major document for the evaluation of *quality of conformance* (to design) — see Total Quality Control (Chapter 13), especially sub-section 13.1.6.

3.2.2 The Conceptual Design Stage

This is the stage of creativity and ideas, and is usually best tackled at the start by individuals working alone rather than in groups. However it may be tackled, the PDS must always be to hand, for unless it meets specification, the most brilliant idea is worthless. Each engineer will have his own way of working and generating ideas, perhaps through one or other of the five processes listed below. After the initial phase, however, it is usually preferable for individual thinking to give way to team endeavour. While individuals are capable of deep and original thought, teams are better at discarding and selecting ideas, the discussion in doing so often leading to refinements or the opening up of new avenues. A few aids to creativity used by both individuals and teams are as follows:

- *Analogy*: Analogies suggest solutions to a problem based on situations and solutions in other areas of engineering and can lead to dramatic breakthroughs — shutters on a camera and Venetian blinds; aircraft carrier ramps and water ski jumps; etc.

- *Attributes Lists*: Sparking ideas by considering lists of contrasting general attributes such as: heavy and light; rough and smooth; hollow, square, and oblong.

- *Checklists*: A standard checklist may be useful if the design is an extension of the company's existing range of technology. Generalised checklists have also been developed and published for general use.[3]

- *Inversion and Combination*: If a product or design already exists, what can be done if we try the opposite of it? — inside out; on the top, not the bottom.

- *Brainstorming*: The rapid generation of key terms for later perusal (usually only by teams).

Ideas must not proceed too far before they are tested, either by practical engineering work, the generation and examination of computer simulation models or — more likely at this stage — through the scrutiny of a group or team as discussed above. The problem-solving techniques associated with total quality control (TQC) may also prove valuable for teams, especially use of the Ishikawa (fishbone) diagram — see sub-section 13.2.4 in this volume and Chapter 17 in *Managing Quality* (footnote 1 above).

The wrong choice of concept or idea can never be made up for in later stages of the design process, no matter how well they are done. Great attention must be paid, therefore, to the way the group

---

[3] A. Osborne (1957), *Applied Imagination*.

Product Innovation

sorts out and evaluates the contenders. The chosen technique must be capable of taking into account engineering feasibility and compatibility, and ensuring, so far as it is possible at this stage, that design will meet specification.

Controlled Convergence

A method put forward by Stuart Pugh[4] for evaluating designs is through a matrix of criteria and design contenders, and is referred to by him as a "controlled convergence". Controlled convergence acknowledges that conceptual designs cannot be truly evaluated, since the physical entities to which they relate do not yet exist. It is necessary, therefore, to select a yardstick against which competing designs can be compared, on a simple "better or worse" basis. A yardstick chosen might be a real competitive product or, if none exists, simply the apparently best conceptual design of those being compared.

Step 1 of controlled convergence consists of the formulation by an evaluation team of 20 or 30 "attributes" against which the contending designs are to be considered. The attributes must be derived from the PDS and must be clear and unambiguous. Examples of attributes that might be covered are: *resistance to corrosion in the open air; ease of maintenance; ease of achieving 1000–2000 Hz; response time.*

At Step 2, each design is considered in turn, the likely potential performance and characteristics of each one being considered under the headings of the attributes formulated in Step 1. If it is believed that the eventual product would be superior to the yardstick with regard to a given attribute, it is marked "+", if inferior it is marked "–" and if the same, "0". If, at the end of Step 2, any designs turn out to be inferior *and cannot be improved by modification*, they are rejected.

An alternative to Pugh's controlled convergence for assessing each contending design is the familiar *weights and marks* method. Each attribute is considered in turn by the team, each team member voting it a *weight* (out of ten) according to its importance as he sees it. The weight finally assigned to the attribute is the average of

---

[4] Stuart Pugh (1991), *Total Design*, Addison-Wesley.

the votes cast. Next, each contending design is considered by the members of the team, à propos the potential product's likely fulfilment of each of the attributes that have been weighted. Each team member *marks* the design (out of ten) in relation to each attribute, the final marks arrived at again being the averages. A score is an attribute weight × the design mark, each final design's score overall being the sum of the individual scores. It has been said that the weights and marks method masks an inexact process with spurious exactitude, and perhaps so.[5] On the other hand, the necessity to assign numbers out of ten forces each team participant to think most carefully about the issues, and any team member casting a vote very different from those cast by others is identified and is able to explain his reason.

To return to Pugh's method, Step 3 is iterative and consists of going into greater and greater detail with a shorter and shorter list of design contenders. It is important that if one design is investigated in greater detail with respect to a particular feature that the other designs are similarly further investigated with regard to that feature.

Pugh claims that controlled convergence eliminates bias and irrational preferences, especially those supported by pushy individuals or by those who have become over-enthusiastic champions of just one particular contender. He also claims that the attempt to modify designs before otherwise discarding them is a valuable long stop.

The Outcome of the Conceptual Design Stage

The outcome of the conceptual design phase is a design that has been engineered sufficiently far down the path to determine its "validity" — i.e. whether it will work, how it will work and what its likely attributes will be. The end result of the phase includes a drawing, either on paper or in CAD form, and, if it is technically and financially feasible to produce one, a physical model or prototype.

---

[5] The value of weights-and-marks is the direction it gives to the process of choice, certainly not the individual scores arrived at. In reality, these can never be reproduced and are therefore best not published in any final team report.

3.2.3 Detail Design

Detail design constitutes 75 per cent of the design work and in practice is usually concerned with the major and minor components to be incorporated in the final product — circuits, beams, bearings, capacitors — *traditional engineering*. Poor detail design will destroy an excellent design concept, although brilliant detail will never rescue a poor concept.

While it is clearly essential to carry out detailed design in the context of the conceptual design to which it relates, what is just as important is to have regard to the interfacing of each component in the final product to all other components, especially those in close proximity. In short, in defining one component, a constraint is placed on all others.

Individual components are treated like the main product. That is, each one must also be specified and designed, albeit that its context within the overall design is an important factor to be taken account of in so doing. The required characteristics of a component can be listed in a way similar to the listing of characteristics in the product design specification. Also to be included is its housing in the main machine and its proximity to other working parts. Examples of characteristics that might be included are: *environment, safety, maintenance, reliability, shelf life, ergonomics, weight* and *material*.

Detail design is the hub of design engineering and there are numerous aids to conducting it. The best known of them is CAD (computer aided design). CAD systems have their origin in the aerospace and automotive industries of the 1950s and were originally conceived as being means of modifying existing designs (say, for scaling them up). They are now used for 3D modelling, geometric analysis, drafting and quantitative analysis (e.g. parts lists). It is acknowledged as being easier to break off and pick up again detailed design work through CAD than when done manually. CAD is limiting and less than wholly useful before the detailed stage.

Perhaps the most important precept of detailed design, however, is to strive for simplicity. Reasons for this are given in Section 3.3. In particular, the engineer must bring to bear the theory of structures and the analysis of load paths that are part and parcel of structural engineering, instead of concentrating always on the function of components.

3.3 "*Design for*" Manufacture

Aims of design for manufacture are to minimise component and assembly costs, to minimise the development cycle time and to enable eventual high levels to be achieved of conformance to specification (i.e. high levels of quality). That is, in this context, "manufacture" includes not only production itself but these other associated matters.

In the past — the recent past for rather too many companies — manufacturing issues were hardly considered until design was complete, with a consequence often then of unduly high costs, difficult quality problems and very long cycle times from product inception to product launch. In this Section, a number of "design fors" relating to manufacture are discussed. But first, a word of caution. If the engineer *designs for* one characteristic X, it is possible he may impact another characteristic, Y, in doing so. If he designs for quality, the result may be higher cost, and so on. A balance must be struck. All the "design fors" must be considered together.

3.3.1 Design for Low Cost

All product costs have their origin in design. However, any method of costing the future final product applied at the design stage will clearly give only an approximate result. A reasonable goal is to be able to estimate cost to within, say, 10 per cent of what it turns out finally to be, and to be able to do so quickly. A starting point for the company is a good knowledge of the costs of existing products in relation to their power and performance (see Section 17.4). Also to be taken into account when either the product or the process is new is the *learning curve*, or *experience curve*.

The learning curve expresses quantitatively a phenomenon that consumers frequently experience, namely that novel products which are initially expensive to buy become cheaper over time and eventually reach stable prices considerably lower than their original ones. In other words, and since prices are usually a reflection of costs, the more that is manufactured of a given product, the better the manufacturer becomes at doing so. By "better" may be

Product Innovation

meant faster or with fewer non-conformances or with fewer resources or with quicker set-ups — any number of improvements may be brought about, each one having an effect on the cost of production.

In order to estimate future cost levels of a manufactured item after costs have been determined for initial production, advantage can be taken of a general relationship between cost of manufacture and the number of items made. This states that *each time the total quantity of items produced doubles, the average cost to produce each one of them (i.e. the average of all of them made so far) decreases by the same constant percentage.*

For example, suppose that we make the very first batch ever of 10 aeroengine parts for £100.00 — this being the direct, or prime, cost as calculated through the company's cost reporting system.[6] The average cost per part is thus £10.00. Now we make another 10 parts. The cost to make them turns out to be £60.00, so that the total cost to make the first 20 parts is £160.00. The average cost per part for the first 20 parts is thus £8.00. If the learning curve rule applies, then the "constant percentage" referred to in the last sentence of the paragraph above, in this particular case, is 80 per cent, i.e.:

$$\frac{\pounds 8.00 \ (average \ cost \ of \ the \ first \ 20)}{\pounds 10.00 \ (average \ cost \ of \ the \ first \ 10)} \times 100$$

This means that, for these particular parts, if we manufacture 40 of them in total (i.e. doubling up from the present total of 20), then the average cost for all 40 parts will fall to £6.40 each (£8.00 x 80 per cent). Now if the average per part for all 40 parts is £6.40, the total cost for them all is £256.00. But the first 20 parts cost £160.00, so that this last 20 will cost £96.00.

Learning curve relationships are not particularly easy to write down in a straightforward table, but one very satisfactory way of expressing them in any given situation is through a log–log graph. This is illustrated in Figure 3.2 for the aeroengine parts and the learning rate of 80 per cent. Note the log scale of the vertical axis (average cost per unit of all those made so far) and the log scale of the horizontal axis (the total number made so far).

---

[6] A.J. Tubb (1977), *Cost Accounting*, Hodder and Stoughton.

Figure 3.2: The Learning Curve

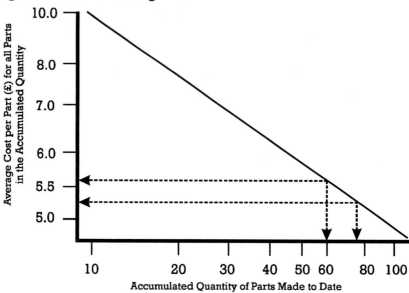

Use of the learning curve can be valuable in assessing future costs and product selling prices, and hence the likely changes in market appeal and manufacturing volumes over time. Besides the technique's incorporation in many software suites, two further practical means of making the calculations are by graph and by formula. In both cases, if costs are to be well estimated at the design stage, a learning curve slope must be decided upon, perhaps chosen from experience with similar products or processes. Naturally, after the product has entered production, the slope of the line can be determined by observation. Here, note that the specific cost of manufacturing the first item should not be used as the basis of the calculations in the equation (see Equation 3.1), because of possible errors or abnormal conditions prevailing during this first manufacture. Instead, the costs of the first "few" should be studied and the cost of the first one worked out from them.

Graphical Solution

As soon as a number of points have been obtained relating to real total costs and total quantities made, a graph can be drawn on a log–log scale as illustrated in Figure 3.2 above, fitting the best straight line to the points plotted.

Product Innovation

The use of the graph in Figure 3.2 is demonstrated by considering the requirement to cost a future parcel of work for 15 of the aeroengine parts, the batch of work to start when it is calculated that 60 parts will by then have been made.

From the graph, we can read off the average cost per part (i) when 60 parts have been made, and (ii) when 75 parts have been made. Thus:

(i) When 60 parts have been made, the average per part is approximately £5.60 each. Consequently the total cost to make all 60 is 60 × £5.60 = £336.00.

(ii) When 75 parts have been made, the average per part is approximately £5.25 each. Consequently the total cost to make all 75 is 75 × £5.25 = £393.75.

From (i) and (ii) we see that the cost to make the last 15 parts is the difference of the two totals, i.e. £57.75 in all (i.e. on average, £3.85 each).

Computer/Calculator Solution

Computer solutions are based on the mathematics of the learning curve as given in Equation 3.1.

$$C_n = c_1 n^{-r} \qquad \text{Equation 3.1}$$

where C_n = the average cost per unit to make the first n units;
c_1 = the cost of making the first unit;
n = the number of units made;
r = an expression for the learning curve, derived by logarithms as follows:

$$r = \frac{\log L}{\log 2}$$

. . . and where L is the learning rate as defined earlier, but expressed as a fraction rather than a percentage. A small selection of values is given in Table 3.1.

Table 3.1: Learning Rates Relating to the Learning Curve

L%	L	r
90%	0.90	0.152
85%	0.85	0.234
80%	0.80	0.322
75%	0.75	0.415
70%	0.70	0.515

In the aeroengine problem, the first task is to calculate r. As before, we first calculate the learning rate L as:

$$\frac{\text{The average cost per part for 20 parts}}{\text{The average cost per part for 10 parts}} = 0.80$$

... whence r = 0.322 from consultation of Table 3.1, giving the relationships between values of L and r.

The second task is to calculate c_1, the cost of the first part. Thus using the data for 10 parts,

$$10.00 = c_1 \times 10^{-0.322}$$

whence c_1 = 20.83 (£)

This is an important result, which enables us to calculate any average cost per aeroengine part at once. For example, we can now readily calculate the average cost per part for making 60 parts and 75 parts:

$$C_{60} = 20.83 \times 60^{-0.322} \text{ (£)} = £5.57$$

$$C_{75} = 20.83 \times 75^{-0.322} \text{ (£)} = £5.19$$

The total cost for 60 parts is thus 60 × £5.57 (£334.20) and for 75 parts is 75 × £5.19 (£389.25) The difference to be attributed to the 15 parts in the package of work under discussion is thus £55.05, a cost of £3.67 each, the difference from the cost obtained graphically being due to the graphical approximations.

In practical terms, a useful extension of the mathematics is shown by Equation 3.2, which is valid when n is greater than 10. In the Equation, c_n is the cost to manufacture the nth object and C_n is the total cost to make the first n objects.

Product Innovation

$$c_n = C_n (1-r) \qquad \text{Equation 3.2}$$

Equation 3.2 is useful if there is a dispute between two parties — say, between the manufacturing company and its customer — as to the value of the learning rate. By measuring (say) the cost to make the 40th unit, and making sure that cost is representative, and knowing from production records the total cost of manufacture of these parts up to that point, the value of r can be recalculated.

3.3.2 Design for Piece Part Producibility

A critical formula through which to express complexity is given by Equation 3.3, in which N_p is the number of parts, N_t the number of types of parts, N_i is the number of interconnections and/or interfaces, and f is the number of functions the product must perform. The lower the complexity factor, the greater the product's reliability[7] and quality and the lower its cost.

$$\text{Complexity} \propto \frac{\sqrt[3]{N_p N_t N_i}}{f} \qquad \text{Equation 3.3}$$

3.3.3 Design for Assembly

Guidance on design for assembly from the viewpoint of what will physically happen in production has been provided as the result of a joint study undertaken by the University of Massachusetts and the University of Salford, the guidelines produced being in the form of a checklist named the UMASS system.[8] Of interest to the manufacturing manager, and notwithstanding comments on tolerances made in sub-section 3.3.5, is the question of tolerance analysis. Tolerance analysis addresses the possibility of assembling a part such that all of the tolerances of the components which have to

---

[7] Although the reasons for it are imperfectly understood, there is also a well-known relationship between product reliability in the field and the number of process interruptions during manufacture. Contributing reasons may be design afterthoughts or corrections of earlier mistakes.

[8] The UMASS system is a checklist of factors to be taken into account to minimise production assembly difficulties, and is described in G. Boothroyd *et al. Design for Assembly: A Designer's Handbook*. See also G. Boothroyd, "Design for Producibility: The Road to Higher Productivity", *Assembly Engineering* magazine, March 1982. See also G. Boothroyd and P. Dewhurst (1987), *Product Development for Assembly*, published by RI Boothroyd and Dewhurst Inc.

mate will stack against each other. That is, all the components will be at the limits of their tolerances in such a way that the tolerance of the mated assembly is exceeded. There are two ways to examine the possibility:

(a) Ensure the stacked tolerances do not exceed the assembly tolerance

Suppose that four mating tolerances are:

>T1 = +0.003" to -0.003" (spread of 0.006")
>
>T2 = +0.004" to -0.004" (spread of 0.008")
>
>T3 = +0.001" to -0.001" (spread of 0.002") and
>
>T4 = +0.005" to -0.005" (spread of 0.010")

The maximum spread is 0.026", so that either the assembly tolerance must be ±0.013" or, the more usual route, an attempt must be made to reduce individual tolerances.

(b) Assume tolerances will not stack

Essentially, engineers trust to luck that tolerances will balance out, or, as they would put it, to the laws of probability. Provided two conditions hold, it can be shown that the tolerance of mating parts such as the four above is T_n, where T_n is given in Equation 3.4.

$$T_n = \sqrt{T_1^2 + T_2^2 + T_3^2 + T_4^2} \qquad \text{Equation 3.4}$$

Using the previous values of T_1, T_2, T_3 and T_4 this gives (in thous):

$$T_n = \sqrt{6^2 + 8^2 + 2^2 + 10^2} = 0.014", \text{ or } \pm 0.007"$$

The tolerance of ±0.007" is almost half of the one previously worked out. The two conditions mentioned above in order to apply the formula are that all mating parts must have a normal distribution of tolerance (so no rework, for example) and that they should be manufactured on different machines, so that they do not have the same bias. Note that whether using method (a) or method (b), the analysis of tolerances in assembly allows the designer to make the easiest tolerance reduction. For example, reducing T_4 above to

±0.004" will be more effective — and possibly easier — than reducing T_1 to ±0.002".

A study of tolerance fittings fully illustrating the foregoing principles and involving the clearance between a socket (female) and an attachment (male) is given by W.B. Rice.[9] The study involves the use of SPC, dealt with in Chapter 14, and as such reminds the design engineer that in reality analysis of a quality dimension or tolerance shows a probability distribution (frequency histogram) — see especially sub-section 14.2.3.

3.3.4 Design for the Production Process

As implied throughout, thought must be given from the start to the process by which the product is to be manufactured. If the product can be made on existing plant, costs and risk are reduced and lead time to manufacture shortened, so much so that compromises may be made in design so that product and existing process will indeed fit. If the process required is new, it is designed, if possible, in parallel with the product itself. This may not be possible if the design of the product is fluid, but where it is possible, the carrying out of the two activities together is referred to as *simultaneous engineering*, or *concurrent engineering*. Simultaneous engineering avoids the mismatches and long delays that often result when the activities are performed serially. The parallel sets of steps involved are illustrated in Figure 3.3, although it must be admitted that process design will always lag product design to some extent.

The emphases in product and process design and the appropriateness or otherwise of a fully-fledged simultaneous engineering project depend on the relative maturity of the product idea and the relative maturity of the process. For example, if product design is in fact the design of a further version of an already existing product, process design is paramount in order to achieve cost savings over the old method. These emphases and relationships are illustrated in Figure 3.4.

---

[9] W.B. Rice (1944), "Setting Tolerances Scientifically", *Mechanical Engineering* (US Journal), Vol. 66, December. See also Eugene L. Grant and Richard S. Leavenworth (1996), *Statistical Quality Control*, Seventh edition, McGraw-Hill, Section 9.6.

Figure 3.3: Parallel Steps in Simultaneous Engineering

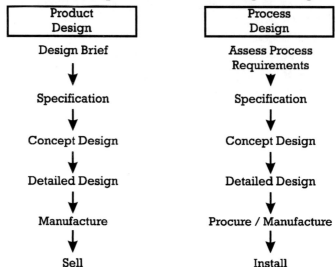

Figure 3.4: Priorities and Response — Product and Process Design

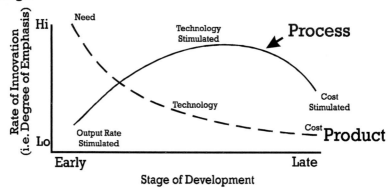

3.3.5 Design for Quality

Chapter 14 deals with Statistical Process Control, where it is explained that the variation in a product's physical attributes following manufacture is caused by the interplay of a number of factors detracting from the perfect operation of the process. Thus a particular dimension — say, the product's diameter — may be sometimes rather less and sometimes rather more than the target value, or ideal value, each time a unit is made, due to minute, random changes in the operating conditions of the machine of manufacture — conditions such as temperature, voltage and pressure, for example. At the design stage, one method of anticipating and alleviating this problem is to design and carry out experiments with a prototype product and process, in an attempt to identify and, if possible, deal with process fluctuations which will indeed have an effect on critical aspects of the product's quality. Isolating the effects of individual possible causes of process fluctuation, however, is a time-consuming and difficult matter. Even when it is accomplished, the problem still then remains of tackling the causes.

An alternative approach is now taken that is due to the Japanese statistician and engineer Genichi Taguchi.[10] Taguchi's method involves the investigation of alternative product or component designs and the selection of that design which results in the minimum range of functional performance of the product in use (subject, of course, to the range being within the limits required by the customer). The range of functional performance, from one product to the next, even though the production output is all to the same design, is the result of the variation in the physical dimensions of the manufactured articles. In turn, these differences are caused by the continual changes in operating conditions affecting the process, as explained above. Note, importantly, that with Taguchi it is not necessary to isolate the individual effects of the operating conditions, as it is in experimental design mentioned in the paragraph above.

Figure 3.5: Quality Variability of Three Alternative Designs

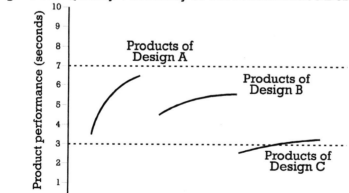

---

[10] G. Taguchi (1986), *Introduction to Quality Engineering*, UNIPUB — Kraus International Publications.

The principles of Taguchi's method are illustrated for ranges of performance relating to three alternative product designs A, B and C in the graph in Figure 3.5. The vertical axis of the graph is a measure of a particular aspect of the product's performance relating to time, expressed in seconds. The required performance limits of the product are from 3.0 seconds to 7.0 seconds. The variability in output of products of Design A is from 3.5 seconds to 6.5 seconds. While this is within requirements, the span of 3.0 seconds occupies virtually the whole of the permitted range, so that the user would potentially experience a considerable difference in performance from one manufactured unit to the next, even though each measure is, strictly, acceptable. The production of 100 per cent product quality through the process for A is also particularly vulnerable to the smallest problems in manufacture, so that extreme vigilance would be necessary to ensure that the process was maintained under control and that non-conformances (i.e. units with a performance outside the 3.0 to 7.0 range) were not produced. Design B is far more satisfactory. The susceptibility of these products to variations in manufacture is such that the span of performance is only 4.5 seconds to 5.5 seconds. Users will experience greater uniformity in the performance of the items produced and manufacturing control will be easier. Products made to Design C have a performance span of 2.75 seconds to 3.25 seconds and so are not within the range specified. However, it is noted that the span of 0.5 seconds is the lowest of the three. Before rejecting Design C, therefore, an investigation might be carried out to see if changes could be made to bring products of this design nearer to the mid-target of 5.0 seconds, perhaps, say, by the use of an alternative material.

The following definitions are encountered Taguchi terminology:

- *Tolerance design*: the extent of variability permitted in component parts;

- *Loss to society*: by society is meant the body of consumers constituting the supply marketplace, but denied satisfaction on receipt of bad quality;

- *Consumer tolerance*: the limits or range demanded by the product consumer, and equal to the following expression:

$$\sqrt{\frac{A}{A_0}} \times \frac{T}{2}$$

  where A is the price of the product, A_0 the cost to the consumer of obtaining a non-conforming unit and T the physical tolerance limits in manufacture;

- *LD50 (live/die 50:50)*: A yardstick used in drug testing, and the limit of functional performance at which 50 per cent of consumers will refuse to buy the product. By analogy, there is no absolute cut-off point for quality acceptable to the consumer, as there is for quality in physical manufacture. Taguchi's view is that as the difference between achieved manufacture and target value increases, the loss to society (above) increases exponentially;

- *Off-line quality control*: tests to assess the sensitivity of design to potential conditions in future manufacture;

- *On-line quality control*: control of the process during manufacture itself (Chapter 14).

It has been pointed out by the Institute of Statisticians (1987) that Taguchi's ideas are not new from the statistical and physical quality viewpoints. What is new and important is the bringing of them to bear at the stage of product and process design. Genichi Taguchi gained the individual Deming prize in 1960 for his work in this field (see sub-section 13.1.4). Training courses in Taguchi methodology are available in the UK.[11]

---

[11] See (1) ASI Quality Systems Ltd., Bletchley, Milton Keynes, Bucks., and (2) Smallpeice Enterprises Ltd., Leamington Spa (www.smallpeice.co.uk). Smallpeice have many short training courses in the area of design, FMCA, QFD, AutoCAD etc.

3.4 FAILURE AND RELIABILITY

3.4.1 Failure

Early in product design it is necessary to obtain some measure of the product's tendency to fail, so that special effort can be applied to reduce it through reliability analysis. The activity is known as *failure mode, effect and criticality analysis*, or FMECA, or again, FMEA. Definitions of the terms used are as follows:

- *Failure Mode*: "what happened?" — reaction of the component to whatever failed (e.g. circuit failure, loose stopcock);
- *Failure Mechanism*: "why?" — what was amiss that created the failure mode? — what was the cause? (e.g. incorrect assembly, wrong part supplied, forming temperature too high);
- *Effect of Failure*: "what then happened?" — the effect of the failure on the component, including also on the surrounding components (e.g. loss of control, leakage);
- *Corrective Action*: "what can be done about it?" — tighter tolerances, redesign, better conformance to instructions (e.g. new cutting machine, better operator training).

It should be stressed in FMECA that it is likely to be difficult to determine many of the causes, effects and corrective actions. In addition, it may not always be possible to make and test sufficient prototype products, or to test what are available for sufficiently long periods to induce failure or otherwise produce clear-cut results.

The FMECA results are normally set out as shown in Table 3.2. The columns P, D, S and I have the following meanings: P = probability of occurrence; D = likelihood of damage to the surrounding environment; S = the seriousness of the failure; $I = P \times D \times S$. The scale for P, D and S are typically: 1 = very low; 2 = low; 3 = likely; 4 = high; 5 = catastrophic.

Table 3.2: Failure Mode, Effect and Criticality Analysis Form

Component	Failure Mode	Failure Mechanism or Cause	P	D	S	I	Effect of Failure	Corrective Action
Control Module	Circuit failure	Incorrect component inserted	2	3	4	24	Loss of Power	Better labelling of circuits
Storage Hopper	Tap jammed	Incorrect metal processing	5	4	4	80	No product function	Higher metal temperature
Outflow Filter	Filter clogged	Carbon particles in oil	4	1	3	12	Pump stopped	Re-specify oil
Packaging	Wrong Label	Wrong label supplied	1	4	3	12	Delayed despatch	Operator training

If critical failures cannot be eliminated or circumvented by redesign, the design concept may be challenged or, at the very least, severe strictures of sale contemplated or prepared for, such as through the setting up of a lot traceability and product recall system.

3.4.2 Reliability

Reliability is an overriding demand of the modern consumer and a matter of high concern in product design. An intuitive definition of a "reliable product" is one that will work correctly and consistently, time after time, throughout its expected life. Observations of reliability, or rather, observations of failure, typically reveal the "bath tub" curve illustrated in Figure 3.6. The burn-in phase shown in the graph is also called "infant mortality". Next, there is a long period of normal operation and low, constant failure due to chance causes (i.e. common causes). And finally, old age.

Figure 3.6: Reliability Curve (Bath Tub Curve)

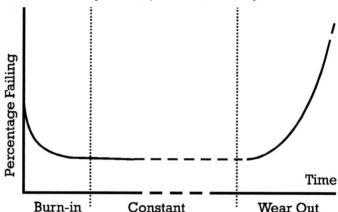

A definition of reliability given by Armand Feigenbaum[12] is *the probability that a unit will perform a required function under stated conditions for a stated time*. An expansion of these and other terms is as follows:

- *Probability*: the recognition that some units will have a relatively short life, others a long one and a great many will have a life close to average length, the distribution of life expectancy being capable of description by one or other of the standard statistical functions;

- *Unit*: a component (a single object which cannot be repaired) or a product (an assembly of replaceable components);

- *Performance*: the unit has a certain job to do and may not be fitted to do others;

- *Time*: time itself is one factor, whether elapsed time or time in actual use, but substitutes for it might be the number of cycles or operations performed etc.;

- *Conditions*: the total life environment from the point of manufacture to stock, and thence to the consumer's hearth;

- *Inherent reliability*: the reliability embodied in marketing's original concept (normally 100 per cent);

---

[12] *Total Quality Control*, A.V. Feigenbaum (Third edition, 1983) McGraw-Hill.

- *Achieved reliability*: this is always less than inherent reliability, so that the difference between the two is the scope for improvement.

Figure 3.7: Failure of Components over 16 Periods, $\lambda = 0.8$

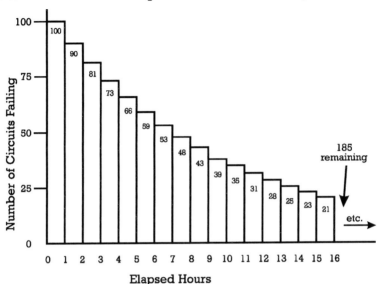

To develop a method of measuring reliability, consider 1,000 electronic circuits. It is observed that 10 per cent of them fail every hour. That is, after 1 hour, 100 of them fail, leaving 900 circuits, so that after 2 hours a further 90 fail, leaving 810; then 81 fail in the third hour, leaving 729; and so on. A histogram of these observations is given in Figure 3.7. It can be seen that this seems to follow the exponential probability density distribution function. Calculations related to the particular example, and general expressions and formulae related to an exponential distribution,[13] are as follows:

a) The probability that a circuit will fail in the third hour, expressed as a fraction of the total original number, is 81/1000 or

---

[13] In practice, the Weibull distribution is often used instead in reliability analysis, this being a generalisation of the exponential distribution.

0.081. In general terms, the *probability of failure per unit time as a fraction of the original number of circuits* = f(t);

b) The cumulative number of failed circuits by the end of the third hour, as a fraction of the original total, is (100+90+81)/1000 or 0.271. In general, the cumulative distribution up to time t as a fraction of the original number is:

$$F(t), \text{ or } \int f(t)dt$$

c) The cumulative number of survivors after the third hour, expressed as a fraction of the original, is (1000–271)/1000 or 0.729. This is known as the *survival rate*, R. In general terms, the cumulative number of survivors at time t is R(t) or 1–F(t);

d) The number of failures in the third hour, expressed as a fraction of the number of survivors, is 81/729 or 0.111. This is known as the *failure rate*, λ, and is a constant for any particular type of unit under stated conditions. In general terms, the failure rate, or number of failures at time t, as a fraction of the number of survivors, is:

$$\lambda(t) \text{ or } \frac{f(t)}{1-F(t)}$$

Two critical measures of reliability derived from (a) to (d) above are, first, the *mean time to failure* (MTTF), θ, given by Equation 3.5, and, second, from (c), the survival rate R up to a particular time T, and given by Equations 3.6(a) and 3.6(b).

$$\theta = \frac{1}{\lambda} \qquad \text{Equation 3.5}$$

$$R_T = 1.0 - \int_0^T \lambda e^{-t\lambda} dt \qquad \text{Equation 3.6(a)}$$

$$= e^{-T\lambda} \qquad \text{Equation 3.6(b)}$$

Note that the reliability of a product with n components having individual failure rates of $\lambda^1, \lambda^2, \lambda^3 \ldots \lambda^n$ and individual reliabilities $RT^1, RT^2, RT^3 \ldots RT^n$ is given by Equations 3.7 (a) and 3.7(b).

$$RT = RT^1 \times RT^2 \times RT^3 \times \ldots \times RT^n \qquad \text{Equation 3.7(a)}$$

Product Innovation

$$= e^{-T(\lambda^1 + \lambda^2 + \lambda^3 + ... + \lambda^n)} \qquad \text{Equation 3.7(b)}$$

A final definition is product availability, given by:

$$\frac{(mean\ time\ to\ failure)}{(mean\ time\ to\ failure) + (mean\ time\ to\ repair)}$$

Sketches of the probability of failure over time f(t), the survival rate R and the failure rate λ are shown in Figure 3.8 (see also Curve Q in Figure 15.15).

Figure 3.8: Reliability Parameters — Exponential Distribution

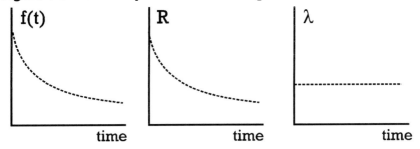

The pattern of failure during the wear-out phase is clearly of particular importance, and in practice is often Gaussian, or normal. Consequently, during this phase only, the probability of failure, the survival rate and the failure rate λ may be as shown in Figure 3.9 rather than Figure 3.8 (see also Curve P in Figure 15.15).

Figure 3.9: Possible Failure Pattern during the Wear Out Stage (Gaussian)

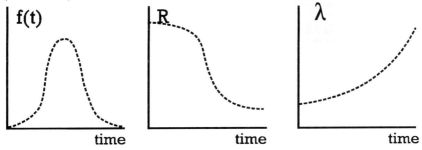

Four approaches to achieving reliability in the potential product are (1) to establish the technical data described above, so that parts liable to high burn-in can be scrutinised; (2) to give special attention to parts most likely to fail during normal operation; (3) to simplify design where possible, since reliability problems are magnified as complexity increases (see $e^{-T(\lambda^I\ldots}$ above); and (4) to develop techniques to improve reliability, such as through FMECA. To achieve the foregoing, it is necessary to manufacture prototypes and trial batches, and to analyse test results rigorously, applying the formulae above. Other actions to improve reliability are to incorporate a safety factor by considering the components with the lowest strengths in conjunction with the highest corresponding stresses they will encounter, to select components of higher duty than otherwise necessary (*derating*) and to incorporate *redundancy* (for example, standby bulbs in overhead projectors and spare tyres in cars).

3.4.3 Spares for Discontinued Machines

There is an unexpected corollary of reliability analysis that concerns materials management, and which has been put forward by Robert Goodell Brown.[14] It relates to the demand for spare parts for models of machines that have themselves been discontinued.

Most companies which discontinue particular sales models undertake to supply spares for them for periods of time dependent on the nature of the products (cookers, cars, locomotives . . .), declared policy and, perhaps, the spares' functional importance. Brown observes that for a short number of years after the model has been withdrawn, demand for spares is likely to be steady, as they are needed in the normal course of events. Soon, however, as reliability analysis shows, the machines for which the spares are required begin to be taken out of service, scrapped or run into the ground by their owners. From this point, it is found that the year-on-year decline in the demand for spares for the survivors is a constant fraction of the demand in each preceding year. The phase can be detected by taking logarithms of each year's demand for each variety of spare: nearly constant values indicate its onset.

---

[14] R.G. Brown (1977), *Materials Management Systems*, John Wiley & Sons; R.G. Brown (1982) *Advanced Service Parts Inventory Control (ASPIC)*, Second edition, Materials Management Systems Inc. (This book is available through Mercia Software, Birmingham.)

Product Innovation

Because the fraction of demand is constant each year, the total demand remaining can be calculated as the sum of a geometric series. Thus if the demand for a variety of spare parts in the current year is D units and the fractional rate of decline is Λ, the total remaining demand ever — what Brown calls the "all-time supply" — is given by:

$$D \times \frac{\Lambda}{(1-\Lambda)} \text{ units}$$

For example, if demand in the past 12 months to date for a spare has been 100 units and the rate of decline is the fraction 0.8 per annum, the total remaining demand is:

$$100 \times \frac{0.8}{(1-0.8)} \text{ units, or 400 units}$$

If the prediction is valid, the number arrived at must exceed the supply needed to fulfil demand over the policy availability period. The amount by which it exceeds it might well be considered protection against running out before the period has ended, were the firm to manufacture the all-time supply at the outset, as a single lot. If the policy period in the foregoing example had a further five years to run, the demand expected in this time is 269 units (i.e. $(100 \times 0.8) + (64 \times 0.8) + \ldots$). The "safety stock" for the period is thus 131 units. Any units out of the original 400 which are still unsold at the end of five years simply provide a welcome, longer spares availability period.

It will normally be well worthwhile for the company to manufacture the all-time supply as one final lot, notwithstanding the capital tied up in the stock and the possible need to store it under special conditions, such as under vacuum. One reason is that manufacturing will be spared the need to make repeated, disruptive small batches over the years. A second is that customers will be provided with a quick and impressive service for otherwise out-of-date parts.

3.5 BILLS OF MATERIALS MANAGEMENT

As the new product moves from design to actual manufacture, facts relating to it must be formally recorded in official company files for the purposes of technical control; materials planning and scheduling; and standard costing. By far the most important of these files is the *bill of materials*. Responsibility for data entry onto the bill of materials and for the bill's subsequent control are normally in the hands of a cross-departmental group, often called *the engineering change committee*. The committee will almost always be headed by a manager from the engineering or technical department. Members will include representatives of, or managers from, manufacturing, purchasing, planning and accounts.

Before entering details about the new product onto the bill of materials, it will be necessary to assign a code to it and to assign codes to each of its constituent components and raw materials, where these are novel. Although a number of companies have developed their own materials coding schemes, a popular system in the public domain used by many others is the Brisch classification system. In the Brisch system, each part (i.e. each product or component) is given a primary code dependent on its shape and dimensions. The primary code in Brisch can be tailored by each company, this being done after undertaking a company-wide survey of needs. After the primary code, secondary codes are attached which describe other relevant aspects of the product — say, the machining operations, how the product is used, the metallic finish, etc. An advantage of a thorough system such as this is that it makes any subsequent analysis of operational activities readily possible (say, the analysis needed to assign products to "manufacturing families" when establishing manufacturing cells as part of group technology (sub-section 15.4.3 and Figure 15.5), or the general analysis of factory plant layout for management purposes). Because the Brisch code is not especially convenient for computer input and in everyday parlance, a unique, simple code is also assigned for common use.

The many roles of the bill of materials and alternative ways of manipulating it are described throughout the book. Concern in this section is with its basic format and, particularly, with the procedures for making alterations to it — i.e. with the bill's management.

Product Innovation

A popular view of the bill of materials is as a *structure*, showing how one thing is made from another. The pictograph on the left in Figure 3.10 represents a very simple case: there is a sales product S, and this consists of (i.e. is made from) two sub-assemblies A1 and A2. Sub-assembly A1 is made from component C1. Component C1 is made from two bought-in parts BIP1 and BIP2, and so on. An alternative way of saying the same thing is through an *indented bill of materials*, a type of list,[15] illustrated on the right in Figure 3.10.

Figure 3.10: The Pictorial and Indented Bills of Material

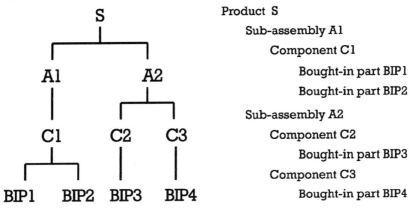

For most products, in reality, their representation by, or at least, comprehension as, pictographs is likely to be virtually impossible. For instance, the structure of products involved in fine chemicals manufacture will typically include tens of thousands of cross-linkages between the various intermediates. Instead of holding the bill of materials data as a structure on the file, therefore, it is organised as simple, separate records, one per product, each record indicating its relationship to the remainder of the file only through the codes of the products that are directly and immediately used in its manufacture. The bill of materials in Figure 3.10 is consequently replaced by a file of 10 records. The records and the bare bones of the data each contains are shown in Table 3.3.

---

[15] The list of materials needed for immediate manufacture and presented by the machine operator to those responsible for issuing stock to the shop floor is the origin of the term "bill" of materials.

Table 3.3: Ten Records in a Bill of Materials File

1.	S (made of 1 of A1 and 1 of A2)	6.	C3 (made of 1 of BIP1)
2.	A1 (made of 1 of C1)	7.	BIP1 (made of --)
3.	A2 (made of 1 of C2 and 1 of C3)	8.	BIP2 (made of --)
4.	C1 (made of 1 of BIP1 & 1 of BIP2)	9.	BIP3 (made of --)
5.	C2 (made of 1 of BIP3)	10	BIP4 (made of --)

Because data on the file relating to structure are so limited, such questions as "what is this product ultimately comprised of?" and "what does this product go into next?" — questions, in other words, having to do with materials planning, standard costing, and so on — must be answered through the separate application of individual computer programs. With one exception ("levelling" — see Section 9.3), the various analyses performed by these programs are made afresh each time the results from them are required.

To illustrate such an analysis, suppose that it was required to draw a pictograph, as in Figure 3.10, armed only with the bill of materials file data in Table 3.3. To begin the drawing, it is necessary to find what product is at the top of the structure. The attribute of a product that is at the top, an attribute not shared with any other, is that, while it *uses* other constituents of the bill, it is not itself *used by* any of them. It is therefore necessary, one-by-one, to investigate each product and find whether any of the other nine products uses it, this being done by accessing each of the other nine records in turn. If any of the nine is found to use the product under investigation, then the product under investigation is not at the top.

For example, consider product C2. Does any product use C2? Yes, product A2, so C2 is not at the top. Eventually, we come to the record for product S. Does any product use S? No! None of the other nine uses S, so S is at the top. Having found the top of the structure, it is a straightforward matter then to determine lower and lower levels. The level numbers are recorded on the products' records as explained in Section 9.3. The drawing stops with the bought-in parts because they do not "use" anything. The computer tools employed are indexes, disk search algorithms and "recursion" (see Section 9.3). Data processing speeds are extremely fast.

The full data in each record of the Bill in practice consist of four sections, regardless of whether the entry in the file is an end product, component or raw material. The sections are:

- **Section 1** (Main): product code; unit of measure; standard manufacturing lead time; planning rules; the product's level number; work centre (place of manufacture); routing; and so on.

- **Section 2** (Direct Constituents): as described in Table 3.3, namely the codes of between zero and n direct constituents. Note, importantly, however, that associated with each of these constituents is its usage in manufacture. Thus associated with a bicycle wheel, the wheel being a direct constituent of a bicycle, is the usage "2".

- **Section 3** (Costing Data): the cost centre of manufacture; the costs associated with manufacture directly at this site; and the costs accumulated from prior stages of manufacture of products used at this site (see sub-section 17.4.3 and Figure 17.28).

- **Section 4** (Engineering Change): see below.

The duties of the engineering change committee or its agents include authorising new entries, amending and deleting entries on the bill of materials file, and generally ensuring the validity of the data. The bill must be 100 per cent correct, for financial as well as technical reasons, and the integrity of its support must be assured. In many companies, the file is subjected to spot audits by an independent team.

Engineering Change

An *engineering change* is an alteration to the bill of materials Section 2 data — that is, an alteration to the bill's structure. Possible reasons for making it include the entry of a new product into manufacture, the discontinuation of an old one, the substitution of one component by an alternative and, in the process industries certainly, a revision in the usage of an existing product constituent. Change should be purposeful and marketing-oriented, not technical tinkering. Because the bill is used to plan physical manufacture, the effect of the change will be to alter the amounts of material that would otherwise be produced or would otherwise be used. Consequently, unless engineering change is well planned, stock imbalances are likely, leading all too often to material write-offs. For example, component A may require raw material X for its manufacture, X being used exclusively for this purpose. There is substantial stock of X and a contract to purchase more over the next six months. Component A is now replaced by a superior component B, which employs raw material Y instead, the engineering change to take place "forthwith".

The most important safeguard against minor disasters such as the foregoing is alert cross-departmental representation on the engineering change committee. Alternative schemes for control are also provided by bill of materials software packages. One such is the *effectivity quantity*, whereby the bill will switch from component A to component B but only when stock of raw material X reaches zero. Because of difficulties with this — stock quantities falling below the standard amount needed for a manufactured batch, and, for raw materials, the supplier contract position — a more popular alternative method is through an *effectivity date*. For example, the switch from A to B will take place on 28 November, this being the date by which planners have separately estimated raw material X will be used up. Facilities are also provided for making mass changes to the Bill (all occurrences of A to be replaced by B wherever they are found) and for making temporary changes to both product constituents and usages.

Chapter 4

Sales Forecasting

4.1 INTRODUCTION TO SHORT-TERM FORECASTING

Sales forecasts of every product on the company's selling range from the current period at least up to the master plan horizon are essential inputs to the manufacturing planning process, whether for make-to-stock, make-to-order or assemble-to-order. In assemble-to-order, forecasts of customer preferences for options are also needed. If the company operates its own distribution network, the forecasts are required at the *SKU* rather than product level, an SKU (stock keeping unit) being a product qualified by the location at which it is stocked. In all cases, forecasts must be generated consistently through a well-maintained, robust short-term forecasting system.

Such a system these days will almost certainly be built around a proprietary sales forecasting package. Much will depend on the statistical technique or techniques at the heart of it. Thus, elementary methods used to analyse sales demand capable of many changes in character over time will produce poor results, unless ancillary supporting activities, including the constant amendment of mathematical parameters, are employed in support of them. By contrast, methods of forecasting capable of the self-adaptation typically needed to cope with sales demand data are mathematically sophisticated. And so we come to a forecasting paradox. Companies that pay the greatest attention to sales forecasting and regard the activity as a high priority could, if they so wished, make do with relatively simple systems and models, because it can be guaranteed that they will receive the ongoing statistical and other support necessary. The great majority of companies, however, neither able nor willing to invest time in their systems, and lacking in-house statistical expertise, must employ systems and models which are sophisticated and capable of self-adaptation if they are to obtain good forecasts over time, for, in the long run, these are the systems that will have to look after themselves.

The generation of short-term forecasts depends in the main on the application of statistical techniques. There are two jobs to be done. First, the ongoing pattern of sales demand must be represented by a mathematical formula, or "modelled", so that the formula can be extended to future periods. Any value so calculated for a future period is a "forecast". For example, suppose that statistical analysis showed that sales demand in any current period was 1.2 times the demand in the previous period, plus 50 units. The model representing this relationship might be written as follows:

$$X_t = 1.2X_{t-1} + 50$$

Having established the model, the term X_t may now be replaced by F_t, meaning the forecast for period t. Consequently, if demand in June is 1,000 units (X_{t-1}), the forecast for July is 1,250 units (F_t) and for August is 1,550 units (F_{t+1}). The second job is particularly important in the volatile world of industrial and consumer sales. This is to detect any permanent change in the ongoing pattern and to reformulate the model accordingly, with the minimum delay.

In the terminology of forecasting, data relating to the quantities of a product sold are said to be *quantitative*. Although the market is affected by the process of change and sales demand is liable to be affected by isolated, unpredictable events, it is held that, in general, data about previous demand will have a bearing on future demand — *the assumption of constancy*. Since forecasts are prepared for the sales of a product based on data relating to the sales of the same product, the data are said to be *dependent*. Data are *independent* when the forecasts of one thing (e.g. carpets) are based on previous sales of something else (e.g. newly built house completions). Housing starts, however, are a *leading indicator* of carpet sales. Since forecasts are required for distinct periods up to a certain point ahead, the familiar way of assembling past data in

Sales Forecasting

readiness for the process of forecasting is, naturally, in distinct periods, period by period, in chronological sequence, so the data constitute a *time-series*. When the forecasts are prepared wholly by statistical means, forecasting is said to be *intrinsic*. If they are determined, say, by marketing knowledge, forecasting is *extrinsic*.

4.2 Patterns of Data

Analysis of time-series shows there to be a small number of "patterns" of sales demand, caused by the passage of time, the operation of the market and the nature of the products in question. Principally, these are *stationarity*, *trend*, *step change* and *seasonality*.

4.2.1 Stationarity

The sales demand for a product during the maturity phase of its life is likely to be relatively stable from one period to the next, as illustrated in Figure 2.1 and in the left-hand sketch in Figure 4.1. In the sketch, the "actual data" is denoted by a solid line. An objection might be raised, of course, that a flat line rarely represents reality; that reality is better represented by the jagged (up and down) solid line in the right-hand sketch in Figure 4.1.

Figure 4.1: The Pattern of Stationary Data

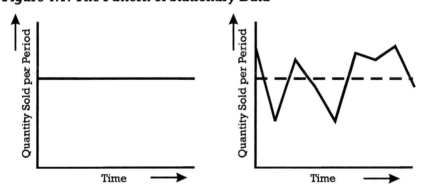

Suppose, however, that the differences are measured between the jagged sales peaks and troughs in the second sketch and the flat broken line through the middle of them. If the broken line were the forecasts, the positive and negative differences would be the forecast errors. Now, there is a well-known statistical test for determining whether data are random. Suppose, further, that this test is applied to these errors, and they are found to constitute random data, i.e. that it is found that the actual demand is randomly distributed about the broken line forecast. Random data cannot, by definition, be forecast.

Consequently, the unchanging, stationary forecasts are the best possible forecasts that could be made. Since the company takes forecasts into account in setting its manufacturing plans, and on 50 per cent of occasions forecasts are smaller than actual demand, the company may wish to protect its customer service in make-to-stock against frequent stock-outs. Protection is achieved either through holding safety stock or by rapid production rescheduling — quite separate concerns dealt with in Chapter 5 and elsewhere.

4.2.2 Trend

Because of favourable circumstances in the sales market or a market that is itself growing, or because of increasing acceptance of the product by customers or effective sales management, sales demand for a product may grow, perhaps at an accelerating rate. For opposite reasons, it may decline. The left-hand sketch in Figure 4.2 illustrates sales growth that is accelerating.

4.2.3 Step Change

Change in the level of demand for a product will normally occur only gradually.[1] Reasons for it are given in the preceding paragraph. Reliance on consistency of level, or at least on only gradual change to it, is a major feature of many forecasting techniques. It is indeed considered a strength of them that the forecasts should not be disturbed by "unusual" high or low sales demand values.

---

[1] Where a large change in the level of demand takes place over three or four periods, rather than one or two, it is often referred to as "ramp change", rather than "step change".

Figure 4.2: The Data Patterns of Trend and Step Change

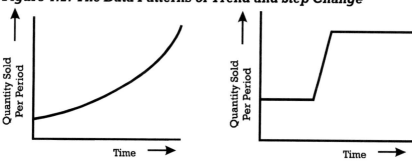

Occasionally, however, consistency of level is broken by a "step change", the step up, or step down, in the level of sales being permanent and "significantly" large. The phenomenon is illustrated in the right-hand sketch in Figure 4.2. Step changes are not predictable statistically, but, in rare cases, a step may be anticipated by marketing staff if there is a relatively small product range and an effective means of system intervention exists (see Section 2.5). Mostly, then, when a step begins, it goes unrecognised and the large upwards or downwards movement in demand is taken to be a single random fluctuation from the normal sales level. Reasons for steps include the loss (or gain) of a major customer, or, at least, the scaling down of his requirements, a change in government regulations and, for products with high elasticity of demand (typically, luxury goods which customers are readily willing to forgo in difficult times), the advent of a sharp economic downturn (see sub-section 16.4.1).

When large deviations occur between forecasts and actual sales, a small number of companies which have committed considerable staff resources to forecast management and which may have a relatively small product range are able, if they choose, to investigate them vigorously. First, the fact of the large deviations will be brought to the attention of product managers by the system administrator, himself warned by an error tracking signal (see sub-section 4.6.1). Next, the managers will undertake investigations to determine whether the errors are due to abnormal, temporary factors or to permanent step changes. Lastly, if due to step changes, the administrator will make the necessary adjustments to the forecasting parameters of the various product time-series in question. (For each product involved, all demand data previous to the step may be disregarded in future forecast analysis.) The great majority of companies, by contrast, will do nothing. Staff can spare neither the time nor other resources for speculative investigations into a handful of isolated products when much needs to be done elsewhere. If any deviation turns out to be a step change, its recognition is expected to be made promptly through the normal operation of the system and the necessary adjustments to the model effected without staff intervention. For the forecasting system to be capable of doing so — not overreacting to random fluctuations yet not carrying on for many months without suitable adjustment — requires of it a high degree of internal sophistication — a return to the forecasting paradox spoken of above.

4.2.4 Cyclicality

Cyclical variation in sales demand is a repeating, consistent variation in level caused purely by the relative point in time in each cycle that sales relate to, the cycle being one in a continuous succession of cycles. In this sense, cyclicality is similar to seasonality, but there are important differences. One is that, whereas in sales forecasting, each season, in a succession of seasons, is identical in duration, the duration of each successive cycle is liable to variation: say, four years, then three years, then six years and so on. A major difficulty in forecasting cyclical demand is consequently the determination of a cycle's start and finish. Thus, world textile cycles, which affect the sales of textile machinery, cloth and dyestuffs, are of five to seven years' duration. Cyclicality is too long-term and diffuse to be recognised as such in short-term statistical forecasting, but it may be taken note of in marketing department intervention and in the sales and operations planning stage of master plan formulation (see Section 2.5, sub-section 6.1.2, Sections 6.4 and 6.5).

4.2.5 Random Variation ("Outliers", "White Noise")

Variation in sales demand, up or down, caused by random, non-repeating events in the marketplace is not, of course, a *pattern* of demand. It is recorded here as a reminder of its continuous presence in time-series data and the need to take it into account in devising methods for recognising and describing genuine patterns.

4.2.6 Seasonality

As stated, in sales forecasting a "season" is a fixed interval comprised of a specified number of periods — it might be a week of five trading days but is more usually considered to be the year and its 12 months. Figure 4.3 illustrates monthly seasonal fluctuation of product demand over three years, imposed on an upwards trend in demand. Relatively higher demand for the product can be expected in the spring months and relatively lower demand in the autumn. The isolation and treatment of seasonality are important if periodic overloads of the master schedule and overloads of warehouses are to be avoided. Because seasonality is a subject apart, it is dealt with in its entirety in this sub-section. Two approaches are described. The first is the application of *decomposition* and the calculation of *seasonal factors*. The second is the application of *harmonic analysis* and the generation of a set of sine equations. Note that in the text which follows, it is assumed that prior allowance is made for the different number of trading days in calendar months. A simple way of doing this will be described in Section 4.3.

Figure 4.3: Seasonality over Three Years, Combined with an Upwards Trend

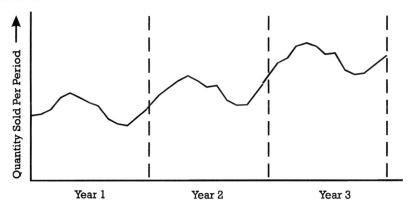

1. Seasonal Factors and Decomposition

Seasonal factors are an intuitive way of expressing seasonality. For example, the seasonal factors for a given product may be as shown in Table 4.1. When they are added up, the total is 12. The "average" seasonal factor is 1.0.

Table 4.1: A Product's Seasonal Factors for 12 Months

Jan	Feb	Mar	Apr	May	Jun	Jul	Aug	Sep	Oct	Nov	Dec
0.9	0.9	1.1	1.2	1.3	1.2	1.1	1.1	0.8	0.7	0.7	1.0

Consider the month of June, when the seasonal factor is 1.2. This means that actual sales in June are expected to be 1.2 times greater than any normal underlying pattern, simply because it is June. Consequently, when we consider historic data relating to any June sales, we should divide it by 1.2 to see its real, "non-June", or neutral, underlying significance. When we divide the data by the seasonal factor in this way to get rid of the seasonal effect, we *deseasonalise* them. Conversely, when we multiply a basic forecast by its seasonal factor in order to obtain the actual forecast for that month with seasonality duly incorporated in it, we *seasonalise* it. The procedures of deseasonalising raw data before using it to prepare a forecast and seasonalising a forecast before issuing it for actual use in the company are followed whether seasonal factors are employed or whether the seasonality has been described through a set of harmonics, as below.

Seasonal factors are arrived at through the decomposition of the data, this meaning its breakdown, in a way to be described, into the sub-patterns of stationarity, trend, seasonality and cyclicality, together with randomness.

The pivot of the process is the initial breakdown of each occurrence of sales demand in the time-series into two separate constituents: (1) *seasonality × randomness;* and (2) *trend × cyclicality.* The method of doing so is referred to as the *ratio of actual to moving averages method.* In Equation 4.1, it is assumed that sales product demand in period t (X_t) is made up of the arithmetic product of the seasonality of period t (S_t), the randomness in period t (R_t), trend in period t (T_t) and cyclicality in period t (C_t).

$$X_t = S_t \times R_t \times T_t \times C_t \qquad \textit{Equation 4.1}$$

To see how we proceed from this point, we turn for a time to an example involving a five-day trading week and sales demand over nine consecutive trading days, rather than the 12 months of the year. The reason for doing so will become clear in due course. Ta-

Sales Forecasting

ble 4.2 gives the sales demand from Thursday of Week 1 to Tuesday of Week 3.

Table 4.2: Sales Demand of a 5-Day Season (A Trading Week)

Week 1		Week 2					Week 3	
Thurs	Fri	Mon	Tues	Wed	Thurs	Fri	Mon	Tues
7	10	5	4	4	8	9	4	5

Any five consecutive days in Table 4.2 constitute a complete season, not simply Monday of Week 2 to Friday of Week 2. Consider, therefore, the complete season from Thursday Week 1 to Wednesday Week 2. The middle period of this season is Monday Week 2. A single moving average of this mid-point is now calculated from the five days in the particular season under consideration, and this is 6.0 ((7 + 10 + 5 + 4 + 4)/5). In having chosen a span of one complete season, the single moving average must have eliminated the day-by-day seasonal effect, i.e. the big selling days and low selling days must have cancelled out. In addition, because we have taken a full five days' demand, we might also suppose for a moment that the ups and downs of randomness have also been cancelled out. Consequently, the mid-point, single moving average consists only of the patterns of trend and cyclicality. Thus, if the single moving average is M and the sub-script t denotes the period "Monday Week 2", then Equation 4.2 follows.

$$M_t = T_t \times C_t \qquad \textit{Equation 4.2}$$

Dividing Equation 4.1 by Equation 4.2 gives Equation 4.3, i.e. the isolation of "seasonality × randomness".

$$\frac{X_t}{M_t} = S_t \times R_t \qquad \textit{Equation 4.3}$$

Since the value of X_t is 5 (i.e. sales demand on Monday Week 2, given in Table 4.2) and the value of M_t is 6.0, (from above), then $S_t \times R_t$ is 0.83 (5 / 6.0).

If the further subscript T denotes Tuesday Week 2, we may similarly find the value of $S_T \times R_T$. This is X_T/M_T, where X_T is 4, the sales demand on Tuesday Week 2 (from Table 4.2) and M_T is the single moving average of the mid-point of the season from Friday

Week 1 to Thursday Week 2, this being 6.2 ((10 + 5 + 4 + 4 + 8)/5). Table 4.3 gives the seasonality × randomness, S × R, values of each day of the season Monday Week 2 to Friday Week 2. We note, incidentally, that to calculate the figures we have required data from almost half a season before Week 2 — (i.e. Thursday Week 1) to almost half a season after (Tuesday Week 3).

Table 4.3: "S × R" Values for One Season of Five Trading Days

Week 1		Week 2					Week 3	
Thurs	Fri	Mon	Tues	Wed	Thurs	Fri	Mon	Tues
—	—	0.83	0.65	0.67	1.40	1.50	—	—

We now leave the five-day trading week and return to the consideration of seasonality and sales demand relating to the months of a year. Table 4.4 gives the sales demand X_t for 24 consecutive months, from July 2000 to June 2002.

Table 4.4: Sales Demand for a Product over 24 Consecutive Months

2000						2001					
J	A	S	O	N	D	J	F	M	A	M	J
8	9	4	4	3	7	8	9	8	10	12	10

2001 cont'd						2002					
J	A	S	O	N	D	J	F	M	A	M	J
8	8	6	5	5	10	10	11	12	12	11	9

One difficulty in applying the technique that has just been employed for the five-day seasonal span becomes immediately apparent when considering a 12-month year: a single moving average of the mid-point period M_t cannot be found, because there is no mid-point of a season with an even number of periods. To overcome this problem, the following three-step convention is normally adopted, termed the *12×12 single moving average method*.

1. First, a mid-point of the season of N months (N is even) is chosen by convention as Month ((N+1)/2) + ½. For the 12-month season January 2001 to December 2001, the mid-point period

Sales Forecasting

is thus declared to be July 2001. From Table 4.4, the single moving average of this mid-point is 8.25.

2. Instead of the convention of choosing $((N+1)/2) + ½$ as the mid-point, we might just as well have chosen $((N+1)/2) - ½$. If so, a second single moving average for July 2001 may be calculated, being the mid-point $((N+1)/2) - ½$ of the 12-month season February 2001 to January 2002. From Table 4.4, this is 8.42.

3. An average is taken of the two values from 1 and 2. The value here is 8.33.

Equations 4.1, 4.2 and 4.3 can now all be applied as before, where the subscript t now takes on the value "July 2001". Consequently, X_t/M_t, the seasonality × randomness value for July 2001, is 0.96 (8/8.33). Table 4.5 gives all the seasonality × randomness values for a complete season (i.e. year) January 2001 to December 2001, obtained from the data in Table 4.4 and using the 12×12 centred moving average method as described. Note that in order to derive these values, it has been necessary to employ data from July 2000 to June 2002 — an extra six months each at the beginning and the end of the data span for which the values are being calculated.

Table 4.5: Seasonality ×Randomness Values for a 12-Month Season

2001					
Jan	Feb	Mar	Apr	May	Jun
1.04	1.23	1.09	1.28	1.52	1.23

2001 cont'd					
Jul	Aug	Sep	Oct	Nov	Dec
0.96	0.94	0.69	0.56	0.55	1.12

The next step is to separate seasonality and randomness, S_t and R_t. In order to do so, it is first necessary to obtain S×R values for a sufficiently lengthy time horizon. What constitutes a "sufficiently lengthy horizon" will depend on the sales market and the product under consideration. Even if a great deal of data are available, as eventually they will be, it is likely that changes in the market and the marketing approach itself will make the seasonality element of the oldest data uncharacteristic of current sales. It is indeed frequently an objective of the Marketing department to enhance product appeal and boost sales during off-peak periods.[2] In the absence of guidelines, five years past data might seem reasonable, remembering with the 12×12 centred moving average method that S×R factors are not calculated for six months at the beginning and six months at the end of the sequence. Having calculated, say, $S_t \times R_t$ values for 48 months, each value is placed in one or other of the 12 groups "January", "February", "March" . . . "December" to which it corresponds. Consider now the January group. The seasonality factor is the same for each of the four values placed in this group. By taking the average of the four values, it is assumed that the elements of randomness will cancel out, so that the average will be the seasonality factor alone for January. The seasonal factors for all 12 groups are obtained in this way. Each factor is finally adjusted so that the total of all 12 of them equals 12.

The objection to decomposition and the derivation of seasonal factors from a comparatively limited horizon of sales demand data stems from assumptions made at two stages. First, in order to arrive at Equation 4.2, it is assumed that a mid-point moving average of just one season has totally eliminated seasonality and randomness. If this is untrue for any mid-point period, because of unusual demand in that season, the further derivation of S×R through Equation 4.3 leads to a doubtful result. Secondly, for the same reason of possible unusual demand, the final averaging of merely three or four S×R factors (say, three or four values in the "January" group) may not have eliminated randomness.

To help counter the objection, the validity of the seasonality factors can be examined by the *adjacent months test*. First, the original month-by-month sales demand values of the complete time horizon are deseasonalised by the newly found seasonal factors.

---

[2] One should beware, in seasonality, of self-fulfilling prophecies. It is well-known by sports shop retailers in Lytham St Annes that the fathers of boys born in November, a month well outside the cricket season, would never wish to give their sons cricket bats as birthday presents.

Working from this point entirely with deseasonalised data, a notional value for the sales demand in each period in the horizon is arrived at by averaging the actual sales demand of the month immediately before the month in question and the actual sales demand of the month after. That is, the notional value for May 2001 is obtained from (April 2001 + June 2001)/2. Next, the actual deseasonalised data for the month in question, May 2001, is divided by the notional value just found. One would anticipate that the value of this fraction would be very close to 1. Finally, the fractions for each distinct month January, February, March, etc. are placed in one of 12 corresponding groups, and the average of the values in each group then found. By convention, the nearer each group's average is to 1, the more likely it is that the seasonal factor for that group is valid.

2. Fourier Analysis

In 1822, the French mathematician Joseph Fourier showed that any consistent, repeating pattern of data over a fixed interval (for example, a season) can be represented by a set of sine waves. When there are 12 data points in the season, Henry Nyquist has further shown that the maximum number of sine equations necessary to do so is 6. This second approach, then, to the treatment of seasonality is distinctly different from decomposition and the derivation of seasonal factors. Variously referred to as Fourier analysis, line spectrum analysis and harmonic analysis, it consists of the fitting by least squares regression techniques of the required sine waves to sales demand data extending over several seasons. The resulting grand equation, the composite of the sine equations obtained by the regression fitting, represents the oscillating pattern of sales over the season, and is used, as seasonal factors are, to deseasonalise raw data and seasonalise forecasts.

In its simplest form, a sine wave may be represented by the expression in Equation 4.4, where θ ranges from 0° to 360° (i.e. 0 to 2π radians).

$$Y = \sine \theta \qquad \text{Equation 4.4}$$

The oscillating form of the sine wave is familiar even to those with no technical background and is illustrated in Figure 4.4.

The simple expression in Equation 4.4 may be expanded to give Equation 4.5.

$$Y_t = A \sin\left[\left(\frac{ft}{n}\right)2\pi + \phi\right] \qquad \text{Equation 4.5}$$

In Equation 4.5, A equals the amplitude of the wave, or extent of oscillation, and is 2.0 in Figure 4.4; f and n are the frequency f over n observations, i.e. the number of oscillations over the number of periods covered. In Figure 4.4, there are two oscillations over 24 periods (which is the same as saying the wavelength is 12 months); t is the time period (in the Figure, one month); and ϕ is the "phase angle" or "phase shift" — i.e. the extent to which the wave is displaced from 0° along the horizontal axis, in Figure 4.4 being 30° (one-twelfth of one wavelength).

Figure 4.4: A Sine Wave with Amplitude 2 and Wavelength 12 Months

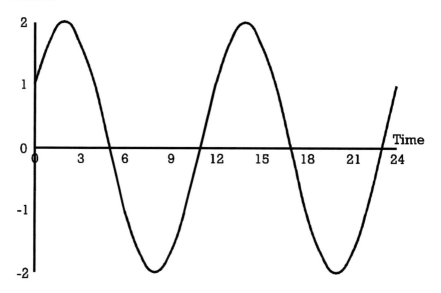

In fitting a single sine wave to the seasonal sales demand data, it can be seen from Equation 4.5 that f, n and t are known. Least squares regression is employed to determine the remaining variables, amplitude A and phase angle ϕ. The least squares technique is extended to find the six amplitudes A_i and six phase angles ϕ_i for each of the complete set of sine waves needed to describe the seasonal oscillation fully.[3]

When the analysis of a product's sales demand has been made and the sine equations derived, the subsequent use of this method for dealing with seasonal fluctuation may be more satisfactory than the alternative use of seasonal factors because of the greater degree of stability offered — the greater degree of resistance to random, individual fluctuations from month to month. This comes about because each sine wave in the final set is obtained by considering all of the data over the 12 months together — the values are interdependent, not independent. Very careful attention must be paid, however, to the derivation of the equations in the first place. If there are abnormal monthly sales demand levels in the original data, the least squares fitting process will naturally cause the fitted curves to pass close to them, creating false peaks and troughs which cannot later be screened out in the way that abnormal months can be screened out in decomposition. It is essential, therefore, to vet the raw data to determine and deal with unusual values before their analysis.

4.3 SALES DEMAND DATA

4.3.1 The Origin of Demand

Notwithstanding the title of this chapter, its subject is not the prediction of what the company will sell but what its customers will ask to buy — i.e. it relates to customer *demand*, not to actual sales. Demand for a product arises from a potential customer willing and able to purchase it, and who has in mind both its physical attributes and the commercial terms (especially price). Factors that affect demand include, say, reliability, service back-up, salesmanship and technical standing, but not availability. Availability is the company's capability for meeting *patent* demand. If marketing is ineffective or if customers are constantly disappointed because of the product's unavailability so that they no longer approach the firm, demand will become *latent*.

---

[3] Peter Bloomfield (1976), *Fourier Analysis of Time-Series Data: An Introduction*, John Wiley & Sons.

It follows from this that in order to forecast sales demand by statistical means, the historical data that should be used in the process should be reflective of past demand, not of past sales or of some other activity. Gaining a true picture is not always straightforward, however. There are two classes of obstacles to being able to do so: informational and organisational.

1. Informational Obstacles

Many of the problems here arise in sales order processing itself, forcing order entry clerks to act as unofficial market researchers. The customer of a paint manufacturer who requires 100 five-litre tins of primrose yellow may be persuaded to take the last remaining stock of 65 five-litre tins of primrose and the balance in jonquil yellow. The demand and the sale are different and it is the original customer request that must be recorded for forecasting purposes. If shortages are widespread, the problems of capturing the data become insuperable — the same customer's demand recorded as lost at each of several company sales outlets and the placing of excessively large orders by customers who expect to be given a partial allocation are examples of the difficulties that may exist.

As we realise with the primrose and jonquil shades of paint, orders accepted for second choice products, yet recorded as true demand, not only gave rise to poor quality data for forecasting, but leave the company vulnerable to competitors who discover the gaps in the market for first choices. Note, however, that second choices here mean the reluctant acceptance of what is on offer and must be distinguished from genuine consumer substitution. Many examples of genuine substitution arise in clothes and giftware — shades, patterns and designs not in the customer's mind prior to a purchase. In these cases, demand forecasting may be performed at the group level (patterned shirts of size 12; figurines from £10 to £20, etc.). Group forecasts are discussed in sub-section 6.3.1.

The system from which a satisfactory file of sales demand history is likely to be potentially obtainable is clearly sales order processing (SOP), but in many companies an amendment may be necessary to create such a file specifically for demand forecasting purposes. The history data file normally associated with the SOP system holds sales statistics, being summaries of actual orders, with payment and despatch details, but typically available only

Sales Forecasting 103

many weeks after the orders are placed. The creation of an additional file of demand statistics might be accompanied by the dissemination of demand statistics analyses for the Sales and Marketing department staff well before the official sales statistics become available (see sub-section 2.3.2).

2. Organisational Obstacles

In his autobiography, one of the founding fathers of General Motors, Alfred Sloan,[4] recalls that in the early months of 1924 the company was experiencing apparently buoyant sales although the American financial press was talking of recession. Sloan undertook a train journey to see for himself, stopping off at major dealers and finding unsold cars stockpiled at all of them. The young GM was pulled from the brink of oblivion by a three-day week. To ensure dealer optimism would never again obscure consumer reality, Sloan then instituted a scheme whereby a dealer was required to send Detroit a postcard within 10 days of each real sale. It is understood that General Motors has now moved on from the postcard arrangement, but over 75 years later a number of companies, due to organisational and business obfuscation, still do not have as good a picture of demand as the postcards then provided.

The usual reason for this obfuscation is the existence of one or just a few semi-autonomous sales and marketing operational units standing between the final user of the product and the manufacturing division. The units may be organisational divisions, subsidiary companies or agents, and the problems the arrangements cause may be compounded by allowing the selling operations to place replenishment orders on the manufacturer without effective restrictions on stock holding costs. To overcome organisational obstacles requires the application of high politics, technology and systems. Politics are needed to end the secretiveness of the selling units and, possibly, to convert the entire operation from one in which stock replenishment orders are placed by autonomous outlets on manufacture to one in which the replenishment of stocking outlets is determined by central planning (see Section 20.2). Technology and systems are needed to communicate data throughout

---

[4] Alfred P. Sloan (edited by John McDonald and Catherine Stevens) (1963), *My Years with General Motors*, Doubleday.

the distribution and supply network and to process them in a consistent fashion.

4.3.2 Time Lags and the Supply Chain

An interesting study into the effects on stock levels and production rates of delays in recognising shifts in sales demand has been carried out by Jay Forrester, employing an early continuous simulation model.[5] Forrester's findings accord with the experience of manufacturers at the start and finish of periods of recession. Manufacturers, especially those at the start of the supply chain making basic chemicals, steel and so on, find that quite small downturns in the consumer market as reported through Government statistics are felt a few months later in massive fall-offs in business, runaway stock levels and crises. Recoveries may be characterised by numerous stockouts in the supply marketplace.

The basis of Forrester's model lies in the graphs in Figure 4.5. The broken line in the top graph denotes sales demand. There is a 10 per cent decrease in demand at Period 2. The reduction is not recognised and responded to by production until the start of Period 3 (the continuous line, top graph). Consequently, from Period 2 to 3, the stock level illustrated in the bottom graph in Figure 4.5 begins to rise. The response in production starting in Period 3 (back to the top graph) is gradual, not sudden and immediate, so that it is not until Period 4 that the levels of production and demand are equal. Because the company is now greatly overstocked, the level of production must fall further to reduce the stock mountain. The model is finally back in equilibrium by Period 6.

---

[5] J.W. Forrester (1961), *Industrial Dynamics*, MIT Press, Boston; the continuous simulation model was DYNAMO. (An edition was published in 1994 by Productivity Press — see footnote 2 in Chapter 15.) Jay Forrester of the Massachusetts Institute of Technology is better known for his invention of magnetic core memory for computers and his development of symbolic instructions (of machine language), also for computers.

Figure 4.5: The Effects on Production and Stock of a 10 per cent Change in Demand

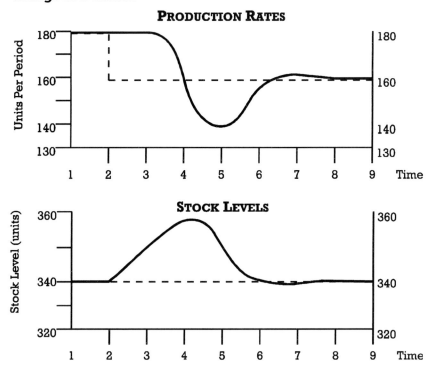

Figure 4.6, the culmination of Forrester's demonstration — though not, in fact, a reproduction of his own model — shows three pairs of graphs as follows: (1) a retailer; (2) a distributor; and (3) a manufacturer. As in Figure 4.5, each pair of graphs denotes demand and production (top) and stock level (bottom). Attention should be paid to the different time ranges that relate to each of the three pairs. The first pair (the retailer) is identical to Figure 4.5, with the same 10 per cent downturn in demand and the one period delay in recognising and responding to it. The demand now placed by the retailer on the distributor is correspondingly less than 10 per cent because of the retailer's wish to reduce their excessive stock. Again, the distributor fails to recognise the downturn for one period, so that their stocks rise to even greater levels. Finally, the reduction in demand by the distributor on the manufacturer is greater yet again, and again goes unrecognised for one period, creating the massive overstocking seen in the bottom graph in the third pair.

Figure 4.6: The Effects on Production and Stock of Communication Lags in the Supply Chain

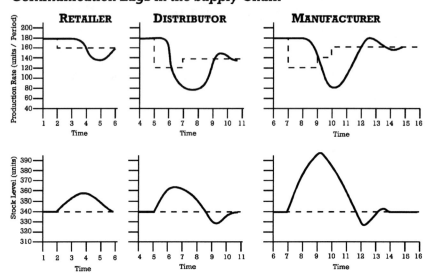

4.3.3 Trading Days Adjustment

Because the number of "trading days" or selling days in each calendar month is potentially different, an "average month" must be decided on and an adjustment made to the raw sales demand figure in each month to take account of the difference in the number of days between that month and the average. Conversely, after the preparation of a forecast based on the average number of days, the output issued to the user must first be adjusted to take account of the actual number of trading days in the calendar month to which the forecast applies. Table 4.6 gives the number of trading days per month in 2001, taking into account public holidays in England, Scotland and Wales. The figures for other countries including Northern Ireland and the Irish Republic are somewhat different.

Table 4.6: The Trading Days in each Calendar Month in 2001

2001											
Jan	Feb	Mar	Apr	May	Jun	Jul	Aug	Sep	Oct	Nov	Dec
22	20	22	19	21	21	22	22	20	23	22	19

The average number of days per month from Table 4.6 is 21.0. Consequently, raw sales data of 500 units for February 2001 should be treated as 525 units ((500/20) × 21.0), and an unadjusted forecast of 500 units for March should be converted to 524 ((500/21.0) × 22). Note that although, as an option, all proprietary forecasting packages permit forecasts to be prepared for weeks, in this Chapter it is assumed that months will be chosen in preference; forecasts expressed in calendar months are far more clearly understood by staff, and fit better with the monthly MPS cycle. Besides, for the great majority of sales products, the uneven receipt of demand from week to week does not justify the precision implied in weekly forecasting. However, there are two points. First, if there is a distinct pattern over the typical month to the receipt of orders, allowance can be made for it in planning, as explained in the next sub-section. Secondly, the effect of the uneven arrival of demand on the planning system can be mitigated for make-to-stock products in the way shown in sub-section 7.1.2.

4.3.4 Using Forecast Data in Planning

1. Make-to-stock

Forecasts are prepared by calendar month but are required to be entered in planning systems as daily quantities. If there is no information regarding the pattern of order receipt over a month, the only recourse is simply to divide the monthly forecast by the number of trading days to arrive at a trading day forecast. If the forecast for February 2001 (20 days) was 1,000 units, the trading day forecast would be 50.0 units per day. Similarly, if the forecast for March 2001 (22 days) was 800 units, the trading day forecast would be 36.4 units per day. Table 4.7 shows the forecast entries in the first week of a master schedule running from Monday, 26 February 2001 onwards.

Table 4.7: Sales Forecasts from Two Overlapped Calendar Months, used in Master Planning

Monday, 26 Feb	Tuesday, 27 Feb	Wednesday, 28 Feb	Thursday, 1 March	Friday, 2 March	Monday, 5 March
50.0	50.0	50.0	36.4	36.4	36.4

If seasonal analysis of the day-by-day demand over a month shows there to be a pattern to the arrival of orders, this should be taken into account, since it will be helpful in the day-to-day assessment and management of the master production schedule. If the company's credit period is linked to the month (say, payment being required by the end of the month), there is likely to be a peak of orders in the first week. There may also be peaks of orders when salesmen's commission is attached to discrete periods.

2. Make-to-order (and assemble-to-order)

Sales forecasts in make-to-order are forecasts of the receipt of new orders, not forecasts of the despatch of completed orders. Consequently, in addition to considerations of overlapping calendar months and the uneven arrival of demand just discussed, there is a further requirement to offset the sales demand forecast by the average order manufacturing lead time before its entry into the planning system. For example, if the forecasts of 1,000 units for February 2001 and 800 units for March 2001, illustrated in Table 4.7 for make-to-stock, were to have applied to a make-to-order product with an average manufacturing lead time of two weeks, Table 4.8 would have resulted.

Table 4.8: Sales Forecasts from Table 4.7, offset by a Two-Week Production Lead Time

Monday, March 12th	Tuesday, March 13th	Wednesday, March 14th	Thursday, March 15th	Friday, March 16th	Monday, March 19th
50.0	50.0	50.0	36.4	36.4	36.4

4.4 THE NAÏVE FORECASTING FAMILY

All forecasting techniques capable of analysing quantitative data and thus available for possible incorporation into a sales forecasting system belong to one or other of two "families", the *naïve family* and the *causal family*. Members of the naïve family are also referred to as *averaging*, or *smoothing*, techniques. The essence of them is that there is only one type of variable — i.e. sales demand — and that each of its values in the time-series contributes to the entire statistical relationship in a way that depends only on its age. During the analysis, the data are considered all together, as a homogeneous set, from a viewpoint determined solely by the arithmetic values of the numbers involved and their times of arrival into the system. These numbers then take part in a unified set of mathematical processes so as to produce the required forecast. When the event being forecast has taken place, to yield another data value, the whole set of data including the new value is considered again in exactly the same way, the mathematical processes being repeated identically to produce the next forecast.

Causal or, sometimes, regression techniques differ markedly from members of the naïve family. In these, a cause-and-effect relationship is described between one type of data and another. Causal relationships of this nature are analogous to the scientific laws of the physical world. For example, Ohm's Law relates electric current I, voltage V and resistance R as follows:

$$I = V/R$$

Once the interrelationship is known, any range or value of data and any combination of the variables can be explored. Unlike natural laws, causal relationships established in this way have no basis of scientific proof. They are nevertheless almost as useful in the broad, exploratory way they can be used. In everyday life, for example, the causal relationship discovered by Sir Richard Doll between cigarette smoking and lung cancer is accepted and used as if it were a rigorously proved fact of medical science.

4.4.1 Single Moving Averages

The averaging or "smoothing" of data is an intuitive process and is the basis of the naïve forecasting family of techniques. The continuous line in the graph in Figure 4.7 shows customer demand for a sales product over 10 periods of time. The broken line gives one-ahead forecasts calculated by the *four-point single moving averages method*. That is, the forecasts are obtained simply by adding the previous four demand values and dividing the total by four. The forecast series is called a "moving average" because, when a new demand value is received, it moves along one period by adding the new value and dropping the oldest.[6]

Figure 4.7: One-ahead Forecasts by the 4-Point Single Moving Average Method

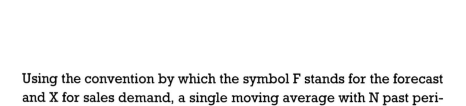

Using the convention by which the symbol F stands for the forecast and X for sales demand, a single moving average with N past periods is given algebraically in Equation 4.6.

$$F_t = (X_{t-1} + X_{t-2} + \ldots + X_{t-N})/N \qquad \text{Equation 4.6}$$

4.4.2 Single Exponential Smoothing

A feature of single moving averages is that equal weight is given to all data points incorporated in the forecast. Such a system clearly fails to provide any particularly effective means of responding to change in the sales pattern and additionally runs counter to the intuitive belief that the more recent behaviour of demand is likely to be a better representative of the current state than is the more distant past. The weighting of data observations in favour of pro-

---

[6] There are two extreme variations of the single moving average. The first is where the number of previous data points equals the total number of points in the whole time-series. The forecast is then the mean, or arithmetic average. The second is known as *Naïve One*, being the single moving average with only one past point. *Naïve One* is used as a yardstick for judging the relative effectiveness of other forecasting methods.

Sales Forecasting

gressively more recent readings is the principal feature of *exponentially weighted moving averages*, or *exponential smoothing*. Suppose, therefore, that to calculate a forecast: (1) we take a fraction β of the latest demand, where β is between 0 and 1; and then (2) we take a smaller fraction $\beta \times \beta$ of sales demand one period older; and then (3) we take a still smaller fraction $\beta \times \beta \times \beta$ of sales demand one period older still . . . and so on. The forecast for Period (t + 1) is as shown in Equation 4.7.

$$F_{t+1} = \beta X_t + \beta^2 X_{t-1} + \beta^3 X_{t-2} + \ldots \qquad \text{Equation 4.7}$$

The sum of a geometric progression, $\beta + \beta^2 + \beta^3 + \ldots + \ldots$ where β lies between 0 and 1 is given by Equation 4.8.

$$\beta + \beta^2 + \beta^3 + \beta^4 \ldots = \frac{\beta}{1-\beta} \qquad \text{Equation 4.8}$$

To be a mathematically valid average, the sum of the weightings in Equation 4.7 must equal unity. To achieve this, the geometric sum in Equation 4.7 may be made equal to 1 by dividing each of the individual, weighted past demand values in the expression by $\beta/(1-\beta)$. That is, each individual term may be multiplied by $(1-\beta)/\beta$ to give Equation 4.9 and thence Equation 4.10.

$$F_{t+1} = \frac{(1-\beta)}{\beta} \times [\beta X_t + \beta^2 X_{t-1} + \beta^3 X_{t-2} + \ldots \qquad \text{Equation 4.9}$$

$$F_{t+1} = (1-\beta) X_t + \beta(1-\beta) [X_{t-1} + \beta X_{t-2} + \beta^2 X_{t-3} + \ldots \qquad \text{Equation 4.10}$$

Since F_t, rather than F_{t+1}, can be obtained in the same way as in Equation 4.10, Equation 4.10 can be rewritten as Equation 4.11.

$$F_{t+1} = (1-\beta) X_t + \beta F_t \qquad \text{Equation 4.11}$$

Conventionally, $\alpha = (1-\beta)$, so that Equation 4.11 is usually given in the form of Equation 4.12.

$$F_{t+1} = \alpha X_t + (1-\alpha) F_t \qquad \text{Equation 4.12}$$

4.4.3 Double Exponential Smoothing

A problem with single exponential smoothing is the technique's poor ability to cope with trend in the time-series. When trend is present, forecasts lag the data. A development that goes some way to correcting this particular deficiency is *double exponential smoothing* or *linear exponential smoothing*. In double exponential smoothing, trend is assumed to take the simple linear form $X = a + b_t$. That is, a fixed quantity of demand b is added or subtracted in each successive forecasting period. If more complex trend is anticipated and it is the intention to deal with it by one of the naïve techniques, double smoothing can be extended to triple, or quadratic, exponential smoothing.[7]

In order to discover the lag between the data and the moving average caused by linear trend, it is necessary to test how well the moving average is performing. This can be done by using the technique a second time, with the same value of α, to take another moving average — but this time *a moving average of the first moving average already taken* (hence the term double exponentiation). By analogy, the amount by which the second moving average lags the first one is the amount by which the first moving average lags the original data. Put another way, remember that we have assumed that the trend is a fixed amount each period, not an accelerating rate. Consequently, although the first moving average is indeed lagging behind the sales demand data, the amount of the lag is consistent — the first moving average and the sales demand data are "in parallel" — the extent of the lag is keeping pace. Consequently, what is true for the parallel relationship between the first moving average and the sales demand data must also be true of the relationship between the second moving average and the first moving average. This second lag must be identical to the first lag. Again, because the trend is linear, the slope of the second moving average must be parallel to the slope of the first moving average, which in its turn is parallel to the slope of the original sales demand data. The position of all three trend slopes is illustrated in Figure 4.8.

---

[7] See S. Makridakis, S.C. Wheelwright and R. Hyndman (1998), *Forecasting: Methods and Applications*, Third edition, John Wiley & Sons ("the bible of forecasting"); R.G. Brown (1963), *Smoothing, Forecasting and Prediction*, Prentice-Hall.

Sales Forecasting

Figure 4.8: Principle of Linear Exponential Smoothing

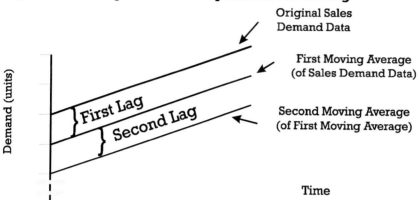

If S represents the original moving average and S' represents the second moving average, then from Equation 4.12 for single exponential smoothing we have Equations 4.13 and 4.14.

$$S_t = \alpha X_t + (1-\alpha) S_{t-1} \qquad \text{Equation 4.13}$$

$$S'_t = \alpha S_t + (1-\alpha) S'_{t-1} \qquad \text{Equation 4.14}$$

Note that although S_t and S'_t are in effect forecasts, they are not to be used as such directly, and are considered here merely as algebraic expressions. For this reason they are subscripted t, not (t+1). The corrective value for the lag between the original moving average and the moving average of the moving average is simply the difference between them. Because this is known, it can now be used as the corrective value for the lag between the original moving average and the sales demand time-series. In other words, the lag between the two moving averages, represented by $(S_t - S'_t)$, is used to adjust the original moving average, represented by S_t. This allows a new expression a_t to be formed, where a_t represents the corrected moving average of the sales demand data, and is given in Equations 4.15 and 4.16.

$$a_t = S_t + (S_t - S'_t) \qquad \text{Equation 4.15}$$

hence $\qquad a_t = 2S_t - S'_t \qquad \text{Equation 4.16}$

Although a_t is a systematic approximation for the data that corrects the lag between moving average and data, it cannot be used as a forecast because no account has yet been taken of the potential increment, in the next period, due to the on-going trend itself.

The lag $S_t - S'_t$ between the first moving average forecast (of the data) and the second moving average forecast (of the moving average) is caused by the presence of trend in the data. In order to make a forecast, it is necessary to find the extra contribution to the lag, caused by this trend, which occurs *in each individual period*. This is not, however, $S_t - S'_t$ since that is the accumulated difference between all of the lags which have been incorporated into the forecasts over all periods of time. In other words, the individual periodic trend lag is wanted, which will be called b, but it is the accumulated total $(S_t - S'_t)$ which is available. Clearly, the *number and proportions* of the individual occurrences of b in the forecasts equal the number and proportions of the data points which are themselves present. However, because trend is constant each period, each of the various values $X_t, X_{t-1}, X_{t-2} \ldots$ in Equation 4.7 (the original exponential smoothing equation) can be replaced by b to give the expression in Equation 4.17 for the accumulated trend $(S - S')$.

$$S - S' = \beta b + \beta^2 b + \beta^3 b + \ldots \qquad \text{Equation 4.17}$$

Summing the geometric series gives Equation 4.18.

$$S - S' = b \frac{\beta}{(1-\beta)} \qquad \text{Equation 4.18}$$

Substituting $(1-\alpha)$ for beta and rearranging terms gives the value for b in Equation 4.19.

$$b = \frac{\alpha}{(1-\alpha)}(S - S') \qquad \text{Equation 4.19}$$

Equation 4.19 gives an expression for the effect of trend b at time t. When the trend is to be used in "bootstrapping" a forecast (projecting it more than just one period into the future), b can be multiplied by the number of periods ahead m to give Equation 4.20.

$$mb_t = m\frac{\alpha}{(1-\alpha)}(S_t - S'_t) \qquad \text{Equation 4.20}$$

It is now possible to obtain a forecast for any period ahead (t + m) by combining Equations 4.16 and 4.20 to give the final Equation 4.21.

Sales Forecasting

$$F_{t+m} = (2S_t - S'_t) + m\frac{\alpha}{(1-\alpha)}(S_t - S'_t) \qquad \text{Equation 4.21}$$

The time-series previously shown in Figure 4.7 and forecast by a four-point single moving average is tackled again with double exponential smoothing and α set to 0.40. The results are illustrated in Figure 4.9, where, as before, the time-series is the continuous line and the one-ahead forecasts the broken line. The improvement in results is evident to the eye.

Figure 4.9: One-ahead Forecasts derived by Double Exponential Smoothing (α 0.40)

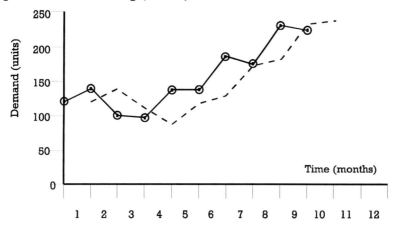

4.4.5 Adaptive Exponential Smoothing

There are two difficulties in using exponentially weighted moving averages. The first is deciding the value of α for each sales product in the first place and the second is determining how then to vary α, if at all, to achieve the right degree of response to the changing states of the data series. Adaptive exponential smoothing represents a mathematical attempt to overcome these difficulties.

Adaptive exponentially weighted moving averaging is derived from a method described in sub-section 4.6.1 for tracking and reporting forecast errors. Very broadly, the errors found between the demand data and the forecasts are themselves used to calculate successive new values of α, in order to make the forecasts respond more quickly or slowly to the most recent demand data points. Two terms are needed initially in the development of the procedure. The first is E_t, the "smoothed forecast error". This is simply obtained by smoothing the successive errors in the forecast e_t, where $e_t = X_t - F_t$. Equation 4.22 shows how E_t is calculated and updated.

$$E_t = \delta e_t + (1-\delta)E_{t-1} \qquad \text{Equation 4.22}$$

δ is a smoothing constant used only for the purpose shown. A likely but arbitrary value is chosen, and remains fixed, and so to that extent is a measure of unsatisfactoriness that remains with this method. The second term is M_t, the smoothed mean *absolute* deviation of the forecast error, obtained by smoothing successive absolute errors in the forecast $|e_t|$. M_t is given in Equation 4.23.

$$M_t = \delta |e_t| + (1-\delta)M_{t-1} \qquad \text{Equation 4.23}$$

A smoothing factor, which is the equivalent of alpha but is called A to avoid confusion with normal exponential smoothing, is then calculated as shown in Equation 4.24. Note that A is subscripted t, denoting that its recalculation takes place at every period.

$$A_t = \left|\frac{E_t}{M_t}\right| \qquad \text{Equation 4.24}$$

It can be seen that when large changes in the data occur, resulting in large forecast errors, e_t will also be large. Thus, e_t will approach or exceed the values for E_{t-1} and M_{t-1}, so that its weight predominates in the expressions for E_t and M_t given in Equations 4.22 and 4.23. Consequently (because e_t is the same as $|e_t|$ except for sign), $|E_t|$ will approach the value M_t. Thus $|E_t/M_t|$, will approach the value 1.0. Similarly, if forecast errors are small, the values of E_t and M_t will be relatively undisturbed, and $|E_t/M_t|$ will stay steady. If the expression A_t is now used instead of $|E_t/M_t|$, adaptive smoothing can be seen merely as the use of A_t in place of α in the original single smoothing equation. The technique was originally proposed in the form shown in Equation 4.25.

$$F_{t+1} = A_t X_t + (1-A_t)F_t \qquad \text{Equation 4.25}$$

There are now found to be two difficulties with adaptive smoothing itself, which arise from the behaviour of A_t. The first is the reactivity of the forecasts resulting from Equation 4.25 to an outlier in the data. Such an occurrence causes the high value of A_t to be compounded with the unusually high value of the outlier at that point,

Sales Forecasting

resulting in overreaction. To alleviate this, Equation 4.25 is rewritten with A_t one period behind, as shown in Equation 4.26.

$$F_{t+1} = A_{t-1}X_t + (1-A_{t-1})F_t \qquad \text{Equation 4.26}$$

The effect of this lag is that the value of A used in forecasting immediately following an outlier is a normal low one, whereas the high value of A resulting from the error with the outlier is applied to data occurring after the period of the outlier has past.

The second difficulty with adaptive smoothing is not cured by the lagged version. This is that while large forecast errors result in high values of A_t, subsequent small errors result in *steady*, rather than *low* values. In a word, A_t becomes stuck at a high value. This is illustrated in Figure 4.10, where the same time-series data (solid line) as in Figures 4.7 and 4.9 are forecast by adaptive smoothing (broken line). The changing values of A_t are shown in the graph. The consequence of A_t staying at a high value is that it will cause over-reaction to all subsequent outliers as if there were no time lag for them. One way of dealing with this may be to supplement adaptive smoothing with software logic, rather than further mathematics, to trap outliers and persistently large values of A. Better yet is to solve the problem of setting and changing α entirely through software as described in 4.4.6 below.

Figure 4.10: Adaptive Exponential Smoothing Showing Changing Smoothing Values

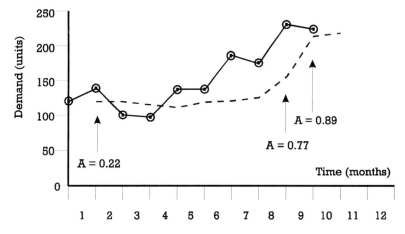

4.4.6 Software and Forecasting

It has been said that the enormous popularity in the 1960s and 1970s of the many variants of exponential smoothing was in part due to the modest demands they made on the equally modest computing resources then available. As Equation 4.12 shows, a product forecast can be calculated from three stored data variables, and even double exponential smoothing in Equation 4.21 requires only six. Now that the power of the computer is what it is, a new approach to forecasting has emerged in which *ad hoc* software procedures and algorithms are applied to boost the operation of the standard methods. For example, in the matter of the choice of α in exponential smoothing, it is possible, using an optimising routine such as Solver in Excel, to determine a value for it which will result in a minimum *mean squared error* as it applies, say, to half a dozen given past data observations.

(The mean squared error, MSE, is a common way of expressing the degree of accuracy of a product's forecasts over a span of time. Calculation of the mean squared error is shown in Equation 4.27, where n is the number of past data observations/forecasts; X_i is the actual sales demand in the ith period over the n months; and F_i is the forecast made for that month.

$$MSE = \frac{\sum_{i}^{n}(X_i - F_i)^2}{n} \qquad \text{Equation 4.27}$$

To determine "best" when judging the operation of a number of models such as those in Table 4.9, the MSE relating to the forecasts of each of them might be calculated and compared over the past six periods.)

Exploitation of the computer's power may be extended still further by the insertion into the software of many forecasting models, each with a different basis of operation. Each model may then be run each month, the particular forecast chosen to be issued to the user being the one emanating from the model that proved to be the "winner" the previous month. When sales demand for a new month becomes known, a potentially new winning model is determined by calculation and comparison afresh of each model's mean squared error. The models are again run in parallel, the forecast issued this time being that relating to the new winner. Thus, consider the three forecasting models in Table 4.9, run in parallel over five months. In April, we shall suppose that Model 1 has been shown to yield the smallest MSE over the previous six months (marked in the Table *Best*). In May, all three models are run as usual, but the forecast issued is that emanating from Model 1 (denoted by *). Model 2, however, is the winner, and so in June the forecast from Model 2 is issued to the user.

Table 4.9: Month to Month Model Switching in Multi Model Software

	April	May	June	July	August
Model 1	Best	*2nd	Best	*2nd	Best
Model 2	2nd	Best	*Last	Last	2nd
Model 3	Last	Last	2nd	Best	*Last

* Denotes that it is the model selected for issue by the software in the particular month.

It would not be unusual for multi-model software to have incorporated within it as many as twenty alternative models, many being of the same type but having alternative parameters — e.g. different values of α and δ. (Note that rather than leaving model selection each month to the operation of the standard procedure of choice as above, the user may optionally nominate a particular model to be used in a given month for a particular product/SKU forecast.)

There are two concerns with multi-model forecasting. First, forecasts are potentially calculated each month by a different procedure, so that the forecasting system controller has neither opportunity nor incentive to refine the operation of a specific technique.[8] Secondly, for long lead time products, because the basis on which bootstrapped forecasts are prepared is potentially changing each month, there may be unacceptably erratic varia-

---

[8] See Deming's funnel experiment in W. Edwards Deming (1986), *Out of the Crisis*, MIT Center for Advanced Engineering Studies, Cambridge, MA, p. 327 *et seq*. The experiment shows the chaos that results when a process is adjusted after each operation — reacting each time to common causes. See especially Chapter 13, Section 2.

tions in month-to-month raw material requirements — see sub-section 4.6.2. In contrast to multi-model forecasting, it may be thought that Bayesian forecasting (sub-section 4.5.3) provides the same adaptive capability, but that its use ensures that each month the forecasts are prepared on a basis consistent one with another.

4.5 THE CAUSAL FORECASTING FAMILY

In the causal techniques, a "model", or mathematical representation, is constructed from the time-series data, rather than the data considered afresh each time. The model is essentially a representation of the pattern of the data.

The essence of the modelling process is to find sets of cause-and-effect relationships between the various data points in the time-series. The relationships are worked out using the statistical techniques of regression. The normal use of regression in statistics is to explore the possible relationship between *different* phenomena through *correlation* (for example, the relationship between smoking habits and contracting cancer). In sales forecasting, the possible existence is explored of relationships within data relating to the *same* phenomenon, through *autocorrelation*. Although the sets of cause-and-effect relationships concern the same type of data (i.e. the sales demand for a particular product), the individual data values naturally occupy different places within the product's time-series. For example, consider the past three years' annual sales demand for a particular product:

$$X_{t-1}, X_{t-2} \text{ and } X_{t-3}$$

It seems commonsensical that the annual sales of this product in the current year, X_t, will be related to the sales in the immediately preceding year X_{t-1}, related somewhat less strongly to the sales in the year before that, X_{t-2}, and perhaps related quite weakly to the year X_{t-3}.

The general mathematical notation expressing a relationship between the sales demand data at time t and the sales demand data at time (t–1) is given by Equation 4.28, where γ and ϕ are constants (i.e. parameters) for this particular product time-series, and a_t denotes some degree of randomness (i.e. non-relationship).

Sales Forecasting

$$X_t = \gamma + \phi X_{t-1} + a_t \qquad \text{Equation 4.28}$$

In practice, as just discussed with regard to the annual sales of a product, the data point X_t is likely to be related to a number of the past annual sales points, not just that corresponding to (t–1). Thus, if we extend Equation 4.28 to still earlier periods (t–2), (t–3) ... we obtain Equation 4.29.

$$X_t = \gamma + \phi_1 X_{t-1} + \phi_2 X_{t-2} + \phi_3 X_{t-3} + \ldots + a_t \qquad \text{Equation 4.29}$$

4.5.1 Autoregressive Moving Averages (ARMA)

Equation 4.29 shows a possible autocorrelation between the values in a time-series depending on different factors ϕ_1, ϕ_2, ϕ_3 ... Suppose, however, that the weighting of these factors decreased in some fixed way, the older the data. The period-by-period decrease might be by a factor θ, where θ is between 0 and 1. So instead of writing ϕ_1, ϕ_2, ϕ_3 ... therefore, we might write a single term ϕ decreased each time by the fixed amount θ as follows: $(\phi - \theta)$, $\theta(\phi - \theta)$, $\theta^2(\phi - \theta)$. Thus at time t we derive Equation 4.30 and at time (t–1) we derive Equation 4.31.

$$X_t = \gamma + (\phi - \theta)X_{t-1} + \theta(\phi - \theta)X_{t-2} + \theta^2(\phi - \theta)X_{t-3} + \ldots + a_t$$
$$\text{Equation 4.30}$$

$$X_{t-1} = \gamma + (\phi - \theta)X_{t-2} + \theta(\phi - \theta)X_{t-3} + \theta^2(\phi - \theta)X_{t-4} + \ldots + a_{t-1}$$
$$\text{Equation 4.31}$$

We can now go through a number of steps that are not dissimilar to those in the workings out of linear exponential smoothing, recalling there that the technique was based on taking decreasing proportions of past sales demand based on the smoothing factor β. The first step is to multiply Equation 4.31 throughout by θ to obtain Equation 4.32.

$$\theta X_{t-1} = \theta\gamma + \theta(\phi - \theta)X_{t-2} + \theta^2(\phi - \theta)X_{t-3} + \ldots + \theta a_{t-1} \qquad \text{Equation 4.32}$$

Next, we subtract Equation 4.32 from Equation 4.30 to obtain Equation 4.33.

$$X_t - \theta X_{t-1} = \gamma(1 - \theta) + (\phi - \theta)X_{t-1} + a_t - \theta a_{t-1} \qquad \text{Equation 4.33}$$

Rearranging Equation 4.33 and replacing $\gamma(1-\theta)$ with a revised value of γ gives Equation 4.34.

$$X_t = \gamma + \phi X_{t-1} + a_t - \theta a_{t-1} \qquad \text{Equation 4.34}$$

Equation 4.34 shows the relationship between X_t and X_{t-1}. It would have been quite possible, however, to have derived a relationship between X_t and X_{t-2} instead of X_t and X_{t-1}. That is, Equation 4.34 may be rewritten for X_{t-2} as shown in Equation 4.35.

$$X_t = \gamma + \phi_2 X_{t-2} + a_t - \theta a_{t-2} \qquad \text{Equation 4.35}$$

We therefore write in all additional terms such as these to derive the basic ARMA expression in Equation 4.36. This is limited to n past terms. In practice, there will be as many terms as are shown to be relevant (and no more). In a times-series with monthly sales demand data, there are likely to be several dozen past time points; demand data more than (say) three years old may be unrelated or simply discarded.

$$X_t = \gamma + \phi X_{t-1} + \phi_2 X_{t-2} + \ldots + \phi_n X_{t-n} + a_t \qquad \text{Equation 4.36}$$

4.5.2 Box-Jenkins (ARIMA Models)

The technique described in the previous sub-section is known as an *autoregressive moving average model,* or ARMA model. If, instead of dealing with actual data values, such as annual sales of litre cans of primrose yellow paint of 2,500, 3,500 and 4,100, we deal with *differences* from one period to the next (0, +1000, +600 in the case of the paint), the technique is called autoregressive *integrated* moving averages, or ARIMA. The ARIMA model was popularised in the 1970s by George Box and Gwilym Jenkins, who described how a practical system could be set up to use it.[9] It is now universally referred to as the *Box-Jenkins Method.*

Box and Jenkins described a three-stage iterative technique for fitting an ARIMA model to a particular time-series. The stages are: (1) model selection; (2) estimation of the parameters; and (3) model checking. If Box-Jenkins were to be applied outside the context of a proprietary forecasting software system, all stages in

---

[9] G.E.P. Box and G.M. Jenkins (1970), *Time Series Analysis, Forecasting and Control,* Holden-Day.

its application would demand a thorough knowledge of the technique and its associated mathematics if they were to be followed to full effect by the user. Stage (1) also requires experience — for example, in how to manipulate the time-series to take account of non-stationary data. Stage (2), the choice of the parameters to be used (i.e. γ, ϕ and θ), is carried out either by trial and error or by effecting iterative improvement using a computer routine. Stage (3) of the process is particularly important. It consists of examining the *residuals* — the differences between the actual data points in the time-series and the "fit" of data achieved by the ARIMA model. The residuals can be thought of as the forecast errors. If they can be shown to consist of completely random data, the original modelling process has exactly represented the pattern of demand and has been totally successful. But if the residuals themselves can be shown to have a pattern — for example, being predominantly positive or predominantly negative — then this is the extent of the pattern *not* represented by the application of the technique. (The pattern in forecast errors is a better yardstick for measuring forecast merit than the mean squared error.)

When used by an everyday industrial user employing one of the several proprietary forecasting software packages which incorporate it, rather than by a trained statistical expert as described above, Box-Jenkins allows the company's forecasting administrator to select an appropriate model from a range of about a dozen. The choice is made informally by comparing the "shape" of the actual past sales demand for each product, displayed as a line graph on the VDU, with the models available in the package. The non-expert user receives maximum help from the system in such matters as parameter fitting. Even so, problems can arise in the application of Box-Jenkins when the nature of the time-series changes. Unless the analyst subsequently "refits" the model — selecting an alternative and refitting the parameters — forecasts may subsequently be poor. In other words, Box-Jenkins needs looking after.

The left-hand graph in Figure 4.11 shows a time-series (continuous line) and forecasts prepared by exponential smoothing (dotted line). It can be seen that smoothing is discounting the past data, including the sales demand peak at about Period 14. The right-hand graph in 4.11 shows the same sales demand data and the application of Box-Jenkins forecasting (dotted line). The Box-Jenkins model that has been fitted specifies that the nature of the sales demand is as we see in the data, namely a very sharp rise to a peak (Period 14) and then a pronounced decline. The Box-Jenkins forecasts are consequently indicating the start of another climb to a peak.

Figure 4.11: Comparison of Exponential Smoothing and Box-Jenkins

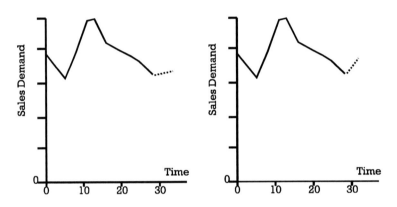

4.5.3 Bayesian Forecasting

With the exception of adaptive exponential smoothing, the forecasting models dealt with so far have been *fixed models* with *fixed parameters* and *fixed variances*. In other words, the changes in the level of demand from period to period as time progresses must be consistent. Or rather, if the pattern of change itself changes — for example, from a steady upwards trend in sales suddenly to an accelerating decline — the fact must be detected through error tracking (sub-section 4.6.1) and the model then adjusted through the personal intervention of the system controller.

Bayesian forecasting is quite different. The method is based on Bayesian probability theory,[10] and is capable of dealing with variable models, variable parameters and variable variances. From the practical point of view, this is of immense importance in manu-

---

[10] Named for its inventor, the Rev. Thomas Bayes (1702–1761), a nonconformist minister of Tunbridge Wells. Note that Bayesian forecasting is synonymous with the *Kalman Filters*, a term originating in engineering science.

facturing and sales; a company typically sells many hundreds of products and customer preferences and requirements change continually. Bayesian probability theory is essentially *experiential*, and consists of combining a *prior probability* (i.e. a probability made before the event or sales period) and the *outcome* of the event (i.e. the actual sales demand), to form a new, *posterior probability*. The posterior probability (in Bayesian forecasting terms) then becomes the prior probability to be used in the next forecast.

The difference between classic probability theory and Bayesian can be illustrated by the tossing of a coin. Suppose that a coin is tossed but it is not known whether it is "fair" or whether it has a bias towards Heads. After two tosses, the results are H, H, and by Bayes' theorem the probability that the coin is biased is 80 per cent. When a third Head is obtained, Bayes' theorem allows us to recalculate the odds, which now rise to 89 per cent biased. After a fourth Head, the odds are 94 per cent, and so on. In sales forecasting, the behaviour of the coin becomes the behaviour of the time-series, and the fairness, bias to Heads, etc. are the various states of stationarity, trend, step change and randomness. The Head or Tail result of the toss corresponds by analogy to the actual sales demand after the forecast has been made.

An important advantage of Bayesian forecasting, as we see from the example of the coin, is its ability to deal with multivariate data rather than simply univariate. A univariate model would be capable of dealing with the prior estimate (actual sales demand) and posterior estimate (forecast) from one viewpoint only — say, from the viewpoint that a pattern of trend existed in the time-series. By employing a multivariate model, it is possible to deal with several states simultaneously. As intimated, the states considered are stationarity, trend, step change and randomness. (Though note that in software implementations, if it is possible from extrinsic knowledge to discount the possibility of a given state, it is generally possible to nullify it in the model.) The patterns were previously illustrated in Figures 4.1 and 4.2. The probabilities of the time-series being in these various states are incorporated in the mathematics, as indicated. The subsequent calculations therefore take place using matrix algebra, not scalars.

One power of the technique is illustrated by its ability to distinguish between and deal with random data points and step change.

Consider the sales demand Q in a single month in Figure 4.12, and which is considerably greater than the previous level of demand (P). The Bayesian model calculates two probabilities based on the previous behaviour of the time-series: (i) that a step change has occurred; and (ii) that Q is a random point. Assuming that step changes are rare, the forecast for the next period is likely to be S. If the next month's demand turns out to be R, the Bayesian equation of *Prior Probability + Outcome = Posterior Probability* comes into effect to change the view of the original data point Q, so that the forecast is revised rapidly upwards in line with Q having been a step change.

Figure 4.12: Bayesian Forecasting dealing with Step Change/ Random

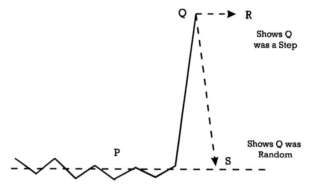

The development of Bayesian forecasting was initiated in 1948 by David Champernowne, his work being subsequently refined by Jeff Harrison and Colin Stevens. Figure 4.13 is derived from an illustration of Bayesian forecasting in action given inHarrison and Stevens' original paper in the *OR Quarterly*.[11] Sales demand is represented by the dotted line in the graph; the one-ahead Bayesian forecasts are given by the continuous line. The model concludes at Point A (month 20) that there is insufficient evidence yet of a step change, but shortly afterwards (month 22) this view is revised and a downwards step is initiated. The slope upwards from point B (month 440 is quickly recognised, even though there is little history of the demand pattern at that period.

---

[11] *Operations Research Quarterly*, Volume 22 (1971), Figure 3, page 355, Pergamon Press.

Sales Forecasting 127

Figure 4.13: Bayesian Forecasting in Action

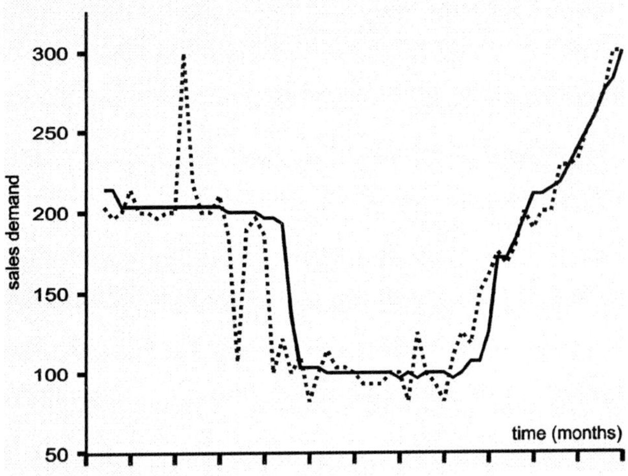

A number of large UK companies, able to call on their own resources for the considerable statistical expertise needed, have employed in-house Bayesian systems since the early 1980s, but, despite its manifest appropriateness for sales demand forecasting in manufacturing industry, seen particularly in its ability to "look after itself", it is only since the mid-1990s that the technique has been commonly incorporated in proprietary off-the-shelf forecasting packages.[12]

4.5.4 Correlation and Dummy Variables

It is possible to have a time-series in which the data values for each month are simply either "0" or "1"; 1 (one) indicates that some particular feature or event was present and active in that month, while 0 (zero) means it was absent. For example, suppose demand is thought to be affected by Easter, and Easter in two successive years was in March and then April. The time-series would be 0 0 1 0 0 0 0 0 0 0 0 0 (first 12 months) 0 0 0 1 0 0 0 0 0 0 0 0 (second 12 months). That is, the presence of the Easter weekend in the month has been denoted by 1 (Month 3 in the first year, and Month 4 in the second year). The absence of the Easter weekend in a

---

[12] A number of software companies are now installing Bayesian capability into their forecasting packages. The IBM Maapics DB sales forecasting module combines Bayesian and a naïve technique in parallel.

month has been denoted by 0. Regression analysis can now be used to determine whether and to what extent the level of sales demand is related to the presence or absence of Easter.[13]

The variable 1 or 0 to represent the presence or absence of an event is known as a *dummy variable*. In practice, several dummy variables might be set up, one for each of the conditions X1, X2, X3 thought to be relevant, to give an equation of the form shown in Equation 4.37.[14]

$$Y = b_0 + b_1X_1 + b_2X_2 + \ldots + b_nX_n + \ldots + e \qquad \textit{Equation 4.37}$$

4.5.5 Neural Networks

An idea similar to dummy variables, but employing rather more esoteric technology than humble regression mathematics, is to be found in the use of *neural networks*.[15] Neural networks and neural computers have their origin in the series of cells in the human brain known as *neurons*. The cells are interconnected as a group, or, put in alternative words, the neurons are interconnected as a network. A neuron may be stimulated by a chemical or electrical impulse, and if it is, will pass on this signal to its neighbours in the

---

[13] If the effect of Easter is very pronounced, as it is for the sale of chocolate, simple dummy variables will not do. Because the date of Easter can vary by six weeks, special procedures must be undertaken.

[14] Events occurring in the social and natural worlds are usually well enough taken care of in industrial sales forecasting by the application of seasonal analysis. Products where dummy variables might be used to effect, however, are those whose sales are particularly sensitive to extremes of weather — prolonged frost, deluges, heat waves . . . but it is not sufficient merely to say *heat wave*. A heat wave must be carefully defined: *so many consecutive days in which the temperature at 12.00 p.m. exceeds 90 ℉ over 70 per cent or more of the British Isles*, etc. The problem then becomes one of predicting the event's future occurrence, not fitting a regression series. In this case, past weather summaries and long-range forecasts may be purchased from the conjurers in the Meteorological Office, but they must be correctly interpreted. They are likely to be useful only at the group forecast level.

[15] Neural computers came to the attention of the public in 1996 through the Magnus "thinking" computer developed at Imperial College, London. Computers, however, have some way to go before they merit their 1950s nickname "electronic brains": the human brain contains some 10 billion neurons, each one capable of receiving hundreds of thousands of connections and sending signals at some 250mph.

network, thus stimulating them in turn. What is important is that if several adjacent neurons are stimulated by the original chemical or electrical impulse, the signals then passed on are progressively accumulated by the neighbours, leaving them, also, stimulated to various magnified degrees. These neighbours will then affect others in the neural network. The complex combinations of these signals resulting from various possible original external impulses constitute unique patterns, each one of which can be learned and — if it occurs again — can later be recognised by the brain. The brain can consequently recognise previous situations without the need each time to analyse the situation afresh.

The power of the computer has now grown sufficiently to be able to simulate the essential idea of the network of neurons. The neural computer consists of a series of data processors. Each processor is connected to an input and an output device. A particular processor is dedicated to a particular type of input data, and, if that input data is received, will in turn generate an output signal. The strength of the output signal is decided on by the people setting up the computer, having regard to the phenomenon itself and the response it is being programmed to mimic. When the programming is complete, the data submitted to the computer overall are sorted out and switched to the corresponding input ports of the processors. The nature, or "weighting", of the output that results from each processor is determined by the program incorporated in the particular processor. The signals that are then output from all the processors are interpreted together, to complete the analysis which the neural computer has been programmed to perform.

The inherent effectiveness of the neural computer depends critically on its correct set-up, or programming. That is, the output from each internal processor must be a correct interpretation of the input — *correct*, that is, to achieve the analysis required. Since there is no connection in mathematics or logic between the data input and output of each processor, the link between the two is at least in part interpretive.

Neural networks applied to sales forecasting have as inputs to their processors much the same *type* of information as regression models based on dummy variables. A dummy variable model might have "*sunshine* or *no sunshine*" (1 or 0) where the neural processor would have "hours of sunshine". Again, a "*major pro-*

gramme on TV or *nothing special on TV*" (1 or 0) versus "a scale estimate between 1 and 10 of the interest in the evening TV programmes". The outputs must each be considered and experimented with so that, when put together, the result is always consistent with the historical record of sales demand for the product in question. (By all accounts, this takes some doing.) It is then hoped that by anticipating the events that affect sales and inputting the data about them in the required way, the neural computer will produce outputs that will in turn lead to a correct product sales forecast.

What the neural network is attempting to represent are the events and conditions in the market and the market's reaction to them in the form of product purchases. The market, however, is a big place and individual product purchases are very numerous, suggesting immediately that statistics are the right tool. As for neural networking, many of the stimuli to buy are unobserved, and some are unobservable, and so cannot be represented as inputs to the network (the individual mood, impulses and feelings of each consumer, for example). Nevertheless, even if neural networking's future in time-series forecasting does not look bright, its potential use in providing an insight to the motivation and influences affecting the final purchasing decision by the individual consumer may be very valuable to the manufacturer in market research, marketing and product design.[16]

4.6 FORECASTING MANAGEMENT

4.6.1 Forecast Errors

Forecast errors are the differences between the sales demand forecasts and the actual sales demand values that come about, not mistakes in the forecasting process as such. There are two parts to their analysis. One is the tracking of them so as to monitor individual products and if necessary correct the operation of the forecasting algorithm. The other is reporting them, in a summarised form easily understood by management, as a means of keeping watch on the performance of the forecasting system itself. Schemes for

---

[16] The software package *4 Thought* from Right Information Systems, London, is based on neural networking.

Sales Forecasting

performing each task can conveniently be carried out as part of data pre-processing, since this takes place at the point where the latest demand becomes available for comparison with previous forecasts.

The means for following individual product forecasts was developed by Derek Trigg, and is known as *Trigg's Tracking Signal*. When each demand data reading is received at the end of Period t, the error in the forecast is obtained for each product as $e_t = (X_t - F_t)$. Values of e_t are smoothed by single exponentially weighted moving averages in the way described for adaptive smoothing in sub-section 4.4.5, using a smoothing factor δ of appropriate size. The equations that are applicable are Equations 4.22 and 4.23.

Rather than speak of an adaptive smoothing constant A_t, which is the absolute value of E_t/M_t (see Equation 4.24), we derive a simple *tracking signal* S_t, given in Equation 4.38. Note that S_t is not the absolute value, since sign is helpful in indicating whether forecasts are too high (S_t negative) or too low (S_t positive).

$$S_t = \frac{E_t}{M_t} \qquad \text{Equation 4.38}$$

Possible loss of forecasting control is indicated when the tracking signal for any product falls beyond limits set for it, or, more likely, limits set for the whole system. The limits and the best values for δ will be found by a company from time and experience. Those selected will depend on the degree of control required, the behaviour itself of the products' data series and the number of individual forecast interventions that staff can deal with in one period.

The normal purpose of the tracking signal is to bring forecasts that are possibly out-of-control to the personal attention of user staff, who can then examine the situation from line graphs on the VDU for each product. Consequently, its operation over the life of the forecasting system must be considered in all its aspects at the design stage. Error tracking is one of those encouragements to good management which, in time, can so easily fall into disuse. In order to prevent this, procedures should be instituted so that it is impossible for staff looking for quiet lives to rig δ and S_t. It may be wise to place control of the parameters in management's hands. In addition, if the forecasting of a product's data series has been signalled as being out-of-control, the consideration and possible adjustment of the forecasting by the system's standard means must be mandatory, perhaps by requiring a file of the signalled products to be serially scanned at a computer terminal. These strictures are all the more important if one of the more limited naïve forecasting techniques has been selected largely on the understanding that it is to be supported by extraneous error tracking of this kind. Use of error tracking is always available as support for a central technique, although there are some instances, such as with multi-model forecasting or with Bayesian forecasting, where it is surely superfluous.

In contrast to error tracking, the simple reporting of forecast accuracy has a managerial, rather than operational, purpose. Of all the threats to the forecasting system's continuing effectiveness, by far the greatest will be any development of belief by staff that, ultimately, good forecasting is expendable to more visible action such as expediting production and general fire-fighting. To guard against such a belief, selected managers including the master scheduler should receive a simple statement of achieved accuracy, in quantitative terms. They should also from time-to-time be reminded of the costs of inaccuracy, especially as manifest in the need to carry higher safety stocks because of it.

4.6.2 Multi-period Forecasting

Even when production lead times and the master scheduling horizon are short, an MPS review frequency of one month will always take the forecasting horizon into two periods.

The calculation of forecasts beyond one period is known as *bootstrapping*. The reason for the term stems from the procedure used in the naïve techniques. Thus, in making the calculations, the first period-ahead forecast itself contributes a "substitute" sales demand value to the second period-ahead forecast. Then the first and second period values contribute to the third forecast, and so on. The forecasting technique for one-ahead forecasts and for the equivalent multi-period (bootstrap) forecasts are clearly one and the same, both to ensure consistency and minimise the effort of developing and maintaining the system.

There is an obvious problem to be overcome when the forecasts prepared in one month are displaced in due course by those prepared in the subsequent month, particularly with regard to purchasing plans formulated on the basis of bootstrapped forecasts. For example, the forecasting performed after Period 1 may give a forward value of 400 units for Period 5, but the next forecasting run (performed after Period 2) may yield a forward value of 600 units forecast for the same Period 5. As mentioned in subsection 4.4.6, significantly large changes may be especially likely when operating a multi-model system, where the software is potentially switching the basis of the forecasts each month. It is, however, an objective of the system's operation to provide the best forecasts possible — ones based on the most recent available data. All decisions and actions to resolve the discrepancies, or at least to mitigate their potential impact on manufacturing and purchasing plans, must be consequently taken at the appropriate points in these systems on just the same bases as decisions are taken in dealing with other disturbances.

Bootstrapping with the causal techniques is simply a matter of extending the horizon of the model's calculation to cover the desired number of months. Optionally, the forecasts can be presented with ranges of values based on various statistical confidence intervals (95 per cent, 90 per cent, etc.).

4.6.3 Field Reports

Field reports consist of information about sudden, unusual market conditions, which it is known will have an immediate, very major effect on demand. Examples are: (1) *cold weather periods out-of-season and their effect on demand for soup;* (2) *plagues or mystifying absences, some years, of agricultural and horticultural pests;* and (3) *prolonged, unusually hot weather and its effect on sales of soft drinks and lager.*

Field reports ("concurrent market intelligence") are clearly not as useful as advance notice. The input and processing of concurrent information is best dealt with through the master scheduling system by converting it at once to "advance notice actual orders". See "Consuming the Forecast", Section 7.1.

4.7 DEALING WITH SPORADIC (INTERMITTENT) DEMAND

A phenomenon in very many companies is the presence of "sporadic", or intermittent, demand in the data series of certain sales products. The products concerned are often spare parts for assemblies sold by the company, though not replacements for wearing parts — i.e. they may be car seat runners and steering wheels rather than brake and clutch cables. Sales demand data for these "lumpy" products are likely to contain a few outliers of high magnitude, with the remaining values between the high points being zero or very low. (The big orders may be stock replenishments of major customers or overseas agents.) It is not possible to obtain satisfactory forecasts for lumpy products using standard techniques. Instead, the problem may be tackled by first ensuring that sporadic behaviour in demand is duly recognised when it is present, and then either (1) determining stock replenishments on the basis of forecasts prepared by a special procedure such as that put forward by John Croston (see below), or (2) managing the replenishment of the product's stock by a modified order point system, perhaps that suggested by Robert Brown. The natural place within the forecasting system for detecting products with intermittent demand and calculating either the parameters relating to the special procedure or those relating to the order point modification is clearly in data pre-processing. The product range might be re-analysed (say) every year to identify the parts and calculate the parameters necessary as described below.

A sales product data series exhibiting sporadic behaviour may be detected by applying the following rule-of-thumb. First, data forecasts F_t are required to be calculated through the system's standard technique. Next, the standard deviation of the forecasts, σ_1, over the number of periods n being examined, is determined as shown in Equation 4.39.

$$\sigma_1 = \sqrt{\frac{\sum (F_i - \mu_i)^2}{n}} \quad \text{where} \quad \mu_i = \frac{\sum F_i}{n} \qquad \text{Equation 4.39}$$

Then, a second standard deviation σ_2 is obtained of the errors between the data series values X_t and the forecasts F_t. If $(X_t - F_t) = e_t$, this is as given in Equation 4.40.

Sales Forecasting

$$\sigma_2 = \sqrt{\frac{\sum(e_i - \mu_2)^2}{n}} \quad \text{where} \quad \mu_2 = \frac{\sum e_i}{n} \qquad \text{Equation 4.40}$$

The rule now is that if σ_2 is greater than σ_1, intermittent or sporadic behaviour may be suspected of being present in the time-series over the n periods; visual examination of a line graph of the demand series may be carried out to confirm this suspicion.

Croston's Method

In 1972, J.D. Croston proposed a method for dealing with the lumpy demand problem by separately obtaining two values, employing the exponentially weighted moving average technique explained in sub-section 4.4.2, and summarised by Equation 4.12, the equation being reproduced here for convenience.[17]

$$F_{t+1} = \alpha X_t + (1 - \alpha) F_t \qquad \text{Equation 4.12}$$

The two values to be obtained are (1) the smoothed *size* of the intermittent customer orders when they are received, and (2) the smoothed *interval of time* between the moments of receipt of such orders. A third value calculated is a moving average of the absolute errors relating to the order size, and is used to obtain a safety stock level (see sub-sections 5.4.1 and 5.4.2). The order size and order interval forecasts are used in conjunction with the chosen safety stock level and the replenishment lead time of the product to determine from period to period whether a replenishment order should be placed.

To illustrate the method, suppose that the following data were to apply to a given lumpy product: the exponentially smoothed value of the customer order sizes = 70 units; the smoothed value of the order receipt intervals = 5 weeks; and the product replenishment lead time = 10 weeks. Then the number of lumpy orders ex-

---

[17] J.D. Croston (1972), "Forecasting and Stock Control for Intermittent Demand", *Operations Research Quarterly*, Volume 23, Pergamon Press. Also see a critique of this paper by F.R. Johnson and J.E. Boylan in the same journal, Volume 47 (1996). Croston explains in his original paper how the various values of α might be calculated in the three uses of Equation 4.12 and what assumptions are to be made as to the probability distribution of the interval of arrival of the sporadic orders. (The Bernoulli distribution is often used.)

pected over the lead time = 10 weeks / 5 weeks, or 2.0. In this case, the order point is 70 × 2.0 = 140 units, plus safety stock.

Brown's Order Point Method

The method described here is attributed to R.G. Brown, and is one of a number of ideas variously published in the academic press or by way of proprietary software for tackling this difficult problem.[18]

Brown's replenishment method comprises three *ad hoc* modifications to the order point procedure to make it suitable for the control of the stock replenishment of products in these circumstances.

Order point itself applied normally is fully described in Section 9.1. As explained there, a new replenishment is ordered when a product's stock level falls to:

(*Demand over the replenishment lead time + Safety Stock*)

where safety stock is calculated as described in Chapter 5, being based on the forecast error and the replenishment interval.

The first modification relates to the matter of detecting when the order point has in fact been reached. At one point, the product stock level is just above the order point; the receipt of a single customer order then takes the level below it. In other words, the subsequent stock replenishment order is requested *after* the order point has already been reached — i.e. after the *lead time demand + safety stock* level has been passed. If the average size of a customer order is C, then, from the expression above, on average the stock of the product in question will be c/2 below its order point when the new replenishment is called for. We might call the amount c/2 the "*overshoot*". Strictly speaking, therefore, under the order point system, a re-order should be made when stock reaches the following level:

---

[18] The Mercia LINCS suite of software, from Mercia Software, Birmingham, was originally developed from R.G. Brown's LOGOL system, and early versions incorporated Brown's ideas described here and in Chapters 5 and 20. The master scheduling module contains the seven rate-based planning rules given in Section 9.5. See also R.G. Brown (1977), *Materials Management Systems*, John Wiley & Sons; R.G. Brown (1982, Second edition), *Advanced Service Parts Inventory Control (ASPIC)*, Materials Management Systems Inc.

Sales Forecasting

(Overshoot + Demand over the replenishment lead time + Safety Stock)

For normal products, the average deficit c/2 hardly matters and is ignored — quite justifiably, if demand is made up of a stream of small orders. But with lumpy products, it does matter, since the lumpy order will be very large of itself and, by definition, very large in relation to the other parameters in the order point system (i.e. the forecast over the replenishment lead time).

Robert Brown recommends that the expression in Equation 4.41 should be used to calculate the overshoot, where the numerator $\overline{c^2}$ is the mean of the square of customer order quantities in the previous 12 months and the denominator c is the simple average of the order sizes.

$$\text{Overshoot} = \frac{1}{2} \times \frac{\overline{c^2}}{c} \qquad \text{Equation 4.41}$$

The second modification addresses the difficulty inherent with intermittent demand, as stated, that normal forecasting methods cannot be successfully applied to forecast the demand over the replenishment lead time. Two alternative solutions are suggested. The first is simply to estimate the annual total sales demand — say, A units. (Good estimates of A can usually be arrived at even for products with demand of this nature.) If the replenishment lead time is T days, the lead time demand D is (A / 250 days) × T units, assuming 250 trading days per year. The second solution is to forecast the expected lead time demand in time (t + 1) directly, using a simple exponential smoothing technique. If d_t is the average lead time demand at time t, β is a smoothing constant (say, 0.8) and D is the current actual lead time demand, $d_{(t+1)}$ is given by Equation 4.42.

$$d_{(t+1)} = \beta d_t + (1-\beta) D \qquad \text{Equation 4.42}$$

The final modification concerns the calculation of safety stock in the special circumstances prevailing, and acknowledges the difficulty in arriving at a safety value based on the methods described in Section 5.4. Brown suggests that the three-step process following should replace the calculations in standard procedures:

a) At the end of Period t, determine the smoothed forecast value d_{t+1} for the sales demand in the next period as given in Equation 4.42.

b) Also at the end of Period t, calculate a smoothed forecast M_{t+1} of the *mean square* of the sales demand in the next period (t+1) as shown in Equation 4.43, where M_t is the previous smoothed mean square of the demand in Period t, D is the latest demand in Period t as before, and where β is the smoothing constant.

$$M_{(t+1)} = M_t + (1-\beta) D^2 \qquad \text{Equation 4.43}$$

c) The standard deviation of the sales demand of the lumpy product is σ, as given in Equation 4.44.

$$\sigma = \sqrt{M_{t+1} - d_{t+1}^2} \qquad \text{Equation 4.44}$$

The standard deviation is now multiplied by a safety factor k (see sub-section 5.2.1 and Table 5.4(a)), chosen by management, to give a targeted percentage cover as shown in Equation 4.45.

$$S = k \times \sigma \qquad \text{Equation 4.45}$$

In summary then, the order point system can be used for sporadic products, but the order point OP itself is greatly modified as shown in Equation 4.46.

$$OP = d_{t+1} + \frac{\overline{c^2}}{2\overline{c}} + S \qquad \text{Equation 4.46}$$

Chapter 5

Safety Stock

5.1 JUSTIFICATION FOR SAFETY STOCK

At first thought, it appears that the notion of a safety stock, or buffer stock, held in reserve to guard against running out of sales stock, is contrary to such principles of good manufacturing practice as constant improvement, total quality control and "working to the numbers". Even though the counsel of perfection may be less than helpful in a busy manufacturing concern, it is true that every effort must be made to improve, and that better procedures and more accurate data should be the first responses to stock availability problems, not stock put to one side as a contingency.[1]

While we can endeavour to be more sure of raw material supplies and the production of component and intermediate products, at the very last link in the chain there is an uncertainty which is not capable of being eliminated, namely the potential activity of customers. We can make a forecast of the behaviour of customers in

---

[1] The contingencies which are guarded against by safety stock relate to the factors defined in this Chapter and are not connected with corporate strategy or policy other than customer service. Stock held as a buffer against the occurrence of some unlikely but potentially catastrophic event may be referred to as *policy stock*. An example in the past has been 12 months' supply of insulin held by the drug's then sole manufacturer against the possible destruction of its plant by fire (12 months being the time estimated as being needed to resume production). The decision to hold policy stock is usually taken by senior management and the quantity held is decided on by considering cost and likely scenarios should the catastrophe occur.

the marketplace, but, because of the factors at work there, that forecast will be in error.

The justification above says merely that one should provide a buffer of stock to guard against error but does not imply that any special care should be taken in calculating the amount. The buffer is there to prevent the manufacturer running out, so he provides enough needed to do the job, say, "three weeks' supply". This means that, if the monthly forecast of a product's sales demand is 800 units, 600 units of safety are to be held. If experience shows stock can still occasionally run out and there is a particular requirement with this product to provide excellent levels of availability, the amount can be increased, say, to five weeks (i.e. 1,000 units if the old forecast prevailed).

This finger-in-the-air approach to the provision of customer service is grossly unsatisfactory because it fails to relate customer service costs to quantitative objectives and quantitative achievement and, therefore, also fails to provide a means for their ongoing control. For example, it will be found that if customer service levels were indeed to be measured, what is actually achieved by the three weeks' supply all-round is, unsurprisingly, inconsistent from product to product. A frequent consequence of this is that safety stock is universally increased, as above, until the most difficult products are sufficiently well protected, but with massive overprovision on the "easy" ones. Again, because the company has no underlying rationale for relating customer service to safety stock levels, the effect on service of altering the safety amounts cannot be predicted. Change is hit and miss. In practice, it is rarely contemplated at all, even in response to new company conditions and objectives, except in such urgent circumstances as cash crises. Yet again, if the factors involved in setting safety levels are not understood, there are no pointers to potential lines of investigation or areas that might warrant improvement. Examples here, as we shall see, are the complex relationships between safety stock levels, customer service targets, sales forecast accuracy, lead times of manufacture, replenishment lot sizes and the costs of expediting the master production schedule.

In short, safety stock is a vital area of concern. The practical control of this stock must be thoroughly understood. And the operation of the safety stock system must be regarded as paramount

Safety Stock

in providing a targeted customer service level at the most obvious, visible point in the entire supply chain. The objective of the system is to overcome the hit-and-miss problem. It is to be able to calculate and set a level of safety stock on a product that then results in the achievement of a *previously defined*, quantified standard of customer service. If this can be done, a great many practical benefits will follow. For example, it will then be possible to use simulation to show the alternative financial investments in safety stock needed to provide alternative standards of service, or to show the effect that changes in master plan lot sizes or rescheduling capability will have on stock availability standards.

Achievement of the objective is far from easy. Target standards of customer service that make sense to customers and Sales and Marketing department staff are expressed in terms that cannot possibly be used in making calculations of stock quantities. To make such calculations, as we shall see, requires the mathematical treatment of a number of variables such as sales forecast errors and replenishment frequencies. What is needed, therefore, is a definition of customer service in these mathematical terms that will lead to safety stock amounts which, when applied, give results close to the sales and marketing target being aimed for. The successful formulation of such a definition is the heart of the subject.

The remaining four sections of this chapter deal with the following matters: (i) the identification and description of the variables, or data, likely to be needed in order to calculate safety stocks; (ii) customer service targets as they are defined by sales and marketing management; (iii) alternative definitions of customer service in "theoretical" terms — i.e. in terms that employ the data identified in (i) and allow the safety stock amounts to be arrived at — *the heart*; and (iv) system activities, particularly those which monitor and exploit the link between the practical target and the theoretical definition.

5.2 FACTORS INVOLVED IN SAFETY STOCKS

5.2.1 The Sales Forecast Error

The alternative patterns of sales demand for specific products in a month — trend, stationarity, seasonal variation and so on — have already been described in Section 4.2. The factors that together give rise to a pattern in a particular time-series are not infinite in number. Only a few of them will make any substantial contribution to it. Each one, however, is itself subject to social, economic and physical influences that are constantly changing in an unpredictable way. The effect of each of these influences on an individual factor will in some instances be to aggravate it (to a greater or lesser degree) and in others to alleviate it. The overall effect of all of them together on any factor will be such that aggravations and alleviations will often largely cancel each other out. Occasionally, however, influences will reinforce each other, increasing or decreasing the importance of the factor on sales demand substantially. Finally, the variations in the degrees of importance of the different factors will again tend to cancel out to leave the *status quo* — i.e. sales demand arising according to an established pattern — but, again, there will be occasions of reinforcement, giving rise to peaks and troughs in demand. In summary, there is an inescapable element of randomness in a product's sales demand due to the interplay of those *common causes of variation* in the relevant market. If the degree of randomness in demand is large, so that forecast errors are potentially large, it will be necessary to carry a commensurately large quantity of safety stock to protect stock availability. If the degree of randomness is small, the amount of safety stock needed to give the same level of protection will similarly be small. To take matters further clearly requires the extent of the forecast errors to be described in exact terms, and this in turn requires the application of statistics.

Consider the monthly forecast errors for a given product obtained over three years.[2] The 36 errors are individually enumerated in Table 5.1 in ascending order of size. Next, each of them has been assigned to one of nine classes or ranges. The nine classes and the number of errors in each are given in Table 5.2. Finally, a histogram illustrating the frequency of the forecast errors in the different classes is given in Figure 5.1.

---

[2] In fact, the errors should relate to the master plan freeze period or, in distribution, to the lead time of depot supply, but discussion of this is deferred until sub-section 5.2.2.

Safety Stock

Table 5.1: 36 Forecast Errors in Units (from Three Years' Data), Arranged in Ascending Order

−220	−138	−90	−38	−24	−8	12	26	55	80	112	166
−152	−105	−74	−32	−18	−4	18	38	70	88	125	214
−140	−101	−38	−25	−15	12	25	40	74	110	151	225

Table 5.2: The Distribution of the 36 Forecast Errors in Table 5.1, in units, by Class

Class No.	1	2	3	4	5	6	7	8	9
Error Classes	≤ -175	> -175 ≤ -125	> -125 ≤ -75	> -75 ≤ -25	> -25 ≤ 25	> 25 ≤ 75	> 75 ≤ 125	> 125 ≤ 175	> 175
Number of Errors	1	3	3	5	9	6	5	2	2

Figure 5.1: Histogram of 36 Forecast Errors, from Table 5.2

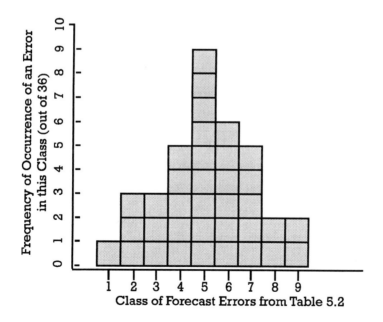

If the individual forecast errors in the classified data are denoted by x_i, the mean $\bar{x}$ is given by Equation 5.1 and the standard deviation s is given by Equation 5.2.

$$\bar{x} = \frac{\Sigma x_i}{n} \text{ for } i = 1, 2, \ldots, n \qquad \text{Equation 5.1}$$

$$s = \sqrt{\Sigma \frac{(x_i - \bar{x})^2}{n}} \text{ for } i = 1, 2, \ldots, n \qquad \text{Equation 5.2}$$

It can generally be supposed for goods sold directly by the manufacturing concern that the statistical distribution of forecast errors about the mean is normal, or Gaussian. As we saw in sub-section 3.4.2, however, there are other statistical distributions besides this. Colin Lewis points out that others known sometimes to be applicable to forecast errors are the Poisson, negative exponential and gamma distributions.[3] It is believed that one or other of these, rather than the normal distribution, is particularly likely to be present in wholesale when there have been supply difficulties: in a period when sales demand has in any case been heavy, buyers, seeing that stocks are low and remembering the difficulties, compound the situation by ordering or buying more than they need while they can still get it.[4] This phenomenon would clearly affect the manufacturer controlling a network of distribution depots or supplying customers in a limited consumer products market. A sketch of the Poisson distribution (when the mean $\lambda = 2$) is given in Figure 5.2, showing the skew to the left (forecasts too large) and the long tail to the right (forecasts too small). If such a distribution were true of a product's forecast errors, since the calculations involving safety stock involve probabilities at the far end of the distribution where the differences between the normal and Poisson are very considerable, then clearly quite wrong answers would result from use of the normal distribution. It is as well to be sure which type is involved, therefore. Thus, if the company manufac-

---

[3] C.D. Lewis (1975), *Demand Analysis and Inventory Control*, Saxon House (see Chapter 12 for simulation of inventory problems). See also *Demand Forecasting and Inventory Control* by Colin Lewis (1998).

[4] Safety stock calculations as described in this chapter are not applicable to safety stock at retail outlets. Apart from very large volume operations and very tiny operations, the stock quantities provided for customer service in retail are best determined by the simulation of queues (see Lewis (1975), op. cit., Chapter 12), assuming the pattern of arrival of customers for each product line to conform to the Poisson distribution. See also intermittent demand, Section 4.7.

Safety Stock

tures consumer goods, the forecast errors for a small number of representative products in each of the various sales groups should be subjected to the chi-squared tests, or "goodness of fit" tests, to find what form the distribution of errors takes or, at least, to confirm that it is indeed normal.[5] The chi-squared test for normality requires the mean and variance (s^2) to be known, and estimates of these are obtainable from Equations 5.1 and 5.2. (Also see the Poisson distribution in sub-section 14.3.1 in relation to the c and u attribute charts.)

Figure 5.2: Sketch of the Poisson Distribution, with Long Tail (when the mean of the distribution $\lambda = 2$)

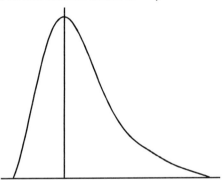

We proceed on the basis that the distribution of the forecast errors is normal, or Gaussian,[6] as it usually will be. The normal curve is also known as the bell curve, and the beginnings of a bell can be seen in the histogram in Figure 5.1. What the histogram is illustrating is the *probability distribution* of the 36 forecast errors.

---

[5] To test the forecast errors to confirm normality may seem a little overcautious. On the other hand, it is extremely baffling and dangerous to set a level of safety stock by a sophisticated method only to find that the customer service actually achieved is quite different from what was intended. The danger arises from the frustration of sales and marketing staff in these circumstances, who abandon science and return to five-weeks' supply.

[6] Despite the name, the mathematics of this distribution were worked out not by Carl Friedrich Gauss (1777–1855), but by Abraham de Moivre (1667–1754). A Huguenot refugee living in London, de Moivre is also responsible for Stirling's Formula. (His considerable talents seem not to have included picking PR agents.) De Moivre also initiated the formulation of what is now known as the *central limit theorem* (see sub-section 14.1.1).

Before dealing with the probability distribution of the normal curve, which is complex, let us first consider a simple, familiar parallel, namely the probabilities and scores resulting from the throwing of two 6-sided dice. There are 36 possible combinations of the dice (6×6) and 11 possible scores. The frequency with which each score can occur is given in Table 5.3. The third line of the table gives the probability of the corresponding score.

Table 5.3: The Scores and Probabilities from throwing Two Six-Sided Dice

Score	2	3	4	5	6	7	8	9	10	11	12
Frequency of Occurrence	1	2	3	4	5	6	5	4	3	2	1
Probability of this Score	$\frac{1}{36}$	$\frac{2}{36}$	$\frac{3}{36}$	$\frac{4}{36}$	$\frac{5}{36}$	$\frac{6}{36}$	$\frac{5}{36}$	$\frac{4}{36}$	$\frac{3}{36}$	$\frac{2}{36}$	$\frac{1}{36}$

The score from throwing two dice is a *discrete* random variable, "discrete" meaning that only a limited number of outcomes is possible, in this case the 11 values. Rows 1 and 3 of Table 5.3 allow us to see at a glance the various probabilities of each score in throwing the dice, and is known as a *discrete probability density function*, the term "function" meaning a reference table, as in this case, or a mathematical formula. (Note and remember that the total of all 11 probabilities is unity.) The table might now be used, say, to find the probability of throwing either a 7, 8 or 9 with the dice. The total of the three probabilities for these scores in Row 3 is 15/36. Again, the probability of the score of 9 being exceeded can be readily obtained from the Table by adding the probabilities for 10, 11 and 12 to obtain 6/36. The frequencies and scores in Table 5.3 are further illustrated in Figure 5.3 as a histogram. The histogram, as well as the Table, can be used to find the probabilities of the various dice scores directly. It will be recalled that the *areas* of the vertical bars of a histogram are meaningful, not just their heights. Thus to find the probability once more of throwing either a 7, 8 or 9 with the dice, we simply add the areas of the vertical bars to which these scores correspond and compare the result to the total area of all 11 bars. The area for the scores totals 15 and the total area is 36, so that the chance of any of these three scores is again 15/36. To

Safety Stock

find the probability that the score of 9 will be exceeded, we add up the complete area to the right of the value 9. This totals 6, so that the chance of throwing better than 9 is 6/36. Probabilities, then, are represented by the areas of the histogram. (The extent of the area is the origin of the term "density".)

Figure 5.3: Probability Distribution for a Score from the Throw of Two Six-Sided Dice

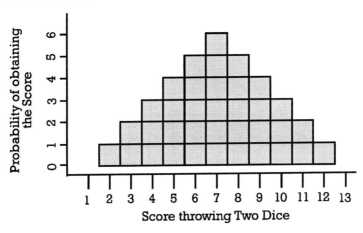

We return now to sales forecast errors and the 36 errors illustrated by the histogram in Figure 5.1. Because they can take any value, forecast errors constitute a *continuous* random variable, rather than a discrete one. As we have discussed, the distribution of the errors is held to be normal, or bell-shaped. Figure 5.4 shows the normal distribution as a thick, smooth curve superimposed on the original histogram from Figure 5.1.

Figure 5.4: The Normal Curve Replacing the Histogram of Forecast Errors

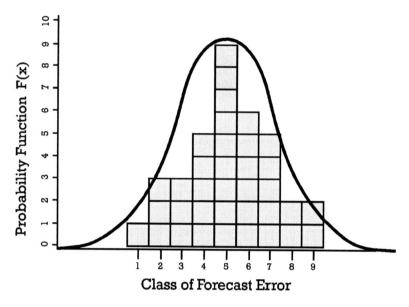

We may consequently abandon the histogram of the forecast errors and substitute for it the formula for the probability distribution of the normal curve, this being a *continuous probability density function*. The function, or formula, which describes the normal curve is given in Equation 5.3, where x is the continuous random variable (i.e. the forecast error), μ is the mean of x and σ is the standard deviation.

$$F(x) = \frac{1}{\sigma\sqrt{2\pi}} e^{-(x-\mu)^2 / 2\sigma^2} \qquad -\infty < x < \infty \qquad \text{Equation 5.3}$$

Just as we could find the probability of specified values in the throwing of two dice by adding up areas of the histogram in Figure 5.3, so can we find the probability of a forecast error lying between any two values p and q, these being points on the horizontal axis of the normal curve, by finding the area under the curve between them. (The total area under the curve is unity.) Again, remembering that in reality the horizontal scale of the normal curve lies between $-\infty$ and $+\infty$, the probability that a forecast error is less than the value p is obtained by integrating (i.e. adding up) the probability density function in Equation 5.3 from $-\infty$ to p to find the

Safety Stock

corresponding area under the curve from the extreme left up to the point p.

Because, mathematically, integrating Equation 5.3 is very difficult to do, and because also we would prefer an expression that will directly give results general for all curves to one dependent on specific instances, a simplification is made. This is to "standardise" the normal curve (i.e. standardise "X" — the values which constitute x in Figure 5.4) by subtracting µ and dividing by σ, to yield a substitute for the forecast errors, called "Z" — i.e. new values z in place of the previous values x. That is, we substitute Z for X as shown in Equation 5.4.

$$Z = \frac{X - \mu}{\sigma}$$ Equation 5.4

There are two consequences of standardisation. The first is that Equation 5.3 is very considerably simplified, as shown in Equation 5.5 for the revised probability density function F(z).

$$F(z) = \frac{1}{\sigma\sqrt{2\pi}} e^{-\frac{1}{2}z^2} \quad -\infty < z < \infty$$ Equation 5.5

The second consequence is that the normal curve in Figure 5.4 must be redrawn with a new horizontal scale. This is shown in Figure 5.5. There are two differences from before. First, because we have subtracted µ in performing the standardisation, the mean is now centred at zero. Although it cannot be seen by eye, the mean previously was centred at 8 units (this value may be calculated from Equation 5.1 and Table 5.2). In other words, the horizontal scale has been shifted along slightly to the right. The second difference is the scale itself. Although the scale lies, in reality, as stated above, between $-\infty$ and $+\infty$, we could see previously that the vast bulk of the curve's area lay between values of approximately 100 units less than the Class 1 forecast errors and approximately 100 units more than the Class 9 forecast errors (in fact, from −283 units to +299 units). To obtain the standardised version, however, we have divided by σ, and σ has a value of 97 units (from Equation 5.2 and, again, Table 5.2). Consequently, and also making allowance for the revised mean of zero, the new scale, illustrated in Figure 5.5, shows the bulk of the re-scaled curve lying between −3 and +3 (these numbers are not "units"; they are dimensionless.)

Figure 5.5: The Normal Distribution of Forecast Errors (Standardised)

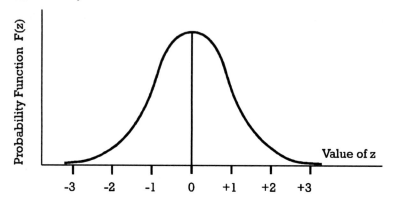

The safety stock calculations gone through in Section 5.4 involve the standardised forecast errors, Z. In particular, they employ the term "safety factor". The safety factor in Section 5.4 is synonymous with the dimensionless scale of the standardised normal curve — a safety factor of 2.0 means the provision of safety stock to guard against forecast errors up to +2.0 on the scale in Figure 5.5. As a consequence of working with the standardised normal distribution, it is necessary ultimately to reverse the standardisation by converting the limited, dimensionless scale of Z and the safety factor (Figure 5.5) to the previous scale of forecast errors and the previous mean. The equation to reverse Z to the original X is given in Equation 5.6, and is obtained from Equation 5.4 by rearranging terms.

$$X = \sigma Z + \mu \qquad \text{Equation 5.6}$$

It is seen from Equation 5.6 that, first, the scale and unit measure of X are restored by multiplying by σ. In the example of the 36 monthly forecast errors illustrated in Figure 5.4, and a safety factor of 2.0, this means 194 units of safety (97 units × 2). Second, the mean is restored to its original value of 8 units by shifting the complete scale back somewhat to the left. While the first adjustment is obvious, the second to accommodate the mean should not be omitted either. Remembering that a forecast error is $(X_t - F_t)$, if the

Safety Stock

mean is positive there is consistent underforecasting. This must be allowed for in any safety stock quantity calculated by adding to it the amount of the underforecast (in our example, by adding 8 units to the 194). Similarly, if the mean is negative so that the forecasts are consistently too high, an adjustment might be made in the opposite direction. It is recalled from Section 4.1, however, that consistent underforecasting or consistent overforecasting is a mark of failure in the forecasting process itself and arises because the pattern of data is not fully being represented in the forecasting model. The parameters of the model should therefore be adjusted or a new model selected, so that the mean of the forecast errors is zero, or very close to it. When this has been done, the safety stock variables relating to the product should be promptly remeasured and recalculated. (See also the remeasuring of forecast errors of seasonal products during peak months in sub-section 5.5.2.)

In conclusion, the first factor involved in safety stocks, the forecast error, has been fully described by the probability density function $F(z)$, σ and μ, and these terms are thus available for use in definitions of customer service in Section 5.4. The calculation of the variables from the product's forecast errors for each sales product is one of the first tasks of a proprietary safety stock software module.

5.2.2 The Master Plan Freeze Period or Lead Time of Re-supply

As we shall see in Chapters 6 and 7, the company's master plan for the production of sales products is usually reformulated once per month, among other things taking into account the latest sales forecasts. The simple technique for incorporating forecasts in master planning was described in sub-section 4.3.4. Because of changes, especially forecast changes, there will usually be a need to reschedule the production of many sales products following the new master plan's release. Immediately afterwards, however, two *time fences* are placed at points on the plan's horizon, creating *frozen* and *semi-frozen zones* from the current period up to a period in the future at least one month away, and preventing the master scheduling software from automatically rescheduling plans occurring in them (see sub-section 6.5.1). Although authority must be held in order to do so, and different companies have different rules, the master planner may himself reschedule plans in the frozen and semi-frozen zones interactively at the VDU. The system, as stated, may not do so, even though arithmetical calculations of projected stock balances may indicate potential negative stock balances or potential excess stock holdings. In the event that a negative or excess stock is detected, the system instead issues a message *recommending* that the master schedule plan be rescheduled, but human judgement must then be exercised as to the actions to be taken. Note that messages are not issued by the system when projected stock balances simply fall to between the products' safety stock levels and zero — the safety stock is there to be used.

The forecast errors $(X_t - F_t)$, described at length in sub-section 5.2.1, are the differences between the actual demand X in period t and the forecast F for that period, the period t being a forecasting month. In practice, for sales products held at and supplied from the master scheduling source, $(X_t - F_t)$ should be modified as shown in Equation 5.7, where L is the interval of time, in fractions of a month, from the calculation of the forecast to the end of the next complete master plan period (after which, plans will again be readjusted and rescheduled).

Freeze or Lead Time Error $= L \times (X_t - F_t)$ Equation 5.7

In short, for sales products at the master scheduling source of supply, what should be considered is not simply the forecast error as discussed in sub-section 5.2.1, but *the forecast error over the period from forecast preparation to the end of the next complete master planning month*. (Hence, somewhat obviously, the master plan review and reformulation should be timed to start as soon after forecast preparation as possible. If it takes place, say, one week afterwards, L will be approximately 1.25.)

Where they concern products held at the point of master scheduling, therefore, the safety stocks calculated by the various methods in Section 5.4 are slanted to the protection of customer service and stock availability over the master plan month, seemingly obviating the need to reschedule production during that period due to higher-than-usual demand. As a matter of policy, however, in some circumstances and for some products, the company may both finance the holding of safety stock and further increase the cost and quality of customer service by authorising the master production scheduler to reschedule the production of sales products in the freeze periods if stockouts seem to be looming. The trade-off between the cost of safety and the cost of rescheduling must be carefully considered. It is explicitly addressed in sub-section 5.4.3. (There is one extreme case of production rescheduling. In the Just-in-Time system, production control and physical production are organised so that a quantity of every sales product, amounting to one day's sales demand, is produced every day. Actual production quantities for each product are then varied each day in accordance with the previous day's sales, so reducing the safety stocks needed to negligible amounts.)

Forecast errors relating to sales from points in a distribution network — regional warehouses, depots and so on, each remote geographically from the source of manufacture or supply — should similarly be modified as shown in Equation 5.7. In this case, the term L is the lead time of re-supply of the sales product from its source, i.e. the factory or central warehouse. Specifically, if the sales outlet is being replenished through a centrally operated distribution planning system such as "Fair Shares" or DRPII (see Section 20.2), this being integrated with the master schedule, L is calculated from the point of detection of the need to re-supply the depot, to the receipt and putting away of the replenishment stock when it arrives. If the sales outlet is operating a re-order point system (see Section 9.1), L is the time from the stock level falling below the order point at the sales outlet, to the placing of the order, and then, finally, to the eventual receipt and putting away of the goods.[7] In this last case, in order to determine L, each of the elements which go to make it up must be identified and measured by the methods used in work study or even by time-based process mapping (sub-section 8.7.1). They include the raising and sending of the order; order receipt and processing at the factory; packing and despatch; transit of the load; and the processing and putting away of the delivery. When this has been done, it is likely to be

---

[7] Note what the text says: *the stock level falling below the order point* — not someone noticing that it has already done so. If stock levels are only checked by the system once per week, a full week must be added to L in addition to any delay after this in placing and receiving the replenishment order itself.

found that the durations of many of the activities are capable of being shortened by relatively simple changes in procedures. If the lead time L can be reduced, the lead time forecast error will similarly be reduced so that less safety stock will be needed to achieve the same level of customer service. In other words, the small cost of shortening the lead time will have a disproportionate effect on the cost of stockholding in the distribution network. The ultimate goal is the same as in Just-in-Time: *fast response to the market* — fast response to what the market is actually doing, not to an error-prone prediction of what it might do.

When dealing with lead time forecast errors and the supply of stock from an independent source, such as with the purchase of sales goods by a wholesaler or merchant, consideration should be given to the variability of the lead time itself. There are two classic approaches to this problem, both assuming there to be no relationship between the variability of sales demand over the replenishment period and the variability of the lead time of the replenishment. In the first approach, the mathematics simply combines the mean and standard deviation of the variation in the demand and the mean and standard deviation of the variation in the lead time. In the second, the probabilities of various lead times being achieved by a supplier are each combined with the various supplier service levels, to calculate an overall supplier service level. R.G. Brown refutes the assumption that the variability of lead time is independent of the variability of demand, advancing a number of convincing anecdotal arguments in doing so,[8] and advocates quite a different solution to the problem. As an activity separate from recording sales demand during the month, demand can also be recorded over the supply lead time directly. Demand over the lead time is simply defined as sales demand year-to-date when the replenishment order from the supplier is received and put away, minus sales demand year-to-date when the order is

---

[8] When things are busy and a manufacturer's production capacity is under pressure, his lead times of supply are likely to increase. When business is slack, a distributor might delay despatching goods until he has a full load. See R.G. Brown (1982), *Advanced Service Parts Inventory Control (ASPIC)*, Second edition, Materials Management Systems Inc.

originally placed. An analysis of these data would seem to end all argument.

Variable lead times for the supply into stock of its own sales products will hardly be a problem affecting the competently managed manufacturing company in full control of its own production and distribution operations. The purchasing manager in manufacturing, on the other hand, can experience variable lead times of supply even when all effort has been made to weed out suppliers who fail to deliver on time. Achieved UK delivery dates of foreign purchases of raw materials seem especially uncertain, even when supplies are coming only from Europe. In the case of raw materials, however, it should be the lead time only which might be the problem, not lead time combined with the delivery quantity. Assuming its variability follows the normal distribution, the mean and standard deviation of the lead time of each raw material in the risk category can readily be measured. A safety factor of (say) 3 standard deviations might then be allowed for in the timing of the order placement and delivery request date from each such supplier.

5.2.3 Protection of Service by Working Stock

The "working stock" that arises because of the manufacturing lot size of a sales product, or that arises because of the delivery quantity to a warehouse or depot, is available as a buffer against forecast error. If a product is replenished 12 times per year, there are 12 times when its stock is low and service is at risk. If the same product were to be replenished just once per year (with 12 times as much stock, of course), there is only one chance of running out — immediately before the big replenishment is due. In any theoretical calculation of safety stock, therefore, one might expect to see the protection offered by working stock accounted for by the inclusion in it of the expression A/N, where A is the annual sales demand for the product and N is either the annual number of manufactured lots or the annual number of depot deliveries.

5.2.4 The Cost of Stockholding and the Cost of Rescheduling

Because there are alternative ways of providing high stock availability other than by holding safety — for example, by rescheduling the master plan; through fast response; or through JIT — the value of the stock and, therefore, the cost of the stockholding have a bearing on the quantity arrived at. The cost must be considered alongside the cost and feasibility of rescheduling or fast response.

5.2.5 The Physical Nature of the Stock

In distribution, one way to provide additional customer service is to trans-ship stock between depots: if Depot A runs out of stock of a given product, excess stock at Depot B can be transferred in. Trans-shipment arrangements work well in certain circumstances but are unsuccessful in others — see Section 20.3 (footnote 23). In the absence of a viable trans-shipment option, therefore, distribution logisticians might consider increasing the safety stock on such products.

5.3 CUSTOMER SERVICE TARGETS

Customer service in this context refers to stock availability; before discussing how it might be defined, we should first crook the knee to other marks of good service besides this. The importance of sales order processing and such concomitant activities as packing, despatch and transportation have already been mentioned in Section 2.4. Measures of performance which might be used to monitor them were also given. Above all, the goods themselves should be delivered on the right day, in the right quantity and at the standard of conformance to quality agreed and promised.

Customer service targets in terms of stock availability will clearly vary widely depending on the nature of the business — a number of alternative suggestions are given in Magee et al. (1985).[9] If a customer order typically consists of ten or a dozen lines (i.e. the specification of ten or a dozen different sales products, one product per line), the company might set a target thus: *90 per cent of all orders to be fulfilled in respect of every line, the items to be delivered within the limits of 36 hours to 48 hours of order receipt by the company.* If an order more typically is for a single

---

[9] John F. Magee, William C. Copacino and Donald B. Rosenfield (1985), *Modern Logistics Management*, John Wiley & Sons. The authors are senior executives with Arthur D. Little Inc., Cambridge, MA. (Note that the transport topics in this book are discussed from a US point of view. For a UK treatment of transport and distribution, see John L. Gattorna (Editor) (1994), *Handbook of Logistics and Distribution Management*, Gower Publishing.)

Safety Stock

product only, a target might be set: *95 per cent of all orders fulfilled completely from stock within 24 to 36 hours.* (It will be appreciated in the foregoing that the percentage figures in the definitions are determined by safety stocks and material availability, while the delivery efficiencies are concerned with sales order processing and system capability — see, particularly, Section 2.4, but also sub-section 13.2.2.) Whatever target is formulated by the Sales and Marketing manager, its achievement or otherwise should be readily capable of measurement through the SOP system. Consequently, subtleties should be avoided. All the data needed to evaluate service achieved and produce summaries of it in the terms of the definition should be fully recordable by a computer program entirely through the system's transactions and files.

It will be noticed in the mild, half-complete suggestions for targets above that they are expressed in terms of total service from all products. (In practice, there might be different targets set for different product groups.) The Sales and Marketing manager considers service in this way, which coincides with the view and experience of the customer. The term *subjective availability* has been used, as opposed to strictly objective availability. A customer service definition in theoretical terms should consequently, if possible, similarly be expressed as the service provided by the sales range as a whole. To achieve this, the service provided for from each individual product should be consistent from one to the next.

5.4 DEFINING CUSTOMER SERVICE IN THEORETICAL TERMS

We recall from the introduction that the heart of the subject of safety stocks is to find a definition of customer service in mathematical terms that will lead to safety stock amounts which, when applied, give results close to the Sales and Marketing target being aimed for. Four alternative definitions are examined. The first is not a serious candidate, but serves to illustrate an important point about the normal probability distribution. The second is the standard method, first published in 1959 by R.G. Brown and included, perhaps with others, in all safety stock software systems. The third and fourth were also devised by the ubiquitous Brown, in conjunction with George Gerson,[10] and are appropriate respectively for setting safety stocks at the master scheduling source of supply, where rescheduling is a viable alternative to safety stock, and for setting them at locations where rescheduling is impractical or unduly costly — say, at geographically remote depots. Note that in this Section we continue to use the forecast errors "z" for the sake of clarity, though in practice these should be adjusted to the freeze or lead time errors "Lz" as discussed in sub-section 5.2.2.

5.4.1 Percentage Forecast Errors

The standardised normal curve in Figure 5.5 is reproduced twice in Figure 5.6. The first illustration shows the area under the bell-curve shaded from the extreme left of the curve (i.e. $z = -\infty$) up to the value of z equal to +1.0. The second illustration shows the shading up to the value of z equal to +1.5.

Figure 5.6: The Standardised Normal Curve with (top) 84.13 per cent shaded, and (bottom) 93.32 per cent shaded

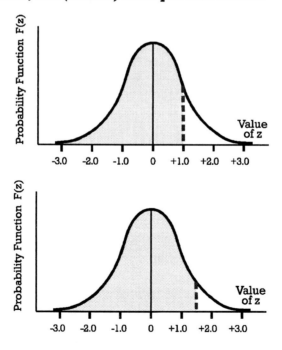

[10] G. Gerson and R.G. Brown (1970), "Decision Rules for Equal Shortage Policies", *The (US) Naval Research Logistics Quarterly*, Vol. 17, No. 3.

Safety Stock

The shaded area under the first curve is 84.13 per cent of the curve's total area, and the shaded area under the second curve is 93.32 per cent of the total. The first percentage is calculated by integration of the probability density function of the standard normal distribution from $z = -\infty$ to $z = +1.0$ — see Equation 5.8 (which is derived directly from Equation 5.5). The second percentage is similarly calculated, to the value $z = +1.5$.

$$\Phi(z) = P(Z < 1.0) = \int_{-\infty}^{+1.0} \frac{1}{\sqrt{2\pi}} e^{-\frac{1}{2}z^2} dz \qquad \text{Equation 5.8}$$

In the first instance, with z equal to +1.0, if a buffer of stock equivalent to "z = +1.0" were always to be available as a safety contingency, it would be sufficient to cover underforecasts up to this magnitude. Now Figures 5.5 and 5.6 are derived from Figure 5.4, an unstandardised distribution with a standard deviation and σ calculated from Equation 5.2 and Table 5.2 to be 97 units. That is, the value "z = +1.0" is equivalent to a quantity of 97 units of the product in question. Clearly, therefore, a permanent safety stock of 97 units (to cover against underforecasts up to 97 units) will protect us against 84.13 per cent of forecast errors. (Naturally, for 50.00 per cent of the 84.13 per cent — i.e. the instances when the forecasts are too large — none of the safety stock reserve will need to be used at all.) In the second example, with z = +1.5, a permanently available safety stock of 146 units (97 units × 1.5, rounded) will ensure that there is a sufficient contingency to protect the product's sales against 93.32 per cent of forecast errors.

Several percentage areas of the normal curve calculated from Equation 5.8 from $z = -\infty$ to various values of z other than +1.0 or +1.5 have been entered in Table 5.4(a) and Table 5.4(b). Table 5.4(a), on the left, gives round numbers of the value z and Table 5.4(b), right, gives round numbers of the calculated area. The full set of probability values (F(z)) is widely available in statistical text books; values can also be obtained through statistical computer packages and many pocket calculators. See also Table 5.9.

Tables 5.4(a) and 5.4(b): The Cumulative Normal Distribution

(a)				(b)			
z	Area %	z	Area %	z	Area %	z	Area %
0.0	50.00	2.7	99.65	0.842	80.0	2.326	99.0
1.0	84.13	2.8	99.74	1.282	90.0	2.576	99.5
1.5	93.32	2.9	99.81	1.645	95.0	3.090	99.9
2.0	97.72	3.0	99.87	1.880	97.0	3.291	99.95
2.5	99.38	4.0	99.997+	2.055	98.0	3.891	99.995
2.6	99.53	5.0	99.9998+	2.170	98.5	4.417	99.9995

The definition now of customer service is simplistic. It is to define service as the percentage of errors covered — that is, the percentage area covered of the normal distribution of the forecast errors. Tables 5.4(a) and 5.4(b) give 24 instances of customer service percentages and their equivalent safety factors — i.e. values of z. Employing the definition, when the value of z has been obtained for the particular percentage service required for a product, it is multiplied by the standard deviation σ of the product's forecast errors to find the safety stock needed to give the targeted protection.

What sinks this method as a useful way of setting customer service is the failure to take account of working stock (sub-section 5.2.3). Consider again the product replenished once a year with a large quantity of stock. The forecast error will assume importance only once in the year, either in the master planning month for which the new stock is scheduled or in the period for which the depot delivery has been ordered. If 90 per cent service had been selected, once every 10 years the company might on average run out of stock before the replenishment arrives because the forecast was too small. The product replenished once per month with a correspondingly smaller quantity of stock will be at risk 12 times a year, and with the same 90 per cent service may stock out once or perhaps twice per year.

While the wild inconsistency between stocking out once a year and once every ten years with the same specified service rules out the idea in our quest for an ideal "theoretical" method and definition, the various percentage coverages of forecast errors illustrated in Tables 5.4(a) and 5.4(b) reveal why holding more and more safety is useless and wasteful. As we see from the Tables, the

Safety Stock

increases in the percentage areas become increasingly small as the amounts of safety are increased (increases in z). In the example with 97 units, 98.0 per cent coverage requires 200 units (97 units × 2.055), while 99.5 per cent coverage, an increase merely of a further 1.5 per cent, requires 250 units (97 units × 2.576).

5.4.2 Percent Annual Demand

The standard method has been widely published and has been included in software since its publication.[11] It is based on the following definition of service:

$$\text{Percent Service} = \frac{\text{Quantity of sales demand for a product per year filled from stock}}{\text{Total sales demand for the product per year}} \times 100\%$$

Derivation of the expression needed to calculate the safety stock giving a particular percentage service requires the use of a further statistic to augment the probability density function introduced in sub-section 5.2.1. This is the *partial expectation*.

The *expectation*, rather than the *partial* expectation, is also referred to as the *theoretical mean* and is a straightforward statistical concept. Returning to the example of two six-sided dice, the "expectation", or expected score, resulting from the throw of the dice, is obtained by multiplying each possible score by its corresponding probability, and then summing the results. From Table 5.3, each of the 11 possible scores in Line 1 is multiplied by its probability in Line 3. The 11 numbers are then totalled to give an expectation, or theoretical mean, of 7.0 from the throw of the dice. In such a simple, symmetrical example, the result of 7.0 can be read at once from either Table 5.3 or the histogram in Figure 5.3. However, in considering the dice earlier, we concluded that the chance of throwing better than a score of 9 was 6/36. If we do indeed throw better than a 9, what score might we expect? What is the theoretical mean for the throw of 2 dice if the score is either a 10, 11 or 12? This expectation, confined to a partial range only of

---

[11] R.G. Brown (1967), *Decision Rules for Inventory Management*, Holt, Rinehart & Winston. Note that Brown's original publication of the safety stock method described in sub-section 5.4.2 was first published in his earlier work, *Statistical Forecasting for Inventory Control* (McGraw Hill, 1959). The first software to incorporate the method was IBM's IMPACT system, also in 1959.

the full results, is the *partial* expectation. The answer in this instance can readily be worked out from Table 5.5 and is the sum of the three probabilities in Line 3, which is 10.67. (That is, in practice, we could anticipate a total score of 1067 if the results of 100 qualifying throws of the dice were to be added.)

Table 5.5: Probabilities relating to the Partial Expectation of throwing a 10, 11 or 12 with Two Dice

Score	10	11	12
Probability of the Score	$\frac{3}{6}$	$\frac{2}{6}$	$\frac{1}{6}$
Score × Probability	$\frac{30}{6}$	$\frac{22}{6}$	$\frac{12}{6}$

Figure 5.7 is a section of Figure 5.3 illustrating the histogram of dice scores and probabilities. Although it is not in fact mathematically valid to say so, and the value cannot be calculated directly, the partial expectation may be thought of as a point on the horizontal axis denoted by the broken line and arrow in the Figure such that the qualifying area of the histogram representing the scores 10, 11 and 12, is bisected — i.e. 50 per cent of the area lies below the partial expectation and 50 per cent lies above it.

Figure 5.7: A Section of the Histogram of Dice Scores (Throws of 10, 11 and 12)

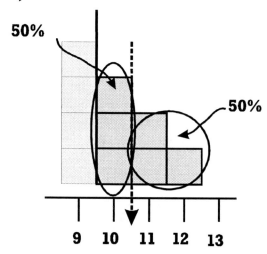

Safety Stock

As we did before, we now turn to the distribution of a continuous random variable, namely the standardised forecast error illustrated in Figure 5.5 and described by the probability density function Equation 5.5. The *expectation* of z is E(z), the value calculated as being most likely to occur, and is given by Equation 5.9, where f(z) is shorthand for the probability density function fully set out previously in Equation 5.5.

$$E(z) = \int_{-\infty}^{+\infty} zf(z)dz \qquad \text{Equation 5.9}$$

The result is μ, the mean of z, and in the case of the standardised forecast errors is, of course, zero, as we can see by eye from the illustration of the curve itself. Again as before, suppose now that we consider just part of the normal curve from a point on the horizontal scale where z equals the value "k" up to the extreme right where z equals $+\infty$. As before, adapting Equation 5.8, the *probability* of a forecast error being greater than k is obtained by integrating the probability density function from z = k to z = $+\infty$, to find the area under the curve between these points, as shown in Equation 5.10. Similarly, adapting Equation 5.9, the *partial expectation* E'(z) of *what the actual error will be* is given by Equation 5.11.

$$P(Z > k) = \int_{k}^{+\infty} f(z)dz \qquad \text{Equation 5.10}$$

$$E'(z) = \int_{k}^{+\infty} (z - k)f(z)dz \qquad \text{Equation 5.11}$$

Figure 5.8 is a sketch of the standardised normal curve taken from Figure 5.5, focusing on the tail-end of the value of z, from z = k to z = $+\infty$. The probability of an error being greater than k, from Equation 5.10, is denoted by the total shaded area. The partial expectation which bisects the shaded area — i.e. the expected value of what an error actually will be if it is indeed greater than k — is indicted on the z scale by the broken line arrow.

Figure 5.8: The Partial Expectation of z for Forecast Errors greater than k

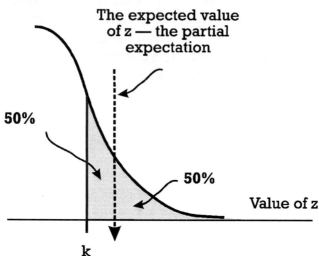

Returning to the definition of customer service given at the start of this sub-section, but working in fractions rather than percentages, if the fraction of annual demand for a product "i" to be filled from stock is "p" and the quantity of annual demand for the product is A_i, then the total annual demand *not* filled from stock is given by Equation 5.12.

$$\text{Total annual demand not filled from stock} = (1-p) A_i \text{ units} \quad \textit{Equation 5.12}$$

The probability of satisfying a fraction of annual demand equal to p is the same as the probability of satisfying the fraction p of every replenishment order for the product. Now, if an amount of safety stock "k" is provided to protect customer service, the *probability* that demand will exceed k is given by Equation 5.10, and the *amount* by which the demand exceeds k is given by the partial expectation $E'(z)$ in Equation 5.11. $E'(z)$, however, applies to the standardised normal distribution, so that the actual amount is $E'(z) \times \sigma_i$ units, where σ_i is the standard deviation of the forecast errors of product i. If there are N_i replenishments per annum for this product, the annual quantity by which demand exceeds the safety provided is given by Equation 5.13.

Safety Stock

$$\begin{array}{c}\text{Annual quantity by which} \\ \text{demand exceeds the safety stock k}\end{array} = N_i \times E'(z_i) \times \sigma_i \text{ units}$$

Equation 5.13

The annual quantity by which demand exceeds the safety stock k in Equation 5.13 is the same as the annual demand not filled from stock given in Equation 5.12. This is shown in Equation 5.14, which leads to an expression for the partial expectation in Equation 5.15.

$$N_i E'(z_i) \sigma_i = (1-p) A_i \qquad \text{Equation 5.14}$$

$$E'(z_i) = \frac{(1-p)}{\sigma_i} \times \frac{A_i}{N_i} \qquad \text{Equation 5.15}$$

All of the terms on the right hand side of Equation 5.15 are known, so that the partial expectation E'(z) of the product can be obtained that will give a level of service equal to p. Equation 5.11 can now consequently be used to find the value of k (i.e. to find the value of the safety factor) which is equivalent to the partial expectation having this value. Note that because the partial expectation is a statistic normally encountered only in dealing with safety stocks, tables of equivalent partial expectations and values of k are not found in statistical textbooks or packages. They are, of course, shown in texts dealing exclusively with materials management and the calculations to obtain them are central to safety stock software. Table 5.6 gives a small number of partial expectations and their equivalent safety factors (i.e. values of z). Many of the values of z in the Table have been selected because of their applicability in later worked examples.

Table 5.6: Values of Safety Stocks z and the Equivalent Partial Expectations E'(z) (a small selection)

Safety Factor z	Partial Expectation E'(z)	Safety Factor z	Partial Expectation E'(z)
-1.24	1.2887	0.90	0.1000
0.00	0.3989	1.26	0.0500
0.22	0.3000	1.63	0.0215
0.32	0.2577	1.73	0.0172
0.47	0.2062	2.00	0.0086
0.49	0.2000	3.36	0.0001

It will be seen from Equation 5.15 that the term A_i/N_i, which is equivalent to the product's average replenishment stock quantity Q_i, reflects the working stock which we know is also able to contribute to customer service. To illustrate that this is so, suppose that the original product with a standard deviation of forecast errors of 97 units from Table 5.2 had annual sales demand of 1,000 units and that a target level of service is set for it of 97.5 per cent according to the definition in this sub-section. Then: (i) if the product is replenished once per year, from Equation 5.15 we calculate that $E'(z) = 0.2577$, and so from Table 5.6 the required safety is 31 units (97 units $\times$ 0.32); but (ii) if the product is replenished once per month, from Equation 5.15 we calculate that $E'(z) = 0.0215$, and so from Table 5.6 the required safety is 158 units (97 units $\times$ 1.63).

5.4.3 Customer Service with Master Plan Rescheduling

When stocks of sales products are held at the source of manufacture as opposed to at warehouses and depots geographically remote from it, customer service provided through safety stocks can be augmented by the rescheduling of the master production schedule during the freeze period. The method of defining safety stocks in this sub-section is by the application of a so-called *management variable* to the complete range of sales products. A management variable is an expression or factor able to be changed by management to achieve changing objectives as different circumstances arise. (For example, the rate of interest set by the Bank of England is in a sense a management variable used by the Monetary Policy Committee as different monetary conditions arise.) Provided it is rationally based, the management variable can literally be anything, as we shall see. However, in the context of this sub-section, we should like a variable which reduces the amount of safety stock when the company is more willing to reschedule the master plan over the freeze period and increases safety stock when it finds it preferable to keep the master plan stable over the freeze. Consider two opposite situations. During a recession when money is short and the rescheduling of production is readily achievable because of plentiful capacity, the company might wish to reduce safety stocks considerably in favour of rescheduling. In busy times when money is far less of a problem but production capacity is under much pressure, it would tolerate an increase in

Safety Stock

safety stocks so that it rarely became necessary to disrupt the production programme. The management variable which Brown and Gerson suggest is given by Equation 5.16, where "r" is the rate of interest to apply to money tied up in stockholding and "c" is the cost ascribed to a stockout. Referring ahead to Equation 5.24, we see that it is used directly in the calculation of the probability density of the normal curve.

$$\text{The "Safety v. Stockout" Management Variable} = \frac{r}{c} \qquad \text{Equation 5.16}$$

From the probability density calculated through Equation 5.24, the corresponding value of safety factor z may be obtained from subsequent use of Equation 5.5. Tables of values of the probability density and equivalent values of z are also published in statistical texts as before. Table 5.7 shows a small selection.

Table 5.7: A Small Selection of Probability Density Values and Safety Factors

Safety Factor z	Probability Density P(z)	Safety Factor z	Probability Density P(z)
0.00	0.3989	2.01	0.0536
0.50	0.3207	2.32	0.0269
1.00	0.2420	2.50	0.0175
1.34	0.1617	3.00	0.0044
1.50	0.1295	3.50	0.0009
1.79	0.0808	4.00	0.0001
2.00	0.0540	5.00	0.000002

From Equation 5.24 and Table 5.7, we see (i) the greater the rate of interest r, the bigger becomes p(z) — i.e. the less the safety stock, since holding it becomes unduly expensive; and (ii) the greater the cost ascribed to a stockout, the smaller becomes p(z) — i.e. the greater the safety stock. In case (ii), if a stockout is deemed to be expensive (c large, p(z) small), larger safety stocks will be set, so resulting in fewer potential stockouts and a more stable master plan. If, on the contrary, a stockout is deemed to be inexpensive (c small, p(z) large), safety will be reduced, giving rise to more potential stockouts and requiring the company to protect service by more frequent rescheduling of the master plan. (In short, there is an informal inverse relationship between the cost of a stockout and the cost of rescheduling the master plan during the freeze.)

It is most important to understand the *general* effect of Brown and Gerson's management variable from the calculations below, i.e. the effect regardless of the actual values chosen by management for the two variables. This is to set comparatively less safety stock on expensive products which are frequently replenished and comparatively more safety on inexpensive ones which are infrequently replenished. Savings in stockholding on the small number of "A class" products in effect pay for the additional safety — and hence master plan stability — on the large number of "C class" ones. *More* safety on slower moving products is the opposite result to the ones obtained by use of the definitions in both sub-sections 5.4.2 (above) and 5.4.4 (below). At the master scheduling source, however, rescheduling the plans of frequently made products which are already in the current month's schedule is clearly likely to be more easily accomplished than rescheduling infrequently manufactured products. However, given the financial importance of the Class A products, the onus is very much on the master scheduler and manufacturing manager to ensure that all is well done.

If a safety factor of z_i is set for a product i and the standard deviation of the product's errors is σ_i, the quantity of safety stock is $z_i\sigma_i$ and the probability that sales demand will exceed the safety is $f(z_i)$, where $f(z_i)$ is given by Equation 5.10. If there are N_i master schedule replenishment plans for the product in a year, the total number of stockouts in the year is $N_i f(z_i)$. If it is now decided to reschedule the master plan in each case of a near stockout, the annual number of such reschedules is thus the same, i.e. $N_i f(z_i)$. For all products on the master production schedule range, the total annual number of reschedules is given by Equation 5.17.

Company Rescheduling Load $= \sum N_i f(z_i)$ *Equation 5.17*

Safety Stock

If the unit value of product i is v_i, the value of the safety stock on product i is $v_i z_i \sigma_i$. For all products on the master production schedule range, therefore, the total value of the safety stock is given by:

$$\sum v_i z_i \sigma_i$$

If the total value of safety stock is called I, then the calculations shown in Equations 5.18, 5.19 and 5.20 follow, where λ in Equation 5.20 is a Lagrange multiplier. Use of Joseph Lagrange's theory of multipliers is in effect the employment of a mathematical trick — as we see in Equation 5.20, the expression in the brackets is zero; consequently it can be multiplied by anything at all, since anything multiplied by zero still gives a result of zero. Equation 5.20 must therefore be true if Equation 5.19 is true. (At the end of the calculations, we will, in fact, substitute our management variable for λ.)

$$\sum v_i z_i \sigma_i = I \qquad \text{Equation 5.18}$$

$$\text{or} \quad \sum v_i z_i \sigma_i - I = 0 \qquad \text{Equation 5.19}$$

$$\text{or} \quad \lambda \left(\sum v_i z_i \sigma_i - I \right) = 0 \qquad \text{Equation 5.20}$$

We now add together the rescheduling load in Equation 5.17 and the cost of safety stock in Equation 5.20 to form a composite of rescheduling load and safety stock value called $R(z,\lambda)$, given in Equation 5.21.

$$R(z,\lambda) = \sum N_i f(z_i) + \lambda \left(\sum v_i z_i \sigma_i - I \right) \qquad \text{Equation 5.21}$$

Next, we differentiate R with respect to the safety factor z to obtain Equation 5.22. (Note that by differentiating $f(z_i)$ we obtain the probability density $p(z_i)$ — i.e. the reverse effect of Equation 5.10.)

$$\frac{dR}{dz} = -N_i p(z_i) + \lambda v_i \sigma_i \qquad \text{Equation 5.22}$$

The minimum of the expression in Equation 5.22 — i.e. the minimum of the rescheduling and safety stock composite cost — is found where the differential is set to zero, as given in Equation 5.23 after rearranging terms.

$$p(z_i) = \frac{\lambda v_i \sigma_i}{N_i} \qquad \text{Equation 5.23}$$

We can replace λ with any constant, but we substitute for it the management variable spoken of above, to derive the final expression in Equation 5.24.

$$p(z_i) = \left[\frac{r}{c}\right] \times \frac{v_i \sigma_i}{N_i} \qquad \text{Equation 5.24}$$

In a literal sense, the management variable is meaningless, so that, when considering the values to ascribe to r and c, what should be looked for are ones that will generate safety amounts that meet the company's objectives in the trade-off between stockholding cost and rescheduling. The company might well have half a dozen alternative values for r/c, ranging from one at the recession end of the scale (minimum safety, maximum rescheduling) to one for booms (reasonably high safety, minimum rescheduling).

Table 5.8 shows the safety stocks that would be set on the product from Table 5.2 with a standard deviation of forecast errors σ of 97 units, assuming it was replenished once per month (i.e. N = 12). The probability densities p(z) and their equivalent values of z are obtained from Table 5.7.

Table 5.8: Four Safety Stocks set at the Master Schedule Source of Production

Unit Cost	r (£ per £ p.a.)	c	r/c	v×σ/N	p(z)	Safety Factor z	Safety Stock
£10	0.20 (hi)	£200 (lo)	0.0010	80.83	0.0808	1.79	174 units
£10	0.10 (lo)	£300 (hi)	0.0003	80.83	0.0269	2.32	225 units
£20	0.20 (hi)	£200 (lo)	0.0010	161.66	0.1617	1.34	130 units
£20	0.10 (lo)	£300 (hi)	0.0003	161.66	0.0536	2.01	195 units

5.4.4 Specified Time between Stockouts

The fourth method of setting safety stocks offers an improvement over the standard method in 5.4.2 through achieving greater consistency of customer service. It might be employed at the master scheduling source of supply if the rescheduling of the master plan over the freeze period was not an option, but is perhaps more generally associated with safety stocks at warehouses and depots geographically remote from the source where the expediting of re-supplies is too troublesome or too costly.

Safety Stock

The "per cent forecast errors" method in sub-section 5.4.1 was superseded by the standard definition in 5.4.2 because of the inconsistencies which were thrown up by it. By incorporating the term A_i/N_i, account was taken of the protection of customer service provided by manufacturing or delivery lot sizes. The term A_i/N_i, however, brings its own troubles. Even though the same "annual per cent service" (p) is specified for all products, inconsistencies in actual service are liable to arise from product to product. They do so because the service provided *by working stock alone* on many products is already higher than the value of p being aimed for. That is, even though the standard technique assigns such products zero safety stocks, the annual per cent service given by them is already in varying degrees superior to p.

Suppose, for example, that the product with $\sigma = 97$ units, replenished once a year, had an annual demand of 5,000 units rather than 1,000 units. Then with service p at 97.5 per cent, annual demand filled from stock, $E(z)$, from Equation 5.15, is 1.2887. From Table 5.6, this is equivalent to a *negative* safety stock of 120 units (97 units $\times -1.24$). The safety stock that would be set in this case is zero, but the "hidden negativity" of -120 units is a true reflection of the imbalance in the service really being provided and a measure of its superiority over the 97.5 per cent being aimed for.[12]

In short, the term A_i/N_i in the standard definition, while doing a good job in many respects, introduces two elements of chance which create potential inconsistency in the per cent annual service delivered from product to product. Because the method does not result in uniform service all round, close correspondence with the Sales and Marketing manager's target is less likely to be achieved.

The annual quantity by which demand exceeds a safety stock k involves the partial expectation $E'(z)$ and is given by Equation 5.13. If v_i is the unit value of this stock, the annual value of stocked out (backordered) sales demand is given by Equation 5.25 and the annual value of all stocked out demand for all products by Equation 5.26.

---

[12] Negative safety stock might be set in wholesale distribution if the danger existed of being left with valuable but unsaleable stock at the end of a sharply defined season: expensive fashion goods, for example. If safety stock is negative, stock replenishments are purposely set at less than forecast.

Annual value of stocked out demand for the ith product $= N_i \times E'(z) \times \sigma_i \times v_i$ units   Equation 5.25

Total annual value of stocked out demand for all products $= \sum N_i \times E'(z) \times \sigma_i \times v_i$ units

Equation 5.26

The total value of the safety stock employed which gives rise to the value of stocked out demand in Equation 5.26 is given by Equation 5.27.

Total value of the safety stock employed $= \sum v_i \times z_i \times \sigma_i$ units   Equation 5.27

If the total value of safety stock in Equation 5.27 is I, then Equations 5.28, 5.29 and 5.30 follow, where λ' is a second Lagrangian multiplier.

$$\sum v_i z_i \sigma_i = I \qquad \text{Equation 5.28}$$

or $$\sum v_i z_i \sigma_i - I = 0 \qquad \text{Equation 5.29}$$

or $$\lambda'(\sum v_i z_i \sigma_i - I) = 0 \qquad \text{Equation 5.30}$$

If the composite value of the stocked out demand in Equation 5.26 and the safety stock employed in Equation 5.30 is $S(z,\lambda')$, then Equation 5.31 follows.

$$S(z,\lambda') = \sum N_i E'(z) \sigma_i v_i + \lambda'(\sum v_i z_i \sigma_i - I) \qquad \text{Equation 5.31}$$

By differentiating S with respect to z, we obtain Equation 5.32.

$$\frac{dS}{dz} = -N_i f(z) \sigma_i v_i + \lambda' v_i \sigma_i \qquad \text{Equation 5.32}$$

Note that f(z) is the reverse of E'(z), as shown in Equations 5.9 and 5.11. To find the minimum value S — i.e. the minimum of the cost of stockouts and the cost of safety in Equation 5.31 — we set the differential to zero and obtain Equation 5.33.

$$0 = -N_i f(z_i) \sigma_i v_i + \lambda' v_i \sigma_i \qquad \text{Equation 5.33}$$

By rearranging terms and cancelling, Equation 5.34 is obtained.

Safety Stock

$$f(z_i) = \frac{\lambda'}{N_i} \qquad \text{Equation 5.34}$$

Suppose we now assign the management variable 1/T to take the place of λ', where T is a time between stockouts to apply to *each and every* product i on the sales range (or rather, T is informally related to the time between stockouts — see below). Our final expression is given by Equation 5.35.

$$f(z_i) = \frac{1}{T N_i} \qquad \text{Equation 5.35}$$

Values of the safety factor z and corresponding values of f(z) from statistical tables are given in Table 5.9. Table 5.9 is related to Tables 5.4(a) and 5.4(b) — if the fractional probabilities in Table 5.9 were converted to percentages, then each percentage value X would be seen as (100% − X) if it were to be entered in Tables 5.4(a) and 5.4(b).

Table 5.9: Values of z and corresponding Values of Probabilities

z	f (z)	z	f (z)
0.00	0.5000	2.00	0.0228
0.43	0.3333	2.13	0.0167
0.84	0.2000	2.35	0.0092
1.00	0.1587	3.00	0.0013
1.22	0.1111	4.00	0.00003
1.99	0.0278	5.00	0.000002

Although the management variable T has been called *the time between stockouts*, as implied above this should not be taken literally. Its purpose is to produce *consistency of service* from product to product, consistency of service being manifest by an approximately equal incidence of stockouts. Thus, setting T equal to 3.0 years will not result in safety stocks such that products stock out literally approximately once every three years, but that the stockout rate that does result will be more-or-less uniform across the product range. The value of T which is to be used and the effect it then really has on stock availability and customer service must be experimented with and will depend on the frequency of replenishments of the products generally and the magnitude of their forecast errors. Values of T equal to 3.0, 5.0 and 9.0 might be tried first to find reasonable boundaries.[13]

Table 5.10 shows the safety stocks that would be set on a product with a standard deviation of forecast errors σ of 97 units by the "time between stockouts" method for three values of T, assuming, first, that the product was replenished yearly and, second, that it was replenished monthly. The value of safety factor z which corresponds to the value of f(z) calculated through Equation 5.35 may be read from Table 5.9.

Table 5.10: Safety Stocks set using the "Time between Stockouts" Method

T	N	$\frac{1}{TN}$	f (z)	Value of z from Table 5.9	Safety Stock $z \times \sigma$
3	1	0.3333	0.3333	0.43	42 units
5	1	0.2000	0.2000	0.84	81 units
9	1	0.1111	0.1111	1.22	118 units
3	12	0.0278	0.0278	1.99	193 units
5	12	0.0167	0.0167	2.13	207 units
9	12	0.0092	0.0092	2.35	228 units

5.5 THE SAFETY STOCK SYSTEM

The safety stock system consists of far more than the software vendor's safety stock module and the procedures laid down to generate safety stock quantities through it. First, a facility must be developed to enable the Sales and Marketing manager or his agent to choose the best method by which to calculate the safety stocks in the first place. Once the system has been initiated, easy experimentation and simulation with alternative methods and

---

[13] "Experiments" are not performed by setting and using actual safety stock on real products. Investigations into the potential effects of safety stocks with various values of T are made employing simulation, using data relating to real past demand, and comparing the results to historical records of stockouts — see Section 5.5.

Safety Stock 175

management variables must be possible. Secondly, periodic reports are essential throughout the year on the customer service actually being achieved, and, for the master scheduling source, the degree of supplementary rescheduling proving necessary. Lastly, extensive simulation capabilities must be provided to enable choices to be made by sales product group managers and others of possible new service targets, targets having associated with them their costs in the form of safety stock investment and estimates of the likely pressure, or relief of pressure, on production rescheduling.

5.5.1 Choosing the Technique

The three contending alternative methods for setting safety stocks dealt with in sub-sections 5.4.2 to 5.4.4 are summarised in Table 5.11.

Table 5.11: Summary of the Three Methods for Determining Safety Stocks

No.	Sub-Section		Management Variable	* Formula to obtain Safety Factor z_i	Notes
1	5.4.2	p	Percent annual demand filled from stock	$E'(z_i) = \dfrac{(1-p)}{\sigma_i} \times \left[\dfrac{A_i}{N_i}\right]$	Standard (MPS or isolated depots).
2	5.4.3	$\dfrac{r}{c}$	$\dfrac{Cost\ of\ stockholding}{Cost\ of\ a\ stockout}$	$p(z_i) = \left[\dfrac{r}{c}\right] \times \dfrac{v_i \sigma_i}{N_i}$	Only at locations where the rescheduling of supply is an option.
3	5.4.4	T	$\dfrac{1}{"Time\ between\ stockouts"}$	$f(z_i) = \dfrac{1}{T N_i}$	For uniformity of service (MPS or isolated depots).

* Notes: $E(z_i)$ = the partial expectation of the ith product; $p(z_i)$ = the probability density; $f(z_i)$ = the probability function; σ_i = standard deviation of forecast errors of the ith product; A_i = annual demand; N_i = number of replenishments per year; v_i = unit value of the product in £.

Although the text of Section 5.4 gives strong indications as to the appropriateness of the various techniques, their actual effects will depend on the particularities and mixture of σ, A, N, and v of the products to which they are applied. To begin the investigation that will lead to a choice of method and choice of management variables, the analyst might set up a datafile of 50 or so representative products, complete with the required data and sales demand history. The demand history is needed to generate forecasts through the parent forecasting system so that the standard deviations of the forecast errors can be derived.

Repeated runs of the data with the alternative methods and alternative management variables will generate alternative safety stocks. Analysis of these should be carried out by attempting to gauge the effect they would have had, had they been applied, on two measures of service. The first is the theoretical measure inherent in the technique itself: *Has application of the technique achieved what it claims for itself, and do the calculated safety stock amounts appear to be self-consistent?* The second is the measure of service in his own terms set by the Sales and Marketing manager: *Is this truly a close link between theory and practice?*

5.5.2 Data Processing throughout the Year

It would be unusual and something of a trouble, but not "wrong", to obtain a sales forecasting system and safety stock module from different software vendors. As it is, the single vendor will provide complete integration of forecasting and safety stocks so that the collection and filing of forecast errors of all products each month needed for safety stocks are transparent to the user. (It follows from this that the evaluation of forecasting software should normally include consideration of vendors' optional safety stock modules.) Besides systematic collection of forecast errors, the package will provide for periodic recalculation of the standard deviation of forecast errors and hence the resetting of safety stock quantities because of the new values. This facility should be invoked for seasonal products at the start of peaks and troughs of demand, since the characteristics of forecast errors and hence the magnitudes of appropriate safety stocks may be quite different over the different periods.

Reports of stock availability actually achieved, including various summaries, must also be produced in terms of the customer service goals set by the Sales and Marketing manager (Section 5.3). In addition, for locations close to the master scheduling source where the rescheduling of sales product manufacture during the MPS freeze period has taken place, reports on the extent of such rescheduling must also be collected. If they are not so col-

Safety Stock

lected, quite a misleading picture may be obtained of the apparent efficacy of the safety stocks: good service may be due to heroic efforts in manufacturing, not to safety stock. Finding a quantitative measure of the degree of rescheduling will require some thought. Since any rescheduling of the MPS during the freeze period is performed by the master scheduler at the VDU, one way to do so may be through the recording of each instance of production expediting, recorded on a simple background history file set up for the purpose.

5.5.3 Simulation and New Choices

A formal review by the Sales and Marketing manager of stock availability and the customer service aimed for and achieved is likely to take place before the start of the company's financial year when budgets and sales targets are being agreed. The summary analyses required to perform these tasks will include the past and proposed financial investments in safety stock by product group and the required degree of rescheduling spoken of above.

The mark of the safety stock system's success is that the customer service targets originally aimed for by the manager and product group managers have, more or less, been achieved. If they have been achieved, it would seem that there is an excellent correlation between the managers' targets and the chosen theoretical definition and management variables. It is consequently a relatively straightforward matter for the analyst to provide simulation capabilities to help company managers arrive at future targets. Simulation will enable answers to be obtained to such questions as: *How much better would the customer service be on product group X if a further £100,000 were to be provided as safety?* and *How much extra would it cost in safety stock to go from "97 per cent of all order lines..." to "99 per cent of all order lines..."?*.

If there is not a good correlation between targets and achievement, the analyst must undertake a thorough investigation either to find a better method of setting the stocks or to come up with better values of the management variable, probably by returning to the experimental file of 50 products mentioned in sub-section 5.5.1. The link between the practical customer service target and the theoretical definition and its accompanying variables in reality is rather a matter of feel and experience. When the link has been established, the company has at its disposal an extremely powerful tool.

Chapter 6

Master Plan Formulation

Master plan formulation and master plan management are pivotal activities within the manufacturing company and of vital concern to the manufacturing manager. The master plan defines the company's stance with regard to customer demand and service. The master plan governs the required production and purchasing responses. Communication, analysis and the development of company-wide procedures are important activities in master planning, but, important though they may be, they are not at its centre. At the centre of master scheduling are the commitment and unity of personnel.

6.1 DEFINITIONS

A short definition of the master production schedule (MPS), or master plan, is *a time-phased set of plans to acquire products that will thus be available for sale or despatch to customers.*[1] As a corollary, we might add that while "acquiring" the stock could imply simply buying in for resale, to the manufacturing manager it will usually mean production. If it means production, then the MPS gives rise to the supporting material and purchase plans, although

---

[1] Darryl Landvater and Chris Gray prefer to define the master schedule as relating to products which it is necessary to control through human intervention, perhaps because of their impact on further material needs or plant capacity, not because they are "based on some location in the product structure", as they rather dismissively put it. See D.V. Landvater and C.D. Gray (1989), *MRPII Standard System*, Oliver Wight Limited Publications Inc. The publication is less a textbook than a defining manual of MRP requirements and "best practice".

it does not itself constitute those plans. For companies that make to stock, the MPS is a set of manufacturing plans for the company's finished goods only. That is, it excludes all required supporting schedules for components and raw materials.[2] The purpose of the MPS in the case of make-to-stock is to satisfy future sales demand, whether placed by customers directly on the source of manufacture or indirectly through warehouse outlets and depots. For companies that make to order, the MPS may be the schedule of manufacturing plans representing the final completion of the orders, generally referred to as the "order book". However, if customer orders are configured from product options and common parts in what is termed a "final assembly schedule" (FAS — see Chapter 8), the MPS will instead be a set of manufacturing plans for these option variants and common parts. But again in both instances, the master schedule excludes any plans for the manufacture of items at levels in the bill of materials lower than the final products or lower than the options themselves. The purpose of master planning in make-to-order companies is to ensure effort is reserved for the final manufacture of customer orders and so ensure that they are then duly completed on time. For assemble-to-order, it is to ensure that option varieties and common parts are available in readiness for the final assembly process.

As a general statement, therefore, the master production schedule consists of manufacturing and purchasing plans at one level only in the bill of materials. It is not a direct statement about the lower level plans needed to support this manufacture or purchasing, even though the feasibility of these secondary actions in support of it is essential. Nor is it a statement about the customer demand for the products, or the products' deployment by the firm to provide customer service.

---

[2] Lower level components being manufactured for sale as spare parts should be master scheduled, whether the main product is make-to-stock or make-to-order. If they are lower in the bill of materials than the product option level, the question then arises as to how total manufacture is finally to be planned, i.e. both for spares and components. This may be answered by entering the spares' identities in the bill of materials as sales products, with new product codes, each with a product structure relating it to its corresponding lower level component. That is, Spare Part C123S, sold directly as a spare, has a zero lead time and zero capacity requirements, and consists of one unit of C123 (the originating component).

Master Plan Formulation

Further salient points relating to the master plan are as follows.

6.1.1 Manufacturing and Inventory Strategies

The master plan is a statement simply of intended production, not a forecast of customer demand. For products made to stock with uneven monthly forecasts, it is consequently possible to weigh the relative merits of steady production rates, with peaks and valleys of stockholding, and frequently adapted production rates with permanently low stocks. The strategy chosen will depend on the economics of production, the cost of stock and other factors. In companies that experience particularly seasonal demand, stock build-ups before the start of the season will be the normal method of operation. (An extreme case in the UK is surely the master planning of fireworks production throughout the year in preparation for Guy Fawkes' Night on 5 November.)

One method of illustrating production strategy and stock holding simultaneously is by way of cumulative figures. Table 6.1[3] gives the forecast sales and cumulative forecast sales of a certain product over 12 months, and the MPS and cumulative MPS. Line 6 of the Table is the cumulative MPS less the cumulative forecast, showing the stock build-up to July and the rapid depletion from that point.

Table 6.1: Stock Build-Up (Cumulative MPS less Cumulative Sales Forecast)

Month	J	F	M	A	M	J	J	A	S	O	N	D
Sales Forecast	10	10	10	10	10	20	50	100	40	10	10	10
Cumulative Forecast	10	20	30	40	50	70	120	220	260	270	280	290
MPS	30	30	30	30	30	30	30	30	30	10	10	10
Cumulative MPS	30	60	90	120	150	180	210	240	270	280	290	300
Stockholding	20	40	60	80	100	110	90	20	10	10	10	10

---

[3] The drawing of bar charts is sometimes advocated to show cumulative forecasts and cumulative production such as in Table 6.1, the bar charts (it is said) giving a more easily grasped picture than simple figures. In practice, because of their vertical scales, cumulative bar charts are awkward to present without converting values to logarithms, which then rather subtract from their comprehensibility.

6.1.2 The MPS Horizon

A self-evident feature of any plan to manufacture end-products (or option varieties and common parts) is the need to express the plan over a significant period of time into the future. Since the manufacture of the MPS must be supported by prior manufacture of components and the acquisition of raw materials, two constituents which go to make up the master schedule horizon are: (i) the maximum purchasing *plus* cumulative component manufacturing lead time; and (ii) the master plan review period. Note that care must be taken in defining the raw material purchasing element of (i). While this is generally taken to be the time to re-order and receive material from the supplier, it is necessary to distinguish between a delivery as part of a close supplier relationship, such a relationship already well-established, so that changes to the raw material schedule may be made with only a few hours' or days' notice, and a normal supplier delivery made in response to an unexpected order. (When a contract with a supplier is initially being agreed, special "long horizon" master schedule runs will often be requested by the buyer to assist him in his negotiation.) Finally, the master schedule horizon will be very considerably added to by the ordering and delivery of very long lead time supplies from certain foreign sources, especially, perhaps, many in the Far East. If there are only a small number of such supplies, it may be worthwhile managing them separately, outside the main system. Other considerations relating to the master plan horizon are as follows.

Make-to-Stock

Time must be added to place goods in front of the customer — whether a day or so to move items to a central warehouse, or several weeks or even months to replenish a complex distribution chain with foreign outlets. Many make-to-stock items are the subject of advertising campaigns and other promotional activities. If these involve the requirement to build up stocks or to arrange for additional capacity or temporary labour, as they frequently do, the times needed to do so must be taken into account in setting the MPS horizon.

Master Plan Formulation

Make-to-Order

Products made to order are scheduled to be manufactured at a time in the future equal to the normal "build" time, plus any delay because of late availability of effort at the time of placing the order (see "available-to-promise", sub-section 7.2.1). Two characteristics of the master scheduling of final make-to-order products, however, are the guardianship required of the existing promised position on customer orders and the need carefully to schedule the plant capacity that will be required to manufacture the final goods. (This last may be a more difficult task than ensuring that capacity is available for make-to-stock items, where stock build-ups are a possibility.) The uncertainty of demand for items made to order must be dealt with continually by careful day-to-day master schedule and capacity management.

Assemble-to-Order

Option varieties and common parts are made to stock, so that the considerations above apply to these constituents of the MPS horizon. In addition, however, the planning horizon of the final assembly schedule itself must be taken into account.

A sketch of the constituents of the master schedule horizon is shown in Figure 6.1.

Figure 6.1: Constituents of the Master Production Schedule Horizon

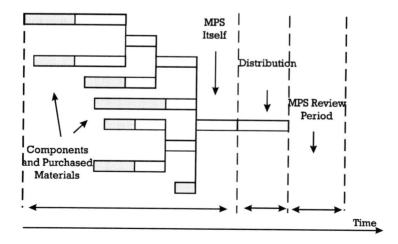

If the duration of the horizon is set too short, the error will be realised at once, since explosion of the plan will reveal a number of raw material requirements to be "past due". If the duration is made longer than it need be, the explosion will create certain raw material and component plans with action dates well into the future. If so, the plans will not need to be examined, but the master scheduler should be aware that they are adding unnecessarily to the data processing burden.

6.2 Overview of the MPS Process

The subject of master scheduling can conveniently be regarded as comprising two areas, though these have certain common ground. The first concerns the *formulation* of the master schedule, an activity carried out over a few days once a month and followed by the simultaneous launch of the new plan and its displacement of the old. The second has to do with the *management* of the new plan over the month, an eye being kept particularly on its continuing appropriateness in the light of actual customer orders (against what was forecast) and on its achievement by manufacturing.[4] Although it is not essential that the cycle of formulation–management–reformulation should be monthly, in the vast majority of cases its relationship to the monthly recalculation of forecasts and to reviews of business and production generally will suggest this to be best.

A final point on time periods is the need to express and monitor the plan in divisions of a day — to use the jargon, in "daily buckets".[5] That is, a particular product plan will have a start *day* and a finish *day*. The inexactitude of any longer period brings uncertainty with regard to the actual sequence of plans in the same time bucket and will mean that work schedules eventually created will

---

[4] In the mythology of MRPII (*manufacturing resource planning*, defined in Section 10.1), "Class A" status requires a 95 per cent or better achievement of the master schedule, measured each week or month and meaning that 95 per cent or more master scheduled plans are manufactured and delivered into stock on the days stated in the master plan. See Section 10.4 (end) and Landvater and Gray (1989), op. cit.

[5] The term "bucket" goes back to computer disk management of the 1960s and the storage of all plans relating to a particular division of time on a segment of the disk's surface having the shape, literally, of an everyday bucket.

Master Plan Formulation 185

need to be heavily and unnecessarily edited to ensure that the dates of specific manufacture are correctly aligned to real needs.

6.2.1 Formulation of the Master Schedule

The mix of factors taken into account in master plan formulation includes sales forecasts, economics of production, finance, seasonality, plant capacity and marketing strategy. Because of this, the formulation process is at the centre of the business and its control should clearly rest in the hands of senior management — the MD, the production and marketing directors, finance and purchasing directors, etc. It is not usually possible for management at this level, however, to deal individually with particular products even though ultimately the MPS must be expressed in product terms. Consequently, formulation of the MPS is a two-step process.

Step 1 is referred to as *sales and operations planning* (S&OP), or sometimes as *business planning*.[6] The term denotes broad planning carried out at the product group, or product "family", level. Senior management will usually consider the firm's business as relating to a small number of product groups aimed at particular market sectors (*small electrical kitchen goods, washing machines, tumble driers* etc), and will express production targets in financial terms over time. Primary inputs to sales and operations planning are forecasts of demand for each product group, expressed in appropriate units (usually monetary, but occasionally other, such as tons or cubic volume). A means must consequently exist for aggregating individual product forecasts over time into forecasts at the product family level. The forecasts are reviewed by senior management to take account of economic and market trends and will sometimes be revised by them, at least in the longer term. An attempt is also made at this stage to assess the demands that the sales and operations plan will make on manufacturing capacity.

Step 2 is detailed formulation of the MPS. Because it is ultimately necessary to manufacture the individual products themselves, a mechanism must be provided for disaggregating product group plans down to the product level. Such disaggregation is not the re-

---

[6] In the United States, S&OP is also referred to rather confusingly by an old US heavy industry term "production planning". This usage is still frequently found in American MPS literature and software.

verse of the forecast accumulation referred to above; sales and operations plans and detailed master schedule plans may be vastly different from sales forecasts, because of production levelling and stock building explained in sub-section 6.1.1. Because of the detail involved, the creation of product master schedules is clearly more demanding of time and close analytical effort, effort usually provided by middle managers including the manufacturing manager. The final plans must, however, lie within the boundaries agreed at the sales and operations planning stage for finance and general volume production. Finally, before the detailed master production schedule can be released, its viability must be assessed in manufacturing capacity terms, a step referred to as *rough cut capacity planning*. Viability of the master plan necessarily includes viability of the consequential supporting plans for lower level components and for the purchase of raw materials. Testing the potential master plan for capacity feasibility at all levels of the bill of materials is a major task of plan formulation.

6.2.2 Management of the Master Schedule

The "achievement" of the master schedule means the manufacture of the plans and the delivery of the material into stock or to customers, on time and in the quantities stated. (Such achievement naturally requires the timely manufacture of components and the acquisition of purchased parts, although the progressing of lower level production is not part of master schedule management.) More is involved than the simple monitoring of final production, however. For each product made to stock, a continuing analysis must be made of its likely future stock balance, bearing in mind the level to date of customer demand and the forecast originally worked to when the MPS was formulated. The master scheduler may decide to reschedule the plans of certain products if major deviations have occurred from the sales demand expected for them. For products made to order, each master plan will have been formulated against a forecast of future order completions. Consequently, it is necessary to evaluate the plan's position simultaneously against these forecast future completions and *actual* orders received for future completion and delivery. A further element of master schedule management for products made to order is the requirement to accept and book customer orders in the

Master Plan Formulation

first place against the published master plan. Just as it is unacceptable in make-to-stock to promise to fulfil customer orders without reference to the on-hand stock position, so is it unacceptable in make-to-order to promise to fulfil orders for delivery without reference to the master schedule.

The Hierarchy of Capacity Planning

The need to ensure the viability of the potential master plan in terms of the resources that will be available for its manufacture and support was mentioned earlier. During plan formulation, action is taken and changes are made to ensure that all stages of planning and manufacture later will be readily feasible. The telling sketch in Figure 6.2 summarises the differences in the discretion and concern of the manufacturing manager between sales and operations planning and production itself.

Figure 6.2: Differences in Manufacturing Emphasis

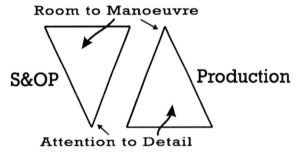

A sequential list of the stages involved in resource and capacity planning from master plan to manufacture and the terms commonly employed are given in a *hierarchy of capacity planning* in Table 6.2. The passage from Stage 2 to Stage 3 is from formulation and hypothesis to commitment and actuality. At any point up to Stage 3, therefore, it must be possible to draw back, review and revise. Consequently, computer processing and data file manipulation at the two master plan formulation steps are in simulation — work is done on copy and temporary files and with special computer programs reserved for the purpose. It is not until the moment of the plan's release from Stage 2 to Stage 3 and beyond that the "live" manufacturing system is affected.

Table 6.2: The Hierarchy of Capacity Planning

	Stage	Planning Terminology	Techniques typically used	Degree of Detail	People involved	Main book Reference
1.	MPS Stage 1 – Sales & Operations Planning	Resource Requirements Planning	Historical Data; Simple Models; Supply Chain Simulators	Not Detailed	Senior Managers	Section 6.4
2.	MPS Stage 2 – Master Scheduling	Rough-Cut Capacity Planning	Simple Models; CRP; Finite Schedulers; Supply Chain Simulators	Some Detail	Middle Managers	Section 6.6
3.	MRP1 or Materials Planning	Capacity Requirements Planning	Input/Output Control	Detailed	Production controller	Section 11.2
4.	Materials Planning &/or in Shop	Advanced Planning & Scheduling	Manual planning; APS systems	Very detailed	Production controllers & planners	Sections 12.2 and 12.3
5.	Hour-to-Hour in actual Manufacture	Shop Floor Control	Job despatching and lead time management	Closely detailed	Foremen, supervisors & team leaders	Sections 11.3 and 11.4

6.3 S&OP I: BUSINESS REVIEW

Inputs to the sales and operations planning process are demand forecasts (at the product group level) and the current master schedule summarised in financial terms. Analyses used by senior management in coming to a decision on the plan are their own business judgment; a quantitative evaluation of the plan's repercussions in terms of stockholding; and an assessment of its viability from the capacity viewpoint. Assessing and dealing with capacity at this level is referred to as *resource requirements planning* and is described separately in Section 6.4.

6.3.1 Sales Forecasts at the Group Level

Because senior management in sales and operations planning work at the product group level, a means must be provided for accumulating product sales forecasts into groups, usually in financial terms. The relationship between three products P1, P2 and P3 and a group G1 is illustrated by the very simple example in Figure 6.3 and Table 6.3. Management may also wish to see long-term accumulations of the group forecast — say, a rolling six-month forecast (£657 in Table 6.3) or a "remainder-of-the-year" forecast.

Figure 6.3: Hierarchical Forecasts

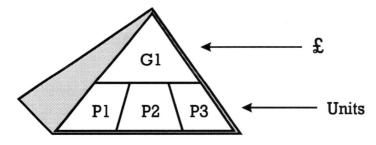

Table 6.3: Three Products' Forecasts Summarised as a Group

	Period					
	1	2	3	4	5	6
P1 — £3/unit	8	9	9	10	8	8
P2 — £5/unit	15	14	12	12	10	10
P1 — £2/unit	10	12	12	10	12	12
Group G1 (£)	£119	£121	£111	£110	£98	£98

Although senior managers should perhaps be discouraged from making changes to group forecasts in the near term — say, in the first two months — if they have evidence suggesting a probable upturn or downturn in economic or market activity beyond this, the means must be provided to override the statistical figures. In the example in Table 6.3, the view may be taken that business will improve beyond what is forecast, leading management to increase the totals for Months 5 and 6 to £135 each. In the next stage of master plan formulation, at the product level, it will be necessary to "force" this increase onto the individual products by amending their original forecasts *pro rata*, as follows:

P1: $8 \times (£135 / £98) = 11$ units;

P2: $10 \times (£135 / £98) = 14$ units;

P3: $12 \times (£135 / £98) = 17$ units.

Further methods of intervention will typically be provided, such as ones which allow particular products to be excluded from a forced group change or which enable a single financial increase or decrease to be shared out over several periods.[7]

6.3.2 The Current Master Plan in Financial Terms

The master schedule consists of a set of plans for each master scheduled product, a plan being a manufacturing lot qualified by the date it is due to be completed. The standard cost of each product is then applied, to convert plans to financial terms. The resulting sums are collected into weeks or months and summarised by product group. Table 6.4 illustrates the procedure for three products in a group and summaries of the plans for two weeks.

---

[7] The Sales Forecasting module of the Amsoft system has particularly strong capabilities in "multi-level" forecasting (allowing for any number of levels, not just products and groups), although it is principally intended for the forecasting of products with very high degrees of substitution (giftware, clothing, etc.). It is marketed in the UK by American Software Ltd., Weybridge, Surrey.

Table 6.4: The Master Schedule by Group and Value

Unit Cost	Master Plan (Units)	Week 1					Week 2				
		D1	D2	D3	D4	D5	D1	D2	D3	D4	D5
£1			20					20			20
£2				30					30	30	
£3		10				10			10	10	
Group Plan per Week by Value		£140					£220				
		(20 ×£1) + (30 ×£2) + (20 ×£3)					(40 ×£1) + (60 ×£2) + (20 ×£3)				

6.3.3 Future Levels of Stock

Master plan formulation is the focal point of inventory control within the company — or rather, it ought to be. Until recently, it has not been practical in the context of S&OP to assess and compare the implications of alternative master plan strategies in terms of the financial costs of stockholding. For senior managers at the sales and operations planning stage, *practicality* means obtaining and being able to compare reasonably precise figures interactively at the VDU. The arithmetical task to be carried out to evaluate a master plan in financial terms is to explode the plan through the bill of materials down to its components and raw materials over the complete time horizon, valuing the projected balances as shown in Table 6.4.

Even though computer processing times required to explode a materials plan have been getting progressively shorter, they are still not negligible.[8] Previous impracticality has, however, now been ended with the advent of Supply Chain Simulators.[9] A Supply

---

[8] Although, as stated in the text, processing times are now far shorter than they were in the 1990s, very high occupation of the computer's input/output channels may freeze out all other jobs on the machine as large volumes of data are transferred between disk and memory. However, see *continuous net change* under "Total Regeneration and Net Change", Section 10.4.

[9] A Supply Chain Simulator available in the UK at the time of writing is web-PLAN, supported by Plexus Software Ltd. of Burston, Stafford. The package is originally from Enterprise Planning Systems of Kanata, Ontario, Canada (website: www.webplan.com). Note that there is in fact no standard universal term for what is referred to here as a "Supply Chain Simulator". Current users of the facility are applying this tool, as in the text, to obtain very fast results within the context of MRPII, APS, ERP, etc.

Chain Simulator is able to perform a complete MPS/MRP explosion over time and present summaries or detailed results in financial terms at the VDU, all in less than a minute. The Simulator does not replace the company's materials planning software. Instead, it is used first to extract data from the conventional system data files. Once the data is in the new format, the Simulator is then capable of processing and manipulating it in seconds.[10] Besides producing financial summaries and any level of financial detail, the subject of this sub-section, the Simulator may be employed for CRP (*capacity requirements planning*) and rough-cut capacity planning (Section 6.6) and for solving broad materials planning problems generally (Chapters 9 and 10). Typically, different simulations made with alternative assumptions are run and quantitatively compared through graphics on the VDU. At the conclusion of a simulation session, the revised planning system data may either be transferred directly by the Simulator to the files of the company's original system or simply input directly into the planning system in the standard way, the system then run conventionally from that point.

A very small fragment of the output resulting from the financial valuation of the projected stock balances relating to an MPS under formulation is illustrated in Table 6.5. Table 6.5 is derived from Table 6.9, which shows the generation of a master schedule and the calculation of the product's *projected stock balance*, a term to be explained in Section 6.5. There are two differences in this Table from Table 6.9. First, a unit value of £5 has been ascribed to the product, and secondly, because individual daily figures would be impossible for the manager to assimilate or work with, the value of the average daily projected stock balance for each week has been shown. (The value of the stock at the end of each week might have been given instead, being £120 and £95 for Weeks 1 and 2 in Table 6.5.)

---

[10] The suppliers of Supply Chain Simulators state that the fast times are obtained through object-oriented computer programming and by the processing of data entirely in the computer's memory (see *Industrial Management & Data Systems*, No. 4, 1996 (magazine, MCB University Press), Nick Chambers). The Lancashire consultant Graham Barton believes that the systems also separate the products' BOM (bill of materials) structure into many individual "chains", which are then each able to be processed independently instead of all together by the standard method described in Chapter 9.

Master Plan Formulation

Table 6.5: The Financial Evaluation of Stock over Two Projected Weeks (derived from Table 6.9)

Master Schedule	PD 0		25			25			25		25
Projected Stock Balance	OH 19	10	26	17	8	24	13	2	16	5	19
	On Hand		Week 1						Week 2		
Average Financial Value	£95		£85						£55		

The breathtaking feat of arithmetic performed in a few seconds by the Simulator is to calculate and value the projected balances over an extensive time horizon, for every master scheduled product, through every level of the bill of materials, and to summarise the results, in time divisions specified by the user, according to user-defined classifications. For finished stock in make-to-stock manufacture, the classifications will naturally include product groups and sub-groups, but for stock at lower levels of the bill of materials, where product families may be meaningless, they are likely to comprise work-in-progress attributable to particular factory areas and, of course, total raw materials. The summaries are presented on the VDU screen, with the opportunity (there and then) to "drill down" to the detailed figures at the sales product, component or raw material product levels.

6.4 S&OP II: Resource Requirements Planning

The effectiveness of the checks carried out at each stage of master plan formulation on the viability of the potential master plan from the resource and capacity viewpoints will have a decisive effect on subsequent manufacturing operations. Use of the term "resource requirements planning" in sales and operations planning, however, was originally intended to reflect actions relating to capacity that only senior managers could take. Thus if additional manufacturing capability is required, actions they might take include those in the list below. (If capability is to be reduced because a long-term downturn is anticipated, the actions to be taken will be the reverse of many in the list.)

- Authorising overtime (where previously it might have been banned);
- Sub-contracting work to external companies,[11]
- Arranging for short-term bank loans to finance stock piles;
- Withdrawing products from the range to free capacity for other products;
- Recruiting staff;
- Re-sourcing the supply of raw materials;
- Buying additional capital equipment to increase capacity directly.

While it is perfectly true that these steps can and may be taken by senior management, the question remains as to how the senior group is to assess the potential capacity requirements of plans under consideration in the first place, including the requirements for supporting components, in the comparatively short period of time occupied by the sales and operations planning meeting. Note that senior managers are not being called on to *solve* any capacity problems, other than by the measures in the list above, but simply to confirm whether a desired sales and operations plan is feasible or not, and, if not, the extent of the infeasibility.

In some instances, assessing whether a plan is feasible may be a simple matter of judgement based on its comparison with other plans formulated and achieved in the past. The yardstick used might be very broad, such as total output by value, or the number of pieces made, or tons produced. Confidence that the plan is feasible will also be very considerably affected by the company's ability or otherwise to "manage" capacity. *Capacity management* means the allocation and reallocation of mobile resources — principally labour — to different parts of the factory in response to plan requirements — *changing capacity to mould it to the plan*. If capacity management is not possible, so that the plan must fit (fixed) capacity, assessment of feasibility and the task of planning are far more difficult.

---

[11] In the chemical industry, work that is sub-contracted is referred to as *toll manufacture* — see Footnote 28, sub-section 16.3.2.

Master Plan Formulation

Two techniques for capacity assessment that have been used successfully in the past are given below. Their days are numbered, however. As the use of Supply Chain Simulators and APS Systems (Chapter 12) becomes more prevalent, the easy ability with the new tools to perform full capacity analysis in a very short time will consign them to obsolescence.

6.4.1 The Load Profile

A load profile is a computer-based table that is similar in appearance and method of use to a spreadsheet, and which relates given levels of production (for distinct product groups, by their financial values) to the demands the manufacture of them will make on each of the company's work centres. If only a few "key" work centres are ever of any concern, the load profile analysis may be confined to these. All of the work centres must be examined, however, if the phenomenon of "wandering bottlenecks" is observed. Wandering bottlenecks are temporary capacity bottlenecks occurring sporadically and liable to arise at any work centre. They are typically associated with fixed capacity plant and large manufacturing lot sizes, and are caused by the uneven materials plan and the coincidence of several plans requiring the same work centre at the same time. Creation and re-creation of the load profile in the first place require very considerable amounts of data processing and are carried out on an occasional basis at convenient times by the master scheduler. To start, master plan quantities in financial terms are selected for each product group, the amounts being related to a chosen time span — a month, or perhaps a week — and regarded as being typical for each group. Thus if there were three product groups G1, G2 and G3, and an example, using highly simplistic figures, of the procedure for the creation of a load profile was desired, the values chosen might be as follows:

G1: £1,000

G2: £2,000

G3: £4,000

Next, on the basis of historical data, each group value is disaggregated to individual master product quantities in one of the ways described in Section 6.5. The master plan quantities are then exploded through the bill of materials, as described in Chapter 9, to obtain the complete materials requirements, including those for components and raw materials, but without regard for their lead times of manufacture. Continuing with the simple example, Table 6.6 shows that the production of £1,000 of G1 involves four products and components in all, and gives the quantities of them required and their work centres of manufacture.

Table 6.6: Creating a Load Profile — Step 1

Products, Components and Raw Materials in £1,000 of Group G1				
Product Code	P9	P14	P5	P21
Quantity (Units)	15	18	6	16
Work Centre	W4	W4	W8	W8

Access is next made to the capacity database to find the capacity requirements of the quantities of production needed for the group. This step is, in essence, identical to the procedures in CRP. For the sake of the example, the assumption is now made that the production rate of W4 is to manufacture products at 3 units per hour and the rate of W8 is 1 unit per hour, both rates applying regardless of the product being manufactured. This being so, the calculated demand of the product quantities in Table 6.6 on the capacities of W4 and W8 are as shown in Table 6.7, which also gives the total demands of the £1,000 of G1 on the company's work centres in the final column.

Table 6.7: Creating a Load Profile — Step 2

Work Centre Requirements in Hours to Manufacture £1,000 of Group G1						
Code	Name	P5	P9	P14	P21	Total
W4	Lathe No. 2		5	6		11
W8	No. 7 Drill	6			16	22

Master Plan Formulation

The final step in the load profile's creation is to bring the various "product group + work centre requirements" figures together in a single table which also includes the individual capacities of the work centres themselves (for the time span selected). In order now to use the load profile, the simple assumption is made that any proposed product group master plan amount will have an effect on the capacities of the work centres involved that is *pro rata* the effect of the standard product group amount used in the load profile's creation. For example, the standard quantity of £1,000 of G1 produced a load on work centre W4 of 11.0 hours. It is consequently assumed that a plan for £1,500 of G1 will produce a load on W4 of 11.0 × (£1,500 / £1,000) hours, or 16.5 hours. Table 6.8 shows the full load profile for all three products groups G1, G2 and G3. Proposals in sales and operations planning are to increase G1 to £1500 (+50%), to increase G2 to £2500 (+25%) and to decrease G3 to £3000 (–25%). In practice, load profile input typically allows for several time periods to be entered, and displays the calculated work centre loadings on the VDU over time as bar charts, one work centre per screen of data.

Table 6.8: Use of the Load Profile

Group Value		G1	G2	G3	Capacity
Standard		£1,000	£2,000	£4,000	Standard
Proposed		£1,500	£2,500	£3,000	Available (*)
Work Centre Load					Required
W4	Standard	11.0		60.0	71.0 80.0*
W4	Proposed	16.5		45.0	61.5
W8	Standard	22.0	20.0		42.0 50.0*
W8	Proposed	33.0	25.0		58.0
W12	Standard		40.0	20.0	60.0 75.0*
W12	Proposed		50.0	15.0	65.0

6.4.2 Special Bill of Materials

The second resource planning technique also requires a good deal of data pre-analysis, this time in order to formulate a simplified bill of materials capable of being very quickly exploded by computer. The capacity requirements of the exploded products are then found in the standard way by CRP. Unlike with the load profile, to achieve the required degree of simplification, use of a special bill is confined to the examination of only a few key work centres.

Step 1 in the establishment of the special bill is the determination from the full, normal bill of materials of the identities of the products which are manufactured on work centres nominated as being "key". (Again, a key work centre is one known to be troublesome to plan or liable to become overloaded.) The only eventual entries in the special bill will be these products, plus, of course, the master scheduled products themselves. Step 2 again involves the full bill, and is the calculation of the usages of products made on key work centres in the manufacture of one unit of each master scheduled product. For example, suppose that in the manufacture of a Model A bicycle, the only constituent bicycle part made on a key work centre is a wheel spoke, and that there are 32 spokes per wheel. The only entry in the usage section of Model A's record on the special bill of materials file (see Section 3.5) will then be:

Model A Bicycle (1 unit)

Usage(s): Wheel Spoke (64 units)

Use of the special bill for resource requirements planning at the sales and operations stage first requires the product group amounts for each time period being investigated to be disaggregated to master scheduled products as described in Section 6.5. Next, the disaggregated product quantities must be exploded through the special bill of materials. Finally, access to the capacity database enables the times required on the key work centres to be determined for each period. Because of the simplifications made, the complete procedure can be performed in a very short period of time. Again, as with the load profile, where this facility has been provided by the master scheduling software vendor, bar chart graphics are usually made available on the VDU.

There are a number of criticisms that can be directed at both the load profile and the special bill of materials. The one that is most obvious and most severe stems from the necessary separation of each model used from live data. The criticism is the failure of the methods to take account of on-hand stock and partly completed work in progress (at all levels of the bill of materials, not just at the

Master Plan Formulation

master schedule level). As a consequence of failing to do so, it is very common to see overloads falsely indicated on work centres in the first period. A second criticism is the *pro rata* assumption — the assumption that the proportional mix of master scheduled products in a product group of standard value will continue to apply at some other group value. It should be said, however, that many companies with manufacture that is relatively easy to assess in capacity terms use the techniques described not at the S&OP stage for resource planning, but at the next stage of MPS formulation for rough cut capacity planning. If they do so, a final comment should be made that the techniques are purely reactive — seeing whether a plan will fit, rather than positively formulating a plan in conjunction with capacity known to be available.

6.5 DETAILED MASTER SCHEDULING I

Even if it is not the intention ultimately to create a master schedule that directly mirrors the sales forecast, perhaps because of a wish to even out production or to build up stock, the first task in detailed master scheduling is nevertheless to input revised forecasts and, perhaps, revised safety stocks to each master scheduled product's data record. As we shall see, forecasts provide essential yardsticks in master plan analysis. If sales forecasts have been amended at the product group level by senior management, the group forecasts will be converted to product forecasts as described previously. If senior management have made no interventions, forecasts can be obtained immediately from the sales forecasting system. Entry of monthly forecasts to a daily bucketed master planning system is as described in sub-section 4.3.4.

Reasons why the company might not wish to master schedule the forecast have already been given. Companies which make to order, of course, where stockpiling is an irrelevance, have no option but to master schedule the forecast directly. A principal concern in revising master schedule plans at the product level in make-to-order is the existing position of order promises to customers. As we shall see (section 7.2), the available-to-promise analysis allows incoming customer orders in master schedule management to be booked against specific master plan effort. Increases or decreases in the master schedule at this stage must consequently be made keeping a careful eye on the current promised position. No gratuitous change can be contemplated that would result in the late completion of a customer's order. In practice, however, many companies which make to stock do in fact also choose to master schedule the forecast. The procedure for calculating master production schedule plans from sales forecasts through the projected available stock balance is described in sub-sections 6.5.1 and 6.5.2. Techniques for generating master schedule plans at the product level directly from a proposed master schedule at the product group level (not via the projected stock balance) are described in sub-section 6.5.3.

6.5.1 Master Scheduling and the Projected Stock Balance

When a master production schedule is to be created for each product purely through software, the standard method of doing so is by way of the projected stock balance. That is, the stock holding of the product at the end of each forward period is calculated based on the stock holding at the end of the previous period less any forecast of sales demand for the period under consideration. Then, if the projected balance is calculated to have fallen below the product's safety stock quantity, a master schedule plan is generated for the period in accordance with the planning rule specified for the product. The addition of this master plan stock restores the product's stock balance, and the arithmetical procedure continues.

The preceding explanation is summarised in Equation 6.1 and illustrated by Table 6.9 and Figure 6.4. Table 6.9 is part of the standard master schedule table given in full in Chapter 7 and throughout the book. Several terms, or rows, found in the full table, have been omitted.

$$\begin{array}{c} \text{Projected} \\ \text{stock in this} \\ \text{period} \end{array} = \begin{array}{c} \text{Projected stock} \\ \text{at the end of the} \\ \text{previous period} \end{array} - \begin{array}{c} \text{Sales} \\ \text{forecast for} \\ \text{this period} \end{array} + \begin{array}{c} \text{MPS quantity} \\ \text{scheduled for} \\ \text{this period} \end{array} \quad \textit{Equation 6.1}$$

Master Plan Formulation

Table 6.9: Creation of a Master Plan through the Projected Stock Balance

On-Hand (OH): 19 units
Past Due (PD): nil
Plan: Lots of 25 units
Safety Stock: 2 units

		Period								
		1	2	3	4	5	6	7	8	9	10
Sales Forecast		9	9	9	9	9	11	11	11	11	11
Master Schedule	PD 0		25			25			25		25
Projected Stock Balance	OH 19	10	26	17	8	24	13	2	16	5	19

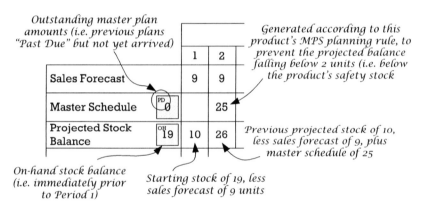

Figure 6.4: Explication of the Arithmetic of Master Plan Creation

Occasionally, manufacturing managers in companies that make to order have some difficulty with the notion of the "projected stock" of items as it applies to their own products. The phrase sounds as if one is planning to build and hold stock without reference to a customer, which is a contradiction of the term make-to-order. There are two responses to this puzzle. In considering them, it must be recalled from sub-section 4.3.4 that the sales forecast against which the master schedule is calculated in make-to-order is offset by the manufacturing lead time of the product. That is, if the forecast for the *receipt* of orders for Day 1 is so-many units and the lead time of manufacture is 10 days, the forecast is entered into the MPS table for *Day 10,* not Day 1. The two responses are as follows:

1. The projected stock balance up to the lead time of the product is simply the means, or mechanism, through which master schedule plans are generated, and which in turn lead to the derivation of lower level plans to manufacture components and acquire raw materials, all so that customers' orders really will finally be made available on the dates determined.

2. *Beyond* the lead time of manufacture, the existence of forecasts and consequent future MPS quantities are essential to the formulation of plans to retain or acquire labour and machines in anticipation of the eventual need to manufacture when orders are finally placed. (However, being beyond the manufacturing lead time, no work actually starts.)

In both cases, the phrase *projected stock balance* is misleading, though not as such wrong, since the "stock" in question, when it is ready, will be despatched promptly and directly to the customers for whom it has been made. That is, it is not "free", as stock is free in a make-to-stock environment. In almost all cases, the MPS planning rule in make-to-order will be "lot-for-lot". That is, the manufacturer will be planning to make precisely what is forecast, and, if so, the projected stock balance will be nil. This is illustrated in Table 6.10, which is similar to Table 6.9, except that the row of sales forecasts is replaced by a composite row of figures incorporating both sales forecasts and "actual demand" (i.e. customers' actual orders — but see *Consuming the Forecast*, Section 7.1).

Table 6.10: The "Projected Stock" of a Product Made-to-Order (Lot-for-Lot)

On-Hand (OH): 0 units
Past Due (PD): nil
Plan: Lot for Lot
Safety Stock: nil

		Period									
		1	2	3	4	5	6	7	8	9	10
Sales Forecast *plus* Actual Demand		55	50	50	50	50	50	50	50	50	50
Master Schedule	PD 0	55	50	50	50	50	50	50	50	50	50
Projected Stock Balance	OH 0	0	0	0	0	0	0	0	0	0	0

Master Plan Formulation

Occasionally, however, it may be convenient for operational reasons to manufacture in lot quantities, rather than lot-for-lot. The implication of this is that part of the projected stock balance will consist of the early manufacture of customers' orders. That is, again, the stock is not free as it is in a make-to-stock environment. The manufacture of make-to-order in lots is illustrated in Table 6.11, this being similar to Table 6.10 but assuming lot quantities of 70 units. The early manufacture of many customer orders requires first rate order management — for example, in Table 6.11, all of the orders for delivery in Period 4 will be made in Period 3 or earlier.

Table 6.11: The "Projected Stock" of a Product Made-to-Order (Lots of 70)

On-Hand (OH): 0 units
Past Due (PD): nil
Plan: Lots of 70 units
Safety Stock: nil

		Period								
		1	2	3	4	5	6	7	8	9	10
Sales Forecast *plus* Actual Demand		55	50	50	50	50	50	50	50	50	50
Master Schedule	PD 0	70	70	70	0	70	70	70	0	70	70
Projected Stock Balance	OH 0	15	35	55	5	25	45	65	15	35	55

6.5.2 Master Plan Time Fences

The projected stock calculation described above generates a product master plan entailing minimum stockholding. At any time during detailed master plan formulation, however (and at any time during master schedule management, Chapter 7), the master scheduler may wish to override the results emanating from the pure application of arithmetic, creating novel alternative plans of his own or directly modifying the system-generated plans in some particular way. Thus, suppose he was faced with the need to meet the sales forecasts shown in Table 6.12, with their strong anticipated seasonal uplift from Periods 5 to 8. For capacity levelling purposes, the master scheduler may formulate a plan such as that given in the Table, building up stock ahead of the peak periods.

Table 6.12: A Master Plan formulated at the VDU by the Master Scheduler

On-Hand (OH): 20 units
Past Due (PD): nil
Plan: Lots of 40 units
Safety Stock: 5 units

	PD/OH	|	Period									
		|	1	2	3	4	5	6	7	8	9	10
Sales Forecast		|	10	10	10	10	20	50	120	40	10	10
Master Schedule	PD 0	|	40	40	40	40	40	40	40			
Projected Stock Balance	OH 20	|	50	80	110	140	160	150	70	70	60	50

If the forecast and other plan data in Table 6.12 were later to be subjected to the normal projected stock arithmetic, however, the master plan would be immediately converted to the one shown in Table 6.13.

Table 6.13: Destruction of the Plan in Table 6.12 by the Projected Stock Arithmetic

On-Hand (OH): 20 units
Past Due (PD): nil
Plan: Lots of 40 units
Safety Stock: 5 units

	PD/OH	|	Period									
		|	1	2	3	4	5	6	7	8	9	10
Sales Forecast		|	10	10	10	10	20	50	120	40	10	10
Master Schedule	PD 0	|		40			40	40	120*	40		
Projected Stock Balance	OH 20	|	10	40	30	20	40	30	30	30	20	10

* i.e. 40 x 3

In master schedule formulation, and especially in master schedule management, to prevent the regression of plans exemplified by conversion of those in Table 6.12 to those in Table 6.13, a *time fence*, or plan boundary, may be imposed by the master scheduler after a period nominated by him. Once this has been done, regardless of the projected stock position, the plan position within the time fence will not be changed by any arithmetical or computer procedure. In the example given, if a time fence had been imposed at the end of Period 7, the results would have been as shown in Table 6.14. Note that the plan for 40 units in Period 8, Table 6.12, ap-

Master Plan Formulation

pears not to be required. Since it falls outside the time fence in Table 6.14, it has been eliminated.

Table 6.14: Preservation of most Plans from Table 6.12 by a Time Fence between Period 7 and Period 8

On-Hand (OH): 20 units Past Due (PD): nil Plan: Lots of 40 units Safety Stock: 5 units					Period			Time Fence		
	1	2	3	4	5	6	7	8	9	10
Sales Forecast	10	10	10	10	20	50	120	40	10	10
Master Schedule	PD 0	40	40	40	40	40	40	40		
Projected Stock Balance	OH 20	50	80	110	140	160	150	70	30	20	10

In practice, it is usual in master scheduling software to be able to set two time fences and so define three periods, or "zones". The current moment to the first time fence is referred to as the *frozen zone* or *freeze period*; the first time fence to the second is the *semi-frozen zone*; and beyond the second, where all changes dictated by the projected stock logic are implemented, is the humorously named *liquid zone*. From the system viewpoint, there is no difference between the frozen and semi-frozen zones except that messages (see below) relating to plans in the frozen zone usually employ more urgent phraseology (*expedite*, rather than *reschedule*, for example). Although there may be no system differences between the frozen and semi-frozen zones, the company itself may institute quite different operational rules and procedures regarding them. For example, the frozen zone might be set at one week ahead, with the master scheduler forbidden to make any changes to plans in it at the VDU without the express agreement of the manufacturing manager.[12] During master schedule management at

---

[12] Slicker replanning through the use of advanced planning systems, and faster set-ups, enable freeze periods to be considerably reduced, with consequently better response to changing customer requirements. (Just-in-Time with a zero freeze period is an extreme example of responsiveness.) Nevertheless, most manufacturing managers welcome the degree of production stability obtained from a freeze period, even though they may be faced with a political fight as to its duration.

least, the second time fence should be placed beyond the maximum purchasing plus component manufacturing lead time as defined in sub-section 6.1.2, to avoid uncontrolled and unnecessary changes to raw material and other lower level plans.

Finally, any discrepancies between the master scheduled plan dates within the frozen and semi-frozen zones and plans and dates that would prevail if the strict logic of the projected stock balance were to apply without restriction are brought to the attention of those responsible for master schedule formulation in the form of *rescheduling messages*. That is, a message will typically advise the master scheduler to alter the *due date* of a specified master plan lot of manufacture to bring it into line with the requirements calculated through the projected balance. MPS rescheduling messages as they apply to master schedule management are dealt with fully in Section 7.1. At the master plan formulation stage, however, message requirements are different from those in master schedule management, although it is a difference rarely provided for in software. First, *reschedule out* messages should be capable of suppression (since the planner may be stockbuilding), and secondly, *reschedule in* messages should be generated if projected stock balances fall below safety stocks (since at the formulation stage, the planner is specifically seeking to make provision for safety stock).

6.5.3 Generating Product Plans from Groups

In the two preceding sub-sections, product master plans were considered to be generated by reference to the sales products' individual forecasts. Individual forecasts, in turn, were obtained by disaggregation of forecasts at the product group level as demonstrated in Table 6.3. In this sub-section, we deal with the situation where there is a major imbalance, throughout the whole range of MPS products, between the sales forecasts and master schedule plans, just as there is a local imbalance between sales forecasts and the master schedule for a single product in Table 6.12.

In these circumstances, rather than generate new master plans each month by reference to forecasts in the standard way, with the necessity then of having to substitute the preferred alternatives in place of those created through the projected stock balance arithmetic, it may be preferable to generate the master plans by reference instead to the schedules of plans already in existence.

Master Plan Formulation

However, the view of senior managers as to the continuing appropriateness of the old plans formulated the previous month may well have changed in the light of recent circumstances. Provision must therefore be made: (i) to allow the level of the current plans to be conveniently reviewed at the group level; and (ii) if required, to permit this level to be changed.

The financial value of current plans can be shown at the product group level through the process described in sub-section 6.3.2 and demonstrated in Table 6.4. When the plans have been so reviewed, senior management may wish to substitute alternative ones, perhaps expressing the alternatives in terms of those being replaced. For example, a revised group plan may be expressed as 130 per cent of the current one, or 85 per cent of it, and so on.

In order to translate the revised group level of manufacture to individual products, new product master schedules can be generated automatically through the standard projected stock calculation from sets of *pseudo forecasts*. A pseudo forecast is one where the master schedule itself has taken the place of the original sales forecast, but where the quantities involved have been adjusted by the percentage increase or decrease to the revised overall level now thought to be more appropriate. Tables 6.15 and 6.16 are derived from Table 6.12. The master schedule figures in Table 6.12 have been made the sales forecasts in the new Tables, except that in Table 6.15, a 10 per cent increase has been applied to them and in Table 6.16, a 10 per cent decrease has been applied. (Because of lot sizing, the percentage changes to the new master schedules finally calculated are not exactly +10 per cent and −10 per cent.)

Table 6.15: Applying a 10 per cent increase in Production to a Master Plan

Plan: Lots of 40 units	Period									
	1	2	3	4	5	6	7	8	9	10
Pseudo Forecast	44	44	44	44	44	44	44	44		
Revised Master Schedule	40	40	40	40	40	80	40	40		
Projected Stock Calculation (OH 20)	16	12	8	4	0	36	32	28	28	28

Table 6.16: Applying a 10 per cent decrease in Production to a Master Plan

Plan: Lots of 40 units		Period									
		1	2	3	4	5	6	7	8	9	10
Pseudo Forecast		36	36	36	36	36	36	36	36		
Revised Master Schedule		40	40	40	40		40	40	40		
Projected Stock Calculation	OH 20	24	28	32	36	0	4	8	12	12	12

6.6 Detailed Master Scheduling II (Rough Cut)

Feasibility of the master plan from the capacity viewpoint at all levels of the bill of materials is essential if staff are to be fully committed to its achievement. The carrying out of some form of *rough-cut capacity planning (RCCP)* to assess its potential requirements would therefore seem to be imperative, to be undertaken before the plan's release to the live system. It is well known, however, that many companies have trusted to luck, and that capacity and raw material needs have not been investigated until after release. In part, this course has been taken because of the long computer run-times required in the past to perform the only thorough rough-cut planning method hitherto open to them, namely *capacity requirements planning*. CRP (see below) entails a full materials explosion, and companies were not prepared to perform this both in simulation at this point and again after plan release in the live system. In part also, they have taken the risk of early release because experience has shown them, in their particular cases, that capacity management and resource switching will always find a way — the manufacturing manager as firefighter.

If master production scheduling is to be expertly and effectively done, the manufacturing manager should undertake some form at least of rough cut capacity planning, even if this consists only of the use of one of the less rigorous methods associated with resource requirements planning. In practice, the technique chosen by most companies for RCCP will be CRP. In a few cases, where there are critical, fixed-capacity machines and sporadic bottlenecks, an advanced planning system will be the preferred tool, run in simulation over the full MPS planning horizon.

Master Plan Formulation   209

6.6.1 Capacity Requirements Planning (CRP)

In a nutshell, CRP consists of the explosion of the potential master schedule by materials planning techniques (Chapter 9), followed by access to the capacity database to determine the periods of time that manufacture of the required materials will occupy on the various work centres.[13] Although material plans are expressed in daily buckets, capacity requirements are analysed in weeks (or even in months). Typically, the results of the analysis are presented as sets of bar charts, one work centre per VDU screen and, within that, one bar per planning period, distinctive colours being used to bring overloads and other deviations to the attention of the master scheduler. Analysis of the results at any level of detail is nowadays available on the screen as required. In the past, but today only as a user-requested option, a full printed report of very considerable volume was produced, making study of the results tedious and haphazard. Note that even though CRP is performed in simulation, direct, up-to-date copies of the live database are used in doing so, so that, unlike with resource requirements planning, all current stocks and work-in-progress are fully taken into account (see sub-section 6.4.3).

Not surprisingly, realistic illustration of the process of CRP is hardly possible here, but an explanation with extremely simple figures is given in Tables 6.17 and 6.18 and Figure 6.5.

Table 6.17 relates to 10 products involved in a complete explosion of a company's potential master schedule through materials planning procedures over the MPS horizon (here, four weeks, though only the figures for Week 1 are visible). The Table shows the quantities of material required to be manufactured, the work centres of manufacture and the number of hours required per week on each.

---

[13] Assessing the load on a work centre by considering the total demands of the succession of individual jobs all requiring service on it in a given period is referred to as *vertical loading*. "Vertical" refers to the disposition of individual bars in the bar graph illustrated in Figure 6.5. It should, perhaps, be better thought of as related to *time* and as being opposite in meaning to *horizontal loading* — the individual work loads demanded by a single job on many work centres, period after period, over the job's life. See sub-section 12.2.1.

Table 6.17: CRP Step 1 — Product/Work Centre Requirements

WEEK 4
WEEK 3
WEEK 2
WEEK 1

PRODUCT	QUANTITY IN WEEK 1	WORK CENTRE CODE	W/C RATE mins/unit	HOURS REQUIRED
P1	240	W60	5.0	20.0
P2	100	W30	45.0	75.0
P5	80	W80	30.0	40.0
P9	60	W60	10.0	10.0
P12	300	W75	2.0	10.0
P13	900	W75	2.0	30.0
P14	20	W80	45.0	15.0
P20	50	W30	30.0	25.0
P22	500	W60	6.0	50.0
P30	400	W30	3.0	20.0

Following on from Table 6.17, the hours of work needed for manufacture in each of the four work centres in each week can be totalled. They are shown in Table 6.18. Again, only the figures for Week 1 are visible. Note that the term "demonstrated capacity" refers to the normal capability of the work centre, and, in this case, "maximum capacity" means the capacity with overtime (see subsection 11.2.3).

Table 6.18: CRP Step 2 — Total Work Centre Requirements by Time

WEEK 4
WEEK 3
WEEK 2
WEEK 1

WORK CENTRE CODE	WORK CENTRE HOURS	CAPACITY	
		DEMONSTRATED	MAXIMUM
W30	120.0	110.0	130.0
W60	80.0	85.0	90.0
W75	40.0	45.0	55.0
W80	55.0	35.0	41.0

Figure 6.5 illustrates individual full summaries of each of the four work centres. Only work centre W30 is visible, and this shows the potential loads on it in each of the four weeks. In practice, details of the products and quantities to be manufactured at the work centre in each period would also be given, and, if any week were overloaded, an indication of the master scheduled products contributing to the overload.

Figure 6.5: CRP Step 3 — Work Centre Summaries

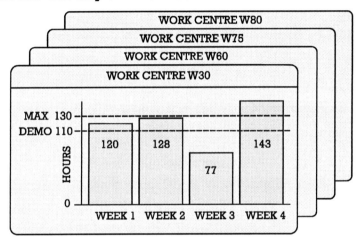

Figure 6.5 shows the potential load in Week 4 to be beyond Work Centre W30's maximum capacity (143 hours v. 130 hours). Because the mechanisms for generating materials plans in this way — and, indeed, throughout MRP — take no account of the capacity of plant, leaving capacity checking to be done separately afterwards, they have been referred to as *infinite loading* systems. This jocular term is intended to highlight their difference from *finite loading* methods, which create plans by the simultaneous consideration of material needs and the resources available to satisfy them (see APS, Chapter 12).

As previously mentioned, in reviewing plans at the detailed stage of MPS formulation, many companies know they will be able to respond to a potential overload indicated by CRP by employing capacity management — making arrangements to change capacity itself, say, by the reallocation of labour between manufacturing departments or by the hire of contract staff.[14] Thus, if it seems certain that capacity management would enable the master plan to be executed if it were to be released, the formulation stage is complete. Other activities which are associated with capacity planning generally are short term rather than concerned with master plan formulation. They include the management of manufacturing job lead times; the assignment of work and overtime planning; the reduction of production lot quantities; and, of course, job scheduling itself. They are not as such part of master schedule formulation except so far that they may be used in the examination of the detailed requirements relating to a CRP overload at the rough cut stage, and so may permit the conclusion to be reached that the potential plan is impossible or that a particular alternative would be better.

In general then, the response in master plan formulation to potential work centre overloads revealed by CRP is rather broad brush. For example, decisions relating to the early manufacture of stocked end-products prior to a seasonal sales peak are likely to be made in the very general way indicated in Table 6.1. Again, here, the Supply Chain Simulators can have a major impact on the procedure. As well as exploding an alternative master plan and valuing the stockholding associated with it in a few seconds as described in sub-section 6.3.3, the Simulator can very quickly produce CRP displays and provide access to capacity detail as here.

6.6.2 Advanced Planning Systems and RCCP

Capacity requirements planning does not take account of such matters as job sequence, set-up times, the coincidence of several jobs requiring a work centre on the same day or competition among production jobs for a limited resource. CRP is concerned with the assessment of general viability. Important though the aforementioned subjects are, they are the everyday detail of

---

[14] The question must be asked, if work centre capacities can be readily altered, as to what capacity figures are to be used in CRP in the first place. If a single, standard value is recorded for a work centre, which then indicates an overload that the manufacturing manager has, in fact, already addressed, CRP may become an irritation and its use may decline. Following any capacity management arrangements, therefore, it seems desirable to allow different capacity figures to be entered on each work centre's capacity data record to reflect the arrangements made, one for each period.

Master Plan Formulation

manufacturing planning. There are, however, a small number of companies where the everyday detail can dictate strategy and where this detail would be best examined before the master plan is released. Companies likely to fall into this category are those with limited common resources such as bottling lines, large-scale process flows and other critical operations.

In such cases, the tool that might be used to check potential master plan feasibility is an advanced planning system. As explained in Chapter 12, APS software is specifically geared to making simulation easy to do. Although the systems are associated in normal use with planning a couple of weeks ahead, not several months, the longer horizon can certainly be handled. Except for "constraints-based" systems, which are relatively fast to run (see Section 12.1), computer processing times for many months ahead may be lengthy. (Various tricks can be performed to shorten times, such as temporarily simplifying planning rules or running the systems in infinite loading mode.) As pointed out at the conclusion of the preceding sub-section, the use of an APS system at this point is to test feasibility prior to a go/no-go decision, not to pre-empt planning intended to be done at a later stage.

6.7 COMMITMENT, RELEASE, COMMITMENT

The dominant place which the master schedule is now to occupy in the company's operations is depicted in Figure 6.6. Before final release, every company manager and member of staff who will have a role in the activity must understand what is required of him and truly agree that he can fulfil it. To repeat the phrase used at the start of this Chapter: ***At the centre of master scheduling are the commitment and unity of personnel.***

Figure 6.6: Master Planning and Company Operations

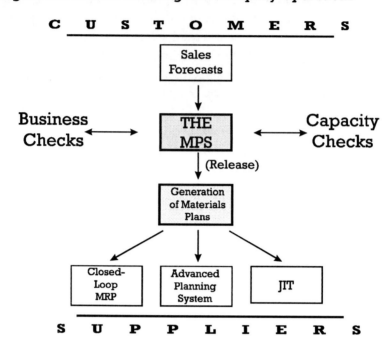

The mechanics of master plan release are straightforward. The newly planned requirements for each master scheduled product overwrite the old requirements and the complete plan is exploded through the bill of materials to determine revised component and raw material needs. If an advanced planning system is being used now to control manufacture, rather than closed-loop MRP, an APS run for the next few weeks will also be necessary.

The continuing fulfilment of the master schedule, day after day, notwithstanding the vicissitudes of manufacturing life, involves managers and staff from sales, manufacturing, purchasing and other functions besides. The resolve of the manufacturing manager to ensure that his own part in the undertaking is well done is accepted without question.

Chapter 7

Master Plan Management

After the formulation of the MPS, it is released to become the prime source of reference for all subsequent planning and operations. Despite the best endeavours of marketing, manufacturing, purchasing and other staff, however, it is inevitable that a few at least of the expectations which were acted upon when building it will not turn out to be the case and even that things will simply go wrong. It is consequently important that the ongoing validity of the master schedule be constantly checked against current conditions and events. Although it is the general wish that the plan should remain stable, to achieve the company's business objectives and to stabilise manufacturing and supply activities, if it seems that serious deviations are occurring, change to it must be considered. In addition, as we shall see, in companies that make to order, referral to the ongoing master schedule is a prerequisite of order acceptance. All of these activities are collectively known as MPS management.

The primary instrument of MPS management as customer demand unfolds is the projected stock balance described in sub-section 6.5.1, its analysis being the responsibility of the master production scheduler, not the manufacturing manager.[1] Other in-

---

[1] In some companies, the title *master production scheduler* may be synonymous with *materials manager*. In small companies it may be synonymous with *production controller*. In very small companies, the master scheduler and the manufacturing manager may in fact be one and the same person. The question of the master scheduler's job description has been addressed in human resources (see sub-section 19.2.1 and sub-section 19.2.3 (footnote 28)).

formation through which the plan must be analysed comes from manufacturing (completed MPS plans and news about capacity); from orders already accepted; and, if relevant, from the distribution network (depot replenishment needs). The pivotal position of the process can be seen in the pictograph in Figure 7.1.

Figure 7.1: The Place of Master Plan Management

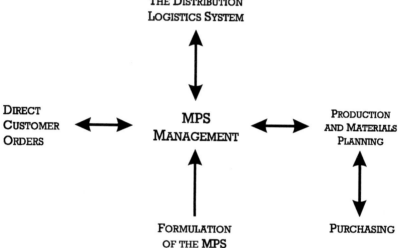

7.1 CONSUMING THE FORECAST

The projected stock analysis is run against plans for all master scheduled products typically every night, after the processing of data relating to completed master plan production and regardless of the nature of the planning system used to control lower levels of the bill of materials. If the planning system is closed-loop MRP, of course, the projected stock analysis at the MPS level is extended all the way down to the raw materials.

Because of the existence of the frozen and semi-frozen time zones (see sub-section 6.5.2), that part of the master plan within the second time fence remains unchanged after computer analysis, but, as explained, differences between the plan and the logical ideal are brought to the master planner's attention through printed or on-screen messages. The list below shows six typical messages. Note again, as explained, in sub-section 5.2.2, that for a make-to-stock product, no reschedule-in message is issued when the pro-

Master Plan Management

jected stock balance falls to a level below the product's safety stock, and down to zero.[2]

- *Reschedule in MPS plan X from Date 2 to Date 1;*
- *Reschedule out MPS plan X from Date 1 to Date 2;*
- *Master scheduled planned lot X is due for manufacture;*
- *Master schedule manufacturing lot X scheduled for receipt on Date D is past due;*
- *Unsatisfied sales forecasts from Date 1 to Date 2;*
- *Delete master plan order X.*

One problem with the projected stock messages, touched on in sub-section 6.5.2, is the repetitious generation of reschedule-out messages when stock build-ups are taking place. Two further problems are as follows, and are dealt with in sub-sections 7.1.1 and 7.1.2:

1. For products made to order, the projected stock analysis takes place in the presence of both sales forecasts and actual orders; and

2. For products made to stock, the analysis may give rise to an excessive number of messages because of the unevenness of customer order quantities received each day.

The subject matter in both of the sub-sections is referred to as *consuming the forecast*. In the first, its "consumption" is by actual demand as the demand is received, to prevent the double counting of both the original sales forecast and the customer demand itself.

---

[2] In addition, no message is issued to reschedule the master plan out when the projected stock exceeds the manufacturing lot quantity by up to the safety level. For example, with a manufacturing lot size of 100 units and a safety stock of 10 units, no reschedule-out message would be output unless the projected stock quantity was greater than 110 units. Note that a number of software systems do permit messages to be displayed on falling below safety, but as a user option, or permit messages to be displayed as an option if the projected stock has remained below the safety level for a certain number of days.

The phrase was coined by Richard Ling.[3] In the second subsection, its consumption, or, at least, manipulation, is so as to suppress rescheduling messages. In both, it may also be said that the passage of time itself consumes the forecast. That is, as the master plan month progresses day by day, the sales forecast of each day past is eliminated — time *rolls over* the forecasts — it *consumes* them.

7.1.1 Consuming the Forecast I: Make-to-Order

First, it will be recalled that the sales forecast quantities and dates in the master schedule of a product made to order relate to the quantities and dates of planned completed manufacture. That is, as explained in sub-section 4.3.4, the forecasts of order receipt are *offset* by the average order lead time prior to their employment in master planning. Method I, then, of consuming the forecast is for products made to order, and is concerned entirely with the simultaneous treatment of remaining (offset) sales forecasts and accepted customer orders in the master schedule. Accepted customer orders, due for completion at the various future dates, are referred to here as "actual demand". The method serves two purposes. First, initially, it permits the projected stock arithmetic to proceed in the presence of both the offset sales forecasts and actual demand. The principal value of this, of course, is in generating the master schedule at the formulation stage. Secondly, again through the projected stock mechanism, it provides the master scheduler during the master planning month with warnings of possible shortfalls in, or excessive provision for, master planning effort. In the first instance, even though customer orders have been satisfactorily booked into the master planning system by the available-to-promise technique (to be explained in Section 7.2), there may be difficulty in meeting further orders which are forecast still to be received. In the second, the presence of a positive projected

---

[3] R.C. Ling and K. Widner (1974), *Master Scheduling in a Make-to-Order Plant*, (proceedings of the 1974 APICS Annual Conference). APICS is the American Production and Inventory Control Society and was once associated with what is now The Institute of Operations Management in Warwick Business Park, Coventry. Richard Ling is one of the gurus of MRPII. See also *The APICS Dictionary*, Seventh edition, published by APICS; James H.Greene (ed.) (1997), *Production and Inventory Control Handbook*, Third edition, McGraw-Hill.

Master Plan Management

balance at the end of the semi-frozen zone may suggest there is overplanning within it.

The consumed forecast is not always explicitly displayed in master scheduling system output, the master scheduler being left to work out the position for himself. It seems more helpful, however, to introduce a new line, or row, into the master schedule display termed "Consumed Forecast". The consumed forecast row shows the total figure now to be used in calculating the projected stock balance in place of either the original offset sales forecast or the actual demand.[4] Its nature is an amalgam of actual demand and part of the original sales forecast. As a general rule, it is arrived at very simply by taking the greater of the two figures "sales forecast" and "actual demand".[5] But different considerations prevail depending whether planning is at the formulation stage or in MPS management.

Table 7.1 shows the consumed forecast and allied data relating to a master plan under formulation.

Table 7.1: Consuming the Forecast (MPS Formulation)

On-Hand (OH): 0 units
Past Due (PD): nil
Plan: Lot for Lot
Safety Stock: 0

	Period									
	1	2	3	4	5	6	7	8	9	10
Sales Forecast	5	5	5	5	5	5	5	5	5	5
Consumed Forecast	4	7	6	5	5	5	5	5	5	5
Actual Demand	4	7	6	3	1					
Master Schedule [PD 0]	4	7	6	5	5	5	5	5	5	5
Projected Stock Balance [OH 0]	0	0	0	0	0	0	0	0	0	0

---

[4] An alternative to the method given here which is more in accordance with Ling's terminology is to introduce a row instead which is, literally, the offset sales forecast as reduced by actual demand. Thus, if the original (offset) sales forecast in a period is 5 units and actual demand in the period is 3 units, as they are in Period 4, Table 7.1, the alternative consumed forecast figure in the period would be 2 units. The projected stock balance is then calculated by taking into account this alternative consumed forecast *plus* the actual demand.

[5] Strictly speaking, the rule for calculating the Consumed Forecast as defined in this text is to take the greater of the two figures: (1) *(sales forecast − actual demand) + actual demand*, and (2) *actual demand*.

Although nine of the consumed forecasts in the ten periods have been derived according to the rule above, the master scheduler has specifically and individually amended the consumed forecast in Period 1 from 5 units to 4 units. He intends to master schedule only 4 units in the period and no further customer orders will be taken for completion before Period 4. If he did not amend the consumed forecast in this way and the software was permitted to insert 5 units in Period 1, in accordance with the "greater of the two" rule, even though the master plan was for 4 units, the projected stock calculation would arrive at −1 (minus one) in Period 1, and a reschedule-in message would be issued following its release.

We now turn to consumption of the forecast during MPS management as new orders are received. A consumed forecast for a particular period is potentially revised after plan release only if additional demand is booked into the period or by direct intervention by the master scheduler.[6] Although in the first case the greater-of-the-two rule continues to operate, there will be a change (an increase) in the consumed forecast only if the revised total actual demand is greater than the sales forecast. Clearly, if the total actual demand is less than (or equal to) the sales forecast, the consumed forecast will remain at the same value as the sales forecast.

The foregoing is illustrated by Table 7.2, which is derived from Table 7.1. When comparison is made with Table 7.1, it is seen that an additional 5 units of demand have been accepted for completion in Period 5, 6 units of new demand have been accepted for completion in Period 6, and 3 units for Period 7. The consumed forecasts in Periods 5 and 6, but not in Period 7, have therefore increased from 5 units to 6 units each, in accordance with the rule. As a consequence, the projected stock balance has fallen below zero. Messages are therefore generated to deal with the negative balance by rescheduling in the master plan quantities to cover it. They may provide a valuable warning to the master scheduler that sales demand for the product is stronger than was allowed for when the plan was first formulated and released. (Alternatively, when they are read in conjunction with information relating to available-to-

---

[6] Allowance should also be made for order cancellations. These may cause the consumed forecast to fall from some previous level above the sales forecast back down to the sales forecast in accordance with the rule.

promise, they may merely serve as a reminder that actual completion of two of the units to be made must be scheduled to earlier dates — see Figure 7.4.)

Table 7.2: Consuming the Forecast and the Generation of Messages through Negative Projected Stock

On-Hand (OH): 0 units
Past Due (PD): nil
Plan: Lot for Lot
Safety Stock: 0

					Period					
	1	2	3	4	5	6	7	8	9	10
Sales Forecast	5	5	5	5	5	5	5	5	5	5
Consumed Forecast	4	7	6	5	6	6	5	5	5	5
Actual Demand	4	7	6	3	6	6	3			
Master Schedule [PD 0]	4	7	6	5	5	5	5	5	5	5
Projected Stock Balance [OH 0]	0	0	0	0	−1	−2	−2	−2	−2	−2

A further scenario involving a positive projected stock balance is presented in Table 7.3, which is again derived from Table 7.1, but here demand has been reduced. First, there has been an order cancellation of one unit in Period 3, so the consumed forecast is reduced automatically from 6 units to 5. Secondly, because of recent poor sales, the master scheduler has overridden the previous consumed forecast of 5 units in Period 4 with 4 units. Messages are accordingly produced to reschedule the master plan out and serve as a memorandum to him that he might in due course take action to scale back production somewhat, perhaps before the end of the MPS month.

Table 7.3: Consuming the Forecast (Positive Projected Stock Balance)

On-Hand (OH): 0 units
Past Due (PD): nil
Plan: Lot for Lot
Safety Stock: 0

	Period									
	1	2	3	4	5	6	7	8	9	10
Sales Forecast	5	5	5	5	5	5	5	5	5	5
Consumed Forecast	4	7	5	4	5	5	5	5	5	5
Actual Demand	4	7	5	4	2					
Master Schedule [PD 0]	4	7	6	5	5	5	5	5	5	5
Projected Stock Balance [OH 0]	0	0	1	2	2	2	2	2	2	2

Non-Consuming Demand

Underlying the process of consuming the forecast just described is the natural assumption that demand when it is received is indeed the forecast become manifest. Actual orders take the place of predicted orders. When they are examined, however, a number of individual customer orders may be found to be very different from the ordinary, say, with regard to their source or size. For example, the company's sales may be thought of as UK-only, with sales forecasts prepared on that basis, when an order arrives surprisingly from France. Alternatively, product orders may typically be for 1 or 2 units, from industrial customers, but one is now received from the Ministry of Defence for 10 units.

Unusual orders of this nature should not be allowed to reduce the expectation of further normal demand. They constitute *non-consuming* demand. Reduction of the original sales forecast should be by *consuming* demand only. The text following describes how the two types of demand appearing together are distinguished and treated in forecast consumption.

As before, there are different considerations in the treatment of non-consuming demand depending on the stage of master scheduling. In the master plan formulation stage, the non-consuming demand is allowed for directly in the master schedule. Consider Table 7.4, which contains the same sales forecasts and actual demand figures as Table 7.1, but it is now supposed that 2 units of the

Master Plan Management

actual demand in Period 3 and 1 unit of the demand in Period 4 are non-consuming. The consumed forecast in Period 3 is now 7 units, not as shown in Table 7.1. The sum of 7 units is made up of two elements. The first is 5 units, this being the normal consumed forecast — i.e. the greater of the sales forecast (5 units) and the *consuming* actual demand (4 units). The second element is the 2 units of the non-consuming demand. Similarly, the consumed forecast in Period 4 is 6 units. Again, this is made up of the normal consumed forecast (5 units) and the non-consuming demand (1 unit). To meet these additional requirements, it will be seen that the master schedule under formulation is greater in these two periods than it is in Table 7.1.

Table 7.4: Formulating an MPS and Non-Consuming Demand

On-Hand (OH): 0 units
Past Due (PD): nil
Plan: Lot for Lot
Safety Stock: 0

					Period					
	1	2	3	4	5	6	7	8	9	10
Sales Forecast	5	5	5	5	5	5	5	5	5	5
Consumed Forecast	4	7	7*	6*	5	5	5	5	5	5
Actual Demand	4	7	6	3	1					
Master Schedule (PD 0)	4	7	7	6	5	5	5	5	5	5
Projected Stock Balance (OH 0)	0	0	0	0	0	0	0	0	0	0

* includes non-consuming demand — see text.

During master schedule management, the first question is how unusual incoming sales orders are to be recognised as such and so be declarable as non-consuming. The general criteria to be used to identify them are likely to be decided jointly by the member of staff in charge of the sales forecasting system and the master scheduler. Much will then depend on whether every order can be individually examined by sales order processing staff. If it can, application of the criteria should be straightforward. If it cannot, strict logical tests will need to be introduced into the SOP system software.[7]

Table 7.5 is derived from Table 7.1, and shows the addition of 4 more units of demand in Period 5 and new demand of 1 unit in Period 6 occurring during the master schedule month. However, it has been determined that the 1 unit for manufacture in Period 6 relates to a non-consuming order. Consequently, the consumed forecast in Period 6 is 6 units, not 5, and the projected stock balance has gone negative, warning the master scheduler of the situation.

Table 7.5: MPS Management and Non-Consuming Demand

On-Hand (OH): 0 units
Past Due (PD): nil
Plan: Lot for Lot
Safety Stock: 0

	Period									
	1	2	3	4	5	6	7	8	9	10
Sales Forecast	5	5	5	5	5	5	5	5	5	5
Consumed Forecast	4	7	6	5	5	6	5	5	5	5
Actual Demand	4	7	6	3	5	1				
Master Schedule [PD: 0]	4	7	6	5	5	5	5	5	5	5
Projected Stock Balance [OH: 0]	0	0	0	0	0	−1	−1	−1	−1	−1

7.1.2 Consuming the Forecast II: Make-To-Stock

It will be recalled from sub-section 4.3.4 that in order to use sales forecasts prepared for monthly periods in a master planning system with daily buckets, the monthly figure is simply divided by the number of working days to arrive at a "daily forecast". (If there is a known pattern of sales over the month, allowance might be made for it.) There are surely no businesses, however, where the sales demand for a product is the same one day to the next, or even approximately the same. On certain days there are substantial excesses of demand over the average, or daily, forecast and on other

---

[7] A test for an order of unusual size for a product is to calculate the mean order size and its standard deviation, and tag as non-consuming any order which is, say, 4 standard deviations or more larger (or smaller) in size than the mean.

days there are shortfalls. Suppose now that, starting with the master plan's release, excesses and shortfalls are accumulated day after day. In the main, excesses (positive) and shortfalls (negative) will cancel out. But now suppose that they do not, and the (absolute) value of the accumulated total comes to exceed the product's safety stock. In such a case, if the value is positive, a reschedule-in message will be generated for every one of the product's master plans, regardless of how near or distant it is within the frozen and semi-frozen time zones. If the value is negative, reschedule-out messages will be generated.

This is seen in Table 7.6 and Table 7.7. Table 7.6 shows a manufacturing plan scheduled for a product in Period 10 at the MPS formulation stage. If the master plan semi-frozen zone extends to 90 periods, there will be further planned lots for Period 50 and Period 90. Table 7.7 gives the actual demand occurring in the first five periods after release. In the first period, the excess of demand over the forecast is +20 units, in the second it is +5 units, in the third the shortfall is −6, and so on, so that the accumulated total of the excesses and shortfalls by the end of Period 5 is +34 units. This exceeds the product's safety stock of 28 units, and, as a result, the projected stock balance has fallen below zero. A message to reschedule in the planned lot from Period 10 to Period 9 is therefore generated. There will also be messages to reschedule in the later plans to Period 49 and Period 89.

Table 7.6: Management of a Product Master Schedule I (Formulation)

On-Hand (OH): 120 units Past Due (PD): nil Plan: Lots of 400 units Safety Stock: 28 units	Period									
	1	2	3	4	5	6	7	8	9	10
Sales Forecast	10	10	10	10	10	10	10	10	10	10
Master Schedule [PD 0]										400
Projected Stock Balance [OH 120]	110	100	90	80	70	60	50	40	30	420

Table 7.7: Management of a Product Master Schedule II (High Demand)

On-Hand (OH): 120 units (start)
Past Due (PD): nil
Plan: Lots of 400 units
Safety Stock: 28 units

					Period					
		1	2	3	4	5	6	7	8	9	10
Sales Forecast		10	10	10	10	10	10	10	10	10	10
Actual Demand per Period		30	15	4	15	20					
Master Schedule	PD 0										400
Projected Stock Balance	OH 120	90	75	71	56	36	26	16	6	−4	386

If the safety stock assigned to a product is relatively large, the generation of messages for the reason alone of uneven customer demand will be uncommon. However, as we know from Chapter 5, the safety stocks set on infrequently replenished products are likely to be low because of the protection of customer service provided by the large replenishment lot itself. They may even be zero on many products, and, if they are, rescheduling messages will be generated almost constantly. Infrequently replenished products are usually numerous. As a result, a master scheduler with a large number of products to manage may find a significant part of his morning spent following system leads which turn out to be without consequence, time he might have better spent on the important matters of the day.

The second method of consuming the forecast is therefore aimed at suppressing rescheduling messages caused by daily fluctuations in day-to-day demand. Its rationale is that the customer service aimed for through the safety stock sub-system and provided for in master plan formulation when safety stock, which may be zero, is "put into" the plan, is independent of master plan management. In particular, it is independent of master plan rescheduling in response to messages generated through the projected stock balance. This being so, it is legitimate to suppress such messages, but there are two provisos. The first is that the method should not be used for higher value products if rescheduling of the master plan is indeed part of support for customer service as described in sub-section 5.4.3. The second applies when stock is low

Master Plan Management

and a master plan replenishment is due in during the master plan month. In these circumstances, uneven incoming demand may lead to a stockout before the replenishment lot arrives. Consequently, the make-to-stock company employing message suppression would do well to support customer service with an available-to-promise facility, so that customers wishing to place orders during a stockout could at least be promised a firm delivery at some specified time in the near future, and not merely put on backorder.

The method itself of forecast consumption in make-to-stock is simple. (Vollmann *et al* refer to it as the *error addback* method.)[8] A new line, or row, is introduced into the master plan display, termed Consumed Forecast (not having the same meaning as in 7.1.1, of course). The figures in the line are the normal daily forecasts, but either reduced or added to as follows. If, at a moment in time, the accumulated excesses and shortages described above are positive, this positive value is *subtracted* from them. If, at a moment in time, the accumulated total is negative, its absolute value is *added* to them (i.e. the negative value is also subtracted).[9] The projected stock balance is now calculated from the consumed forecast, not the original sales forecast.

Table 7.8 is derived from Table 7.7, where the excess of demand in Periods 1 to 5 was 34 units. The original sales forecasts remaining have been reduced from Period 6 onwards by a total of 34 units and the revised figures placed in the Consumed Forecast line. The projected stock balance is calculated from the new values and so does not fall below the product's safety. As we see, no rescheduling of the MPS plan in Period 10 is now indicated.

---

[8] See Figure 19.10 in T.E. Vollmann, W.L. Berry and D.C. Whybark (1988), *Manufacturing Planning and Control Systems*, Second edition, Dow Jones-Irwin.

[9] A rule governing the way a positive value might be subtracted from daily forecasts, starting with the earliest, is that the maximum reduction of any given daily forecast should be to zero (i.e. not to a negative value), with any remaining reduction carried forward to the next day, as shown in Table 7.8. A rule governing the subtraction of a negative value is to limit the increase in the daily forecast to 100 per cent, again carrying the remainder forward.

Table 7.8: Suppression of a Rescheduling Message in Make-to-Stock

On-Hand (OH): 120 units (start)
Past Due (PD): nil
Plan: Lots of 400 units
Safety Stock: 28 units

		Period								
	1	2	3	4	5	6	7	8	9	10
Sales Forecast	10	10	10	10	10	10	10	10	10	10
Actual Demand per Period	30	15	4	15	20					
Consumed Forecast						0	0	0	6	10
Master Schedule	PD 0									400
Projected Stock Balance	OH 120	90	75	71	56	36	36	36	36	30	420

7.2 AVAILABLE-TO-PROMISE

"Available-to-promise" is concerned with what manufacturing effort or manufactured stock in the master production schedule is available, literally, to promise to potential new customers. That is, it has to do with what remains in the master plan after customer orders already accepted have been taken into account. The technique is a powerful one, and is the cornerstone of master schedule management for products made to order and assembled to order. It is also able to provide a supplementary form of service for products made to stock. Its application and the mechanics of its operation are dealt with below in three sub-sections.

Before turning to the detail, however, consideration should be given to the very point where order enquiries are being made and the available-to-promise position is consequently being analysed. Clearly, a technical (computer) connection is required here between the sales order processing system and the master scheduling system. The SOP system has already been described from the commercial viewpoint in Section 2.4 and Figure 2.5. What must be added now is the ability of the sales order processing clerk or technical salesmen to access the master schedule and the ATP data when order dates are being discussed with the customer. Similarly, the master scheduler must be able to access sales order promises and delivery dates if he is to be able to make decisions on master

Master Plan Management

plan management and potential rescheduling. Unfortunately, integration of the two systems or, at least, the provision of online access to the required data files by each is often difficult because of the origins of the software. Many software houses providing slick SOP systems able to maintain on-hand stock files and perform order allocation in make-to-stock have failed to incorporate a means for accessing the master plan and ATP. Providers of manufacturing system software, who know ATP very well indeed, frequently provide SOP modules of insufficient sophistication. If the company has to fall back on file transfer methods as a means of exchanging data between the two systems, the full value of master schedule management in combination with ATP is most unlikely to be realised.

7.2.1 Available-to-Promise

For companies that make to order, a product's master schedule is a set of plans for the completion of work. Each plan is qualified by the quantity of product finally to be manufactured and the date its completion is intended. Alternatively, although it is not quite the same thing because of the time required for the final manufacturing stage, the master schedule might be thought of as a schedule of final stage manufacturing effort.

In master schedule management, when an order is accepted from a customer for manufacture and delivery in the future, it is not simply "launched into the factory" — that is, entered into the list of jobs to be undertaken in the hope that it will be finished by the time promised. Instead, it is booked individually and in calculated fashion into the master schedule; a particular part of the master schedule, qualified by the order's quantity and date, is reserved exclusively for it.

At any particular moment, therefore, assuming the existence of outstanding factory orders which have already been accepted and booked in, and which are scheduled to be completed at various dates in the future, part of a product's master schedule is said to be "promised". That part of it that is not promised remains "available to promise" for orders still to be received.

The management of incoming orders through available-to-promise therefore comprises, first, the review of the promised and still available to promise positions of manufacturing effort master scheduled for each product. Secondly, for a particular product and a particular potential new customer order, it comprises the consideration of alternative ways of inserting the order into remaining effort in the master schedule. By definition, the final decision on doing so will determine the order's promise date. A date may have to be individually negotiated with the customer, but, if it does not need to be, insertion of the customer order gives considerable scope to the sales order processing clerk to ensure, say, that an order known to be routine is promised for a later rather than an earlier date and that effort therefore remains in the master schedule for customers with more urgent requests.[10] Finally, as the order is confirmed and booked into the MPS, comes the updating of the ATP position. It will be noted in the foregoing that the master schedule remains stable throughout the process, but that the lead time quoted for orders is liable to variation, being longer when business is busy and shorter when things are slack. Lead time variation is, in a sense, the make-to-order company's equivalent to safety stock.

In order to work out a product's available-to-promise position, it is necessary to start with the quantities and dates of its master schedule and the current state of orders already accepted. These data can be set out in a table, as shown many times in Section 7.1. Calculation of the ATP then proceeds from right to left, not left to right. It does so because, although it is perfectly acceptable to complete an order early, it cannot be completed late without breaking the promise to the customer. By working from right to left, we see that even though there may be insufficient effort available to complete an order on a given date, earlier effort may be available for it "to the left".

The right-to-left requirement is illustrated in Figure 7.2, which relates to a product manufactured in lots of 40. The actual demand to be completed in Periods 8 and 9 amounts to 29 units. The planned effort of 40 in Period 10 ("on the right") is not relevant because it is later than the promise dates of the demand. It is the con-

---

[10] If urgent orders do not materialise, orders can always be brought forward. For example, available-to-promise can be used for accepting repair work via capacity available-to-promise (7.2.2), always reserving a certain amount of effort for possible emergencies. If an emergency job does indeed arrive, the company will wish to charge a premium rate for it.

Master Plan Management

vention in ATP, for the sake of clarity, for the actual demand to reduce the first master plan which is available to be used. Consequently, what is "available still to be promised out of the MPS" in Period 7 has been reduced from 40 to 11 units and the ATP in Period 6 continues to be the MPS's full 40 units.[11]

Figure 7.2: Available to Promise I

Period	6	7	8	9	10	
Actual Demand			12	17		End of Plan Horizon
Master Schedule	40	40			40	
Available to Promise	40	11			40	

Figure 7.3 is similar to Figure 7.2 except for 25 units of additional demand in Period 7. The total of 54 units of actual demand in Periods 7, 8 and 9 use up all of the MPS plan of 40 units in Period 7 and 14 units of the MPS plan in Period 6. Another way of saying this is that the actual demand of 14 units in Period 7 which cannot be satisfied by the MPS in Period 7 is "passed back" (i.e. to the left), to be satisfied by the plan in Period 6.

Figure 7.3: Available to Promise II

Period	6	7	8	9	10	
Actual Demand		25	12	17		End of Plan Horizon
Master Schedule	40	40			40	
Available to Promise	26	0			40	

Figure 7.4 shows the available-to-promise situation in the first five periods of a product made lot-for-lot. If a customer wished to place

---

[11] In practice, the orders that constitute the demand in Periods 8 and 9 of Table 7.2 may, in the event, be manufactured in Period 6.

an order for 5 units for delivery in Period 3, we realise that although there is nothing available to promise in Period 3 itself, it can be accepted because earlier effort is available in Periods 1 and 2. (One way of seeing this more obviously would, perhaps, be to display "–2" ATP in Period 3, with the full 5 units ATP in Period 2, as discussed below in relation to Figures 7.8 and 7.9.)

Figure 7.4: Available to Promise III

Period	1	2	3	4	5
Actual Demand	16	15	22	9	8
Master Schedule	20	20	20	20	20
Available to Promise	4	3	0	11	12

←⎯⎯⎯⎯⎯⎯⎯

An alternative presentation again is to display what is available to promise *cumulatively*. That is, after calculating the single figures from right to left in the standard way, we might proceed back again, from left to right, starting in the first period, accumulating the available effort from one period to the next. The same available-to-promise position in Figure 7.4 is given again, cumulatively, in Figure 7.5.

Figure 7.5: Available to Promise IV (Cumulative Display)

Period	1	2	3	4	5
Actual Demand	16	15	22	9	8
Master Schedule	20	20	20	20	20
Cumulative ATP	4	7	7	18	30

⎯⎯⎯⎯ *First*
Next ⎯⎯⎯⎯→

A cumulative display is usually available as a user-specified option in master scheduling systems. The majority of sales order processing clerks and master schedulers prefer the single figure display, however. It is thought easier with single figures to see what has

Master Plan Management

happened, especially if the volume of production is high such that the accumulated MPS quantity is very large (see sub-section 6.1.1, footnote 3).

Next, suppose that an ATP situation is as shown in Figure 7.6. If a customer here now wished to place an order for 10 units for delivery in Period 2, we see that there is insufficient effort in the master plan to satisfy this — that is, 4 units only are available. The earliest date for which the sales order processing clerk or master scheduler can promise full delivery of the potential order is Period 3.

Figure 7.6: Available to Promise V

Period	1	2	3	4	5
Actual Demand	14	12	11	3	9
Master Schedule	30		30		30
Available to Promise	4		16		21

If the clerk or master scheduler were to book the order for completion in Period 2 (4 units) and Period 3 (6 units), the new position would be as shown in Figure 7.7.

Figure 7.7: Available to Promise VI

Period	1	2	3	4	5
Actual Demand	14	16	17	3	9
Master Schedule	30		30		30
Available to Promise	0		10		21

Naturally, a master scheduler might be pressed to reschedule the master plan in Period 3 to the earlier date of Period 2 so that the order could indeed be met as originally requested, but many would consider such an action disruptive and extreme.[12] It is sometimes remarked that make-to-order companies which boast that they will accept all orders and the completion dates demanded of them without question are usually the worst at fulfilling their promises. Whatever the truth of the matter, in the instance in Table 7.6, a decision to reschedule the MPS is certainly not one that can be taken by a sales order processing clerk or technical salesman. Sales and Marketing must consequently regard the available-to-promise position in make-to-order as they are forced to regard the on-hand stock balance in make-to-stock.

Suppose now, for illustration, that the order for 10 units in Period 2 were nevertheless to be taken, despite the fact that effort is not available for it. The position would then be as shown in Figure 7.8.

Figure 7.8: Available to Promise VII (Overpromised Master Schedule)

Period	1	2	3	4	5
Actual Demand	14	22	11	3	9
Master Schedule	30		30		30
Available to Promise	−6		16		21

←———————

The 6 units short in Period 1 cannot be passed to the left because we have reached current time. Any negative figure in Period 1 of an available-to-promise display indicates an *overpromised*, or *overloaded*, MPS. Such a situation is one that must be avoided, of course. If it occurs, its gravity is such that the presence of the negative sign alone is sufficient warning, without the need for a message from the system.

Note that many software systems show the ATP position of an overpromised MPS somewhat differently from Figure 7.8. The

---

[12] Notwithstanding this, it is noted that a number of software systems provide what they refer to as a *capable-to-promise* facility, this being an analysis of what would be available to promise if production were based on maximum output rather than the committed master schedule — see capacity available-to-promise below.

Master Plan Management 235

amount by which the MPS is overloaded — i.e. the 6 units here — is "reserved" to satisfy the overload at the first point that effort becomes available. This is done by deducting the overpromised amount from the otherwise spare effort at the first period that it occurs. For example, in Figure 7.8, the first point that stock is available is seen to be Period 3. The available total in Period 3 is accordingly reduced from 16 units (Figure 7.8) to 10 units as shown in Figure 7.9. Software adopting this convention usually also shows negative figures wherever they occur, rather than zero. For example, in Figure 7.4, the "–2 available-to-promise" rather than 0 referred to earlier would be inserted at Period 3. The advantage of doing so is that the master scheduler's attention is drawn to the situation.

Figure 7.9: Available to Promise VIII (Alternative Display of Overpromising)

Period	1	2	3	4	5
Actual Demand	14	22	11	3	9
Master Schedule	30		30		30
Available to Promise	–6		10		21

Although available-to-promise is normally associated with make-to-order and assemble-to-order, when used in make-to-stock, the technique provides a new facet of customer service during a temporary stockout, one that is certainly a significant improvement on the simple acceptance of orders into a backorder file. In some make-to-stock environments relating to industrial rather than consumer sales, the use of available-to-promise in conjunction with an effective safety stock system would obviate the need ever to reschedule the master plan. Consider Figure 7.10. First note that the on-hand stock of 20 units in this instance is itself available to promise and is conventionally included in, or added into, the available-to-promise figure in the first period.

Figure 7.10: Available to Promise IX (Make to Stock)

On-Hand (OH): 20 units

Period		1	2	3	4	5
Actual Demand						
Master Schedule			30			
Available to Promise	OH 20	20	30			

⬅

If an industrial customer now wished to place an order for the immediate delivery of 25 units, we see that there is insufficient stock on hand to meet it. However, we can satisfy 20 units now and give him a specified day, namely Period 2, when the outstanding units will be available. (The SOP clerk might even persuade him to take a single delivery of all 25 units in Period 2.)

It is seen that no account is taken in available-to-promise analysis of sales forecasts or consumed forecasts. ATP is essentially an operational tool, not a planning one. Forecasts are the province of the projected stock balance. In practice, available-to-promise and the projected stock balance must be used in conjunction for fully effective master schedule management. An example of this is given in Table 7.9, a full master schedule display with the available-to-promise line now added, and with figures taken from Table 7.5. While the order for 1 unit in Period 6 was perfectly acceptable from the viewpoint of available-to-promise, it caused a negative projected stock balance because it was unusual and non-consuming. This perhaps threatens the company's ability to satisfy its regular customers in due course. All the evidence must be reviewed together in order to make the best decision.

Master Plan Management

Table 7.9: Full MPS Display for Master Schedule Management

On-Hand (OH): 0 units
Past Due (PD): nil
Plan: Lot for Lot
Safety Stock: 0

	Period									
	1	2	3	4	5	6	7	8	9	10
Sales Forecast	5	5	5	5	5	5	5	5	5	5
Consumed Forecast	4	7	6	5	5	6	5	5	5	5
Actual Demand	4	7	6	3	5	1				
Master Schedule [PD 0]	4	7	6	5	5	5	5	5	5	5
Projected Stock Balance [OH 0]	0	0	0	0	0	-1	-1	-1	-1	-1
Available-to-Promise	0	0	0	2	0	4	5	5	5	5

Figure 7.11 shows the "profile" of each of three products: made-to-order, assembled-to-order and made-to-stock. By *profile* is meant the extent to which each product's master schedule is promised (shaded area within the time limit indicated) and the extent to which it remains available-to-promise (outside the shaded areas), over the entire MPS horizon.

Figure 7.11: Promised/Unpromised Profiles of Three Products

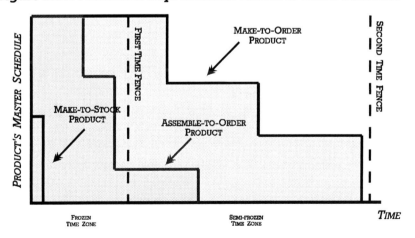

If sketches such as those in Figure 7.11 were to be made for every master scheduled product on a company's range and the sketches then combined, the general result for each of the three types manufacture would be as shown in Figure 7.12.

Figure 7.12: Promised/Unpromised Profiles of Three Companies

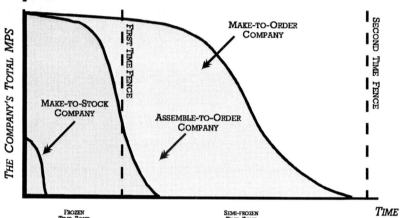

7.2.2 ATP and Capacity Allocation

A variation of available-to-promise gives some weight to Landvater and Gray's definition of master scheduling (see 6.1.1, footnote 1). This is the requirement of many companies to book customers' orders against the capacity of critical machine resources, and to track the continued ability to promise time on those resources, rather than employ available-to-promise on the master scheduled products themselves. A few companies, indeed, sell time itself on critical machines, without reference to their customers' particular products. The concern of an aluminium extrusion company, for example, is the time that an incoming order will take on one of its extruders, hardly the profile of the particular die that will be used.

In cases such as these, it is necessary to translate each incoming order into its requirement for capacity on the resource, and monitor "capacity available-to-promise". This is illustrated in Tables 7.10 to 7.12 and Figure 7.13. In the example, Product A and Product B are the only two products made on the critical resource Work Centre X. Product A requires 1 hour per unit and Product B requires 3 hours per unit. The MPS and order positions of the two products are given in Tables 7.10 and Table 7.11. Table 7.12 exists purely to

Master Plan Management

record the capacity planning and control of Work Centre X. Note that the time periods for A and B are one period out of synchronisation with the time periods for X. This is because Tables 7.10 and 7.11 for Products A and B show when manufacture of the products is due to be completed (i.e. Periods 2 to 11), and Table 7.12 for Work Centre X shows when manufacture itself is due to commence (Periods 1 to 10). That is, the lead time of manufacture of each product is one period. To illustrate the mode of procedure more clearly, the pictograph in Figure 7.13 shows how the actual demand for the two products in Period 5 leads to the capacity available to promise value in Period 4.

Table 7.10: Master Schedule of Product A (Occupying Time on Resource X)

On-Hand (OH): nil Past Due (PD): nil Plan: Lot for Lot Safety Stock: 0	Leadtime 1 period; 1 hour per unit									
	Period									
	2	3	4	5	6	7	8	9	10	11
Sales Forecast	5	5	5	5	5	5	5	5	5	5
Consumed Forecast	5	7	5	5	5	6	5	5	5	5
Actual Demand	5	7	4	4	2	6	3			
Master Schedule [PD 0]	5	7	5	5	5	6	5	5	5	5
Projected Stock Balance [OH 0]	0	0	0	0	0	0	0	0	0	0

Table 7.11: Master Schedule of Product B (Occupying Time on Resource X)

On-Hand (OH): nil Past Due (PD): nil Plan: Lot for Lot Safety Stock: 0	Leadtime 1 period; 3 hours per unit									
	Period									
	2	3	4	5	6	7	8	9	10	11
Sales Forecast	4	4	4	4	4	4	4	4	4	4
Consumed Forecast	4	4	4	4	4	4	4	4	4	4
Actual Demand	4	3	4	3	2	1	1			
Master Schedule [PD 0]	4	4	4	4	4	4	4	4	4	4
Projected Stock Balance [OH 0]	0	0	0	0	0	0	0	0	0	0

Table 7.12: Capacity Available-to-Promise

On-Hand (OH): 120 units (start)
Past Due (PD): nil
Plan: Lots of 400 units
Safety Stock: 28 units

	\multicolumn{10}{c}{Period}
	1	2	3	4	5	6	7	8	9	10
Hours Required for the MPS	17	19	17	17	17	17	17	17	17	17
Hours Required for Actual Production	17	16	16	13	8	9	6			
Maximum Capacity (Hours)	20	20	20	20	20	20	20	20	20	20
Available to Promise	3	4	4	7	12	11	14	20	20	20

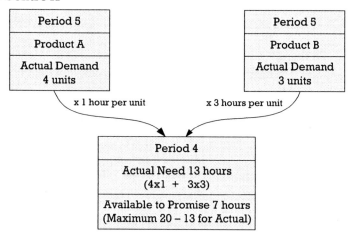

Figure 7.13: Explication of Capacity Available to Promise on Work Centre X

The capacity available-to-promise of Work Centre X is calculated from its maximum capacity less the capacity required to manufacture the actual demand for Product A and Product B, allowance being made for the lead time of manufacture, and might therefore be regarded as another version of "capable-to-promise" mentioned in footnote 12 above.

A small variation of capacity available to promise may be useful when the length of time jobs will occupy on the resource cannot be finely judged in terms of hours. Instead, the time available on the resource might be considered to consist of a number of "slots" (say, 100 slots/week). Jobs under consideration at the point of order acceptance are then allocated "tariffs" based on their perceived complexity — say, 1 slot, 2 slots ... 5 slots. It may be easier for or-

Master Plan Management

der reception staff to think in these terms rather than in literal hours.

Capacity planning and capacity available-to-promise can be extremely valuable tools in make-to-order and assemble-to-order companies, especially when accompanied by simulation capabilities. As well as tracking capacity promised on critical machines, the techniques can readily be used to keep track of the load being accepted for whole manufacturing departments. As with ATP in general, however, it is feared that the dull medium of the printed page hardly conveys the vibrancy of the living system and its operation in the hands of skilled, experienced clerks, planners and negotiators.

7.2.3 The Overpromised and Overstated MPS

Figure 7.8 in sub-section 7.2.1 shows an overpromised master schedule. The negative value in Period 1 indicates that the orders accepted are greater than the company's intention to manufacture. It is frequently the fate of an overpromised master schedule that it should become an *overstated* one. This term means that while orders may have been correctly booked against the MPS, the MPS itself cannot be manufactured because there is insufficient capacity to do so. There are not just arrears: there are missed delivery dates and angry customers; heated discussions; interminable meetings; and all of the accompaniments of the firefighter's life.

The advice to the manufacturing manager that he should not get into this extremely difficult position will not be considered helpful if he is already in it. Nevertheless, before discussing very briefly how he might extricate himself, it must be given. The cause of the overstated master schedule must be determined by going through each step in the hierarchy of planning described in sub-section 6.2.2 and investigating what has gone amiss.

One start that might be made in tackling the overload may be to re-establish data accuracy if this is thought to be at an insufficiently high level. Effective day-to-day control cannot be exercised unless stock and production records are accurate and capacity limits and standard job times have been correctly recorded. A second step may be to adopt input/output control, and so take charge of work-in-progress and shop floor queues as described in Section 11.2. But the main advice for a cure is that there must be a return to order and systematisation. The weapons required to overcome arrears and shortages have been described in this Chapter and Chapter 6. The motto heard in Total Quality Management applies to master scheduling also: *work smarter, not harder!*

The Master Scheduler's Remit

One way to avoid arrears or an overstated master schedule is to look carefully at the remit of the master scheduler and the authority given him, and how in practice the job is done.

The conflict that must be resolved by the master scheduler is between sales, pressing for flexibility and change, and manufacturing, pressing for stability. The primary quality required of the job holder, therefore, is the ability to cope under pressure from both sides and cope with the pressure of events as well. Having weighed the facts and taken a view, the master scheduler must be of the resolution to carry things through. He must also be a practical, self-disciplined worker. This is not a post for dreamers.

The master scheduler's job remit will clearly cover a great many of the tasks implied in this Chapter and Chapter 6, and, if applicable, Chapter 8. What is more pertinent is the authority that is to go with it. As made clear, master scheduling intrudes on a number of sensitive areas, areas relating to stock and production strategies, customer relations, finance and the rest. It is not the business of the master scheduler to decide policy in these areas. That will be decided by senior managers or cross-functional committees. But it is his business to help execute policy and, in the hurly-burly of everyday, the danger then exists of treading on toes or becoming caught up in company politics. Perhaps the area most fraught with risk here lies in his relationship with the Sales and Marketing department. To forestall accusations by Sales that he does not understand their concerns, senior management might well consider the appointment of the master scheduler in the first place from the ranks of sales and marketing staff. See sub-section 19.2.3, footnote 28.

7.3 MASTER SCHEDULING NEW PRODUCTS

This Section is something of an appendix to master schedule management and deals with the first creation of a master plan for a new product prior to its launch in the marketplace. The method described was developed by R.G. Brown,[13] who identifies two components of the stock needed from the initial manufacture. The first is what is initially required to satisfy day-to-day sales demand itself before resupply can be effected through the next master schedule plan. The second component is "pipeline fill". In a distribution network, pipeline fill includes stock at various points in the supply chain other than at the points from which customers are directly supplied, such as at the central warehouse or in transit, as well as stock for merchandising purposes and, perhaps, for salesmen's samples (see Equation 20.1). There are three difficulties:

1. Despite prior market research and testing, there remains great uncertainty as to what sales actually will be after the product is launched and the rate at which they will be achieved.

2. If sales turn out to be high — if they turn out to be far better than predicted — communication of this fact may be slow, and the rescheduling of the master schedule difficult. Running out of stock would be expensive in lost sales and would give a poor impression of the launch to the market.

3. If sales are poor — much lower than predicted — product may remain on the shelf and may eventually need to be scrapped.

In order to determine the amount of product to master schedule by Brown's method, the Sales and Marketing department must submit two sets of weekly forecasts of demand for a period ahead following the launch approximately equal to the product's shelf-life. One set should relate to an optimistic, though realistic, view of what sales will be; the other to a pessimistic view. To illustrate the logic of the procedure, we now plot the *cumulative* values of the two different sets of forecasts on the same graph. (That is, plot (Week 1),

---

[13] R.G. Brown (1982), *Advanced Service Parts Inventory Control* (ASPIC), Second edition, Materials Management Systems Inc.

then (Week 1 + Week 2), then (Week 1 + Week 2 + Week 3), and so on.) An example is shown in Figure 7.14.

Figure 7.14: Cumulative Plots of Optimistic and Pessimistic Forecast Sales

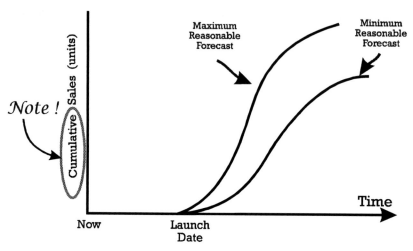

Two points in time following the product's intended time of launch are now considered. The first is the date when the second master scheduled plan will be available for resupply of the stocks, assuming the master schedule is based on the optimistic view. The second is the date when stock will have exceeded its shelf-life or will have become otherwise unsuitable for sale, assuming the master schedule is based on the pessimistic view. Two stock quantities are also now considered, thus:

Quantity 1: The cumulative forecast of sales demand at the point in time when the second MPS resupply occurs, assuming the optimistic forecasts;

Quantity 2: The cumulative forecast of sales demand at the point in time when the shelf-life expires, assuming the pessimistic forecasts.

Caution and logic say, first, that Quantity 1 is the minimum amount of stock to manufacture, plus what is required for the pipeline.

Master Plan Management

Secondly, they say that Quantity 2 is the maximum amount to manufacture, plus pipeline stock.[14]

We next turn to the cumulative demand forecasts supplied by Sales and Marketing, and calculate Quantity 1 and Quantity 2 according to the definitions above. There are now two alternative situations.

The first is that Quantity 1 really is less than Quantity 2. That is, the minimum which should be manufactured really is less than the maximum which should be manufactured, as illustrated in Figure 7.15.

Figure 7.15: Cumulative Plots with Maximum Greater than Minimum

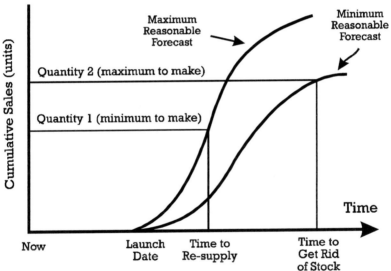

If this is the case, any amount can be master scheduled between the two values (plus pipeline stock) and the launch seems very safe from this point of view.

The second situation is that Quantity (1) is greater than Quantity (2). That is, for the demand forecasts given, the minimum amount to

---

[14] In considering the maximum stock and the pessimistic outcome, an allowance should be made for the need to get rid of stock from the pipeline by finally feeding it through to the points of sale.

make is greater than the maximum that it is safe to make. This is illustrated in Figure 7.16.

Figure 7.16: Cumulative Plots with Minimum greater than Maximum

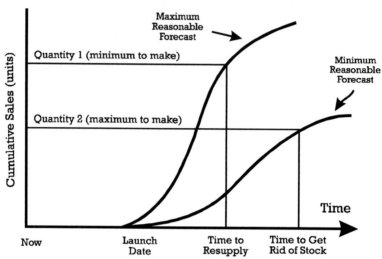

Forewarned is forearmed. Three actions may now be taken to nullify or, at least, reduce the risks attendant on the product's launch. First, arrangements may be made for special feedback on sales following the launch date, so as to reduce the time to resupply the distribution chain if sales are in the optimistic class. This is equivalent to moving the "Time to Resupply" in Figure 7.16 to the left, so reducing the "minimum quantity to make" amount. Secondly, steps can be taken to block the supply of stock to parts of the pipeline. For example, orders may be satisfied only directly from the centre, rather than from every depot. Thirdly, the launch of the product can be timed to occur, say, a couple of weeks before a master schedule formulation date, so that, if rescheduling is required, it is easier to accomplish.

Chapter 8

Assemble-to-Order ("Quick Response")

8.1 INTRODUCTION

The term *assemble-to-order*, or *quick response* (QR),[1] means the provision of a manufacturing service whereby a customer may specify a highly differentiated product, which is then manufactured on his behalf in a very short time. The product is not made for the customer from start to finish in a very short time. Instead, preliminary manufacture of basic parts and alternative product options has already taken place and these are being held in stock. When the customer's particular order is received, the basic parts and the option variants corresponding to it are selected and assembled so as to produce the required final specification. This final activity is universally referred to as *final assembly* and the plan for it as the *final assembly schedule* (FAS). In practice, the FAS will often involve a good deal more than simply assembly and, despite the foregoing, will frequently take place over many days or, in a few instances, even weeks.

There are a number of reasons why a company not offering an assemble-to-order manufacturing service might wish to do so. First, customers — different lifestyles, different needs — want differentiated products and are willing (up to a limit) to pay for them and are willing (up to a limit) to tolerate the delay in getting them.

---

[1] Assemble-to-order is also widely referred to as *two-level master scheduling*, although the term is not quite correct. As stated in the text, the final product is "final assembled". Only the product options are master scheduled.

Secondly, for the manufacturing company, product differentiation means harder selling prices. Thirdly, for companies which currently make to stock but whose customers, it is judged, do not in fact require instant product availability, assemble-to-order may be seen as a means of exchanging finished goods stockholding for stockholding at a lower, less expensive level in the bill of materials. Furthermore, whereas with make-to-stock the risk exists of certain of the less popular varieties being left on the shelf, with assemble-to-order the company is able to offer a greater choice than ever with the possibility only of a few unassembled component options being left. Lastly, companies which now require the customer to wait while the product is made completely to order see in quick response enormous advantages in competitiveness and more economic production. QR and the argument for it are summarised in the sketch in Figure 8.1.

Figure 8.1: A Summary of Assemble-to-Order (QR)

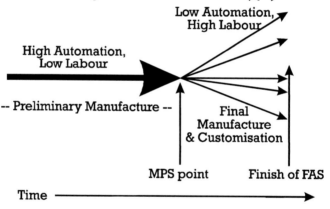

Throughout this Chapter, many aspects of assemble-to-order will be illustrated by reference to a simple, fictitious product, namely an electric pencil sharpener. The electric pencil sharpener is available with either an electroplated or painted sharpener unit and with a red, white or blue casing — six possibilities in all. The sharpener unit and the casing are referred to as *option types*. The electroplated and painted versions, and the three casing colours, are referred to as *option variants*. An attempt has been made to draw the physical bill of materials of the pencil sharpener in Figure 8.2, but even with this simple example, recourse has been necessary to annotation and arrows.

Assemble-to-Order

Figure 8.2: Electric Pencil Sharpener (Physical Bill of Materials)

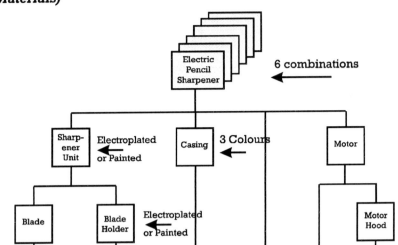

Alternative representations of the make-up of a product assembled-to-order in forms other than the traditional physical bill of material play a major part in the treatment of the subject and will be dealt with in Sections 8.3 and 8.4. Before this, ways and means are described as to how a company might re-engineer a product currently made to stock or made to order into one suitable for assemble to order (or, indeed, how the company might design such a product *ab initio*).

8.2 REDESIGN FOR ASSEMBLE-TO-ORDER

The redesign or design of a product for assemble-to-order, or its "modular design", and the adoption of quick response methods affect many aspects of the business — engineering, manufacturing, assembly, production control, master planning, finance, sales, marketing, etc. It is, naturally, a team endeavour, typically undertaken by a team of some eight to ten members in all, drawn from these areas of the company. The remit must similarly be broad — to question everything from conceptualisation to field service. Two aspects of the task to be accomplished are described in this Section, the analysis of common parts and product redesign itself.

8.2.1 The Analysis of Common Parts

The importance of identifying common parts in assemble-to-order is that once it has been achieved, the production planner is able to co-ordinate plans for matched sets of the parts regardless of the mix of option variants ultimately chosen by customers. And because common parts are uncommitted to any particular combination of option variants until actual assembly in the FAS, safety stock otherwise associated with assemble-to-order is also dispensed with (the provision of safety stock in assemble-to-order is commonly referred to as *option overplanning* — see sub-section 8.6.2).

There are two types of common parts in the context of this subsection. First, a component part or sub-assembly may be common to the product itself and independent of all option types. It is simply present in all of the products manufactured, regardless of the particular option types and option variants specified. Such a one is referred to here as a *general* common part. In the pencil sharpener, the motor and base unit are general common parts. Secondly, a component part or sub-assembly may be common to all option variants of one particular option type only. This is referred to here as an *option* common part.[2] In the pencil sharpener, the blade and blade strip are common to both the electroplated and painted sharpener units. However, we see from Figure 8.2 that it is unnecessary to designate the blade strip as a common part, since it is a component part of the blade. In other words, once the blade has been identified and planned, further explosion of the physical bill of materials from that point will ensure that the blade strip is allowed for in the normal way.[3]

---

[2] If an option type with common parts can simply be omitted altogether in a customer's specification, the set of its common parts should be qualified by the forecast probability that the customer will specify that option type — see also super bills and product families, Section 8.4 and footnote 10.

[3] It appears from Figure 8.2 at first glance that the blade holder blank is also a common part. In fact, the blade holder blank is a component part of the electroplated blade holder and, separately, a component part of the painted blade holder. The gross requirements from which blade holder blanks are planned are made up of two constituents — the requirement for them for the manufac-

Assemble-to-Order

Procedures for identifying general and option common parts are described in due course. Meanwhile, a preferred method of organising the parts so identified is illustrated in Figure 8.3.

Figure 8.3: The Organisation of Common Parts

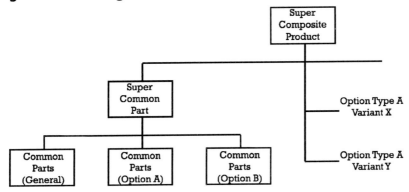

In Figure 8.3, the *super common part* is an artificial entity the purpose of which is to provide a route from the product itself (i.e. the super item, described in Section 8.4), to the general and option common parts shown at the next level down. There are two advantages in the arrangement. First, it is made clear which option common parts are assembled with which option types. Secondly, it is possible thereby to assign different lead times of manufacture to the different sets of option common parts. Consequently, if final assembly work on a particular option type needs to be started earlier than work on others, the common parts required for it are automatically planned for the earlier time.

It is self-evident from Figure 8.3 that the super common part, the general common part set and the various option common part sets are not "real" products. They are simply conveniently categorised collections of common parts. Each collection, or entry, in the representation of materials in Figure 8.3 is referred to as a *pseudo item*. For example, the set of general common parts in the electric pencil sharpener, consisting of a base unit and motor, is not a single

---

ture of electroplated blade holders and the requirement for them for painted blade holders — see "Low-level Coding", Section 9.3 and "Gross Requirements", sub-section 9.4.1. It is important that the requirements for these otherwise "common" components, for each option variant, are dealt with separately, since different quantities for each will be required at different times.

physical entity. It is a pseudo item. An everyday example is the collection of option common parts constituting a car sports pack — leather covered steering wheel, alloy wheels, spoiler, etc. These do not constitute an object but are a collection of items which together enable the manufacturing manager to create a sales feature (in this instance, see footnote 2).

Although the various collections of common parts are simply convenient categorisations, each individual component within them has a direct link to the physical bill of materials. These links lead to the reality of manufacture when the bill of materials is exploded in the way described in Chapter 9. For example, as mentioned earlier, the blade, the only constituent of the sharpener unit's common parts set, has a direct link to the blade strip (Figure 8.2). Similarly, the motor in the general common parts set of the electric pencil sharpener itself has direct links to the battery and motor hood in the physical bill (Figure 8.2).

If the product in question is being designed from the start, the identification and categorisation of general and option common parts is straightforward as specification proceeds. If an existing product is being redesigned for assemble-to-order, these tasks can be achieved through one of two approaches.

1. Matrix Analysis

For less complex products, a semi-computer, semi-manual method can be followed involving a matrix as illustrated in Table 8.1.[4] Table 8.1 involves the electric pencil sharpener. The columns and rows of the matrix are as follows:

Columns The major, or parent, columns each correspond to an option type (in Table 8.1, the sharpener unit and casing). The column sub-divisions are the option variants within each option type.

Rows Each row relates to the component parts and sub-assemblies as they appear in the physical bill of materials. (An obvious difficulty is the need, later, to recognise

---

[4] L.R. Kneppelt (1984), "Product Structuring Considerations for Master Production Scheduling", *Production and Inventory Management*, magazine of APICS, Vol. 25, No. 1, as amended by Vollman et al. (1988), op. cit., Chapter 14.

and remove the blade strip, blade holder blank casing blank, battery, motor hood and motor hood blank.)

For each row in turn, an "X" is placed on the row and in the option variant column if the part is present in the overall product when that option variant is specified by the customer.

Table 8.1: Matrix Analysis to find Common Parts

	OPTION TYPES BY VARIANT				
	Sharpener Unit		**Casing**		
Components	*Electro*	*Painted*	*Red*	*White*	*Blue*
Blade	X	X			
Blade Strip	X	X			
Holder (electroplated)	X				
Holder (painted)		X			
Blade Holder Blank	X	X			
Casing (red)			X		
Casing (white)				X	
Casing (blue)					X
Casing Blank			X	X	X
Base Unit	X	X	X	X	X
Motor	X	X	X	X	X
Battery	X	X	X	X	X
Motor Hood	X	X	X	X	X
Motor Hood Blank	X	X	X	X	X

Now, any component part or sub-assembly which has an X in every option variant of every option type is a general common part. If it has an X simply in every option variant column relating to one particular option type only, it is a common part corresponding to that option type.

2. Computer Analysis

Analysis of the bill of materials by computer has previously been described in Section 3.5. In this instance, a relatively straightforward two-stage programming routine might be employed, such as the "CCAS" method below, developed by William Tallon.[5]

1. *Stage One: Creation of a Component Data File for each Option Type.* Deal with each option type in turn as follows. Suppose that there are *n* option variants in the option type. Then, for each of these option variants, find and record which components are used in its manufacture and each component's usage. Write the results as a separate data file. For example:

    Variant: electroplated sharpener unit;

    Components: Blade (usage 1.0);
    Blade strip (usage 1.0);
    Electroplated blade holder (usage 1.0);
    Blade holder blank (usage 1.0);

    Variant: painted sharpener unit;

    Components: Blade (usage 1.0);
    Blade strip (usage 1.0);
    Painted blade holder (usage 1.0);
    Blade holder blank (usage 1.0).

2. *Stage Two: Checking for Commonality.* Take each component on the option type's data file in turn and find whether it appears *n* number of times, each time with the same usage. If it does, the component qualifies as being potentially common, and, if it does not, it is particular to an option variant. In the ex-

---

[5] See Chapter 14 in T.E. Vollmann, W.L. Berry and D.C. Whybark (1988), *Manufacturing Planning and Control Systems*, Second edition, Dow Jones-Irwin, which includes a detailed example of the analysis by William Tallon of seven families belonging to a materials handling vehicle super super item (see Section 8.4). Although there were 1,279 unique parts, 4,319 common parts (including sub-components of common parts) and 19,645 combinations of vehicle sold, Tallon found that the average vehicle was made up of 76 per cent common parts and sub-components of common parts. The computer method developed by W.J. Tallon was called by him "CCAS" — Component Commonality Analysis System — and published as *The Design and Performance of Master Planning Scheduling Techniques for Assemble-to-Order Products* (1986, PhD dissertation, University of Iowa). A software routine to perform common parts analysis might be a module element in a master production scheduling system, or might be available as a free-standing program from another source.

Assemble-to-Order

ample, n is 2 and we see that the blade, blade strip and blade holder blank all appear twice, each time with usage 1.0. Further data processing would next be necessary to eliminate potentially common components which are, in fact, simply lower level sub-components of common parts or lower level sub-components of option specific parts. (In the example, the blade strip and blade holder blank are to be eliminated.)

Alternative computer methods for ascertaining common parts might also be developed using bill of materials implosion routines.

8.2.2 Modular Design

Six approaches are described for moving to assemble-to-order. The first four are entirely manufacturing and modular design solutions.[6] The last two are marketing solutions.

Solution 1: Extend the FAS Lead Time

Consider the partial physical bill of materials for the sharpener unit assembly of the electric pencil sharpener, which may be either electroplated or painted depending on the customer's specification. Although the construction of the sharpener unit is part of Figure 8.2, it has been reproduced for convenience in Figure 8.4.

---

[6] Evidence of the effectiveness of redesign for assemble-to-order, or modular design, was given by Stoves plc (formerly Valor), a Merseyside company which manufactures ovens (*Manufacturers Organising for Rapid Response*, a two-day conference in February 1995, held in London and organised by ICM, Guildford). Before modular design, Stoves introduced only five new variants per annum to its product range, each taking some 18 to 24 months to develop. Following modular design and QR, the company creates three new variants per day, each taking about two weeks to develop. Previously, Stoves had 15 variants and a three-months make-to-order manufacturing lead time. After implementation of QR, they have 1,500 variants and deal with 75 per cent of orders from their wholesalers and retailers within 10 days. Also see subsection 8.7.3.

Figure 8.4: The Sharpener Unit and the "Embedded" Blade Holder

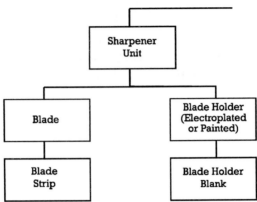

Suppose, now, that for certain technical reasons, it is not possible to hold electroplated and painted sharpener units as stocked option variants. Instead, the "level" at which stock of either of the two option variants can be held is the blade holder. The blade holder is, as it were, "embedded" at the lower level of the bill of materials.[7] Consequently, in this case, it is possible to master schedule electroplated and painted blade holders and hold them as stock, but it is not possible to master schedule and hold electroplated and painted sharpener units. Suppose further that the time currently to build the electric pencil sharpener from the sharpener unit, casing, base unit and motor is two days and the lead time to manufacture either an electroplated or painted sharpener unit from the blade and corresponding blade holder is four days. Then, in order to be able to "assemble" to order without knowing beforehand whether the customer wants an electroplated or painted unit, it becomes necessary, at least theoretically, to extend the FAS time to six days to give enough time to manufacture the specified sharpener unit and then complete the final build. That is, sharpener unit manufacture has become an activity within the FAS itself.

However, the calculation of the lead time above is based on manufacturing data relating to make-to-order. When the electric

---

[7] As we know, embedded options are common. There are numerous real-life examples in make-to-order manufacture of the need to start work at a relatively early stage on particular optional features required by the customer — see Solutions 2 to 4 in the text.

Assemble-to-Order

pencil sharpener was made to order, the manufacture and purchase of all items were required to be co-ordinated by extensive, complex procedures involving the battery, motor, base unit, blade strip, blade holder etc. With assemble-to-order, the nature of the manufacturing process has changed from the viewpoints of required planning, stockholding and production itself. A great many of the previous activities have already been completed before the customer's order is received. In particular, the manufacture of the sharpener unit and the immediate subsequent final manufacture of the electric pencil sharpener might be capable of considerable streamlining.[8] If they are, the theoretical lead time of these activities is unlikely to be incurred in practice. Changed methods and slicker, simpler procedures may very considerably reduce the time.

The prior manufacture of common parts and option variants and the streamlining of FAS activities may between them sufficiently reduce the assemble-to-order response time as to be fully acceptable to the Sales and Marketing department member of the modular design team. On the other hand, options may be so deeply embedded in the bill of materials that FAS activity is seen as unacceptably complex and the time required for it unacceptably lengthy. If so, the team must proceed to Solutions 2 to 6.

Solution 2: Hold Partially Manufactured Inventory

The embedded option may be such that its physical form and the manufacturing operations needed to make it can be redefined as a two-stage manufacturing process as follows:

Stage 1: Manufacture the option to a halfway stage up to, but not beyond, the point at which the option variant is formed. The semi-finished fabrication is no longer considered a semi-finished option, of course. It has become a common part.

Stage 2: Later, in final assembly, form the sales feature (or "option variant") particular to the customer's requirement from the "half manufactured" entity from Stage 1.

---

[8] The sharpener unit (electroplated or painted) has a transitory existence in the changed circumstances of assemble-to-order. Delays, such as those described in sub-section 11.2.1, are minimal. In the jargon, the part is known as a *phantom*.

Examples of the above will often be relatively straightforward manufacture in which part formation and part finishing are readily identifiable stages. None could be quite as straightforward as a pack of insoles for shoes. The pair of insoles might be sold as "men's size 6 to 12" with size outlines printed on each insole to enable the customer to cut them himself with scissors to his own shoe size. A touch more involved than this is the recent development in the manufacture, distribution and sale of cars. The manufacturer makes a range of cars with a spread over the range of such fundamental features as engine size and gear transmission type, and with a very low degree of other fitted options. These cars are held as stock at a number of "vehicle holding centres". When a customer makes his choice of options in the dealer's saleroom, the corresponding model is moved from the nearest holding centre to a regional "rapid specification centre". There, it is modified, or finished, as appropriate and fitted with the required options prior to delivery to the customer's dealer.

Solution 3: Interconnecting Components

Case 1: A component, such as a cable that secures or connects one option type to another type, may not be a common part. Instead, the connecting component might be specifically and uniquely associated with one of the two option types being connected. In this case, for planning purposes, the connector should be included with the parts making up the particular option variant with which it is associated.

Case 2: The component connecting two option types may be unique to the particular combination of variants connected. That is, at the extreme, however unlikely, if there are n option variants of one type and m option variants of the second option type, there may be $n \times m$ possible connector components. Three alternative solutions present themselves:

a) *Hold all possible connecting components as stock.* In practice, the number of valid combinations of connecting components is likely to be far fewer than $n \times m$, perhaps making this solution acceptable.

b) *Partially manufacture connecting components (as in Solution 2).* If this is feasible, the acceptability of the solution may turn on the additional time needed to finish the component when the actual connection is made in final assembly.

c) *Re-design the option variants being connected, and the form of the connector between them.* Suppose Part A was connected to Part B using Connector C. Then part of the function of Connector C is transferred to Part A, and part of the function of C is transferred to Part B. The re-engineered configuration of the revised parts are as illustrated in Figure 8.5 and described below.

   1. *Sub-component (A).* This comprises the function transferred to Part A from Connector C. The new sub-component is now included in Part A's components list.

   2. *Sub-component (B).* This comprises the function transferred to Part B from Connector C. Analogously to the above, the new sub-component is included in Part B's unique bill of materials.

   3. *The new component.* This comprises the remaining function of Connector C after the two transfers above, and is a new general purpose connector capable of connecting any variant of option type 1 and any variant of option type 2. The new component is a common part.

Figure 8.5: Re-Engineering of an Interconnecting Component

Solution 4: Feature Redundancy

Different option variants may require different, specific preparatory modifications to have been undertaken. However, instead of performing the work on an individual basis for each particular variant, a feasible and economic alternative may be to make wide-ranging prior modifications in a single operation, between them able to accommodate any variant that may then be selected.

For example, different option variants may require different configurations of holes to be drilled in a metal plate, the metal plate with the special holes being embedded low in the bill of materials.

The manufacturing process is now changed: many holes are drilled, which between them will cater for any option variant later chosen. The redesigned metal plate becomes a common part.

The provision of feature redundancy is very widely carried out in engineering design and seems an intuitive solution to the problem it solves. Holes and brackets to cover many later alternative option variant preferences are found in many machines. In electronics, a great many possible circuit layouts may be provided for in the general layout of a circuit board, to cater for any function of the device eventually specified.

As stated, the possibility of feature redundancy should be addressed during the design process. It is a simple, commonsense way of streamlining manufacture generally and also of streamlining maintenance and repair. In short, it has far wider applicability and appeal than simply in assemble-to-order and master scheduling. Thus throughout manufacture, we see common housing for components; standardisation of sub-components; and interchangeability of parts (see Section 3.3).

Solution 5: Popular Choices of Product Variant Combinations Made to Stock

Analysis of the customer off-take of assemble-to-order preferences may reveal either relatively high sales of a few specific combinations of option variants ("our popular models") or repeated substantial sales of a specific combination to one particular customer. The make-to-order company may therefore elect to hold these particular models as stock.

The decision to do so is a partial solution only, and clearly has no bearing on the re-structuring of the bill of materials for assemble-to-order. Nevertheless, when a restructuring solution is eventually found, it may be easier to implement if the volume of manufacture by the new method is substantially less than before because the popular combinations and repeat orders are being dealt with separately.

If it is decided to make-to-stock and assemble-to-order in parallel, care is required to ensure that the master scheduling of the make-to-stock combinations takes place at the same level as the FAS of the remaining products being assembled to order, so that all combinations of products place a demand together on their common part equivalents. Total visibility is required in the planning of common parts so that the master scheduler can make the best decisions regarding them. If make-to-stock master planning is not at the FAS level, the common part component requirements for it will simply be buried within the materials planning calculations.

Solution 6: Desirable Options as Standard

The offering of desirable options as standard is not uncommon in many consumer goods markets and has been especially associated over the years with automobiles — PAS, ABS, radio, etc. The options must indeed be universally desirable and the customer must be willing to pay (although an option that so becomes standard may not add to the product price in an obvious way). On this last point, it should be noted that the car manufacturer has detected and exploited a consumer base of steadily increasing affluence over the years.

8.3 THE MODULAR BILL AND OPTION CHOICE

In this Section, we deal with the representation of an assembled-to-order product from the viewpoints of the customer and the salesman. The issue is a real one — because of the multiplicative effect of different options in combination, the total possible number of choices of the final end-product may be astronomical. Even the most modest range of option types and option variants can yield large numbers of possibilities — a machine available in any of ten colours of external paint, five styles of bodywork, five alternative engines, feature X or not, feature Y or not, and feature Z or not, has 1,600 possibilities ($10 \times 5 \times 4 \times 2 \times 2 \times 2$). It is possible, of course, that many of the theoretical combinations are technically not possible or are simply not offered. For example, in the purchase of a lawnmower, certain option variants may require the larger engine sizes, and these may in addition be sold only with such accessories as ride-on seats and gears. If this applies, simple multiplication of the numbers will be invalid. (Companies in a few cases may confine choice to such a small number of combinations that they can be successfully forecast and offered from stock in the normal way.) Sub-section 8.3.1 is concerned with the organisation and representation of data relating to option types and option variants so that the choices made can be accurately recorded. Sub-section 8.3.2 describes two very different ways through which the salesman might assist the customer in making his particular selection of variants.

8.3.1 The Modular Bill of Materials

The purposes of the modular bill of materials are: (1) to make clear to the customer, salesmen and manufacturing manager alike what options are available to be selected, and, then, which ones have indeed been selected; and (2) to enable data relating to customer preferences to be easily recorded and filed.

Before describing it, two comments are necessary regarding the bill's name. First, the word *modular* relates to *module*, which is here synonymous with *option*.[9] Secondly, the modular bill is not a bill of materials in the sense used elsewhere in this book — that is, a representation of an object's physical constitution. Non-physical bills such as this are usually called *planning bills of materials*, shorthand for a product's representation for purposes other than physical manufacture. In the case of the modular bill, however, that epithet rather stretches the meaning of "planning".

The modular bill of materials omits any reference to the end-product itself. The top of the bill simply comprises the option types and option variants to be considered and selected as required features by the customer. The recording of customers' choices in terms of the modular bill enables option preferences to be analysed for the purposes of forecasting and option overplanning (i.e. the provision of safety stock). As we shall see in Section 8.4, forecasts of option preferences are required in the construction of the super bill.

The identity of the components that directly make up each option variant may be included in the variant's data record. Since the data records of the components themselves are also stored on the bill of materials database, it can be said therefore that a direct link is possible between the options on the modular bill of materials

---

[9] Perhaps the originators of the term *modular* bill of materials would have preferred *optional* bill of materials had this phrase not suggested that the bill was a matter of choice, not one of choices. The terms *bill of configurations* and *bill of features and options* are also used by certain software vendors.

Assemble-to-Order

and the physical bill. Consequently, it may be said further that the planning of component requirements is possible through the modular bill. Strictly speaking, such a statement is correct. In practice, however, the master scheduling of option variants and the subsequent planning of the supporting manufacture of components are effected through the super bill of materials. In addition, it must be appreciated that the option variant entries on the modular bill (and on the super bill as well) are potentially pseudo items as defined in sub-section 8.2.1. While their planning will result in the production of the correct quantities of components, manufactured at the correct times, it will not necessarily indicate how final manufacture is to take place. We recall the leather covered steering wheel, alloy wheels and spoiler making up the car sports pack. The car sports pack is self-evidently a sales feature, represented as such on the car's modular bill of materials. The creation of this feature on the customer's car itself involves three quite separate activities, the organisation of which is a matter for the manufacturing team in final assembly.

Figure 8.6 shows a modular bill for the electric pencil sharpener. The option variants have been drawn separately and only one level of components beneath the variants has been shown.

Figure 8.6: The Modular ("Option") Bill of Materials

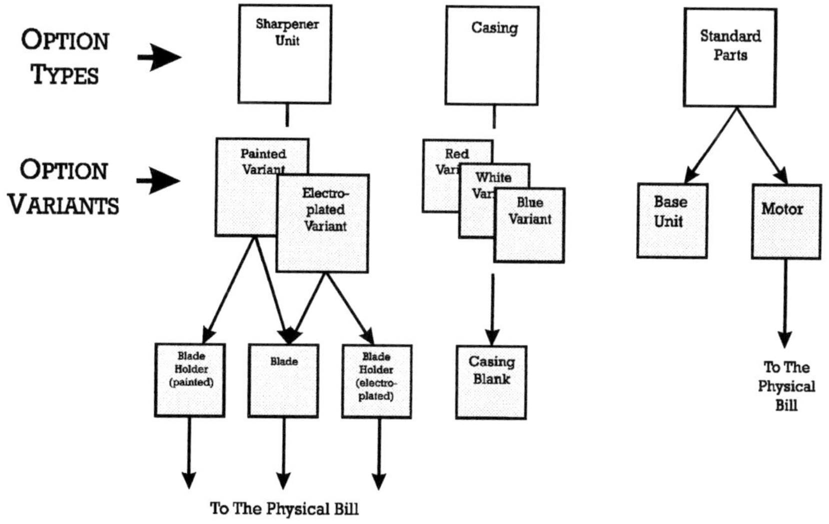

OPTION TYPES → Sharpener Unit | Casing | Standard Parts

OPTION VARIANTS → Painted Variant, Electro-plated Variant | Red Variant, White Variant, Blue Variant | Base Unit, Motor

Blade Holder (painted), Blade, Blade Holder (electro-plated) → To The Physical Bill

Casing Blank → To The Physical Bill

Base Unit, Motor → To The Physical Bill

8.3.2 Customer Specification of Options

The manner in which the customer makes his choice of the features and options available to him and the assistance he receives in so doing are clearly important from a number of viewpoints. First, the combination he chooses may be technically valid but could lead to a poorer final performance of the purchased product than he expects, and consequently to his disappointment in it. On the same lines, the customer may specify options he does not need, so that he acquires a product inappropriate to his use of it and more costly than was necessary. The provisions made by the company to guide the customer in the selection of his choice will naturally vary depending on the nature and cost of the product. Two examples are given below. Note that in all instances, the company must give thought to order alterations by the customer after the choice has been made. It is in the interest of both parties that order alterations due to a change of mind by the customer should be permitted and feasible until as late as possible.

The Total Package

The manufacturing company may regard the manufacture and delivery of the product — say, an executive jet — as merely two elements in a whole range of services making up a total package. The choice of "options" may therefore take the form of a lengthy discussion, perhaps lasting several days and involving teams, in which the technical and commercial specifications are gone over in relation to a detailed statement prepared by the customer concerning his intended use of the product and his expectations of it from both the viewpoints of technical performance and commercial payback. Means of finance of the purchase might be included, such as the terms of an operating lease.

Hi-tech Presentation of Options

If a detailed discussion with the customer is unnecessary because the product and its use are well-known, the company may present the options using a menu-driven, multimedia computer facility, perhaps with photographic displays of alternative options on the VDU via CD or the Internet. If the customer is an end-consumer, as he is for a private motor car, the option menu might include alternative financing schemes.

8.4 THE SUPER BILL

The tool central to the planning and ongoing management of assemble-to-order manufacture is the *super bill*. The super bill is a second planning bill of materials, which solves two problems. First, the multiplicity of option combinations which prevents the practical representation of a physical bill is replaced by a single generic, or "composite", entity termed a *super item*. The super item takes the place of all finished products regardless of their many possible alternative option combinations. The plans to final assemble the diverse orders placed by customers are replaced by plans to final assemble super items. Similarly, general forecasts of levels of manufacturing effort in final assembly are replaced by specific forecasts of demand for the generic super item. The second problem is the difficulty of planning many option variants within an option type and doing so simultaneously. This is solved by assigning a "usage", or "quantity per", decimal fraction to each option variant. The fractions for the option variants of a given option type are arrived at by calculating the probability of each variant being chosen.[10] For example, analysis of historical data may lead to the estimation (i.e. forecast) that the preference for electroplated sharpener units in electric pencil sharpeners is 0.75 and the preference for painted sharpener units is 0.25. Consequently, the usage, or quantity per, of the electroplated sharpener unit in the super bill is 0.75 and the usage of the painted unit is 0.25. The electric pencil sharpener is the super item in this case. If its forecast sales are 200 units, explosion of the super bill will result in planned requirements for 150 electroplated sharpener units and 50 painted units.

Figure 8.7 shows the super bill for the electric pencil sharpener and is derived from Figure 8.2. Besides the sharpener unit option variants, decimal fractions have also been made up and assigned to the casing variants. Note that a fractional preference of 1.0 has been placed on the common parts pseudo item.

---

[10] Clearly, if an option type is mandatory in the manufacture of a product, the total of the option variant probabilities will equal unity. If an option type is not mandatory, the sum of the probabilities assigned to the option variants within it will equal the probability that the option type is specified by the customer.

Figure 8.7: The Super Bill

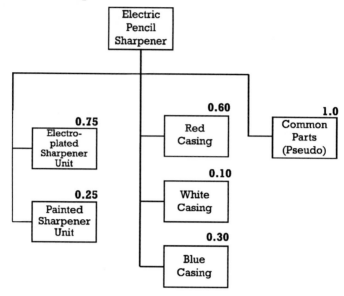

The role of the super bill in the final assembly scheduling of customer orders and the way in which it helps determine the master schedule plans of the option variants are described at length in Section 8.5. Determination of the super bill fractional usages is briefly described in sub-section 8.6.1.

A refinement to the organisation of a super bill is likely to be worthwhile if the company is able to place its final products in one or other of a number of "families", within an overall generic classification. An overall classification might be "lawnmowers", with three families *electric, small petrol* and *large petrol*.

The arrangement is known as a *super super bill* and requires first the creation of separate super bills, one for each family. Next, the super item of each family is made subservient to a single top-level entity termed a *super super item*. The super super item is a composite product having the same relationship to the super items as they in turn have to the lower level options. Decimal fractions, or usages, adding up to 1.0 are now assigned to the super items at the second level of the super super bill. The fractions are based on the probabilities that customers' orders will be for products in one or other of the families. The super super bill for lawnmowers is illustrated in Figure 8.8. The probabilities will be derived from the individual product family forecasts.

Figure 8.8: The Super Super Bill of Materials for Product Families

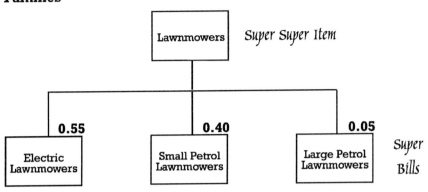

The advantage of employing the super super bill is the clarity obtained in master scheduling. In some circumstances, if a single super bill only is used, a great many option types and option common parts may not be applicable across the complete range of customer choices. There may even be some instances where there are no general common parts at all. By creating families and linking them via the super super bill, a clearer picture may be obtained of the master plan requirements of the various families and their competing demands on resources.

8.5 THE FAS AND MASTER SCHEDULING

8.5.1 The Final Assembly Schedule

The final assembly schedule and the individual master schedules of option variants and common parts are separate plans, though formulated in conjunction with each other. The final assembly itself is derived from the consumed forecast of the super item (sub-section 7.1.1), using the projected stock mechanism described in sub-section 6.5.1. The consumed forecast is obtained from actual customer orders being assembled or waiting to be started (near in) and forecast sales of the super item (far out). Table 8.2 shows the final assembly schedule for the electric pencil sharpener at a moment in time.

Note that the bottom row of the table has been given two labels. The first is *available-to-promise*. This has the meaning explained in Section 7.2. It is calculated from the FAS, less the actual demand already accepted. Its purpose is to assist in order acceptance by showing how much final assembly effort is available in Periods 1 to 10 for assembling future orders. The second label is *FAS less actual demand*. Arithmetically and in fact, this is the same thing as available-to-promise, of course, but because the figures are put to a different use, described in sub-section 8.5.2, it is right that the description of this alternative use should also be given.

Table 8.2: The Final Assembly Schedule before a New Order for four units

On-Hand (OH): 0 units
Past Due (PD): nil
Plan: Lot for Lot
Safety Stock: n/a

	Period									
	1	2	3	4	5	6	7	8	9	10
Super Item Sales Forecast	20	20	20	20	20	20	20	20	20	20
Consumed Forecast	24	20	20	20	20	20	20	20	20	20
Actual Demand	24	19	16	8	4	0	2	0	0	0
Final Assembly Schedule [PD 0]	24	20	20	20	20	20	20	20	20	20
Projected Stock Balance [OH 0]	0	0	0	0	0	0	0	0	0	0
Available-to-Promise, or ... FAS less Actual Demand	0	1	4	12	16	20	18	20	20	20

20 - 8 = 12, and shows we can accept a new order to assemble 4 super items here

Let us now suppose that a new customer wishes to place an order for four electric pencil sharpeners for completion in Period 4, all with the electroplated sharpener unit. From the viewpoint of final assembly, the order is acceptable and has been booked into the FAS as shown in Table 8.3. The joint line *Available-to-promise, or FAS less actual demand* has been amended.

Assemble-to-Order

Table 8.3: The Final Assembly Schedule after acceptance of a New Order for four units in Period 4

On-Hand (OH): 0 units
Past Due (PD): nil
Plan: Lot for Lot
Safety Stock: n/a

					Period					
	1	2	3	4	5	6	7	8	9	10
Super Item Sales Forecast	20	20	20	20	20	20	20	20	20	20
Consumed Forecast	24	20	20	20	20	20	20	20	20	20
Actual Demand	24	19	16	12	4	0	2	0	0	0
Final Assembly Schedule [PD 0]	24	20	20	20	20	20	20	20	20	20
Projected Stock Balance [OH 0]	0	0	0	0	0	0	0	0	0	0
Available-to-Promise, or ... FAS less Actual Demand	0	1	4	8	16	20	18	20	20	20

(20 less 12)   (8 + 4 (new order))

A discussion of the final assembly schedule from the viewpoints of personnel, management control and costs is deferred until Section 8.7.

8.5.2 The Master Scheduling of an Option Variant

We now turn to the master schedule of an option variant, namely the electroplated sharpener unit with a usage of 0.75 in the super bill. At the moment in time corresponding to the FAS in Table 8.2, let us suppose that the actual demand for electroplated sharpener units was as shown in Figure 8.9. That is, the unit quantities given in Figure 8.9 show clearly the period-by-period customer orders which specify this option variant (and which might be confirmed by reference to the file recording customers' orders for this product). These amounts are definite requirements, which must be planned and manufactured in readiness for incorporation into the FAS.

Figure 8.9: The Actual Demand for an Option Variant

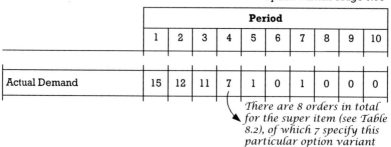

Consider the new order referred to above for 4 pencil sharpeners in Period 4, all of which specified the electroplated sharpener units. If we assume for now that the units will be available for the FAS at the required time, Figure 8.9 is revised as in Figure 8.10.

Figure 8.10: Actual Demand for an Option Variant after a Further Order for four units

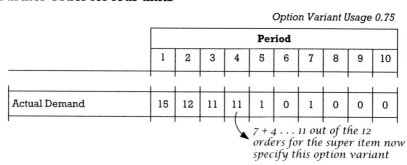

At this point we conclude that we have dealt with, and are dealing with, actual demand satisfactorily both in the FAS and in the master schedule of the option variant. Among other things, we are making full use of new information about orders as they arrive. Real sales data is being used about what each customer is actually ordering. But what has not yet been addressed is *demand which is still to come* — orders which we forecast will be received but which have not yet been placed.

We return briefly to consideration of the FAS. The FAS is calculated from the super item's consumed forecast using the lot-for-lot planning rule, not directly from its sales forecast or from actual demand for the product. The consumed forecast is the greater of

Assemble-to-Order

the super item's sales forecast and actual demand, and largely remains constant (although change is possible, as explained in subsection 7.1.1).[11] The FAS therefore comprises actual demand and forecast demand together. The two elements that go to make it up are, however, available separately. One of them is directly given, namely the "actual demand" on Line 3 of Tables 8.2 and 8.3. The other constituent is, of course *FAS less actual demand* on Line 6 of the Tables. That is:

FAS = FAS less actual demand + actual demand

The *FAS less actual demand* is the key to the forecast elements of the option variants being master scheduled in support of it. It determines how much forecast demand in total must be incorporated into the forecast elements of the option variants' master schedules. The question now is how it should be apportioned among them.

The planning assumption made in the management of the super bill is that future demand for the various option variants will be proportional to the option variants' usages. The method of apportioning the *FAS less actual demand* is, therefore, according to the individual super bill usages. That is, in master scheduling an option variant, the forecast element to be planned for, alongside actual demand, is the super item's *FAS less actual demand* multiplied by that particular variant's usage in the super bill. Note that assemble-to-order software packages follow this rule regardless of the relative proportions of the option variants already specified over time by customers. That is, no correction is made to compensate for short-term deviations of actual orders from the standard super bill fractional usages. The standard super bill usages are used to apportion the *FAS less actual demand*, the forecast element of the FAS, no matter what has happened in the month so far.[12]

---

[11] Because of the consumed forecast methodology, continual modification to the FAS as orders come in is unnecessary. The manufacturing manager and the teams in the assembly department for their part will assemble any valid mix of option variants they have to. Concern there is only with the number of assemblies to be built.

[12] The uneven arrival of actual demand was discussed in sub-section 7.1.2. If the option variant's safety stock, or overplan amount, is zero or low, an excessive number of messages will be received to reschedule it during the freeze period. To suppress these, the software should "consume the forecast" along

The forecast demand element of an option variant derived as stated above is referred to in master planning as its *production forecast*. Continuing with the electroplated sharpener unit, we know the actual customer demand for these units and we also now know how to calculate their production forecasts. The position of the production forecast and actual demand elements to be master scheduled in support of the electric pencil sharpener before the acceptance of the new order for four more electric pencil sharpeners referred to earlier is illustrated in the bottom section of Figure 8.11. The top section of the Figure is taken from data in Table 8.2.

Figure 8.11: Calculating the Production Forecast of an Option Variant

Super Item (Electric Pencil Sharpener)

	Period									
	1	2	3	4	5	6	7	8	9	10
Actual Demand	24	19	16	8	4	0	2	0	0	0
Available to Promise, or ... FAS less Actual Demand	0	1	4	12	16	20	18	20	20	20
Production Forecast	0	1*	3	9	12	15	14*	15	15	15
Actual Demand	15	12	11	7	1	0	1	0	0	0

12 × 0.75

Electroplated Sharpener Unit (0.75 option variant)

*rounded

After acceptance of the new order for four pencil sharpeners for Period 4, all specifying the electroplated sharpener unit, the revised position is as shown in Figure 8.12. The top section of Figure 8.12 is taken from Table 8.3.

---

the lines described in 7.1.2 by compensating for short-term imbalances in the variant mix. From Table 8.2 and Figure 8.11 in the text, the total forecast preferences for the two types of sharpener unit in the first four periods are 63 (84 × 0.75) and 21 (84 × 0.25). The demand up to this point has been 45 units and 22 units. Consequently, rather than split the remaining 17 units 75:25 in the standard way, all 17 should be allocated to the electroplated unit.

Assemble-to-Order 273

Figure 8.12: Recalculating the Production Forecast after an Order for four units in Period 4

Super Item (Electric Pencil Sharpener)

	Period									
	1	2	3	4	5	6	7	8	9	10
Actual Demand	24	19	16	12	4	0	2	0	0	0
Available to Promise, or ... FAS less Actual Demand	0	1	4	8	16	20	18	20	20	20

8 × 0.75

Electroplated Sharpener Unit (0.75 option variant)

Production Forecast	0	1*	3	6	12	15	14*	15	15	15
Actual Demand	15	12	11	11	1	0	1	0	0	0

*rounded

Demand for the option variant has been collected and the production forecast calculated, so that the option variant's master schedule can be calculated. Note that although the considerations in this Section show there to be major differences in formulating and managing the master schedule of an option variant from standard master scheduling procedures described in Chapters 6 and 7, there are many similarities as well. They are:

- The option variant's master schedule is reformulated once a month in a two-step process: (1) sales and operations planning; and (2) detailed master scheduling;
- The potential practicality of the master schedule is tested by resource requirements planning and RCCP;
- Once it has been released to the live system, each master plan is managed by freeze periods, available-to-promise, the projected stock balance and (possibly — see footnote 12) consuming the forecast;
- The master plan is exploded through the bill of materials to create time-phased plans for components and raw materials. As with standard master scheduling, assemble-to-order master scheduling is then indifferent as to the technique employed for progressing these plans (i.e. MRP or APS).

The master schedule of the electroplated sharpener unit after the receipt of the new order for four units in Period 4 is illustrated in Table 8.4.[13]. Note that *sales forecast* in the standard display (see Table 7.9) has been replaced by *spares forecast*, the requirement for spares, or service parts, being the only likely direct demand for an option variant. The standard consumed forecast line is omitted — the master schedule is calculated so as to satisfy the production forecast and the actual demand in their entirety.

Table 8.4: The Master Scheduling of an Option Variant (Complete Figures)

On-Hand (OH): 9 units Past Due (PD): nil Plan: Lots of 40 Safety Stock: 2 units	Period									
	1	2	3	4	5	6	7	8	9	10
Spares Forecast	0	0	0	0	0	0	0	0	0	0
Production Forecast	0	1*	3	6	12	15	14*	15	15	15
Actual Demand	15	12	11	11	1	0	1	0	0	0
Master Schedule PD 0	40			40			40		40	
Projected Stock Balance OH 9	34	21	7	30	17	2	27	12	37	22
Available-to-Promise	11			28			39		40	

*rounded

8.6 FORECASTS AND OPTION OVERPLAN AMOUNTS

8.6.1 Forecasts

Forecasts of sales demand at the top level must be prepared for super items and the various sets of option common parts, at least up to the MPS horizon of the longest lead time option variant. Forecasts of general common parts and the decimal fractions which split any super super item are directly derived from the foregoing. All of the principles discussed in Chapter 4 apply here as well. In particular, because the super item is at the level it is, the company

---

[13] The electroplated sharpener unit is referred to in the text as an option variant made to stock for the sake of illustration, notwithstanding the note in subsection 8.2.2, Solution 1, that sharpener units cannot be stored "for technical reasons".

must ensure that forecasts for it are not hijacked by the Sales and Marketing department to become sales targets. The remarks in Section 2.5 apply with double force.

Forecasts are also required of the customer demand for the various option variants. Note that if an option type can be omitted altogether, the probability that it will be so omitted by a customer can be derived from the forecasts for the option variants chosen and the forecast for the higher super item. Super bill fractional usages are simply obtained as shown in Table 8.5.

Table 8.5: Converting Forecasts to Super Bill Usages

Option Variant	Forecast	Usage
Electroplated Sharpener Unit	333 units	0.75
Painted Sharpener Unit	111 units	0.25
Total	444 units	1

The relative preferences of customers in quantitative terms for alternative option variants within an option type are unlikely to be well known, making the use of a formal statistical forecasting package most advisable. A particular problem here stems from a shortcoming in almost all master scheduling packages. Normally, assemble-to-order super bill software will allow only one set of option variant usages to be entered on the super bill for an option type, despite the fact that relative usages change and are capable of being derived from forecasts up to the variants' MPS horizons. (The customer's choice of option variants is often strongly seasonal, for example.) To make up for this deficiency, the master scheduler may need to intervene in the calculated option variant master schedules at the MPS formulation stage and ensure that super bill usages are brought up-to-date on a regular basis.

A further problem relates to the treatment of option variants which are "unusual" — i.e. specified by customers relatively infrequently. It is possible that the demand for these will qualify as sporadic, or lumpy, as defined in Section 4.7. If so, as described in 4.7, either forecasts must be prepared by Croston's procedure or else master plan replenishments will need to be governed by an order point system such as Brown's (see Equation 4.46). The treatment of sporadic demand also has an impact on option overplanning.

8.6.2 Option Overplanning

As we have seen from the previous sub-section, super bill usages are derived from sales forecasts. As such, and not surprisingly, they are liable to be in error when compared to the split of option variants which transpires in practice. If the actual demand for an option variant exceeds the usage assigned to it in the super bill, the company may exhaust its stock during the MPS month unless service is protected by safety stock. In assemble-to-order, the provision of safety stock on option variants is termed *option overplanning*.

The way in which safety stock is introduced into the master plan at the MPS formulation stage and the rules governing the generation of rescheduling messages when the projected stock balance falls below it during MPS management have already been described in sub-section 7.1.2. There is a further consideration relating to the safety stock of an option variant during MPS formulation, however.

During MPS formulation, provision need only be made for safety stock if the possibility exists of more orders being accepted at the final assembly level. If the final assembly schedule has been "used up" in a particular period, the provision of safety stock against further orders is clearly counter to logic. Consider Figure 8.13, which we suppose shows the position of the electric pencil sharpener super item and the electroplated sharpener unit option variant at the time of formulation of the variant's MPS (i.e. MPS Formulation Stage II).

The projected stock balance is here allowed to fall to zero in Period 3, notwithstanding the option variant's safety stock provision of two units. This is because, as we see, the available to-promise position of the super item from Periods 1 to 3 is zero — for this reason no new orders can be accepted and so no safety is needed for the electroplated sharpener unit. By contrast in Period 6, however, an MPS plan for 40 units is generated to prevent the projected stock balance falling to zero. Sixteen super items are available to promise at this point. It is true that 12 are apportioned to the electroplated sharpener unit, but doubt still remains about four of them.

Figure 8.13: Safety Stock and the FAS in Master Plan Formulation

Super Item (Electric Pencil Sharpener)

	Period									
	1	2	3	4	5	6	7	8	9	10
Actual Demand	24	20	20	16	8	4	4	0	0	0
Available to Promise, or FAS less Actual Demand	0	0	0	4	12	16	16	20	20	20

On-Hand (OH): 38 units
Past Due (PD): nil
Plan: Lots of 40
Safety Stock: 2 units

Electroplated Sharpener Unit (0.75 option variant)

		1	2	3	4	5	6	7	8	9	10
Production Forecast		0	0	0	3	9	12	12	15	15	15
Actual Demand		15	12	11	12	4	0	1	0	0	0
Master Schedule	PD 0				40		40			40	
Projected Stock Balance	OH 38	23	11	0	25	12	40	27	12	37	22

The safety stock to be applied to each option variant should be determined through a formal method, preferably the one described in sub-section 5.4.3, with careful consideration given to the level of customer service actually provided (Section 5.5). Regretfully, the very name "option overplanning" says how too many managers currently set them — by intuition and "feel". Pending the implementation of a formal forecasting and safety stock system and one step ahead of intuition and feel, use might be made of the formula in Equation 8.1.[14] The equation is based on the simplistic technique described in sub-section 4.4.1 and applies if the number of super items to be final assembled is 50 or more.

$$\text{Safety Stock} = k\sqrt{S \times u_i \times (1 - u_i)} \qquad \text{Equation 8.1}$$

where k = the safety factor corresponding to a chosen probability density, as given in Tables 5.4(a), 5.4(b) and 5.9;
S = the number of super items; and
u_i = the super bill usage of the ith option variant.

---

[14] Equation 8.1 is valid given that the sum of all i values of u_i is unity.

For example, suppose that 99 per cent safety cover was required on the electroplated sharpener unit (u = 0.75). Then, from Table 5.4(b), the value of k equivalent to 99 per cent is 2.326. If the number of super items was 444, then the safety stock required for the electroplated sharpener unit is:

$$2.326\sqrt{444 \times 0.75 \times (1-0.75)} = 21 \text{ units (rounded)}.$$

8.7 QUICK RESPONSE

The establishment of assembly to order in a manufacturing company requires other activities to be undertaken besides modular design and the master scheduling of option variants. One that is desirable rather than essential is compression of the options' master schedule plan horizon. A shorter manufacturing lead time is always a target to aim for, of course, but, in assemble-to-order, reduction means increased responsiveness to change in the market's preferences for the various option types and option variants. (A corollary of this is reduced option variant safety stocks, as well as lower work-in-progress.) An activity widely regarded as essential, by contrast, is the setting up of empowered teams in the final assembly department. Empowerment and teams are discussed in sub-section 19.3.1. Whatever their merits elsewhere in the company, in final assembly, with its focus on the customer, its concern with quality and initiative and its demand that those responsible should take control from start to finish, many practitioners contend that they are absolutely necessary to its success.

8.7.1 Compression of the MPS Horizon

The broad components of the master schedule horizon are the purchasing, manufacturing and distribution lead times illustrated in Figure 6.1. In order to achieve their overall reduction, one approach is to analyse and review at a detailed level all of the processes which go to make them up from the viewpoint of the time each one takes, subdividing time into "value added" time and "non-value added". The causes of delay — i.e. the reasons for non-value added time — can then be investigated and dealt with by whatever method seems appropriate. The rationale for this approach is that since the goal is to reduce overall duration — *to*

Assemble-to-Order 279

compress time — it makes sense first to look at the problem as a whole, in timely terms, so that individual targets can best be chosen.[15] Advocates of time compression state that what must be examined and heightened is the responsiveness of the supply chain itself — *the supply chain dynamics*, to use time compression jargon. Processes, procedures and communications must be simplified and, where possible, reduced in number or redefined with fewer interfaces between different working groups.[16] Just as causes of excessive duration in the manufacturing chain may include unnecessarily complex product design and lengthy machine change-overs, so the causes of delay elsewhere may lie in areas less familiar to the manufacturing manager. Examples are poor external communications; an absence of trust in supplier relationships; and, from the outsourcing of services and even manufacture, the laggardly conduct of these activities by those responsible for them. Other familiar factors influencing supply chain dynamics are EMQs;[17] machine breakdowns; poor performance measures, such as "keeping machines busy"; the incidence of non-conformances and rework; repeated and unnecessary engineering changes to the bill of materials; and a climate of distrust and poor performance that leads to excessive stock holding all the way from raw materials to finished goods.

A valuable means of achieving time compression is through the use of *time based process mapping* (TBPM),[18] an activity whereby the processes, sequence and interfaces of the whole supply chain are analysed from the viewpoint of time and set out as a type of Gantt chart. The starting point to time compression itself is the

---

[15] See A.P. Beesley (1996), *Time-Compression Self-Help Guide* (publication available from the Warwick Manufacturing School); and Stalk and Hout (1990), *Competing against Time*.

[16] Time compression experts also stress that its employment is not a once-only matter. The company, they assert, must repeatedly reassess and challenge how things are and how they are done in order to remove yet further time from the total supply chain.

[17] Economic Manufacturing Quantities — see Economic Delivery Quantities, Section 9.6.

[18] The time-based process mapping methodology described in the text was developed in 1995 by the Warwick Manufacturing Group, University of Warwick (see A.P. Beesley (1996), op. cit.)

drawing of the process map. This is usually carried out by gathering data relating to a "generic customer". A generic customer is simply a typical customer, representative of the company's principal business. An example might be a textile mill, the mill being the customer of a company manufacturing dyestuffs from basic chemicals. (In gathering the data, it does not do to become embroiled in detail highly specific to a particular, actual customer.)

The "core processes" and principal support activities involved in ultimately supplying the customer should next be identified. A core process is one which adds value to the product. Examples are the receiving of goods, manufacture, technical analysis and moving material to a retail outlet. Core processes should include critical core activities immediately outside the control of the company itself, such as the delivery of raw materials to its supplier's distribution depot or the selling of the company's own goods through independent wholesalers. A support activity is one which does not affect the supply chain duration because it can be scheduled "off line", such as the carrying out of a plant cleanout. The data to be associated with core and support activities are the identities of those responsible for them (wholesaler, own company distribution department, own company manufacturing department . . .) and their durations in appropriate time units (say, days for distribution, hours for manufacture and minutes for packing). The upper and lower limits and average may have to be recorded if there is a significant variation in the duration of any activity (see sub-section 13.2.2). Finally, the core processes and the rest are flowcharted as in Figure 8.14. Note that, for ease of working, the direction of time is from right (the past) to left (the future), this being the opposite of the Gantt Chart; note also that the flowchart is not a time-based process map itself, but a half-way stage to one.

Assemble-to-Order 281

Figure 8.14: Stage I in the development of a Time-Based Process Map

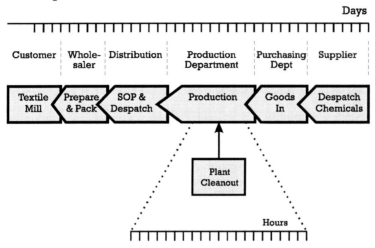

The next stage in TBPM will take many weeks to complete. This is the breaking down of the core processes into sub-processes, the identification of the personnel responsible for each of them and the gathering of facts, usually by one-to-one interviewing, relating to each sub-process.[19] The facts relate to activity and duration. They must clearly include time spent in "null" activities such as queuing at machines, waiting for transport or waiting for information to be communicated or processed. To ensure that all sub-processes have been identified, special care is taken to account for all sub-process to sub-process linkages. As previously, some durations may need to be recorded with upper and lower limits. Finally, the individual activities and the time spent on them in each sub-process can be designated value-adding or non-value-adding. Value-adding activities are characterised by one or a combination of three properties: (1) the activity physically changes the nature of the product or one of its components; (2) the change produces something valued by the customer; and (3) the activity is not a second attempt to perform something that was previously done wrongly. Examples of non-value-adding activities include scheduling and expediting, re-packing, checking, queuing, reworking

---

[19] It is suggested by Warwick Manufacturing Group that an effective way of gathering facts is to get the interviewee to imagine "a day in the life of the product".

and training. Auxiliary data that should be gathered at this stage include inventory quantities (e.g. batch sizes) and resource capacity. Resource capacity conventionally relates to physical plant, such as throughput, scrap or yield and operational times of work centres. In time compression, however, it should include other facilities — clerical units, computer I/O, etc.

It is now possible to draw the final time-based process map, perhaps on a wall chart using markers of different colours. The map's value is its visual exposure, in an obvious and simple way, of where time really is consumed, all in the context of the total supply chain. One of its drawbacks, however, is the difficulty of incorporating some of the information gathered and analysed. A number of conventions have been adopted, therefore, to illustrate variable lead times (i.e. those with a minimum and maximum), processes that are performed in parallel and the production of stock, and to distinguish value-added and non-value-added time itself. Nonetheless, it is important in time compression and TBPM not to become transfixed by methodology. If there is any doubt about what to do, any commonsense, clear convention can be adopted. The value of time-based process mapping is simply as a means of identifying and focusing on sub-processes which can be simplified or changed or otherwise addressed, so as to reduce non-value-added time and with it the overall supply chain time. A very simple time-based process map expanding the example of the dyestuffs manufacture and the textile mill is shown in Figure 8.15.

Figure 8.15: A Simple Time-Based Process Map (TBPM)

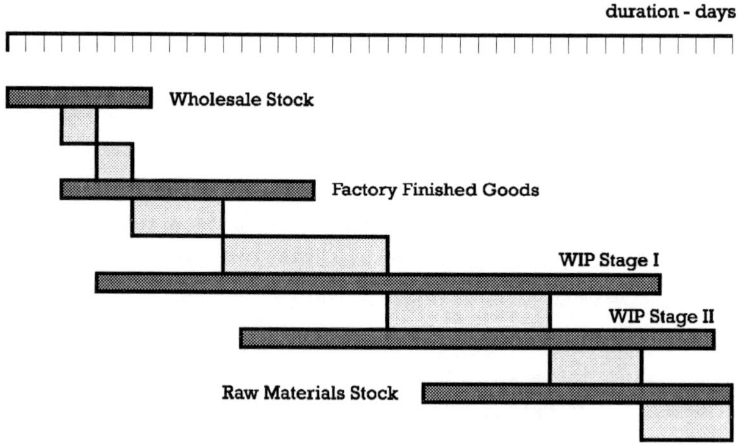

Assemble-to-Order 283

Processes identified and discussed in this book which may contribute to unnecessary duration of the master planning horizon of option variants are as follows:

- Time lags and errors in communicating to the centre data relating to sales activity in the field (sub-section 4.3.2);

- The diverse components of the distribution lead time (Section 20.1);

- The components of the sales order processing lead time (Section 2.4 and sub-section 5.2.2);

- Choice of an inappropriate Incoterm in either selling or purchasing (Section 16.3.1);

- Unduly lengthy machine changeover times, and unduly large manufacturing and purchase lot sizes (Sections 15.3 and 9.6);

- Poor communication with suppliers (Section 16.1.3).

8.7.2 Order Receipt and Final Assembly

The specification by the customer of option preferences has been discussed in sub-section 8.3.2. The data processing necessary on order receipt by the company's sales order processing section entails four steps as follows:

1. The customer's requirements for option variants and his requested date of delivery are formally recorded in the system;

2. The available-to-promise position of the product's FAS is checked to determine whether the order can be assembled by the required date. The order is tentatively booked ("earmarked") for the required date if effort is available, or on the earliest date effort is available afterwards if the first choice date cannot be met;

3. The available-to-promise position of each of the option variants specified is next checked to ensure the specified variants will all be available to support the earmarked final assembly effort. (The available-to-promise of the common parts may also be double-checked.) As in 2, the option variants and common parts are earmarked;

4. If everything is in order and a satisfactory date can be negotiated with the customer, the order is confirmed. That is, the tentative allocations are converted from earmarked to "accepted" status and the revised *actual* and *production forecast* positions for the FAS and the various option variant master schedules are confirmed. The master scheduler will wish to review the projected stock position and consider any rescheduling messages as soon as possible afterwards — typically, each morning after an overnight computer run.

In discussing empowerment and team working in Chapter 19, it is stated that there is a need to redesign work so that participants can gain confidence, feel in control. The importance of taking on responsibility for a job from beginning to end is also brought out. In final assembly and quick response, we see that the work requires no redesign because it already has all of the properties looked for in empowered working and team working. Into the bargain, we also see in final assembly that because there is no stockpiling, problems must be resolved on an individual "part" basis, taking the best action to hand and doing so without involving management. The requirement within empowerment for the plentiful provision of education and training is also self-evidently a requirement in assemble-to-order.

8.7.3 Costs

Quick response cannot succeed if the results are higher costs and unacceptably high prices. Yet the widely acknowledged truths of cost and manufacture are:

Increased Volume.. Decreased Costs

Increased Capacity Utilisation .... Decreased Costs

Increased Variety ....Increased Costs

Increased Process Variation ....Increased Costs

At first glance, the mission in quick response then seems impossible: to increase flexibility to meet customer specifications but maintain cost. But as we have seen, modular design, master scheduling and final assembly enable us to achieve these goals.

Dominant though these may be, they should not be the only methods employed to reduce cost. Other lines of attack are production engineering to increase productivity and reduce production costs; value analysis applied to the company's own products (and an insistence that worthwhile programmes are undertaken on bought-in parts by suppliers); and, particularly, an unremitting drive on quality. The cost advantages of quality are dealt with in sub-section 13.1.3. They affect quick response specifically in two areas: (1) at the option manufacturing stage, where improved levels of quality will decrease costs because of fewer mistakes and better use of machines; and (2) in final assembly where quality methods and precepts have the potential to make a major impact on cost if they are undertaken in the environment of empowerment and teams.

An example of the economics of modular design and assemble-to-order is given below. It is adapted from a case study presented by the Lancashire manufacturing company Stoves PLC.[20]

Tooling and Production Costings in Quick Response

Twenty different control knobs are required for one gas cooker, each having a different shank depending on its mechanical function. To provide customer variety, the knobs are offered in 18 different shapes and 10 different colours. The cost of a tool for this manufacture is £5,000, the manufacturing time for one knob is 2 seconds and the set-up time for a tool is 12 minutes. The tooling costs and manufacturing time are compared for: (1) making 25 knobs of each colour, for each shank/shape variety, in one operation; and (2) making 25 knobs of each colour, for each shank/shape variety, in two parts (i.e. modular design and assemble-to-order). Thus:

---

[20] See sub-section 8.2.2, footnote 6, and the *Manufacturers Organising for Rapid Response* conference.

(1) One Part

(a) Number of tools = 20 × 18
    Cost of tools = 20 × 18 × £5,000
                  = £1,800,000

(b) Production time = (20 × 18 × 10) × 25 × 2 secs
                    = 180,000 secs

    Set-up time = (20 × 18) × 12 minutes
                = 4,320 minutes

    Total production + set-up = *7,320 minutes*

(2) Two Parts (modular design and assemble-to-order/quick response)

(a) Number of tools (shanks) = 20
    Number of tools (shapes/colours) = 18 (not 18 × 10)
    Cost of tools = (20 + 18) × £5,000
                  = £190,000

(b) Production time (shank) = (20 × (18 × 10)) × 25 × 2 secs
    (i.e. 180 shanks are needed for each of the 20 shank types, to match the 180 shape/colour combinations, × 25 for the required production output)
                              = 180,000 secs

    Production time (shape/colour) = ((18 × 10) × 20) × 25 × 2 secs
    (i.e. 20 shape/colours are needed for each of the 180 shape/colour combinations, to match the 20 shank types, × output (25))
                                   = 180,000 secs

    Set-up time (shanks) = 20 × 12 minutes

    Set-up time (shapes/colours) = 18 × 12 minutes

    Total production + set-up = *6,456 minutes*

Chapter 9

Materials Planning

Materials planning in this chapter means the formulation of a set of plans to manufacture components and acquire raw materials in support of the company's master production schedule. The plans are time-phased. That is, each is qualified by the day the required manufacture is to start and to finish (or in the case of raw materials, the day delivery is to be made). The data required to be taken into account in creating the materials plans are the bill of materials records, lead times of manufacture, on-hand stock, work-in-progress and manufacturing and purchasing lot sizes.

Again in the context of this Chapter, there are two things materials planning is not. First, it is not a means of tracking progress in the carrying out of the plans and making plan adjustments in response to day-to-day events by rescheduling. A means to do so is indeed needed, but progressing and rescheduling are performed either by closed-loop MRP (Chapter 10), through local shop floor control or an APS (Chapters 11 and 12) or through Just-in-Time (Chapter 15). In other words, just as master scheduling is a precursor to materials planning, so is materials planning a precursor to one or other of these further activities. Secondly, except in a few instances, despite the fact that the materials plans are time-phased, they do not constitute what is generally referred to as a *schedule*. In manufacturing, a schedule is a plan of work that incorporates start and finish times of operations (i.e. hours of the day, not calendar days), work centres and machines to be used, work sequence and priorities. It is true, however, that in a few companies the coarse detail within a materials plan serves the same purpose that the fine detail of a schedule serves in most others. Companies that can commence actual manufacturing operations from materials plans alone are characterised by relatively lengthy production times (days or weeks) and disjunctive manufacturing stages that are usually further separated by discrete, easily identified materials movement activities. Examples are to be found in the process industries — say, in the manufacture of heavy chemicals, dyestuffs or glass — and it is significant that these are the industries where closed-loop MRP has been successful.

For the manufacturing manager, then, this Chapter describes a required introductory step, a step that must be followed by a second activity, dealt with in later chapters, to turn materials plans into practical working plans and effect a means of day-to-day plan management.

9.1 ORDER POINT

A modification to the *order point system*[1] of stock replenishment has already been described for dealing with sales products with lumpy demand (Section 4.7). In practice, order point has relatively little applicability in manufacturing, although the manufacturing manager should be aware of the technique. Because it assumes that stock levels fall in a gradual, even way, its use is largely confined to operations involving the sale of finished goods. It might, however, be used within the factory for managing the ordering of certain "consumables" or fuel.

Suppose that we wish to control the replenishment of a material through the order point system, and that we currently hold Q units of stock. Suppose also that the lead time of resupply is T days.

Because we must order the material T days before it is received, it is necessary to forecast the quantity of stock that will be used up in that period — a quantity known as the "lead time demand", D units. A sales forecast usually relates to a *month*, while the lead time demand is the anticipated offtake over a certain number of *days*. Consequently, it is necessary to convert the monthly forecast

---

[1] Order point is also variously known as re-order point (ROP) and the min-max system. In the last name, the "min" is either the order point itself or the safety level (take your pick), while the "max" is the replenishment quantity R + safety S (see text).

Materials Planning

to a daily one. This is simplistically done by dividing it by the number of trading days in the month to which it relates (see sub-section 4.3.4). Thus if the monthly forecast is F units and there are d days in the month, the daily forecast is f, where f is:

$$\frac{F}{d} \text{ units per day.}$$

The lead time demand D is therefore:

$$T \times f \text{ units.}$$

This would be the order point — the level to which stock falls and at which a new order is placed — were it not for forecast error. To guard against forecast error over the replenishment period T, we therefore add safety stock S to the lead time demand to obtain the order point OP as given in Equation 9.1

$$OP = (T \times f) + S \text{ units} \qquad \textit{Equation 9.1}$$

Note that if the replenishment quantity is R units, then before delivery there are S units in stock and afterwards there are R + S units. Regardless of the forecast or delivery time, therefore, the average stockholding is given by:

$$\frac{R}{2} + S \text{ units}$$

The order point system and the various stock levels are illustrated in Figure 9.1.

Figure 9.1: The Order Point System of Replenishment

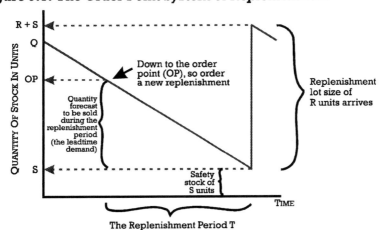

To operate the order point system as above, it is necessary to monitor stock levels continually to see whether any product's stock has fallen to its order point. Suppose, however, that the company wished simply to read stock levels once a month and initiate the delivery of all required orders then. If the stock level of a product at the start of the month is Q units, then it will fall to its order point in:

$$\frac{Q - OP}{f} \text{ days}$$

If this number of days is less than the number of days in the month, advance notice can be given of the need for the replenishment. Theoretically, it is also possible to give notice of the requirement for all resupplies after the next delivery, since a replenishment lot of R units will last for R/f days — the *time-phased order point, TPOP*. TPOP however ignores the fact of bootstrapped forecasts — i.e. different forecasts applying to different months ahead (see sub-section 4.6.2). Because of the awkwardness of making the calculations to obtain a time-phased order point replenishment schedule, it is necessary to revert to standard projected stock calculations and the standard format for making them given in sub-section 6.5.1, Section 9.5 and elsewhere.

9.2 Planning and Manufacturing

Orders that are placed by customers directly on the final source of their supply, whether at the factory itself or at a local distribution depot, are said to constitute *independent demand*. The demand is independent in the sense that it is independent of the materials planning or logistics system which governs the production or distribution of the stock.

To support the manufacture of customers' orders, it is necessary to manufacture components and acquire raw materials. The requirements for these other materials are said to constitute *dependent demand* — i.e. demand dependent on plans for the sales products and the operation of the system.

Manufacturing plans to satisfy independent demand are referred to as the master plan or master production schedule, a subject dealt with at length in Chapters 6, 7 and 8. Manufacturing plans

Materials Planning

to satisfy dependent demand are *materials plans*, calculated by reference to the bill of materials and other data. To create them, it is necessary to start with the master schedule at the top of the bill of materials and work down, level by level. The notion of the bill of materials having a top, and levels, has already been introduced in Section 3.5. Levels themselves are dealt with fully in Section 9.3.

Independent and dependent demand and levels of the bill of materials are illustrated in Figure 9.2, representing an electric toothbrush made to stock and clearly designed by the engineer responsible for the electric pencil sharpener in Figure 8.2.

Figure 9.2: Bill of Materials — an Electric Toothbrush Made to Stock

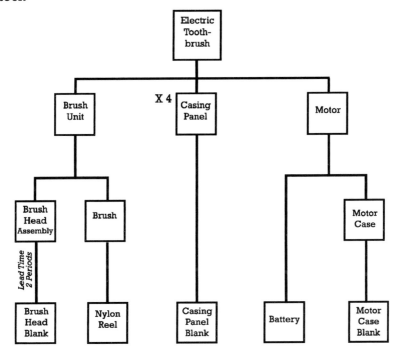

Suppose the master scheduler chooses to plan the electric toothbrushes in batches of 100. By reference to Figure 9.2, in order for the manufacturing manager to make a batch, he must have available 100 brush units, 400 casing panels and 100 motors, all of them one "manufacturing lead time" before the toothbrushes are required. (The usage of casing panels is 4.0 — i.e. four panels per toothbrush.) Similarly, if brush units are manufactured in lots of

150, 150 brush head assemblies and 150 brushes must be available one further lead time before the units are required also. The replenishment needs for all the foregoing and for all other materials shown in Figure 9.2 must take into account the data mentioned in the introduction to this Chapter — stock-in-hand, work-in-progress, lead times of manufacture and so on.

The picture would be complex and even confusing were it not for the discipline and logic established within the rules of dependent demand. As stated, we start at the top of the bill of materials and calculate what is needed to fulfil manufacture of the MPS, and the dates the materials are needed. When *all* products at the top level have been dealt with, only then do we proceed to the next level down and calculate what is needed there, and again the dates. When every product at this level also has been dealt with, and not until, we proceed to the next level down, and so on. Eventually, the bottom of the bill of materials is reached and the requirements and dates of all raw materials are calculated. A picture of the progress of these calculations for the electric toothbrush is given in Figure 9.3. From the viewpoint of planning, the Figure is read from right to left — i.e. starting at the top of the bill, and Period 7, and moving to the raw materials at the bottom, and Period 2. From the view of manufacturing progress, it is read from left to right. Each anticipated supply and manufacturing activity — i.e. each expected physical outcome of planning, the reality of manufacture — is denoted in the pictograph by a thick arrowed line. The first, involving the delivery of brush head blanks, starts in Period 2 and is to be completed in Period 3. The last, involving final assembly of the toothbrushes, starts in Period 6 and is to be completed in Period 7. There are 12 plans in all, identified by the name or names of starting material and the name of the finishing material, and there are 12 physical undertakings to supply or manufacture material, denoted by the arrowed lines. Responsibility for the physical undertakings are split between the purchasing manager and the manufacturing manager. The purchasing manager must ensure the on-time delivery of the correct quantities of raw materials on five occasions. These are at Period 3 (once), Period 4 (twice) and Period 5 (twice). He must therefore requisition five raw materials supplies so that they are duly delivered by suppliers — Period 2 (one), Period 3(two) and Period 4 (two). The manufacturing man-

Materials Planning 293

ager must ensure materials are made on time on seven occasions. These are at Period 5 (three times), Period 6 (three times) and Period 7 (once). He must therefore begin production on the seven corresponding plan start dates.

Figure 9.3: Representation of Plans and Manufacturing Activity

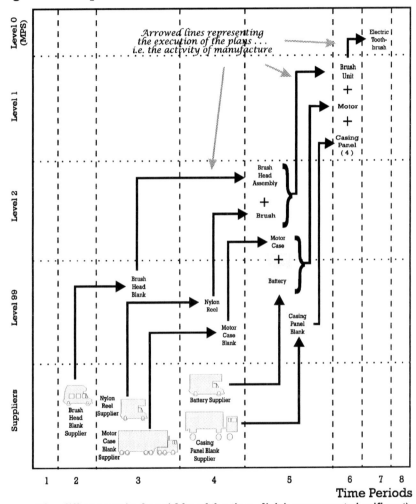

(the differences in the widths of the time divisions are not significant)

9.3 LEVELS IN THE BILL OF MATERIALS

As explained, to create materials plans it is necessary to start at the top of the bill of materials and work downwards, level by level. To be able to do so, it is first necessary to determine the level at which each product is held within the overall bill of materials structure, and record it in the individual product's database record. It is then possible in plan creation (described in Section 9.5) to identify and deal with all products together at each succeeding level.

By convention, the number of the level given to the top of the bill is "0". That is, "Level 0" is assigned to the master scheduled items. The level number is increased by 1 as each deeper level is reached. The level of raw materials, the bottom of the bill, is however designated 99. This is done for consistency; by doing so, no matter which product is involved and however deep or shallow its bill, raw materials will be at Level 99. The number 99 is chosen as being on the safe side, since the chance of any bill having 100 levels is surely nil.[2] Thus the levels in a bill of materials with five levels will be designated 0, 1, 2, 3 and 99.

It will be recalled from Section 3.5 that the data relating to the bill of materials structure is confined, for each product's record, simply to the materials which are directly used in its manufacture, plus the level number as later determined here. Again from Section 3.5, we recall that the original determination of which products are at Level 0 is accomplished by finding which products are *used by no other*. When this has been done, levels are next assigned one after another by following the linkages to the materials directly used, recorded on each product's record, and then the materials directly used by these in turn, and so on. To do so, the computer programming technique of *recursion* is employed.

The technique of recursion involves a programming routine — say, Program X — which contains a programming instruction which invokes itself (i.e. an instruction in Program X which calls Program X). Similarly, this second execution of Program X just initiated may

---

[2] If the bill of materials is never re-levelled and there have been a great many engineering changes to products over the years, the effect of low-level coding might be to create very high level numbers — though still hardly 100. The deepest bills of materials are likely to be found in the chemical industries, where every manufacturing stage adds a level and there is little or no use of a routings file. In engineering, there may be a great many distinct technical steps in manufacture, but the consecutive, individual steps on the shop floor are recorded in the routings file and together will contribute only one level to the bill of materials.

Materials Planning

also invoke itself (i.e. yet a third execution of Program X). The first use of the program in levelling is to deal with Level 0 of the bill. Then the routine calls itself whenever a new level lower down has to be dealt with. Thus to deal with a bill with five levels by recursive programming, there will be five invocations of the programming routine. Not all programming languages support recursion; for example, PL/1 and Pascal do, COBOL and FORTRAN do not.

As we shall see in Section 9.5 where materials planning itself is described, all of the requirements for a component must be planned together, taking account of the component's stock and creating a single set of time-phased plans. Consequently and obviously, therefore, a component may be assigned only one level in the bill of materials. If the analysis of one sales product P shows it uses a component X lower in the bill at Level 1 and later analysis of a second sales product A shows that it also has component X as an ancestor, but at Level 2, the level number assigned to component X is "2", the lower occurrence.

The principle of assigning items to the lowest level at which they occur is embodied in the levelling routine first used to determine levels, and is referred to in the jargon as *low-level coding*. The program supporting low-level coding is permanently resident in the planning system, and is automatically invoked if any change is made later to the structure of the bill of materials by adding records or changing the identity of a product's direct components. On detecting such a change, the program determines the levels of the items involved in the alteration by the method described above, and then checks to see whether there is a clash between the newly worked-out levels of the materials involved and those previously assigned. If there is, the lower level is chosen and adjustments are made elsewhere as necessary. Because low-level coding never assigns a component to a higher level in the bill following an alteration to it, at very infrequent intervals the manufacturing manager might request the complete re-levelling of the bill using the original levelling program, to reduce unnecessarily high level numbers and so assist clarity when dealing with data relating to products (see footnote 2).

The principle of low-level coding is illustrated in Figure 9.4 by three sketches. The left hand sketch shows the original levels assigned to three components Q, X and S on analysis of sales product

P. Sales product A is then analysed, centre sketch, and component X is now seen to be at level 2, not level 1 as previously. Component X's level is duly changed to 2 (low-level coding) and the sub-components which are dependent on X are also allocated to lower levels — sketch three in the Figure. When a lower-level component (level n) must also be master scheduled at level 0 for subsequent sale as a spare, the situation is dealt with as described in Footnote 2, Section 6.1.

Figure 9.4: Low-level Coding affecting two Components X and S

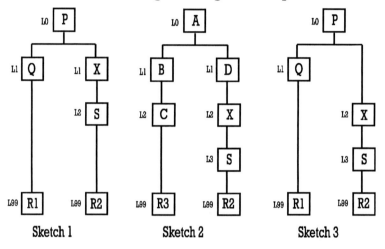

Sketch 1   Sketch 2   Sketch 3

A complication that can arise very occasionally in levelling is the occurrence of loops. A loop exists when a product directly or indirectly contributes to its own manufacture. For example, a certain oxide may be used as a coating in the early stages of manufacture of videotape. At a later stage when the tape is cut, a very small quantity of the oxide flakes off. Because it is expensive, it is recovered and fed back into the earlier coating process.

Two examples of loops and their effect on low-level coding are given in the bills of materials sketches in Figure 9.5. In the left-hand example, component B already exists at Level 2 but is entered in the bill again at a lower level, Level 4. When this is done, the original Level 2 is changed to Level 4 by the low-level coding rule. Consequently, C is changed to Level 5 and the new occurrence of B is changed to Level 6 ... and so on round the loop. In the right-hand example, B already exists at Level 5. When it is now added higher in the bill as a component of product C, it is therefore forced by the

Materials Planning 297

low-level coding rule to assume Level 5 also. However, on re-levelling, E becomes Level 6 and the original occurrence of B is now changed to Level 7 ... and so on round another loop.[3]

Figure 9.5: Two Instances of introducing Product Loops

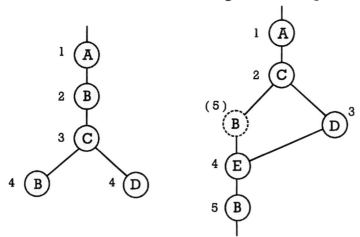

Although product loops are valid physically, computer-based materials planning systems cannot deal with them and they must be eliminated by giving the products whose second occurrence gives rise to them distinct, separate identities through the assignment of new codes. The original product and the recoded product are then dealt with by the planner on a semi-manual basis in a similar way to "equivalent products" (sub-section 9.4.9). The question concerning loops, then, is purely one of detecting them. A common means of detecting any loop which already exists in a bill of materials is to institute a software trap to monitor levels being calculated by the low-level coding routine and terminate any calculation with a message if the level reaches, say, 50. A method of ensuring a loop is not created in the first place when a bill of materials alteration is being made is for software to make a check,

---

[3] Despite the easy example of videotape oxide in the text, loops are rare. In the old ICI Dyestuffs division in the 1960s, with 2,000 chemical raw materials and 7,500 chemical stage manufactured products, made in 250 work centres distributed among 10 factories, there were only eight loops in a bill of materials comprising some 35,000 cross-linkages. See I.M. Milne (1968), *A Description, including Historical Summary and Calculation Methods, of the Normal Costs Computer System*, ICI Dyestuffs division memorandum, MSD/68/12.

online, to ensure each product being added or amended does not already exist either higher or lower in the product chain.

9.4 THE CALCULATION OF MATERIAL REQUIREMENTS

Before materials plans themselves can be formulated for a product, it is first necessary to calculate the quantities of the product to be supplied — the *material requirements* — and then, by application of the *planning rule*, to determine the quantities to be manufactured in order to satisfy these requirements. Material requirements are dealt with in this Section and planning rules in Section 9.6.

9.4.1 Gross Requirements

The term *gross requirements* is widely used in materials planning and means simply the total requirements for a product before any stock on-hand or in-progress manufacture is taken into account. Gross requirements for a product are qualified by a specified time period, that is — *gross requirements for Product P on Day D*. The gross requirements for a product on a particular day may spring from the product's intended use in a number of different manufacturing jobs. The requirements for use in each of the individual jobs constitute *partial requirements*, the sum of all partial requirements being equal to the gross requirements.

The partial or gross requirements for a component arise because of the existence of a plan for manufacture of a further product at a higher level in the bill of materials, the planned manufacture requiring the direct use of the component in question. The planned manufacture must clearly take into account the usage of the component and the lead time of manufacture. For example, suppose the lead time for the assembly of an electric toothbrush was two days and a plan existed to assemble 100 toothbrushes, to be available on Day 10. Then from the usage of four casing panels per electric toothbrush given in Figure 9.2, such a plan would give rise to partial requirements for 400 casing panels on Day 8.[4] This is illustrated in Figure 9.6.

---

[4] If casing panels were used only in the manufacture of the electric toothbrush and not in the manufacture of any other product, the partial requirements in this case would also equal the casing panel's gross requirements.

Materials Planning

Figure 9.6: Partial Requirements

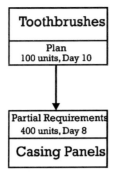

Figures 9.5 earlier, and Figures 9.6 and 9.8 to 9.12 are deliberately made simple to achieve their purpose of illustrating various aspects of materials planning, but, as in the case of Figure 9.6, they fail to show the potential arithmetical complexity of gross requirements calculations. A very distant glimpse of this complexity is caught in Figure 9.7. Figure 9.7 shows the calculation of gross requirements over eight periods for the motor used in the electric toothbrush, but which is used also in an electric pepper mill. The toothbrushes have an assembly lead time of two days and the pepper mill three days.

Figure 9.7: The Creation of Time-phased Gross Requirements

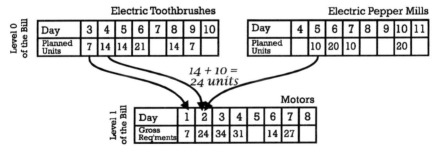

In MRP systems as described in Chapter 10, the time-phased gross requirements are not simply calculated when there is a need to use them, and then discarded. For reasons related to "pegging", described below, they are held in discrete fields allied to each product's data record and are assigned identification numbers. Consequently, to ensure that higher level plans and the supporting lower level gross requirements are always in balance, as described, it is necessary to amend the gross requirement accordingly if any change is made to the quantity or timing of any higher plan. Doing so is referred to as *gross requirements maintenance*.[5] Note that a change to the gross requirements does not imply the automatic recalculation of plans formulated lower in the bill of materials to meet them (Sections 9.5 and 10.4). That is, while gross requirements maintenance ensures that plans for a product are always matched by corresponding lower level gross requirements of components, any newly calculated gross requirements may themselves not always be matched by correct lower level plans formulated to fulfil them, until further action is taken through the system (see *net change*, Section 10.4).

The data record stating the relationship between a plan and the gross requirements for a lower-level material required to fulfil it is known in the jargon of materials planning as a *peg*. In the past, before the advent of sophisticated techniques for searching the bill of materials online, it was necessary to print the entire *pegging file* to enable the planner, if needs be, to trace higher level plans giving rise to a material's gross requirements. Tracing gross requirements to plans giving rise to them one level higher in the bill is referred to as *single-level pegging*; tracing gross requirements all the way up to the master schedule plans is referred to as *full pegging*.[6]

9.4.2 Multi-site Gross Requirements

In describing the relationship between plans and gross requirements of lower-level components in sub-section 9.4.1, the tacit assumption was made that the plans and requirements related to a single site. A number of companies, however, especially those

---

[5] Ideally, gross requirements maintenance should take place immediately following a plan change. Software application systems differ. In MRP, immediate change can be guaranteed only with a "continuous net change" system. With continuous net change, the calculations are made immediately, in real time. With a "batch net change" system, gross requirements maintenance may be effected from time to time when a net change update is run. With a "total regenerative" MRP system, gross requirements maintenance is likely to be carried out only when the system parameters and data are completely recalculated, *ab initio*. See Section 10.4.

[6] D.V. Landvater and C.D. Gray (1989), *MRPII Standard System*, Oliver Wight Limited Publications Inc, Chapter 10.

Materials Planning

employing purpose-built, specialised plant, manufacture material at one factory site for use in the manufacture of a further material at a second factory site. The material manufactured at the second factory site may in turn be sent on for use at yet a third site, and so on.[7] The arrangement is not at all uncommon in the process industries. Figure 9.8 illustrates such a chain, though limited to two sites. A component material M is manufactured at the first site, denoted in the Figure as the *originating site*. Material M is used in the manufacture of product Q, made at a second, remote site, denoted in the Figure as the *consuming site*. The quantities shown in Figure 9.8 relate to the three circumstances described in the text below.

Figure 9.8: Multi-site Netting

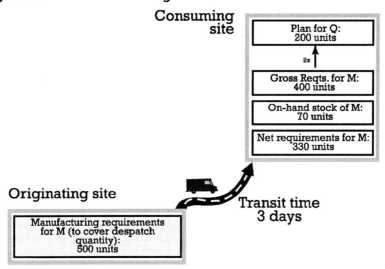

Firstly, there may already be a certain amount of stock of the material involved in the transfer to the consuming site being held there. If it is, the amount required to be transferred from the originating site to the consuming site should be reduced by the quantity so held. For example, suppose that it was planned to manufacture 200 units of Q at the consuming site, and that each unit of Q requires

---

[7] The "third site" may be the original site — i.e. the material may be returned after a specialised operation at the second site. A return trip is logically no different from a despatch to a further site, however. Although the process industries make the greatest use of multi-site netting, many engineering companies send work to external suppliers for specialised treatment and return.

two units of M according to its bill of materials, M being manufactured at the originating site. The requirements for material M in order to commence this manufacture are therefore 400 units. However, if 70 units of M are already being held at the consuming site, the net requirements from the originating site are 330 units only.

Secondly, there may be a rule determining standard quantities of stock which are to be transferred from the originating site to the consuming side (i.e. a despatch quantity rule). If so, the transfer quantity to be sent from the originating site to the consuming site may be greater than is actually needed there, in order to comply with the delivery lot size rule. For example, if the despatch rule for material M in Figure 9.8 is 500 units, one lot of 500 will be despatched to cover the consuming site's need for 330 units.

Thirdly, the time taken to effect the transfer of stock from the one site to the other must be taken into account in calculating the date the requirements on the originating site are to be available and despatched.[8] In the example, suppose that the manufacture of Q at the consuming site is due to start on Day 10, but that the transfer duration of material M is three days. The 500 units of M must consequently be available and despatched from the originating site on Day 7.

If there were to have been yet a third site directly or indirectly requiring the use of material Q, thus extending the reach of Figure 9.8, the calculations would need to have started with this further site in order to ascertain the planned needs for Q at the second site.[9] Since the plans for Q affect the final requirements for M at the original manufacturing site, we see that a complicated chain of calculations results. In the jargon of materials planning, the required planning is referred to as *multi-site netting* or *multiple netting*. Materials planning software providing this feature is usually dedicated to process industry materials planning despite its occasional requirement in engineering industry.

---

[8] Note that despatch plans from one site to another are quite different in character from manufacturing plans, even though both types of plans specify start and finish dates and quantities.

[9] To say that we must start with the most "distant" transfer material in multi-site netting is merely to say again that the calculations must begin at the highest level of the bill of materials and proceed downwards. See DRP, subsection 20.2.1.

Materials Planning

9.4.3 Requirements and Recoveries

A material may be required as a component, or ingredient, in a manufacturing process but then be partly or wholly recovered at the end of it. For example, solvents used in processes are usually largely recovered. Catalysts are entirely recovered.

In materials planning, the required starting amount of the material and the subsequent recovered amount should be shown separately. To do so, the material recovery is entered as a component in the process, but with a negative usage. The three reasons for doing this are:

1. The reality of manufacture is better represented;
2. The separate entry of the starting materials shows the need for the full amount at the commencement of manufacture, not merely the net amount finally consumed; and
3. The negative usage ensures that the recovered stock is credited to the material's stock balance at the end of the manufacture when the plan is signified as having been fulfilled.

The schema is given in Figure 9.9. Figure 9.9 shows 200kg of product P manufactured from 300kg of product C, the process of manufacturing employing solvent S. The starting amount of S is 1,000kg. The recovery of S is entered as a further constituent of –600kg. Provided it has been modified to do so, the materials planning system will ensure that the starting quantity of S of 1,000kg is duly planned for. At the end of the manufacture, the 600kg recovery will be added back into the stock of S.

Figure 9.9: Materials Planning and Recoveries

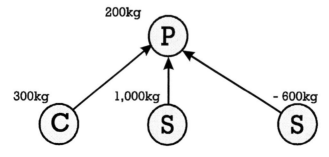

9.4.4 Materials Planning and By-products

The manufacture of one product may result in the accompanying but unwanted production of a particular by-product. Instances occur mainly but by no means exclusively in the chemical industry. Figure 9.10 illustrates the manufacture of 100kg of a principal product Q from 200kg of component A and 150kg of component B, and the side-by-side manufacture of 50kg of by-product R.

Figure 9.10: Manufacture of a By-Product (physical representation)

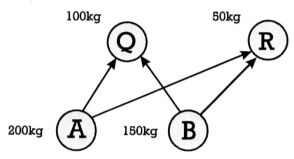

Although Figure 9.10 may be a helpful picture of the physical process, representation of it in this way in the bill of materials database is invalid from the viewpoint of materials planning. In planning terms, Figure 9.10 states that products Q and R may each be planned and made in isolation from each other, each of them being made independently from components A and B. (See however co-products, sub-section 9.4.5.)

For materials planning purposes, by-product R should be entered in the bill of materials as a component of product Q, but with a negative usage, as in a recovery. Figure 9.11 shows the required schema. It is seen from Figure 9.11 that product Q can be directly planned but by-product R cannot be. Provided it has been modified to do so, following the manufacture of 100kg of Q, the materials planning system will subtract 200kg from the recorded stock quantity of component A and 150kg from the recorded stock quantity of B. But it will also subtract −50kg from the stock of R, thereby increasing the stock quantity of R on the record by 50kg.

Materials Planning

Figure 9.11: Materials Planning and By-products

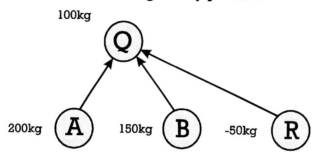

It was stated earlier that the by-product is unwanted. If so, it is presumably not used by any further process so that its physical stock will build up over time. It will consequently have to be disposed of on an occasional basis either by one-off sales or as waste. One way of initiating this through the materials planning system is to generate fictitious independent demand for it when the level of its stock reaches a certain quantity.

9.4.5 Co-products

The relatively straightforward treatment of the simultaneous manufacture of a main product and a by-product is possible because the by-product is unwanted. The by-product does not need to be planned. Concern is only with its disposal.

When two (or more) products are produced by a process simultaneously and both are required in further manufacture, or are required to fulfil regular sales demand, the situation is very much more complicated. Products that are independently required in materials planning but are made simultaneously by a single process are known as *co-products*.

The first complication is representing them on the bill of materials. Figure 9.12 illustrates a process whereby an acrylic sheet (one foot square) is stamped to produce 4½" circles and 4½" squares of acrylic shapes simultaneously. The number of shapes produced by stamping one sheet is three circles and five squares. The demand for circles and the demand for squares are about equal. The two sources of this demand are independent of each other.[10]

---

[10] The manufacturing manager may wonder why the stamping process described in the text cannot be modified to correct the imbalance between the

Figure 9.12: Co-Products (Two Acrylic Shapes)

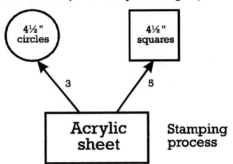

Conceptually, Figure 9.12 is no different from Figure 9.10, and the same criticism can be made as there that the representation of the process in this way wrongly shows that the circles and squares may each be planned and manufactured independently. In the case of co-products, the materials planner has no option but to do so. No harm is done, however, since the whole treatment of co-products and the parent product from which they are derived must be separated from the flow of mainstream planning and carried out with the assistance of special software. In short, planning must be done by the planner himself at the VDU, having simultaneous access to the products' requirements and plans as described below.

To illustrate the planner's actions and the data required, consider the relationship between the requirements for acrylic circles and squares needed to fulfil higher level plans for these two products, and the plans to stamp one-foot acrylic sheets. In order to keep track of the production both of circles and of squares and the separate requirements for them, *two* projected stock balances must

---

ratio of production and the ratio of demand. Action possible with acrylic shapes, however, cannot be taken with chemical processes, where the ratio of co-product production is determined by chemistry. An example of such is the production of sodium and chlorine by the electrolysis of salt. In engineering industry, machines which have reached the end of their lives may be "disassembled" to reclaim valuable components which have a continuing use. In this last case, however, the proportions of the components (co-products) recovered may vary if some are found to be not fit to be further used. Differing proportions of co-products (petrol, oil, etc.) may also be obtained from crude oil by varying the cracking process employed to obtain them, although in this case production planning is effected through linear programming, not as described in the text.

Materials Planning 307

be maintained, one for each co-product. This is shown in Figure 9.13. When an acrylic sheet is processed, the stock of both circles and squares is increased: circles by three units and squares by five units, per one acrylic sheet processed. But the stock of circles in a given period is reduced only if there is a requirement for circles in that period, and the stock of squares is reduced only if there is a requirement for squares.

Figure 9.13: Simultaneous Planning and Consumption of Two Co-Products

Period	1	2	3	4	5	6	7	8
Reqts. for Circles	6	2	0	1	0	8	0	4
Reqts. for Squares	2	1	11	7	5	1	2	0

Stock of Circles [OH 0]	0	1	1	6	9	1	1	0
Stock Squares [OH 0]	8*	12	1	4	4	3	1	6

Acrylic Sheets	2	1	0	2	1	0	0	1

* *2 acrylic sheets produce 6 circles and 10 squares; 2 squares are needed for the requirements in Period 1, leaving a stock of 8 squares.*

The circumstances of each instance of co-product production must be examined carefully. If necessary, the straightforward logic above may need to be modified. An example of such modification is given by Landvater and Gray, where a disassembly into co-products occurs on a regular basis which is independent of the periods in which the co-products are actually needed.[11]

9.4.6 Materials Planning and Grades of Quality

The normal quality of a batch of materials manufactured by a particular process will naturally be satisfactory — say, "grade 1". When so, the material can be used in further manufacture in the usual way. On occasions, however, the process may proceed imperfectly, resulting in the production of batches of sub-standard

---

[11] D.V. Landvater and C.D. Gray (1989), op. cit.

material — say, grades 2 or 3.[12] One sub-standard grade may be saleable to certain customers for special purposes while the other may have to be disposed of as waste. An example is the potential variation in colour and strength output from batch to batch inherent in the manufacture of dyestuffs.

In these circumstances, the quantities of the sub-standard stock should not be held on the product's stock record, categorised by grade (i.e. grade 2 stock . . . grade 3 stock . . .), since to do so wrongly suggests that sub-standard grades of material can be specifically planned for.[13] Instead, a separate bill of materials record should be set up for each of the product's sub-standard categories, making each sub-standard grade a "product" in its own right, the record having no linkages with any other record in the BOM database and having no planning rule. When a sub-standard batch of material is made, the completed plan must be removed by the materials planning system as having being fulfilled, in the normal way, but the materials planner himself must then transfer the sub-standard stock quantity on the computer to the stock account of the sub-standard material on its standalone record. Sub-standard stock of each grade must be disposed of from time to time by sale or as waste as described in sub-section 9.4.4 for by-product stock.

9.4.7 The Non-standard Batch Size

A planning problem in some process industries results from the discretion necessarily given to the manufacturing manager with

---

[12] The occasional production of sub-standard stock as in the text will cause temporary shortages of grade 1 material. Although the method outlined will initiate replanning as soon as the data about events have been communicated, the manufacturing manager may feel justified in holding buffer stock, notwithstanding the remarks in Section 5.1. As a general point which applies to sub-sections 9.4.7 and 9.4.8 also, if there are problems with a production batch — say, a missed scheduled manufacture date, material past due — problems relating to the quantity ultimately expected — the facts must be posted at once to planning via the shop floor information system, so that plan adjustments can be made.

[13] The assignment of quantities of stock to such categories on the stock record as *allocated, obsolete, deteriorated* and so forth (see sub-section 17.2.1) is done either under system control or by the manufacturing or stores manager, and is a different matter from the chance, accidental production of non-standard physical grades.

Materials Planning 309

regard to the sizes of the batches of production he makes. For example, a batch size rule in the materials planning logic might be to manufacture in lots of 1,000kg. If net requirements are 1,600kg, materials planning will generate two plans for 1,000kg. In practice, the manager on the day may decide instead to make two batches of 800kg, reducing the lower level gross requirements and the need for stock to be used in the production process. Alternatively, in other circumstances, the manager may elect to manufacture three batches of 700kg, increasing the lower level gross requirements. See sub-section 9.4.6, footnote 13, once more.

9.4.8 Alternative Bill of Material Usages

In certain companies in the chemical and food industries, plans of manufacture are occasionally formulated employing temporary, special component usages rather than the standard. Reasons for doing so include the one-off purchase and intended use of non-standard raw materials and the prior manufacture of non-standard product. Non-standard usages clearly present a difficulty in materials planning. A method of overcoming it is first to calculate component material requirements in the normal way and then to change the material quantities directly by a special computer transaction, overriding the standard calculated amounts.

9.4.9 Equivalent Products

It is not uncommon in the chemical industry for two or more products with different product codes, made on different work centres, to be physically identical. It is quite possible for the identical products to be manufactured by different processes and with different bills of material. Products identical in this way are often referred to as *equivalent products*.[14] For materials planning purposes, it is clearly necessary for data relating to a group of equivalent products to be recorded such that the totalities of

---

[14] Notwithstanding the chemical identicalness of equivalent products, their alternative locations of manufacture will ensure that they have different standard costs. It is possible, however, to calculate the likely individual annual values of production of each equivalent, based on forecasts and budgets, and, from this, to calculate an *average* cost. The average cost can then be used to value the total work-in-progress recorded under the key product.

requirements, stock and plans can be readily seen as single figures.

A simple way to achieve this is to designate one product in a group of equivalents as the "key", or central, product and all other equivalent products in the group as "non-key". When this has been done, for each equivalent group, every occurrence of a non-key product code as a component, or constituent, of manufacture elsewhere throughout the bill of materials database is changed to the code of the key product. (The bill of materials will not now reflect the truth of actual manufacture, of course.) Consequently, the various requirements for the product under all its previous codes, or aliases, then become simply partial requirements for the key product. The sum of the partial requirements constitutes the key product's gross requirements. Next, in order to formulate plans for the key product, it is first necessary to net off any existing key product stock. A further planning procedure must then be put in place. This is that all stock produced of non-key material must be credited to the stock account of the key product, not to the stock accounts of the non-key products actually produced. The gross requirements for the key product minus this augmented grand total of key product stock give the net requirements for the key product. Finally, the surprising planning rule "do not plan" should be assigned to the key product. As a result of doing so, no plans will be generated by the computer software to fulfil the net requirements for the key product, thus resulting in the output of a standard system warning message following planning calculations: *unsatisfied net requirements for Product X*. The warning message draws the attention of the planner to the situation so that he himself can formulate plans to satisfy the net requirements directly at the VDU. The plans he formulates will be for both the key and non-key products, as judgement dictates and bearing in mind the manufacturing capacity of the work centres involved.

9.4.10 Scrap and Yield

In the manufacture of certain discrete parts in a great many industries, a percentage of the parts under manufacture may eventually be scrapped because of imperfections in the process or in its operation by staff. The *scrap factor*, as it is commonly called, must clearly be allowed for in materials planning. If a scrap factor of 1

Materials Planning 311

per cent relates to a particular manufacture and 1,000 units output are required, the number of units planned must be 1,010 (1,010 × 0.99 = 1,000 rounded). The equivalent of scrap in the process industries is *yield*. If 1,000kg of production are required and the process yield is 90 per cent, 1,111 kilograms must be planned for.

If a scrap factor or yield applies to a product, it is held on the data record and is typically re-set each year during the calculation of standard costs, the revised figure being based on the evidence of the previous year's production records (sub-section 17.4.3). The scrap or yield which actually turns out in practice is very likely to be different from the target, requiring prompt shop floor data submission. (Variances between target and actual production quantities are used by the cost accountant to track manufacturing performance — see sub-sections 11.5.3 and 17.4.3.)

To complicate matters further, in the chemical and food industries the proportions of material actually used in manufacture will often differ from the proportions implied in the bill of materials usages. As with yields, the required stock adjustments to the consumed materials' stock records must be made via the shop floor information system when details of the manufacture are notified (again, 9.4.6, footnote 13).

9.5 GROSS REQUIREMENTS TO PLANS

To satisfy final material requirements, account is first taken of on-hand stock — in the jargon, stock is "netted off" (i.e. subtracted) to arrive at the material's *net requirements*.[15] Account is next taken of any work-in-progress. Plans are finally generated, in accordance with a planning rule assigned to the particular product, to satisfy the requirements remaining using the projected stock balance mechanism originally described in sub-section 6.5.1. The calculation of plans through the projected stock balance to satisfy the gross requirements for the motors in Figure 9.7 is illustrated in Table 9.1.

---

[15] If the stock quantity on the record is inaccurate, the material plans subsequently formulated will be invalid, simultaneously destroying both the credibility and the usefulness of the planning system — see sub-section 18.3.2.

Table 9.1: The Calculation of Plans to meet Gross Requirements

On-Hand (OH): 2 units
Past Due (PD): 35 units
Plan: Lots of 35 units

	Period							
	1	2	3	4	5	6	7	8
Gross Requirements		7	24	34	31		14	27
Scheduled Receipts [PD] 35								
Projected Stock Balance [OH] 2	30	6	7	11	11	32	5	5
Plans to finish Manufacture			35	35		35		

$35 + 2 - 7 = 30$ units

Although the principles of plan generation here are the same as those employed in generating a master schedule given in sub-section 6.5.1, comparison of Table 9.1 and Figure 6.9 shows there to be a small number of differences. One of these is the introduction in Table 9.1 of a line entitled "Scheduled Receipts". Scheduled receipts are also termed "open orders", and are manufacturing plans currently in progress on the factory floor. They are separated from future planned manufacture, which is placed on the last line, in part to make the position clear to the planner, in particular reminding him that components or raw materials at the next level lower in the bill required for the manufacture in question have already been issued to the factory and do not need to be allowed for in planning the lower level stock. In Figure 6.9, by contrast, master schedule plans actually in progress are not directly distinguished from those that have not yet started. (The information as to whether or not a master plan has started is, of course, readily available from other sources.) A further reason for separating scheduled receipts relates to their treatment in closed-loop MRP (see sub-sections 10.2.1 and 10.3.2). In Table 9.1, a scheduled receipt is shown as *past due*. That is, according to the planning data, if the 35 units involved had been made on time, they would have already been booked into stock. Final production is presumed to be imminent, however. Consequently, the materials planning system takes the 35 units into account in calculating the projected stock balance in Period 1. The projected stock balance at the end of Period 1 is therefore 30 units — i.e. 35 units past

Materials Planning

due (a scheduled receipt) *plus* two units of on-hand stock *less* seven units gross requirements for the motors.

It should be noted that the principles of plan generation from gross requirements are no different if planning rules specify a *rate* of output rather than discrete batches. If this is done, the planner will nominate the particular rate-based rule and the period over which it is to apply, while the arithmetic in the software calculates the rate. The following seven rules have been implemented:[16]

1. *Net requirements by period;*
2. *Smoothed production rates;*
3. *Full shift capacity;*
4. *Fixed production rate;*
5. *Maximum rate as late as possible;*
6. *Smooth production within a time period;*
7. *Limit the percentage change in rates between periods.*

Table 9.2 shows the generation of a plan of production in which Rule 6 above is applied, specifying the time horizon Period 1 to 8 inclusive. (The gross requirements in Table 9.2 are taken from Table 9.1.)

Table 9.2: Generation of a Rate-Based Manufacturing Plan

On-Hand (OH): 12 units
Past Due (PD): 0
Plan: Smooth rate, Periods 1 to 8

		Period							
		1	2	3	4	5	6	7	8
Gross Requirements		7	24	34	31		14	27	
Scheduled Receipts	PD 0								
Projected Stock Balance	OH 12	26	23	10	0	21	28	22	43
Plan of Manufacture		21	21	21	21	21	21	21	21

---

[16] These seven rate-based planning rules are given in the master scheduling module of the MERCIA LINCS suite of software (see Chapter 4, footnote 18).

9.6 Planning Rules

In order to formulate plans for a product from its net requirements, a rule must be assigned governing the lot sizes of material to be manufactured. In a number of cases, the physical process itself may entirely dictate the planning rule. Autoclaves and centrifuges are items of plant with single, fixed capacities which determine the batch sizes of products made on them. Again, in engineering, a tool such as a grinding wheel may have a very short life before it is finished with, effectively determining the running time of a machine. The delivery quantity of many raw materials may also be fixed through suppliers' packaging decisions.

In the main, however, planning rules, or rather, manufacturing and purchasing lot size rules, are decided by the manufacturing and purchasing managers. The decisions they reach have a major impact on two very important company matters. The first is the relative level of work-in-progress in the factory and all of the costs incurred in supporting it — the value of capital tied up in stock (representing money that could be employed elsewhere), and such expenses as storage, insurance and stock deterioration. The second is the tempo of manufacturing operations. If small batch quantities are made or bought very frequently to reduce the amount of WIP held, the company will incur commensurately greater costs in machine set-ups, potentially with consequent losses in productivity, greater purchase order placement and delivery costs and greater costs of other administrative tasks connected with order receipt, payment, batch recording and the rest.

The origination and assignment of standard planning rules to be applied to manufactured and purchased material that will have the effect of minimising the sum of the stock and operations classes of cost above, overall and for the entire company, is not feasible for three reasons. First, the trade-off between WIP and operating stability cannot be permanent. In one month, when things are busy, higher WIP may seem a good price to pay for more stable schedules. In another, when things are slack, the opposite may be true. Secondly, even if a trade-off between the two classes of cost were to be agreed, calculations of the batch size would then depend on an assumption as to the net requirements for each material over the planning system's time horizon. Yet in the event, requirements are certain to change. Thirdly, calculations of batch sizes, again, would have to take account of the many thousands of relationships between planned amounts, level to level, over time, so as to minimise "remnant stock" — the stock left over from batches of production after what is required in further manufacture at the next stages has been used. For example, in Figure 9.7, the planning rules for electric toothbrushes, electric pepper mills, motors and all remaining components in the bill of materials not illustrated must be assigned so as to minimise the sum of the WIP costs implied in every material's projected stock balance and the costs of initiating and managing each of the manufacturing plans giving rise to it. (Even if such an awesome task were to be accomplished, the validity of the calculations would not survive even the mildest change.)

Just-in-Time deals with this Gordian Knot in Alexandrine fashion. By rearranging the physical layout of machines, by greatly reducing set-up times and by reorganising the flow of work, Just-in-Time enables the manufacturing manager to make very small batches of material very frequently, but economically, directly in response to customer demand. The purchasing manager is required to support the new pattern of production by arranging for small, frequent deliveries from suppliers. But as we shall see in Chapter 15, the full applicability of Just-in-Time is limited. Nevertheless, the ideas, or "philosophies", of JIT do have a bearing on the planning rule problem. It must always be advantageous to the company to eliminate delay, eliminate stock and streamline its operations. We shall speak more of this later in the Section.

Although the goal of determining perfect lot sizes cannot be attained, some rationale at least must be adopted if chance and disorder are to be avoided. A number of procedures have been developed for calculating lot amounts. Five of the most important of them are described in the sub-sections that follow. The fifth is concerned with purchase lot quantities and the question of discounts. An assumption relating to all of them is that the net material requirements for each particular period being planned for must be satisfied in full, and that plans relate to one product only, in isolation and therefore at one level only of the bill of materials. That is, the complexity of multi-levels and remnant stock touched on above is not considered. Although this may be so, one or other of the first four methods can be used in practice throughout the material range by following a simple two-step procedure:[17]

1. Starting at Level 0 of the bill of materials, calculate the lot size for each product at this level, using the lot size rule chosen from sub-sections 9.6.1 to 9.6.4;

2. Match the lot sizes of the components at the next lower level with the lot sizes just calculated in (1), taking into account the component usages. (For example, if the lot size of electric toothbrushes in Figure 9.2 turns out to be 75 units, the lot size of casing panels is set to 300 units.) Go to the next lower level and do the same thing. However, if any component at a lower level has two or more descendants, the rule breaks down for that particular component. (For example, the motor in Figure 9.7 has two descendants, the electric toothbrush and the electric pepper mill.) Where this occurs, the lot size of the component concerned should be calculated by reverting to the original standard chosen method.

9.6.1 The Economic Order Quantity

The *economic order quantity*, EOQ, refers to the physical size of an order the company places on a supplier for the delivery of raw material, consideration being given to the commercial ordering and payment processes; the handling of the delivered material; and the financial value of the material while it is in stock.[18] The materials planning technique for calculating the EOQ is the oldest in current use, having been devised in 1915.[19] The word *economic* in its

---

[17] From an *Inventory Control & Logistics Workshop*, presented by R.G. Brown at the London Business School, September 1988, organised by GMCS Ltd. of Lytham St Annes (http://www.gmcs.co.uk).

[18] The EOQ is not to be confused with the *economic manufacturing quantity*, EMQ, or *economic batch quantity*, EBQ. The EMQ is a somewhat hazy notion involving a supposed trade-off between the value added to stock by production, i.e. the direct stage cost × batch size (see 17.4.3), and the cost of the manufacturing set-up.

[19] R. Mennel (1961), "Early History of the Economic Lot Size", *APICS Quarterly Bulletin*, Vol. 2, No. 2, quoted in R.G. Brown (1982), *Advanced Service Parts Inventory Control (ASPIC)*. Levin et al. give Ford W. Harris as the originator of the EOQ formula (R.I. Levin, C.A. Kirkpatrick, D.S. Rubin (1982), *Quantitative Approaches to Management*, Fifth edition, McGraw-Hill.

Materials Planning

name simply means *least cost*. An important assumption in the procedure for the EOQ's calculation is that the use of the net material requirements to be acquired are uniform over the time period under consideration. Consider, for example, the gross requirements of the motors shown in Figure 9.7, given again in Figure 9.14 for convenience. If the stock of motors is zero, the gross requirements in Figure 9.14 are also the net requirements. However, because they are uneven from period to period, the EOQ calculations would need to proceed on the basis of the average net requirements for each period and so could not be expected to produce an optimal result. (The total net requirements in Figure 9.14 amount to 137 units, giving an average of 17.1 units per period.)

Figure 9.14: The Unevenness of Period-by-Period Requirements for Motors

Motors

LEVEL 1 of the BILL	Day	1	2	3	4	5	6	7	8
	Gross Req'ments	7	24	34	31		14	27	

Suppose that the quantity of a material ordered or manufactured over a year is q units. Then two classes of cost are incurred, given in (1) and (2) below:

1. Let the cost of placing the order be O (letter O, given in £). This cost includes the cost of an order delivery, its receipt and other associated administrative costs mentioned at the beginning of this Section. Suppose that the demand for the material over the year is A units. Then the number of orders placed in the year is A/q and the annual ordering cost is given by:

$$\frac{A}{q} \times O \quad (£)$$

2. If the demand for the material over the year is uniform, then, from Section 9.1, if q units are ordered, the average amount of stock held is $(q/2 + S)$ units, where S is the safety stock. Suppose the annual cost attributed to stockholding is a fraction i of the value of the stock quantity held. Then, if the unit value of the material is v (£), the annual cost of stockholding is given by:

$$\left(\frac{q}{2} + S\right) vi \quad (£)$$

The total annual cost C of ordering q units and subsequently holding material is consequently the sum of the two costs in (1) and (2), and is given by Equation 9.2.

$$C = \left(\frac{A}{q} \times O\right) + \left(\frac{q}{2} + S\right) vi \quad (£) \qquad \text{Equation 9.2}$$

Differentiating C with respect to q gives Equation 9.3.

$$\frac{dC}{dq} = \frac{AO}{q^2} + \frac{vi}{2} \qquad \text{Equation 9.3}$$

Setting the differential dC/dq to zero and rearranging terms gives q', where q' is the value of q in which the sum of the two classes of cost is minimum — Equation 9.4.

$$q' \text{ (i.e. the EOQ)} = \sqrt{\frac{2AO}{vi}} \quad \text{(units)} \qquad \text{Equation 9.4}$$

The expression on the right-hand side of the equation is sometimes given purely in financial terms (i.e. for the economic order value, not quantity). There have been numerous other extensions to the standard formula. These include:

a) The economic order quantity in which the replenishment is delivered over a short period, rather than in one lot;

b) The EOQ in which consumption of the material is concurrent with its delivery or manufacture;

c) The EOQ in which stockouts are allowed; and

d) The EOQ when there is a risk of sudden obsolescence of the material ordered.[20]

In addition, two ingenious variations have been developed in which a lot size is computed that (1) minimises stockholding for a

---

[20] See Chapters 6 and 11 in R.G. Brown (1982), op. cit.; Chapters 12 and 14 in T.E. Vollmann, W.L. Berry and D.C. Whybark (1988), *Manufacturing Planning and Control Systems*, Second edition, Dow Jones-Irwin; Chapter 12 in N. Slack, S. Chambers, C. Harland, A. Harrison and R. Johnston (1995), *Operations Management*, Pitman Publishing; and Chapter 14 in Ray Wild (1980), *Production and Operations Management*, Holt, Rinehart and Winston.

Materials Planning 319

fixed number of orders per annum, or (2) minimises the number of orders placed for a fixed stockholding, both calculations avoiding the need to specify O and i at all.[21]

The terms O and i in Equation 9.4 are management variables of the same class described in sub-section 5.4.3. That is, they can be altered to achieve different results in different company circumstances. To give one example, if the company wishes to release money tied up in WIP by purchasing and manufacturing a larger number of smaller batches, i might be reset from (say) 0.20 (i.e. 20 per cent per annum) to 0.40 (40 per cent per annum). Initially, however, O should be set by reference to actual purchasing cost data, and i set to the company's target figure for rate of return on investment.

The two components of the cost of ordering and holding stock given in (1) and (2) above can be represented graphically. This is shown in Figure 9.15. The sum of the components, or the total cost, is also drawn on the graph as a third curve. Corresponding to Point P on this other curve are the lowest total cost, c (on the vertical axis of the graph) and the EOQ, q' (the value of q on the horizontal axis).[22]

Of particular interest and importance in Figure 9.15 is the shallowness of the total cost curve at Point P. We see from the vertical axis of the graph that the cost difference between the EOQ cost c and a close but arbitrarily chosen slightly higher order cost c^1 is quite small. There are two alternative order quantities corresponding to, or giving rise to, order cost c^1. As we see from the horizontal axis of the graph, the sizes of the two quantities are p^1 and p^2. But as we see further, the difference between p^1 and p^2 is relatively large. That is, the large difference between order quantities p^1 and p^2 results in only a small difference in cost between c^1 and the optimum c. This suggests that precision in such matters as the choice of A, O and i is not required in connection with the EOQ and that use of the formula will give generally good results. As a rule of thumb, it has

---

[21] Chapter 7 in Levin et al. (1982), op. cit.

[22] Note in Figure 9.15 that the vertical line from Point P to the horizontal axis does not pass through Point X where the two cost components bisect. This *can* occur, but only in the special case where the two components of the total cost are equal.

been suggested that any value between the following extremes will be satisfactory:[23]

$$\frac{EOQ}{\sqrt{2}} \text{ and } \sqrt{2}EOQ$$

Figure 9.15: Graphs of Costs relating to the EOQ Formula

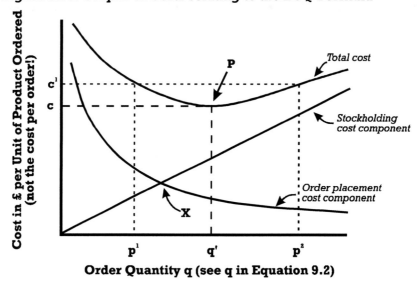

9.6.2 The Period Order Quantity

The *period order quantity* (POQ) refers to an economic, or least cost, *time interval* between order placements, rather than to an economic lot size. The time interval is fixed for the material in question, and is derived from the EOQ as given in Equation 9.5.

$$POQ \text{ Time Interval (days)} = \frac{EOQ}{\text{Average Daily Net Requirements}} \qquad \text{Equation 9.5}$$

On calculation of the POQ time interval, the rule then operates by creating a plan on the first day of each period, the plan covering all of the period's requirements.

---

[23] See S. Eilon (1969), *Elements of Production Planning and Control*, Collier-Macmillan.

Materials Planning 321

For example, suppose that the EOQ for motors in Figure 9.14 was 40 units, the average daily requirements over the eight days being 17.1 units. Then, from Equation 9.5, the POQ time interval is:

$$\frac{40 \text{ units}}{17.1 \text{ units per day}} = 2 \text{ days (rounded)}$$

Four plans will now be generated to cover the net requirements of motors over the 8 days in Figure 9.14, namely on Day 1 (to cover Days 1 and 2), Day 3 (3 and 4), Day 5 (5 and 6) and Day 7 (7 and 8), as shown in Figure 9.16.

Figure 9.16: Generation of Plans for a two-day POQ Time Interval

Motors

Day	1	2	3	4	5	6	7	8
Gross Req'ments	7	24	34	31			14	27
Stock [OH] 0	24	0	31	0	14	0	0	0
Plans	31		65		14		27	

The POQ rule effects an improvement over EOQs when net requirements over the planning horizon are uneven, since the quantities planned are allowed to vary.[24] That is, the plans calculated for periods when net requirements are low are themselves commensurately low. Comparison of the POQ stock balance in Figure 9.16 with the stock balance in Figure 9.17 arising from plans in fixed lots of 40 units shows the difference at a glance, albeit that the example is indeed simplistic.

---

[24] W.L. Berry (1972), "Lot-Sizing Procedures for Requirements Planning Systems", *Production & Inventory Management*, Second Quarter, or see Chapter 12 in Vollmann, Berry and Whybark (1988), op. cit.

Figure 9.17: The Stock Balance with Fixed Lots (for Comparison with Figure 9.16)

Motors

Day	1	2	3	4	5	6	7	8
Gross Req'ments	7	24	34	31		14	27	
Stock $\boxed{0}^{OH}$	33	9	15	24	24	10	23	23
Plans	40		40	40			40	

The considerable value of the POQ rule in planning is not to be found in economical stock balances, however. The POQ rule, whether formulated via Equation 9.5 or not, confers very welcome stability on the delivery schedules to be followed by suppliers of raw materials. When change occurs in the net requirements for a raw material, if a POQ rule has been employed, the schedule stays fixed even though the quantities required may vary.[25]

A comparison of the effect of a change in net requirements between the POQ rule and a fixed lot planning rule is made in Figure 9.18. Figure 9.18 is based on the gross and net requirements in Figures 9.16 and 9.17. However, the requirements in Day 2 have been increased by 11 units, from 24 to 35 units. The change in the POQ (top table in the Figure) is, obviously, to increase the delivery requirements on Day 1 by the 11. Changes in the delivery pattern for fixed lots of 40 units are wholesale. A supplier who was able to

---

[25] A fixed schedule but varying delivery quantities with the POQ rule is no different in principle from daily, and possibly varying, quantities required from JIT suppliers (see sub-section 15.5.1). The ability to fix a schedule through POQs would also be required if DRP were chosen as the basis of a distribution system, to enable shipments to be dovetailed with fixed transport schedules (see sub-section 20.2.1). It is sometimes suggested by proponents of closed-loop MRP that variable planning quantities such as those generated by the POQ rule, part-period balancing (9.6.3) and Wagner-Whitin (9.6.4) may give rise to numerous MRP rescheduling messages because of constant change to gross requirements. Such might be the case only if the plans concerned had been made "firm" by the planner. Because of the complexity of the variable plan calculations, the dynamic nature of their application and the reason for creating firm planned orders in the first place, which is usually to override standard planning, this is unlikely to be the case (see sub-section 10.2.3).

Materials Planning

accommodate change in the first instance might have considerably more difficulty in the second.

Figure 9.18: New Plan Positions with the POQ and Fixed-Lot Rules following a Change in Requirements (compare with Figures 9.16 and 9.17)

Motors

POQ of 2 Days	Day	1	2	3	4	5	6	7	8
	Gross Req'ments	7	35	34	31		14	27	
	Stock [OH 0]	35	0	31	0	14	0	0	0
	Plans	42		65		14		27	

Lots of 40	Day	1	2	3	4	5	6	7	8
	Gross Req'ments	7	35	34	31		14	27	
	Stock [OH 0]	33	38	4	13	13	39	12	12
	Plans	40	40		40		40		

9.6.3 Part Period Balancing

As we shall see, the improvement over the EOQ and POQ effected by *part period balancing* arises because the method allows for any unevenness over time in the net requirements of the product being planned. In the phraseology, the term *part period* is the carrying of one unit of stock for one period. For example, if the duration of the period concerned is a day, then carrying 34 units of stock from the beginning of Day 1 until its consumption in manufacture in Day 3 involves $34 \times 2\frac{1}{2}$, or 85, part periods. That is, 34 units are carried for 2 whole days, and then the 34 units are said to be used up in a uniform way during Day 3. The *balancing* term in the expression refers to the method by which the rule works. This is to calculate a schedule of plans, from the current period to the planning horizon, such that the cost of holding stock for the duration of each plan is balanced by (i.e. equals) the plan's ordering or manufacturing set-up cost. To illustrate the use of part period balancing for a single plan, consider the plan requirements for electric motors in Figure 9.14, reproduced for convenience in Figure 9.19.

Figure 9.19: Period-by-Period Requirements for Motors (as Figure 9.14)

Motors

	Day	1	2	3	4	5	6	7	8
LEVEL 1 of the BILL	Gross Req'ments	7	24	34	31		14	27	

Let us assume the cost to place or initiate an order is £250, and that the cost of stockholding is £1 per part period (i.e. 1 unit of stock held for 1 day costs £1). On the basis of £1 per part period, Table 9.3 shows the total part period costs of an initial plan to cover the requirements in Table 9.19 for 1 day, 2 days, 3 days . . . up to 8 days ahead.

Table 9.3: Calculations of Stockholding Costs for various Periods in Part Period Balancing

	Cost of Holding Stock for n days							
	1 day	2 days	3 days	4 days	5 days	6 days	7 days	8 days
Day 1 (7 units)	7 x ½ £3.50							
Day 2 (24 units)	7 x ½ £3.50	24 x 1½ £36.00						
Day 3 (34 units)	7 x ½ £3.50	24 x 1½ £36.00	34 x 2½ £85.00					
Day 4 (31 units)	7 x ½ £3.50	24 x 1½ £36.00	34 x 2½ £85.00	31 x 3½ £108.50				
Day 5 (0 units)	7 x ½ £3.50	24 x 1½ £36.00	34 x 2½ £85.00	31 x 3½ £108.50	0 x 4½ £0.00			
Day 6 (14 units)	7 x ½ £3.50	24 x 1½ £36.00	34 x 2½ £85.00	31 x 3½ £108.50	0 x 4½ £0.00	14 x 5½ £77.00		
Day 7 (27 units)	7 x ½ £3.50	24 x 1½ £36.00	34 x 2½ £85.00	31 x 3½ £108.50	0 x 4½ £0.00	14 x 5½ £77.00	27 x 6½ £175.50	
Day 8 (0 units)	7 x ½ £3.50	24 x 1½ £36.00	34 x 2½ £85.00	31 x 3½ £108.50	0 x 4½ £0.00	14 x 5½ £77.00	27 x 6½ £175.50	0 x 7½ £0.00

Materials Planning

Thus the stockholding cost incurred in ordering a lot size of 96 units to cover the first five days of the net requirements for the motors is £233.00 (£3.50 + £36.00 + £85.00 + £108.50 + £0.00). A lot size of 110 units to cover requirements up to Day 6 would cost £310.00 in stockholding (i.e. an extra £77.00). Since the first sum is the nearer to the given order cost of £250, 96 units becomes the first lot size, to cover Days 1 to 5. (To calculate the amount and duration of cover of the second lot, we start completely afresh, making Day 6 the "first day" — that is, the second lot would only *arrive* into stock on Day 6 — it is not necessary to bear any stockholding costs relating to it from Day 1 to Day 5.)

If the gross requirements for electric motors were to be extended (say) to 30 days ahead, with continued uneven day to day requirements over the complete time span, the durations of the plans generated to satisfy them will similarly be uneven. The uneven spread of plans is illustrated in Figure 19.20, in which four plans for electric motors are ranged over the time span from the current period to the end of Period 30. Plan A is the plan for 96 units to cover the first five days, as calculated from Table 9.3. The values and workings out for Plans B to D would require Table 9.3 to be greatly extended and are not given. However, a number of comments relating to them and Plan A follow.

Figure 9.20: Four Plans created through Part Period Balancing

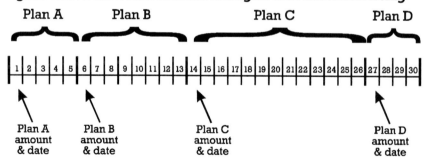

Plan A The cost of acquiring the stock in Period 1 is balanced by the cost of holding it, and eventually consuming it, in the satisfying of net requirements from Period 1 to Period 5, as demonstrated in Table 9.3.

Plan B The cost of acquiring the stock in Period 6 is balanced by the cost of holding it, and eventually consuming it, in the satisfying of net requirements, the requirements and the stockholding costs starting in Period 6 and finishing in Period 13.

Plan C The cost of acquiring the stock in Period 14 is balanced by the cost of holding it, and eventually consuming it, in the satisfying of net requirements, the requirements and the stockholding costs starting in Period 14 and finishing in Period 26.

Plan D The cost of acquiring the stock in Period 27 is balanced by the cost of holding it, and eventually consuming it, in the satisfying of net requirements, the requirements and the stockholding costs starting in Period 27 and finishing in Period 30.

9.6.4 The Wagner-Whitin Algorithm

The *Wagner-Whitin algorithm* employs the mathematical technique of dynamic programming to compute an optimal schedule of planned lots to cover the net material requirements of the complete planning horizon.[26] To begin, the stockholding cost and order cost are evaluated of one replenishment lot for the complete horizon, to arrive in the first period. (The same method of evaluating a stockholding cost is used as in part period balancing and Table 9.3.) Then, the stockholding costs and order costs of 2 replenishment lots are evaluated. However, although one lot of some particular size must arrive in Period 1, there are numerous ways of scheduling the second. All are evaluated and the cost and arrangement of the most economic one are put to one side as interim working figures. (In the case of Figure 9.14, two lots of 7 units and 130 units could be scheduled for Day 1 and Day 2, two

---

[26] Dynamic programming is one member of the family of techniques termed *mathematical programming*. Other members of the family are linear, integer and mixed-integer programming. The term "programme" refers to the mathematical procedure used, not to computer software. An "algorithm" is a set of rules by which a calculation is performed. See H.M. Wagner and T.M. Whitin (1958), "Dynamic Version of the Economic Lot Size", *Management Science* magazine (US), October. See also Section 12.1 and sub-section 12.4.2.

lots of 31 units and 106 units for Day 1 and Day 3, two lots of 65 and 72 for Day 1 and Day 4 . . . seven combinations in all.) Next, the stockholding costs and order costs of three replenishment lots are dealt with, and each of the various ways of arranging the replenishment orders again evaluated. As before, the cost and arrangement of the most economic schedule of the three lots are put to one side as further interim working figures. (In the case of Figure 9.14, although one lot of some size must be scheduled for Day 1, in all there are 21 ways of scheduling the other two.) Clearly, as we proceed from one lot to two lots, two lots to three lots, and so on to n lots, selecting the most economic schedule at each step, less and less cost is incurred in stockholding because the lots are increasingly small. However, at some point as we go from n lots to (n + 1) lots, the resulting decrease in the stockholding cost will be more than offset by the additional cost of placing the one extra order. The optimal order schedule, with the n lots, will consequently have been found.

Before proceeding to sub-section 9.6.5, which is concerned solely with purchase discounts, a word should be said about the relative merits of the four lot sizing rules above. Computer simulation experiments with the various models indicate that the Wagner-Whitin algorithm gives results which are markedly superior to (i.e. more economic than) those obtained through the EOQ rule when the net requirements being planned are particularly uneven. As might be supposed, Wagner-Whitin's superiority over the POQ and Part Period rules is much less pronounced.[27] In the wider context, the manufacturing manager should remember the JIT philosophies referred to earlier. Constant pressure should be brought to bear on set-up times, delivery delays and the rest. Small lots and a dynamic schedule are synonymous with responsiveness in manufacturing and planning. Their achievement should be pursued with vigour.[28]

---

[27] See Chapter 12, Figures 12.1 to 12.7 in Vollmann, Berry and Whybark (1988), op. cit. R.G. Brown appears somewhat sceptical of the more sophisticated of the lot-sizing methods — see Chapter 10, Appendix in Brown (1982), op. cit.

[28] Smaller batch sizes and more flexible, more dynamic scheduling mentioned in the text are prime advantages stemming from the use of Advanced Planning Systems — see Chapter 12.

9.6.5 The Least Unit Cost Ordering Procedure

The *least unit cost ordering procedure* may be used for determining whether additional purchased material should be ordered so as to take advantage of a discount being offered by a supplier. It revolves round the calculation of the unit cost of material for various quantities which might be ordered to satisfy requirements over a succession of future periods, taking into account (a) the amount ordered, (b) the price to be paid, (c) the cost of placing the order, and (d) the cost of holding stock not required until later. What is of interest is whether the eventual cost per unit of the material finally incurred is smallest if the buyer orders sufficient material to qualify for the supplier's discount. The procedure is illustrated in Table 9.4. The eight columns in Table 9.4 have the following meanings:

PER: Period number. Typically for purchased material, periods are weeks. Note that Period 4A denotes a point during Period 4 at which the cumulative requirements exactly equal the quantity which must be purchased to qualify for the discount, taken here to be 100 units.

REQ: The requirement for the purchased material in the period specified, in units. Note the lumpiness of the period-by-period needs.

C. REQ: The cumulative requirements (i.e. the accumulation of REQ, period by period),

£ORDER: The cost to place an order, taken here to be £8.00, and fixed regardless of the quantity ordered.

£PRICE: The unit price of the goods, taken here as £10.00 each up to 100 units ordered, and £9.50 each for orders of 100 or more. (As stated, the discount price break occurs during Period 4.)

£CARRY: The stock-carrying burden at the end of each period, accumulated from period to period. The value is calculated from the amounts of stock and the lengths of time it is held until needed. The cost of stockholding is here put at 0.03 of the value of the

Materials Planning

units held, per period. (Thus £500 of stock held for two periods = £500 × 2 × 0.03 = £30). Note that unlike part period balancing in sub-section 9.6.3, all of the material is assumed to be consumed at the start of the period in which it is required. So, for example, the stockholding cost in Period 1 is zero, not £100.00 x 0.30 x ½, since the 10 units needed in Period 1 are deemed to be consumed immediately.

£C. COST: The cumulative total cost at the end of each period, being the sum of the ORDER cost, the CARRYing cost and the acquisition cost (i.e. REQuirements × PRICE).

£C. PER UNIT: The cost per unit of the goods — i.e. the cumulative total cost divided by the quantity purchased.

Table 9.4: The Least Unit Cost Procedure for evaluating a Discount

PER	REQ	C. REQ	£ORDER	£PRICE	£CARRY	£C. COST	£C. PER UNIT
1	10	10	£8.00	£10.00	£0.00	£108.00	£10.80
2	30	40	£8.00	£10.00	£9.00	£417.00	£10.40
3	50	90	£8.00	£10.00	£39.00	£947.00	£10.50
4A*	10	100	£8.00	£9.50	£45.60	£1,003.60	£10.00
4	40	140	£8.00	£9.50	£79.80	£1,417.80	£10.10

* At some point during Period 4, it does not matter when, the unit price of the material drops to £9.50 because of the discount.

To illustrate the workings out, consider Period 3 (i.e. the third row of figures in Table 9.4). Fifty units of the material are required in the period, so that the cumulative total requirements up to this point are 90 units (10 + 30 + 50). The cost to place the order is £8. The carrying cost at the end of Period 3 is:

i) For Period 1: zero (all 10 units are used up at the start of Period 1);

ii) For Period 2: 30 units x £10/unit x 0.03, carried during Period 1 = £9.00;

iii) For Period 3: 50 units x £10/unit x 0.03, carried for Periods 1 & 2= £30.00;

iv) **Total:** £39.00.

The total cumulative cost at the end of Period 3 is consequently the purchase price (90 units at £10.00 each) + the ordering cost (£8.00) + the carrying cost (£39.0), or £947.00. This is £10.50 per unit ordered. Looking at the complete results, the cheapest unit cost is obtained when 100 units are ordered, obtaining the supplier's discount.

Whatever the figures may show, the ordering of more purchased material than is needed in order to obtain a discount should be done with great caution. Larger quantities than are needed can engender uncaring attitudes to quality if "there is always material to work on", and there are dangers previously mentioned regarding engineering change (Section 3.5). On the other hand, danger or no, the purchase of extra material at a discount may be astute business, whether arising from a one-off opportunity, whether made normally in the supply marketplace or whether secured at the negotiating table. But it does mean that the cost of raw material stockholding attributable to each company buyer should be monitored month by month and regarded as one of the measures of his performance.

Chapter 10

Closed-Loop MRP

10.1 Defining Closed-Loop MRP

The outcome of materials planning is the creation of manufacturing and purchasing plans, each tagged with its required start and finish date.

In a small number of companies, those with relatively lengthy, distinctive manufacturing steps, such a materials plan is sufficient to enable actual manufacturing and purchasing to proceed at once.[1] But for most companies, the materials plan is merely the starting point to the further creation of a manufacturing schedule specifying work centres, operations, priorities and times. This activity is described in detail in Chapters 11 and 12. The final schedule of manufacture at this more detailed level may well differ somewhat from the broader materials plan. Clashes between manufacturing jobs in competition for common resources and the requirement to control the day-to-day workload, perhaps making use of input/output analysis (11.2.3), may lead the production planning manager to bring some jobs forward and push others back (though always with one eye on the master schedule in doing so). Whether the company has fine-tuned the materials plan in this way or not, the passage of time in all companies, not simply in those required to prepare schedules, will inevitably give rise to certain departures from the original expectations: customer de-

---

[1] See Chapter 9, opening remarks (paragraph 2).

mand not as forecast, manufacturing jobs completed early or late, supplier difficulties, machine breakdowns, and so forth.

One means of response in planning to the passage of time and the events of manufacturing and purchasing is to update the materials data accordingly and simply formulate a new plan, the reformulated plan naturally taking into account the latest stocks and the latest state of work in progress on the factory floor. The differences between the new plan and the former plan are drawn to the manufacturing manager's attention in the form of messages and instructions — that is, changes to previous dates and quantities that have been made or are now required to be made by the planner in the new plan are output on the VDU screen and in printed reports. In a nutshell, the system of feeding back data, then reformulating the materials plan and displaying messages relating to differences from the superseded plan constitutes the famous *closed-loop MRP*. "Closing the loop" refers to the feeding back of data to the MRP system, especially data relating to stock balances, manufacturing plans that have been started and plans that have been completed. The "MRP system" is a stringent canon of rules that has been developed over many years governing materials planning, plan management and — above all — plan rescheduling.

Strictly, the acronym MRP is derived from *materials requirements planning*, and is the closed-loop system described in this Chapter. The term originated in the United States in the 1970s, where its subject matter acquired a considerable following.[2] The addition of further components to MRP by 1980, especially the master schedule, and a belief by its exponents that it represented the way forward for American industry, led to its rechristening as MRPII, *manufacturing resource planning*.[3] The promotion of MRPII in litera-

---

[2] The first reference to materials requirements planning appears in an IBM publication in 1971 by Joseph Orlicky, George Plossi and Oliver Wright, while the first reference to closed-loop MRP was by Oliver Wright in 1974 (*Production and Inventory Management in the Computer Age* – known as "The Orange Book"). Preceding all publications, however, was the development by IBM from 1965 of its PICS system and the later application of PICS facilities within a number of companies in Racine, Wisconsin.

[3] Oliver Wight (1981), *MRPII: Unlocking America's Productivity Potential*, Oliver Wight Publications Inc. The late Oliver Wight is regarded as the father of MRPII (and therefore of ERP, *enterprise resource planning*). This book may be obtained through the Oliver Wight Organisation (UK Office in Gloucester).

ture and by consultants, training companies and software houses was subsequently carried out with a zeal that was not to be well-matched by the system's success. MRPII is heavily supported by software —there are over 100 proprietary packages on the software market. The term itself has now become something of a catch-all, so much so that it is impossible to know what a manufacturing manager quite means when he says he "uses MRP".

A subject somewhat apart from the logic of closed-loop MRP is the way in which data relating to manufacturing and purchasing "events" are indeed fed back into the system — i.e. the mechanics through which the loop is closed. Here, in order to update the system's database, data relating to an event is entered by the person responsible onto a VDU screen corresponding in format to the type of activity that has taken place. That is, there is a different VDU screen layout for each type of event that requires to be notified — for example,

- *Activity type 11* — the withdrawal of stock for a job;
- *Activity type 14* — start of job;
- *Activity type 17* — receipt of raw material from a supplier;
- *Activity type 21* — the return of material to stores ... etc.

The formatted data and its transmission to the computer are each referred to as a *transaction*. A pictograph depicting transaction processing and the conveyance of information from a shop floor to a system database is given in Figure 11.10. Pitfalls in the general procedure for doing so are discussed in sub-section 11.5.1 and Section 18.3. To anticipate that discussion, attention is drawn here to the essential disconnection of the physical world and the computer system. If those responsible for entering transaction data fail to do so, or do so wrongly, or do so late, the real world continues unchecked. The system, by failing to reflect that world, then rapidly loses credibility and usefulness.

10.2 PLAN TYPES IN MRP

Refer back to Chapter 9. Figure 9.3 illustrates 12 plans involved in the manufacture over six periods of an electric toothbrush. Discussion at the end of Section 9.2 to which the Figure relates centres around manufacturing responsibility: one of the 12 plans is for a master scheduled item, six are for other manufactured components and five are for purchased materials.

MRP also classifies plans into three types, but their nature, names and purposes are very different from the familiar ones in Section 9.2. In MRP, plan classification is solely concerned with the rules applied by the system and to be applied by system users with regard to plan manipulation including, particularly, plan rescheduling. A full appreciation of the three MRP plan types and the differences between them is essential to an understanding of closed-loop MRP. The three plan types are: (1) a *scheduled receipt* (also known as an *open order*); (2) a *planned order*; and (3) a *firm planned order* (also sometimes known as a *fixed planned order*). They are described in sub-sections 10.2.1 to 10.2.3.

10.2.1 The Scheduled Receipt (Open Order)

A *scheduled receipt*, or *open order*, is a plan that has been released, physically, for execution — a plan now under manufacture on the shop floor or in transit from a supplier. Data held by the computer relating to a scheduled receipt include the product code; the quantity of material involved; the plan identification number; the date the plan was started, or released; the date manufacture or supplier delivery is due; and the date manufacture or delivery is needed (these last two dates might be different for reasons explained in due course). The scheduled receipt might be created by the planner at the VDU from scratch. More usually, however, it will be created by "releasing" a planned order or firm planned order (i.e. releasing for manufacture). That is, on its commitment to physical manufacture, the classification of the planned or firm planned order is changed to that of a scheduled receipt.[4] (In effecting the release, the planner may take the opportunity, if he so wishes, to change the dates, quantity or lead time of manufacture of the original plan. The identity of the components re-

---

[4] In some MRP systems, the creation of a scheduled receipt from a firm planned order leaves the firm planned order extant. If so, the planner must himself delete it. It is never necessary to delete planned orders since the system itself will do so, as explained in Section 10.3.

Closed-Loop MRP 335

quired for manufacture may also be changed if material substitutions are to be made or a special bill of materials used.)

The manufacturing manager may also change the date a scheduled receipt already in progress is due for completion, or the quantity associated with it that is expected to be manufactured. If a manufacturing job on the shop floor is to be split (see 11.4.2), the scheduled receipt on the system must also be correspondingly converted into separate plans. When the manufacturing job has been finished, a transaction relating to the stock produced and the identification number of the scheduled receipt now completed must be transmitted to the system. When this has been done, the scheduled receipt on the system is "downdated", an amusing jargon term in MRP meaning that it is deleted (downdated being the opposite of updated).

Note that while the manufacturing manager or shop floor supervisor is permitted, through the system, at the VDU screen, to make any change he wishes to a scheduled receipt, the logic, or arithmetic, of the MRP system itself is not. In particular, and most importantly, *the system cannot directly change the due date or quantity of a scheduled receipt.* Consequently, the date a scheduled receipt is due to be completed may differ from the date the system calculates that it is needed — see Section 10.3.

Shortly before the moment of actual release of a scheduled receipt for a manufactured item on the system, the planner will normally make a check online at the VDU as to the availability of the component materials needed for actual manufacture. (Note, however, that a scheduled receipt can still be released even if certain of the required components are shown on the stock records to be unavailable. For one thing, there may be a *lead time offset* on a particular component, meaning that it is not required until the manufacturing job has been underway for a specified time. A further exception to the general rule relates to rework.[5] A rework job is

---

[5] *Rework* means the machining of components again to correct nonconformances in the original manufacture, or the reworking or re-treating of substances, including food and chemicals, to correct a quality problem. In industry generally, because it is a tiny part of manufacturing activity and does not have a place in mainstream procedure, rework is all too often dealt with casually, leading then to occasional blunders. An example might be a failure to subject a reworked item to analytical or performance checks.

represented in MRP by a scheduled receipt but one generally having no component allocations at all.) After the component availability check, the component quantities are moved from *available,* or *free, stock* status on the stock record to *allocated stock* status. (In this sense, scheduled receipts are to allocations what planned and firm planned orders are to gross requirements.) The identification number of the scheduled receipt is associated on the stock records with the quantities of stock so allocated. Following allocation, the MRP system will generate a picking list for the stores supervisor to enable the physical withdrawal of stock to proceed. Note that removal of the need to kit parts physically until they are needed for imminent manufacture cures a major operational headache. Kitted parts require additional space and security, and items in kits are frequently subjected to unauthorised and disruptive "robbery" for jobs other than the ones for which they are intended. Kitting on the computer by means of available and allocated stock categories is hardly an exclusive feature of MRP, of course. It is a facility easily provided when the very difficult matter of obtaining high stock records accuracy has been achieved — see Sections 18.3 and 18.4.

For purchased parts, a scheduled receipt is released by the buyer prior to the raw material due date, the buyer taking into account the time needed to communicate the data to the supplier and the delivery lead time of the material. Naturally, for convenience, all requirements from a particular supplier are collected by the MRP system into a single multi-line purchase order.

In MRP, if a plan is not a scheduled receipt, it is either a planned order or a firm planned order.

10.2.2 Planned Orders

As we shall see in the rules of MRP rescheduling, to be dealt with in Section 10.3, *planned orders* are created to satisfy a product's remaining gross requirements only after account has first been taken of the product's on-hand stock and any scheduled receipts and firm planned orders that may be in existence. The planned orders are generated by the system automatically, as described in Sections 9.5 and 10.3, and as illustrated in Tables 9.1 and 10.2. The planning rule which is to be applied in determining the plan quantities is associated with the product's basic data, having been assigned by the manufacturing manager from a small library of alternative rules provided as part of the overall system.

The mechanism of automatic plan generation ensures that from the viewpoints of logic and the projected stock balance, the due date and the need date of a planned order are one and the same. (The planned order's required start date is its due date offset by the product's standard manufacturing lead time.)

When MRP is run to produce a new materials plan, *all planned orders from the previous plan are deleted and a new set is formulated automatically through the logic of the projected stock balance.* The production control manager and manufacturing manager should review the differences between the new plan and the old one to assure themselves that the new plan is feasible. (To assist in this task, a small number of MRP systems generate messages highlighting any such differences.) Any subsequent reconversion of a plan to its previous form by a manager will necessarily involve the reconverted plan having firm planned order status. One reason for reverting may simply be that the new plan is technically impractical while the old one was not. A reason for going some way to reconversion might arise because a small change in gross requirements has caused a quite disproportionate change to plans that will be a trouble to deal with. This "partial reversion" is discussed further in sub-section 10.2.3 and illustrated in Figure 10.1.

In MRP, if a plan is not a scheduled receipt or a planned order, it is a firm planned order.

10.2.3 Firm Planned Orders

While a planned order is generated by the system, a *firm planned order*[6] by contrast is created by a planner at the VDU. In doing so, the planner is able to specify a non-standard manufacturing quantity and other non-standard plan attributes, and to determine the start and due dates of the firm plan himself. The planner may also specify the use of an alternative bill of materials, that a product

---

[6] A misunderstanding not uncommon in manufacturing industry is to confuse an MRP firm (planned) order with a *customer firm order* (i.e. a sales order from a customer that may have been confirmed in writing). The two phenomena are not connected. If the company wishes to ensure that a firm customer order will definitely be met on the date promised, it should book it into the available-to-promise schedule as described in sub-section 7.2.1.

normally made in-house is to be purchased, or that a purchased product is to be made in-house. (If an alternative or new bill of materials is to be used, the planner must determine and manage the firm planned order's demands on the required lower level components himself.) The data relating to a firm planned order held on the computer include a unique plan identification number.

A firm planned order is normally created by the planner *ab initio*, although it is quite possible for him to change the status of a planned order to firm planned, perhaps so as to bring the plan's start and due dates under his own control. Control comes about because, as with a scheduled receipt, *the firm planned order's dates and other attributes cannot be changed in any way by the logic or arithmetic of the MRP system itself*. The planner may himself make any change he wishes to it, but the system cannot. (Consequently, again as with a scheduled receipt, a firm planned order may have a due date that is different from the date the system calculates is needed — Section 10.3.)

The principal reason the planner may create firm planned orders, overriding planned orders and circumventing standard planning rules, is so as to impose his own schedule on the materials plan.[7] By using the information presented through the system, but in addition bringing to bear his own knowledge of plant, priorities and capacity, the planner is able to formulate a better shop floor plan or overcome a problem anticipated in fulfilling ordinary planned orders generated by the system. Because of the rule that firm planned orders cannot be changed or rescheduled by the system, any such imposed local schedule can be guaranteed to be preserved following the generation of a new materials plan when the MRP system is rerun.

A further reason mentioned in sub-section 10.2.2 for creating a firm planned order is to undo the disproportionate effects of a

---

[7] The principal reason given in the text for creating a firm planned order (i.e. to achieve a more practical schedule) is different from the reason for placing a time fence on the master schedule horizon, freezing MPS plans (to stabilise the business plan) — see sub-section 6.5.2. The firm planned order and the frozen MPS plan are treated similarly by the logic of the projected stock balance in their respective systems, however. A frozen MPS plan is commonly, if not quite correctly, referred to as being "firm" in master scheduling software output.

Closed-Loop MRP

small change in gross requirements. An example of such a change was given in Figure 9.17 and in the second table in Figure 9.18, which are reproduced for convenience as the top and second tables in Figure 10.1. Disregarding for a moment the immediacy of the dates, the change which has occurred in the second table is that the gross requirements in Period 2 have increased from 24 units (top table) to 35 units (second). Rather than persevere with the disrupted schedule in the second table brought about by the change, the planner decides to create a firm planned order in Period 1 for 51 units (i.e. 40 + 11), to replace the previous planned order for 40 units. This is shown in the bottom table, and is denoted by the superscript "F" attached to the plan quantity of 51. On rerunning the system, the schedule of plans in Table 3 is obtained, in which the planned orders from Period 2 to Period 8 are identical to those in the original schedule in Table 1.

Figure 10.1: The Creation of a Firm Planned Order (Table 3) to Reverse the Effects of a Change in Gross Requirements

Period	1	2	3	4	5	6	7	8
Gross Req'ments	7	24	34	31		14	27	
Stock ^{OH} 0	33	9	15	24	24	10	23	23
Plans	40		40	40			40	

Period	1	2	3	4	5	6	7	8
Gross Req'ments	7	35	34	31		14	27	
Stock ^{OH} 0	33	38	4	13	13	39	12	12
Plans	40	40		40		40		

Period	1	2	3	4	5	6	7	8
Gross Req'ments	7	35	34	31		14	27	
Stock ^{OH} 0	44	9	15	24	24	10	23	23
Plans	51^F		40	40			40	

10.3 THE MRP RESCHEDULING LOGIC

As explained in Section 10.1, the essence of closed-loop MRP is the feeding back of data about stocks and work-in-progress and the subsequent calculation of a revised materials plan. The general principle of plan generation is the same as described at length in Chapter 9. That is, starting at the top of the bill of materials, plans are formulated to meet gross requirements according to a given planning rule for each product, using the logic of the projected available stock balance. The plans so calculated at one level give rise to gross requirements for manufacturing components at the next level down in the bill, and so on.

What is different about closed-loop MRP from generic materials planning is the possible presence of scheduled receipts and firm planned orders, and the immutable rules stated in the preceding Section that the system is not allowed to alter the details of such plans, including, particularly, their quantities and timing.

10.3.1 The MRP Standard Display

Before showing how scheduled receipts and firm planned orders take part in materials planning within MRP, what must first be described is the format in which the data are presented and manipulated. The so-called *MRP standard display* is given in Table 10.1. It will be seen that the layout and terminology are very similar to the layout and terminology previously employed in Table 9.1, Section 9.5. The difference between the two is in the last line. In the MRP standard table, what is shown are the dates manufacture is to *start*, not the dates, as in Table 9.1, when it is to finish. "Planned order release" means the commitment of manufacture to the shop floor so that work can begin. Consequently, in the standard display, it is necessary to offset the proposed, or intended, manufacturing quantities from the plan starting dates to see when the manufacture will be finished and the completed stock will be available for use. Thus in Table 10.1, from the information displayed at the top left of the Table, we see that the lead time of manufacture is one period. Consequently, the planned orders for 35 units each shown in the last line in Periods 1, 4 and 7 are due for completion and ready for use in Periods 2, 5 and 8. The one-period offsets of all three plans have been indicated in the Table by small arrowed lines to illus-

Closed-Loop MRP

trate what is meant. The advantages of showing the plans at their release dates rather than at their completion dates are that it brings the attention of the planner to the durations of time over which manufacturing activities are to take place, and shows clearly the dates by which lower level components must be available.

Table 10.1: The MRP Standard Display

Plan Lead Time: 1 per.
On-Hand (OH): 12 units
Past Due (PD): 0
Plan: Lots of 35 units

		Period							
		1	2	3	4	5	6	7	8
Gross Requirements		9	13	17	8	6	15	5	10
Scheduled Receipts	PD: 0								
Projected Stock Balance	OH: 12	3	25	8	0	29	14	9	34
Planned Order Release		35			35			35	

$35 + 3 - 13 = 25$ units

Although it is important, the MRP standard display is unfortunately not readily memorable except by rote learning. As an aid to this, Figure 10.2 gives the terms in the display alongside their meanings in common parlance.

Figure 10.2: Terms in the MRP Standard Display and their Common Meanings

Standard Display	Meaning
Period	Daily or weekly time bucket (see Section 6.2)
Gross Requirements	What is needed (for the next level up)
Scheduled Receipts	What is already coming (from the shop floor)
Projected Stock Balance	What is available (at the end of this period)
Planned Order Release	What (and when) production is planned to start

10.3.2 The Rescheduling Assumption

If a materials requirement for a product is generated in closed-loop MRP and there are scheduled receipts or firm planned orders in existence relating to it, the system invokes what is known as the *rescheduling assumption*. The rescheduling assumption states that planned orders will not be created to fulfil a product's gross requirements until use has been made, first, of existing scheduled receipts (considered in chronological sequence) and, second, of existing firm planned orders (considered again in chronological sequence). Thus, after taking account of on-hand stock in the normal way, the projected stock balance calculations begin by regarding the existing scheduled receipts and then firm planned orders as being in two "pools" or "repositories" of potential production plans. In calculating the product's projected stock balance, the procedure determines the ideal period when each scheduled receipt is needed, considering them one after another in sequence, and then the ideal period for the release of each firm planned order, again considering them one after another in sequence.[8] Only when the consequences have been determined of deploying all scheduled receipts and firm planned orders at the calculated ideal times does the system turn to the normal generation of planned orders to satisfy any gross requirements that may remain. Since the system cannot, of course, change the actual dates when the scheduled receipts and firm planned orders are due, the differences between their current due dates and the dates that it has calculated that the plans are ideally needed are brought to the planner's attention by way of rescheduling messages (see sub-section 10.3.3).

There are two important corollaries of the rescheduling assumption. The second corollary is dealt with in sub-section 10.3.3.

The first corollary is that although the system assumes that the scheduled receipts and firm planned orders will be rescheduled in accordance with the messages, the reality is that until the planner does so reschedule them, they remain precisely where they are. As a result, pending the planner's action, the projected stock will show either a negative or excess balance.

One example of the rescheduling assumption and a negative stock balance is given in Table 10.2. A scheduled receipt is due for

---

[8] It is possible in closed-loop MRP for a scheduled receipt to have a due date later than the due date of a firm planned order. In the operation of the rescheduling assumption, however, any such scheduled receipt is still considered for use and rescheduling in priority over the firm planned order.

Closed-Loop MRP

completion in Period 2, but it is ideally needed to be completed in Period 1 to cover the negative stock balance at that time. The rescheduling assumption holds that this will be done. (The requirement to reschedule the plan in by one period is indicated by an arrow pointing to the left, before the number 50 in Period 2 of the Table.) Since the scheduled receipt, in fact, remains in Period 2, the projected stock balance has fallen to –2 units in Period 1.

Table 10.2: The Rescheduling Assumption and a Scheduled Receipt

Plan Lead Time: 1 per. On-Hand (OH): 16 units Past Due (PD): 0 Plan: Lots of 50 units		Period						
		1	2	3	4	5	6	7	8
Gross Requirements		18	20	19	20	18	10	11	17
Scheduled Receipts	PD 0		←50						
Projected Stock Balance	OH 16	–2	28	9	39	21	11	0	33
Planned Order Release				50				50	

In the case of a scheduled receipt, the rationale for making the rescheduling assumption is that it "must" be easier and more practical to reschedule a plan already on the shop floor than to overcome the problem of the unsatisfied gross requirements and negative stock by creating and releasing a special firm planned order *ab initio*.

A second example of the rescheduling assumption and a negative stock balance is given in Table 10.3. A firm planned order is due for receipt into stock in Period 3, but it is ideally needed for completion in Period 2 to cover the negative stock balance in Period 2 of –8 units. Rather than create a planned order in Period 1 to deal with the –8 units, the rescheduling assumption comes into play and holds that the required rescheduling of the firm planned order will take place. The requirement to reschedule the FPO is indicated by an arrow pointing to the left before the number 50 in Period 2 of the Table. Since the firm planned order, in fact, still remains due for release in Period 2 and receipt into stock in Period 3 until action is eventually taken by the planner, the projected stock balance in the Table falls to –8 units in Period 2.

Table 10.3: The Rescheduling Assumption and a Firm Planned Order

Plan Lead Time: 1 per.
On-Hand (OH): 30 units
Past Due (PD): 0
Plan: Lots of 50 units

		Period						
	1	2	3	4	5	6	7	8
Gross Requirements	18	20	19	20	18	10	11	17
Scheduled Receipts [PD: 0]								
Projected Stock Balance [OH: 30]	12	–8	23	3	35	25	14	47
Planned Order Release		50^F		50			50	

One reason for making the rescheduling assumption in the case of a firm planned order is, again, that it "must" be easier and more practical to reschedule a plan already in existence, and for which components have been planned, than to deal with the situation by generating a new planned order with an earlier date. A second reason is that if such an earlier plan were indeed to be formulated for the standard manufacturing lot size, excessive stock would be created. This is illustrated in Table 10.4, derived from Table 10.3, in which a firm planned order has been initiated and inserted by the planner for release in Period 1 to overcome the shortfall of 8 units seen in Period 2. Although there is now no longer a negative stock balance, comparison of the projected stock balances in Tables 10.3 and 10.4 shows considerably higher stock holding in the second case.

Table 10.4: Failure to Follow the Rescheduling Assumption and the Creation of Excess Stock

Plan Lead Time: 1 per.
On-Hand (OH): 30 units
Past Due (PD): 0
Plan: Lots of 50 units

		Period						
	1	2	3	4	5	6	7	8
Gross Requirements	18	20	19	20	18	10	11	17
Scheduled Receipts [PD: 0]								
Projected Stock Balance [OH: 30]	12	42	73	53	35	25	14	47
Planned Order Release	50^F	50^F					50	

Closed-Loop MRP

The new order created by the planner in Table 10.4 for release in Period 1 must be firm planned, as stated, since this is the only way of overriding the normal materials planning logic. It is characteristic of the use of firm planned orders in closed-loop MRP that once firm plans are employed in one part of a product's schedule, their use is likely to become progressively widespread elsewhere in order to prevent the materials planning logic from taking over and disrupting the position the planner has worked out. Note in this case that the original firm planned order due for release in Period 2 is not now required for release until Period 4, so that a "reschedule out" message will be output by the system when MRP is rerun (see the arrow pointing to the right in the Table).

10.3.3 The MRP Messages

The second important corollary of the rescheduling assumption relates to the importance of the rescheduling messages. As the negative and excess stock balances in Tables 10.2, 10.3 and 10.4 attest, such messages in closed-loop MRP to reschedule plans due to changes in requirements are not polite suggestions. They are important obligations either to follow the directives indicated or, at least, to evaluate the situations individually and embark on alternative courses of action that will resolve the problems revealed.

After the materials plan is reformulated under MRP, system messages are generated at the VDU and as a printed report. As implied in the preceding paragraph, the most important of them are those relating to the required rescheduling of scheduled receipts and firm planned orders. One might add to these, in many systems, the highlighting of differences between the new planned orders and the previous ones. Rescheduling directives and warnings of change are most important because they concern the balance of supply and demand of materials into and within the company and the ultimate achievement of the master production schedule. (It should be noted that "rescheduling out" and planned order cancellations are as important as "rescheduling in" if the subsequent plans at all levels are to constitute a valid representation of real needs. Besides which, rescheduling out releases capacity for plans that are to be rescheduled in.) Messages individually identify the plans concerned, distinguishing between manufacturing and purchasing, and typically employ different phraseology depending on the immediacy of the action recommended ("expedite" v. "reschedule", for example).[9]

The manufacturing manager contemplating the use of closed-loop MRP rather than APS as described in Chapter 12 should think most carefully about the nature of the MRP rescheduling messages. Their appropriateness to his manufacturing and planning environment is a mirror of the appropriateness of the MRP system itself. *Appropriate* does not mean *logically correct*. It means suitable to the tempo and reality of actual manufacture. Rescheduling imperatives issued in manufacturing environments with lengthy, disjunctive materials processing steps, each occupying many days, may be adhered to closely, and are one thing. Daily messages relating to manufacturing in short steps, organised in a complex way that necessarily must take careful note of machine availability and intricate planning rules, are another. It was said before the advent of Advanced Planning Systems that "much of the value of MRP is derived from its rescheduling capability".[10] Compliance with the rescheduling messages is the instrument of that capability.

The closed-loop MRP system also outputs messages relating to scheduled receipts which are past due, and planned orders and firm planned orders which have reached their start dates but which have not yet been released to manufacture. Even if the activities to which they relate have in fact taken place, the messages will, of course, result if staff responsible have failed to submit data transactions about them.

Warnings are also issued about "unsatisfied" gross requirements, these being requirements for which no plans have been created, and other planning oddities capable of detection by the

---

[9] The degree to which scheduled receipts and firm planned orders require to be rescheduled is known in the jargon of MRP as system "nervousness". Most proprietary MRP systems allow the planner to suppress individual messages if any of them relate to a reschedule of less than a certain number of days.

[10] Oliver Wight (1981), op. cit., Appendix 5, p. 533.

Closed-Loop MRP

scanning of data by the system.[11] (See the non-creation of plans in the treatment of equivalent products in sub-section 9.4.9.)

10.3.4 Rescheduling and the Firm Planned Order

Despite the value of the firm planned order described in sub-section 10.2.3 for overcoming local scheduling difficulties, its use in MRP should be sparing. For one thing, small or large changed requirements within the system are liable to arise continually throughout the bill of materials. When they do, it is quite likely that the need dates of very many firm planned orders will similarly change, each one then giving rise to a rescheduling message. Reading and evaluating messages and subsequently taking the required rescheduling action at the VDU may become burdensome if there are a great many of them to attend to.

There is also the matter of delay. Since the firm planned order is by definition concerned with manufacture in the future, it might be argued that the comparatively short period between the recalculation by the computer that rescheduling is required and the subsequent processing by the computer of the planner's response via the VDU is of little practical importance — change in manufacture is inevitable. If the materials plans at levels lower in the bill of materials than the product being rescheduled by the planner are all ordinary planned orders, all lower plan changes will subsequently be calculated and communicated immediately the re-run of the system takes place. However, if plans at lower levels are also firm planned orders, there may be a one-day hold-up at each such level for the planner to reschedule the firm plans at that level as well. It is true that a hold-up at each level is not inevitable. Thus a minor change in the gross requirements for a product may be absorbed because of the work-in-progress associated with the manufacturing plans formulated to meet them. This is illustrated in Figure 10.3, which is taken from the top two tables of Figure 10.1, but with a

---

[11] In an article "Reschedule the Reschedules you just Rescheduled — Way of Life for MRP?" for the *APICS* magazine, Hal Mather, the popular American educationist and speaker on MRP and production control, suggests that the manufacturing manager should investigate the ultimate causes of rescheduling messages and eliminate those causes having their origin in over-sophistication of the system and poor data accuracy (see also sub-section 9.6.2, Footnote 25).

planning rule applied of 200 units rather than 40 units. The change in gross requirements in Period 2 from 24 units to 35 units makes no difference to the need for the single plan in Period 1.

Figure 10.3: A Change in Gross Requirements but no Change in Plan

Period	1	2	3	4	5	6	7	8
Gross Req'ments		7	24	34	31		14	27
Stock [OH] 0		193	169	135	104	104	90	63	63
Plans		200						

Period	1	2	3	4	5	6	7	8
Gross Req'ments		7	35	34	31		14	27
Stock [OH] 0		193	158	124	93	93	79	52	52
Plans		200						

Nevertheless, if firm planned orders are heavily used throughout the system, many delays will result and a number of them could be very severe. In the worst cases, as many runs of the MRP system as there are levels in the bill of materials may be needed to evaluate change fully. Inevitably in such cases, especially if MRP replanning takes place infrequently, such as only every week or every half week, the manufacturing manager will turn away from the closed-loop MRP system to informal methods and MRP will lose credibility and usefulness.

It might be thought that the use of the firm planned order is at least free of problems at the purchased materials level. Because there is no level lower in the bill, the hold-ups just warned against cannot occur. Even here, however, widespread use of firm planned orders brings its problems. Buyers can become overwhelmed by rescheduling messages and may lose control in evaluating and communicating changed requirements to suppliers. Ideally, then, in purchasing, leaving aside use of the period order quantity rule described in sub-section 9.6.2, purchase requirements should be planned orders, communicated to suppliers by electronic means. A freeze period and semi-freeze period might be agreed with each supplier. A freeze period means that no changes will be made to the supply schedule, say, for the immediate week ahead. A semi-freeze period (perhaps for one week beyond the freeze) permits change, but with the purchasing company bearing any extraordinary costs the supplier may incur in making it (see sub-section 16.1.3, Step 4).

Note that the potential for delay in rescheduling firm planned orders, caused by changes to gross requirements at successively lower levels of the bill of materials, does not have its equivalent in the rescheduling of scheduled receipts. The components required for the manufacture of scheduled receipts have already been allocated and so are unaffected by changes to the due dates of the products under manufacture.

10.4 TOTAL REGENERATION AND NET CHANGE

In Section 10.1, the need was mentioned for promptness and accuracy in closing the loop by the submission of data transactions relating to the completion of manufacturing plans and the completion of similar events. An allied matter is the question of the subsequent replanning of the system in the light of the revised data. Three options offered by MRP software vendors are *total regeneration*, *batch net change* and *continuous net change*.

Total regeneration of the materials plan means what it says. All previous planned orders and previous gross requirements are deleted, and the materials plan is rebuilt, completely, level by level, starting with the master plan at Level 0, and taking account of available and allocated stock balances, scheduled receipts and firm planned orders. In the sweep through the system down to the raw materials, messages are also assembled relating to scheduled receipts past due and firm planned orders not reported as having started but which have passed their start dates. Although it is a factor of rapidly diminishing importance, total regeneration of the system occupies considerably more time on the computer than net change. More pertinent is that until the system is indeed rerun, the plans, stocks and gross requirements maintained by it are somewhat out of date and the system thus has correspondingly less value as an online source of data. The importance of that will depend entirely on the use the manufacturing manager, planner, shop floor supervisor and purchasing manager put it to with regard to short-term planning and scheduling during the day, after the overnight MRP run.

Under net change, whether batch or continuous, replanning and recalculation are confined to elements of the materials plan which have changed or which may have changed. If a transaction is processed that affects such data relating to a product as its available stock balance, allocated stock, planning rule, scrap, scheduled receipts and so forth, or which may have done so, or which may give rise to a rescheduling message, the product is "marked" for net change. Net change itself is simply the subsequent localised replanning of the product: the deletion of its planned orders; the netting off of its available stock; employment of the rescheduling assumption; and the final calculation of new planned orders. The replanning is followed by the recalculation of the gross requirements for the product's lower-level components and the plans to meet them, in case they have been affected by the change as well, and the processing if necessary of any such further lower levels.[12]

Because net change processes only those products that are affected directly or indirectly by recent transactions, special procedures must be provided to ensure that the identities are obtained and reported on of all scheduled receipts that are past due and all firm planned orders that have missed their start dates.

In *batch* net change, a list of products marked for localised replanning is accumulated. On initiation of the procedure — say, every hour or every half-shift — the list of data is processed as a batch. MRP systems capable of batch net change can also be run in total regeneration mode.

---

[12] Identification of a product's lower level components in net change is obtained by immediate access to them on the bill of materials file, not by the normal level-by-level method described in sub-section 9.4.1.

Closed-Loop MRP

In *continuous* net change, the replanning of a product is performed immediately after it has been marked.[13] Continuous net change systems can be run as batch net change and in total regeneration mode.

THE ABCD CHECKLIST

The late Oliver Wight suggested, not entirely seriously, in 1977 that MRP users might be assigned to one or other of four classes A, B, C and D with regard to their success in implementing and running the system. An original checklist of 20 questions to determine a company's class was expanded to 25 in 1981, the revised questions covering technical capability; the standards maintained of data accuracy; the degree of education undertaken by the company's staff; and — most importantly and obviously — evidence relating to how well MRP really was working at the company whose class was under determination.[14] In a nutshell, the criteria that distinguish the Class A user are that senior management use MRP to "run the business" and that the MRP plans produced through the system really do represent the company's day-to-day working schedule. Class B users see MRP as a production and in-

---

[13] Darryl Landvater and Chris Gray report that users who are familiar with total regeneration and the two modes of net change "are convinced" that continuous net change is superior to total regeneration, although, as the authors point out, there has been no migration by companies from MRP software offering only total regeneration to software with net change (D.V. Landvater and C.D. Gray (1989), *MRPII Standard System*, Oliver Wight Limited Publications Inc., Chapter 2 and Appendix 4). The data files maintained by MRP continuous net change are clearly more accurate and therefore potentially more useful sources of online data. Nevertheless, data enquiries on these files must be *ad hoc* or, at least, limited in scope. A full-scale, online simulation requires the use of a Supply Chain Simulator (Nick Chambers, *Industrial Management & Data Systems*, No. 4, 1996, MCB University Press). A Supply Chain Simulator is capable of performing total regeneration of MRP in just a few seconds (see sub-section 6.3.3).

[14] See Oliver Wight (1981), op. cit., Appendix 2. The original list of 20 questions has now been expanded (with something less than the original humour) to an astonishing 382 questions covering almost every aspect of control within a manufacturing company (Landvater and Gray (1989), op. cit., Appendix 19). The scope of a system encompassing the activities and features in the latest list is far beyond even the original boundaries set for MRPII, and nowadays appears to warrant the title *Enterprise Resource Planning*, ERP.

ventory control tool, rather than for business. Limited use only is made of the system by Class B users for shop floor scheduling. Companies assigned to Class C have not really closed the loop. They use MRP as a means of stock ordering rather than manufacturing planning. Class D companies are the outright failures. For them, MRP is working only in the IT department, even though it is observed that a Class D company will have spent as much money in implementing the system as a Class A company.

Chapter 11

Shop Floor Control[1]

11.1 Work Scheduling

The materials plan derived from explosion of the master production schedule consists of individual plans each with a start day and due day and the quantity of material to be manufactured. An assessment of the capacity needed to fulfil it will have been made through rough-cut capacity planning during the formulation of the MPS (Section 6.6). The method used for making the rough-cut assessment will depend on the nature of the company's plant. If capacity is plentiful or capacity management can be extensively deployed, a simplistic tool such as the load profile may have been used (sub-section 6.4.1). If capacity is short or if capacity management is not an option because of fixed output quantities, capacity requirements planning or an APS in simulation will have been used to assess the potential material plan's viability (Section 6.6). As also explained previously, the preparation for limited, broad brush capacity management may have already taken place because of rough-cut planning by the time the new materials plan is launched.

As stated in the opening remarks of both Chapter 9 and Chapter 10, a number of companies are able to use the materials plans

---

[1] Note that the following topics, which might equally have been covered in this chapter, are dealt with instead in Chapters 12 and 15: advanced planning and scheduling (Chapter 12); job sequencing (sub-sections 12.2.3 and 12.3.4); fast changeovers (Section 15.3); plant organisation (Section 15.4); and equipment maintenance (Section 15.6).

as a direct work schedule (though always subject first to input/output analysis, as described in sub-section 11.2.3). A small number of modifications to ease local capacity difficulties may be made by the production control manager before the manufacturing jobs, or manufacturing orders, are finally released to the plant. An illustration of the use of a typical materials planning trick to solve a potential capacity problem by plan modification is given in Figure 11.1. In Figure 11.1, the work centre making Component C has insufficient capacity for 2,000 units in a particular time period. By investigating the on-hand stock position of C and its gross requirements, it is seen that a manufactured lot reduced to as little as 600 units would be sufficient to support overall requirements. In different circumstances, Figure 11.1 might have shown a more complex solution to the overload on the work centre manufacturing C through reduction of the plan amounts for A or B, so effecting a reduction in turn of Component C's gross requirements.[2]

Figure 11.1: Gross and Net Requirements before a Solution of the Overload on Capacity for Component C

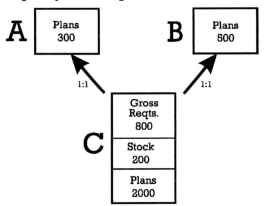

In the majority of companies, generation of the materials plan leads at once to the preparation of a work schedule that encompasses the jobs which are to be undertaken and the suitability and

---

[2] The purchasing manager as well as the manufacturing manager should take note of the example in the text illustrated by Figure 11.1. If a supplier announces that a delivery will be late, the buyer should be able and willing to attempt to solve the problem through the planning system after investigating gross and net requirements and after pegging up to the manufacturing plans giving rise to them, as well as by traditional supply expediting.

Shop Floor Control

availability of planned resources and labour. In small companies with comparatively few jobs and resources to juggle, preparation may be sufficiently straightforward that it can be done adequately by the shop supervisor or foreman after the jobs' release to the shop floor. For the rest, the schedule must be built in the planning office and will include as a minimum requirement the identities of the jobs to be started; their start times; the jobs to be completed; their required completion times; the processing operations to be performed; and the expected durations of the jobs at each operation. The principal data file used in schedule preparation is the *routings file*, described further in sub-section 11.5.3. Also required are machine capacities, rules relating to running jobs at the various work centres, set-up times and other data relevant to a particular shop environment. If schedule preparation is done manually, a company may develop special forms and worksheets over the years to assist in the process. Manual scheduling requires experience and a certain agility of mind.

A new schedule is usually produced each week by the production control manager and his staff following a materials planning run, the schedule typically extending two weeks into the future. The time required for the task of preparation varies considerably from company to company: a few hours, a day, two days . . . Shorter times are likely to be associated with manufacturing that progresses along fixed routes or with jobs that take predictable times. If manufacturing routes are diverse or very lengthy, or if likely processing times are difficult to calculate, or if there are complex rules, such as ones relating to job sequencing, preparation time is longer and the work schedule finally formulated will be less stable — *less confident*. Less confident means that stated job arrival times and lead times are less likely in the event to be adhered to. This does not imply a free-for-all, but it does mean that the disciplines of job release to the shop, input/output analysis and the application of job despatching rules, described in Sections 11.2 and 11.3, assume considerable importance in schedule management and in the general control of the shop. If the planner is not to escape this regime by turning to an APS, as described in the paragraph following, he may at least wish to exert top-down control over the situation by the adoption of closed-loop MRP, since the essentially simple techniques described in this Chapter are not sufficient alone to ensure that what is being done continues to relate closely to the master schedule.

The task of scheduling is now rapidly being taken over by computer-based *advanced planning systems*. The job of scheduling is changing accordingly to the management, manipulation and support of such systems. Characteristics of a work plan produced by computer are the exactitude of the calculated schedule, even when the manufacturing environment is complex, and the closer adherence to it achieved by the shop floor supervisor and operators. (Many of the rules described in Sections 2 and 3 may in fact be incorporated in the scheduling software.) APS systems are dealt with separately in Chapter 12.

Typically in many factories, the manufacturing manager will hold a meeting towards the end of the week with the production control manager, shop floor supervisor or foreman and others to determine finally which jobs are to be released the following week and to confirm arrangements, especially those concerning the deployment of staff. Issues discussed at the meeting may include the transfer of staff between manufacturing departments; overtime and annual leave; and the contracting of work to outside companies.

11.2 THE RELEASE OF ORDERS TO THE SHOP

11.2.1 Lead Time and Queue

Manufacturing lead time is the time which elapses between a job's being released to the shop floor and the subsequent availability of the manufactured items at the place they are required. As we have seen previously, especially in Chapter 9, product lead time is a central item of data in planning. Hitherto, however, it has simply been assumed that lead time is "known". It is now necessary to take a closer look at it.

Although there are exceptions and special cases, the principal components of lead time are *queue time* (waiting for the machine to become free), *set-up time*, *machine running time* (i.e. making the items), *wait* (waiting to be moved) and *move* (moving the items to where they are next required). The second and third of these are governed by technical considerations not of concern in this Chapter. The fourth and fifth are of some concern to shop floor control to

Shop Floor Control

the extent that poorly organised materials handling in the shop will needlessly add to lead time. But to a very great number of manufacturing personnel, especially those familiar with the job shop, it seems that the dominant and often troublesome component is queue time. It is not unknown in certain engineering job shops for queue to comprise 80 per cent or more of total lead time.

The justification put forward by the manufacturing manager or shop floor supervisor for maintaining extensive queues on the shop floor, and making no attempt to reduce them, is that the release of work to manufacture from planning is uneven, or that it is liable to unevenness. Efficient manufacture requires a steady flow of work if an alternation of idle machines and temporary bottlenecks is to be avoided. If queues of jobs are held in the shop, the supervisor can himself guarantee that his workload will be steady and that idle machines and unemployed labour will be avoided.

Even in a well-controlled manufacturing environment employing rough-cut capacity planning, available-to-promise and the rest, there is truth in the contention that uneven manufacturing requirements can exist, if these are judged purely by the succession of orders required to be made and their start dates and need dates. Put in different words, if the workload to be undertaken by the plant were to be set down in tabular form for each successive day, based entirely on the dates calculated through materials planning, the variation in the magnitude of the productive effort required from one hour to the next would very likely be unacceptable to the shop supervisor, or, at least, would be difficult for him to cope with efficiently without the maintenance of a queue of jobs already on the shop floor to act as a buffer.

11.2.2 The Vicious Circle

The action required to smooth the flow of work to gateway work centres[3] and nullify the reason for maintaining queues of them is for the production controller himself to manage the rate of job release to them in the most careful manner, sometimes holding jobs up, sometimes bringing them forward. The mechanism for managing this process is *input/output control*. Before illustrating it

---

[3] A gateway work centre is one where a starting operation is performed, immediately following job release — say, a turret machine or press.

through the input/output control table, some cautionary tales must be told of lead time inflation and hyperinflation in companies which did not understand the fundamental link between lead time and queue and which therefore failed to adopt the simple corrective procedures necessary.

The ABC Company quotes a six-week lead time for its range of products. A flurry of orders is received, all of them being released to the shop floor on receipt. As a result, the observed lead time rises to eight weeks. That is, customer orders placed on the promise of the six weeks lead time are now beginning to fall behind schedule. Enter Manager. Manager addresses the lead time and customer delivery problems by adopting what in practice is the worst course of action possible: he increases the standard lead time of the company's products from six weeks to eight weeks. The materials planning data is revised and customers are informed. *Think, Manager, think!* Customers' own planning systems, primed with the revised lead time for supply from the ABC Company, immediately generate a rush of new purchase orders, since the outcome of their calculations now indicates that the orders which were to have been placed over the next two weeks have become past due. On receipt of this influx at ABC, the new orders are released to the shop floor, increasing the queue of work still further, and forcing the observed product lead time up from eight weeks to ten weeks — and so on, round the vicious circle. Only the pressure of competition and lost business brings a halt to the process. Competitive pressure will be removed if there is a shortage of capacity in the industry generally, since companies with shorter lead times which gain business because of them will themselves then become overloaded, so that in turn they also will start to quote longer lead times. In a heartfelt article in 1970 about this phenomenon, Oliver Wight rebukes the then management of American gray iron foundries:

> It is not uncommon for gray iron foundries to be quoting lead times of 36 to 48 weeks to make castings that can easily be produced in five working days.[4]

---

[4] Oliver Wight (1970), "Input/Output Control: A Real Handle on Lead Time", *Journal of APICS* (see Chapter 7, footnote 3), Third Quarter.

Lead time inflation does real harm in a number of ways. Planning and control are more uncertain, in part because of the longer master schedule and sales forecasting horizons needed to support them. Jobs in the mighty queues of work are rescheduled by the foreman and the progress chaser, not by the production control manager, perhaps in response to the pleas of individual customers to expedite their orders. The priorities of jobs in the queues do not reflect up-to-the-minute needs. Formal scheduling collapses. Also harmful is the creation of a great burden of stock on the shop floor. It is harmful because physical manufacturing problems and solutions to them are less easily seen when there is excessive work-in-progress on hand, especially problems related to quality. (An occurrence that is also not unknown is an old job becoming lost because new ones have been piled up in front of it.) And, as we saw in sub-section 9.6.1, stockholding costs money.

The problems spoken of above clearly also have their equivalent in the purchased materials area when the company's own suppliers notify increases in their standard delivery lead times. Long supply lead times caused by lead time inflation are often not well understood by buyers. Many mistakenly believe that a quoted lead time is solidly devoted to manufacturing itself, unaware that an order will merely join an extremely long queue. Indeed, they may believe a lengthy time is, somehow, a good thing, since (they think to themselves), *with all that time to devote to the order, there can be no doubt that delivery will be precisely on time as promised.* (They are also unaware that their suppliers' queues are constantly subjected to reshuffling by progress chasers and the rest.) Further harm is done here: at least in one's own manufacturing facility, a most urgent, unanticipated requirement even with a long lead time can be rushed to the heads of queues and fulfilled. This action cannot be forced on a supplier when an unanticipated raw material requirement arises.

When the standard, official lead time of a product is reduced, there is an exact reversal of the effect above. The shorter time is input to the materials planning data and customers are informed. In the case of ABC above, a lead time reduction from six weeks to five weeks will mean that new orders will dry up for a week, with a commensurate effect on ABC's shop floor queues. (Since customers now also find that they have placed their more recent orders with ABC too soon, they could in fact cancel them, though this is rarely done.) The virtuous circle of lead time deflation must, however, be accompanied by the installation of input/output control to stabilise and control the future flow of work into the shop.

11.2.3 Input/Output Control

The purpose of input/output control in the engineering job shop is to control queues, and thereby simultaneously to control manufacturing lead time, work-in-progress and the utilisation of machines. The relationship between queue, WIP and machine utilisation for intermediate (i.e. non-gateway) work centres is described in sub-section 11.2.4. The question of target queues at intermediate work centres is also discussed there. However, the assumption made in 11.2.4 about the pattern of arrival of jobs at these work centres is not valid for gateway work centres, since the release of jobs to the gateway work centres is directly controlled by the production control manager through the input/output table. Consequently, queues serve no purpose at starting operations on the shop floor and should therefore be non-existent or, at least, very small.

Figure 11.2 is a simple diagram illustrating the rationale of input/output control and the terminology employed. To maintain a level of queue (denoted by the level of liquid in the funnel), input and output must match. Input can be increased only if output is increased correspondingly.

Figure 11.2: Analogy of I/O Control and Terminology

Shop Floor Control

The input/output table is a convenient device for arranging and analysing the data needed to manage shop floor loading and queues. The format of the table is given in Table 11.1, as it relates to a certain work centre. The figures are standard hours of work and the time periods weeks. Four past weeks (–4 to –1) and the current week (0) are shown, and, in this case, four future weeks (+1 to +4). It is supposed that the planned inputs of hours of work for Weeks 0 to +4 have been obtained by averaging the total materials planning load for each of these five weeks. Actual inputs (Weeks –4 to –1) will have been obtained from transactions relating to work completed at this work centre, submitted through the shop floor data collection system. The planned outputs for Weeks 0 to +4 are the week by week totals of standard hours of work the shop floor supervisor or foreman has specifically agreed to produce. Every possible effort must be made in input/output control to avoid using an output rate based on wishfulness rather than on cold calculation. A maximum output rate often used is an average of recent confirmed output achievement, referred to as the *demonstrated output*, or *demonstrated capacity*. The actual outputs will again have been obtained through the shop floor data collection system. (If the shop undertakes relatively lengthy jobs, data should be collected and included for partial job completions.) The queue in standard hours at the end of a period is calculated according to Equation 11.1.[5]

$$\text{Queue at the end of this period} = \text{Queue at the end of the previous period} + \text{Input over the period} - \text{Output over the period} \qquad \textit{Equation 11.1}$$

---

[5] In a very real sense, Equation 11.1 is self-fulfilling, since all times relating to input and output over the period are standards, recorded on the database. If the output of a work centre deviates from plan, and yet it is properly manned and appears to have been running normally, it is possible that the standard times of jobs have been poorly estimated and should be re-estimated.

Table 11.1: Input/Output Table Showing Hours of Work at a Work Centre

	GATEWAY WORK CENTRE NO. 250									
	Week beginning DD/MM/YY; all figures standard hours									
Week		−4	−3	−2	−1	0	+1	+2	+3	+4
Planned input		100	100	105	105	106	110	110	100	100
Actual input		102	100	114	101					
Planned output**		102	102	102	102	104	104	104	104	104**
Actual output		98	100	110	108					
Planned queue		5	3	6	9	10	16	22	18	14
Actual queue	7	11	11	15	8*					
Cumulative input variance		+2	+2	+11	+7					
Cumulative output variance		−4	−6	+2	+8					

* To begin the calculation of the planned queue from weeks 0 to +4, the actual queue at the end of week −1 is used. ** The planned output in weeks 0 to +4 is the average output "demonstrated" to have been achieved in weeks −4 to −1.

Note that Table 11.1 also shows the cumulative variances of planned inputs v. actual inputs and planned outputs v. actual outputs, each for Weeks −4 to −1. The cumulative variances are a quick indication of whether a work centre is running consistently ahead of plan or behind. "Control limits" are usually set for the cumulative variances of each work centre. If the cumulative variance then exceeds the control limit (say, ±20 hours in the case of Work Centre 250 in Table 11.1), the shop floor information system draws the fact to the production controller's attention so that he can investigate the matter. Control limits should be tightly set so that potential problems can be addressed early on, before they become crises. The normal way of scrutinising the input/output table is, first, to examine output — is the work centre executing its capacity plans? If input is as planned but output is down, there may be a technical problem.

11.2.4 Queues at Intermediate Work Centres

In a number of manufacturing environments with a regular pattern of work — i.e. not in engineering job shops — the queue element of job lead times may be readily controllable through careful work scheduling, as intimated in Section 11.1. In the job shop, with manual scheduling, the synchronisation of job arrival times and departure times at intermediate rather than gateway work centres may be difficult to accomplish, so that strict adherence to such a schedule, even if formulated, may be particularly difficult to maintain. Nonetheless, even though there is some loss of control regarding work centre input because of the seemingly sporadic arrival of work from other work centres, input/output reports and plans should still be prepared for intermediate work centres just as they are for the gateway work centres. The main values of the I/O table for an intermediate work centre are as a monitor of the target queue there (see below) and as a monitor of the general equilibrium between input and output. In this last regard, if the table indicates the work centre is starting to run out of work, the shop floor supervisor may be able to expedite jobs due into it from other work centres. If it seems that it is beginning to fall behind, it may be possible to relieve the pressure on its capacity by some means such as by the authorisation of overtime; by the transfer into it of additional labour; or by the diversion of work due into it to some alternative work centre.

Although a degree of input and output management is thus possible, the pattern of arrival of jobs into the intermediate work centre remains liable to unevenness, justifying the maintenance there of a queue to ensure a steady rate of work and the satisfactory utilisation of physical resources. The question is: *how much queue should there be?* To answer it, it is necessary, briefly, to turn to queuing theory.

In the terminology of queuing, the situation of jobs waiting for processing on a machine constitutes a *single-channel* system with one *server*. Suppose that the rate of arrival of jobs into the queue for the machine is in accordance with the Poisson distribution, as usually it will be. (This distribution was previously encountered in sub-section 5.2.1 and Figure 5.2 in connection with the receipt of sales demand. It will be met again in sub-section 14.3.1 in relation to quality.) Suppose further that the various lengths of time the jobs occupy on the machine are exponentially distributed (the distribution usually encountered). For the single server case, it can be shown that in these circumstances the relationship between size of the queue (in terms of the number of jobs waiting) and the percentage utilisation of the machine takes the form illustrated in the graph drawn in Figure 11.3. Queue size is given on the vertical axis and percentage utilisation of the machine on the horizontal axis.

Figure 11.3: Trade-off between Queue and Machine Utilisation (Single Channel Queue with Poisson Arrivals and Exponential Service Times)

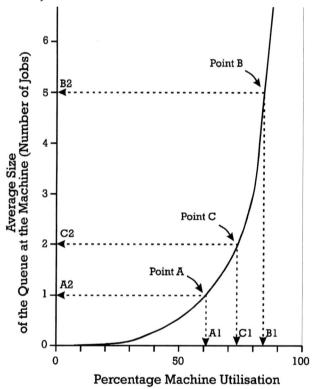

Consider Point A on the curve in Figure 11.3. It will be seen here that the percentage utilisation of the resource denoted by A1 on the horizontal axis is somewhat poor (about 61 per cent). Point A corresponds to a queue size of one job, denoted on the vertical axis by A2, so that it is seen that an average queue of less than this might not be thought economic in terms of machine utilisation. Consider next Point B on the curve. Here, the high, satisfactory utilisation of the machine is denoted on the horizontal axis by B1 (about 84 per cent). However, we might believe that the corresponding size of queue required to give this utilisation, an average

Shop Floor Control

of five jobs, denoted on the vertical axis by B2, is beyond what is acceptable in terms of cost of work-in-progress and the lengths of job lead times that would result. Consequently, we may conclude that to achieve a reasonable compromise between satisfactory machine utilisation and acceptable work-in-progress in the queue, the shop supervisor should aim to be between Point A and Point B on the curve — say, to be at Point C, just before the rapid upwards acceleration of the curve. The percentage utilisation corresponding to Point C is denoted by C1 on the horizontal axis (about 74 per cent), and the queue size, or queue length, by C2 (an average of two jobs).

It will usually take quite some time, involving trial and error and management debate, to establish a happy balance between queues at the intermediate work centres, overall machine utilisation, work-in-progress and manufacturing lead time. To assist the process, it may be useful to express input, output and queue in terms of jobs rather than standard work hours. Table 11.2 is an input/output table similar to Table 11.1, but in which figures have been expressed in terms of jobs not hours. The demonstrated capacity figures have been obtained by averaging and a queue of two jobs is being aimed for.

Table 11.2: Input/Output Table in terms of Jobs (Target Queue is Two Jobs)

INTERMEDIATE WORK CENTRE NO. 350									
Week beginning DD/MM/YY; all figures are numbers of jobs									
Week		−4	−3	−2	−1	0	+1	+2	+3	+4
Planned input		20	18	20	21	17	19	20	19	18
Actual input		21	17	20	19					
Planned output		20	20	20	20	19	19	19	19	19
Actual output		22	18	18	18					
Planned queue		3	1	1	2	2	2	3	3	2
Actual queue	3	2	1	3	4					
Cumulative input variance		+1	0	0	−2					
Cumulative output variance		+2	0	−2	−4					

If the demand on a manufacturing resource exceeds its capacity in the short term, the problem can be overcome by stock building (planned through the master schedule, sub-section 6.5.1), available-to-promise (sub-section 7.2.1) and the controlled release of jobs using input/output analysis.[6] If the demand for a resource exceeds capacity on a sustained basis, the problem is normally resolved, ultimately, by the acquisition of further capacity — for example, through sub-contracting, by the purchase of more machinery or by staff recruitment. Short term or long, the means by which the facts are examined is the input/output table, not by the presence of shop floor queues.[7] Until the problem of capacity shortage is resolved, jobs which cannot be released because of the rules of I/O must be held back, in production control, and prioritised as described in the next sub-section.

Personal responsibilities must be amended to support the new regime. The production control manager, who in the past may have been judged by whether or not the work schedule was met, should instead take up the more important duty of maintaining a steady balance between shop floor input and output. Responsibility for meeting schedule must pass to the shop floor supervisor or foreman. There is a joint responsibility held by all managers, including the manufacturing manager, to maintain the agreed and established four-way balance of queue, machine utilisation, WIP and manufacturing lead time spoken of above. The changes must also be explained carefully to shop floor operators, who should have access each week to the I/O data corresponding to their own work centres. Unless such explanation is given, small queues may be interpreted by them as meaning poor customer orders, and they may by subtle means decrease their rates of output.

---

[6] There are close similarities of principle between available-to-promise and input/output control. With available-to-promise, customer orders are booked against a given master schedule (equivalent to a given demand on capacity). With input/output control, shop orders are similarly booked against a given shop capacity.

[7] The OPT advanced planning system dealt with in Section 12.4 could be used to address long-term bottlenecks. Rather mischievously, one must wonder how many companies have turned to OPT and similar sophisticated tools to overcome capacity bottleneck problems that were, in fact, illusory, and might have been solved rather more simply by lead time deflation.

Shop Floor Control 367

11.2.5 Final Order Release

Candidate jobs for release to the shop floor and actual manufacture are clearly those in the planning schedule which have reached their start dates, the proviso being that the total workload is in accordance with planned input as described above. Even though the company may not be employing closed-loop MRP, the same steps are followed as those described for scheduled receipts in sub-section 10.2.1. That is, the availability of the required components is checked on the stock records and the stock quantities involved are transferred to allocated status. Picking lists for the physical marshalling and transfer of the parts to the shop floor are prepared for use by stores staff. As before, unavailability of components may not mean the abandonment of a job if there is a lead time offset, i.e. if they are not required until part way through manufacture. Far more usually, all components are required in order to start the job. If a particular component is not available in full because of a mistake (often caused by inaccurate stock records) or, say, because of the failure of a supplier to deliver on time, the manufacturing manager and production control manager must decide whether to abandon the job or to proceed, but producing a smaller manufacturing lot than originally intended. Tool availability may also be checked at this stage by reference to a tools database (sub-section 11.5.3). Advance notice of the requirement for job set-up may be conveyed to the shop floor (see sub-section 15.3.1).

Shop floor documentation is also generated as the job is released. The paperwork typically accompanying a job on its journey through the shop comprises a *production route card* and a *shop order identification card*.[8] The route card shows the operations and work centres of the job and the sequence in which operations are to be performed. Other information may include the machines and tools to be used and the operations' expected running times. The shop order identification card constitutes a permanent record for

---

[8] The shop order identification card generated at the time of order release may be bar-coded. The most important advantage of bar-coding seems to stem not from fast or error-free recording (welcome though they may be), but from the very capture of the data, and the consequent elimination of errors due to lost transactions or their late submission. See Error 4, Table 18.2.

identification, authorisation and traceability purposes. Provision may also be made at this point for retrieving and printing engineering drawings from a drawings database.

If analysis of the work schedule in conjunction with the planned workload destined for a particular work centre shows that not all jobs can be released, because of the restrictions of input/output control or, perhaps, because of a clash of requirements for a single resource, it is necessary to hold some jobs back. To determine which jobs are to proceed and to determine the order of job release if this is to be different from the chronological order of their start dates, it is necessary to assign release priorities. The prioritisation of jobs for initial *release* is not the same thing as the despatch or prioritisation of *jobs in queues*, actually on the shop floor, dealt with at length in Section 11.3. It is true that job release priorities may in the event be decided by the job queue priority criteria described in 11.3. However, for initial job release, broader issues are often considered, such as whether the order is for further production or is for spares; or whether there are a number of later orders dependent on this order's completion. If the release of the jobs involves final end-item production, commercial factors may be important, such as the identities of the customers for whom the jobs are intended; each job's eventual contribution to company profits; or whether any of them carries a financial penalty for late delivery. Clearly, a problem in attempting to include commercial considerations such as these is the concomitant need for a weighting scheme in order to balance the factors involved. If a breakdown in a commercial priority system occurs — if the system is clearly seen to be allowing individuals to release their favourites, regardless of their "true" priorities — it is advisable to abandon it and adopt the rules for despatching jobs in queues on the shop floor.

Note that to sustain an even flow of work into the shop according to the I/O plan, it will also be necessary to release jobs earlier than their start dates as well as to delay them. The same scheme as above is used for prioritising jobs for early release, although, before prioritisation takes place, the earlier required availability of the components needed for their manufacture must be checked.

11.3 JOB DESPATCHING RULES (JOB PRIORITISING)

First, a number of distinctions are made in terminology. *Scheduling* is defined here as the process of deciding the start times and finish times of manufacturing jobs in a programme of future work and allocating (finite) manufacturing resources to those jobs. *Sequencing* is the determination of the order in which jobs are to be manufactured on a given resource. Sequencing is therefore included in the activity of scheduling. *Despatching* is the prioritisation of jobs waiting in a queue for a common resource and the selection of each job for manufacture when its turn is reached. Scheduling and sequencing must consider all jobs and all resources simultaneously and are complex activities calling for the use of quantitative procedures. They are dealt with in Chapter 12. Despatching involves the application of rules, for the most part simple, in which some attribute of one job is compared to that of another in order to assess the jobs' relative claims on precedence. In a number of companies employing informal despatching, application of the "rules" might be nothing more than the exercise of the personal judgement of the shop supervisor or foreman. Although no doubt shop floor performance will be better improved by the company's adoption of an APS system or, at least, by reducing the causes of variance through the techniques recounted below, if manual despatching at all is to be undertaken, it is better that a formal despatching rule be applied than the hit-and-miss of an informal one.[9] Job despatching is dealt with in this Section.

The 1960s and 1970s saw very extensive investigation into despatching rules, investigation almost entirely conducted through computer simulation, such that, by the early 1980s, conclusions as to the relative merits and applicability of the alternatives were

---

[9] Dramatic improvements in due date performance are cited when formal despatching rules are employed alongside input/output control — see Figure 11.4 and A.O. Putnam, R. Everdell, G.H. Dorman, R.R. Cronan and L.H. Lindgren (1971), "Updating Critical Ratio and Slack time Priority Scheduling Rules", *Journal of APICS*, Fourth Quarter. The late Arnold Putnam was one-time president of Rath & Strong, long-established management consultants of Lexington, MA.

largely agreed.[10] The four rules now regarded as the principal ones are described in sub-sections 11.3.1 to 11.3.4. "Classic despatching", as it might be called, makes the assumption that there is a certain degree of variance in the performance of activities in a "normal" shop floor environment — for example, that job processing times are likely in the event to be shorter or longer in duration than those assumed in planning, that times to move jobs between operations will deviate from plan and that machines are liable to break down. The correct choice of a despatching rule in these circumstances makes a considerable difference to the performance of the shop floor. Shop floor performance is defined here simply as the degree to which completed jobs are early or late (alternative measures of performance are discussed in sub-section 12.2.3). To analyse performance, data are collected relating to the numbers of jobs so-many days late and so-many days early, and plotted as a frequency polygon as illustrated in Figure 11.4. Figure 11.4 has been adapted from results given by Putnam et al. (footnote 3), and shows the due date performance of a precision components manufacturer before the use of I/O control and formal despatching (11.4(a)) and after their adoption (11.4(b)). In accordance with the precepts of common and special causes of variation, explained in Section 13.2, Figure 11.4(b) shows shop floor performance to be controlled with a due date performance apparently normally distributed around a mean of 0 days (i.e. zero days late / zero days early). In the past ten years, it has come to be accepted by many workers in the field of manufacturing science that the key to high achievement in shop performance as just defined is indeed removal of the factors causing variance in the first place. That is, it has been shown that the removal of variance in the carrying out of shop activities results in improvements in performance which are far greater than those gained by an acceptance of the *status quo* in these matters and the adoption of a best despatching rule. Activities which can contribute to the elimination of causes of variance are thoroughgoing rough-cut capacity planning (Section 6.6), total productive maintenance for machines (TPM, sub-section 15.6.2)

---

[10] J.H. Blackstone, D.T. Phillips and G.L. Hogg (1982), "A State-of-the-Art Survey of Dispatching Rules for Manufacturing Job Shop Operations", *International Journal of Production Research*, No. 20.

and the adoption of SMED and "pull" production scheduling techniques (Sections 15.3 and 15.5).[11] When the shop floor schedule has been well put together and the performance of activities is on time, and all is as planned, job despatching is a mere formality. If everything is done to plan and to schedule, there is no reason to give further consideration to jobs' priorities than is accorded them in formulating the schedule in the first place. Since the manager may believe the day when everything is done to plan to be a little way off in his own factory, however, we turn to classic job despatching.

Figure 11.4: Frequency Polygons illustrating Shop Floor Due Date Performance

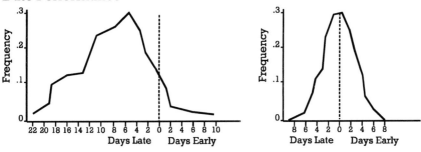

(a) **No formal system**

(b) **Employing I/O control and a despatching rule**

---

[11] In a study using simulation published in 1992 comparing the performance of the four rules in sub-sections 11.3.1 to 11.3.4, and FCFS (*first come, first served*) as a "base line", Steven Melnyk et al. showed that when variance was present, SPT (*shortest processing time* — see sub-section 11.3.4) performed best and FCFS worst (by far) (Steven A. Melnyk, David R. Denzler and Laurence Fredendall (1992), "Variance Control v. Dispatching Efficiency", *Journal of the American Production & Inventory Control Society*, Third Quarter 1992 (date relates to its printing in the Journal of the then British P&ICS, now the Institute of Operations Management)). When variance was removed — i.e. when the environment was controlled — huge improvements were gained in performance as measured by minimum job tardiness, except for performance under SPT. SPT performed worst of all five with no variance because of its lack of logicality in a controlled environment. There is no *reason* to process the shortest job first other than to get the maximum number of jobs through in a relatively *uncontrolled* environment. The authors' conclusion to this study is that researchers in the field would do best to turn their attention to the relative effects on shop performance of eliminating the various elements of variance and away from the development of refinements to despatching rules.

A number of simplifying assumptions are made in the application of job despatching rules — for example, that an operation once started must be completed, that no resource can process more than one job at a time and that all operation times are known in advance. A further assumption that is made, which may be less than acceptable to the supervisors of many shops and which illustrates the difference between scheduling/sequencing and job despatching, is that the set-up times of the various jobs are independent of the order of despatch. If the set-up time of each job is in fact dependent on job sequence, the fact must be taken account of in scheduling and sequencing itself. (The method of so doing is illustrated by Figure 12.8.) Consequently, it is essential for the supervisor in this instance to adhere to the job schedule. Non-adherence to the schedule and the reliance instead on a despatching rule would be quite unacceptable.

An important distinction is made in the descriptions in subsections 11.3.1 to 11.3.4 as to whether each despatching rule is a *static rule* or a *dynamic rule.* A static rule means that the release priorities of jobs are worked out from data inherent in the jobs themselves, independent of activities taking place. Examples of inherent job attributes are the total standard job processing time, from beginning to end, and the total number of operations the job must go through, from beginning to end. With a dynamic rule, priorities are assigned based on data relating to each job's current status, such as the work already completed on it or the time remaining to its due date. The distinction is important because the despatch priorities of jobs under a static rule can be calculated at a moment in time — say, at the start of a day or the start of a week — and require only the most limited feedback of data from the shop floor. The principal static rule is based on jobs' relative processing time requirements, so that if this rule were to be used, the processing time of each job might be conveniently printed for shop floor staff on the job's production route card. The despatch priorities of jobs under a dynamic rule depend for their calculation on the collection and feedback of shop floor data at the time the rule is to be applied.

There are many more despatching rules than the four described below — "earliest release date", "earliest due date", "minimum total float", "fewest operations remaining" and "first

Shop Floor Control

come, first served" are examples of others.[12] The fact that there is not a comprehensive list here does not mean that others should not be considered by the manufacturing manager for his own factory. The suitability and efficacy of a despatching rule is dependent to some extent on the nature and mix of jobs in a particular manufacturing environment. While the four rules given have been found to be superior generally, their potential effect in a particular environment should be analysed through computer simulation before adoption. The member of staff conducting the investigation should have no hesitation in introducing variations and refinements in order to deal with his own shop floor's special characteristics.[13]

11.3.1 Slack Time

Slack time is defined as follows:

(Time due – Time now) – (Processing time still remaining)[14]

Note that the first part of the expression (the time the job is due *minus* the time now) refers simply to elapsed time, and the second part (processing time remaining) refers to machine set-up time and machine running time. Importantly, note further that job queue time, job wait time and job move time are not directly incorporated in the rule.

---

[12] See Ray Wild (1980), *Production and Operations Management*, Holt, Rinehart and Winston, p. 267; and James R. Evans, David R. Anderson, Dennis J. Sweeney and Thomas A. Williams (1984), *Applied Production and Operations Management* (International Edition), West Publishing Company, p. 613.

[13] Examples of refinements to both the slack time per operation and critical ratio rules in the late 1960s by Hughes Aircraft; Stromberg-Carlson; Jones & Lamson Machine; Moog; and Black & Decker are given by Putnam et al. (1971), op. cit. A number of the refinements are not in fact particular to these companies, but simply to make the rules' operation robust under all general circumstances.

[14] Rather than "time", the terms "date due" and "date now" are very often used in the definition of slack time, although doing so may suggest, incorrectly, that periods of a day are implied. The definition given in the text, the method of calculation used and the conclusions drawn are independent of the denomination of the periods. A period will be chosen for a shop floor that is appropriate to that particular manufacturing environment. Periods in practice might be days or shifts or hours.

Suppose that the time now is Day 1 and that a job is due on Day 10, and that there are five days of work remaining to be done on it. Then the job's slack time is:

$$(10 - 1) - (5) \text{ days} = 4 \text{ days}.$$

In other words, there are four days in hand with regard to this job. Greatest priority rests with jobs with the smallest slack time. If there are three jobs A, B and C with slack times of 1 day, −3 days and 4 days respectively, they would be ranked in priority order B, A, C. Slack time is a dynamic rule.[15]

11.3.2 Slack Time per Operation

If two jobs each had slack time of four days, but the first had only one operation remaining and the second had two remaining, it would seem that the second job should have a higher priority. Each operation to be gone through brings its own delays, especially if there is a queue at the machine. Slack time per operation is therefore defined as:

$$\frac{\text{Slack time}}{\text{Number of operations remaining}}$$

Greatest priority rests with jobs with the smallest slack time per operation. For the two jobs with slack time of four days but with one and two operations remaining respectively, the slack time per operation quotients are 4.0 days per operation and 2.0 days per operation. The second job therefore has the higher priority. Slack time per operation is clearly also a dynamic rule.

11.3.3 Critical Ratio

Critical ratio is the basis of a further dynamic rule, and is defined as follows:

---

[15] Slack time is the basis of the PERT project scheduling technique for ranking project activities in order of priority. PERT (Programme Evaluation and Review Technique) employs network scheduling, and is used for analysing and managing the interrelated activities involved in large projects. It enables the project manager to answer questions, say, relating to the priorities of the various tasks and the identity of tasks which should be "crashed" (i.e. expedited). PERT was developed in the 1950s in part by the United States Navy from the "Set Back Charts" used in Line of Balance methodology.

Shop Floor Control 375

$$\frac{\textit{Time due - time now}}{\textit{Lead time remaining}}$$

As with the two slack time rules, *time due minus time now* in this expression is simply elapsed time. But what is different and important is that the denominator, the "lead time remaining", is the sum of all five of the elements which go to make up a job's remaining duration, given in sub-section 11.2.1, not just two of them. In applying the rule, jobs with the lowest critical ratios have the highest priorities.

The incorporation of queue time in the critical ratio gives the rule an advantage over slack time per operation. The reason for this is that the standard, or target, length of queue decided for each job, as implied from the target queues and I/O analysis discussed previously, will contribute to the determination of the job's start time and due time (along with set-up, run, wait and move). It is because of queue's contribution to the establishment of the start time and due time that the critical ratio rule is claimed to be superior to slack time per operation. In operation of the rule, if the job is on schedule to meet its due time, so that, among other things, its target queue is being maintained, the job's critical ratio will be 1.0. If the job falls behind (critical ratio less than 1.0), the rule will cause its priority to increase until it catches up. When it has caught up, the balance of the elements set-up, run, wait, move and, of course, queue will have been restored. If the job's progress is too fast (critical ratio greater than 1.0), the rule will cause its priority to decrease until, eventually, the critical ratio is back to 1.0, thus again restoring the queue element of the job's remaining duration.

An argument against slack time per operation is the inconsistency of the priorities calculated resulting from the variability of the durations of the elements of a job's lead time from operation to operation. This is illustrated for a job in Table 11.3, which is on time throughout its life (all figures refer to "periods"). Despite being continually on time, the job's slack time per operation is different at each step. Critical ratio is consistent at 1.0.

Table 11.3: Comparison of Calculated Despatching Priorities when there is an Uneven Spread of Times from Operation to Operation

	Operation 1	Operation 2	Operation 3	Operation 4
Time due *minus* time now (i.e. total remaining lead time)	40.0	34.0	14.0	5.0
Set-up + run time	2.0	8.0	5.0	3.0
Total remaining set-up + run time	18.0	16.0	8.0	3.0
Queue + wait + move	4.0	12.0	4.0	2.0
Total remaining queue + wait + move time (same as the slack time, in the s-t/op rule)	22.0	18.0	6.0	2.0
Slack time per operation	22.0/4 = 5.5	18.0/3 = 6.0	6.0/2 = 3.0	2.0/1 = 2.0
Total remaining lead time (as above)	40.0	34.0	14.0	5.0
Critical ratio	40.0/40.0 = 1.0	34.0/34.0 = 1.0	14.0/14.0 = 1.0	5.0/5.0 = 1.0

11.3.4 Shortest Processing Time (SPT)

SPT is a static despatching priority rule, and if the objective is to process and complete as many jobs as possible, regardless of their relative due dates, it is also an intuitive one. The SPT rule says simply that jobs should be prioritised in order of their total processing times (i.e. set-up time *plus* running time), jobs with the shortest times having the highest priorities. If there are three jobs A, B and C with processing times of ten hours, five hours and one hour, the SPT priority order is C, B, A. Table 11.4a shows the processing times under SPT for the three jobs and the times they must consequently queue, waiting for their turns. The queuing times should be compared to the queuing times in Table 11.4b, in which the jobs are despatched in the opposite order to SPT, i.e. A, B, C.

Shop Floor Control

Table 11.4a: SPT Priority Order

Job	Processing Time	Queuing Time
C	1	0
B	5	1
A	10	5 + 1
Total	16	7

Table 11.4b: Reverse of SPT

Job	Processing Time	Queuing Time
A	10	0
B	5	10
C	1	10 + 5
Total	16	25

Not surprisingly, SPT consistently outperforms other despatching rules in simulation studies in which jobs are considered to arrive in no particular sequence, when measured by the yardstick of minimum job lateness. Two caveats must be entered before its adoption, however. The first is that SPT is liable to give poorer performance in a controlled environment in which adherence to the schedule is important. As remarked earlier, there is, after all, no rationale to SPT other than the objective of processing the maximum number of jobs.[16] The second caveat very obviously relates to long-running jobs. In the standard treatment of queues in queuing theory, the assumption is made that "the calling population", or members of the queue, are dealt with on a first come, first served basis. Because this is not the case when jobs are being despatched by SPT, long-running ones will be pushed to the bottom of the priority list in every queue they join. They will not become totally stuck in a given queue — we see from Figure 11.3 that with a target queue of two jobs, on average a machine is idle for about 25 per cent of its time, meaning that all jobs have been cleared then, long-running and short. However, if the job is a long runner, it will be at the bottom of the priority list at each operation when it joins the queue, regardless of the processing time at that particular operation, and is liable to become progressively more late. And although it falls further and further behind, there is nothing in the SPT rule even to recognise the fact, let alone do anything about it. If SPT is to be adopted, therefore, it is essential that it should be augmented with a supplementary scheme aimed at ensuring that the lateness of long-running jobs does not become un-

---

[16] See Melnyk et al. (1992), op. cit.

acceptable. A simple idea that has been used in practice is to apply the SPT rule for despatching jobs, say, from Monday to Thursday of the week, switching to first come, first served on Friday! Another method that has been employed is to calculate job priorities first by critical ratio, despatching those jobs beyond a certain level of criticality, and then to recalculate the priorities of the remainder by SPT.

The ease of application of despatching rules in the planning office or on the shop floor clearly has a bearing on their relative suitability. Consequently, in choosing a rule, as well as analysis of the simulation investigations mentioned earlier, this matter also should be most carefully considered. The manufacturing manager may conclude that the rule that theoretically would give excellent results when applied is nevertheless beyond his factory's current ability to operate correctly, whether for technical/IT reasons or others, and that experience should first be won with a simpler though less theoretically effective method. An even better course of action than developing expertise in the application of despatching rules might be to follow the advice quoted earlier, and install an APS capability, or, at least, concentrate on eliminating causes of variance in shop floor performance so that formal despatching fades in importance — see Footnote 11, Section 11.3 above and Melnyk et al. (1992), op. cit.

11.4 LEAD TIME MANAGEMENT

The creation of a work schedule from a materials plan requires the use of standard data in order to calculate the potential durations of operations and jobs and hence determine their required start times and due times: *it takes X minutes to set up this machine, the manufacture of those items proceeds at the rate of Y per hour.* As we have seen, queue time is a management variable. Obtaining valid data for the remaining elements of lead time and keeping them up-to-date are extremely important matters, and are considered in the next Section (The Shop Floor Information System). (Standard data may be used for more than work planning. They may be used to

Shop Floor Control

measure labour efficiency or they may form the basis of a bonus and remuneration scheme.)[17]

When calculations show that a planned job will be late, or when a job is becoming increasingly late because of a shop floor problem — a machine breakdown or the production of non-conforming parts, for example — it may be possible for the supervisor or foreman to take special action to help the job catch up. The action might be to overlap operations, to divide one step of manufacture among two or more machines or to expedite the job's interoperation queue, wait and move times. Such action is referred to here as *lead time management*.

11.4.1 Operation Overlapping

Operation overlapping means sending pieces ahead — starting the next operation before the present one has finished. The action has the advantages of clearing space at the location of the first operation and, potentially, utilising idle capacity at the second. The principal reason for taking it, however, is to reduce the standard lead time. The reduction achieved will depend on whether the first operation is shorter than the second or whether it is longer.

First Operation Shorter than the Second

Suppose that the first operation begins at time 0 and has a duration of L1. Under normal circumstances, the second operation will start at time L1. If the first units are sent ahead to the second operation at time T instead, however, the lead time saving is (L1 − T). The saving is illustrated in Figure 11.5, which shows the original durations of the jobs (top sketch) and the revised ones (bottom sketch).

---

[17] Bonus schemes such as those referred to in sub-section 19.2.2 (Footnote 21), based on the achievement or otherwise by operators of standard operation and job times, are less commonly found than they once were, notwithstanding the current vogue for variable pay (see sub-section 19.2.4). When a scheme is in place, it is usually hedged about with complex rules to discourage staff from completing jobs in a time the manufacturing manager or quality control manager believes to be unreasonably short. For example, there may be an "efficiency" limit of 140 per cent of standard, beyond which further bonus is not payable. (The completion of a standard ten-hour job in eight hours would be said to be 125 per cent efficient — i.e. 10/8 × 100 per cent.) A severe problem with bonus schemes dependent on job completion is that shop floor operators are likely to report work to the shop floor information system in a way that is to their own best financial advantage even though it may be contrary to the facts.

Figure 11.5: Operation Overlapping (Operation 1 shorter than Operation 2)

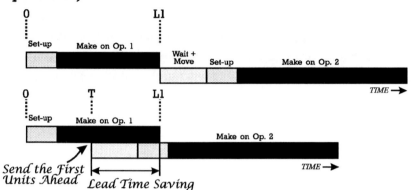

First Operation Longer than the Second

Although the second operation clearly cannot be completed until the last units to be made on the first operation have been moved, received and processed, at least a start can be made at the second operation on the first units before the last ones arrive. One element of the lead time saving is therefore the set-up time of the second operation, since set-up has obviously already been done as the last units arrive. The second element is that proportion of the machine processing time at the second operation that corresponds to the proportion of the units sent ahead and already processed. For example, suppose that the set-up time at the second operation is one hour, and that the total standard processing time at the second operation for a standard manufacturing batch of 10 units is 20 hours. Then if eight, or 80 per cent, of the units are sent ahead from the first operation, such that they will have been processed by the time the last two units arrive, the lead time saving will be 17 hours (1 + 20 hours × 80 per cent). The saving is illustrated in Figure 11.6 for the batch of 10 units, where the wait + move time from Operation 1 to Operation 2 is four hours. It is necessary to take this time into account in order to work out the start time of manufacture of Operation 2. Operation 2 should start so that it is ready for the final lot of two units just as they arrive. As in the previous Figure, the top sketch gives the original situation and the bottom one the revision, showing the timely arrival of the final units.

Figure 11.6: Operation Overlapping (Operation 1 longer than Operation 2)

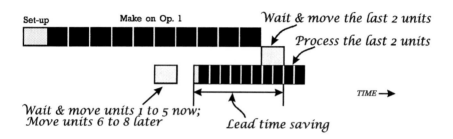

11.4.2 Operation Splitting[18]

If an operation can be carried out at a second, alternative machine and this is free, the job can be split between the two machines. Duplicate tools and a qualified operator must also be available, of course. Because operation splitting entails a further machine set-up, it may be uneconomic to split the job between three machines. Duplicate shop floor paperwork must be obtained from the shop floor data system when the action being taken is notified to it. In addition, materials planning data must be amended, as must the schedule data in the formal shop schedule. The effect on lead time of operation splitting is illustrated in Figure 11.7. The top sketch shows the original operation duration, and the second and third sketches show the durations of the two split operations.

---

[18] Operation splitting is not the same thing as job, or batch, splitting, which refers to holding back part of a manufacturing batch so as to be able to expedite the remainder. Batch splitting is very definitely an emergency procedure only. First, it means double set-ups at every remaining operation. Secondly and more seriously, the part batch left behind is sometimes forgotten or mislaid. Because of this, job splitting is a practice banned in some shops.

Figure 11.7: Operation Splitting

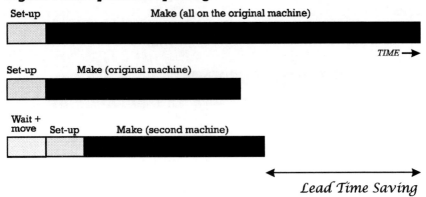

11.4.3 Interoperation Time Compression

If a job is behind schedule but it is particularly important that its due time should be met, it can be flagged as urgent, say, by the attachment of a coloured ticket. When this is done, the job will be automatically assigned top priority in every queue and its movement following each operation accorded special treatment. There is, of course, a limit to the number of jobs that can be handled in this fashion before numerous top priority jobs are found to be competing against each other for preferment and the breakdown of shop floor discipline is threatened.

Theoretically, if it is required to reduce the job time by a certain amount, it is possible to reduce each interoperation queue, wait and move time by a certain percentage to achieve this target.[19] Thus, if the total remaining queue, wait and move time is 20 hours and a reduction of 15 hours is sought, each queue, wait and move element might be reduced by 75 per cent. In practice, the more practical method is simply to eliminate all wait elements, and re-

---

[19] The manufacturing consultant Nick Murphy (formerly with Aurora Ltd., Co Wexford, Ireland) uses the term *window scheduling* for interoperation time compression. The possibility of reducing all interoperation times by a calculated fixed percentage is given in IBM COPICS (Vol. V, Chapter 6, pp. 31–32). COPICS stands for *Communication Oriented Production Information and Control System*, published by IBM in eight (slim) volumes (1972). The IBM order numbers are G320-1974 to G320-1981. Although entitled COPICS, this publication is not a reference manual to the IBM MRPII system of that name. It is a very impressive work on manufacturing control, written from the perspective of a computer system implementation.

Shop Floor Control

duce queue elements by the maximum time possible, until the required lead time reduction has been achieved.

Figure 11.8 shows the reduction of the first three interoperation times in a job in order to bring it back on schedule. The top sketch is the original situation, back scheduled from the required due time and showing the degree of potential lateness. The bottom sketch represents the planned situation if maximum compression of queue, wait and move time is achieved on the first three interoperation times, the reductions achievable having been first estimated by the shop floor supervisor.

Figure 11.8: Interoperation Time Compression

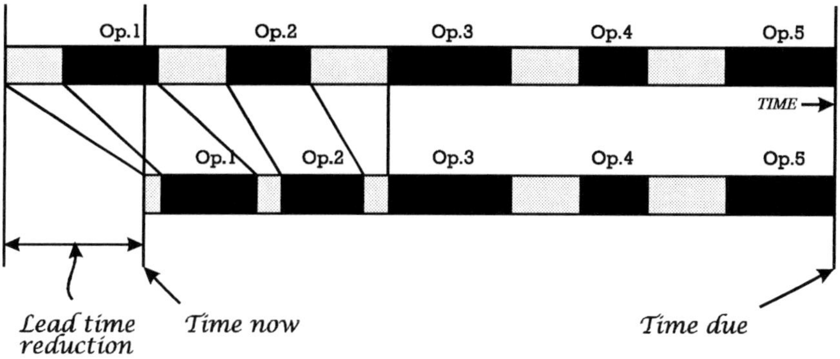

11.5 THE SHOP FLOOR INFORMATION SYSTEM

It is self-evident that shop scheduling, job release, prioritisation and the rest must be supported by a shop floor information system based on accurate and up-to-date data. The design and development of such a system are activities demanding prescience and a high order of capability, however. Experience too often shows that although the technological side of things may be successfully installed — bar-coding, data networks, RDTs[20] and so on — the value of the system in such matters as achieved shop control and the

---

[20] RDTs (radio data terminals) are free-standing, hand-held devices measuring about 8" × 5" × 2" with a two-way data communication capability with the computer provided by means of radio rather than co-axial cable. An RDT is equipped with a VDU monitor (about 3½" × 3½") and, optionally, a bar-code wand.

provision of support for decision-making turns out to be poor in relation to the time and money spent, at least as judged by many manufacturing managers and shop floor supervisors.[21] There are a number of reasons for this disappointment, dealt with mainly in sub-sections 11.5.1 and 11.5.2 below. Sub-section 11.5.3 describes the data files that form the basis of the system.

11.5.1 The Nature and Scope of the System

The first challenge to management in the design and building of this difficult system is to ensure that its qualities will be well matched to what is required of them, and in particular that its complexity will be no greater than it has to be. Three matters are considered: data volume, intended system use and the *tempo* of the manufacturing environment in which it is to be installed. The conclusions reached by a company regarding the effect of each of them on the system's nature must have a determining influence on design and development.

The extent of the volume and breadth of data that are required to be processed is one obvious factor dictating whether a system can be simple or must be complex. In manufacturing, a company with shallow bills of material and short lead times may need to track and control fewer than a hundred shop orders at any one time. The support technology and the scope of the computer transactions that thus need to be provided may be quite modest. A major company with deep bills of materials, complex operation routes and long lead times may need to control as many as 5,000 shop orders at any time, requiring that it employ more powerful technology to capture data and that it provide a wider range of transac-

---

[21] One reason for failure in the installation of shop floor information systems in the past was the availability of government grants in this area. A small company accepting a grant may have believed it was to "acquire" a shop floor information system simply by obtaining the hardware and installing a software vendor's package. Government hand-outs distort judgement. If shop floor information objectives are clear and there is management commitment, as described in sub-sections 11.5.1 and 11.5.2 of the text, the system will finance itself; if not, it will not. For a reflection on the role of government in industry at a somewhat higher level, see Sir Geoffrey Owen (1999), *From Empire to Europe*, Harper Collins, Chapter 17.

tions within the system to deal with the very great diversity of shop floor events liable to be encountered.

A more important differentiator between the need for a simple system and a complex one is its intended mode of use by the shop floor supervisor or his staff. Is the system to be used merely for limited data collection and record keeping? Or will it constitute essential support for decision taking from hour to hour throughout the day on the shop floor? If the company generates work schedules by computer or has fixed route manufacturing plant, the informational demands made on the system are likely to be small. So far as supervisory plan control is concerned, little more is required than to ensure that staff adhere to schedule and report due achievement. If, however, there is a need to review and manage input/output tables; to prioritise job release; to prioritise jobs in queues by dynamic despatching rules; and to split or overlap jobs and then monitor the resulting changes — the shop floor information system that is provided in support must be comprehensive and sophisticated, so much so that it can take three to five years to develop.

There is a final influence on the shop floor information system that may force the company to adopt a simple approach, notwithstanding high volumes of data and the wish of shop floor supervision for decision support. This is the tempo of manufacturing activity. The speed of shop floor events might be such that data relating to normal manufacturing control points simply cannot reasonably be captured (other than by direct machine monitoring). An illustration of potential control points relating to a two-operation job, Job P, is given in Figure 11.9. If the duration of Job P from start to finish is less than (say) two hours, it might be difficult indeed, even with the friendliest technology, to persuade shop operators to submit any transaction in a timely fashion other than "job complete". If the duration of Job P was five days, it would not be unreasonable to require transactions to be submitted relating to all 12 control points if it was agreed that these data were required to support shop floor decision taking.

Figure 11.9: A Succession of 12 Manufacturing Shop Floor "Events"

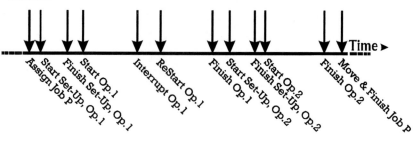

The reason for failure by the shop operator to submit data transactions in a timely way in a fast-moving production environment hardly stems from hostility to the system. It comes about because data recording is very much a secondary task, and one might say something of a chore, compared to production itself. Under the pressure of normal work and job deadlines and, here, the requirement to attend to many things seemingly all at once, the task of data recording is put to one side until time is convenient.

The vulnerability of the shop floor information system in general to human failing arises because, ultimately, there is no actual compulsion even to report a manufacturing event, let alone to do so accurately and promptly. This problem was first mentioned in relation to transaction processing in closed-loop MRP (Section 10.1) and will be encountered again in the maintenance of accurate stock records (Section 18.3). In almost every other computer-based system installed in the manufacturing company except these three, data processing of one sort or another, whether in accessing a file or submitting data via the VDU, is a necessary precursor of action. For the shop floor system, however, action — the activities that lead to and constitute manufacturing itself — has already taken place, and is irreversible, by the time data relating to its reality are to be raised. In summary, data recording is after-the-event and, notwithstanding rules, exhortation and the convenience of technological data recording devices, is in its essence voluntary. The situation is illustrated by the pictograph in Figure 11.10.

Shop Floor Control

Figure 11.10: Schema of the Transmission of Facts from the Shop Floor to the Database

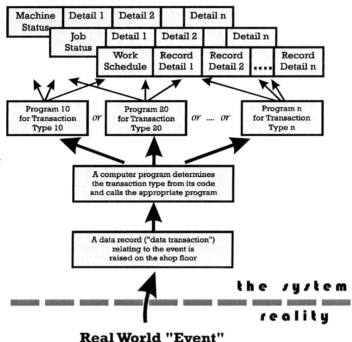

One means of avoiding the dangers of wrong, late or missing transactions, at least for certain manufacturing operations, was mentioned in passing earlier in the sub-section. This is to monitor processes directly by the incorporation within them of switches, sensors, counters or other instruments, these being further connected to a computer. Direct machine monitoring and control is associated in the minds of many manufacturers only with technical process control — for example, with the regulation of machine temperature and pressure — but the attachments can just as well monitor machine running times, stoppages, output rates and the numbers of pieces produced. With the caveat below, their value in prompt, error-free data gathering may be as important as it is in more usual circumstances.

The caveat entered is that fast-moving manufacturing events may defeat even direct machine monitoring, since the information system is not being required to make a technical machine adjustment but to assist a foreman in a decision-making process that also requires reflection and the application of personal judgement. If, in the circumstances of fast manufacture, the system's usefulness will be necessarily confined to providing background facts only, this must be very carefully taken into account when deciding which transactions are to be provided as part of the system — i.e. which events it is necessary to know about and which it is not, or which cannot be assimilated so as to form the basis of timely action.

11.5.2 Design and Development

As previously said, the qualities of the shop floor information system must be well matched to what is required of them. To ensure that this is so, particular attention must be paid in design and development to the involvement of manufacturing staff and to the use of open-ended system architecture.

As we have already seen in sub-section 11.5.1, there is no universal model for a shop floor information system and there are no universal rules. The system to be designed and developed must be attuned to the particular personnel who are to use it and to the particular environment in which it is to operate. It is essential therefore that the system design produced following initial systems analysis by IT staff should be regarded strictly as a draft, to be subjected to the closest scrutiny by shop floor staff including representatives of shop floor operations. Two alternative methods of scrutinising and amending a draft design are by a *structured walkthrough* and by the *inspection method* developed by Michael Fagan.[22] The first involves a detailed, lengthy presentation of the draft system to a sizeable group of potential users by the system designer, centred round dataflow diagrams and structured flowcharts (see Figure 2.5 for an example of a dataflow diagram). Destructive criticism is invited at a structured walkthrough as well as constructive, as an effective means of testing the potential system. Fagan's inspection method is now generally thought to be superior. It first requires the draft system to be meticulously documented by the designer. The

---

[22] Michael Fagan, formerly of IBM and now of Michael Fagan Associates, Palo Alto, CA, has published a number of papers describing his methodology. See especially Michael Fagan (1987), "Advances in Software Inspections", *IEEE Transactions on Software Engineering*, Vol.12, No. 7. The IEEE (Institute of Electrical and Electronics Engineers Inc.) is the world's largest technical professional society. *Inspection* is now accepted as a mainstream tool of quality assurance in software development.

design document is then "inspected", in isolation — i.e. not in the presence of the designer — for correctness, consistency and clarity by a small team led by a "moderator". (The method is now regarded as having far wider applicability as a means of quality control than its use in system verification.)[23]

Convincing evidence that initial designs must be regarded as drafts and submitted either to walkthroughs or inspections is evinced by Figure 11.11.[24] Figure 11.11 is a bar chart showing the relative cost to correct an error in a computer system as the system progresses from design to implementation. In this context, "error" encompasses the misinterpretation of requirements; the creation of potential operational demands on the user which will be difficult to fulfil; failure to provide for needed information; and so on, not simply a gross mistake. The bar chart should be read in conjunction with the fact that some two-thirds of the mistakes and misconceptions lying behind the errors in a typical final system are made at the design stage, and that only 15 per cent of IT project implementations are wholly "successful".[25] The incidence of poor return on investment and disappointment in the development of a shop floor information system in the ordinary course of events was mentioned at the beginning of this Section.

---

[23] Nowadays, in systems engineering terms, obtaining a catalogue of the user's "real needs" and ensuring eventual compliance of the completed project is referred to as *requirements capture*. Requirements capture, it is true, is associated with undertakings very much grander in scale than a shop floor information system — with the development of new aerospace and railway systems, for example — and encompasses such matters as contract bidding, legal and regulatory compliance and project management. Although practitioners are of two minds as to the value of software tools in this field, Ed Yourdan's Cradle Requirements Management System is very well regarded. Ed Yourdan has long been associated with structured design and data flowcharting methodology and was at one point closely connected with Gane and Sarson (see footnote 11, Chapter 2). Cradle is sold in the UK by Structured Software Systems Ltd (3SL).

[24] See Tom Gilb (1988), *Principles of Software Engineering Management*, Addison-Wesley Publishing Co., p.221, and other many other systems engineering authorities.

[25] On software errors, see T.A. Thayer et al. (1978), *Software Reliability*, TRW Series, North Holland, NY. On IT project failures, see Andrew Taylor (2000), "IT Projects: Sink or Swim", *The Computer Bulletin* (Magazine of the British Computer Society), January.

Figure 11.11: Relative Costs in £ to Fix an Error during Development

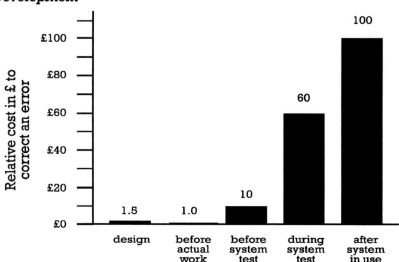

It goes without saying that the final introduction of the system must be preceded by ample, well thought out training and education, including lengthy spells for each potential system user on training versions of the database files described in sub-section 11.5.3. Project leaders consistently place the providing of more training for user staff at the top of their lists of things which, in retrospect, they would have done differently.

One method of building the system is by the employment of *open-ended system architecture*. Advocates of open-ended system architecture point out that as time progresses, system goals, ideas and requirements are liable to change, especially as experience is gained of the new ways of working. Consequently, such advocates go on to say, analysts, designers and programmers engaged in the system's development must continually select methods and adopt solutions which are amenable to change, extension, enhancement and the application of alternative technology.

At the simplest level, open-ended architecture might mean the adoption of object-oriented programming and the writing of small program modules; making provision for very large expansion of data volumes; the setting up of flexible codes and parameters; building networked databases rather than a single, integrated DBMS; and using standard data interfaces. A more radical way yet of pursuing the goal of system adaptability is to embrace the technique of *evolutionary systems development*.[26] The development of a system by evolutionary methods rather than in two or three large stages entails the identification of some 20 or so system delivery steps, each step then broken down to perhaps 100 standalone small tasks. It is claimed for evolutionary development that it avoids the risks inherent in the "big bang" approach. *Evolution not revolution* allows continual review and adaptation and, because of them, the minimisation of risk.

11.5.3 The Information System Datafiles

Four files are central to the operation of the shop floor information system and will be described in turn. They are the *routings file*, the *work schedule file*, the *job status file* and the *machine status file*. They are not, of course, the only ones to play a part in the system.[27] The bill of materials has already been encountered in Sections 3.5 and 9.3, and implicit in its use is a product, or parts, master file, typically holding such commercial data as product name, marketing group membership and the rest. The names of other files not explicitly dealt with here give a further idea of the information system's complexity: the *work centre master file*, *stock records file*, a file for *standard job times* and the *shop calendar*. Two further files again not directly described are the *operations file* and *tools database*. It is usual for systems designers to link these two particular files and the routings file in the way shown in Figure 11.12 in accordance with the IT principle of storing data in one place only. Adherence to the principle simplifies file updating and ensures that all possibility is eliminated of non-matching values occurring for the same item of data stored in two places.

---

[26] Tom Gilb (1988), op. cit.

[27] See *COPICS* (1972), op. cit., Volume VIII, for a comprehensive list of shop floor data files, the data fields likely to be associated with each of them and the principal technical considerations.

Figure 11.12: Cross-Linkages between Three Datafiles

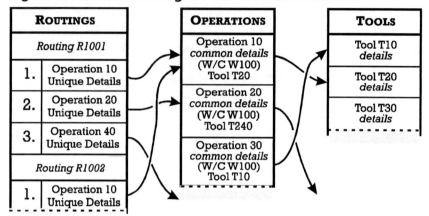

Note, incidentally, that the transactions themselves, which convey data relating to shop floor events to the system's database as illustrated in Figure 11.10, also constitute a file. The data connected with old transactions that have done their work may be arranged as a set of records and displayed on the VDU or in a printout as a *transaction trail* or *audit trail*. Analysis of the transaction trail reveals the activity that has taken place regarding, say, a particular job. Common uses of this information are for the control of costs in large-scale process industry manufacture and for the control of costs in the manufacture of major products made to order. The factory's cost accountant may require to know the set-up and running times for the job in question; the production yield or amount of scrap; rework time; the cost value of consumed components; and the value of expenses and services such as indirect labour (see sub-section 17.4.3). Provided, of course, that the related data are recorded through transactions as part of the shop floor information system, the cost of the job can be calculated through an analysis of the transaction trail. The transaction trail format and its interrogation and interpretation are described in sub-section 18.4.2 in the context of cycle count reconciliation.

The Routings File[28]

Each record in the routings file is keyed on a route code, and specifies a set of manufacturing operations and their sequence. Other data may be held directly on the record (for example, the code of any alternative, equivalent routing). Further data are associated with the record indirectly, via links to the operations file as illustrated in Figure 11.12.

The task of setting up and maintaining the routings file usually falls to the production control manager. If the company is to make use of an Advanced Planning System as described in Chapter 12, the accuracy of the data held must be 100 per cent. Considerable difficulty can be experienced in reaching and maintaining this level, however. Manufacturing operations staff usually know informally "what happens", but cannot always be relied on to record it accurately or may be reluctant to notify changes that have occurred. Two steps must be taken to assert and maintain control over the file if it is accepted that the 100 per cent target must be achieved. First, responsibility must be formally vested by senior management in the manager concerned. Secondly, someone with a detailed knowledge of plant operations and, preferably, with skills in work study must be available to act on behalf of the manager to observe and record routes directly. Such a person cannot be everywhere, so it should be made known to operations staff that when routes change, they have a serious responsibility to follow the notification procedures laid down.

A particular routing code is associated with the product record of a manufactured part. Consequently, when the product code of the part to be manufactured is known, the route of manufacture is accessible from the corresponding routing record on the routings file — that is, the identity and sequence of the manufacturing operations which are to be performed can be retrieved. Figure 11.13 shows the machine/operation sequences of two routes with codes R1001 and R1002.

---

[28] The routings file is also known as the manufacturing routings file, the route file and the process flow file. The term *bill of resources* is also used, to mean the routings file together with the bill of materials.

Figure 11.13: Two Routings File Routes and the Operations Specified

Product Route	Sequence	W/C / Machine/Operation
R1001	1st	W100 M1 Op. 10
	2nd	W100 M2 Op. 20
	3rd	W100 M4 Op. 40
R1002	1st	W100 M1 Op. 10
	2nd	W100 M3 Op. 30

The Work Schedule File[29]

The work schedule file is ultimately derived from the materials plan and the routings file. That is, it is derived from the requirements for various lots of manufactured material and the operations routes involved in fulfilling them. In practice, for the reasons given in Section 11.1, the materials plan must be modified to take account of the practicalities of production. A schedule of jobs is therefore formulated, either manually (in conjunction with such other tools as I/O analysis) or through an Advanced Planning System.

Figure 11.14 shows a manufacturing schedule for the next couple of days relating to two products P50 and P51. It can be seen that one manufactured lot is required of each product. In anticipation of the release of these two plans to the shop floor as manufacturing jobs (or as scheduled receipts, or open orders, in closed-loop MRP parlance), they have been assigned job numbers J200 and J201.

Figure 11.14: The Product Routes associated with Two Products and Jobs

Product	Product Route	Quantity	Start Date/Time	Job
P50	R1001	500	001/08.00	J200
P51	R1002	250	001/11.00	J201

---

[29] This file is also known as the work sequence file (or list); the despatch file (or list); the operations schedule file; and the manufacturing schedule file.

Shop Floor Control

The work centre, machines and operations involved in this manufacture are obtained from the routings file (plus operations file), so that the schedule in Figure 11.14 can be expanded as illustrated in Figure 11.15. Note in Figure 11.15 that the durations of the operations are split between set-up time and job running time, and are obtained by calculation involving standard hours and the quantities to be manufactured. Note also that for the sake of clarity, no allowance has been made in the calculations of durations in Figures 11.15 to 11.17 for staff rest periods and the like.

Figure 11.15: An Expansion of Figure 11.14 Incorporating Operations and Durations

Product	Work Centre	Machine/ Operation	Quantity	Start Date/Time	Duration (hh.mm)			Job
					Set-Up	Run	Total	
P50	W100	M1/10	500	001/08.00	0.30	2.30	3.00	J200
"	"	M2/20	500	001/11.00	0.00	7.00	7.00	"
"	"	M4/40	500	001/18.00	0.30	3.30	4.00	"
P51	W100	M1/10	250	001/11.00	1.00	9.00	10.00	J201
"	"	M3/30	250	001/21.00	0.00	3.00	3.00	"

Further data commonly included in the work schedule VDU display by the designers of shop floor information systems are the identities of the work centres previous to and following each operational step, and the status of the job. Job status may be obtained directly from shop floor data transactions or read from the job status file. It need hardly be said also that the English descriptive names of products and operations are also displayed. As seen from Figure 11.15, the work sequence file is displayed in work centre/equipment/operation sequence order. At the point in time that it is prepared, the schedule will typically extend for two weeks into the future. Then, as time moves on, operations which have passed their expected completion times may be automatically removed from it and the data transferred to a history file, or may be flagged for deletion by the shop floor supervisor. By the end of the first week, the work schedule horizon will have shrunk to a week, and the schedule will be reformulated.[30]

---

[30] When a work schedule is prepared manually, the first amendments to it are likely to be made within a day or two of its issue, and thereafter such that, by the end of the week, it will look very different from its form at the begin-

The Job Status File[31]

The job status file is essentially a rearrangement of the data constituting the work schedule file, augmented however by data captured from the shop floor system transactions relating to each job's reported progress (*job assigned, set-up started* and so on, as sketched in Figure 11.9). It is assumed here that the only jobs to be carried out at Work Centre W100 are J200 and J201. Figure 11.16 is therefore a complete display of the status of jobs at the work centre, four hours after the arrival of J200. Since that event, transactions have been received relating to both jobs as follows: (1) for Job J200, confirmation that all steps involved in Operation 10 have been completed, and that Operation 20 is now running, and (2) for Job J201, confirmation that set-up has been started for Operation 10.

Figure 11.16: The Status of each Job at Work Centre W100

WORK CENTRE W100 : STATUS OF JOBS ON DATE D, 12.00 HRS

Job J200, Product P50, Quantity 500 units

Machine/ Operation	Start Date/Time	Duration (hh.mm)			Status
		Set-Up	Run	Total	
M1/10	001/08.05	0.35	2.30	3.05	Completed
M2/20	001/11.10	0.00	7.00	7.00	Running
M4/40	001/18.10	0.30	3.30	4.00	not started

Job J201, Product P51, Quantity 250 units

Machine/ Operation	Start Date/Time	Duration (hh.mm)			Status
		Set-Up	Run	Total	
M1/10	001/11.10	1.00	9.00	10.00	Set-Up
M3/30	001/21.10	0.00	3.00	3.00	not started

ning. Nevertheless, full recalculation of the schedule even in these circumstances is still likely to be made only once a week, because of the pressure of time and the need to minimise disruption.

[31] The job status file is also known as the shop order status file; the open shop orders file; the open orders file; the scheduled receipts file; and simply as the status file.

Shop Floor Control

Other data are associated with each job record. For example, tool references may be included and, if relevant, details relating to action to be taken in lead time management.

The Machine Status File[32]

A unique code is assigned to each machine in each work centre on the factory floor, and is used as the key to records on the machine status file. The principal purpose of the file is to record which jobs/operations have been assigned to which machines in each work centre by the foreman. (It will be appreciated that a given operation on a job may be capable of being performed at two or more alternative machines in a work centre, and that in some cases a particular machine may be capable of performing two or more operations.) The identity of the shop floor operator assigned to the machine for each operation is also recorded. (Jobs are assigned to machines and operators are assigned to machines, ergo jobs are assigned to operators.)

As well as holding job assignment details, the machine status file is used to record each machine's status as conveyed to the system through shop floor transactions. In the majority of cases, status is inferred directly from the status of jobs — say, *set-up* and *running*. In others, machine status will be the direct subject of the transaction itself. Examples are *start of planned maintenance* and *awaiting repair*. Figure 11.17 shows the machine status file for all machines M1 to M4 at Work Centres W100 at the point in time corresponding to Figure 11.16.

Figure 11.17: Machine Status — Work Centre W100

WORK CENTRE W100 : STATUS OF MACHINES ON DATE D, 12.00 HRS								
Machine	Operation	Status	Operator	Current Job		Next Job	
				Code	Time	Code	Time
M1	10	Set-Up	A.N.Artisan	J201	10.00		
M2	20	Running	M.K.Moiler	J200	7.00		
M3	30	idle	none			J201	3.00
M4	40	idle	none			J200	4.00

---

[32] The machine status file may be referred to as the machine assignment file or the load status file.

An indication of the complexity that underlies the support of the four files described is obtained when even the most limited list is read of the subjects not covered in this sub-section: *job reassignment; lot splitting; operation resequencing; the transmission of requests for assistance; end-of-shift routines; partial job completions; changed time standards; changed routing;* and so forth.

Yet a further aspect of shop floor information that must be considered in the development of the system is the control of materials movements on the shop floor — wait time and move time are, after all, two of the five elements of lead time. The objective of materials handling control is to ensure that the priorities of the jobs to which waiting time and movements relate are upheld and adhered to. Consequently, transactions relating to movements must be input to the system with the same accuracy and promptness as they are to other events. The control of materials movements through the shop floor information system is particularly valuable, though more difficult, when job routes do not follow a predetermined sequence. In many process industry companies, control of material movements is of such high importance that it may justify its own separate, separately developed information system. Justification becomes necessitation when materials planning encompasses multiple sites, as described in sub-section 9.4.2 and illustrated in Figure 9.8.

The permutations and combinations of data obtainable from the system files which might form the bases of reports providing assistance in shop floor control are endless. The task of identifying which to provide is part of the system development process. Examples of reports that might be required were encountered in sub-sections 11.2.3 and 11.2.4 — that is, reports on job queue limits exceeded, obtained through input/output analysis, and on the identities of intermediate work centres likely to run out of work. Assistance in shop control for the foreman is commonly provided in proprietary shop floor information systems for the assignment of jobs to machines through a VDU display of work sequence data and machine status data. The substance of the display is a combination of Figures 11.15 and 11.17. The foreman is able to make the assignment by moving job numbers with the mouse from the left-hand half of the screen (= the work schedule) to the right-hand half (= machine status).

Shop Floor Control

When jobs are assigned to machines in the way described, the foreman himself can be sure that local rules and conditions and quirks of production are taken into account by application of his own knowledge. When the assignment of jobs to machines is being made through the scheduling capability of an APS system, it is necessary to support the process by the provision of a computer library of work centre/machine assignment rules held in the form of executable program code. The identification and enunciation of the rules and quirks which apply to job assignment and the coding of logic to represent them in the software library are major tasks in the set-up and management of an Advanced Planning System, and will be addressed in sub-section 12.2.3. It is to advanced planning that we now therefore turn.

Chapter 12

Advanced Planning Systems

12.1 INTRODUCTION

Although the software systems known as *advanced planning systems* (APS), or *advanced planning and scheduling systems*, typically comprise a number of functional modules — for example, demand forecasting, master scheduling, materials planning and others — and are promoted as integrated solutions to company-wide manufacturing control, at the centre of each one lies a capability to create a practical, detailed plan of work for achieving the company's manufacturing objectives.[1] In short, what is at the heart of an advanced planning system is a finite scheduling capability, just as what is at the heart of an integrated MRPII system is closed-loop MRP.

The role of scheduling in manufacturing is self-evidently to translate the master plan and materials plan into a practical programme of operations — job start and finish times, operations to be completed, their durations and the anticipated occupancy of machines. The presumption in Chapter 11 was that the task of

---

[1] The majority of APS vendors in the market by 2001 seemed to be companies with previously well-established and substantial MRPII/ERP systems which had taken over or merged with vendors of successful third generation "finite scheduling" systems. The work of data integration required to form their unified APS systems was reportedly more difficult and protracted than they had anticipated. See *The Software Users' Year Book*, published by VNU Publications Ltd, or, perhaps better in this fast-moving area, search the Internet, being sure to qualify the acronym APS with a secondary search term such as "manufacturing" or "scheduling".

schedule creation and the management of subsequent events was traditional, or manual. In this Chapter, the presumption, as stated in Section 11.1, is that the task of scheduling is to be performed through an advanced planning system, or, at least, through that part of an APS concerned with the creation of a "finite schedule". (*A finite schedule* is jargon used frequently in the past for a schedule in which the limited availability and nature of manufacturing resources needed to execute it have been explicitly recognised in its creation.)

One result of the taking over of the planning office's role in scheduling by software has already been mentioned in Section 11.1: the job itself of scheduling is thereby changed — *to the management, manipulation and support of the APS*. Three other results of rather greater significance are that:

1. Because of the superiority of APS schedules over those created manually, work-in-progress and material throughput times are very considerably reduced;

2. Because of the speed of schedule generation, simulation of the results of operational decisions is readily performed, enabling the relative merits of alternative courses of action to be compared; and

3. Because of schedule quality, speed of calculation and the provision within the system of interactive, graphically based facilities, the responsiveness of the factory to changes in customer requirements is greatly enhanced.

Advanced planning systems, scheduling and connected issues are considered here under two headings: *discrete job systems* and *continuous flow systems*. Discrete job planning systems (Section 12.2) are directed at the scheduling of many distinct jobs through many work centres and machines. Continuous flow planning systems (Section 12.3), as the name suggests, are concerned with rates of manufacture, the rise and fall of stocks and (often) final production on packing lines. This said, it should be noted that there is, now, a sizeable area of overlap in capability between systems from the two families, which is getting larger each year. That is, many discrete job systems are capable of dealing with rates of production and flows, while most continuous flow systems can schedule individual jobs.[2] The last Section of the Chapter deals with the special case of scheduling and production bottlenecks.

From the description of continuous flow systems, it seems clear that their use will principally be in certain large-scale process industries — in the manufacture of food and drink for the mass consumer market; in oil and petroleum; in the manufacture of polymers and similar chemicals; and so on. As well as general flow APS systems used widely in these industries, a number of them on the market are aimed at specific sectors of it (at papermaking companies, for example, or at steel manufacturers). Industry-specific software may incorporate the particular features required in the relevant type of manufacture in a more easily usable form than in the more general purpose software, and may further be supported by literature and VDU graphics more obviously geared to the specialist user.[3] Industry specificity is, not surprisingly, absent from the discrete job systems, although attention is drawn by proponents of the Theory of Constraints (see sub-section 12.4.1) to alternative structures of the bill of materials and "VATI analysis".[4] The V, A, T and I of VATI ingeniously refer to certain "shapes" of bills of materials, as sketched in Figure 12.1. V means few starting products and many sales products (for example, the basic chemical aniline giving rise to many hundreds of different dyestuffs); A means many starting materials and few sales products (components into lawnmowers, say); T represents standard basic parts but with a multiplicity of final option combinations (the electric pencil sharpener illustrated in Figure 8.2 and described in Section 8.3, for example); and I is the bill of materials found in continuous flow. VATI analysis has been used in the literature of Theory of Constraints to

---

[2] An example of a prominent APS system with discrete job scheduling capable of handling rates is Provisa, from Lanner Group, Redditch; a prominent flow scheduler capable of handling discrete jobs is Schedulex, now incorporated in software from J.D. Edwards Ltd.

[3] A number of well-known general advanced planning systems in the flow manufacturing class have been adapted from models developed many years ago for a particular industry — MIMI, for example, was originally written for the scheduling of oil and gas production at Exxon Inc., Texas. MIMI is available from Chesapeake Decision Sciences (Aspen Technology Inc.).

[4] M. Umble and M.L. Srikanth (1990), *Synchronous Manufacturing: Principles for World Class Excellence*, South-Western Publishing, Cincinnati.

illustrate differences between one industry and another as regards manufacturing control points, types of equipment employed and relative difficulties in achieving material synchronisation, but beyond this role appears to have limited value. Notwithstanding VATI and the application of flow systems to particular process industries, the one and only question that matters to a company, regardless of its particular industry, is whether the APS to be used can absolutely accurately represent and deal with the physical reality of production scheduling and production control. If it can, its declared industry class is irrelevant; if it cannot, the system itself is irrelevant to the company in question.

Figure 12.1: Illustrating Bill of Material Structures through "VATI"

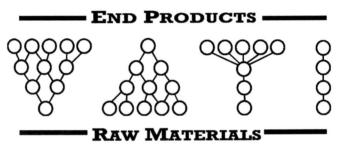

Given the supremacy of the previous point, a company that believes that the problems and complexities and quirks inherent in planning its own work and resources are beyond the capabilities of a standard APS from either the discrete job or continuous flow category may turn instead to in-house development.

It is most unlikely nowadays that a manufacturing company would contemplate the development of the scheduling component of an APS *ab initio*. Instead, the company will turn to tools on the software market which enable a bespoke scheduling capability to be built up in a relatively easy way using a kitbag of facilities supplied as part of the package. The first task to be undertaken in doing so is common to the establishment of a standard advanced planning system as described in Sections 12.2 and 12.3. This is to record the facts and rules relating to the resources that constitute the factory's manufacturing capability. What then follows is different. Instead of relying on the standard model, the user creates a tailor-made model himself within a module specially provided for

Advanced Planning Systems

the purpose. Let us call such a model, say, *Schedule-Builder*.[5] The elements of the model to be defined by him in *Schedule-Builder* might be: (i) time periods; (ii) the manufacturing activities required to be scheduled; (iii) the available resources of various types; and (iv) rules, or *constraints*. The computer code on which *Schedule-Builder* is based will typically be obtained from a C++ development library within the system. The programming statements to be written, which are needed to define the time periods, activities, resources and constraints, are straightforward. Straightforward though they may be, the skills of the programmer must be brought to bear in setting out the many thousands or even tens of thousands of lines of code in a lucid, well-organised fashion that is amenable to future maintenance and change. (It was not unknown in the 1980s for self-developed scheduling models based on ordinary simulation code to be invalidated overnight by some seemingly simple operational change such as the introduction to the factory of a new employee shift system.) The creation of the schedule itself, based on the statements in *Schedule-Builder*, is carried out separately by a second module, which might be termed, say, *Schedule-Solver*. *Schedule-Solver*, again likely to be based on C++ tools and library functions, constitutes what in the jargon of advanced planning systems is known as the "scheduling engine". (The type of scheduling engine used here has been termed *knowledge-based*.)[6] A procedure involving two activities is employed in order to formulate the final solution. One is the application of standard *constraint programming*, the purpose of which is to reduce the extent of possible solutions to the problem. The generation of constraints to guide the search for a schedule will certainly take place at the start of the

---

[5] APS cognoscenti will be aware that the example given in the text is based on the powerful ILOG development tools and in particular on ILOG-Schedule and ILOG-Solver. ILOG is used in far broader applications than simply manufacturing planning and scheduling — examples of its use are to be found in manpower and military planning, commercial portfolio management, airline scheduling and traffic control at airports and major railway stations. ILOG's UK offices are in Bracknell, Berkshire.

[6] M. Benoy, P. Dewilde, W. Herroelen and M. Voet (1994), *Finite Scheduling: State-of-the-Market*, published by Ernst & Young Management Consultants, Brussels (text in English); 27 packages were surveyed. As previously stated, a finite scheduler is the essential, central component of an Advanced Planning Systems, APS.

procedure, but in fact refinements are generated at every point where possibilities are narrowed through the choice of options at the search stage. The second activity is the conducting of an iterative search, employing one or other variation of a "branch and bound" procedure, to contribute to the building of the schedule by confirming or eliminating alternative courses of action.

Branch-and-bound[7] is one of a number of so-called *backtrack algorithms* employed for solving certain problems, especially those connected with integer programming. (Integer programming is a variant of *mathematical programming*, a family of optimisation techniques that includes linear programming, discussed in subsection 12.4.2. Integer programming constrains the solution reached to one involving whole numbers, not fractions.) The technique of backtracking is centred round the creation of a decision tree used for exploring various schedule alternatives and recording which have been accepted and which rejected, and, if necessary, allowing the search algorithm to backtrack to some previous decision point. Thus suppose that at some point on the decision tree there are two alternative *branches* that might be taken, namely Branch A and Branch B. Based on some previously defined criterion, such as shortest processing time or least cost, the more immediately promising path might be Branch A. However, before finally selecting A and rejecting Branch B, Branch B is explored a little further to see whether there is, in fact, a path further along it that is even more promising than Branch A. If there is, Branch B is taken and Branch A is rejected. If there is not, it is necessary to track back along Branch B to the original decision point, reject B and confirm the choice of Branch A. When any branch is finally decided on, *bounds* are set so that the very large number of possible

---

[7] For a substantial treatment of branch-and-bound and other search algorithms, see Harvey Wagner (1975), *Principles of Operations Research*, Second edition, Chapter 13; see also Ray Wild (1980), *Production and Operations Management*, Holt, Rinehart and Winston. For a short discourse on constraint programming, visit http://www.aiai.ed.ac.uk/links/cons. Note that in scheduling jargon, a search strategy which directs the operation of a heuristic (see footnote 16) is referred to as a *meta-heuristic*. Besides mathematics, heuristics have also been developed from observations of natural, biological and physical processes, including the phenomenon of *annealing* (the controlled heating and cooling of material).

Advanced Planning Systems

schedules not connected with it — i.e. outside its boundaries — need no longer be considered.

In the programming of practical applications of branch and bound, much will depend on how effectively lists of backtrack addresses and deferred alternative pathways are handled. Returning to *Schedule-Builder* and *Schedule-Solver*, procedures have been developed involving "stacks" of solutions and the automatic generation of resource constraints. The result is that after an initial computer run to evaluate and store various parameters, re-runs to create alternative schedules due to changed manufacturing conditions even for very large factory models are extremely fast, typically taking only a few minutes to produce revised output.

To illustrate the side-by-side operation of constraint "propagation" and a search algorithm, consider the scheduling of four jobs A, B, C and D, to be loaded in a furnace over a period of seven days. The capacity and availability of the furnace on each day are illustrated in the pictograph in Figure 12.2(a), where the horizontal axis denotes time periods (in days) and the vertical axis capacity (in "standard batches").[8] The capacity demands of the four jobs are given in Table 12.1 and represented graphically in Figure 12.2(b). In addition, there are four external constraints as to job completion: Job B must be finished by Day 6, and Jobs A, C and D must be finished by Day 7. For simplicity, no sequencing or other technical constraints have been imposed.

Figure 12.2(a) Furnace Capacity Available   ***Figure 12.2(b) Jobs to be Scheduled***

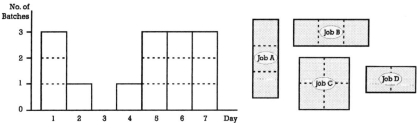

---

[8] The distinctly odd pattern of furnace availability in Figure 12.2(a) has been devised to draw out points in the example without overburdening it with too many complex rules. See also "Developing Scheduling Systems with ILOG Schedule and ILOG Solver", *ILOG Monograph*, September 1994, pp. 23–36, from which the illustration in the text is adapted.

Table 12.1: Amounts and Capacity requirements of Four Jobs to be loaded in the Furnace

Job	Amount Required (standard batches)	Job Duration (days)
A	3	1
B	1	3
C	2	2
D	1	2

The procedure to determine a schedule is an alternating succession of constraint generation and search steps as follows:

1. **Initial Constraint Propagation:** This is the most critical step. Constraints are propagated by the application of special programming tools, including mathematical logic, set theory and truth tables. In the example, it is deduced that (i) Job B must start on Day 4, (ii) Job C must start on Day 5 or Day 6, and (iii) Job C must occupy two out of the three batches of capacity on Day 6.

2. **Initial Solution Search:** Job A can start on either Day 1 or Day 7. As a search rule, we shall select and evaluate the first possible start date for it, namely Day 1.

3. **Constraint Propagation 2:** because Job A starts on Day 1, Job D cannot be completed by Day 7 — i.e. an inconsistency has been detected.

4. **Solution Search 2:** in order to remove the inconsistency above, backtrack so as to remove Job A from Day 1. (In this simple example, it is seen that no other backtracking needs to be done — i.e. no other previous actions need to be reversed.)

5. **Constraint Propagation 3:** start Job A on Day 7. As soon as this action is taken, the further constraint is automatically propagated that Job C must start on Day 5. If so, Job D must start on Day 1.

6. **Solution Search 3:** (all jobs have now been scheduled and there are no further avenues to explore.)

The final schedule is shown in Figure 12.3.

Advanced Planning Systems

Figure 12.3: Furnace Schedule for Four Jobs over Seven Days

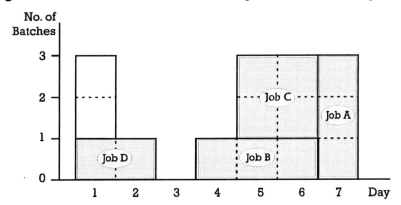

Although the intellectual complexity of schedule generation as seen in the need to maintain stacks of alternative routes and continually regenerate constraints very rapidly accelerates as applications are made more realistic, the computer procedures remain simple and straightforward. Where alternative valid schedules are possible, then as previously mentioned, the choice between them must be decided on some such basis as earliest finish date or minimum cost. (It is noted that even in the simple example given, if the restriction on Job B's finish date is changed from Day 6 to Day 7, a second schedule is possible other than in Figure 12.3 (i.e. Job A, Day 1; Job D, Day 4; Job B, Day 5; and Job C, Day 6). If the capacity availability of the furnace were to be increased to three batches for all seven days, clearly, a very considerable number of alternative solutions would become possible.)

12.2 DISCRETE JOB SYSTEMS

12.2.1 Scheduling Tools and Procedures

I: Simulation

Due to the insurmountable practical difficulties in solving the problem of scheduling jobs through machines by straightforward mathematical means,[9] combined, just as importantly, with the need

---

[9] The general expression to derive the number of possible ways of scheduling n jobs through m machines is $(n!)^m$. Thus the "10 × 10 problem", a yardstick for evaluating the effectiveness of solutions to combinatorial problems — i.e.

to take into account transient operating objectives and priorities in any solution derived, schedules themselves, in both discrete job systems and continuous flow systems, are created by means of simulation.

As a general technique, simulation entails the setting up of a *model*, or representation, of a situation or problem that it is intended to investigate or solve, the model usually taking the form of rules, equations and constraints, held in computer-readable form. In some cases, a means must also be provided to allow direct human intervention — i.e. direct external input. The investigation proceeds by altering in some way the initial conditions governing the model's "state", and observing the effects such an alteration has on other aspects of the situation or problem being studied. One obvious condition certain to be a candidate for change is time. Thus the starting situation may relate to hour-zero, with the investigation intended to see how certain states, such as an amount of stock held or an amount of production achieved, represented in the model, change as time is advanced from hour-zero to (say) hour-24. All of the foregoing — building the model, testing it to ensure that it truly represents what it is meant to represent, changing conditions and interpreting and displaying output — is subsumed in the term *simulation*.

Simulation depends for its existence on the computer, and is by now a mature technique. It is used in many more situations in the manufacturing concern than advanced planning and scheduling. Other areas of use are in product design and FMECA (Section 3.4), customer service evaluation (safety stocks, Section 5.5), capital planning and more besides. Special programming languages have been developed to facilitate the building and running of simulation models (languages, for example, providing an easy means to "advance time", as spoken of above).[10] Almost certainly, therefore, the scheduling engine constituting the basis of a discrete job or con-

---

the scheduling of ten jobs through ten machines — yields some 10^{70} possible solutions, an astronomical number even by astronomical standards and not directly capable of evaluation by practical means.

[10] Two of the best-known simulation languages in the UK are Witness and Hocus. Among many other well-known languages are GPSS, Simcript and Slam. Witness is from Lanner Group (see footnote 2 above) and Hocus is from P-E International.

Advanced Planning Systems

tinuous flow APS system will be written in the simulation language of choice of the software vendor offering the product.

Simulation models are classified according to three criteria. An understanding of these classifications and an acquaintance with the jargon used is essential to an appreciation of the use of simulation in APS and scheduling. Thus:

1. **Human interaction with the simulation model.** Models are said to be either *behavioural* or *operational*. Behavioural models might be representations of strategic business planning scenarios or business negotiations, the characteristics of which are wholly dependent on human decisions and human reaction (which may be irrational). Operational models, which include all models used in advanced planning systems, are dependent only on the operating conditions or mechanisms defined in the model and the logical outcomes of these conditions, not on human involvement.[11]

2. **The effect of chance events on the model.** Classifications here are *deterministic* and *probabilistic*. Deterministic means that the data and assumptions relating to the model are fixed and inviolable, not subject to chance disturbance or random variation. Deterministic simulations depend purely on the conditions defined in the model at the start, together with the strict logic of rules laid down as governing their change. Discrete job and continuous flow system models are deterministic — the interaction of jobs and machines is held to proceed over time absolutely in accordance with the rules and data defined. A probabilistic model, by contrast, deals with conditions liable to sudden change, the probability of such change being capable of statistical representation. Examples of statistics and sudden change are the chance of a machine breaking down and the probability of a new job arriving unexpectedly to join a queue of jobs at a work centre.[12]

---

[11] In the jargon, the overall resources, plant and products represented in a simulation-based APS model are said to constitute its *environment*. In a deterministic model, the environment is not affected by human input, and is said to be *neutral*.

[12] At first sight, there is a conflict between determinism in advanced planning simulation and the maintenance of queues on the shop floor as discussed in

3. **The way in which the progress of the model will be periodically reassessed.** The purposes of the simulation are to track, direct and report on the changes that will take place over time by reference to the rules, equations and constraints which govern the model's behaviour. In a probabilistic simulation, a reassessment would clearly be made whenever probability suggested that a random event might have occurred, such as a machine breakdown or an addition made to the job queue. In a deterministic simulation, there are two alternative ways by which the model's progress might be influenced and reported. First, if there is a reasonable frequency of "events" occurring, as there usually is, for instance, in discrete job scheduling (calculations indicating jobs arriving at work centres and leaving them, set-ups taking place, job processing starting and finishing and jobs being moved from one work centre to another), then the model can be simply reassessed whenever such an event occurs. This seems an ideal strategy for tracking and revising a (deterministic) scheduling model, since changes in its state need be re-examined only when an event occurs; once the state of the model has been directed and recorded at an "event point", a change occurs in accordance with the rules, and the focus of attention transfers to the next event to occur. Simulation which employs this trigger mechanism is referred to as *discrete event simulation*. If, however, interest lies not in individual happenings, but in the overall effect of all the events together — for example, in the total number of units manufactured in a given period or in the

---

sub-section 11.2.4. There is no such conflict. The shop floor situation described in 11.2.4 hardly deals with a scheduling *model*. Scheduling in those circumstances is a very local matter, based on a limited panorama of jobs. In advanced planning systems, the computer is able to manage and schedule all jobs, on all resources, over the complete horizon, and so *determine* the loads at work centres and *determine* the times of arrival of new work. However, it should be said that an argument against determinism in APS is put forward by proponents of the Theory of Constraints and others, who point out the vital need to keep bottlenecked plant constantly fed with work (in the way that the shop supervisor wishes to keep his work centres busy in 11.2.4). It is advocated in bottleneck scheduling that "protective capacity" or "protective WIP" should be established facing the bottleneck, to deal with any failure of supply of work to the bottleneck from the stage prior to it (see sub-section 12.4.1).

Advanced Planning Systems 413

time it will take for a storage vessel to become full, then *continuous simulation* is used. In continuous simulation, it is the aggregated, gradual effect of all events which is tracked, typically by means of continuous variables — e.g. by means of data expressed as *so-many units per hour*, as *maximum capacity of so-many litres* and in such other terminology as is familiar to planners in large-scale process industries.[13] (A definition of process manufacturing is *production that adds value by mixing, separating, forming and/or performing chemical reactions . . . in either batch or continuous mode . . .*)[14] We can see intuitively that the way that such manufacture would best be modelled, or represented, in a simulation would be in terms of continuous variables, and that progress of the model should be influenced and followed by focusing on carefully selected points in the operation of plant. Examples of focal points given in Section 12.3, in connection with a process illustrated there, the manufacture of "Ben's Home Brew", are the start and finish of distillation and the start and finish of the packing of the Home Brew product into one-litre and four-litre containers.

II: Horizontal Loading and Forwards/Backwards Scheduling

In sub-section 6.6.1 and Figure 6.5, the term *vertical loading* was used to mean the assessment and assignment of the total of all demands on a single resource in one particular time period, the various demands potentially stemming from many different jobs. In contrast to vertical loading, discrete job APS systems employ so-called *horizontal loading*. Here, the capacity requirements of a single job are assigned, over the many succeeding time periods constituting the job's overall duration, to all of the resources involved in its completion. Horizontal loading is illustrated by Figure 12.4.

---

[13] In Forrester's curves, described in sub-section 4.3.1, created using a continuous simulation model, the points chosen are the times of maximum and minimum stockholding, and the points where stockholding is restored to its starting values — see Figures 4.5 and 4.6.

[14] *The APICS Dictionary*, Seventh edition, published by APICS.

Figure 12.4: Forward Horizontal Loading of Job J (four steps) on Resource R

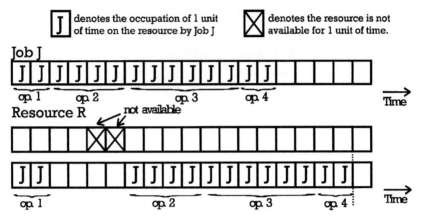

The top sketch in the Figure represents a Job J comprising four operations, and the successive requirement of each of the operations for time on a Resource R over 14 periods (Op. 1, two units of time; Op. 2, four units; Op. 3, six units; Op. 4, two units). In this case, all operations are to be performed on the single resource only, which is available for use from Periods 1 to 19, excepting Periods 5 and 6 (middle sketch of the Figure). The bottom sketch of Figure 12.4 shows the horizontal loading of the job on the resource. (The term "horizontal" in the expression refers to the passage of time, not to the layout itself of the diagram.)

To introduce a further term, Job J in Figure 12.4 is said to have been (horizontally) loaded onto Resource R by *forward scheduling*. Forward scheduling means that the loading process is to start at the first opportunity from the current time, and continue naturally forward in time. Forward scheduling is the more usual procedure in discrete job systems. However, an option is usually provided in software alternatively to permit a job to be loaded by *backward scheduling*. Backward scheduling is the loading of the job's last operation first, usually timed to be completed on the date the job is needed, further loading then proceeding backwards in time to the present. (Materials planning and MRP, described in Chapters 9 and 10, are examples of backward scheduling, from the MPS at its required future date, exploded back in time.) If a priority rule based on slack time were to be employed (see Section 11.3), then in the absence of certain data obtained from a materials planning system,

Advanced Planning Systems

a discrete job system might need to undertake, first, backward scheduling, and then forward scheduling, in order to find a job's slack time.

Figure 12.5: Backward Horizontal Scheduling (Top Sketch) and Infinite Horizontal Backward Loading (Bottom Sketch)

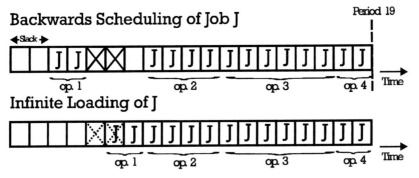

Figure 12.5 (top sketch) shows the previous Job J horizontally loaded on Resource R by backwards scheduling, such that Operation 4 is timed to be completed by Period 19. The bottom sketch in Figure 12.5 illustrates yet a further option typically provided as a feature of advanced planning systems and completes this brief introduction to scheduling terminology — planning by *infinite loading*. This is the loading of work without regard to the limitations of the capacity of the resources concerned. Infinite loading can be most useful in pinpointing the locations, times and extents of shortfalls in capacity.

12.2.2 The Discrete Job Scheduling Engine

Although as explained, the discrete job APS systems are based on the operation of deterministic simulation models, not all implementations are discrete event simulations. The systems on the market can generally be placed in one of two classes: Class I schedulers have been called by Mark Benoy et al.[15] *heuristic schedulers*;[16] schedulers in Class II employ standard discrete event

---

[15] M. Benoy et al. (1994), op. cit.

[16] *Heuristics* are guidelines, or "rules of thumb that work", and which enable a computer to arrive at a decision or solve a problem more quickly than otherwise. In everyday life, the thought the human being takes to reach many deci-

simulation. The Class I heuristic schedulers are historically the oldest of all types[17] and it will be seen below that the way in which they create a schedule is simplistic. Because of this, the schedules so derived are, in general, of an unsatisfactory standard, but before the class is thereby condemned, three points are made. First, the reasons for the inadequacies of schedules produced by basic heuristic schedulers are so well known that it is likely that a software vendor offering an APS incorporating this type of scheduler will have taken some action to improve the function of his own product. Secondly, although the quality of a schedule produced by an advanced planning system is highly important, the ancillary system facilities are also important, and those provided with many heuristics-based APS systems may well be on a par with those available through discrete event simulators — graphical presentations, reports, editing facilities, the provision of interactive operation, etc. Thirdly, again it must be said, the acid test of a schedule is whether or not it is a true representation of the real world. The sophisticated, high-standard schedule that is not valid is an oxymoron: the schedule is no schedule at all. Or rather, a schedule of mediocre standard in terms of optimality which is nevertheless highly accurate from the practical point of view may yet be acceptable and very useful.

---

sions shows them to have been easily and immediately arrived at. But translating this human intelligence to the computer — that is, endowing the computer, so to speak, with a measure of *AI* (artificial intelligence) — is a complex and time-consuming task (see also sub-section 4.5.5).

[17] Many of the scheduling engines incorporated in discrete job APS systems are derived from stand-alone *third generation finite schedulers*. What made these products third generation, rather than second or first, seemed to be the use they made of the ever-increasing power of the computer: for example, in their provision of graphics displays and, especially, in their incorporation of interactive editing facilities as a bridge between the user and the schedule itself. A major, much respected representative of second generation finite schedulers is IBM's Caposs-E, described briefly by Vollmann et al. in connection with the scheduling of engine overhauls. See *Capacity Planning & Operations Sequencing System (Extended)* by IBM. The example in Vollmann et al., op. cit., Chapter 5, relates to scheduling engine overhauls at Swissair, the difficulty of planning work in this environment stemming from the inability to judge the time required to complete the overhaul until the engine has been stripped down and inspected.

Advanced Planning Systems

Class I — Heuristic Schedulers

Heuristic scheduling as it is defined here means the creation of a schedule for a number of jobs or work orders by the following two-step process:

1. *The Heuristics Step*: All jobs waiting to be scheduled are assigned relative priorities according to one or other of such priority despatching rules as are described in Section 11.3 (e.g. slack per operation; critical ratio, CR; shortest processing time, SPT; and others which may be favourites of the software vendor). It is the simple use of a despatching rule which gives rise to the term "heuristics" as the name of the method. As explained in 11.3, despatching rules are rules of thumb, arrived at by trial-and-error, and having no underpinning of mathematics or theory.

2. *The Scheduling Step*: Every step of each job to be despatched is assigned to the planned resources on which it is to be manufactured, by horizontal loading, in accordance with the route for the job recorded on the routing file. The complete job is assigned to the resources required, in its entirety. If a step of a job cannot be assigned over the time required, because an earlier job of higher priority has already earmarked the resource for its own use, the step is assigned to the resource at the first opportunity available. When a complete job has been assigned, the procedure returns to Step 1 and the next highest priority job waiting is dealt with, again in its entirety.

Table 12.2: Priorities, Work Centres and Durations of the Operations in the Three Jobs, J1 to J3, Scheduled in Figure 12.6

Job	Priority	Four Operations and their Durations
J1	1st	w/c A* (2); w/c B (4); w/c C (6); w/c D (2)
J2	2nd	w/c B* (3); w/c C (6); w/c D (4); w/c A (3)
J3	3rd	w/c A (4); w/c B (3); w/c C (4); w/c D (3)

* Note that Job J1/Operation 1 is already in progress on work centre A and will be finished at the end of Period 2, and that Job J2/Operation 1 is also in progress on work centre B, and will be finished at the end of Period 3.

The operation of a simple heuristic scheduler in scheduling three jobs J1, J2 and J3 is illustrated in Figure 12.6. Each of the jobs involves four operations, one on each of the four work centres A, B, C and D. The priorities of the jobs are given in Table 12.2. Thus (to interpret the information in the Table): Job J1 has the highest priority of all three of them, and the sequence, work centres and durations of the four required operations are read as follows:

- 1st operation, on work centre A; operation duration 2 periods;
- 2nd operation, on work centre B; operation duration 4 periods;
- 3rd operation, on work centre C, operation duration 6 periods;
- 4th operation, on work centre D; operation duration 2 periods.

The heuristics scheduler first deals exclusively with the remaining three operations of Job J1, by horizontal loading and forward scheduling as shown in Figure 12.6. Next, the three remaining operations of Job J2 are horizontally loaded by forward scheduling, the job operations yet to be performed fitting onto work centres C, D and, finally, A, as soon as the work centres are free of occupation by J1. Lastly J3 is loaded, the four operations fitting onto A, B, C and D as shown in the Figure.

Examination of the final schedule in Figure 12.6 reveals to the human eye many gaps in utilisation of the four work centres and a number of opportunities whereby simple overriding of the strict job priority order would have produced better work centre loading and an earlier completion of production.

Figure 12.6: Horizontal Loading of the Three Jobs from Table 12.2 (Heuristics Scheduler)

| 1 | denotes the occupation of 1 unit of time on the resource by Job J1 | 2 | denotes 1 unit of time by Job J2 | 3 | denotes 1 unit of time by Job J3 |

work centre A:
| 1 | 1 | 3 | 3 | 3 | 3 | | | | | | | | | | | | | | | | 2 | 2 | 2 | | | | |

work centre B:
| 2 | 2 | 2 | 1 | 1 | 1 | 1 | 3 | 3 | 3 | | | | | | | | | | | | | | | | | | | |

work centre C:
| | | | | | | | 1 | 1 | 1 | 1 | 1 | 1 | 2 | 2 | 2 | 2 | 2 | 2 | 3 | 3 | 3 | 3 | | | | | |

work centre D:
| | | | | | | | | | | | | | | 1 | 1 | | | | 2 | 2 | 2 | 2 | 3 | 3 | 3 | | |

Advanced Planning Systems

Class II — Discrete Event Schedulers

Figure 12.7 shows the horizontal loading of the three jobs J1, J2 and J3 from Table 12.2 by forwards scheduling, this time using discrete event simulation. That is, the three remaining operations relating to Job J1 are *not* simply loaded one after another.

Figure 12.7: Discrete Event Scheduling of the Three Jobs in Table 12.2

| 1 | denotes the occupation of 1 unit of time on the resource by Job J1 | 2 | denotes 1 unit of time by Job J2 | 3 | denotes 1 unit of time by Job J3 |

work centre A:
| 1 | 1 | 3 | 3 | 3 | 3 | | | | | | 2 | 2 | 2 | | | | | | | | | | | | |

work centre B:
| 2 | 2 | 2 | 1 | 1 | 1 | 1 | 3 | 3 | 3 | | | | | | | | | | | | | | | | |

work centre C:
| | | | 2 | 2 | 2 | 2 | 2 | 2 | 1 | 1 | 1 | 1 | 1 | 1 | 3 | 3 | 3 | 3 | | | | | | | |

work centre D:
| | | | | | | | | | 2 | 2 | 2 | 2 | | 1 | 1 | | 3 | 3 | 3 | | | | | | |

Operation 1 of J1 is, as before, already loaded on w/c A, and is completed at the end of Period 2. This completion constitutes the first "event" following the commencement of the schedule. Consequently, the simulation model now intervenes and all loading opportunities are examined on a system-wide basis at this point. Since w/c A has now become free as a result of the event and the first operation of Job 3 is waiting to be loaded, it is duly assigned to work centre A. The next event to occur, and so the next opportunity for action in the simulation, is at the end of Period 3, when Operation 1 of Job 2 finishes. At this point, since w/c B has now become free and Job J1 (Op.2) is waiting, J1/Op2 is duly loaded onto B. The simulation continues, decisions being made on a system-wide basis as event after event occurs (there are 11 events in all, to completion). The final schedule is shown in Figure 12.7. Comparison with Figure 12.6 shows a good improvement in utilisation of the work centres. Table 12.3 gives the finish periods of the three jobs in the two schedules.

Table 12.3: Finish Periods of three Jobs, from Figures 12.6 and 12.7

Job	Finish Period, Heuristics Scheduling	Finish Period, Discrete Event
J1	15	17
J2	26	16
J3	26	22

12.2.3 Scheduling Rules

Regardless of the procedure by which the discrete job work plan is created, a centrally important datafile in the process is clearly the routings file, holding the work centres and operations involved in manufacture and such other detail of manufacture as set-up and running times. The requirement for 100 per cent accuracy of the file, and the difficulties in obtaining and maintaining it, were briefly mentioned in sub-section 11.5.3. In the last paragraph of Chapter 11, the point was also made that in the final assignment of jobs to machines by a foreman executing the schedule, the foreman can personally take account of rules and guidelines to ensure that assigned jobs and machines are compatible and that the progress of work will be smooth, whereas, in advanced planning by computer, *the identification and enunciation of the rules and quirks which apply to job assignment and the coding of logic to represent them in the software library are major tasks in the set-up and management [of the facility]*.

Table 12.4: A Simple Rule Governing the Assignment of Jobs to Three Blanking Machines

	Press 1	Press 2	Press 3
Diameter	200–350	200–500	300–500
Gauge	1.0–2.5	1.0–3.5	1.0–4.0

Rules and quirks may simply be straightforward technical conditions of manufacture (the ranges of diameter and gauge able to be accommodated on a particular press, for example, as shown in Table 12.4). Alternatively, the rules may be empirical and individual-

Advanced Planning Systems

istic, being based on everyday shop floor experience (say, *Press 3 must not operate for more than 120 minutes continuously*). Other rules relate less to jobs and work centres than to the required attributes of the schedule itself. An example here might be the requirement to moderate a schedule because of a corporate objective to minimise work-in-progress. Similarly, many further scheduling rules relate to job sequence. Thus the requirement for a number of jobs to be carried out in a particular sequence may be due to compelling technical factors which nullify the determination of sequence by prioritisation through despatching rules.

Work centre rules must be recorded painstakingly by the person responsible (perhaps the production control manager, as suggested in 11.5.3), and then, separately, translated into the terms required by the APS software, calling on an extensive library of rules that the software vendor will have provided. Eliciting the pertinent operational information in interviews with shop floor staff may be time-consuming and difficult, since staff may not realise that certain facts, which seem commonplace to themselves, are important and may not therefore volunteer them. One later indication that important work centre rules have been missed or misinterpreted is eventual non-adherence to the schedule by shop floor staff. (There may be other reasons for non-adherence, of course: inaccurate stock records, wrong routings, poor supplier or manufacturing performance and simply "not trying".) Instances of non-adherence must be investigated and the causes of them removed.

Although the libraries of rules provided by software vendors grow in size and sophistication continuously as worthwhile additions suggested by their clients are incorporated over the years, inevitably there will be instances where the conditions prevailing in a particular company cannot be accurately represented by one or other rule in a particular vendor's armoury. The ability to model the reality of its manufacture, however, is a *sine qua non* in the selection by the company of an APS.[18] If, therefore, the standard li-

---

[18] As part of the evaluation of his system, a software vendor should be made to show that he can faithfully model the company's plant and *all* of its scheduling rules and requirements, even if he is required to write special programming code to do so. And it is never at all advisable for a company to purchase software on the promise that a facility will be provided at a date in the future

brary of rules cannot deal with all work centres, the logic required to fill the gap must be provided separately. One way this is sometimes done is for the vendor to write the additional program code as part of a package customisation service. A more common solution is for the software vendor to provide the user with a means of writing and inserting the missing logic himself. The programming capability supplied in some instances is C, C++ or Visual BASIC; in others, vendors may provide tailor-made, easy-to-use private compilers specially developed for the purpose. The user is shielded from the need to become involved in computer system technicalities, but must nevertheless be capable of specifying, writing and testing what might be a tricky computer program.

There are a number of reasons why the user might prefer to program his own special work centre rules rather than rely on a software vendor's customisation service. Rules are liable to change and the long-term cost of this aspect of vendor support must be considered. Again, if control over rules is maintained in-house, it is possible to change them on an *ad hoc* basis, perhaps for a special simulation run or, say, to enable the APS system to run faster when long-range investigative schedules are required (run faster by temporarily simplifying the more complex rules). The requirement to write, maintain and amend small programs to accommodate special work centre rules should be borne in mind when the job description of the person who is to manage the advanced planning system is being put together.[19] The software vendor will typically provide training of about one week's duration in programming instruction.

Returning to the straightforward rules governing the assignment of jobs to three presses in Table 12.4, it will be seen that data pertaining to the diameter and gauge involved in the job must be associated with other data relating to it, so that a test can be made

---

(cynically termed "vaporware") — in the event, its provision may prove impossible, either technically or financially.

[19] The requirement to write computer code is not the only job description amendment to be made when an APS is taken on. To support and get the best out of the system requires considerable computer fluency. There is also no longer a requirement for auxiliary staff who are bright at scheduling. The role of auxiliaries under the new regime is to support the system's data files, especially those relating to routings and work centre rules.

Advanced Planning Systems

as to its suitability for assignment. The computer program considering the loading of Job 1 at Press 1 will make the following simple tests, where *Gauge* and *Diameter* are the obvious job data parameters:

- If *Diameter* < 200 or > 350, "Reject"
- If *Gauge* < 1.0 or > 2.5, "Reject"

The attachment of the tag "Reject" to the job marks it as not to be considered for scheduling through Press 1.

Suppose, now, that Job 1 passes the test for Press 1, and that Jobs 2 and 3 also pass the test for this press. Which of the three will be assigned first to Press 1 by the program? How will the three jobs be prioritised?

A very simple way of prioritising available jobs qualifying, according to the rules, for despatch through a work centre would be to fall back on the standard despatching rules mentioned many times previously. However, the power of the computer and of computer simulation can be used to improve very considerably on standard despatching. It is possible to devise and apply a host of alternative, user-controlled rules and tests aimed at achieving local company scheduling objectives. More important, the application of the rules and tests by the program relates to the specific circumstances of the jobs to be prioritised, at the moments prevailing, whereas the effectualities of the standard despatching rules relate merely to standard situations. A system providing local prioritising rules and tests under the user's control is termed (from the viewpoint of sequencing), a *rule-based advanced planning system*.[20]

A typical and commonly employed rule or test applied by the simulation program in the formulation of the schedule will relate to

---

[20] It is as well always to remember that "rule-based APS" means *sequencing*, or *priority* rule-based, as defined in the text, since the term is otherwise a little confusing. Thus advanced planning systems which are not rule-based nevertheless rely on and obey work centre *loading* rules relating to technical and physical manufacturing feasibility (see the earlier text) and may employ the standard despatching rules as well. The rules in a rule-based APS system and the parameters capable of being varied by the user are to the discrete job system what soft and strategic constraints are to a continuous flow system (see sub-section 12.3.3).

work-in-progress and its minimisation. Thus, in words: *If Job J is due to go to work centre W and the amount of work already at W exceeds H hours, do not despatch the job* (where the value of H is capable of variation on a system-wide basis by the production controller prior to executing the simulation run). Other major objectives that are invariably the subject of rules are to minimise job lateness and to minimise set-up time. An obvious difficulty in deciding the despatch order of jobs here, of course, is a clash of objectives — for example, to despatch Job J as top priority will incur a high set-up cost but not to despatch it will make the job late. To resolve such difficulties, the operation of the rules will typically incorporate a point-scoring mechanism. Various numbers of points, or weights, are associated with the different objectives, the sizes of numbers assigned reflecting the production controller's view of the objectives' relative, general importance. The program then evaluates the number of points gained by each job in turn, points being accumulated by reference to achievement of the various objectives and by simulating alternative job despatch priorities. The job that achieves the best score when the simulator assigns it to the highest priority is confirmed as top priority in the schedule being built. This job is then assumed to have been despatched, and the remaining jobs are re-evaluated — i.e. re-scored — in the new circumstance. Again, the job with the best (revised) score is despatched next, and so on.

In any point-scoring system, some ingenuity is required of the software programmer to ensure that the allocation of points results in the best despatch order of jobs under all circumstances, or at least, that it doesn't result in an order that is unfeasible or quite clearly inferior. To illustrate the application of rules and point scoring to determine a despatch order, consider six jobs involving the preparation of snack foods, with two alternative fillings and two alternative flavours, all jobs being available for despatch and all processed on the same work centre.[21] Job details are set out in Table 12.5. Note that "Days Cover" relates to the manufacturer's cur-

---

[21] The snack foods scheduling example is adapted from information and examples supplied by Jeff Woodhams, former technical sales manager for the Provisa APS, a major discrete event system marketed in the UK by Lanner Group.

Advanced Planning Systems

rent stockholding and is a measure of job urgency or degree of lateness. That is, the job with the fewest days cover is the most urgent. In the case of Table 12.5, the rules defined to the simulation program and the points to be applied in the scoring process are the four given below. In this particular simulation, with these particular rules and scores, jobs with the *lowest* total scores have the highest despatch priorities.

1. *Lateness Rule*: If Days Cover ≤ 2.0, Score = Days Cover
   Else Score = Days Cover $\times$ 100;

2. 1st *Set-Up Rule*: If Previous Job = same product filling (rice or noodles)
   Score = Score *minus* 50;

3. 2nd *Set-Up Rule*: If Previous Job = same flavour (beef or curry)
   Score = Score *minus* 100;

4. *Work Centre Rule*: If there is a changeover of either product filling or product flavour, a cleandown must be scheduled.

The points shown in Table 12.5 relate to the initial points allocation, made immediately after considering the number of days cover on each of the six products. (Prior to this starting situation, it is assumed the production line is clean.)

Table 12.5: Rule-based Scheduling — Scores Assigned after Initial Assessment

Job	Customer	Days Cover	Filling	Flavour	Initial Points Allocation
J1	A	3.6	Noodle	Beef	360
J2	B	2.4	Rice	Beef	240
J3	A	3.3	Noodle	Curry	330
J4	C	3.9	Rice	Beef	390
J5	C	3.5	Noodle	Beef	350
J6	B	1.9	Noodle	Curry	1.9

Job J6 is to be despatched first, having the lowest score. If J6 is first, it is possible to apply the second and third rules on product filling and product flavour to evaluate job scores, and so determine the job to be despatched second. That is, each job from Jobs 1 to 5 is evaluated on the basis of whether it has the same filling as Job 6 and/or the same flavour as Job 6. After this second round of scoring, the position is as shown in Table 12.6.

Table 12.6: Rule-based Scheduling — Scores assigned after Second Assessment

Job	Customer	Days Cover	Filling	Flavour	Revised Points Allocation
J6	*B*	*1.9*	*Noodle*	*Curry*	*n/a*
J1	A	3.6	Noodle	Beef	310
J2	B	2.4	Rice	Beef	240
J3	A	3.3	Noodle	Curry	180
J4	C	3.9	Rice	Beef	390
J5	C	3.5	Noodle	Beef	300

The second job despatched in the Schedule is thus J3 with 180 points (330 − 50 − 100). Because of the specifications of the four jobs remaining, whatever the next job is to be, there must be a change of filling or a change of flavour, or both. This being so, the work centre rule is invoked whereby a plant cleandown is scheduled. Consequently, the despatching priority of the third job reverts purely to considerations of lateness and the points in Table 12.5. Of the four remaining jobs (i.e. not despatched) in Table 12.5, the one with the lowest score is J2. This is therefore despatched third. Job 2 is rice and beef, and, on that basis, the points of the three remaining jobs are re-evaluated and are as given in Table 12.7.

Table 12.7: Despatching of the Fourth Job in the Snack Foods Example

Job	Customer	Days Cover	Filling	Flavour	Revised Points Allocation*
J2	*B*	*2.4*	*Rice*	*Beef*	*n/a*
J1	A	3.6	Noodle	Beef	260
J4	C	3.9	Rice	Beef	240
J5	C	3.5	Noodle	Beef	250

*Remember, these revised allocations relate to Table 12.5, not to Table 12.6.

Advanced Planning Systems

From Table 12.7, the fourth job to be despatched is J4 with 240 points (390 – 50 – 100). Since there is now bound to be a change in product filling in proceeding to the next job, the cleandown rule is again invoked and the point scoring position of the two remaining jobs J1 and J5 reverts once more to Table 12.5, the assumption being made that they are following Job J4 (rice and beef). The final despatch order of the six jobs is J6, J3, J2, J4, J5 and J1.

The use of a weighting scheme such as above may be inappropriate and heavy-handed if job sequence is governed by "compelling technical factors", as spoken of earlier. A readily appreciated example here is the sequence of manufacture of successive batches of paint of various colours. Technicalities and commonsense say that to alleviate the difficulty of preparing the plant for manufacture and to reduce the risk of colour cross-contamination, the sequence of manufacture *must* start with white and other light colours and finish with dark colours and black. To give effect to the rule, a colour code of each batch to be manufactured must be carried with the job data so that the APS can correctly sequence them.

In some instances, best sequences are far less easily determined than through a simple descriptive code. One such, requiring the application of mathematics, is the determination of sequence when machine set-up times are dependent on the order of jobs. An example of set-up time dependency is given in Figure 12.8, which shows the times required to set up a machine for each of four jobs (J1 to J4), expressed in minutes in the column beneath each job code, the times varying and being dependent on the identity of the job for which the machine was previously set up (given in the leftmost column). To read Figure 12.8 further, consider the first row of the Table (i.e. the figures ∞; 13; 30; 10). The first entry (∞) relates to the set-up time for J1 when the previous job on the machine was also J1. Since "J1 preceded by J1" is a nonsense condition (introduced to assist in the solution to the problem, in a way analogous to the creation of dummy locations in Figures 20.28 and 20.29), the set-up time to achieve it has been specified as "∞", thus ensuring it will not be part of the final, optimal sequence. The next entry, 13 minutes, relates to the set-up time for J2 when the previous job on the machine was J1. The third entry in the row means that the set-up time for J3 is 30 minutes when the previous job set up was J1. The last entry shows that J4 takes 10 minutes to set-up after J1 has previously occupied the work centre. (Note, incidentally, that the standard set-up time for J1, *ab initio*, if no job had previously been set up, is 16 minutes, given at the foot of the J1 column.)

Figure 12.8: The Set-up Time Dependency Problem (to find the best sequence of four Jobs)

		Alternative Job Set-up Times			
		J1	J2	J3	J4
Job Previously Set Up on the Machine	J1	∞	13	30	10
	J2	12	∞	14	0
	J3	6	15	∞	2
	J4	16	0	34	∞
No Prior Job		16	22	34	26

The set-up time dependency problem is to find the sequence of manufacture of the four jobs whereby the total set-up time is minimised. In mathematical parlance, it is a *combinatorial optimisation* problem and is commonly referred to in the jargon as the *travelling salesman problem*.[22] In this case there are (4!) possible solutions. The working out of the solution is not given here, but is very similar to the mechanics of the transportation algorithm, an almost identical problem described fully in Section 20.3. The optimum sequence arrived at is J1 (16 minutes set-up, from scratch, with no prior job on the work centre); then J4 (10 minutes); J2 (0 minutes); and then, finally J3 (14 minutes); a total of 40 minutes in all (against the sum of the four standard times of 98 minutes).

---

[22] The travelling salesman has to visit n towns, and wishes to find the least-distance route to do so, visiting each town once and starting and finishing at "town 1". The problem translates in the text to finding a least time (= shortest distance) job sequence (= route), involving four jobs J1, J2, J3, J4 (= towns). The travelling salesman problem is described in many operations research texts, such as Wagner (1975), op. cit.

Advanced Planning Systems

Many more facilities than local optimisation algorithms are typically to be found in the software vendor's kitbag. Perhaps surprisingly present, seemingly contradictory to the term *discrete job system*, are usually means to handle rates of manufacture (see Section 9.5 and Table 9.2). That is, jobs can be dealt with involving packing and bottling, and job rules can be specified in such process-industry familiar terms as *"pack X amount of material"*, *"pack at the rate of X litres/hour"* and so forth.

Figure 12.9: Gantt Chart Schedule Display of a Discrete Job Scheduler

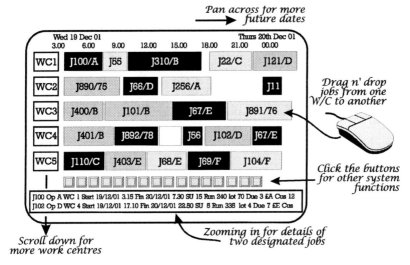

The centre of attention following the creation of the work plan by the APS is its presentation in the form of a Gantt chart on the VDU, as illustrated in Figure 12.9 with a horizontal loading display. Naturally, because of the limitations imposed by the size of the computer screen, facilities are provided to allow the user to scroll (downwards) to view all work centres and pan (across) to view the schedule to its maximum horizon.[23] It is usually possible to edit (i.e. change) the schedule directly by moving jobs on the screen with the mouse. When this is done, the validity of the forced change is

---

[23] The production control manager will typically create a work plan at the weekend for two weeks ahead. The accuracy of the plan and the adherence to it are usually sufficiently exact for its duration to last the complete week. Changes in the materials plan and in shop floor arrangements will require the schedule to be rerun at the next weekend.

checked by the system and internal data files are adjusted accordingly. As might be supposed, colour coding is widely used — for example, to distinguish at a glance jobs ahead from those behind.

The ability interactively to edit the schedule is considered by users of advanced planning systems to be an essential feature of them. Through editing, the production controller can impose his own character on the schedule — for example, by specifying that such lead time management activities as operation overlapping or operation splitting are to be undertaken (section 11.4), or by specifying the use of alternative product routes and work centres, or, again, by arranging for work centres to be kept free for planned maintenance. Also required as part of effective operation of the APS is the ability to conduct simulations in order to investigate and evaluate alternative factory operating decisions (e.g., to evaluate the cost of working X hours overtime, and to determine whether such overtime will enable jobs currently behind time to catch up).

Notwithstanding the facilities of the discrete job APS and its overall quality, Marnix Voet[24] observes that a system may succeed in one company but fail in another. According to Voet, the issues which make the difference between success and failure are:

1. Management commitment to the APS project;
2. The maintenance of high levels of data integrity;
3. The provision of effective scheduling rules;
4. The provision of user training and education at all levels; and
5. **Above all else**, the creation of true representations of reality in the schedules and plans produced, so that staff have confidence in them and a commitment to the system.

12.3 CONTINUOUS FLOW SYSTEMS

Many products such as paper, steel, chemicals, petroleum and food, associated with the process industries, are made by what may be termed *flow manufacture*. The environment of flow manufacture is characterised by fixed plant layout and the ability to deal with high volumes of continuous material (liquids, powders, etc).

---

[24] Benoy et al. (1994), op. cit., Chapter 9.

Advanced Planning Systems

Materials move through the flow environment either continuously or in batches. Very typically, the overlapping of stage-to-stage operations is a permanent feature of a process. And, as it was put in Section 12.1, the scheduling of continuous flow manufacture *is concerned with rates of manufacture, the rise and fall of stocks and (often) final production on packing lines.*

12.3.1 The Influence of the Master Production Schedule

The central role of the master production schedule and its importance to the manufacturing company's operational objectives have been described at length. What is different in continuous flow manufacture, however, is the influence of master planning decisions at the MPS formulation stage (Chapter 6) on final plan formulation. In a very real sense, MPS formulation is the first step of continuous flow advanced planning. For example, when one or several products can be manufactured on a number of alternative production lines, it is at the MPS formulation stage that a decision is taken as to the assignment of production among the various possibilities. The assignment will be influenced by technical suitability, quality, cost, the volumes of production required and plant capacity. (Linear programming may be employed to decide the allocation. If so, minimum cost and maximum throughput volume are likely to be candidates for the choice of objective function.)

Problems of seasonal product demand and the requirement to process seasonally available fresh food with a limited storage life are also dealt with at the MPS level. A manufacturing planning solution to seasonal demand may be to build up stocks ahead of the season, as described in Section 6.5. A common technical answer to the need to process seasonally available fresh food is to dehydrate or freeze it so that manufacture can be levelled out over the year.[25]

Master schedule formulation is a multidisciplinary activity, so that decisions on flow scheduling must be taken by the manufacturing manager in conjunction with others, especially purchasing and distribution. Engineering maintenance is also involved; maintenance may demand full-scale shutdowns for extensive periods.

---

[25] Perhaps these days, the company could add *genetic modification* to its list of technical responses, undertaken in order to extend the harvest period and storage life of crops?

The achievement or otherwise of company objectives in such matters as economic production, customer service, market share and the rest is determined in flow manufacture at the master planning level by striking a balance — a careful, calculated balance — between such various factors as plant suitability, cost, technical operation, quality and seasonality. Continuous flow advanced planning and scheduling must be seen within this context. Scheduling itself is a second step subordinate to Sales and Operations Planning (Section 6.3). It is the finding of a best operating solution, a best production solution, to fulfil the higher master plan.

The master–subordinate MPS/scheduling relationship may become apparent in the resolution of potential day-to-day scheduling conflicts by reference to the higher objectives and balance of the master plan. An example of this would be seen in the determination of response to an unexpectedly large customer order — is response to be its immediate manufacture, and consequential schedule amendment, or is it to be its deferment in order to maintain schedule stability and low-cost operation?

12.3.2 Scheduling Procedure

Continuous flow advanced planning and scheduling involves the creation through the APS software of a deterministic continuous simulation model. What is being modelled is not the successive arrival of jobs at the manufacturing environment, and their despatch, as in a discrete job system, but the manufacturing plant which constitutes that environment, and the manufacturing operations carried out within it.

The manufacturing plant on which the operations take place, in its entirety, in sequence and from start to finish, is often referred to in the nomenclature as a *process train*. The process train is comprised of *stages* and, within each stage, *units*. Units are individual items of plant each capable of one or other of the manufacturing operations. Distillation columns, autoclaves and packing lines are units. One or more units are combined in sequence to form the stage. Stages are thus the main building blocks of the process train, and, importantly, are separated from each other by tanks or similar vessels for the storage of stock. The separation of stages by stocks in the process train allows a limited degree of autonomy to be exercised in each stage's scheduling. The limitations are the need for the stage schedule to dovetail with the process overall (i.e. with other stages), the stockholding capacities of the storage vessels and, perhaps, the storage life of the material being stored.

If two or more units are not separated by stock — that is, if a single stage is made up of two or more units — scheduling of the units must be carried out conjointly. The task of doing so is often complex.[26] A common (complex) situation here, provided for in continuous flow systems, is often termed "pack-from-make" (or "make-and-pack"). As the name suggests, this is a two-unit stage comprising the continuous production of material from the one unit and its subsequent discharge to a continually operating packing line, the next unit, with either no intermediate storage buffer or else a very small one.

Figure 12.10 illustrates a process train comprised of three stages S1 to S2 to S3. The symbols used are those suggested by the BSI for flowcharting process steps: a circle denotes "an operation" and an inverted triangle "storage".

Figure 12.10: A Process Train Comprising Three Stages S1, S2 and S3

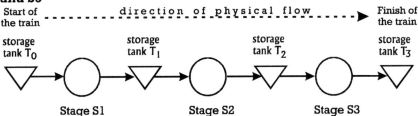

In discrete job planning, as we have seen, the mode of procedure in formulating the schedule is to start with a materials plan and due dates. Next, the impact of materials on capacity is investigated and, if necessary, the materials plan is adjusted accordingly. In a continuous flow APS, by contrast, the schedule is built for a process train stage by stage, stage after stage. As the schedule is cre-

---

[26] Examples and problems of conjoint manufacture were seen in sub-section 9.4.5 (co-products). The pack-from-make algorithms associated with continuous flow advanced planning systems are a mite more complex than those needed to deal with the acrylic shapes in 9.4.5, and are usually closely guarded as important software secrets. New algorithms are published in academic journals from time to time. Mark Fox of the University of Toronto is eminently associated with work in this area.

ated for each stage, the required materials and capacity are considered side-by-side. The joint consideration of materials and capacity encompasses output requirements, the production cycle, stock levels and, perhaps, packing sequences. The objective is to establish a "fit" between all stages of the process train — i.e. an overall plan such that output goals and timings of production at one stage match input requirements and timings at the next stage, all along the way. In the process of establishment, the schedule created for each stage of the process train should properly be called a "trial schedule". This is because, if a stage-to-stage fit cannot be found — if there is a scheduling infeasibility or if a stage schedule is of unacceptably high cost — the previous stage scheduled must be returned to and an alternative trial schedule formulated, going back as many stages as are needed to resolve the problem. If the schedule for the very first stage is unacceptable, the master plan itself must be reformulated.

There are three ways in which the stage-by-stage building of the process train schedule might proceed: (1) by *backwards scheduling*, (2) by *forwards scheduling*, and (3) by *bottleneck scheduling*, or *midpoint scheduling*. Backwards scheduling (or reverse scheduling), is associated with companies that consider packing/bottling to be their major concern. A trial schedule is formulated for the end-product first, and the procedure works backwards stage by stage ultimately to the first processing stage (of raw materials). In Figure 12.10, the backwards scheduling path would be first to create a trial schedule for S3, then a trial schedule for S2, and then a trial schedule for S1. Forward scheduling is often associated with the manufacture of food and drink, and textiles. A trial schedule is first formulated for the processing of the raw (starting) material, and the procedure works forward to the final (output) stage. In Figure 12.10, schedule creation would be first S1, then S2, then S3. Bottleneck scheduling is applied if a stage production bottleneck exists in the process train (other than at the first or last stages). A trial schedule is created for the bottleneck stage, and then forward scheduling is applied from the bottleneck to the end-product, and, separately, backwards scheduling from the bottleneck to the raw material. In Figure 12.10, if Stage S2 were a bottleneck, the two flows would be S2 to S3 and S2 to S1. Discussion of bottleneck scheduling in all its aspects is deferred until Section 12.4.

12.3.3 Scheduling Constraints

Just as there are rules and quirks and schedule objectives in discrete job work planning, so are there in continuous flow. A more apposite word is used, however — *constraints* — better reflecting the nature of the manufacturing plant. Added to various classes of constraints, schedule rules must be available, as with discrete systems, to allow manufacturing sequence to be determined (other natural sequences besides paint colours from white to black, given previously, are *broad to narrow width* and *low molecular weight to high molecular weight*). Two further prescriptives unique to continuous flow advanced planning are production cycles and campaigns (also known variously as *campaign cycles, rotation schedules* and *schedule wheels*). In continuous flow, production of many successive batches of the same material or production of a high, continuous volume, acquires a rhythm of its own as the campaign proceeds, with the attainment of steady, high levels of yield, efficiency and quality.

Note that one situation that does not arise in continuous flow APS systems is the need to make provision for "private rules" for unusual work centres. By now, software vendors claim to be able to represent any continuous flow manufacturing configuration. (The advice given in sub-section 12.2.3 (footnote 18) stands, nevertheless, that a vendor should be required to show that he can faithfully model the company's environment before his system is purchased.)

1. Hard Constraints

Hard constraints are rules stemming from the physical characteristics of the plant and from technical factors relating to the process. That is, they are such limits and restrictions as: the maximum stockholding of a storage vessel; a maximum and minimum processing speed; a maximum and minimum rate of packing; the minimum processing duration required to achieve satisfactory quality; and so on. The rules and parameters corresponding to hard constraints are directly specified within the planning model and software by the production planner and will confine schedule generation accordingly. That is, hard constraints are written into a company's APS as "absolute rules" and cannot then be overridden in schedule generation.

2. Soft Constraints

The interest of the technologist in the progress of flow manufacture is in the transformation of material — its nature, the quality and yield obtained and similar physical matters. The interest of the scheduler lies in the building up and depletion of stock volumes; the durations of times the process and its various stages are to operate; and the economics of the whole manufacture as they are affected, say, by product shelf life, plant changeovers or the periodic need for engineering maintenance. The scheduler is likely to have in mind limits on the volumes of stock or the lengths of production runs or the frequency of changeovers considered by him to be "desirable", and may set target values for them. Limits and targets of this nature are referred to as *soft constraints*, in contradistinction to the mandatory limits of hard constraints.

There is an element of judgement in the setting of soft constraints. For example, based on an assessment of the risk of a supply delivery being late, a lower limit might be set as a buffer on the stock level of a raw material to ensure continuity of the process operation. Or again, a target, or economic, production run length might be calculated, by dividing the so-called "economic manufacturing quantity" by the process rate of production.[27] Yet, as remarked in sub-section 9.6.1, an EMQ is a somewhat hazy concept supposedly representing a trade-off between manufacturing set-up costs and the added value of the production achieved. Even with the more firmly based notion of the EOQ described in 9.6.1, we see that there is conflict calling for management judgement between stockholding and frequency of stock deliveries in arriving at an optimal quantity. In the same way, there is a conflict between stockholding, production run durations, changeovers and other soft operating constraints in arriving at the continuous flow schedule.

The means by which all phenomena can be judged together to arrive at the best schedule overall is through the common denomi-

---

[27] Adapting more than somewhat the illustration of the POQ calculation given in sub-section 9.6.2, if the EOQ is 40,000 litres and the rate of manufacture is 2,000 litres/hour, the economic run length is 40,000/2,000 = 20 hours.

Advanced Planning Systems

nator of money. Thus, a cost per unit of time is ascribed to stockholding so that the stockholding cost element of a possible schedule can be determined. Similarly, a cost is ascribed to changeovers to determine the next element. A cost is ascribed to each further type of soft constraint, many of them likely to be highly particular to the process train being modelled (*the cost of the batch going cold, the cost of the material decaying*, etc.) and its contribution to the total cost of the final schedule duly incorporated. In this way, alternative possible schedules may be evaluated, the schedule incurring the lowest cost being selected for implementation in production.

It should be made clear here that in formulating the process train schedule, the role of costs in soft constraints is to guide and direct, not to optimise. There is a close analogy with the weighting, or point scoring, mechanism described for despatching jobs in discrete job systems, sub-section 12.2.3. Just as the discrete job points are management variables, so are the costs of soft constraints. While it is recommended by practitioners that costs should be set at reasonable, realistic values (and doing so is not regarded as being a matter of great account), they can be altered, like other management variables, to achieve alternative purposes when company circumstances change.

3. Strategic Constraints

Strategic constraints is the term given here to a class of soft constraints derived from commercial and operational rules, or rather, imperatives. Typical rules which must never be broken might be "*the initiation of the process must be in prime shift*", "*work on this plant must be restricted to four hours or less*", and "*production output for Customer X must never be late*". Less strict rules could include "*no plant changeovers at weekends*" and "*no change must be made to the current schedule over the immediate two-day freeze period*". A strategic constraint is imposed on the scheduling process by imputing a prohibitively high, albeit contrived, cost to the inclusion in the schedule of the event it is intended to block. Thus a cost of £10,000 might be associated with the late production of Customer X's job, making any potential schedule in which the job would be late unlikely to be the least cost solution.

12.3.4 Continuous Flow Scheduling in Action

The operation of the continuous flow advanced planning system is illustrated by following the workings out and procedures involved in backwards scheduling a process train producing a simple, fictitious product called "Ben's Home Brew" (BHB).[28] A manufacturing process flowchart of the BHB process train is given in Figure 12.11.

Figure 12.11: Process Flowchart for the Manufacture of "Ben's Home Brew"

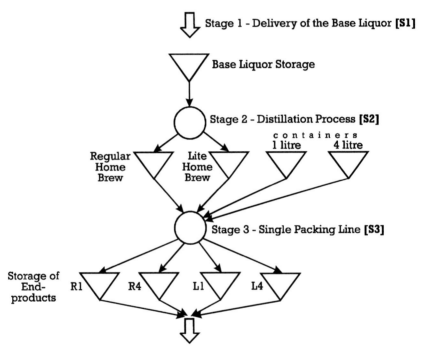

---

[28] Attention is drawn to an earlier, more comprehensive worked illustration of continuous flow manufacture, reference to which is strongly recommended, involving another fictitious material "Polygoo", made in three grades A, B and C and packed in 1 gallon cans and 5 gallon pails, given by Prof. Sam Taylor (University of Wyoming) and Prof. Steven Bolander (Colorado State University). See S.G. Taylor and S.F. Bolander (1994), "Process Flow Scheduling: A Scheduling Systems Framework for Flow Manufacturing", *Journal of APICS*; and James H. Greene (ed.) (1997), *Production & Inventory Control Handbook*, Third edition, McGraw-Hill. This latter *vade mecum* comprises 37 chapters and some 1,150 pages, and is a most useful reference in the manufacturing manager's library.

Advanced Planning Systems

The production flow begins with the delivery of Base Liquor to a storage tank. In Figure 12.11, this is termed "Stage 1", and corresponds to Stage S1 in Figure 12.10. Base Liquor is withdrawn for distillation, the niceties of the distillation process then producing either the "Regular" variety of Home Brew or the "Lite" variety of Home Brew as required. The distillation process in Figure 12.11 is called Stage 2 (corresponding to S2 in Figure 12.10). The finished Home Brew is discharged either to the Regular storage tank or to the Lite storage tank. The distillation process yield is 100 per cent — i.e. one litre of Base Liquor produces either one litre of Regular Home Brew or one litre of Lite. Note that it is unnecessary to define to the APS detail that is not significant to scheduling, such as the rate of discharge of the finished Home Brew to the storage tanks. The objective is to obtain from the model a planning fit between the stages of the process train. Concern is not to create a complete simulation model of the process such as might be required for technical or manufacturing design purposes. (However, it is necessary, clearly, for *planning* purposes to know the process yield.)

Regular Home Brew is withdrawn from storage and packed on the process train's single packing line, into either one-litre or four-litre containers, to form end-products R1 or R4. Lite Home Brew is similarly withdrawn and packed in one-litre or four-litre containers to form end-products L1 or L4. In the process train flowchart, the packing stage is Stage 3, equivalent to S3 in Figure 12.10. The packing line yield for all four packed products is 100 per cent. Labels, one-litre and four-litre empty containers are readily available from store and need not be represented in the model (even though the containers have been drawn for clarity in Figure 12.11). R1, R4, L1 and L4 are stored ready for distribution.

The MPS Requirements

The master schedule for Ben's Home Brew is determined in the normal way by considering demand forecasts and stocks, and by Rough-Cut Capacity Planning (see Section 6.5 and 6.6). The MPS for a certain month is:

- R1: 16,000 units per day (requiring 16,000 litres per day of Regular);

- R4: 3,000 units per day (requiring 12,000 litres per day of Regular);
- L1: 8,000 units per day (requiring 8,000 litres per day of Lite);
- L4: 1,000 units per day (requiring 4,000 litres per day of Lite).

Scheduling Overview

As explained, schedules in continuous flow manufacture are built one stage at a time, following the path of the process (either backwards or forwards). In the case of BHB, because packing is a more critical activity than the receipt and storage of the Base Liquor, the decision has been taken to backwards schedule. That is, three trial schedules will be formulated, one after another. The first will be for the final packed products R1, R4, L1 and L4 and the packing line, to meet the month's daily MPS requirements; the second for the production of Regular and Lite Home Brew at the distillation stage, to meet the packing requirements. The third trial schedule will be for the delivery and storage of Base Liquor, to meet the demands of the distillation process.

First Trial Schedule: Packing

The packing line operates one 12-hour shift per day, five days per week, and is capable of packing 40,000 litres per day of either Regular or Lite. For reasons of productivity, changeovers of the packing line between Regular and Lite or between one-litre and four-litre containers are performed overnight. Consequently, packing runs for R1 or L1 are in multiple lots of 40,000 units (40,000 litres), and packing runs for R4 or L4 are in lots of 10,000 units (40,000 litres).

The minimum packing cycle for packing all four end-products is governed by the requirement to pack the lowest volume product, L4. The daily MPS requirements for L4 are 4,000 litres, giving a minimum cycle of 10 days to pack 40,000 litres (10,000 units) of L4. Exploring a ten-day cycle, we see in Table 12.8 the packing durations and quantities that are feasible.

Advanced Planning Systems

Table 12.8: Exploration of Possible Packing Durations to Determine Cycle Time

R1	4 days	160,000 litres	(16,000 litres/day)
R4	3 days	120,000 litres	(12,000 litres/day)
L1	2 days	80,000 litres	(8,000 litres/day)
L4	1 day	40,000 litres	(4,000 litres/day)
	10 days	400,000 litres	(40,000 litres/day)

The notion of a *schedule wheel* can also be used to help determine cycle periods. The BHB schedule wheel is illustrated in Figure 12.12. The area, and therefore arc, of each segment of the circle represents the time required to manufacture each of the various grades. The cycle time is the area, and therefore circumference, of the complete circle (i.e. "the time" for the wheel to turn one complete revolution). For a more exact treatment of cycle time determination, see Taylor and Bolander's Polygoo model (see footnote 28 above).

Figure 12.12: Schedule Wheel for Ben's Home Brew

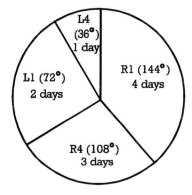

While there is a requirement in determining the sequence of packing of the four end-products to maintain the packing cycle of 10 days, and to adhere to the packing run durations of 4 days, 3 days, 2 days and 1 day above, beyond this, there are 6 (3 × 2 × 1) possible ways of sequencing the order in which the four products are to be packed, given in Table 12.9.

Table 12.9: Theoretical Packing Sequences of Four Products

(1)	R1	L1	L4	R4
(2)	R1	L1	R4	L4
(3)	R1	L4	L1	R4
(4)	R1	L4	R4	L1
(5)	R1	R4	L1	L4
(6)	R1	R4	L4	L1

If there is a required sequence, all that is necessary in setting up a continuous flow APS model is to specify it to the system as a hard constraint. In the case of Ben's Home Brew, we shall suppose that for certain reasons the required packing sequence is the second in Table 12.9, i.e. R1, L1, R4, L4. If a given packing sequence is not mandatory — if there is some flexibility as to sequence — the merits of sequence alternatives may be evaluated in terms of soft constraints and low cost as described earlier. We glimpse here, however distantly, the power of the advanced planning system in its ability to evaluate a large number of alternative sequences, selecting the one giving the best schedule outcome in terms of timely production, minimum stockholding or fewest line changes.

A summary of the trial packing schedule, its sequence and durations is now given in Figure 12.13.

Figure 12.13: Summary of the First Trial Schedule (Packing)

R1	L1	R4	L4

0   1   2   3   4   5   6   7   8   9   10 . Day

The detailed production requirements and stock balances corresponding to this schedule are given in Table 12.10.

Advanced Planning Systems

Table 12.10: Detail Relating to the First Trial Schedule

END-PRODUCT R1 (FIGURES IN '000s) Max 150, Min 20

Day	1	2	3	4	5	6	7	8	9	10
MPS Requirements	16	16	16	16	16	16	16	16	16	16
Production Schedule	40	40	40	40						
Projected Stock OH 32	56	80	104	128	112	96	80	64	48	32

END-PRODUCT L1 (FIGURES IN '000s) Max 100, Min 10

Day	1	2	3	4	5	6	7	8	9	10
MPS Requirements	8	8	8	8	8	8	8	8	8	8
Production Schedule					40	40				
Projected Stock OH 48	40	32	24	16	48	80	72	64	56	48

END-PRODUCT R4 (FIGURES IN '000s) Max 120, Min 20

Day	1	2	3	4	5	6	7	8	9	10
MPS Requirements	12	12	12	12	12	12	12	12	12	12
Production Schedule							40	40	40	
Projected Stock OH 96	84	72	60	48	36	24	52	80	108	96

END-PRODUCT L4 (FIGURES IN '000s) Max 50, Min 5

Day	1	2	3	4	5	6	7	8	9	10
MPS Requirements	4	4	4	4	4	4	4	4	4	4
Production Schedule									40	
Projected Stock OH 44	40	36	32	28	24	20	16	12	8	44

Note that in the calculation of these details, checks are necessary to ensure that the maximum stockholdings of the storage areas available to each of the products are not exceeded, and, where relevant, that stockholdings do not fall short of minimum values (perhaps set, in the case of vessels and tanks, because of pumping operation requirements).

Continuous flow APS systems provide graphical VDU displays of stockholding over time. Figure 12.14 illustrates graphically the stock levels of R1, R4, L1 and L4 given numerically in Table 12.10. The graphical stock display is the centrepiece of continuous flow system output, having, so to speak, the same pride of place as the Gantt chart in discrete job systems. Examples of the use of graphical stock displays, although not apparent in the BHB example, include the perusal of seasonal stock profiles, with stock-build-ups and the end-of-season winding down, easy comparison of stock holdings where there is considerable product mix and easy comparison of stock holdings against maximum limits. The VDU display is also the door through which the user may obtain further detail. Examples of detail available on request to the system are summaries of activity and schedule achievement in any nominated period — say, in the case of Figure 12.14, obtaining the number of units of R1 that will be packed between 10 a.m. and 2 p.m. on Day 2.

Figure 12.14: Graphical Display of Projected Stock Balances, BHB Packing Schedule

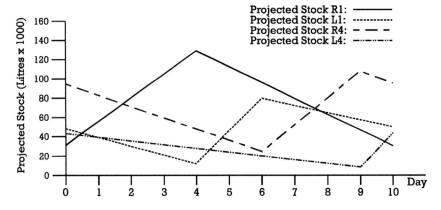

Second Trial Schedule: The Distillation Process

The distillation plant which manufactures Regular or Lite Home Brew operates two shifts per day, five days per week. Over the day, the plant is capable of making 40,000 litres of Regular or 40,000 litres of Lite from 40,000 litres of Base Liquor (i.e. the process yield is 100 per cent). The changeover between Regular and Lite is made at night, out of shift time, but, "for technical reasons", it is desirable to manufacture either R or L continuously for a minimum of two days (four shifts).

The following quantities of R and L are required to support the ten-day packing schedule:

Advanced Planning Systems

- R: 280,000 litres (160,000 for R1, 120,000 for R4);
- L: 120,000 litres (80,000 for L1, 40,000 for L4).

400,000 litres

The production cycle for the distillation process is consequently

- R: 7 days; L: 3 days.

The trial schedule for the distillation process over the ten-day cycle is as illustrated in Figure 12.15.

Figure 12.15: Summary of the Trial Schedule over ten days for the Distillation Process

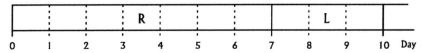

As before, the trial schedule and projected stock balances of the Regular and Lite Home Brews are calculated, and the minimum and maximum stock levels checked, as given in Table 12.11.

Table 12.11: Detail relating to the Second Trial Schedule

REGULAR HOME BREW R (FIGURES IN '000s)   Max 300, Min 50

Day	1	2	3	4	5	6	7	8	9	10
Requirements	40	40	40	40			40	40	40	
Production Schedule	40	40	40	40	40	40	40			
Projected Stock OH 150	150	150	150	150	190	230	230	190	150	150

LITE HOME BREW L (FIGURES IN '000s)   Max 200, Min 20

Day	1	2	3	4	5	6	7	8	9	10
Requirements					40	40				40
Production Schedule								40	40	40
Projected Stock OH 110	110	110	110	110	70	30	30	70	110	110

Again, the stock profiles in Table 12.11 are available from the APS on the VDU as graphical output, illustrated here in Figure 12.16.

Figure 12.16: Graphical Display of Projected Stock Balances: BHB Distillation

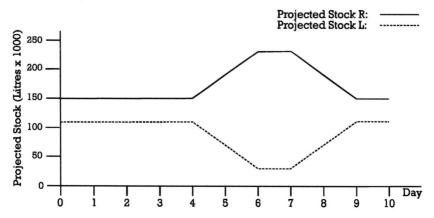

Third Trial Schedule: Base Liquor

Base Liquor is delivered by road tankers in lots of 250,000 litres. The required supply schedule must meet the Distillation Process requirements. The calculation is a standard materials planning procedure, set out in Table 12.12.

Table 12.12: Details of the Base Liquor Delivery & Storage Schedule

BASE LIQUOR (FIGURES IN '000s)   Max 300, Min 20

Day		1	2	3	4	5	6	7	8	9	10
Requirements		40	40	40	40	40	40	40	40	40	40
Delivery Schedule					250						250
Projected Stock	OH 140	100	60	20	230	190	150	110	70	30	240

The stockholding of Base Liquor is illustrated graphically in Figure 12.17.

Advanced Planning Systems

Figure 12.17: Graphical Display of the Projected Stock Balance — BHB Base Liquor

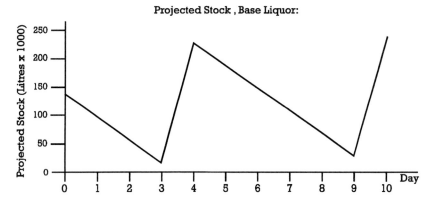

Note that since all three stage schedules S3, S2 and S1 are feasible, they need no longer be regarded as "trial". In practice, the planner would interrogate the model and scrutinise the schedule detail, adding his own know-how and judgement to obtain a refined, improved final version.

When a decision has been made that a schedule is to be put into production, it is typically presented to operations staff in the form of shift or daily work sheets, detailing the action to be followed over continuous time. That is, activity to be undertaken is shown in the form of " 6.00 a.m. to 8.00 a.m.: Action 1; 8.00 a.m. to 10.00 a.m.: Action 2 . . .". The typical horizon of a schedule may be many weeks, but, as with the discrete job Gantt chart, the duration of schedule validity will be curtailed by plan changes and other factors. Companies with fast-moving production, volatile customer orders and difficult master plan management environments — dairies, for example — are known to revise their work plans many times a day.

12.4 BOTTLENECK APS SYSTEMS

A "bottleneck" is shorthand for a manufacturing stage within a process train or a work centre within a discrete job environment which is permanently unable to fulfil the demands for output made of it. One says *permanently* since temporary bottlenecks can also arise. The actions taken to manage the permanent bottleneck are unlikely to be appropriate to the management of the temporary one, or to the management of the bottleneck which can be overcome by judicious stockpiling ahead of a high season. Because the presence of the bottleneck in the materials chain restricts the output of the entire chain (*a chain is as strong as its weakest link,* as they say) two issues dominate bottleneck scheduling. The first, dealt with in sub-section 12.4.1, is commonsensical — ensuring that the output from the bottleneck is at maximum. The second, sub-section 12.4.2, is more complex and has given rise to considerable debate in manufacture — allocating the scarce output from the bottleneck to subsequent manufacture in the best way.

12.4.1 Maximising Bottleneck Output

Reliability in operation and good quality in output are needs identified elsewhere than in bottleneck management. The adoption of total productive maintenance, TPM, in looking after the physical plant, and the establishment of an emergency repair team as a last resort, are described in sub-section 15.6.2. In addition to these precautions, engineers, process workers and shop floor operators responsible for everyday running of the bottleneck might be expected to contribute ideas to its improved operation, especially in the matter of increasing yield (or reducing scrap).

As noted above, output from the bottleneck governs output from the complete manufacturing chain, so that improvements in efficiency have a disproportionately greater effect on company productivity than they would have elsewhere. The notion of identifying bottlenecks and improving their efficiency has been extended very considerably by those who have made this subject their particular concern. By analogy, they point out, there are liable to be constraints other than physical manufacturing plant which stand in the way of the company fulfilling its potential. Examples might be the poor deployment of sales effort; wrong decisions on stocking in a distribution network; and the delays in order handling spoken of in sub-section 5.2.2. The identification and removal of poor practice of this nature may sound simply like good management, or, if it has to have another name, total quality management (Chapter 13), but has been built up into a complete philosophy termed *The*

Theory of Constraints (TOC),[29] incorporating problem solving, motivation analysis and other similar subjects besides. On the factory floor, senior management can put an end to a plant's bottleneck status and the need for the sophisticated systems that may have been developed to direct its output by the obvious expedient of acquiring further capacity through capital construction, purchase or take-over. Under TOC, in contrast, the quest to identify and remove corporate constraints is never-ending.[30]

Returning to the maximisation of physical bottleneck output, two actions can be taken in materials planning besides paying operational attention. The first is to ensure that the bottleneck is never starved of work because of a failure in materials supply from the prior process. It will be recalled that in the brief discussion of advanced planning systems and simulation in sub-section 12.2.1, the assumption was made that manufacturing plans and progress were deterministic — that matters would proceed strictly in accordance with the rules and standards laid down. What if this is not reality, so that a bottlenecked plant or work centre is forced to surrender a portion of its precious capacity because of a failure to deliver material for its use by the prior stage? Or if a bottlenecked plant, for some reason, is temporarily capable of operating at a higher rate than normal, but advantage is unable to be taken of the situation because of insufficient supporting material? One way to protect against these possibilities is to increase the output capacity of the stage prior to the bottleneck. The size of increase should be governed by consideration of the possible shortfall in prior stage rate of supply and the possible increase in the rate of bottleneck demand. To achieve this protection will require a greater increase in capacity at the prior stage than might be supposed at first. Con-

---

[29] See Greene (1997), op. cit., Chapter 9.

[30] Followers of the TOC philosophy may also become temporarily enveloped in an *evaporating cloud*. The analogy of an evaporating cloud has been put forward by Eliyahu M. Goldratt, the Israeli manufacturing guru closely associated with TOC and famous for devising and marketing the OPT system (see 12.4.2). When seeking to resolve a conflict or remove an obstacle to progress, the seeming impossibilities of doing so (= the cloud) should be analysed and expressed in precise terms and the assumptions standing in the way of change identified. The assumptions can then be challenged and, it is hoped, removed, one by one (= evaporation). Goldratt's cloud appears to be a meteorological version of Sakichi Toyoda's *Five Why's* — see Section 15.1, footnote 4.

sider Table 12.13(a), in which the capacity of a constraint C can vary between 10 units/period and 20 units/period, and is matched for throughput by the capacity of a non-constraint NC, which also can vary between 10 units/period and 20 units/period. The third column of Table 12.13(a) is the rate of throughput through C and NC together, in series. That is, the throughputs are the lesser of the pairs of corresponding figures for C and NC. The average is 12.5, even though for half the time constraint C has had a capacity of 20. In order to improve the performance of this mini production line, the capacity of NC must be raised such that, when it is working *below par*, it can, at that time, support C *working above par*. This is shown in Table 12.13(b), where the capacity of NC has been raised from 10/20 to 20/30.

Table 12.13(a) Reduced Output of Two Work Centres in Series

C (Rate)	NC (Rate)	Together
10	10	10
10	20	10
20	10	10
20	20	20
Average		12.5

Table 12.13(b) To Boost Output, disproportionate extra Resource is needed

C (Rate)	NC (Rate)	Together
10	20	10
10	30	10
20	20	20
20	30	20
Average		15.0

The additional capacity needed for NC has been referred to as *protective capacity*.[31]

An alternative approach to the provision of protective capacity is to invest in protective WIP. If the rate of production of the bottleneck is R units per hour, and an estimate of the loss of processing time at the stages prior to the bottleneck due to delay or malfunction is L hours, the protective WIP to be held at the bottleneck to protect against material starvation is clearly $R \times L$ units.

The degree of protection is usually spoken of, however, simply as time, L — so many hours, so many days. In practice, the setting of protective capacity and protective WIP should take account of the reliability of operation of the prior stages and the statistical prob-

---

[31] See Greene (1997), op. cit., Chapter 9.

Advanced Planning Systems

ability of an interruption of supply to the bottleneck. In purely theoretical terms, queuing theory, mentioned in sub-section 11.2.4, and the relationship of queue and resource utilisation illustrated in Figure 11.3, apply. In practice, drawing representative graphs is likely to prove quite impractical, and the amounts needed for protection must be decided by simulation and after observation of supply performance over a reasonable period.[32]

The bottleneck should be managed for output as well as protected for input. If completed production cannot be cleared away, its operation may be impaired or even halted if the stage of manufacture following has broken down. It will be unusual indeed in a job shop environment if space somewhere cannot be found for completed output. The situation is very different when output needs to be cleared, say, by wagon cars or when the bottleneck is a stage in a process train discharging material to a storage tank. As before, the size of buffer for which post-production space should be provided is obtained by multiplication of the bottleneck rate of manufacture, R units/period, and the time L' likely to be lost in after-stage processing, i.e. $R \times L'$.

A final means of maximising output is to minimise the time lost due to set-up. If set-up times are dependent on the sequence of production, we can turn to a sequencing algorithm such as that used to solve the travelling salesman problem. Whether they are dependent or not, set-up times can be very substantially reduced by application of the SMED methodology, described at length in Section 15.3. In the absence of an SMED programme, the manufacturing manager can simply elect to minimise set-up loss by running extremely large batches of production (after first having confirmed, of course, that the value of the additional bottleneck output obtained in doing so will more than cover the costs associated with the extra stock). One danger here, however, is that the production of large batches of bottlenecked material at infrequent intervals may, perversely, starve later, non-bottlenecked stages of

---

[32] It will be recalled that one reason given for building a sophisticated, high performance shop floor information system would be to keep an eye on work centres about to run out of work, so that jobs destined for them and waiting at other work stations could be immediately reprioritised. If the work centres about to run out are bottlenecks, reason for installing such a system is doubly justified.

production, leading to plant idleness and inefficiency in their operation. What is preferable at these later non-bottlenecked work centres is to manufacture in small batches, thereby obtaining reductions in queue sizes, WIP and lead times for the reasons explained in Section 11.2.

To overcome the conflict between large batches at bottlenecks and small batches at non-bottlenecks, the concepts are introduced of *process batches* and *transfer batches* That is, a large process batch of material may be made at the bottleneck, and this material then sent on to further non-bottleneck manufacturing sites in small lots, known as transfer batches.

In the philosophy of bottleneck scheduling, as expounded by proponents of the OPT system, the possibility that small transfer batches at non-bottleneck work centres may be inefficient, in part because they may incur disproportionately large amounts of setup, is lightly regarded. One of the precepts of OPT is that "time saved at a non-bottleneck work centre is a mirage". Advantages (throughput, WIP) and disadvantages (administration, set-up) stemming from many small transfer batches are in most respects the same as those incurred in operation splitting and operation overlapping, described in Section 11.4 under Lead Time Management, even if the underlying reasons for their creation are different.[33]

12.4.2 Allocating Bottleneck Output

Although the repercussions on product availability of only a small number of bottlenecks in the factory may give rise to many problems in the manufacturing company's Sales and Marketing department, a sense of perspective must be retained. The manufacturing programmes of a great many products will be unaffected. For them, the conventional steps of master scheduling, materials planning and work scheduling will be followed as before. One way of identifying products affected by the presence of bottlenecks

---

[33] Vollmann et al (1988), op. cit., Chapter 20, report that simulation experiments with "repetitive lots" of transfer batches, conducted in 1986 by F. Robert Jacobs and D.J. Bragg of Indiana University, do indeed confirm that improvements are gained in flow times and reduced WIP from many small batches, with expected, commensurate increases in set-up times.

Advanced Planning Systems 453

and separating them from those not so affected is through the employment of conventional CRP (6.6.1). Figure 12.18 is a schematic of a company-wide bill of materials, created by explosion of the master plan products (top of diagram) in the normal way.

Figure 12.18: Delimiting the Bottlenecked and Free Areas of the Bill of Materials

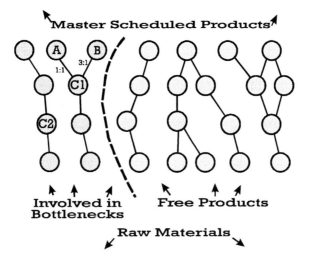

When the capacity demands of materials needed to support the MPS are evaluated by reference to the capacity database, it is found that the requirements for the products marked C1 and C2 cannot be fully satisfied because of a permanent shortage of capacity at the work centres on which they are made. Because C1 and C2 are made on bottlenecks, it is necessary to isolate and consider separately the manufacturing requirements of all the lower level ancestors and higher level descendants of the two products.[34]

Although this sub-section is principally concerned with the decisions to be made in the deployment of material made on bottlenecks — i.e. with the quantities of (limited) output to be allocated

---

[34] It is not safe to ignore the lower level ancestors of bottlenecked products on the grounds that the requirements for them are simply balanced in 100 per cent support of maximum output of the bottlenecked products. The bottlenecked plant may be capable of making several products. Consequently, until the product mix is decided, the requirements for lower level materials cannot be determined.

to subsequent higher-level manufacture — the point is made that the majority of the bill of materials network is unaffected and can be treated normally.

In Eliyahu Goldratt's OPT system,[35] the program responsible for determining bottlenecks and separating the bottlenecked products and those products connected to them from the non-bottlenecked ones is called Split. In the jargon of OPT, products unaffected by and unconcerned in the bottlenecks are termed "free products".

The section of the bill of materials in Figure 12.18 encompassing the two master scheduled products A and B and the bottlenecked product C1 is magnified in Figure 12.19. Figure 12.19 also illustrates the constraint work centre W on which C1 is made, this being represented by a rectangle. The capacity of W is 2,500 hours and the rate of manufacture of C1 is one unit per hour. The usage of C1 by A is one unit of C1 per unit of A manufactured. The usage of C1 by B is three units per unit of B manufactured. Other data relating to A and B are also shown. These data are given again separately in Table 12.14.

Figure 12.19: Focus on Three Products from Figure 12.18

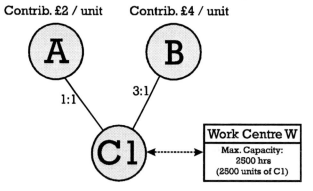

---

[35] Goldratt has now surrendered his proprietorial interest in OPT, which is sold in the UK by Scheduling Technology Group Ltd, Hounslow, Middx. There is a vast literature on OPT; search the Internet with terms +*optimization* (or +*optimisation*); +*scheduling*; and +*OPT*. OPT is not the only system which works the way it does. Benoy et al. (1994), op. cit., report that ST-Point and Goal Systems are also what they call *Theory of Constraints Finite Schedulers*.

Advanced Planning Systems

Table 12.14: Data relating to Products A and B in Figures 12.18 and 12.19

MPS Product	Unit Contribution (£, each)	Sales Demand Requirements (units)	Hours required of the bottleneck (= units of C1)
A	£2	1000	1 hr per unit of A
B	£4	750	3 hrs per unit of B

The term *unit contribution* in Table 12.14 means the financial contribution to company profits arising from the sale of one unit of the product, and is defined as the selling price of a product less the costs of materials, expenses and labour directly incurred in its manufacture (i.e. excluding any and all overhead costs). The direct costs include not only the direct costs at the stage of final manufacture, but the accumulated direct costs incurred in the manufacture of the product's ancestor materials, and, ultimately, the costs of raw materials. (An understanding of product costs and the terms used in costing are essential to the manufacturing manager. They are dealt with at length in Section 17.4.)

The total requirements for capacity from work centre W to support the sales demand fully are 3,250 hours (1,000hrs for A, stemming from 1,000 × 1 units of C1, plus 2,250 hrs for B, from 750 × 3 units of C1), but only 2,500 hours are available because of the capacity limitation. A decision must therefore be made as to the division of the hours available and the allocation of the units of C1. That is, how many hours/units of C1 are to be allocated to Product A's production requirements and how many allocated to Product B's?

Although it is an objective that can be questioned, and will be so at the conclusion of this sub-section, one might suppose that the "best" allocation is one that maximises the total contribution to profit of the master scheduled products.

Allocation by Straight Contribution

As a naïve first attempt to achieve maximisation of total contribution, suppose that master scheduled products A and B are ranked in a "profitability index" according to their straightforward unit contribution, with Product B at the top of the index, since it yields a contribution of £4 per unit sold, and Product A second, at £2 per unit. When this has been done, time on the bottleneck (i.e. output from it) is allocated by giving preference to the products higher in the index — in this case, allocating C1 to Product B until either there is no more C1 to allocate, or until Product B's requirements are fully satisfied. When Product B has been dealt with, allocation of C1 is made to the next product lower in the profitability index, Product A. The result of this method of allocation is given in Table 12.15, showing a total contribution from A and B together of £3,500.

Table 12.15: Allocation of Bottleneck Output to the MPS by Straight Contribution

Bottleneck Capacity 2,500 hours

Product	Rank in Profit. Index	Contrib. per unit	Time needed on B'neck	Demand for this Product (units)	Hours allocated	Hours remaining on B'neck	Contrib. from Product/Alloc.
B	1st	£4	3 hrs/unit	750	2,250	250	£3,000
A	2nd	£2	1 hr/unit	1,000	250	0	£500
Totals					2,500		£3,500

Unfortunately for the method of allocation by straight contribution, in this instance, had the allocation been in the reverse order, the total contribution would have been greater (£4,000). This is shown in Table 12.16. As we see, what straight contribution fails to do is to take account of the demand of the products on the bottlenecked plant. Product B may yield a higher unit contribution than A, but it hogs three hours on the bottleneck for every unit made, compared with A's requirement merely for one hour per unit.

Table 12.16: Allocation of Bottleneck Output to the MPS in Reverse of Straight Contribution

Bottleneck Capacity 2,500 hours

Product	Rank in Profit. Index	Contrib. per unit	Time needed on B'neck	Demand for this Product (units)	Hours allocated	Hours remaining on B'neck	Contrib. from Product/Alloc.
A	2nd	£2	1 hr/unit	1,000	1,000	1,500	£2,000
B	1st	£4	3 hrs/unit	750	1,500	nil	£2,000
Totals					2,500		£4,000

Allocation by Bottleneck Operating Contribution

Instead of ranking products in the profitability index by straight contribution, an alternative method that takes into account each product's demand on the bottleneck is to rank them in order of their *bottleneck operating contribution*. That is, to rank them in order of their contribution per hour of demand on the bottleneck.[36] The figures for A and B are:

- **A:** £2 contribution per 1 hour of demand on the bottleneck = £2.00/hour;

- **B:** £4 contribution per 3 hours of demand on the bottleneck = £1.33/hour.

Product A is now top of the profitability index and B second; the allocation of time and C1, and the total contribution, are as shown in Table 12.16.

Allocation by Excess Contribution

A measure by which sales products may be ranked in the profitability index that has proved superior to bottleneck operating contribution is *excess contribution*, devised by Tom Heywood, a senior accountant and then a member of ICI Dyestuffs division's Commodore project team.[37]

---

[36] See the worked example by James Cox and John Blackstone (Greene (1997), op. cit., Chapter 9). The authors state that the background to their example is from E.M. Goldratt (1990), *The Haystack Syndrome: Sifting Information out of the Data Ocean*, North River Press, NY.

[37] The Commodore project was embarked on by ICI Dyestuffs division in the late 1960s in order to formulate a finite schedule, or APS model, whereby the division's many bottlenecked resources would be allocated to sales products in "the most profitable way", as described in sub-section 12.4.2. (See D.M. Crabtree, R.M. Waugh, E. Atherton and T.E. Heywood (1968), *Commodore: A General Description of a Contribution Maximising Model of Divisional Resources*, 1/1/68, ICI Dyestuffs division memorandum (no ref. number).) A number of methods were experimented with for ranking the profitability index, including straight contribution, bottleneck operating contribution and excess contribution. The method of allocation chosen however was linear programming, described at the end of this chapter. A rigorous comparison and review of the contending methods was made on a closed model involving 60 foodstuffs colours and 320 intermediates and raw materials in 1969, by Ian Milne and Peter Spooner (*Commodore: A Comparison of Different Approaches*

Excess contribution rests on the notion that the company's work centres each have an "operating value" (as well as a conventional capital value). Although only work centres producing sales products may appear directly to generate sales income and contribute to company profits, in truth it may be said that all prior stages of manufacture play their parts. In fact, we may go on to say that it is legitimate to attribute credit for the achievement of sales income and contribution to all these prior stages of manufacture. Focusing only on contribution, an equitable means of apportioning the credit, or apportioning a sales product's contribution, is in accordance with each prior manufacturing stage's value to its final manufacture. A measure of a work centre's value to manufacture is the short-term investment made in the manufacturing process itself. A measure of this, in turn, is the *stage direct expenses* incurred in the manufacture (and, at the gateway work centres, raw material costs). (Stage direct expenses are explained in sub-section 17.4.3; they are the costs of manufacturing activity itself — energy, tools usage, plant services and so on. They exclude labour costs and the stage costs of materials.)

Having found a way of crediting the contribution of each sales product to its ancestor components, the first step in determining work centre operating values is duly to apportion each sales product's contribution, but to do so *based on 100 per cent fulfilment of the desired sales and manufacturing plan* — that is, disregarding the fact that certain work centres are bottlenecks.

The second step is to assign the contribution associated with each product from the first step to the work centre on which it is manufactured, or, for work centres involved in the manufacture of two or more products, to add the individual contributions to obtain summary figures for them.

At this juncture, the total, ideal company-wide sales product contribution, regardless of bottlenecks, has been assigned to the work centres in accordance with their value to end-stage manufac-

---

to the Allocation Problem, 28/5/69, ICI Dyestuffs division memorandum MSD/69/17). Linear programming was, naturally, the clear winner, but excess contribution was a creditable second and well ahead of bottleneck operating contribution.

Advanced Planning Systems

ture. The sum of money assigned to each work centre is referred to as that work centre's "operating value".

Heywood now introduces a further notion, that of *work centre rental*. This is defined as a work centre operating value divided by the total time on the work centre that would be needed to achieve the ideal manufacturing quantities that are involved (*ideal* quantities — that is, again disregarding the fact that required capacity on the bottlenecks is not, in fact, available). Work centre rental might be expressed in £/day for each work centre.

The work centre rental for each work centre can now be regarded as an *opportunity cost*. Opportunity cost is an economic rather than an accounting term. It is the value of something that is foregone by taking a particular action. For example, in everyday life, we might hear a citizen indirectly refer to opportunity cost thus: *Attending the Open Golf Championship has cost me the holiday I had otherwise intended to book to Florida!* Regardless of the financial cost of attending the Championship, given the citizen's limited resources of time, the *opportunity* cost of attending it is the holiday, which must now be foregone. A work centre rental is the opportunity cost of spending time manufacturing any particular sales product. That is, for any work centre, including any bottlenecked work centre, if time is diverted to the sales product, what is foregone is time available for the ideal manufacturing plan, represented in profitability terms by the plant rental. This being so, a plant rental can be associated with the manufacture of each unit of sales product. This is obtained by calculating the demands each unit of sales product makes on all components and their associated work centres lower in the bill of materials, demands being expressed as time rather than as quantities of material. Knowing the demands of the sales product manufactured on the time of the lower level work centres, individual "rents" (£) can be calculated. A rent is defined as the time demand (days) multiplied by the work centre's rental (£/day). The sales product's rental per unit manufactured is the sum of its rents.

Heywood's excess contribution is now defined as a sales product's straight contribution (i.e. sales income per unit *less* variable cost per unit) *less* the sales product's rental per unit. In other words, the financial value to the sales plan of the sales product's income is diminished not only by the variable cost incurred in manufacture, but by the opportunity cost of occupying plant which might have been used more profitably in an alternative way.

A profitability index is now drawn up, ranked in descending order of excess contribution. If the procedure were to be applied to the scenario illustrated in Figure 12.18, clearly a great deal of data relating to all levels of the bill of materials and to stage expenses would have to be assembled in order to calculate the plant rental of sales product A and the plant rental of B. If such data were to be fabricated here, the sum of money to be allocated as rental to lower-level work centres arising from product A would be £2,000 (1,000 × £2) and from B £3,000 (750 × £4). However, the unit plant rental of B would be greater than the unit rental of A, because of sales product B's far greater demand on work centre W. Figures might therefore be concocted to show B having a plant rental more than £2 per unit higher than A's (£2 is the gap between the straight contribution of B and the straight contribution of A). If this were done, the excess contribution of B would be lower than that of sales product A, and the ranking and calculations illustrated in Table 12.16 would prevail.

Allocation by Linear Programming

However sophisticated may be the method for ranking the profitability index and achieving the objective of best deployment of bottlenecked output, it is unlikely to lead to a satisfactory result in the face of many of the complex situations that can arise in reality. Examples of complexities are bottlenecks feeding other bottlenecks, alternative plant sites, the possibility of lead time management (see Section 11.4) and such process industry oddities as co-products and recoveries (Section 9.4).

A technique capable of dealing with these complexities which specifically addresses the problem of how to allocate limited, bottlenecked resources so as to attain an objective such as maximum

Advanced Planning Systems

contribution, is *linear programming*, a term already mentioned a number of times in this Chapter.[38]

Linear programming is a major operations research technique widely used in manufacturing industry in applications as diverse as product mix planning; blending and cutting; skills and manpower planning; sequencing and scheduling; transportation and location planning; activity scheduling; and many others besides. LP is incorporated in numerous software applications, and there is a very extensive literature.[39]

A problem which is to be solved by linear programming must have two properties. It must have constraints and it must have an objective. Constraints in the context of advanced planning systems are clearly the capacity limitations of work centres and maximum sales targets. In the example in Figure 12.18 and Table 12.14, if the quantity of product A to be manufactured using output from bottleneck W is *a units* and of product B is *b units*, then bearing in mind: (1) the products' usages of C1; (2) the limitations of capacity of work centre W; and (3) the maximum requirements for A and B; we may write the three inequalities shown in the three expressions termed Equations 12.1 to 12.3.

$$a + 3b \leq 2{,}500 \qquad \text{Equation 12.1}$$

$$a \leq 1{,}000 \qquad \text{Equation 12.2}$$

$$b \leq 750 \qquad \text{Equation 12.3}$$

---

[38] As previously mentioned in Section 12.1, linear programming is one of a small family of *optimisation* techniques collectively known as *mathematical programming*. Although the method of allocation of output employed by OPT has not been published, it might reasonably be supposed that it employs *mixed integer programming*, a combination of linear programming and integer programming. The initial separation of the bottlenecked section of the bill of materials from free products illustrated in Figure 12.18 is a useful precursor to the application of the technique, since the mathematical model thereafter constructed is confined to the bottlenecked area, substantially reducing its subsequent demand on computing capacity. This trick was used in Commodore and is, presumably, the reason for initially running Split in OPT.

[39] See Ray Wild (1980), op. cit.; C.A. Kirkpatrick, D.S. Rubin (1982), op. cit.; James R. Evans, David R. Anderson, Dennis J. Sweeney and Thomas A. Williams (1984), op. cit.; James H. Greene (ed.) (1997), op. cit.; James Bates and J.R. Parkinson (1969), *Business Economics*; and, especially, Harvey Wagner (1975), op. cit.

An *objective* is some quantity which is to be either minimised or maximised (hence the common term for the technique, *optimisation*). In the case of sales product A and sales product B, it was decided to maximise the total contribution of the output of the two products, so that the equation in Equation 12.4 can be written, where P is the total contribution to profit in £.

$$12 \times a + £4 \times b = P \qquad \textit{Equation 12.4}$$

A lengthy worked example showing the calculations involved in linear programming is given below. The procedure is similar to the transportation algorithm previously mentioned as being used for determining the optimal distribution of excess material in a distribution network (see the worked example in Section 20.3).

To conclude the sub-section, we return to challenge the very premise on which the allocation of bottlenecked output has been built: the goal of maximising sales product contribution. The determination of product mix based on maximum contribution or minimum cost or some similar optimum must presuppose that the customer and the sales manager are indifferent as to the actual mix of products arrived at. In the worked example below, it will be seen there that the customer has indeed no interest whatsoever in the proportions of seven cattlefeed products used to make up a final cattlefeed mix. His interest lies only in the nutritional qualities of the final mix. Where there is discretion in the determination of output from a bottleneck and freedom to choose which sales products are to be made and which are not to be made, such as in the example involving A and B in Figure 12.18, the customer and sales manager must have very powerful voices in determining the product mix to be produced. It is highly unlikely that maximum contribution of the mix to the manufacturing company's profit will be given much weight compared with such issues as allocation to favoured customers, allocation to particular markets, to industrial or geographic segments, support of the company's spares operation and so on. To conclude, in the circumstances of rationed supply, the allocation of resources to output is a major task involving the sales

Linear Programming: Worked Example

A customer of the Troy Cattlefeed Company requires a quantity of cattlefeed which must contain 100, 80 and 120 grams of the nutrients N1, N2 and N3 respectively. The company manufactures seven different standard feeds, each one containing a number of grams per kilogram of each or any of the three nutrients. The quantities of nutrients and the cost per kilogram of each of the seven standard feeds are given in Table 12.17. The problem to be solved by linear programming is to find the mix of standard feeds that will satisfy the customer's requirement at lowest cost.

Table 12.17: Starting Data relating to the Troy Cattlefeed Problem

Grams of Nutrient per kilogram of Standard Product \ Name of Troy's Standard Product	P1	P2	P3	P4	P5	P6	P7	Customer's Requirements
N1	5	0	2	0	3	1	2	100 grams
N2	3	1	5	0	2	0	1	80 grams
N3	1	0	3	1	2	0	6	120 grams
Cost of Product (p per kilogram)	40	10	50	6	35	7	40	

The fundamental premise of linear programming is that in such a situation as the one described, there is a solution to the problem whereby at least four of the seven standard feeds are not in-

---

[40] The misfortune of the inexperienced sheepdog who drove the sheep over the ridge of the hill serves for a warning against the blind use of maximum contribution: ". . . the untoward fate which so often attends dogs and other philosophers who follow out a train of reasoning to its logical conclusion and attempt perfectly consistent conduct in a world made up so largely of compromise." (*Far from the Madding Crowd* (Ch.5), by Thomas Hardy.) The dog was subsequently shot by the farmer, Gabriel Oak.

cluded.[41] An initial solution excluding four or more standard feeds is called a *basic solution*, or *basis*. Linear programming procedure consists of formulating a succession of basic solutions, each having a lower cost than the previous one, until a solution is found that cannot be improved upon (i.e. until a minimum cost solution is found).

If the cattlefeed problem were to be tackled algebraically, it would entail solving 35 sets of three linear equations in seven variables. As we shall see, the repetitive procedure of linear programming is far simpler and ideally suited to computer processing. The superiority of linear programming becomes more apparent as the size of problem grows. A cattlefeed problem involving ten nutrients and 30 standard products would involve the solution of 30 million sets of ten equations in ten variables if tackled algebraically. Solution by linear programming would be a simple matter, performed in seconds by computer.

To begin the solution, we must derive a first basis, remembering that a basis involves three standard products only. Inspection of Table 12.17 shows that 100 kg of P6, 80 kg of P2 and 120 kg of P4 will satisfy the customer's requirements. The cost is 2220p. The solution is the basis and the starting point of the linear programming procedure. The basis was easily derived because three of the standard products contained only one gram of nutrient per kilogram. This will not normally be so. When it is not, artifices are employed, known as *slack variables* — fictitious products with very high costs, introduced to enable the basis to be formulated. This will be explained in due course.

What is now required is a way of moving from the starting basis of P6, P2 and P4 to another basis costing less than 2220p. Clearly, this can be achieved only by introducing another standard product not included in the starting basis. Equally clearly, if another product is so introduced, it will be necessary to remove some of the existing ones.

Consider the introduction to the mixture of 1 kg of standard product P1. If this is done, we automatically introduce 5 grams of

---

[41] An alternative way of stating the remarkable premise in the text is that if there are three nutrients, a mix can be formulated from only three standard products. And since there are many ways of formulating it, one way must be superior to all others as regards lowest cost or some other desired optimum.

N1, 3 grams of N2 and 1 gram of N3. Consequently, to maintain the cattlefeed according to the customer's specification, we must (somehow) remove 5 grams of N1, 3 grams of N2 and 1 gram of N3. From Table 12.17, we can readily see that this can be accomplished by removing 5 kg of P6, 3 kg of P2 and 1 kg of P4. Although the balance of nutrients is the same after taking this action, the cost of the mix has changed. From Table 12.17, we see that the introduction of 1 kg of P1 increases the cost by (1 × 40p), but, again from Table 12.17, the removal of P6, P2 and P4 decreases the cost by (5 × 7p) + (3 × 10p) + (1 × 6p). The net reduction is 31p and is known as the *differential cost*.[42] The same procedure as the foregoing is used to investigate the introduction to the basic solution of 1 kg of P3, 1 kg of P5 and 1 kg of P7. The results of doing so, along with the figures calculated for introducing P1, are given in Table 12.18. The differential costs have also been worked out and are shown in the last column of the Table.

Table 12.18: Changes required in the number of kilograms of Standard Products to compensate for changes shown in the leftmost column (i.e. moving from the initial basis to the second basis)

	P1 kg	P2 kg	P3 kg	P4 kg	P5 kg	P6 kg	P7 kg	Differential Cost
For each 1 kg of P1 introduced...	1	−3	0	−1	0	−5	0	−31p
For each 1 kg of P3 introduced...	0	−5	1	−3	0	−2	0	−32p
For each 1 kg of P5 introduced...	0	−2	0	−2	1	−3	0	−18p
For each 1 kg of P7 introduced...	0	−1	0	−6	0	−2	1	−20p
Cost Row (p)	40	10	50	6	35	7	40	

---

[42] At the conclusion of the linear programming process, a differential cost will have been calculated for every variable, whether or not it appears in the optimal solution. The figures are the amounts by which the costs of the standard products would need to be reduced before they would form part of the optimum. Alternatively, they indicate the loss to the user of including the product in the final solution (perhaps for technical or other reasons) rather than the optimal products.

The next important, albeit obvious, rule of linear programming is to introduce whichever standard product gives rise to the greatest cost reduction. As we see from Table 12.18, this is product P3. The amount of P3 which is to be introduced is that quantity required to eliminate just one of the three products present in the starting basis. Naturally, the quantities of all three of the starting products should be reduced on introducing P3. However, as increasing amounts of P3 are considered, we see that the quantity of P2 will be reduced to zero before P4 and P6 are. This is because there are only 80 kg of P2 in the starting basis, and each 1 kilogram of P3 leads to a required reduction of this starting quantity by 5 kg. In fact, only 16 kg of P3 are required to eliminate P2 completely. The cattlefeed will then comprise 16 kg of P3, 72 kg of P4 and 68 kg of P6. (If the nutrients content of each kilogram of standard product is checked from Table 12.17, it will be seen that the new formulation continues to satisfy the customer's requirement for 100 grams of N1, 80 grams of N2 and 120 grams of N3.) The cost of the formulation is now, however:

$$(16 \times 50p) + (72 \times 6p) + (68 \times 7p) = 1708p$$

This is 512p cheaper than the starting basis of 2220p. However, what is important is that the second, cheaper solution is *itself a basis* and that a procedure has been found that enables us to go from one basis to another, cheaper basis, guided by differential cost.

The procedure can now be repeated by constructing a new table, Table 12.19, similar to Table 12.18, to guide us in making our next move in search of a third basis that is cheaper still. Calculation of the entries for each row of the new Table is not quite as simple as before, however, since one of the products, P3, in the second basis just formulated, contains all three nutrients N1, N2 and N3. Simple algebra overcomes this difficulty as follows:

Consider the first entry to be made in Table 12.19. That is, we wish to introduce one kilogram of P1 to the cattlefeed at the expense of some of the three products currently making up our latest basis (i.e. P3, P4 and P6). Let us say that we will reduce P3 by p kilograms, P4 by q kilograms and P6 by r kilograms. From Table 12.17, we see that introducing 1 kilogram of P1 will introduce 1×5 grams of N1, 1×3 grams of N2 and 1×1 grams of N3. But, again from Table 12.17, reducing P3 by p kilograms will reduce the con-

Advanced Planning Systems

tent of N1 by $2 \times p$ grams, N2 by $5 \times p$ grams and N3 by $3 \times p$ grams. Similarly, subtracting q kilograms of P4 will reduce N3 by $q \times 1$ grams, and subtracting r kilograms of P6 will reduce N1 by $r \times 1$ grams. Consider now the three nutrients in turn. If the additional amount of N1 added by the 1 kilogram of P1 (i.e. 5 grams) is to be matched by the reduction in N1 obtained from removing p kilograms of P3, q kilograms of P4 and r kilograms of P6, then Equation 12.5 holds true.

$1 \times 5g\ N1 = (2 \times p) + (0 \times q) + (1 \times r)$ g of N1   *Equation 12.5*

Similarly, if the additional amount of N2 added by 1 kilogram of P1 (i.e. 3 grams) is to be matched by the reduction in N2 from removing p kilograms of P3, q kilograms of P4 and r kilograms of P6, then Equation 12.6 holds true.

$1 \times 3g\ N2 = (5 \times p) + (0 \times q) + (0 \times r)$ g of N2   *Equation 12.6*

Finally, if the additional amount of N3 added by 1 kilogram of P1 (i.e. 1 gram) is to be matched by the reduction in N3 from removing p kilograms of P3, q kilograms of P4 and r kilograms of P6, then Equation 12.7 holds true.

$1 \times 1g\ N3 = (3 \times p) + (1 \times q) + (0 \times r)$ g of N3   *Equation 12.7*

Equations 12.5 to 12.7 may be rewritten as Equations 12.8 to 12.10.

$5 = 2p + r$ *Equation 12.8*

$3 = 5p$ *Equation 12.9*

$1 = 3p + q$ *Equation 12.10*

Solving for p, q and r, we have

$P = +0.6, q = -0.8$ and $r = +3.8$

In summary then, we have introduced 1 kg of P1 to the cattlefeed, and so must reduce P3 by 0.6 kg, increase P4 by 0.8 kg and reduce P6 by 3.8 kg. The differential cost of doing so will be:

$(1 \times 40p) - (0.6 \times 50p) + (0.8 \times 6p) - (3.8 \times 7p) = -11.8p$

The first row of Table 12.19 can now be completed as given. The remaining rows for P2, P5 and P7 can be completed by repeating the procedure just described and calculating the differential costs.

Table 12.19: Changes required in the number of kilograms of Standard Products to compensate for changes shown in the leftmost column (i.e. moving from the second basis to the third basis)

	P1 kg	P2 kg	P3 kg	P4 kg	P5 kg	P6 kg	P7 kg	Differential Cost
For each 1 kg of P1 introduced ...	1		–0.6	0.8		–3.8		–11.8p
For each 1 kg of P2 introduced ...		1	–0.2	0.6		0.4		+6.4p
For each 1 kg of P5 introduced ...			–0.4	–0.8	1	–2.2		–5.2p
For each 1 kg of P7 introduced ...			–0.2	–5.4		–1.6	1	–13.6p
Cost Row (p)	40	10	50	6	35	7	40	

Observing the differential costs in Table 12.19, we first notice that the value for introducing P2 is positive (+6.4p). That is, moving to another basis by introducing P2 would result in a higher cost than before. (This conclusion is obvious from our previous change of basis, which eliminated P2 from the solution.) Of the three remaining products and their negative differential costs, we choose P7 (–13.6p).

To find how much P7 is to be introduced, we must find how much of it is needed to eliminate each of the current basis's constituents in turn. To do this, we must evaluate the following expression for each of the three products P3, P4 and P6:

$$\frac{\textit{quantity of the basis product in the present basis}}{\textit{quantity of the basis product replaced by one kilogram of P7 (from Table 12.19)}}$$

- For P3, we have 16.0/0.2 kg of P7 required, = 80.0 kg.
- For P4, we have 72.0/5.4 kg of P7 required, = 13.33 kg.
- For P6, we have 68.0/1.6 kg of P7 required, = 42.5 kg.

The greatest amount of P7 that can be introduced is the least amount required to eliminate one of the products completely. Thus

Advanced Planning Systems

by introducing 13.33 kilograms of P7, we eliminate all P4. We also reduce P3 by 2.67 (13.33 × 0.2) kilograms and reduce P6 by 21.33 (13.33 × 1.6) kilograms. The new, third basis of the cattlefeed is as follows: P3 13.33 kilograms (16.0 − 2.67); P6 46.66 kilograms (68.0 − 21.33); P7 13.33 kilograms. The cost of the Troy Cattlefeed Company's potential new cattlefeed mix is 1526.3p.

The procedure is continued, and after a further iteration, the situation is as shown in Table 12.20. The cattlefeed mixture at this point is 11.55 kilograms of P1, 6.05 kilograms of P3 and 15.05 kilograms of P7, at a cost of 1366.5p. Since all the differential costs in Table 12.20 are positive, the basis reached is the cheapest mixture of Troy's standard products which will meet the customer's requirement. In four cycles of simple arithmetical operations, we have produced a result that could otherwise only have been achieved algebraically by solving 35 sets of three simultaneous equations in seven variables.

Table 12.20: *Changes required in the number of kilograms of Standard Products to compensate for changes shown in the leftmost column (the optimal basis)*

	P1 kg	P2 kg	P3 kg	P4 kg	P5 kg	P6 kg	P7 kg	Differential Cost
For each 1 kg of P2 introduced...	0.055	1	−0.257				0.119	+4.11p
For each 1 kg of P4 introduced...	0.073		−0.009	1			−0.174	+1.51p
For each 1 kg of P5 introduced...	−0.485		−0.065		1		−0.220	+3.55p
For each 1 kg of P6 introduced...	−0.248		0.156			1	−0.037	+3.40p
Cost Row (p)	40	10	50	6	35	7	40	

Note on slack variables: Attention was drawn at the beginning of this worked example to the convenience of the numbers in the problem, in that a basis could be immediately established since three of the standard products contained only 1 gram of nutrient per kilogram each. Consider the starting situation in Table 12.21 where this is not true and where a starting basis is not obvious.

Table 12.21: Starting Data relating to the Troy Cattlefeed Problem requiring the Introduction of Three Slack Variables P8, P9 and P10

The artefact used in linear programming to overcome this difficulty is to introduce three fictitious products P8, P9 and P10. The products contain, respectively, 1 gram per kilogram of nutrient N1, 1 gram per kilogram of nutrient N2 and 1 gram per kilogram of nutrient N3. Each product's cost is set at, say, 10,000p per kilogram. A starting basis can now be formulated with 100 kilograms of P8, 80 kilograms of P9 and 120 kilograms of P10. Because the fictitious products have such high costs, they will all have been eliminated from the solution after three cycles and cannot affect the final, optimum solution. They are called *slack variables*.

Strictly, the terms slack and surplus variables used in mathematical programming denote non-negative variables introduced into inequalities to convert them to equalities. For a treatment and example of linear programming in mathematical terms in which the starting data such as those relating to the constituents of the standard products and the customer's specification are expressed as linear equations and linear inequalities, rather than simply written into tables as here, see the Hion Hog Farm Company example and many others by Harvey Wagner (1975), op. cit., section 2.1 et al.

Chapter 13

Total Quality Control

13.1 THE IMPERATIVE OF TOTAL QUALITY

13.1.1 Today's Marketplace

The complexity, sophistication and sheer scale of the modern marketplace have created vast changes in the demand for "quality" compared even to 20 years ago. This can readily be seen in the profile of today's buyer. The buyer is typically careful and knowledgeable and expects the product bought to be satisfactory at all stages — for example, reliable and economic in everyday use. Shoddy goods are unacceptable goods. The buyer's expectations of the future are also different nowadays, especially with regard to advanced technical features. A key term in purchasing is that of *total value*. The cost to the buyer of breakdowns, maintenance, consumables and (say) the use of energy are considered carefully at purchase time.

In retail, buyers stand out as a class apart. Consumers are aware of their power and of the vulnerability of the high street shop. They demand that their complaints and wants be listened to. In practice, the objectives of consumer and manufacturer are identical, since the manufacturer's route to profitable business is the anticipation and satisfaction of consumer demands, particularly in regard to quality (see Section 2.2).

The manufacturing company's response to the new marketplace has similarly changed radically, with the widespread acceptance that it is a primary objective to satisfy the purchaser and, if quality should fail, to make good any defect. Bad quality persists only where the buyer himself can be forced to bear the cost, as he can in command economies where government has a monopoly of supply. The market is also now faster moving — many companies have sales and production rates ten times greater than they had in the 1960s. Greater turnover because of increased size and higher consumption has increased the company's quality target as of necessity. Thus if 0.1 per cent of products were defective out of annual sales of 100,000 units, engineers would need to be available to service 100 machines. The same rate of defective units if sales increased to 500,000 might cripple the company's ability to respond.[1] And with five times the number of dissatisfied customers the "quality initiative" would most likely be lost. The Japanese drive on volume world markets could not have been sustained if a commensurate burden of repair and service needs had also been incurred.[2]

In summary, the impact of quality on our daily lives is immense. From first thing in the morning until last at night, we employ a continuous succession of services and manufactured goods, and we expect every one of them to be trouble-free (we expect *zero redundancy*). In turn, in the daily life of manufacturing, we know we will be out of business if we fail to provide goods of the required quality.

13.1.2 *Caveat Venditor!*

Besides the compelling demands of social and economic change above, the manufacturer is also under a legal obligation with regard to quality, notwithstanding the fact that he may be separated by many links in the supply chain from the ultimate user of the product.

---

[1] The terms *non-conforming* and *non-conformance* are generally used in quality, and in the text of Chapters 13 and 14, in preference to the broader, less exact terms *defective* and *defect* from everyday speech. Feigenbaum, however, makes the distinction that a non-conforming unit is one which does not meet specification, whereas a defective unit is one which fails or is otherwise unsatisfactory in actual use (A.V. Feigenbaum (1983), *Total Quality Control*, Third edition, McGraw-Hill, Section 15.5).

[2] The point might also be made, of course, that even if nowadays the rate of failure of household consumer goods is one-tenth of what it once was, the average householder is now in possession of ten times as many such goods as he used to be!

In common law,[3] the defining case is *Donoghue* v. *Stevenson* (1932).[4] Mrs Donoghue was bought an ice cream and ginger beer in a café by a friend, the ginger beer being in an opaque bottle, to be poured onto the ice cream. After dispensing and consuming half of it, the remainder was poured on to reveal the presence in it of a partly decomposed snail. Mrs Donoghue brought an action against the manufacturer of the ginger beer, Stevenson Ltd, claiming compensation for shock and gastro-enteritis. In a landmark judgment in the House of Lords, it was held that the manufacturer did indeed have a duty of care to the ultimate consumer of the product, even though the ultimate consumer was not a party to the contract to buy from him.[5] Lord Atkin, the presiding judge, stated:

> "A manufacturer of products, which he sells in such a form as to show that he intends them to reach the ultimate consumer in the form in which they left him, with no reasonable possibility of intermediate examination, and with the knowledge that the absence of reasonable care in the preparation or putting up of the products will result in an injury to the consumer's life or property, owes a duty to that consumer to take reasonable care."

To re-emphasise, the phrase *ultimate consumer* of the product means what it says, not merely the contractual purchaser. And nowadays also, the term *manufacturer* is taken to include any intermediary in the supply chain who has had a hand in the final product's preparation or packing. (The term "having *product paternity*" is sometimes used.)

---

[3] Common law is the unwritten law of England, and is based on ancient practice and universal usage. Although unwritten as such, it is embodied in reported court decisions in past cases, such as that of *Donoghue* v. *Stevenson*, and in commentary such as that of Lord Atkin.

[4] *Donoghue* v. *Stevenson* [1932] AC 562. See Margaret Griffiths (1994), *Law for Purchasing & Supply*, Pitman. The case of *Donoghue* v. *Stevenson* is quoted in all British legal texts on contract law.

[5] *Donoghue* v. *Stevenson* is an important (and famous) case for the lawyer as well as for the manufacturing manager. Donoghue was not able to sue the café owner, as she was not privy to the contract to buy the refreshment (the contract was between her friend and the café proprietor). Her only recourse was to take action against the manufacturer, alleging the *tort of negligence*. A tort is the breach of a duty imposed by law other than one where there is contractual obligation.

The judgment delivered went further, going on to define *duty of care* and *neighbour* as follows:

> "The rule that you are to love your neighbour becomes in law, you must not injure your neighbour; and the lawyer's question, *Who is my neighbour?* receives a restricted reply. You must take reasonable care to avoid acts or omissions which you can reasonably foresee would be likely to injure your neighbour. Who then, in law, is my neighbour? The answer seems to be: persons who are so closely and directly affected by my act that I ought reasonably to have them in contemplation as being so affected when I am directing my mind to the acts or omissions which are called into question."

Besides the constraints of civil law, there are very many statute laws. Five principal Acts of Parliament (in the UK) that the manufacturing manager should be aware of are as follows:

1. *The Trade Descriptions Act, 1968.* This Act governs the application of false or misleading trade descriptions to goods and services;

2. *The Consumer Protection Act, 1987.* This is confined to the *supply* of goods, including their hire or distribution in promotional activity, the goods in question specifically being intended for the private consumer, so excluding material provided for business and industry. The provisions of the Act relate to the safety of the goods in use;

3. *The Health and Safety at Work Act, 1974.* This enactment is commented on in sub-section 19.4.2;

4. *The Food Safety Act, 1990;*[6] and

5. *The Weights and Measures Act, 1985,* dealing both with goods sold direct by quantity and with those sold in "regulated packages". It should be remembered here that prosecution in the court for short delivery does not lead to compensation for the customer, who must turn to the civil court and the *Sale of Goods*

---

[6] The first recorded Act in England relating to matters of food is *The Assize (= Edict) of Bread and Ale*, issued by Henry III in 1266.

Act, 1979, for redress.[7] For regulated packages, an extension of the Act in 1986 permits the use of an average weight (denoted on the package by the mark "**e**"). The principle of average weight is new in English law, and has relieved the company of the considerable expense associated with the need previously to bear the burden of overpacking, in order to be sure that packages with short measure were not produced. The quantity of goods stated relates to the average for a complete manufactured batch only. An under-supply (or over-supply) up to 2.5 per cent in individual packages is permitted. The shortfall of 2.5 per cent is referred to as a *tolerable negative error* (TNE), and an offence is committed only if a so-called "inadequate" is supplied — that is, if an individual package is supplied with a shortfall of more than 5.0 per cent. Control of regulated packages by the Weights and Measures Inspectorate essentially lies at the point where the goods are packed.

13.1.3 Quality and Cost

Besides market pressure and the demands of the law, there is an overwhelming economic case for adopting a high quality corporate strategy. In making the case, quality professionals talk of "the hidden factory". The hidden factory comprises the manufacturing resources, shop floor operators and other staff who might otherwise be producing good quality goods or might otherwise be engaged in useful activities, but who instead are spending their time inadvertently creating non-conformances or whose time is diverted to correcting non-conforming work or repairing other damage caused by it. Examples of damage (to the company's financial health) are the need for rework; the costs of warranty and service call-outs; the cost of inspection and audits; clerical corrections; and many more. (*"Quality is free"*, says quality guru Philip Crosby, *"it is bad quality that costs money!"*)[8] Many of the activities performed in the hidden factory may be so widely accepted as stan-

---

[7] The two principal defences in the criminal court to the charge of short supply are (1) that the supplier obtained the goods from a third party and has a *written warranty* from him as to their quantity; and (2) the defence of *due diligence* — that the supplier employs a well-formulated, well-managed dispensing and packing system.

[8] Philip B. Crosby (1979), *Quality is Free*, McGraw-Hill Book Company.

dard practice within the company that their identification with bad quality is far from obvious — operators queuing for parts because of wrongly issued kits, for example. Release of the potential of the hidden factory or, at least, the elimination of its cost, is seen to be elevated to the level of strategy in the flowchart, or *chain reaction*, in Figure 13.1. Nor can the flowchart be dismissed as naïve or simplistic. It was devised by Walter A. Shewhart, the founding father of modern quality control, and introduced to senior Japanese manufacturing executives shortly after World War II. According to W. Edwards Deming, writing in 1982,

> "... the chain reaction became engraved in Japan as a way of life. This chain reaction was on the blackboard of every meeting (of American industrial advisers) with top management in Japan from July 1950 onward."[9]

Figure 13.1: Shewhart's Strategy for Corporate Quality

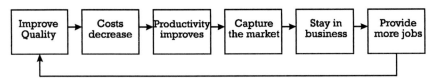

The cost of the hidden factory as a proportion of the whole is unknowable or, at least, difficult to estimate. (Feigenbaum estimates it as 15 per cent to 40 per cent, and other quality writers have made guesses around 30 per cent.)[10] The financial improvements to be gained from a successful drive to total quality come about not only from producing more saleable, good quality units per total resource input, and making more efficient use of resources. They also come about from smoother operational control of the factory

---

[9] W. Edwards Deming (1986), *Out of the Crisis*, MIT Center for Advanced Engineering Studies, Cambridge, MA. See also Walter A. Shewhart, *The Economic Control of Quality of Manufactured Products* (First edition, Van Nostrand, 1931; reprinted as a 50th anniversary commemorative reissue by The American Society for Quality Control, 1980 and again by CEEP Press, The George Washington University, 1986); and Mary Walton (1986), *The Deming Management Method*, Mercury Books and Management Books 2000 Ltd., Chapter 1.

[10] The figures in the text relate to an estimate of "waste" inherent in American manufacturing costs made by A.V. Feigenbaum in *Quality Progress* magazine, November 1977 (article *"Quality and Productivity"*).

Total Quality Control

itself, and greater responsiveness to customer requirements — i.e. better running plans and, with more content customers, improved sales. The result of Shewhart's chain reaction is reflected in greater turnover, reduced expense and higher profits.

13.1.4 Defining Total Quality

It is for the customer, and no one else, to say what determines quality. Thus, based on the customer's experience with the product, and measured quantitatively against his requirements, characteristics of quality will typically include *availability*; *delivery*; *reliability and life*; *attractiveness*; *ability to be serviced*; *cost of operation*; *safety*; *maintainability*; *effect on the environment*; ... and so on. All of these characteristics, and more, come together as a composite, at a particular cost. This composite constitutes "quality" if it thereby creates customer satisfaction. (Of course, customer satisfaction is itself a moving target, since expectations will rise and fall — for example, faults which may be acceptable in completely new goods still at the novelty stage will not be tolerated later in the product's life cycle.)

Notwithstanding universal agreement with the foregoing statements, formal definitions of quality promulgated by the various authorities and experts in the field vary greatly, depending on the views and philosophies of their authors. A number of alternative definitions are given below.[11] Very brief notes are attached to them to give a little colour to their backgrounds and for the sake of interest. References are also given to further reading.

The British Standards Institution (BSI)

> "The totality of features and characteristics of a product or service that bear on its ability to satisfy stated or implied needs." (BS 4778, or ISO 8402).

---

[11] A summary of the various gurus' strengths and weaknesses is given in N. Slack, S. Chambers, C. Harland, A. Harrison and R. Johnston (1995), *Operations Management*, Pitman Publishing, p. 815. A review of each of their "quality positions" and a short history of the changes in perceptions of quality over the years are given by Barrie Dale (ed.) (1994), *Managing Quality*, Prentice Hall Europe, Chapters 1 and 2. See also the article "The Quality Gurus" by Tony Bendell at http://www.dti.gov.uk. The personalities described in the text are American unless otherwise stated.

The BSI is a quasi-governmental body[12] set up in 1901 and based in Milton Keynes and London which devises and publishes standards, often in conjunction with industrial associations, on a very wide range of products and services. Examples are the width of tramlines (its very first standard), the colour coding for the wiring of domestic electrical equipment and the properties of various grades of petrol. The definition of quality issued, which is virtually identical to that given by the American Society for Quality Control, contains more than a hint of an outmoded checklist/prescriptive approach to the subject. In conjunction with the International Standards Organisation (ISO), the Institution has published a series of guidelines for the setting up and maintenance of what it terms a "total quality system", formerly known by its BSI code BS 5750 and now, following the adoption of BS 5750 in 1987 by the International Standards Organisation, by the code ISO 9000. It should be said, however, that a great many practitioners in quality, especially those subscribing to Deming's approach to the subject, regard the BSI's views on these matters to be deeply flawed. ISO 9000 is commented on at length in Section 13.3.[13]

Philip B. Crosby

"Conformance to requirements."

Phil Crosby was quality director of ITT in the 1960s and was closely associated with the US "zero defects" campaign. He measures conformance to requirements by the cost of non-conformance (and talks of conformance/non-conformance rather than of good/

---

[12] Since 1929 the BSI has operated under a Royal Charter. In recent years it has expanded as a testings agency by borrowings and acquisition, and now has a turnover of £106 million per annum and annual profits of £10 million. The flotation of the Institution as a fully-fledged profit-seeking company, in order to exploit further the marketing of its well-known "kitemark" symbol, has been discussed (*The Times*, 29 April 1998).

[13] The British Standards Institution, London and Milton Keynes. BSI Quality Assurance, an operating section of the BSI, originally published BS 5750 in four parts: Part 0: Guide to quality systems; Part 1: Product design; Part 2: Manufacture or the provision of any service; Part 3: Supplies. As stated in the text, the standard has been superseded by ISO 9000 (See Section 13.3). Snapshots of BSI publications and standards are obtainable at the BSI's website at http://www.bsi-global.com.

bad quality). For Crosby there is only one standard of performance: namely *zero defects*. There is no place for acceptable errors and merely adequate standard of compliance, since these in turn imply an acceptance that errors are inevitable and even planned for. The only management standard, says Crosby, is zero defects.[14]

William Edwards Deming

"A predictable degree of uniformity and dependability, at low cost and suited to the market."

The late Dr W. Edwards Deming is by far the best known of the quality elite; to his countless adherents worldwide, he is *The Master*.[15] Deming's philosophy is encapsulated in his *fourteen points*. These assert that the company must reject an approach to quality based on inspection, reward, fear or sole reliance on "best effort". Eliminate slogans and exhortation, says Deming. They are demeaning and adversarial, and show lack of trust. For Deming, the key to quality is an understanding that any manufacturing process or human-centred system is liable to variation in performance due to *common causes* inherent in its operation. Quality is confined by the system that produces it; if it is to be improved, then management must change the system.[16]

---

[14] Philip B. Crosby (1979), op. cit.

[15] See W. Edwards Deming (1986), op. cit. See also Mary Walton (1986), op. cit.; William J. Latzko and David M. Saunders (1995), *Four Days with Dr Deming*, Addison-Wesley Publishing Co. (an account of the "experience" and substance of attendance at one of Deming's renowned four-day seminars that brilliantly captures the occasion); and many other sources.

[16] At the invitation of the Japanese Union of Scientists and Engineers (JUSE), Deming visited Japan in 1950 and again in 1951 to lecture on quality and statistical quality control (SQC, see Chapter 14). The assault on quality which followed the almost national take-up of Deming's quality methods by Japanese industry was accompanied in 1951 by the institution of the now immensely prestigious "Deming Prize", funded by royalties made available by him to the JUSE. Several prizes are awarded, one for individuals, the remainder for company applications in various categories, and all of them centred around the use of SQC in quality. The prize award ceremonies are nowadays shown on Japanese national TV. Deming's lectures were not the impetus that set the Japanese quality juggernaut rolling, however. According to Kaoru Ishikawa, this was the demand by the US Army in 1946 that Japanese industry should adopt modern quality control in effecting the reconstruction of its tele-

Armand V. Feigenbaum

> "The total composite product and services characteristics of marketing, engineering, manufacturing and maintenance through which the product and service in use will meet the expectations of the customer."

Dr Feigenbaum is the former manager of world wide manufacturing operations and quality control for General Electric Co. Inc., and is currently CEO of his own company, General Systems, specialising in the design and implementation of manufacturing operations systems. He is replete with honours worldwide in the field of quality. The State of Massachusetts has given his name to an annual quality award.[17]

Kaoru Ishikawa

> "To practise quality control is to develop, design, produce and service a quality product which is most economical, most useful and always satisfactory to the consumer."

Kaoru Ishikawa spent eight years in industry and in war service before returning to the University of Tokyo in 1949. At the University he took up what was to be a lifelong commitment to quality, initially concentrating on the application of statistical techniques. He has played a major role in the development of Japan's quality ethos and in proselytising Japanese companies to the cause of quality. Ishikawa has helped set up national quality study groups and, particularly, the famed Japanese Quality Control circles. He has been honoured by the creation of a national prize in his name, awarded annually for innovative methods.[18]

---

phone and communication system (Kaoru Ishikawa (1985), *What is Total Quality Control (The Japanese Way)?*, translated by Professor David J. Lu, Prentice-Hall.) See Ishikawa also for an interesting comparison of Western and Japanese quality methods (ibid., Chapter II).

[17] A.V. Feigenbaum (1983), op. cit.

[18] Kaoru Ishikawa (1985), op. cit. This book is not a conventional text, but a stimulating and fascinating reminiscence of the author's life in Japanese quality. It was (understandably) a bestseller in Japan.

Japanese Quality

"A system of production methods which economically produces quality goods or services meeting the requirements of consumers."

The formal definition above is taken from The Japanese Industrial Standard (JIS) and hardly captures what distinguishes the Japanese quality approach from the West's. The Seventh (Japanese) Quality Control Symposium held in 1967 determined that the following six differences marked out Japanese quality: (1) Company-wide quality control, and participation in it by all members of the organisation; (2) Education and training in quality control; (3) QC circle activities; (4) QC audits (Deming Application Prize and presidential audit); (5) Utilisation of statistical methods; (6) Nationwide quality control promotion activities.

Kaoru Ishikawa summarises Japanese quality thus:

"Total quality control, Japanese style, is a thought revolution in management. Therefore the thought processes of all employees must be changed. To accomplish this, education must be repeated over and over again."[19]

Joseph M. Juran

"Fitness for purpose or use."

Like Deming, Juran was also closely associated (from 1954) with the JUSE and the Japanese quality movement. Unlike Deming, however, he places far more open emphasis on the cost aspect of quality. For example, Juran advocates that quality improvement programmes should be selected on the basis of cost reduction opportunities, and that yearly quality cost reduction targets should be set and their achievement closely monitored. Juran also ascribes greater importance to the responsibilities of middle management and the need for control systems than to motivation and the need for endorsement of the TQC programme by staff and the shop floor.[20]

---

[19] Ibid., p. 37.

[20] J.M. Juran (ed.) (1979), *Quality Control Handbook*, McGraw-Hill.

Walter A. Shewhart

Shewhart's monument to quality is less a formal definition than his development of the control chart as a means of ensuring consistent quality output from a stable process.

Walter Shewhart (1891–1967) is the originator of statistical process control (Chapter 14), and so may be said to have had a greater effect on quality in manufacturing than any other person in history. Shewhart spent over 30 years at Bell Telephone Laboratories Inc., setting out his proposal for the famous control charts of his invention in an internal Bell memorandum presented in 1924. He held a number of prestigious US university posts in mathematical statistics and was a guest lecturer at London University. Walter Shewhart was an active contributor to numerous quality associations and an honorary member of the Royal Statistical Society. The Shewhart Medal is awarded annually by the ASQ.[21]

13.1.5 "Total Quality Control" and "Total Quality Management"

Reflecting upon the definitions above, we may conclude that the goal of the manufacturing company is to provide products and services in which quality has been provided for with respect to design, manufacture, marketing and service, all at the most economical cost, and which make for full customer satisfaction over the life of the product. In order to achieve the goal, it is necessary to set up and maintain comprehensive, company-wide procedures, contributed to jointly by the various functional departments. Vital additional activities include making provision for the education and participation of staff, and obtaining their understanding of and commitment to a programme of continuous improvement. All of these procedures and activities, together fulfilling the company's commitment to quality, constitute *total quality control (TQC)*. The determination of quality policy and the carrying out of those management functions required to give effect to TQC are termed *total quality management (TQM)*, an activity, as we shall see

---

[21] Walter A. Shewhart (1931), op. cit.

Total Quality Control 483

again in Section 13.2, that must clearly be led by the company's most senior executives.[22]

A clearly defined, robust *total quality system* is essential for the operation of TQC, although, as intimated, it should be said that what is meant by *system* is a means of focusing on customer needs and, above all, effecting the enhancement of customer satisfaction, not a prescription of controls and procedures. Poor quality, or unnecessarily high expense in providing good quality, comes about from fire-fighting, reaction and failure to agree quantitative measures. The non-quality environment relies on rules, exhortation and threats. The skills of TQC and TQM by contrast depend on two disciplines: systems engineering and human engineering. The first encompasses the devising and carrying through of clear programmes of activity; the measurement of achievement, especially the engenderment of customer satisfaction; and the analysis of variation of achievement from the goals set. The second involves placing action and control in the hands of the people who do the work and are therefore best able to see where improvements might be made in its performance.

13.1.6 Conformity to Customer Requirements

If quality is meeting customer requirements, it follows that critical steps in the process are determining what those requirements are and then assessing whether the company can satisfy them. The first tasks in doing so relate to the process of design and the assessment of *how well* the product or service is designed to meet its stated purpose. In order to accomplish this, it is necessary to discover what characteristics are valued by the customer, using any means at hand, including, especially, market research, as described at length in sub-section 2.2.2. (It is remembered particularly from 2.2.2 that *cost* will be a vital attribute of the final product.) The outcome is a milestone in the process of delivering

---

[22] There are many alternative formal definitions of TQC and TQM than those in the text. For example: TQC — *the operational techniques and activities that are used to fulfil requirements for quality* (BS4778 Part I); TQM — *A management philosophy embracing all activities through which the needs and expectations of the customer and the community, and the objectives of the organisation, are satisfied in the most efficient and cost effective way by maximising the potential of all employees in a continuing drive for improvement* (BS4778, Part II).

quality and the means, amongst other things, whereby the product's eventual conformance to requirements may be judged.[23] It is referred to as *The Design Brief*, and was previously dealt with in Section 3.1.

One method of discerning requirements, other than through the means described in Chapter 2, is to examine the customer/supplier chain. When we speak of a customer/supplier chain, we doubtless have in mind a link between two companies — between the manufacturing company's external supplier and itself, for instance, or between the company and its own customer. But in the world of total quality, a customer/supplier link is any relationship between a provider of goods or service and a receiver. That is, besides external suppliers and external customers, we can suppose that there are a myriad other links between providers and receivers *but within the company itself*. Two examples might be between one operator on the shop floor and the next, in a product route, or between the sales order processing clerk and the warehouse despatch clerk. It is held in TQC that in order to ensure quality for the external customer, it is necessary to provide it at every stage internally as well.[24] Confining endeavour only to such very obvious points as those involving (say) the final production of the product comes down simply to inspection and reaction, and does not amount to TQC. To anticipate a number of considerations in Section 13.2, questions each individual within the company might ask in

---

[23] The degree to which the final product meets customer requirements is termed *quality of conformance,* this being simply shorthand for *quality of conformance to design.* In turn, but only in part, quality of conformance is determined (self-evidently) by the thoroughness and standards which have prevailed in initial research, design and production engineering. For the remainder, of course, it is determined by the verdict of the users in the field, not only as to actual performance, but in regard to operating costs, required service and support, ease of use and the rest. (Finding out the views of customers may not be easy, especially where they relate to very inexpensive items sold in large quantities and used in a casual way.)

[24] Bad quality in an internal supply chain creates further bad quality. Operator 2 will feel demotivated and may be less inclined to work conscientiously if the component passed to him by Operator 1 and that he is now working on is nonconforming. Unless he stops the process (which, of course, he should) no matter how good a job Operator 2 were to do, the article would still be nonconforming at the conclusion of the job. Why bother?

relation to his own contribution to quality might be those in the two lists as follows.

My Customer	My Supplier
Who are my immediate customers?	Who are my immediate suppliers?
What are their real requirements?	What are my real requirements?
How can I discover their real requirements?	How do I communicate my needs?
How can I measure the ability to satisfy them?	How can supplier capability be measured?
Do I have the capability?	Do the suppliers have the capability (in relation to the required standards)?
Do I continue to meet requirements?	How is supplier performance to be evaluated?
How can I monitor changes in needs?	How will changes in needs be recognised and communicated?

Where the customer really is the external customer, we know from Chapter 2 that the Sales and Marketing department takes the lead in establishing his wants and needs, often having to do so in the face of fuzzy objectives or sometimes seemingly none at all. The key characteristics in the eyes of the customer must be established. They must be expressed quantitatively, and will include such attributes as those listed under *Elements of the PDS* in subsection 3.2.1. To reiterate a point made previously: mistakes at this stage that are allowed to persist uncorrected will defeat the very goal of quality. It is essential, therefore, that maximum effort be brought to bear.

To identify customers and suppliers within the company itself is quite a different matter and requires the journey to be commenced from "non-quality organisation" to "quality organisation". In turn, this demands a major re-think by senior management of the way it perceives quality to be determined, delivered and sustained, and then the quiet, sincere commitment of the company to the long road that must be taken. Those elements that it is widely agreed make up the quality organisation are described in the next Section.

13.2 TOTAL QUALITY IN THE MANUFACTURING COMPANY

In TQC, the "system" is the means in its totality by which materials and services are delivered to the customer. There are two never-ending tasks to be undertaken to achieve control over the quality of the materials and services so delivered and to enhance their value to the customer. First, the occurrence of occasional, unusual events that have a destabilising effect on the system's operation and thereby detract from quality must be prevented (or, rather, their effect on the system must be blocked). The result of completing this task will thus be to have stabilised the system so that its operation is impacted only by natural random factors (for example, by the changes in volumes of sales orders received from day to day). In other words, although the system will have been stabilised on completion of the first task, its output, perceived as "quality" by the customer, will still be subject to variation, the variation however being between stable, natural limits. The second task of total quality control is quite different from the first. It is to study and understand the newly stabilised system itself with a view to making changes in its fundamental operation that reduce the effect of the randomness of the natural phenomena on its operation. The consequent reduction in the variation of the materials and services delivered will lead to improved productivity and will be perceived by the customer as constituting improved quality (see 13.1.3 and 13.1.4).

We begin by examining the nature of the system that delivers materials and services to the customer.

13.2.1 The System

The term "system" has been used many times in this book to mean the detailed specification of procedures and data flow implicit in the attainment of relatively narrow objectives. The activities involved in sales order processing, for example, were given in Section 2.4 and a data flow diagram of the SOP system was illustrated in Figure 2.5. The procedures and flow diagram in Section 2.4 and Figure 2.5, augmented with a great deal more detail and paperwork, might be used as the basis for the design and implementation of a complex software system comprising many scores of programs for the processing of sales orders.

Total Quality Control

"System" is used differently in the context of total quality and is broader in meaning. In relation to manufacturing overall, it is broader in so far as it encompasses all direct and supporting means by which raw materials are converted to sales goods. That is, consideration of a system of manufacturing is not confined simply to the machining of parts themselves and their transformation to the finished goods, but is extended (say) to the recruitment of staff; the training of supervisors; sales and distribution; consideration of the impact of government regulations; the working out of costs; the setting of prices; and so on and so on. There is no concern, at least initially, with the examination of close detail, as there is with an incipient computer system. The manager regarding the corporate system from the viewpoint of total quality is interested instead in the broad picture — the way parts fit together and the improvements that might be made.

Concern with activities from the viewpoint of the detailed data processing system is *top-down* — indeed, as explained, the structured flowchart in Figure 2.5 is based on hierarchical principles so that the most minute detail could readily be included if it were thought to be desirable. The system viewpoint in quality, by contrast, is *outside-in* — not concerned with detailed procedures but instead with stepping back and regarding the whole, critically, at a glance and through the eyes of the customer.

The constituent parts of a quality system and how they fit together might typically be drawn on a flipchart by senior managers in a few hours. Their purpose in doing so as part of a quality investigation would be to facilitate discussion among themselves as to how each distinct process contributes to objectives; to spark ideas about what changes might be made to remove sources of trouble; and to change procedures so as to effect improvement in customer satisfaction.

Although it is very simple, the quality flowchart in Figure 13.2 would represent at least a starting point for management debate. Its breadth and informality should be contrasted with the narrowness and precision of the SOP system flowchart.

Figure 13.2: A (Quality) System Flowchart intended to facilitate Management Debate

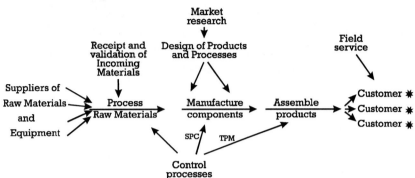

As senior management discusses the various elements that make up the system in Figure 13.2, it will certainly be necessary to break the broadly stated steps into somewhat more detail. For example, if the company employs simultaneous engineering in design, the procedure in Figure 13.2 given as *Design of Products and Processes* might be expanded, on a separate sheet of paper, to the dozen or so steps given for this activity shown in Figure 3.3.

As stated in the introduction to this Section, however, the first task of quality management is to bring the system as it currently stands under control by removing the impact of unusual, destabilising events, known in total quality control by the key term *special causes*. Consequently, senior management must first focus attention on areas of the system where trouble is known to exist, trouble being manifest in unacceptably high costs, a high incidence of non-conformances or numerous customer complaints. Permanent removal of the special causes of variation will bring the system *under control*. An understanding of what is meant by this fundamental quality term is central to an understanding of total quality.[25]

---

[25] It must be said that the "understanding of total quality" in the text, and the treatment of special causes and common causes described in sub-section 13.2.1 and later, is very much according to the Deming philosophy rather than the (opposing) Crosby view. While alternative approaches might be followed, the "golden thread", as it has been put, running through all of them is the adoption by the company of quality as the foundation of its manufacturing and commercial strategy.

13.2.2 Stabilising the System

In TQC, a system is said to be stable and under control when all special causes that affect its performance have been eliminated. Variation still exists in performance, however, but this is due to natural phenomena that are part and parcel of the system itself. These phenomena are referred to in total quality jargon as *common causes*. If the system remains unaltered, the identity and presence of the common causes are also unchanged from one period to the next. Consequently, the variation in performance they give rise to is between constant boundaries. The system at this point is said to be *under control*. It has a defined capability and its performance is predictable.

Variation in system performance arising from special causes can be distinguished from variation arising from common causes only through statistical analysis. It is wrong to assume the presence of a special cause by surmise or opinion. Instead, its presence must be detected by the statistical analysis of some manifestation of the system's behaviour.[26] When this has been done (and before the trail goes cold), an investigation is then carried out to determine the likely cause of it. When this in turn has been carried out and its identity has been confirmed, steps are taken to ensure that it can never affect the system again.

The statistical analysis referred to above is a simple matter, and is carried out by completion and perusal of what is referred to as a *Shewhart control chart*. In order to construct a Shewhart control chart, a critical measure of the system's performance is recorded at regular intervals of time and its value on each occasion plotted on the chart. When this has been done, it will be found that the great majority of the points plotted are relatively close to an average value. That is, the 50 per cent of them that are above the average will be found always to be within a relatively close range above it;

---

[26] The relative extent of variation in system performance due to a special cause might be quite small (albeit erratic in occurrence and outside the limits of a stable system). In another system, the variation due to common causes might be relatively great (and commensurately undesirable from the customer's viewpoint), but nevertheless stable and under control. It is the irregularity and the lying outside limits which define the variation as being due to special causes. These are matters of statistics, not conjecture, so that only statistical analysis can be used for their detection.

the 50 per cent of the values below will similarly be within close reach. The reason for variation about the average and between two close limits is the permanent presence in the system of the same common causes (and, of course, their mutual tendency to cancel out each other's effect, as described in sub-section 5.2.1). But, in addition, in a system which has not yet been brought under control, there will also be a small number of values, occurring at irregular intervals, which are outside the normal limits (i.e. which are above the upper limit or below the lower limit). A variation in the system's performance that occurs at inconsistent intervals and is above or below close, normal limits — being, usually, a long way above the average or a long way below it — is due to the entry into its operation of a special cause.

At this point, in order to begin the task of bringing the system under control, the identity of the special cause must be discerned by a general investigation carried out by staff familiar with its operation. At the start of the adoption of TQC, when the most obvious system areas are being investigated, special causes are likely to be easy to identify. After a few years, especially in regard to the manufacturing process itself, things will be more difficult. At this later juncture, therefore, it is likely to be useful to adopt formal investigative techniques such as those described in sub-section 13.2.4. When agreement has been reached as to cause, procedures are put in place to prevent its recurrence or, if that is impossible, at least to block its effect on the system. The action is usually taken by operational staff, especially where causes relate to production on the shop floor, since they are best placed to decide what to do. Help may also be needed from management, however — if, for example, outside suppliers are involved. When this has been done for all the special causes, the variation in system performance remaining will be due to common causes alone. The system's performance will thus now be predictable and between defined limits. (Constant vigilance is needed, however. A new special cause due to the effect of some extraneous activity not previously anticipated might arise in the future. Its presence will be identified as before by control charts and it too must be investigated and removed by corrective action.)

To illustrate the use of a Shewhart control chart in the analysis of one aspect of system performance, consider the time taken by a

Total Quality Control

manufacturing company to process and deliver customer orders (avoiding here the more complex matter of stock availability discussed under safety stocks in Section 5.3). Table 13.1 gives the number of hours to process and deliver customer orders from the time of order receipt by the company. The data in the Table were obtained by taking the averages of the order times of samples of three consecutive orders each working day in a particular month (so 20 sample averages for each of 20 working days — 60 orders in all).[27]

Table 13.1: The Average Durations (i.e. sample averages) Calculated Day by Day, relating to three Customer Order Delivery Times

Day	Avg. Hours	Day	Avg. Hours	Day	Avg. Hours	Day	Avg. Hours
1	25	6	21	11	23	16	29
2	30	7	31	12	35	17	26
3	31	8	47	13	32	18	28
4	24	9	29	14	27	19	27
5	37	10	29	15	53	20	33

The duration averages and dates in Table 13.1 are now plotted for convenience on a Shewhart control chart, illustrated in Figure 13.3. The axes of the chart are days (horizontal) and averages, or means, of the small samples of consecutive delivery durations

---

[27] The values in Table 13.1 and plotted on the control chart in Figure 13.3 are calculated average order durations each derived from a sample taken of three consecutive orders per day. (Alternative size samples of, say, two or four might have been taken instead — see sub-section 14.2.1, but also see sub-section 14.1.1 (footnote 4)). It is also necessary to calculate the "ranges" of each sample, a range being the difference between the longest and shortest time of the three order times in the sample. Application of Equations 14.8, 14.18, 14.25 and 14.26 then enables the control limits to be plotted, as described in Chapter 14 (*Statistical Quality Control*). Detailed explanation relating to the completion of control charts is not appropriate here, however, justifying the simplifications in calculating the control limits that have in fact been made. The important point about Figure 13.3 is that determination of the capability of the delivery system is made statistically and from observation, not by wishful thinking or the setting of management targets for it.

(vertical). Note the upper and lower "control limits" (horizontal broken lines — see footnote 27).

Figure 13.3: Shewhart Control Chart tracking the performance of a Despatch/Delivery System over a Month

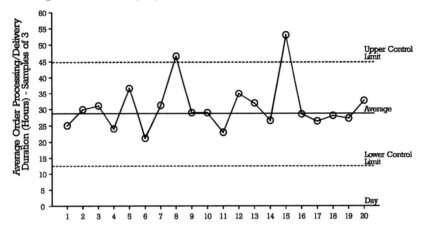

From the completed control chart, it will be seen that the average delivery performance is 28.7 hours, and that upper and lower control limits have been calculated to be 44.8 hours and 12.6 hours. Note the word *calculated*. That is, the control limits are *not* simply set to what might seem to be reasonable values, or set to target values considered by management to be desirable from the customer viewpoint, or targets that might be achievable "if only everyone would just work a little harder". Their values arise purely from calculations involving data relating to the observed performance of the system itself. The observed performance of the system and a statistical procedure explained in sub-sections 14.1.3 and 14.1.4 are together used to calculate the system control limits (see again footnote 27).

The management information that is derivable from the control chart is as follows:

1. The processing and delivery capability of the company's SOP system is between approximately 13 hours and 45 hours. Any duration between these two limits is possible and admissible (although there will be a preponderance of deliveries not far from the average of about 29 hours). If this performance is to be improved, it will be necessary to make fundamental

changes to the way the system operates, so as to reduce the impact of common causes (see sub-sections 13.2.3 and 13.2.4).

2. On two occasions (Day 8 and Day 15), special causes were at work, resulting in delivery performances outside the system's natural capability. The identities of these causes must be found by investigation, and procedures developed (or existing procedures modified) to prevent their occurring ever again.

13.2.3 Improving the System's Capability

Although the performance of a system which is under control is indeed predictable and between defined limits, this is not to say that its standard is acceptable. (In manufacturing, as we know, it is quite possible to have a stable system for the production of non-conformances.)

In order to improve the standard — i.e. improve the quality of goods and services being delivered by a stable system — it is therefore necessary, first, to consider what aspects of them the customer most appreciates and which of these he would like to see improved as a priority. Secondly, it is necessary for management and staff to devise alternative, superior techniques and procedures for delivering the improvement.

Impediments both to selecting targets for improvement and devising alternative procedures for delivering it are the functional organisation of the company itself and the undeniable fact that most individual members of staff have only a restricted view of things. Yet each one of the individual components which go to make up the quality composite is likely to involve activity by many company sections within many functional departments. We have already seen in the book so far instances of cross-functional cooperation having a bearing on some aspect of customer service: new product development; simultaneous engineering; master scheduling; sales order processing. Consequently, the formation of permanent and temporary cross-functional groups, identified by way of the "outside-in" view of systems and each dedicated to some distinctive area of customer satisfaction, is recommended by many quality experts as a way forward in the establishment of TQC. The composition of each group will be made up of staff from the corresponding functional areas involved in that group's specialisation. The groups themselves might simply be called "teams" *(the despatch preparation team; the order pricing and credit team;* and so on).

While teams are charged with identifying aspects of change needed to existing systems and are likely to be well placed to specify what should be done to bring about the improvements sought, final responsibility for approving and authorising the changes clearly lies in the hands of management and is clearly also a long-term job. All quality gurus are in agreement that genuine, long-term commitment to the new quality regime by senior management is an absolute requirement of TQC. In fact, two commitments are needed, not one: a commitment to corrective action that will eliminate special causes; and a commitment to the revision of existing systems and procedures to reduce the impact of common causes. In tracking improvements to quality as TQC progresses, it is observed in a number of companies that progress comes to a halt after a couple of years, leading to disappointment and disillusion. Deming suggests that the reason for this is that the company up to that point has put all of its energies into removing special causes — commitment 1. No further improvement is then possible when this task is complete unless it begins the more demanding one of redesigning and reimplementing its systems to reduce the impact of the common causes — commitment 2.[28]

Much has been written about the need by members of staff including shop floor operators for commitment to the cause of quality and to the success of the new regime. On this question, the quality gurus differ markedly in opinion. A number of them advocate the institution of a high-profile indoctrination programme, starting with the managing director, and proceeding downwards, layer by layer. For example, Philip Crosby talks of signing pledges and holding a Zero Defects Day with family and friends invited along to share the fun.[29] W. Edwards Deming takes the more severe view that staff and the shop floor are as committed to quality as everyone else, and that the only inspiration they need is the sight of management doing something about the systems which constrain their ability to deliver it. As mentioned earlier, in Deming's view,

---

[28] See W. Edwards .Deming (1986), op. cit., Figure 33.

[29] Philip B. Crosby (1979), op. cit., Chapter 11 (see ZD Day, Step Nine).

posters and slogans exhorting people to give of their best, among other things suggesting that management believes they currently do not do so, are at best worthless and at worst derogatory and patronising, and should be removed. This is not to say that Deming does not believe in training and the need for competence. Far from it. These aspects of the subject are deferred until sub-sections 13.2.4 and 13.2.5.

The reaction of the manager to a variation in the system's performance due to the presence of common causes is a telling indication of his commitment to the new way. It is an indication of his true acceptance or not that common cause variation — variation, that is, from the standard of perfection to which, in his heart, he may aspire — is natural and acceptable. Thus, faced with an incidence of variation within a system's natural, stable limits, the manager on the one hand might indeed make lengthy, careful preparation to improve its capability, discussing the changes with all concerned, instituting the new procedures and providing training in them. On the other hand, quite legitimately, due to pressure of time and more urgent priorities, he may do nothing.

Now managers are often appointed to the posts they hold because of their propensity to do, hardly their propensity to do nothing. It requires a deep understanding of the meaning of common causes and the nature of stable systems to accept that a mistake has been made in the operation of the system or that something has gone wrong, the system's variation nevertheless remaining within its normal boundaries, and then *not* to seek out the cause, *not* to hold an inquest, *not* to take corrective action. "Corrective action" on a stable system will, by definition, be destabilising. It will cause more trouble than it cures. Corrective action on a stable system includes telling off or threatening the 50 per cent of staff involved in it whose performance is below average. Provided their performance is within the control limits of the system, threats are ineffective or counterproductive and, above all, *unfair*.

The temptation to take action and the refusal to leave well alone can be illustrated by an example. Consider what the manager is liable to do on the discovery, following a cycle count, of shortfalls of stock for which he is responsible. Even though the overall stock records accuracy reported may be within the percentage boundaries established for the stores, a materials manager may insist that the storekeeper go off on an extraordinary paperchase to account for the negative discrepancy. (*This is the company's money that has gone missing!*) The interest of such a manager is not with the system (for example, he does not chase after stock gains, even though they have arisen through the operation of the same system). The manager believes that by exerting his authority and demanding that staff sort things out — *do a better job and take more care!* — he is fulfilling his rightful role. Under total quality, the manager has a more subtle and a more demanding one, a role calling for creativity and administrative ability. It is to deliver enhanced quality, in this case by way of more accurately maintained stock records obtained through an improved stock recording system, not to present an account of the causes of the discrepancies of the moment (see especially Section 18.3).

13.2.4 Identification and Elimination of Special Causes

In the early days of TQC within the company, special causes of variation are likely to abound throughout its operations. Consequently, when use of a Shewhart control chart indicates a special cause to be present in the carrying out of some system activity, the underlying reason for it is likely to be very obvious and the action needed to remove it equally so. In due course, after the cherries have been picked, identification of the reasons for special cause variation and their subsequent elimination will typically be a good deal more problematical, especially with regard to the operation of the manufacturing process itself. At this point, it will be valuable for the company to be able to employ formal methodologies, governed by standard procedures and in which all staff have received training. Three such that have been found by many to be helpful are as follows and are expanded on below: use of the Ishikawa diagram; the cycle of continuous improvement (PDCA); and Quality Improvement teams. Other techniques at the disposal of the company were given in sub-section 3.2.2 (Conceptual Design and Controlled Convergence).[30]

---

[30] See also Dale et al. (1994), op. cit., Chapter 17.

The Ishikawa Diagram

The Ishikawa diagram (or cause-and-effect diagram, or fishbone diagram) was devised in 1952 by Kaoru Ishikawa to assist in the discussion of possible causes of an effect (manifest in special cause variation) and to enable possible reasons for it to be recorded easily and in a way suitable for the openness of team working. An example of an Ishikawa diagram as it might appear part way through a meeting to discern a cause is illustrated in Figure 13.4. In the Figure, the five categories of cause used to guide the group to a solution are those traditionally associated with manufacturing investigations. When non-manufacturing effects are being investigated, the "fish" will normally have four bones rather than five: policies, procedures, plans and people.

Figure 13.4: Ishikawa Diagram for Investigating Cause and Effect

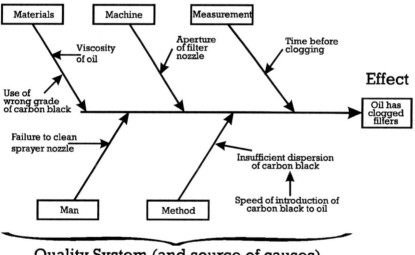

What is being investigated in Figure 13.4 are a number of recent field complaints that a certain lubricating oil, one of the company's products, dispensed by spraying onto engines, has clogged the filters of the spray guns. (The oil is coloured black so that the operator can see where he has sprayed.) As with so many investigations, it is usually possible to write down ten or twenty possible reasons, but, in true Pareto character, only three or four will be serious contenders, and one only will hit the jackpot. The Ishikawa diagram will typically be constructed on a flipchart, with a second diagram next to it illustrating the process itself as a reminder and a common point of reference. The diagrams are often used in conjunction with "brainstorming", the fast and furious outpouring of ideas by the assembled problem solvers, led by a facilitator.

The Cycle of Continuous Improvement [31]

The cycle of continuous improvement, or PDCA cycle, is illustrated in Figure 13.5 as a circle with four quadrants perpetually rotating in a clockwise direction.

Figure 13.5: The Cycle of Continuous Improvement (PDCA Cycle)

The PDCA cycle can be interpreted at the strategic TQM level, rather than the level intended here. When this is done, the starting "Plan" activity is the determination of goals and the devising of alternative methods of reaching them, the goals being directed to the fulfilment of company policy regarding quality. The second quadrant, "Do", then denotes the carrying out of education and training in the field corresponding to the goal selected in 1, so ensuring that all staff can contribute to its achievement effectively and are committed to its success; and finally the making of the

---

[31] The notion of the cycle of continuous improvement was originally put forward by Walter Shewhart in 1939. It is known, however, at least in Japan, as the *Deming cycle*. The Japanese term *"kaizen"* is also used to denote continuous improvement, although the full meaning of *kaizen* as defined by its principal exponent Masaaki Imai also encompasses self-improvement as well as improvement of the work environment.

Total Quality Control

changes necessary to reach the goal set. Quadrant 3, "Check", is verification that the changes implemented in 2 have been well carried out, and that the effects aimed for have occurred (making a note also of any undesirable, unanticipated side effects). The last quadrant, "Action" is the incorporation of the new procedures into the company's way of working (modified to eliminate any side-effects reported in 3).

At the operational level, the cycle of PDCA for determining the reasons for special cause variation and taking action to eliminate them amounts to little more than the scientific process of hypothesis and experiment. At the strategic level, the commitment to continuity — the commitment to keeping the PDCA circle perpetually revolving — accords well with Shewhart's original idea of continually revisiting the system described in relation to Figure 13.1. At the operational level, the four stages are as follows:

1. **Plan**: select the cause of variation which is to be removed (perhaps ranking alternative causes using Pareto principles); plan the changes which need to be made in order to eliminate the cause selected.(Particular emphasis is placed in this step on the collection and study of data from the shop floor and from actual field operations);

2. **Do**: carry out the changes intended to achieve the effect being sought (on as small a scale as possible, commensurate with obtaining realistic results);

3. **Check**: carefully study the results of the change made (among other things, by recompiling a further Shewhart chart to ensure that the special cause variation has been removed);

4. **Action**: review P, D and C and, if the change is to be implemented, take action to incorporate it in the company's procedures, displacing the old ways.

Quality Improvement (QI) Teams

The creation of permanent and temporary teams for examining quality problems requiring contributions from a number of functional departments has already been mentioned. At this point, we consider the setting up of teams, usually with six to twelve members, made up entirely of shop floor staff, for the purpose of identifying and solving special cause variation. Formal work teams in production at the middle management level are common enough, of course — the membership of weekly planning meetings, for example. Formal teamwork at the supervisor/operator level merely recognises that in the drive to attain process stability and eliminate special cause variation, the people best placed to find reasons and devise solutions are those nearest to the work.

There are a number of important general issues relating to teamwork — team mix, leadership, focus, discipline and so forth. Discussion of these is deferred, however, until sub-section 19.3.1 (*Teams and Empowerment*). Two points are raised here particular to quality improvement teams. Firstly, there must be a reasonable degree of management direction of each team's activity overall. A team is responsible for diligently tackling the problems it is asked to address, and its presentation of findings and recommendations at the conclusion of each investigation should reflect best endeavour. Secondly, it is essential that a team whose recommendations are accepted should have the satisfaction of seeing those recommendations adopted — the satisfaction of seeing money spent and procedures changed to bring about the targeted improvement in quality. Unless quality improvement teams are supported in these two respects, their adoption will fail and that failure will be a reflection of lack of company commitment to TQC.

The shop floor quality improvement team occupies a position halfway between a management-led task force and a Japanese-style quality control circle. QC circles began in Japan in 1962 following the first publication there of an educational magazine edited by Kaoru Ishikawa entitled *QC for Foremen*. Meetings were held outside factory hours, time was unpaid and attendance was studiedly voluntary and free of management direction in order to emphasise the company-wide nature of TQC responsibility.[32] It is now estimated that some 10 per cent of the Japanese manufacturing workforce beneath the rank of management belong to QC circles, with meetings still outside factory hours but time now paid. Although attendance remains voluntary, one may imagine the peer pressure to turn up to meetings to be irresistible. The progress and standard of work of each team are, in fact, tracked by management;

---

[32] Kaoru Ishikawa (1985), op. cit., Chapter 8.

each one is expected to complete two or three projects a year. There are national prizes and an annual convention attended by some 2,000 representatives.

Questions that cannot be answered either by the Japanese QC circle or by the more usual QI team in the UK factory are those relating, say, to engineering specifications, design, suppliers, machine maintenance, training or recruitment. Variation due to these factors has its origin in systems and common causes. What has been said repeatedly is said again: these are issues only management can address.

13.2.5 Training and the Introduction of TQC

It is a commonplace to say that if endeavour is to be successful, it must go hand-in-hand with competence. Indeed, Deming's preference for a low-key introduction of TQC and his opposition to a Crosby ZD Day is precisely because of his belief that enthusiasm without competence and understanding cannot prevail. Assurance of a workforce not only committed to TQC but capable of doing its part to achieve it might be considered by senior management under three headings, as follows:

1. *Recruitment.*[33] While a great deal of finesse is possible (and care taken) in assessing the suitability of job applicants for the cerebral work involved in management posts, based on the evidence of educational certificates and previously held positions, frequently little trouble is taken to assess carefully what capabilities are required of shop floor and other staff for the physical work required of them and to obtain hard evidence of each applicant's corresponding suitability. For example, as we shall see in Table 18.2, the two top causes of error in the stock recording referred to in sub-section 13.2.3, between them responsible for over 20 per cent of all errors that are made, are

---

[33] Going "upstream" to seek solutions to quality problems frequently pays off, such as going to recruitment, as in the text. Other examples of *upstream* (and areas for investigation and discussion) are suppliers of raw materials (knowledge of the ultimate use to be made of incoming materials); government offices (say, information needed to avoid mistakes in tax or National Insurance); and software houses (promoting clarity in documentation). The outside-in view is also of immense value in Health and Safety management — see Section 19.4.

incorrect counting and *incorrect recording*. And yet an applicant might be accepted into the stores, his suitability having been judged merely on his ability to drive a forklift truck and the impression he has made at an interview, without any examination of his clerical aptitude, eyesight or colour vision.

2. *Training in total quality control itself.* Leaving aside the matter of SQC in Chapter 14, which requires the institution of a major programme of education, tasks to undertake here are to get over to staff the notion of the multi-function system and its focus on customer satisfaction, to explain the nature of and difference between special and common causes of variation and to give practice and explanation in the techniques in the previous sub-section.[34]

3. *Job training for all staff newly installed in a job.* Learning as one goes along and learning from watching others is an obvious means of perpetuating bad habits in a workforce. The performance of even a simple job will be enhanced by teaching the potential jobholder theory. A formal, well-conceived course of instruction will also add to the jobholder's job satisfaction.

One early critical task for senior management starting down the endless road of TQC is to assure itself of the suitability of the remit, staffing and resources of the Quality Assurance department. In the TQC company, the QA department might be thought of as an extension of the office of the managing director itself, obviating the necessity for it to become involved in the detail. (What it must not be, it goes without saying, is a dumping ground for the MD's responsibility in these matters.)

Deming suggests that the head of the TQC programme ("the leader in statistical methodology", as he calls him) should be a participant in all major meetings of the MD and his board and have the right to question and follow up anything in the company he so

---

[34] Particular caution is needed if the company also feels it must issue a quality statement or mission statement — *the vision thing*, as former US President George Bush Sr. put it. And, as Rhymer Ridley of *Management Today* put it, *for every eagle there are a dozen ground-bound turkeys* (Rhymer Ridley (1998), "Mission Statements", *Management Today* magazine, March 1998).

Total Quality Control 503

chooses. The Master goes rather further. He adds that the manager should hold an MSc in statistics and have published papers to his name. Whatever the practicality of this in a small to medium-size enterprise, Deming nevertheless makes his point — the statistical knowledge and experience necessary to institute and lead an SQC programme as outlined in Chapter 14 is certainly considerable. Deming goes on to warn that "... no plan (to succeed in TQC) will work without the competence of and confidence in the statistical leadership".[35]

The QA department has other work to do besides unifying and guiding the TQC effort. The make-up of the department at the section level suggested by Armand Feigenbaum is as follows: quality engineering; quality information equipment engineering; and process control engineering.[36] Quality engineering relates to the company's quality systems (Figure 13.2) and in essence encompasses all activities described in this Chapter in which QA's expertise and co-ordinating powers are necessary or desirable. Quality information equipment covers the work required to design and develop the technical in-process inspection and test equipment needed for physical measurement, and to analyse and communicate the in-process data recorded. Process control engineering is Feigenbaum's term for the monitoring of QC/SPC application on the factory floor itself, as described in the next Chapter, as the new ways begin to supersede inspection.

13.3 ISO 9000:2000 [37]

The ISO 9000:2000 family of standards is a prescription of controls and requirements which the International Standards Organisation believes must be adopted by a company to give effect to its *quality management system* (QMS). There are three family members. The first is ISO 9000:2000 itself ("Fundamentals and Vocabulary"), comprising general guidelines and definitions, and used as a reference in interpreting the specifications in ISO 9001:2000. The

---

[35] Mary Walton (1986), *The Deming Management Method*, Mercury Books and Management Books 2000 Ltd., Chapter 16.

[36] A.V. Feigenbaum (1983), op. cit., Chapter 8.

[37] For the ISO and further details about ISO 9000 : 2000, visit http://www.iso.ch

second is ISO 9001:2000 ("Requirements"). This is the centre of interest, constituting the actual specification describing the company's QMS, and laying down a number of requirements in eight clauses described below. Of these, Clause 7 (Product or Service "Realisation")[38] is perhaps the most important to the manufacturing manager. Product realisation, which was termed "process control" under the 1994 standard, includes the steps involved in designing, manufacturing and delivering the product or service to the customer. The third member is ISO 9004:2000 ("Guidelines for Performance Improvement"), which is intended for the company that wishes to expand the scope of its QMS beyond the 9000/9001 limits.

The history of the standard began in the 1960s and 1970s and attempts made over that time by the UK government to improve the level of quality in industry, especially as it related to the fulfilment of government contracts. Earlier standards in 1971 and 1974 culminated in the publication in 1979 by the BSI of a quality procedures standard *BS 5750* and its subsequent promotion by roadshows and government funding. Finally, in 1987, BS 5750 was adopted in its entirety by the ISO in Geneva, Switzerland, and renamed ISO 9000. The reasons behind this extraordinary takeover appear to have been, on the British side, a wish to advance the reputation of British quality internationally and, on the ISO side, to facilitate world trade as regards common standards in the field of quality.

A revision to the 1987 standard was made in 1994, to create a family of procedures now referred to as ISO 9000:1994 — ISO 9001:1994; ISO 9002:1994; ISO 9003:1994; and ISO 9004:1994. The present-day standard (i.e. 9000:2000) is a major update of the 1994 edition and was published on 15 December 2000. Companies subscribing to the 1994 standards have until 15 December 2003 to

---

[38] ISO 9000:2000, even more than its 1994 predecessor, is also intended to serve commercial and service companies. The necessary lack of industry specificity, but their wish nevertheless for an industry-wide quality standard that could replace their own individual schemes, led Chrysler, Ford and General Motors in 1994 to issue an alternative, namely QS 9000. QS 9000 incorporates ISO 9000:1994 in its entirety, but with some 60 further provisions mainly relating to the automotive industry. More importantly, QS 9000 includes the need for the elimination of variation in output (see Chapter 14). The standard is supported by a permanent task force and was revised in 1998. Note that in US terminology, ISO 9000:2000 is ANSI/ISO/ASQC Q9000.

change over (noting then that the titles ISO 9002 and ISO 9003 will be obsolete). The ISO have put a great deal of effort into planning the transition to the revised standard, for example in preparing for review of accreditation bodies and for the retraining of auditors (see below). For the manufacturing company, although much additional work needs to be done to effect the transition, it is said that those companies which undertook a thorough and conscientious job in obtaining the 1994 version will be far better placed than the very many others which obtained fast certification merely for commercial reasons.[39] (Nevertheless, an area of difficulty may lie ahead for companies holding ISO 9002:1994. This standard was (is) a subset of 18 of the 20 provisions in ISO 9001:1994, i.e. excluding those related to design. Under the old regime, even if the company did have a limited design function, it could choose deliberately to exclude it from assessment and obtain certification under the lesser standard (i.e. 9002, not 9001). The auditor was not able to object. Under ISO 9001:2000, there is only one standard, and whether there is or is not a design function is itself a matter for audit. If there is so, design cannot be "excluded" from the QMS. Note also that if the company undertakes design, it cannot exclude it even if the customer requiring the certification requests that it does so. Parallel rules naturally also apply to holders of ISO 9003 (Inspection & Testing).)

It is suggested in the new standard that the company should give careful consideration to its stance in eight areas. These are termed *principles*, and are incorporated in ISO 9000:2000 itself and ISO 9001:2000 with explanations and examples of key benefits claimed to stem from their adoption. They are: (1) customer focus; (2) leadership; (3) the involvement of people; (4) a process approach; (5) a system approach to management; (6) continual improvement; (7) a factual approach to decision taking; and (8) mutually beneficial supplier relationships. (Note that Principle 4 means that the organisation's key activities — i.e. "processes" —

---

[39] An immediate start in making the transition from 1994 to 2000 may be made by renumbering and editing existing documentation in the new format. This alone is not sufficient, however, since there are numerous extra requirements, especially in relation to obtaining and evaluating feedback data. On documentation, see later in the text.

should be identified and considered in relation to the resources employed in carrying them out, while Principle 5 is concerned with the activities' interdependency and integration.) Whether or not the company seems to follow the eight principles can be taken into account in assessing its QMS under ISO 9001.

The substance of the new standard is ISO 9001:2000, which sets out requirements in eight clauses. These are given as follows with very brief comments.

1. *Scope.* This defines those corporate activities over which quality may be controlled through ISO 9000 in general, not the specific activities which are the object of the QMS in question.

2. *Normative References.* Standard references.

3. *Terms and Definitions.* From ISO 9000:2000.

4. *Quality Management System Requirements.* General requirements include a statement on the need for continuous improvement and the PDCA cycle as shown in Figure 13.5. Documentation requirements include the need to maintain a quality manual and an explanation of the means of documentation control and quality records control.

5. *Management Responsibility.* Procedures and statements relating to management commitment; customer focus; a corporate quality policy; measurable (and measured) quality targets; senior management representation; the communication of quality matters to staff; and management review, including a review of customer feedback and achieved product conformance.

6. *Resource Management.* Statements relating to determining the need for, and providing, the financial and other resources to give effect to the QMS; the provision and support of the company infrastructure; determining what personnel competencies and skills are needed, and stating how they are secured; how quality awareness is fostered in staff; and how training needs are identified, and training provided.

7. *Product Realisation.* This clause is central to the manufacturing company and covers six broad areas. These are as follows, with examples in brackets: (i) the planning of product realisa-

tion (materials planning and shop floor control); (ii) customer-related processes (determining customer requirements, product legal requirements and customer satisfaction); (iii) design and development (the design brief, conformance to design, value engineering and engineering change); (iv) purchasing (procedures for selecting suppliers, supplier evaluation methods and the verification of incoming products); (v) production and service provision (control of production operations, traceability, product storage and ongoing process control); and (vi) control of monitoring and measuring devices (the means of assuring final product conformance).

8. *Measurement, Analysis and Improvement.* Particular emphasis is paid in this clause to the value of the Plan-Do-Check-Action cycle (described in sub-section 13.2.4). Activities required are the assessment of customer satisfaction; the conducting of internal audits; the control of outgoing non-conforming product (see Figure 14.14); the effecting of continual improvement; and the conduct of preventive maintenance.

As anyone knows who has had even the slightest contact with it, what characterises ISO 9000 is the sheer volume of documentation that must be prepared and maintained in its support. Documentation can be regarded as a hierarchy, typically with five tiers, though perhaps with more in large multinational companies. At the top are statements setting out the company's quality policy and quality objectives (see footnote 34). The next tier comprises the QMS manual itself. (Clause 4 specifies the minimum requirements here. Two examples are the need for descriptions of management responsibilities and for a sketch of the company's organisation.) At the third tier comes the documentation of certain procedures specified by the standard as being mandatory to include. Responding to complaints on all sides about documentation, the committee responsible for ISO 9000:2000 has reduced the number of such specified procedures from 20 in the 1994 version to 6. This may be so, but at Tier 4 next must come documents relating to the planning, operation and control of all the company's processes — i.e. key activities — as they are set out in Clauses 5 to 8. For the manufacturing company, this includes documented procedures on the six areas of product realisation given earlier.

At the bottom of the tree are quality records. Quality records specified as mandatory include those relating to the following activities: the conduct of management reviews; the administration and carrying out of training and education; design; supplier evaluation; calibration and measurement; and internal audit. To demonstrate conformance to the key activities as described at Tier 4, other records, relating to them, must also be completed and filed. It should be noted that since the 2000 standard stresses continual improvement and customer satisfaction, records must duly be made proving their existence — that is, records must be made and kept relating to the effectiveness of actions taken and the satisfaction of those affected by them.[40]

There are three reasons why such heavy emphasis is placed on documentation and records in the ISO standard.

The first is, by now, the entrenchment of mind of officials responsible for it and their constant looking out for opportunity to impose its requirement, quite regardless of its value, or not, for serious reasons of operating guidance or later technical analysis.[41]

The second reason is far more reprehensible. It was always in the minds of the promulgators of BS 5750 and ISO 9000 that a formal means of certification should be provided along with the standard itself. And if so, how else could compliance be judged except through documentation? By imputation, then, the means of managing the QMS under ISO 9000 has its origin in its (commercial) value to the standard's publishers, not in its contribution to the satisfaction of the company's customers, even though the requirement for paperwork and record-keeping at every turn appear to staff foolish and even predicated on an ultimate distrust of their competence and reliability.

---

[40] Some ingenuity may be expected with regard to records describing the effectiveness of training and education (though see sub-section 19.2.4). Even greater ingenuity may be expected regarding the effectiveness of the marketing department's research into customers' aspirations and its formulation of marketing strategy in response (see sub-section 2.1.4).

[41] The standard worksheet takes pride of place on the Toyota shop floor — see Section 15.7. We may suppose, however, that it is not necessary for security guards at the Koromo factory site to sign slips of paper every evening at 9pm certifying that they have checked the gates.

The final reason for documentation that damns ISO is the supposition that, at any given instant, procedures are fixed. There may indeed be strict and unvarying procedures for performing technical tasks, but human-centred activities need room to breathe. In a stable system encompassing human endeavour and operating in manufacturing society, Deming's common causes are the necessary little accommodations that must continually be made to counter the buffets of the environment and provide for the unanticipated requirements of customers. Taking action always to comply with the snapshot reflected in the latest version of the ISO documentation will often be to destabilise the system in just the same way that a system is destabilised when common causes are treated as special causes, as described in sub-section 13.2.3.

For the vast majority of companies, the purpose of taking up ISO 9000 is purely to obtain the ISO certificate, not because the journey down the path to obtain it will lead to their transformation to quality-conscious organisations. Certification means that the company has written down its QMS; that this has been subject to audit through its documentation by an ISO 9000:2000 assessor; and that the documentation and its correspondence with the activities carried out indicate that it complies with the standard's requirements — in short, that the company is *capable*. In the UK, assessors are normally members of staff of companies approved by the National Accreditation Council for Certification Bodies, established by the Department of Trade and Industry. There are currently some 25 companies, one such being BSI Quality Assurance (see footnote 13). There are a further dozen non-accredited companies which also issue certificates. It is not irrelevant to add that assessors charge a fee to conduct the audits and to conduct yearly or twice-yearly follow-up audits to verify continued compliance. When added to the fees of the selfsame personnel advising on the standard in alternative roles they invariably have as consultants, we see why ISO 9000 is such big business for this element of the quality community and why it is so difficult for companies in the UK to obtain measured advice on this and similar quality matters.

TQC and the activities described in Section 13.2 lead to enhanced customer satisfaction and reduced costs. Since ISO leads to neither, it must be asked why so very many companies seek accreditation.

One reason is undoubtedly because "getting ISO 9000" is familiar management territory. A senior manager is appointed by the MD to be project leader and a steering committee is formed to keep watch on progress. The mountainous task of compiling the documentation is organised in systematic fashion, perhaps by documenting current practice and examining the results for gaps. (Shewhart and Deming and the Japanese example, are, of course, forgotten in the meantime.)

A second reason — forgivable — may be that the company's customers, as ignorant of quality matters as were government contract inspectors all those years ago, require of it possession of the standard as a condition of doing business. Because ISO 9000 "guarantees the quality of what they buy", or, perhaps, because the task of obtaining it is seen to serve as a harmless initiation ritual such as might be imposed on a college freshman, they, the customers, are relieved of all requirement to understand quality issues themselves. As well, customers in possession of the standard may believe, wrongly, that their suppliers must also be accredited (and so the standard is propagated, like a malign chain letter).[42]

The culmination of the ISO project is the carrying out of the audit itself by an official outside assessor carefully chosen by the company. D-day is typically preceded by a frantic last-minute rush to put things in order and, somehow, bring records up-to-date. Now there are anxious moments. A mistake here *(will he fail us?)*, a nonconformance there *(will he spot it?)* — but the company passes! The certificate is hung on display; the logo is added to the stationery.

---

[42] Clauses 7 and 8 of ISO 9000:2000 require of the company only that some supplier selection process of its choosing should be documented and duly observed, and records kept relating to suppliers' actual performance. Of the very large number of instances of wasted time and effort resulting from the standard's application, one of the more amusing under ISO 9000:1994 was the demand by Oxford City Council that, since all of its suppliers had to be *quality* suppliers and so have the *quality kitemark*, a troupe of Morris Dancers was to register to ISO, the dancers being engaged by the parks services department of the Council to entertain tourists at its "Oxford in Bloom" flower festival (*Daily Express*, 2 March 1995, p. 23). "The BSI sets the standards for the quality awards and we have to follow these to make sure we keep up with our quality," said a spokesman.

In his powerful and cogent refutation of ISO 9000:2000, essential reading for any managing director or manufacturing manager pondering the value of ISO 9000:2000 or for any purchasing manager contemplating the infliction of the standard on his company's suppliers, the UK quality expert John Seddon states that the most beguiling argument used to justify the standard's adoption is that it would be alright *if only folk would do it right*.[43] "Procedures" (say the standard's supporters) "do after all provide us with order and predictability . . . ISO 9000:2000 is a good start." The evidence of useless endeavour, the demotivation of staff crushed by trivialities and even of direct customer harm turned up by Seddon in his book and exposed in page after page seem to count for nothing against the prospect of doing it right. Yet as he shows, the standard itself is fundamentally flawed, done right or done wrong. Thus he points out that when people are subject to ISO controls and adherence to the controls is duly measured through the ISO documentation, their action will be directed to those matters which affect the measurements directly, to the detriment, if called for, of all else. Seddon supports his argument with six case studies illustrating just how "creative" the recording of data can be and how the action of staff becomes focused on rules and reports, not on customers.

---

[43] John Seddon (2000), *The Case Against ISO 9000*, Second edition, Oak Tree Press. John Seddon is MD of Vanguard Consulting of Buckingham (http://www.vanguardconsult.co.uk).

Chapter 14

Statistical Quality Control (SQC)

The pure application of statistical techniques to quality is termed *statistical quality control* (SQC) and is considered in two divisions: *statistical process control* (SPC) and *raw material and product control*. Each division may itself be sub-divided, as shown in Figure 14.1.

Figure 14.1: The Positions of SPC and Product Acceptance within SQC

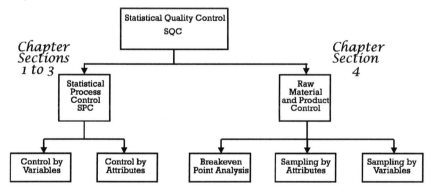

The principal interest of the manufacturing manager is in SPC. This is a means that is at once simple, ingenious and powerful for determining whether an ongoing manufacturing process is operating in a stable and settled manner and for tracking over time the process's continued stability. The methods and procedures of SPC were laid down in 1931 by Walter Shewhart; they have been adopted widely throughout manufacturing industry, largely in their original form.[1] SPC is covered in Sections 14.1 to 14.3 of the Chapter.

Raw material and product control is applied to goods that have already been manufactured. It includes the theory and practice of sampling, and is, for the quality control manager, a subject larger even than SPC. It is especially associated with the assessment for quality of incoming raw materials, but it has also been applied to the assessment for quality of outgoing product, perhaps into finished goods stock or perhaps due for direct despatch to the customer. The subject is covered in Section 14.4.

14.1 SPC — THE STATISTICAL BASIS

14.1.1 The Central Limit Theorem

Despite the name, knowledge of statistics is in no way essential to the everyday application of SPC at the shop floor level, and great efforts have been made by quality control managers to present the subject so that it can be readily applied by shop operators.[2] Nevertheless, for the manufacturing manager, an appreciation of the statistical theory on which the subject is based is surely essential to a proper understanding of its use within the plant. Indeed, knowledge of both the theory and practice of SPC will greatly enhance his understanding of the nature of the productive process and of production itself.

The basis of SPC is the taking of small samples over time of output from the manufacturing process and the measurement of some predetermined physical characteristic of each member of the sample. The samples are taken every so often, perhaps every few hours, and each one is of equal size — say, either four parts or five parts. Because of minute variations in the process — e.g. variations in temperature, voltage, pressure — in short, the common causes

---

[1] Walter A. Shewhart (1931), *The Economic Control of Quality of Manufactured Products* (50th Anniversary Edition published in 1980), Van Nostrand.

[2] For an excellent non-statistical treatment suitable for shop floor staff, see Robert T. Amsden, Howard E. Butler and Davida M. Amsden (1986), *SPC Simplified — Practical Steps to Quality*, Kraus International Publications. For a statistically oriented introductory text, see A.G. Hopper (1969), *Basic SQC*, McGraw-Hill. Many videos and other teaching aids are also available.

Statistical Quality Control (SQC)

introduced in Chapter 13, here associated with a production process rather than a human-centred system — the measurements taken will show variation one from another. If the number of parts in each sample is n and the measurements recorded for the individual parts are $X_1, X_2, X_3 \ldots, X_n$, then the mean of the measurements in a given sample is $\overline{X}$ (X bar), as shown in Equation 14.1.

$$\overline{X} = \frac{1}{n}\sum X_1 + X_2 + \ldots \ldots + X_n \qquad \text{Equation 14.1}$$

If k samples are taken in all over an interval of time, and the mean of each one of them is calculated as in Equation 14.1, the means of all the samples can be written as follows:

$$\overline{X}_1, \overline{X}_2, \overline{X}_3, \ldots, \overline{X}_k$$

For the sake of clarity, the mean of a sample such as one of those above is referred to from this point in hyphenated form as a *sample-mean*.

As a group of numbers, the sample-means themselves have a mean, commonly termed in SPC the *grand average*, or $\overline{\overline{X}}$ (X bar bar). The grand average of the k sample-means above is given by Equation 14.2.

$$\overline{\overline{X}} = \frac{1}{k}\sum \overline{X}_1 + \overline{X}_2 + \overline{X}_3 + \ldots \ldots + \overline{X}_k \qquad \text{Equation 14.2}$$

Although it is not yet under discussion, we know that the sample-means also have a standard deviation, termed here:

$$\sigma_{\overline{X}}$$

This expression (sigma sub X bar) is referred to in statistical textbooks as the *standard error of the mean*.

Textbooks also refer to a *population* (or *universe*, or *parent distribution*) when referring to the collection of items from which samples are drawn, the implication being that the population is large (and in many cases stated as being assumed to be infinite). In SPC, the population is the completed and potential output from the process. (If the process is altered before potential output is achieved, however, the characteristics of the actual output will be different from what otherwise would have been expected. In such circumstances, we may therefore say that the characteristics of the population have similarly changed.) For the population of the manufactured parts here, the mean value of the physical characteristic being measured, X, is referred to as µ, and is, at this point, unknown. The standard deviation applying to the distribution of X in the population is, as is customary, referred to as σ, and is also at this point unknown.

We now summon a powerful and remarkable law of statistics, the *central limit theorem*.[3] The central limit theorem can be stated in three parts, and allows us to relate the mean of the sample-means and the standard deviation of the sample-means to the mean of the population and the standard deviation of the population. Thus:

1. The grand average of the sample-means is the same as the mean of the population from which the samples are taken. That is, Equation 14.3 applies

$$\overline{\overline{X}} = \mu \qquad \text{Equation 14.3}$$

2. The standard deviation applying to the distribution of the sample-means is the same as the standard deviation applying to the distribution of the population, divided by the square root of the size of the samples taken. That is:

$$\sigma_{\overline{X}} = \frac{\sigma}{\sqrt{n}} \qquad \text{Equation 14.4}$$

But it is Part 3 that makes the central limit theorem so astonishing.

3. *The statistical distribution of the sample-means is (approximately) normal, or Gaussian,* **regardless of the distribution of the population**, provided the sample size *n* is sufficiently large. (In fact, *n* does not have to be large at all for the distribution of the sample-means to approximate to the normal distribution

---

[3] The central limit theorem was first formulated by our acquaintance from Chapter 5, Abraham De Moivre, and was subsequently refined and generalised by Pierre-Simon Laplace (1749–1827) and Andrei Nikolayevich Kolmogorov (1903–1987). It has very wide application. It is, for example, especially important in life insurance. An insurance company targeting a particular segment of the market which it believes to be stable need only satisfy itself as to the characteristics of a sample from it to draw conclusions on risk for the whole segment, based on probabilities derived from the normal distribution (see Part 3 of the theorem). Expositions of the central limit theorem can be found in many advanced texts on statistics, and at a great number of Internet sites.

closely enough for all practical purposes. Samples of four are quite all right and samples of two or three give adequate results.)[4]

14.1.2 Shewhart's Bowls

To demonstrate the truth of Part 3 of the central limit theorem, Walter Shewhart, in an internal paper for Bell Telephones, NJ, in 1924, reported the results of three sets of experiments involving drawing samples of various sizes from a bowl (literally, an ordinary kitchen bowl) containing numbered metal-rimmed chips, or tags. Three sets of experiments were conducted, involving populations of chips in which the distributions of the numbers were normal, rectangular and triangular. Four thousand random drawings were made from each type of population. After each sample had been drawn and the numbers recorded, the chips were replaced and the bowl stirred again. The mean of each sample was calculated, and the sample-means from each experiment corresponding to a given sample size plotted as a histogram. Each such histogram showed the familiar bell shape of the normal curve (see Figures 5.4 and 5.5).

Shewhart's bowls have an important (and affectionate) place in the history of manufacturing quality; experiments with chips and a bowl are frequently conducted as part of quality and statistical training courses. (The original kitchen bowl and a number of the metal tags are now in the possession of the American Society for Quality Control at Milwaukee, WI.)

A more modest attempt to illustrate that the distribution of sample-means is normal regardless of the distribution of the population from which the samples are drawn is given as follows. (Part 3 of the central limit theorem, after all, is far from intuitive.)

Figure 14.2 represents a "square" distribution of 16 chips, numbered as shown. It is proposed to consider all possible samples of four chips that might be taken from this population. The sum of the numbers in any sample of four range from a minimum of 4 (1 + 1 +

---

[4] In areas of application other than SPC, rules of thumb for assuming normality are that n can be as low as 10 if the population is known to be symmetrical and that n should be 30 or more if the population is asymmetrical or completely unknown.

1 + 1) to a maximum of 16 (4 + 4 + 4 + 4). There are 13 possible totals in all: 4, 5, 6, 7, 8, 9, 10, 11, 12, 13, 14, 15 and 16. The mean and expectation of these numbers is 10.0.

Figure 14.2: Sixteen Chips having a "Square" Distribution

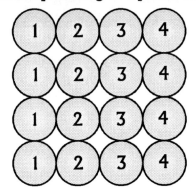

Now of all the very many possible ways of selecting a sample of four chips, there is only one in which the sum of the numbers on the chips is the minimum of 4 and only one way in which the sum is the maximum of 16. However, it will be readily seen from Figure 14.2 that 16 different samples can be chosen in which the numbers add up to 5. (There are four ways of selecting three 1's and four ways of selecting a 2.) Similarly, 16 different samples are possible in which the numbers add up to 15. (Four ways of selecting three 4's and four ways of selecting a 3.) Table 14.1 shows the number of samples possible relating to each of the 13 totals from 4 to 16.[5] Figure 14.3 shows the theoretical frequencies in Table 14.2 set out as a histogram. The bell shape obtained is similar to the bell shapes for the experimental frequencies obtained by Walter Shewhart from his bowls.

---

[5] As verification of the number of possible samples in Table 14.1, it will be found that the sum of the 13 possible outcomes from 4 to 16, each multiplied by its probability of being drawn from the population, is 10.0, the expected value. That is:

$$4 \times \frac{1}{1820} + 5 \times \frac{16}{1820} + 6 \times \frac{52}{1820} + \ldots \ldots = 10.0$$

Statistical Quality Control (SQC) 519

Table 14.1: Theoretical Combinations for Samples of Four Chips from a "Square" Population

Sum of the four chips in the sample	Number of possible samples, or combinations
4	1
5	16
6	52
7	128
8	229
9	304
10	360
11	304
12	229
13	128
14	52
15	16
16	1
Total	1820

Figure 14.3: Histogram of Number of Sample Combinations (Sample Size of 4) (Sum of Sample Values = Sample-Mean × 4)

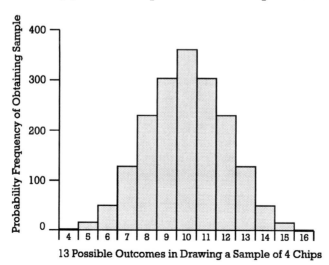

13 Possible Outcomes in Drawing a Sample of 4 Chips

The distribution of the measurements of X in the population from which samples are taken often is normal in manufacturing, but sometimes is not. Statistical distributions mentioned in sub-section 5.2.1 are Poisson, negative exponential and gamma. Others possible in manufactured output are multi-modal and those in which the items involved have been subject to a degree of inspection and screening before machining commences.[6] All this is by the way. What is important is that the distribution of the population does not have to be determined. The normality of the sample-means is all that need be of concern.

To summarise progress in describing the basis of SPC so far: the frequency distribution of the sample-means is bell-shaped with a grand average of $\overline{\overline{X}}$. What is, of course, missing is a measure of the dispersion of this bell — i.e. knowledge of $\sigma_{\overline{X}}$.

14.1.3 Dispersion of the Sample-Means

Two alternative methods are available for determining the standard deviation of the sample-means, $\sigma_{\overline{X}}$. They are: (a) through calculation of the standard deviation of the values in each sample; and (b) by calculation of the *range*. The standard deviation method may be employed with samples of any size but is usually used only when samples are large (15 or more).[7] Calculation involving the range is far easier arithmetically and is preferred for that reason on a busy shop floor. Because of the danger of inaccuracy, however, its use is confined to samples of fewer than 15.

---

[6] The mode is the most frequently occurring value in a distribution; when the value of the greatest frequency is shared by two members of the population, the distribution is said to be *bimodal*. The effect of screening parts before machining might be (say) to remove all of them in which X has a value within a certain range (thus distorting the natural distribution of the values of X).

[7] As we shall see in sub-section 14.1.5 *et seq.*, large samples imply closer control limits, since:

$$\sigma_{\overline{X}} \propto \frac{1}{\sqrt{n}}.$$

That is, the larger the sample size, the narrower the spread of the bell — which is equivalent to saying the narrower the control limits "UCL$_{\overline{X}}$ minus LCL$_{\overline{X}}$". Closer control limits are desirable when it is required to keep one's eye out for small changes in the process average $\overline{\overline{X}}$ on the control chart.

Statistical Quality Control (SQC)

The Range

If the values of X in a given sample are $X_1, X_2, X_3, \ldots, X_n$; then the range R is the difference between the largest value of X in the sample and the smallest value. That is, Equation 14.5 applies.

$$R = X_{max} - X_{min} \qquad \text{Equation 14.5}$$

For k samples taken over an interval of time, the ranges are R_1, R_2, R_3, ..., R_k, and the *average range* $\overline{R}$ (R bar) is given by Equation 14.6.

$$\overline{R} = \frac{1}{k} \sum R_1 + R_2 + R_3 + \ldots + R_k \qquad \text{Equation 14.6}$$

The expression $\overline{R}/\sigma$ is, in words, the ratio of the average range of a number of samples of size n to the standard deviation of the population from which the samples are taken. Statistical theory which need not be pursued here allows this ratio to be calculated for any sample size n. By convention, the ratio is referred to as d_2. Table 14.2 gives values of d_2 for a small number of sample sizes (when the population is normal).

Table 14.2: Values of d_2 for Eight Sample Sizes (Use of the Range to Determine the Dispersion of the Sample-Means)

Sample Size n	$\dfrac{\overline{R}}{\sigma}$ (d_2)	Sample Size n	$\dfrac{\overline{R}}{\sigma}$ (d_2)
2	1.128	6	2.534
3	1.693	7	2.704
4	2.059	8	2.847
5	2.326	9	2.970

Since

$$d_2 = \frac{\overline{R}}{\sigma} \qquad \text{Equation 14.7}$$

and since from previously

$$\sigma_{\overline{X}} = \frac{\sigma}{\sqrt{n}} \qquad \text{Equation 14.4}$$

then Equation 14.8 follows:

$$\sigma_{\overline{X}} = \frac{\overline{R}}{d_2 \sqrt{n}} \qquad \text{Equation 14.8}$$

Standard Deviation

The standard deviation s of the values of X in a sample is given by Equation 14.9. (This Equation was previously encountered in sub-section 5.2.1. See also Equation 5.2.)

$$s = \frac{\sqrt{(X_1 - \overline{X})^2 + (X_2 - \overline{X})^2 + \ldots + (X_n - \overline{X})^2}}{(n-1)} \qquad \text{Equation 14.9}$$

For k samples taken over an interval of time, the sample standard deviations are s_1, s_2, s_3, ... , s_k, and the *average sample standard deviation* $\overline{s}$ is given by Equation 14.10

$$\overline{s} = \frac{1}{k} \sum s_1 + s_2 + s_3 + \ldots \ldots + s_k \qquad \text{Equation 14.10}$$

The ratio $\overline{s}/\sigma$ is, in words, the ratio of the average sample standard deviation of a number of samples of size n to the standard deviation of the population from which the samples are taken. Further statistical theory, which again need not be pursued, allows this ratio to be calculated for any sample size. By convention, the ratio is referred to as c_4. Table 14.3 gives values of c_4 for a small number of sample sizes (when the population is normal).

Table 14.3: Values of c_4 for various Sample Sizes (Use of the Standard Deviation to determine the dispersion of the Sample-Means)

Sample Size n	$\dfrac{\overline{s}}{\sigma}$ (c_4)	Sample Size n	$\dfrac{\overline{s}}{\sigma}$ (c_4)
2	0.7979	6	0.9515
3	0.8862	7	0.9594
4	0.9213	8	0.9650
5	0.9400	9	0.9693

Statistical Quality Control (SQC)

Now since:

$$c_4 = \frac{\bar{s}}{\sigma} \qquad \text{Equation 14.11}$$

and from previously

$$\sigma_{\bar{X}} = \frac{\sigma}{\sqrt{n}} \qquad \text{Equation 14.4}$$

then:

$$\sigma_{\bar{X}} = \frac{\bar{s}}{c_4 \sqrt{n}} \qquad \text{Equation 14.12}$$

14.1.4 Monitoring the Process — First Steps

Since the distribution of the sample-means is known to be normal, with a mean of $\bar{\bar{X}}$ and a standard deviation of $\sigma_{\bar{X}}$, and since both of these values can be calculated from data relating to the various samples being taken from the process output, using either Equation 14.2 and Equation 14.8 or Equation 14.2 and Equation 14.12, then a complete picture of the distribution of the sample means can be drawn as shown in Figure 14.4.

Figure 14.4: Distribution of the Sample-Means showing the three Sigma Limits on either side of the Grand Average

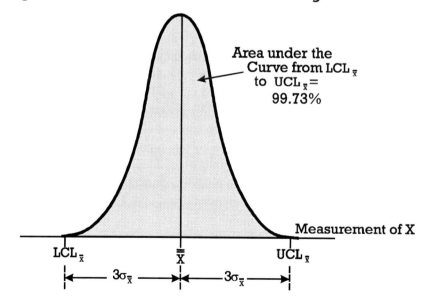

It is seen in Figure 14.4 that two points have been marked on the horizontal axis almost at the two extremes of the normal curve as $LCL_{\overline{X}}$ (Lower Control Limit of $\overline{X}$) and $UCL_{\overline{X}}$ (Upper Control Limit of $\overline{X}$). As indicated in the Figure, the $LCL_{\overline{X}}$ is located on the horizontal axis at position $\overline{\overline{X}} - 3\sigma_{\overline{X}}$ and the $UCL_{\overline{X}}$ is located at position $\overline{\overline{X}} + 3\sigma_{\overline{X}}$. The distance of $6\sigma_{\overline{X}}$ between the two limits, being centred at $\overline{\overline{X}}$, is known to encompass 99.73 per cent of the area under the curve and is shaded in Figure 14.4. (This percentage is obtained from integration of the expression for the normal curve in Equation 5.3. and was discussed at length in sub-section 5.2.1. Values for the areas under the normal curve from $-\infty$ to various points on the normal curve's horizontal axis are given in Tables 5.4(a) and 5.4(b).)

If the manufacturing process responsible for the production of the parts being taken as samples has reached a stable state — i.e. is unchanging — then three consequences seem to stem from the foregoing: (1) as each sample of output is taken one after another and the dimension X of each sample member duly measured, the mean of X (the sample-mean $\overline{X}$) will lie between the values $LCL_{\overline{X}}$ ($\overline{\overline{X}} - 3\sigma_{\overline{X}}$) and $LCL_{\overline{X}}$ ($\overline{\overline{X}} + 3\sigma_{\overline{X}}$); (2) the values of all of the sample-means will be distributed more-or-less equally on either side of the grand average $\overline{\overline{X}}$; and (3) the overall distribution of the sample-means will be more-or-less bell-shaped as in Figure 14.4.

Unfortunately there are two snags.

The first is that it would be possible for the manufacturing process to change and for the distribution of the sample-means to change (while continuing to be normal) even though the grand average remains at $\overline{\overline{X}}$ and the individual sample-means continue to lie between the $LCL_{\overline{X}}$ and the $UCL_{\overline{X}}$. This is demonstrated in Figure 14.5 in which the original distribution of the sample-means (denoted by normal curve A) is displaced due to a change in the process by a second distribution of sample-means (denoted by normal curve B).

Statistical Quality Control (SQC)

Figure 14.5: Two Superimposed Normal Distributions with Different Dispersions but a Common Mean

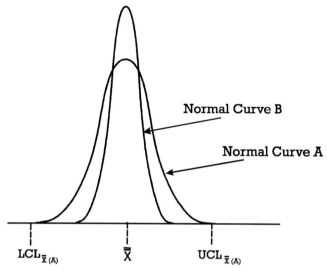

Consequently, in order to detect such a change, it is necessary to track the dispersion of the values in each sample and to set limits on it, either by monitoring the range R of each sample and the average range $\bar{R}$, or by monitoring the standard deviation of each sample s and the average sample standard deviation $\bar{s}$.

Let us consider first the range R. We recall that an average value of the ranges of the samples, $\bar{R}$, has already been calculated (Equation 14.6). To determine upper and lower limits of control of $\bar{R}$, it is necessary to calculate the standard deviation of the average range, σ_R. The two control limits are then given as shown in Equations 14.13 and 14.14.

$$UCL_R = \bar{R} + 3\sigma_R \qquad \text{Equation 14.13}$$

$$LCL_R = \bar{R} - 3\sigma_R \qquad \text{Equation 14.14}$$

Now the expression σ_R/σ is, in words, the ratio of the standard deviation of the range to the standard deviation of the population from which the samples are taken. Once more, statistical theory allows this ratio to be calculated for any sample size n. By convention, the ratio is referred to as d_3. Table 14.4 gives values for d_3 for a small number of sample sizes (when the population is normal).

Table 14.4: Values of d_3 to Enable the Dispersion of the Range to be Calculated

Sample Size n	$\frac{\sigma_R}{\sigma}$ (d_3)	Sample Size n	$\frac{\sigma_R}{\sigma}$ (d_3)
2	0.8525	6	0.8480
3	0.8884	7	0.8332
4	0.8798	8	0.8198
5	0.8641	9	0.8078

Rearranging the expression for d_3 gives σ_R in Equation 14.15.

$$\sigma_R = d_3 \sigma \qquad \text{Equation 14.15}$$

From Equation 14.7 for d_2, we obtain Equation 14.16.

$$\sigma = \frac{\overline{R}}{d_2} \qquad \text{Equation 14.16}$$

From Equation 14.15, substituting σ from Equation 14.16, we obtain Equation 14.17.

$$\sigma_R = d_3 \frac{\overline{R}}{d_2} \qquad \text{Equation 14.17}$$

Since σ_R has now been found, we may rewrite Equations 14.13 and 14.14 as Equations 14.18 and 14.19.

$$UCL_R = \overline{R} + 3\frac{d_3}{d_2}\overline{R} \qquad \text{Equation 14.18}$$

$$LCL_R = \overline{R} - 3\frac{d_3}{d_2}\overline{R} \qquad \text{Equation 14.19}$$

In passing, it should be noted that the right-hand side of Equation 14.19 is negative when samples of six or fewer are chosen. By convention, when $n \leq 6$, LCL_R is set to zero and otherwise ignored.[8]

When the standard deviation s is to be used to track dispersion, rather than the range R, the upper and lower control limits are as

---

[8] The absence of a lower limit for $\overline{R}$ when n is six or less is a statistical phenomenon. In the physical world, some variables may naturally have no lower limit — for example, material impurities. Others may have no upper limit — say, tensile strength.

Statistical Quality Control (SQC)

given in Equations 14.20 and 14.21, where $\bar{s}$ is the average sample standard deviation as given in Equation 14.10.

$$UCL_s = \bar{s} + 3\sigma_s \qquad \text{Equation 14.20}$$

$$LCL_s = \bar{s} - 3\sigma_s \qquad \text{Equation 14.21}$$

The value of σ_s may be obtained from the approximation in Equation 14.22 for samples of size n.

$$\sigma_s = \frac{\sigma}{\sqrt{2(n-1)}} \qquad \text{Equation 14.22}$$

σ itself is obtained from Equation 14.11 involving c_4 and the values previously given for c_4 in Table 14.3, so that the final expression for σ_s is as shown in Equation 14.23.

$$\sigma_s = \frac{\bar{s}}{c_4\sqrt{2(n-1)}} \qquad \text{Equation 14.23}$$

Note, however, that a refinement is necessary to Equation 14.23 for values of n of 25 or less.[9] Note also that LCL_s is set to zero when n = 5 or less.

The second snag is the essentially static depiction of the information within Figure 14.4. Neither the normal curve in the Figure nor any similar histogram, as it might be constructed from calculations of sample-means obtained as the manufacturing process proceeds, albeit with values distributed between two control limits, conveys the dynamics of production or provides for warning signals should the process become unstable. The element of time is absent.

14.1.5 Monitoring the Process — The Control Chart

Time is supplied by the famous control charts. Shewhart now opens up the grouped and vertical data of the normal distribution by casting them horizontally across time. The grand average becomes a horizontal central line, with horizontally drawn control limits above and below it. Room is made across the bottom of the chart for the range and its limits. The sample-means and ranges are plotted one after another across time as the process proceeds.

---

[9] See Eugene L. Grant and Richard S. Leavenworth (1996), *Statistical Quality Control*, Seventh edition, McGraw-Hill, sub-section 4.2.5.

528   The Manufacturing Manager

Figure 14.6 shows a Shewhart control chart in which samples of five parts have been taken every hour over a ten-hour shift. (The Figure is an expanded version of Figure 13.3.) The individual measurement X of each member of the sample is recorded for convenience on the chart itself, with space provided for the calculated sample-means and ranges. The sample-means are plotted over the ten hours, in this case falling satisfactorily between the upper control limit ($\bar{\bar{X}} + 3\sigma_{\bar{X}}$) and the lower control limit ($\bar{\bar{X}} - 3\sigma_{\bar{X}}$). The ranges are also entered at their corresponding times and again, here, fall satisfactorily between the upper control limit for the range, UCL_R, and zero.

Figure 14.6: Shewhart Xbar and R Variable Control Chart

Component: *Blade Holder*				Code: *P50*	Part: *X*	Location: *WC 100. Op. 10*			
Operator: *Andrew Artisan*					Gauge: *Vernier*	U.O.M.: *thou* "			
Date: *19th Dec 2002*									
Time:	8.15am	9.05am	10.00am	11.00am	12.00pm	1.00pm	2.00pm	3.00pm	4.00pm	4.45pm	n/a
	7.1	10.0	5.6	7.9	5.9	7.8	8.9	6.9	7.9	6.0	
	7.8	7.9	8.3	9.9	5.8	6.2	7.2	5.5	10.0	8.2	
	9.1	9.9	8.9	9.7	6.4	9.8	10.0	5.7	7.9	7.0	
	5.9	9.8	5.9	6.8	6.4	10.0	6.9	6.1	8.1	5.9	
	6.2	8.0	7.0	7.9	6.6	9.0	8.0	6.8	9.5	8.9	
Sum	36.0	45.6	35.7	42.2	31.1	42.8	41.0	32.0	43.4	36.0	
Avg.($\bar{X}$)	7.2	9.1	7.1	8.4	6.2	8.6	8.2	6.4	8.7	7.2	
Range	3.2	2.1	3.3	3.1	0.8	3.8	3.1	1.4	2.1	3.0	

Sample-Means (Averages, $\bar{X}$): UCL (9.20), $\bar{\bar{X}}$ (7.71), LCL (6.21)

Range (R): UCL (5.48), $\bar{R}$ (2.59)

The grand average $\bar{\bar{X}}$ of the sample-means in Figure 14.6 is 7.71 thou and the average range $\bar{R}$ is 2.59 thou. Although at least 25 samples should be taken before calculating these pivotal statistics, rather than merely ten, for the sake of illustration these values will be used here to determine the control limits.

First, $\sigma_{\bar{X}}$ is obtained from Equation 14.8, substituting 2.59 for $\bar{R}$ and 2.326 for d_2 for a sample of size 5 (n = 5, from Table 14.2). That is, Equation 14.24 applies.

Statistical Quality Control (SQC)

$$\sigma_{\overline{X}} = \frac{2.59}{2.326\sqrt{5}} = 0.498 \qquad \text{Equation 14.24}$$

The upper control limit and lower control limit for $\overline{\overline{X}}$ are now obtained from Equations 14.25 and 14.26.

$$UCL_{\overline{X}} = \overline{\overline{X}} + 3\sigma_{\overline{X}} \qquad \text{Equation 14.25}$$

$$LCL_{\overline{X}} = \overline{\overline{X}} - 3\sigma_{\overline{X}} \qquad \text{Equation 14.26}$$

The limits are 9.20 thou and 6.21 thou and are shown on the control chart as broken lines. However, the expression $3\sigma_{\overline{X}}$ in Equation 14.25 might be rewritten from Equation 14.8 as:

$$\frac{3}{d_2\sqrt{n}} \times \overline{R}$$

In order to relieve the shop floor operator of an arithmetical chore and help eliminate errors, the left-hand part of this expression is replaced by a single variable conventionally termed A_2. Values of A_2 can be obtained from Table 14.2 by simple arithmetic for samples of the various sizes. They are usually provided in a handy table often printed on the reverse of the control chart. A typical list is given in Table 14.5.

Table 14.5: Values of A_2 for Eight Sample Sizes (for the "One-Step" Calculation of the Xbarbar Control Limits)

Sample Size n	$A_2 \left(\dfrac{3}{d_2\sqrt{n}} \right)$	Sample Size n	$A_2 \left(\dfrac{3}{d_2\sqrt{n}} \right)$
2	1.880	6	0.483
3	1.023	7	0.419
4	0.729	8	0.373
5	0.577	9	0.337

This simplification allows Equations 14.25 and 14.26 to be rewritten as Equations 14.27 and 14.28. The two control limits for $\overline{\overline{X}}$ can consequently be calculated in one arithmetical step only, using the appropriate value of A_2 from Table 14.5. In the case of Figure 14.6, the two control limits are 7.71 + (0.577 × 2.59) (= 9.20 thou) and 7.71 − (0.577 × 2.59) (= 6.21 thou).

$$UCL_{\overline{X}} = \overline{\overline{X}} + A_2 \overline{R} \qquad \text{Equation 14.27}$$

$$LCL_{\overline{X}} = \overline{\overline{X}} - A_2 \overline{R} \qquad \text{Equation 14.28}$$

Simplifications and shortcuts such as this are used very widely in SPC and have contributed greatly to its smooth and efficient application in busy factories.

Two further instances of simplification arise in the calculation of the control limits for $\overline{R}$. Thus, first, Equation 14.18 can be reformulated as Equation 14.29.

$$UCL_R = \overline{R}(1 + 3\frac{d_3}{d_2}) \qquad \text{Equation 14.29}$$

That part of Equation 14.29 in brackets is now replaced by a variable conventionally termed D_4, so that Equation 14.29 may be rewritten as Equation 14.30.

$$UCL_R = D_4 \overline{R} \qquad \text{Equation 14.30}$$

Values for D_4 can be readily calculated using equivalent values for d_2 and d_3 in Tables 14.2 and 14.4. Table 14.6 gives values for D_4 for eight sample sizes.

Table 14.6: Values of D_4 for Eight Sample Sizes (for the "One-Step" Calculation of the upper Rbar Control Limit)

Sample Size n	$D_4 (1 + 3\frac{d_3}{d_2})$	Sample Size n	$D_4 (1 + 3\frac{d_3}{d_2})$
2	3.267	6	2.004
3	2.574	7	1.924
4	2.282	8	1.864
5	2.114	9	1.816

The upper control limit for $\overline{R}$ in Figure 14.6 is given as follows, from the value of $\overline{R}$ previously calculated and D_4 in Table 14.7 for n = 5.

$$2.59 \times 2.114 = 5.47 \text{ thou}$$

In the second instance, we rewrite Equation 14.19 as Equation 14.31.

$$LCL_R = \bar{R}(1 - 3\frac{d_3}{d_2}) \qquad \text{Equation 14.31}$$

Again, that part of Equation 14.31 in brackets is replaced by a variable, this time termed D_3, so that it may be rewritten as Equation 14.32.

$$LCL_R = D_3 \bar{R} \qquad \text{Equation 14.32}$$

D_3 can also be calculated at once from values for d_2 and d_3 in Tables 14.2 and 14.4. Table 14.7 gives a number of values. (It will be recalled from above that negative lower control limits for $\bar{R}$ are ignored and have been set to zero in the Table. In the example in Figure 14.6, with samples of 5, LCL_R is, of course, zero.)

Table 14.7: Values of D_3 for Eight Sample Sizes (for the "One-Step" Calculation of the lower Rbar Control Limit)

Sample Size n	$D_3(1 - 3\frac{d_3}{d_2})$	Sample Size n	$D_3(1 - 3\frac{d_3}{d_2})$
2	0	6	0
3	0	7	0.076
4	0	8	0.136
5	0	9	0.184

Simplifying factors related to the use of the standard deviation rather than the range as a measure of dispersion (Equations 14.20 and 14.21) are A_3, B_3 and B_4. In addition, when a process has reached long-term stability and the mean and dispersion of the sample-means are very well established, the quality manager speaks of a *standard value* of $\bar{\bar{X}}$, termed $\bar{X}_0$, and associated standard measures of dispersion. Factors involved with standard values are A, D_1, D_2, B_5 and B_6. Many reference books contain explanations of these factors and complete tables of values.[10] See also E_2, Table 14.8, sub-section 14.2.3.

---

[10] See A.V. Feigenbaum (1983) *Total Quality Control*, Third edition, McGraw-Hill, pp. 406–407.

14.2 USING THE VARIABLE CONTROL CHART

The principal purpose of the Shewhart variable control chart is to determine whether a manufacturing process is stable and under control and, if it is not, thereby to discover what action should be taken to remove special causes of variation so that stability may be regained. Little formality is needed to initiate its use on the shop floor and, indeed, to initiate a regime of statistical quality control within the company.

14.2.1 Setting up the Chart

The term *variable* in *variable control chart* refers to the measure of a given property of a manufactured part (say, its length, area, impedance, hardness, viscosity, etc.) and which can be expressed quantitatively. The variable chosen for measurement from the many candidates that might present themselves should, if possible, relate to a characteristic agreed to be symptomatic of overall product quality — perhaps some matter currently causing trouble and leading to non-conformance of the component or to the need for rework.

The sample of parts to be measured is referred to more properly in SPC by Shewhart's own term, the *rational sub-group*. As we shall see shortly, an objective in choosing a rational sub-group is to achieve minimum variation among the members that comprise it. Consequently, small groups are preferred, usually of four or five: Shewhart suggested four; shop floor practice emanating from the days before calculators favours five. Although statistical inaccuracy may result if sub-groups have fewer than four members, sub-groups of two or three may nevertheless be used if measurement of the variable is very difficult or expensive. Larger sub-groups are chosen only when close control of the process average is required, as described in footnote 7.

Two most important issues concomitant with sub-group size are how individual members of a sub-group are to be chosen (the *within sub-group* membership) and how sub-groups are to be chosen one to the next (the *group-to-group* membership).

Before dealing with these questions, we should first reflect on the meaning of the central lines and control limits on the variable chart. From the manner in which $\bar{\bar{X}}$ and the average range $\bar{R}$ are

Statistical Quality Control (SQC)

calculated, the two values — the two central lines — represent (by definition) the *averaged* pattern of variation from one sub-group to another. In addition, since the four control limits are derived from these averages, the values of $\overline{X}$ and R plotted on the chart and falling within the limits show a relationship to these averages strictly according to the standard dispersion inherent in the normal curve. In summary, the central lines reflect the averaged *within-sub-group* variation, while the line plotted from point to point across time in the course of completing the chart represents the *group-to-group* variation. The question the control chart is thus answering is: *is this group-to-group variation statistically consistent with the established within sub-group variation?*

In order for the control chart to do its job of keeping watch on the process, the sub-groups, one to the next, should be chosen so as to give maximum opportunity for the natural group-to-group variation to become manifest. If group-to-group variation indicates continuing control, the process is left unchanged. If there is process instability or change, however, this fact will be established when a sample is next taken in accordance with the predetermined sampling schedule. The mean and range of the sample so taken will show what has happened when they are plotted on the control chart. They will not conform to the averages and control limits established for the process and drawn on the chart. The operator will then know that he must take action to bring the process back under control.

However, while the group-to-group variation should give maximum opportunity for differences to be revealed, the variation between the individual readings *within* a given sub-group should do the reverse. That is, within-sub-group variation should be minimal. Each individual variable reading of each individual member of the sub-group is a reflection of the process at the moment that part is produced. And if the parts constituting the sample are, together, to be a reflection of the process, the individual parts themselves will therefore be more-or-less consistent with each other, in so far that they are each (separately) consistent with the process at that time. It is clearly essential that the variation within each sub-group truly reflects the state of the process at a particular time. If it does so, then we can be sure that the group-to-group variation also truly reflects the process at the various corresponding times the samples were taken, including reflecting any changes that have occurred. If such changes are within the control limits, the process remains stable. What is not wanted within a sub-group are parts taken (say) at widely different times, so that the sample-mean and range of the sub-group are merely representative of the average state of the process. Within sub-group variation must be a snapshot of the process as it is, not an average of it.[11]

So far as the membership of a given sub-group is concerned, what this boils down to is a very simple rule. The members of the sub-group should be selected together, one after the other, in order of time as they are made. (It is a common practice to place them in numbered boxes as they are successively produced.) Measurement of successive variables in order of time to obtain within-group variation — i.e. keeping track of the order of production — is without doubt by far the most important factor in the consideration of rational sub-groups.[12]

While the rule for within-sub-group membership is simple and unvarying, such cannot be said for group-to-group membership (the sampling schedule). When SPC is first introduced for a given process, sub-groups might be chosen every hour as shown in Figure 14.6. After a time, when special causes of variation have been

---

[11] Large sub-groups are a particular problem, since they tend to reflect a process average rather than the process itself as obtained from small sub-groups. For this reason, their use is limited as previously stated in footnote 7.

[12] While the sub-group members should show consistency, they should also represent distinct and separate operations of the process. A mistake is sometimes made in choosing members of a sub-group all of which have resulted from a single operation of the process. Consider, for example, a plate stamped out by a machine and which is then cut into four parts. Suppose now that the four quarter-plates produced are used as sub-groups, the variable measured being the individual thickness of each quarter-plate. Not surprisingly, since each quarter plate in any one of these sub-groups is produced by the same process operation, the sample range of each one will be relatively small, and the average range $\bar{R}$ of all the sub-groups calculated will also be correspondingly small. Consequently, $UCL_{\bar{X}}$ and $LCL_{\bar{X}}$, which are dependent on $\bar{R}$ (Equation 14.8), will also be small. When the group-to-group variation is plotted on the control chart, it will inevitably appear that the process is out of control, since the different thicknesses of the plates from one stamping to another will be far greater than the differences in thickness between the four quarter-plates in any particular sub-group. The moral of this is that the statistics of SPC should always be considered in conjunction with the technical process itself.

removed, experience and a wish to reduce the expense of sampling may deem it acceptable to switch to once per day or even less frequently. However, there is also the matter of engineering specifications. When the capability of a process is very close to the specification limits, frequently taken sub-groups, perhaps even every 15 minutes, may be permanently advisable — see Figure 14.11(c).

14.2.2 Monitoring the Process

Indication on the variable control chart that loss of control has occurred and that the shop floor operator should begin the search for a special cause of variation is not entirely straightforward. There are two problems. One is that the chart may falsely indicate that loss of control has occurred when in fact it has not. We note, for example, that 0.27 per cent of the sample-means $\bar{X}$ fall outside the $3\sigma_{\bar{X}}$ limits on either side of $\bar{\bar{X}}$, even though they conform to the distribution of the normal curve.[13] (In practice, rather more than 0.27 per cent are likely to fall outside the control limits, since the distribution of the sample-means is not perfectly normal when the sample size n is small.)

The second problem is that the guidelines laid down to spot trouble may fail to trap the emergence of a special cause when it occurs. Besides the four control limits, there are in fact other pointers to non-control which are used.

The chief of these relates to what is termed the *theory of runs*. Thus, if we consider that there is an even chance that any sample-mean should be either above the centre line $\bar{\bar{X}}$ or below it, then we may use simple probability theory to calculate the chances of so-many successive sample-means being either all above the line, or all below it. For example, using the tossing of a fair coin as analogy,

---

[13] If 0.27 per cent of the sample-means fall outside the control limits, this does *not* mean that there will be 0.27 per cent non-conformances. What the control limits indicate is process *control*. The issue of non-conformance relates to specifications and tolerances. For example, we note in Figure 14.6 that 40 per cent of the individual variable readings lie outside the upper and lower control limits for $\bar{\bar{X}}$, even though the process is in control. Provided the upper and lower tolerance limits are sufficiently distant from the control limits, no non-conformances will be produced. See Figures 14.11(a) to 14.11(d) and supporting text.

the probability of obtaining either seven heads or seven tails from seven tosses of the coin is:

$$\left(\frac{1}{2}\right)^7 \times 2 = \frac{1}{64}$$

Based on probabilities and calculations such as these, the guidelines that are typically used to warn the operator that loss of process control may have occurred are shown in Table 14.8. Note that 0.27 per cent, the chance of a value of $\overline{X}$ being outside the control limits, is 1/370 — about half way between a run of 9 and a run of 10.

Table 14.8: Additional Indicators to Denote Possible Process Trouble (from the Theory of Runs)

Number of Successive Sample-Means	Number of Sample-Means on one side of the central line
7	7
11	10
14	12
17	14
20	16

In practice, it is usually found that sequences and runs are due to common causes rather than special causes, while it is rare for a point outside the upper and lower $\overline{X}$ and R control limits to be due to any other than a special cause.

Additional guidelines sometimes introduced to help detect trouble through the control chart are "warning limits" placed at $2\sigma_{\overline{X}}$ on either side of $\overline{\overline{X}}$ — they say *Be vigilant! Trouble may be on the way!* (It should be added that charts on the factory floor are routinely annotated by the machine operator, recording problems encountered and investigations made in the course of manufacture. Control charts are living documents.)[14]

When the control chart indicates loss of control, the shop operator's interpretation of the story it is telling will depend on his ex-

---

[14] See *A Japanese Control Chart*, a 20-minute video featuring the production of components at the Tokai Rika Company, presented by Don Wheeler and obtainable from Process Management International (www.pmi.co.uk).

perience and perspicacity and, of course, his knowledge of the process. The first line of investigation is usually the range. Reverting for a moment to the bell curve, loss of control of the process's dispersion is represented in the sketch in Figure 14.7.

Figure 14.7: Loss of Control of Process Dispersion (R) over Time

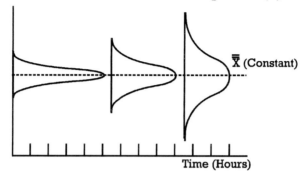

Technical reasons for out-of-control process dispersion include: changes in materials or method; changes in the specification of raw materials; the introduction of mixtures of materials of different quality; and tool wear.

The second line of attack is the $\overline{X}$ chart. Figure 14.8 is a sketch of drift in the process average, again illustrated through the bell curve. Reasons for process drift include: changes in the physical environment, such as temperature; deterioration of equipment; technical modification of the process itself; and gradual deterioration in the environment, such as through the build-up of waste.

Figure 14.8: Loss of Process Control (Change in Average Xbar)

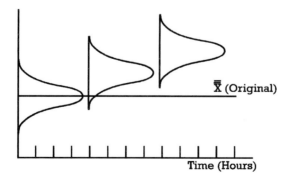

When tool wear is gradual, there may be a linear trend in the measurement of the variable being tracked. Rather than attempt to reset the machine at frequent intervals to correct for it, it may be worthwhile, if the tolerances are sufficiently distant from the control limits, to predict the rate of drift of the process average, and draw sloping control limits on the control chart. This is illustrated in Figure 14.9. It is common in the process industries to take the idea of trend lines still further by calculating moving averages of variables related to the process.[15]

Figure 14.9: Using Sloping Control Limits on the Control Chart to Track Trend caused by Tool Wear

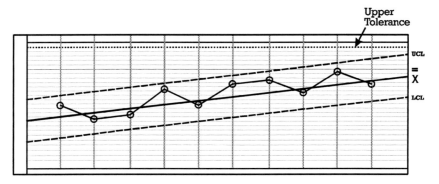

14.2.3 Process Capability[16]

Before discussing process capability, it is necessary to be quite clear as to the differences between (1) the distribution of the sample-means of the variable being measured, represented by $\overline{X}$ and $\sigma_{\overline{X}}$; (2) the distribution of the individual values of the variable

---

[15] It is of interest that Derek Trigg's formulation of adaptive exponential moving averages, described in sub-section 4.4.5 and illustrated in Figure 4.10, was first applied by him not to sales forecasting, but to tracking the progress of the Nylon 8 process at Teesside, then owned by ICI and now owned by Du Pont.

[16] Process capability should be distinguished from machine capability, although the two are calculated in the same way. Machine capability is intended to represent the machine in isolation, and exclude such sources of variation as human operation, incoming materials and the environment. The data from which it is calculated are therefore gathered over as short a period as possible. The data to calculate process capability, by contrast, may be collected over a month or so, so as to absorb all possible common causes of variation.

Statistical Quality Control (SQC)

in respect of the particular parts themselves being manufactured, represented by μ and σ; and (3) the tolerances set by the engineering department on the product characteristic being measured — i.e. the upper and lower specifications of the variable X, often referred to in SPC as USL_X and LSL_X.

The mean and distribution of the sample-means have already been discussed at length. Applying the $3\sigma_{\overline{X}}$ limits, the form of the distribution is as illustrated in Figure 14.4. The mean μ and distribution σ of the individual parts, or population, from which the samples are drawn are now also obtainable at once in the following way. Firstly, from Part 1 of the central limit theorem, the mean μ is the same as the grand average of the sample-means $\overline{\overline{X}}$, and $\overline{\overline{X}}$ is known. Secondly, if we turn to the relationship between the standard deviation of the population, σ, and the average range in Equation 14.16, we see that σ can be obtained once the average range $\overline{R}$ has been established for a given sample size.

$$\sigma = \frac{\overline{R}}{d_2} \qquad \text{Equation 14.16}$$

If we assume that the distribution of the population is normal, then the bulk (99.73 per cent) of the curve lies as ever between the limits of $(\overline{\overline{X}} + 3\sigma)$ and $(\overline{\overline{X}} - 3\sigma)$. These limits may be referred to as UCL_X and LCL_X. (Note carefully that the subscripts in the expressions are X, not $\overline{X}$.) Substituting the value of σ from Equation 14.16, we obtain Equations 14.33 and 14.34 for UCL_X and LCL_X.

$$UCL_X = \overline{\overline{X}} + \frac{3\overline{R}}{d_2} \qquad \text{Equation 14.33}$$

$$LCL_X = \overline{\overline{X}} - \frac{3\overline{R}}{d_2} \qquad \text{Equation 14.34}$$

The expression $3/d_2$ is usually replaced by a shorthand variable as previously discussed, conventionally termed E_2. Values of E_2 are given in Table 14.9. The particular value chosen from the Table will depend on the sample size n originally used to calculate the average range $\overline{R}$.

Table 14.9: Values of E_2 for the Direct Calculation of the Process's Capability Limits (3 sigma limits of X, not 3 sigma limits of Xbar)

Sample Size n	$E_2 \left(\dfrac{3}{d_2} \right)$	Sample Size n	$E_2 \left(\dfrac{3}{d_2} \right)$
2	2.6596	6	1.1839
3	1.7720	7	1.0947
4	1.4570	8	1.0537
5	1.2898	9	1.0101

Substituting E_2 in Equations 14.33 and 14.34 gives Equations 14.35 and 14.36, which may be used in conjunction with Table 14.9 for the direct calculation of the 3σ (99.73 per cent) limits of the process.

$$UCL_X = \overline{\overline{X}} + E_2 \overline{R} \qquad \text{Equation 14.35}$$

$$LCL_X = \overline{\overline{X}} - E_2 \overline{R} \qquad \text{Equation 14.36}$$

Figure 14.10 shows the distribution of the sample-means as a bell curve (Curve A), superimposed on the bell distribution of the population as calculated in Equations 14.35 and 14.36 (Curve B). From the relationship given in Part 2 of the central limit theorem, it comes as no surprise to see that the bell of the sample-means is narrower than that of the individual parts — see Equation 14.4.

$$\sigma_{\overline{X}} = \dfrac{\sigma}{\sqrt{n}} \qquad \text{Equation 14.4}$$

If, for example, the sample-means relate to samples of four (i.e. n = 4), the dispersion of the sample-means will be half the dispersion of the population.

Figure 14.10: The Normal Distribution of the Sample-Means (A) and the Normal Distribution of the Individual Parts (B)

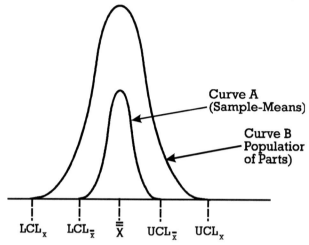

The upper and lower engineering tolerances are in a sense independent of the foregoing considerations. While, clearly, engineering design staff must be aware of the ability of manufacturing to produce parts to various specifications and tolerances, only actual manufacture will prove capability in a given instance. Without SPC, it may be thought necessary to make and inspect many thousands of parts in a series of pilot runs to prove the viability of the process. With SPC, as soon as the process is shown to be within control and values of $\bar{X}$ and $\bar{R}$ have been obtained, the engineering specifications can be readily compared to the grand average $\bar{\bar{X}}$ and the 6σ population limits given by Equations 14.35 and 14.36.

SPC, the variable control chart and the distribution of the sample-means are subjects bound up with bringing a process under control and maintaining that control, so that time after time the parts produced are of a predictable nature (being broadly uniform). Whether or not the parts produced by a stable process conform to the standards demanded by engineering is quite a different matter and must be judged in relation to the engineering specifications and tolerances defined. If a stable process does produce parts that conform to requirements, it is said to be *capable*. Figures 14.11(a) to 14.11(d) each show the 6σ spread of variable values X achieved by the process (i.e. as defined by Curve B in Figure 14.10), the $6\sigma_{\bar{X}}$ spread of sample-means (Curve A in Figure 14.10) and the lower and upper engineering specifications LSL_X and USL_X defined for X.[17]

Figure 14.11(a): SATISFACTORY

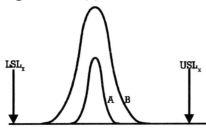

LSL_X is sufficiently below LCL_X and USL_X above UCL_X that it seems that no non-conforming parts will be produced so long as process stability is maintained. The frequency of subgroups to be taken is not likely to be high once control has been achieved.

Figure 14.11(b): NOT CAPABLE

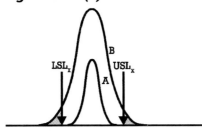

LSL_X is above LCL_X on the horizontal scale, and USL_X is below UCL_X, so that inevitably a fraction of non-conforming parts will be produced (denoted on the diagram by grey shading). It may be possible to improve the operation of the process or change some other aspect of it to make it capable. Alternatively, re-examination of the specifications may persuade the design engineer that the tolerances can be broadened. If nothing can be done, the manufacturing manager must resign himself to the 100 per cent inspection and screening of the final parts.[18] Figure 14.11(b) reminds us once more that although a process may be under control, this is not to say that it is capable of producing parts which conform to requirements.

---

[17] Note that specification limits are frequently omitted from the data given on variable control charts, to avoid possible confusion with the control limits for the sample-means.

[18] The problems with 100 per cent inspection are both human and economic. Human means the inevitable onset of inspection fatigue — non-conformances slipping through due to minds sent to sleep by repetitious work. Economic means what it says — the bearing of wage costs of inspections and repeat inspections, and still with the inevitability of a small fraction of non-conforming parts getting through.

Figure 14.11(c): TIGHT

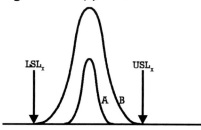

The specification limits are within a very short distance of the control limits (though not actually on them). SPC is essential for the production of conformances, with frequently taken sub-groups for constant vigilance, and immediate and earnest attention paid to the first hint of loss of control. Control limits at 2σ might also be drawn on the chart as warning beacons (see sub-section 14.2.2).

Figure 14.11(d): UNECONOMIC

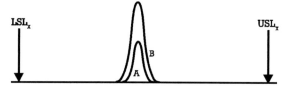

Even with infrequently taken sub-groups, the effort required to keep the process focused on a tiny range in the middle of wide specifications may not seem cost effective as things are. Can engineering design take advantage of narrower tolerances? Can an alternative process be used?

In order to provide a concise and convenient means of expressing the capability of a process without recourse to diagrams such as Figure 14.11, a number of *capability indices* have been developed. An early capability index, C_p, is given by Equation 14.37.

$$C_p = \frac{USL_X - LSL_X}{6\sigma} \qquad \text{Equation 14.37}$$

The process is capable if $C_p > 1.0$ and if the mean μ ($\overline{\overline{X}}$) is centred at $(USL_X + LSL_X)/2$. A minimum target value of $C_p = 1.33$ is usually aimed for. A goal of $C_p = 2.0$ (i.e. a process range of half the specification range), has been popularly referred to as "6 sigma" quality.

A superior index that avoids the need to qualify the calculated figure with a statement about the mean is termed C_{pk}, where C_{pk} is the *lower* of C_{pL} and C_{pU}, as given in Equations 14.38 and 14.39.

$$C_{pL} = \frac{\overline{\overline{X}} - LSL_X}{3\sigma} \qquad \text{Equation 14.38}$$

$$C_{pU} = \frac{USL_X - \overline{\overline{X}}}{3\sigma} \qquad \text{Equation 14.39}$$

The process is capable if C_{pk} in Equation 14.40 ≥ 1.0.

$$C_{pk} = \min(C_{pL}, C_{pU}) \qquad \text{Equation 14.40}$$

Note that refinements must be made to Equations 14.38 and 14.39 if the distribution of X is not symmetrical.[19]

14.2.4 Process Capability Studies

The variable control chart in Figure 14.12 shows the intrusion of special causes of variation in the process at two points. A number of typical special causes were given in sub-section 14.2.2. The first task in SPC is to find and remove such causes so as to bring the process to a stable, steady state. A proper foundation for process improvement does not exist until such a state has been achieved. Tools of investigation include the fishbone diagram, PDCA and the use of Quality Improvement teams, as described in sub-section 13.2.4.

Figure 14.12: Variable Control Chart with two "Out-of-Control" Sample-Means

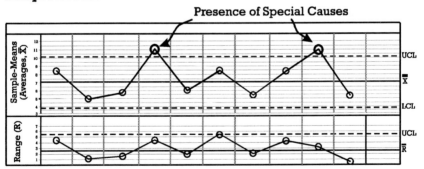

If the process is not capable of meeting specification when under control, the quality control manager, engineering manager and manufacturing manager may embark on a *process capability study*

---

[19] Victor Kane (1986), "Process Capability Indices", *Journal of Quality Technology* (US magazine), Vol. 18.1, January.

Statistical Quality Control (SQC)

in an attempt to adjust the process so that capability is attained. A capability study may be initiated anyway as part of an ongoing programme of improvement. The benefits of enhanced capability include less troublesome manufacturing operation; possible increased productivity; possible reduced operating and material costs; and, it seems, a more smoothly functioning product in the hands of the customer.

Those undertaking the work must have an intimate knowledge of the process itself. Although no two studies are alike, a starting point is usually to attempt to identify all major possible sources of variation, and then to conduct tests and experiments to determine the sensitivity of process output to controlled variation in each identified source.[20] In conducting capability studies, investigations lead to further investigations — it has often been said that SPC is 10 per cent statistics and 90 per cent engineering. Very often, it seems that a single, key, quite unsuspected factor is a major determinant of capability, a small change made to it having a major effect on the entire process. Note that there is no necessity whatsoever to explain the effect of a process change in physical, mechanical or chemical terms.

14.3 THE ATTRIBUTE CONTROL CHARTS

In the jargon of SPC, an *attribute* is a characteristic of a manufactured part associated with non-conformance. For example, blemishes, spots, holes and cracks may be undesirable quality attributes that are either present or not present in the part. Features such as these often reflect aspects of quality regarded as important by customers but are difficult or impossible to describe quantitatively.

Attribute data are typically available to be collected at points within the factory where general inspection of parts takes place. The parts may have been taken from production output every hour or every day, or they may constitute a manufactured batch. Not only

---

[20] A line of investigation that is often fruitful is to find the effect of variation in the inputs to the process. Example of inputs are electrical tension (voltage), raw materials and their characteristics, heat and so forth. It may then prove worthwhile to apply the disciplines of SPC to the input process itself.

is the recording of the data easier and cheaper than the maintenance of data relating to variables, but its presentation in the form of reports is far more easily absorbed by management.

A distinction should be made at this point between a non-conformance and a non-conforming part, or non-conforming item. A non-conformance is some aspect of finished manufacture that is imperfect — the blemish, spot, hole and crack are each non-conformances. A part may be said to be non-conforming if it has one or more non-conformances. That is, a single non-conforming part may have, say, three non-conformances present.[21]

In choosing which attributes to record and analyse, it is customary initially to record as many as possible at the place of inspection — say, 10 or 15. After a time, the less useful ones can be dropped, retaining only those which prove effective in combination with the attribute control charts in the detection and removal of special causes or which are considered to be central to product quality. If a problem persists, an Xbar and R variable control chart may be introduced based on an allied product characteristic in order to get to the root of the matter.

There are four attribute control charts, falling into two classes. Class 1 (sub-section 14.3.2) contains the fraction rejected chart (or percentage rejected chart) and the number rejected chart (the *p chart* and the *np chart*). Class 2 (sub-section 14.3.3) contains the count chart (or number of non-conformances chart) and the count per unit chart (the *c chart* and the *u chart*).

14.3.1 The Statistical Background to the Attribute Charts

The p and np Charts

The testing of attributes involves the taking of repeated samples from a population of parts containing a *constant fraction p* that are non-conforming. Each part in each sample is tested to see whether the particular attribute for the part is conforming or non-conforming.

---

[21] If 10 parts out of 100 have Defect A, the percentage non-conforming is 10 per cent with regard to Defect A. If 20 parts out of the 100 have Defect B, the percentage is 20 per cent non-conforming due to B. Because a part can have both Defect A and Defect B, the overall percentage non-conforming may be anywhere from 20% to 30%.

Statistical Quality Control (SQC)

When the probability of the occurrence of an event X is constant, and a random experiment (such as the testing of a part) can give rise to only two, mutually exclusive, conditions — i.e. the event being true or the event being not true — then the tool of statistics used to describe and explore the situation is the binomial theorem.

The form of the binomial theorem familiar from algebra is given in Equation 14.41 for the expansion of two variables a and b. Equation 14.41 reduces to Equation 14.42.

$$(a+b)^n = a^n + \binom{n}{1}a^{n-1}b + \binom{n}{2}a^{n-2}b^2 + \ldots \ldots + b^n \qquad \text{Equation 14.41}$$

$$(a+b)^n = \sum_{x=0}^{n} \frac{n!}{x!(n-x)!} a^{n-x} b^x \qquad \text{Equation 14.42}$$

If the probability of the non-conformance of an attribute is p, and the probability of its conformance is q, then (p + q) = 1, where (p + q) represents the entire probability of the event, and where q = 1 − p. By substituting (p + q)^n for (a + b)^n in Equation 14.42, the relevance of the binomial expansion to the analysis of the conformance or non-conformance of attributes in a sample of parts becomes apparent. That is, substituting p for a and q for b, and writing the probability density function for the binomial distribution, we obtain Equation 14.43.

$$p_R(r) = \frac{n!}{r!(n-r)!} p^r q^{n-r} \quad \text{for } r = 0, 1, 2, 3 \ldots n \qquad \text{Equation 14.43}$$

To illustrate the use of Equation 14.43, Equation 14.44 gives the probability of finding three non-conforming parts (r = 3) in a sample of five (n = 5), when the fraction of non-conformances in the population is 0.08 (p = 0.08 and q = 0.92).

$$p_R(3) = \frac{5!}{3! \times 2!} \times 0.08^3 \times 0.92^2 = 0.004336 \qquad \text{Equation 14.44}$$

Sampling, the binomial theorem, and the approximation of the normal distribution to the binomial distribution, are dealt with at length in a great many quality and statistical textbooks.[22] The binomial theorem is also central to acceptance sampling and the construction of sample plans in raw material and product control, as described in Section 14.4. It is sufficient to record here that in the use of the p and np control charts, if the fraction of the parts non-conforming in the population is p and the fraction conforming is q, then in a sample of size n, the mean of the number of parts not conforming is p and the standard deviation σ_p is given by Equation 14.45.

$$\sigma_p = \frac{\sqrt{npq}}{n} \qquad \text{Equation 14.45}$$

Equation 14.45 is more conveniently written as Equation 14.46.

$$\sigma_p = \sqrt{\frac{p(1-p)}{n}} \qquad \text{Equation 14.46}$$

On the fraction rejected p control chart, described in sub-section 14.3.2, the mean, or central line, is the average mean $\bar{p}$ (p bar) obtained from many samples, k, of equal size, as given in Equation 14.47.

$$\bar{p} = \frac{\sum p_1 + p_2 + p_3 + \ldots + p_k}{k} \qquad \text{Equation 14.47}$$

The upper control limit, UCL_p, on the chart for a particular sample i of size n_i is given by Equation 14.48, derived from Equation 14.46.

$$UCL_p = \bar{p} + 3\sqrt{\frac{\bar{p}(1-\bar{p})}{n_i}} \qquad \text{Equation 14.48}$$

The lower control limit, LCL_p, for the sample is given by Equation 14.49. If LCL_p is negative, it is ignored.

$$LCL_p = \bar{p} - 3\sqrt{\frac{\bar{p}(1-\bar{p})}{n_i}} \qquad \text{Equation 14.49}$$

---

[22] See, for example, Grant and Leavenworth (1996), op. cit., p. 185; and Paul Newbold (1984), *Statistics for Business and Economics*, Prentice-Hall, pp. 164, 218.

Statistical Quality Control (SQC)

Instead of the fraction of non-conforming items, p, it may occasionally be preferable, with sub-groups of strictly fixed size, to track and control the number of non-conforming parts, np, rather than p. The mean, or central line, of the number chart, or *np chart*, is $n\bar{p}$, and the upper and lower control limits are given by Equations 14.50 and 14.51.

$$UCL_{np} = n\bar{p} + 3\sqrt{n\bar{p}(1-\bar{p})} \qquad \text{Equation 14.50}$$

$$LCL_{np} = n\bar{p} - 3\sqrt{n\bar{p}(1-\bar{p})} \qquad \text{Equation 14.51}$$

Note also that the *percentage rejected* limits are obtained from the *fraction rejected* simply by converting $\bar{p}$ in Equations 14.48 and 14.49 into a percentage by multiplying it by 100 and remembering to write $(100 - \bar{p})$ in place of $(1 - \bar{p})$.

The c and u Charts

The class of attribute control charts described in sub-section 14.3.3 (the count chart, or c chart, and the u chart) track not the number of non-conforming parts in a sample, but the number of actual instances of non-conformance themselves, the sample very often being a single (large) part. The statistical treatment of the actual number of instances of non-conformance is based on a concept which is quite different from the binomial theorem, the latter governing as it does the relative *probabilities* of non-conforming versus conforming items.

In statistics, when there are a very large number of opportunities for an "event" to occur, but the number of actual occurrences of the event is very tiny, the tool used to explore the situation is the Poisson law.[23]

The application of the Poisson law — *the law of small numbers* — has been seen previously in sub-section 5.2.1 and Figure 5.2 (many customers arriving at a retail outlet, but only a few of them request-

---

[23] The Poisson law was formulated in 1837 by the French mathematician Simeon Poisson (1781–1840). The probability function of the Poisson distribution $P_X(x)$ is given by $\dfrac{e^{-\lambda}\lambda^x}{x!}$ for $x = 0, 1, 2, 3 \ldots$ and $\lambda > 0$.

ing to buy a given type of item) and in sub-section 11.3.4 (the arrival of jobs from elsewhere in the shop at an intermediate work centre on the shop floor). In everyday application, the Poisson law is used extensively in analysing the incidence of accidents. For example, many car trips are made year after year on the M6 (very many), but the number of fatalities in accidents in each of the years is (mercifully and surprisingly) very small. The first treatise on the application of the Poisson law and the Poisson distribution published in 1898 by Ladislaus von Bortkiewicz concerned 122 deaths over 20 years of Prussian cavalrymen caused by kicks from horses.

In SPC, the large number of opportunities for an event to occur is represented by the repeated possibilities of the process creating product non-conformances in its operation. The tiny number of actual occurrences of the event is the number of non-conformances that do in fact result.

Clearly, in order to calculate a mean or compare one set of figures, or occurrences, against another, the number of opportunities that present themselves in each case must be the same. For fatalities on the M6, comparisons must relate to equivalent spans of time (say, years) and involve the same stretch of road (say, a specific range of junctions). In von Bortkiewicz's study, the accidents involved the same ten corps of men from one (defined) year to the next. So in SPC, similar properties defining each of the samples in which non-conformances are counted must also be identical. As mentioned, this might be the number of non-conformances on a single part, such as a completed engine or an aeroplane wing. If the incidence of non-conformances is very low, however, the sample may be a fixed number of parts — 10, say, or 20. (These two instances are the principal reasons the c chart may be chosen over the p chart: with large structures, non-conforming items — i.e. items having one or more non-conformances — are likely always to constitute 100 per cent of the sample. When items are of very high quality, the percentage of non-conforming items will be very small, and the number of non-conformances may be a somewhat more helpful indicator of quality.) If the samples differ from one to another, but the "opportunity rate" in each one is the same, the count of non-conformances may be capable of standardisation through the u chart (or unit chart) procedure. For example, after manufacture, there are a number of imperfections on the surface of acrylic sheeting. Sheets are produced in approximate squares measuring between 9' × 9' and 10' × 10'. Since the sheet sizes differ, the number of imperfections per sheet cannot be compared from one to the next, but the number of imperfections per 100 square feet can be so compared.

In order to derive the mean and standard deviation of the number of non-conformances from one sample to the next, one may turn either to the Poisson probability distribution itself (see footnote 23), or one may take the limiting case of the binomial.

Since critical formulae have already been presented for the binomial, for dealing with the np chart, the second route is followed here. In essence, the count, c, of non-conformances is substituted for $n\bar{p}$. The standard deviation σ_{np} of $n\bar{p}$, which forms part of Equations 14.50 and 14.51, is given by Equation 14.52.

$$\sigma_{np} = \sqrt{n\bar{p}(1-\bar{p})} \qquad \text{Equation 14.52}$$

Substituting c for $n\bar{p}$ gives Equation 14.53.

$$\sigma_c = \sqrt{c(1-\frac{c}{n})} \qquad \text{Equation 14.53}$$

Now because $c/n \to 0$ as $n \to \infty$, the standard deviation is simply $\sqrt{c}$. That is, for the Poisson distribution, *the standard deviation is the square root of the mean*. If an average value of c, $\bar{c}$ (c bar), is found in the usual way, then the upper and lower control limits for the c chart are as given in Equations 14.54 and 14.55.

$$UCL_c = \bar{c} + 3\sqrt{\bar{c}} \qquad \text{Equation 14.54}$$

$$LCL_c = \bar{c} - 3\sqrt{\bar{c}} \qquad \text{Equation 14.55}$$

For the unit chart, UCL_u and LCL_u are obtained from Equations 14.54 and 14.55 by substituting for $\bar{c}$ the number of counts of non-conformances per standard chosen unit.

Note finally that because the Poisson distribution is not symmetrical, UCL_c and LCL_c as calculated in Equations 14.54 and 14.55, do not represent exactly equal probabilities on either side of the mean $\bar{c}$. Depending on the circumstances of a particular case, and by reference to the Poisson probability data, the quality control manager may adjust each limit to obtain (symmetrical) so-called 99 per cent control limits.[24]

14.3.2 Using the Fraction Rejected Chart (p Chart)

The p chart may be used as an ongoing check of a process by taking samples of fixed quantities at regular intervals — say, every hour, every shift or every day. Alternatively, the chart may arise from the inspection of output following the completion of a planned job or manufacturing batch, the sample size in this circumstance being the total batch. When regular samples are taken, the sample size should be small enough to reflect the operation of the process at a specific time, but large enough to yield, on average, one non-conforming item. Thus if the average percentage of non-conforming items is 5 per cent, a sample size, say, of 20 items would be satisfactory. Samples of some 200 would be necessary for 0.5 per cent non-conforming items.[25]

Presentation of the results of the fraction rejected chart is usually as a percentage. This is seen in Figure 14.13 showing a chart for samples of 50 items taken over eight days. The centre line ($\bar{p}$) in Figure 14.13 has been calculated as the average of the 15 individual fractions from the daily results seen on the chart, and has a value 0.05467 (plotted as 5.47 per cent). In practice, for the p chart, a *standard fraction* for $\bar{p}$ (represented by p_0) should be calculated, using at least 25 samples, p_0 being revised at periodic intervals.[26]

In Figure 14.13, the upper control limit UCL_p is derived from Equation 14.48, as shown in Equation 14.56. The lower control limit is obtained from Equation 14.49. It turns out to be negative, and so is not used. Note that on the chart for nine of the readings, denoted

---

[24] See Victor Kane (1986), op. cit., Section 7.7.

[25] We see from the text that far less effort is required of the upkeep of the X bar and R control charts than of the p chart. The X bar and R charts are also far more generally useful in process control and process investigation.

[26] The standard fraction rejected p_0 must be based on observation and calculation, not wishful thinking. If management believes the fraction of non-conforming parts to be too high, the means to reduce it are the tools described in sub-section 13.2.4 and sub-section 14.2.4, not exhortation and the imposition of an arbitrary (albeit desirable) lower value of p_0. See other comments on "management targets", sub-sections 13.2.2 and 13.2.3.

Statistical Quality Control (SQC)

by *, the number of actual non-conformances recorded is greater than the number of non-conforming items.

$$UCL_p = 0.05467 + 3\sqrt{\frac{0.05467 \times 0.9453}{50}} \qquad \text{Equation 14.56}$$

$$= 0.1511 \text{ (drawn on the chart as 15.11\%)}$$

Figure 14.13: A Fraction Rejected Chart (p Chart), Illustrated in Percentage Format

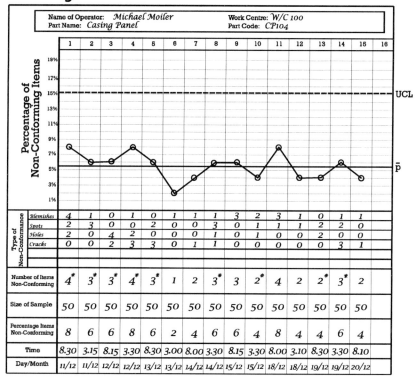

When the p chart is being used to monitor completed production lots of varying quantities, the chief problem is one of presentation, since the control limits for each sample are different (different values of n being used for their calculation in Equations 14.48 and 14.49). Indeed, the results from week to week for each such sample may be more clearly read not on a chart at all, but simply as figures in a table.

14.3.3 Using the Count Chart (c Chart)

The c chart is constructed in much the same way as the p chart, but by plotting the number of non-conformances in a sequence of samples of fixed size, as described in sub-section 14.3.1 (the size perhaps being 1). The numbers of non-conformances from Figure 14.13, as opposed to the number of non-conforming items, are plotted over the eight days and given in Figure 14.14. The average number of non-conformances per day is 4.20, and is used here (prematurely) as $\bar{c}$. From Equation 14.54, the upper control limit on the chart is 10.35, as shown in Equation 14.57.

$$UCL_c = 4.2 + 3\sqrt{4.2} = 10.35 \qquad \text{Equation 14.57}$$

LCL_c is negative and is discarded. (In addition, the upper limit UCL_c has been drawn on the control chart at 10.5, rather than at 10.35, since the value of c in a sample will be integer — i.e. it will be either 10 or below, if the process is in control, or it will be 11 or above, if the process is out of control. Placing the control line at 10.5 makes out-of-control points marginally more obvious).

Figure 14.14: A Section of a Count Control Chart (c Chart) Derived from Figure 14.13

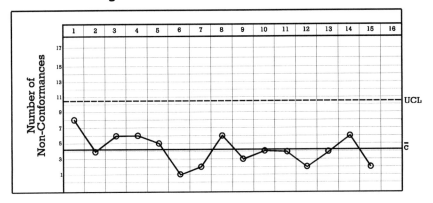

A refinement to the c chart first suggested by Harold Dodge and expanded on by Armand Feigenbaum[27] is to assign "demerit points" to each type of non-conformance, and then to plot not the count of non-conformances, but the count from sample to sample

---

[27] Feigenbaum (1983), op.cit., p. 253.

of demerits. Demerit weightings that have been suggested are: a critical non-conformance, 100 points; major, 40; minor, 20 and incidental, 1. The manufacturing manager may wish to assign his own weightings, peculiar to his own operation's circumstances, perhaps in conjunction with a shop floor quality drive. The purchasing manager may also find the scheme useful as an aid in the difficult matter of assessing supplier performance (see sub-section 16.1.4). Charts of demerits are called *D charts*.[28]

14.4 RAW MATERIAL AND PRODUCT CONTROL

14.4.1 Breakeven Point Analysis

Assessment of the quality of components and assemblies which have already been manufactured is a major concern of every factory, whether relating to its own production or to incoming material from its suppliers. Assurance of in-house quality can be gained by the adoption throughout the plant of SPC, as described in Sections 14.1 to 14.3. For purchased goods also, the most desirable situation is that suppliers should have adopted SPC and should be committed to programmes of product improvement such as described earlier. Indeed, in many industries, especially those in which small suppliers are dominated by large customers, the practice of SPC may be made a condition of supply. Relationships such as these often incorporate so-called *product accreditation schemes* and quality assurance visits by the purchasing manager and quality control manager to suppliers' premises to check that everything is as it should be (see sub-section 16.1.3). Even when such close relationships and formal means of assessment have not been established, there must always be a willingness of supplier and purchaser to exchange quality information — for example, from purchaser to supplier, to convey the relative importance of the various quality characteristics of supplied components and, from supplier to purchaser, to forward the results of technical tests. If

---

[28] The *Q chart* (quality score chart) is a variant of the D chart whereby an attempt is made to weight non-conformances not only by type but also by their intensity of manifestation. For example, a "crack" may earn a demerit of 10 points if it is less than one inch long, 20 points if it is from one to six inches, 30 points if it is . . .

statistical sampling is to be adopted, as we shall see shortly, further mutual quality agreement will be necessary on the *producer's risk* and the *consumer's risk* inherent in any sample plan (see sub-section 14.4.2).

In the absence of information provided through SPC, the question of assessment of the quality of manufactured parts is usually answered on the basis of cost. If the cost of inspecting one part is k_1 and the cost of a non-conforming unit being accepted into production, causing later rework and repair when it is discovered, is k_2, the "inspection versus correction" *breakeven point*, BEP, is given by Equation 14.58.

$$BEP = \left[\frac{k_1}{k_2}\right] \qquad Equation\ 14.58$$

The breakeven point is now compared to the standard fraction of parts non-conforming, $\overline{p_0}$, preferably obtained from the supplier, but otherwise maintained by the receiving company itself (see sub-section 14.3.2 and footnote 28). Replacing $\overline{p_0}$ by p here, the rule is that if p > BEP, it is economical that the parts be 100 per cent inspected, and if p < BEP, it is economical that the parts be admitted into production at once, without inspection.

There are a number of conditions and caveats surrounding the application of the breakeven rule. Indeed, there are well-known situations where the rule simply does not enter into things at all. Thus there may be a requirement that aerospace, medical and safety-critical components be 100 per cent inspected, whether by law or company policy. In contrast, ordnance and other items which are destroyed on test must either be sampled or passed with no inspection.

Two assumptions must be made in order to apply the rule. Speaking now of raw materials, the first is that if a part is manufactured using a non-conforming raw material item, the manufactured part so made is thereby deemed to be non-conforming. The second assumption is that if a part is manufactured from a conforming raw material, the manufactured part is thereby similarly deemed to be conforming.

A more troublesome matter may be ascribing a value to k_2 for use in the calculation of the BEP. If the non-conforming manufactured part produced can be spotted as such and repaired before it leaves the factory, k_2 is readily calculable. If it becomes manifest only in use by the customer, it is likely as a consequence to be far higher and may incorporate such factors as loss of goodwill. Again, the detection and repair or removal of non-conformities in production will cause disruption there, perhaps serious, and will create additional manufacturing costs for that reason, all of which must be debited against k_2.

When there is confidence in the values of p and BEP, and either one greatly exceeds the other, use of the rule and acceptance of its outcome will go unchallenged in a great many cases: 100 per cent inspection versus no inspection. Where p and BEP are about the same, or where the fraction of non-conforming parts is erratic, the company may turn to *sampling*, an amalgam, as it were, of both inspection *and* no inspection. Note that there are no clear cut rules to say how close p and BEP should be, or how erratic p should be, to justify this course. What is important is that the decision to sample should be taken by those concerned, including the supplier's quality control manager, after examination of the risks and costs of sampling and examination of the consequences and costs of the alternative courses of action open.

14.4.2 Sampling — Three Viewpoints

Sampling (or at least, single sampling) in the context of Raw Material and Product Control means taking a randomly selected quantity n units (the sample) from a thoroughly mixed incoming lot of known size, N units, and inspecting each of the n units so selected. The inspection to which each unit is subjected is for conformity or non-conformity of attributes, in the manner described for the n and np attribute control charts in sub-section 14.3.2.[29] If the number of non-conforming items in the sample is less than or equal to the *acceptance criterion* of this particular *sample plan*, the acceptance criterion being conventionally referred to as the quantity c, the lot of N parts is accepted. If the number of non-conforming items is greater than c, the lot is rejected.

---

[29] Note however that the military sampling tables described in sub-section 14.4.4 may be used either for sampling non-conforming items (as in the n and np charts) or for sampling non-conformances (as in the c and u charts).

The cost of operating the sample plan is made up of two components. The first is the cost itself of inspecting the sample, nk_1. The second is the cost of repairing and correcting manufactured parts made from non-conforming items (since these will exist in the unsampled items, and will have a fraction non-conforming p). The sum of the two components is given by C in Equation 14.59.

$$C = nk_1 + (N-n)pk_2 \qquad \textit{Equation 14.59}$$

The manufacturing manager, supplier and ultimate user of the material each has a different interest in sampling, and the purpose and emphasis of a sampling plan will depend on which of these interests is to be served. Thus:

The Manufacturing Manager's Viewpoint

For an incoming lot of material, the manufacturing manager would like the sample plan to give him best assurance that its quality is better than a certain value that he and the supplier have agreed should be regarded as its *limiting quality level (LQL)*. Because sampling by its nature involves probability, if the supplier's actual quality p is at the LQL or is worse, there is a risk that operation of the sample plan will not be successful in leading to the rejection of the lot. This risk (that a lot which it was intended should be rejected is in fact accepted) is referred to in the standard terminology of sampling as the *consumer's risk* (or β risk). If the supplier continues to send material with a fraction non-conforming equal to or worse than the LQL, in the long run, risk will become reality and the cost component $(N - n)pk_2$ from Equation 14.59 will be greater than the manufacturing manager bargained for.

The Supplier's Viewpoint

The supplier would like the sample plan to give him best assurance that a lot which he submits will be accepted if the fraction of non-conforming items therein is equal to or better than a designated level. The level is agreed in consultation with the purchasing company and is known as the *acceptable quality level (AQL)*. (The adjective *acceptable* has the sense of admissible or receivable, or not rejectable; it does not mean welcome or tolerable. See importantly sub-section 14.4.4.) Assuming that the operation of the sample plan does lead to the acceptance of submitted lots when $p \geq$

AQL, the cost of the plan is entirely the purchaser's, and is given in Equation 14.58. As before, however, because sampling by its nature entails risk, there is a probability that lots with a quality equal to or better than the AQL will in fact be rejected. The risk is referred to in standard sampling terminology as the *producer's risk* (or α risk). If risk again becomes reality, the cost element $(N - n)pk_2$ in Equation 14.59 will not be incurred by the purchaser. Instead, the lot will be rejected and the supplier must bear a cost $(N - n)k_1$ for its inspection.

The Ultimate User's Viewpoint

Following the employment of a particular sample plan, the ultimate user of the material sampled has an interest only in the level of quality he receives. (The "ultimate user" is usually the manufacturing manager once more, but he may be the customer if what is being sampled is completed production.) Material that has been subject to sampling is referred to as *outgoing* material. After a period of time, there are two improvements to its quality over the level of quality previously. The first (a very tiny improvement) is due to the sampling inspections themselves, since any non-conforming items in the samples taken are repaired or replaced. The second comes about, with either the LQL or AQL approach, if the lots which have been rejected by the sample plan are then 100 per cent inspected and all non-conformances subsequently repaired or replaced. For example, using percentages rather than fractions, if the incoming material was 1.5 per cent non-conforming (i.e. 100p = 1.5)[30] and the particular sample plan employed led to the rejection of 23 per cent of the lots, which lots were then 100 per cent inspected, with non-conformances repaired or replaced, the *average outgoing quality (AOQ)* would be given by Equation 14.60.

$AOQ = (1.5\% \times 77\%) + (0\% \times 23\%) = 1.15\%$ *Equation 14.60*

Although sampling tables have yet to be introduced, it can be said here that for a particular sample plan, a table allows the probabil-

---

[30] To equate fraction and percentage non-conforming quality levels, the convention is used that $100p \equiv p$ per cent. For example, in the text, p = 0.015 non-conforming, so that 100p = 1.5 per cent.

ity of acceptance (P_a) of an incoming lot to be found for a given level of quality of the incoming material. It can be seen from the small calculation in Equation 14.60, therefore, that average outgoing quality levels can readily be calculated, for a given sample plan, for a complete range of quality levels of incoming material. Table 14.10 shows the probabilities of acceptance of a given lot for a number of levels of incoming quality as it relates to the sample plan from Figure 14.15 in the next sub-section (though the plan is not otherwise pertinent to this explication), and the AOQ level which is associated with each such incoming quality level. The AOQ is derived by application of Equation 14.60.

Table 14.10: Average Outgoing Quality (AOQ) Values taken from a given Sample Plan (from Figure 14.15)

Incoming non-conformances (100p)	Probability of acceptance of the Lot (100P_a)	Probability of rejection of the Lot 100(1–P_a)	AOQ Calculation from Equation 14.60	AOQ (%)
0%	100%	0%		0%
0.5%	98%	2%	0.5% × 98% + 0% × 2%	0.49%
1.0%	90%	10%	1.0% × 90% + 0% × 10%	0.90%
1.5%	77%	23%	1.5% × 77% + 0% × 25%	1.15%
2.0%	56%	44%	2.0% × 56% + 0% × 44%	1.12%
2.5%	38%	62%	2.5% × 38% + 0% × 62%	0.95%
3.0%	25%	75%	3.0% × 25% + 0% × 75%	0.75%
3.5%	15%	85%	3.5% × 15% + 0% × 85%	0.52%
4.0%	8%	92%	4.0% × 8% + 0% × 92%	0.32%

The results in Table 14.10 are plotted as a graph in Figure 14.15.

Figure 14.15: Level of Incoming Quality v. Outgoing Quality after Inspection, showing Worst Quality (i.e. max. AOQ value) of 1.20 per cent (The "AOQ Limit")

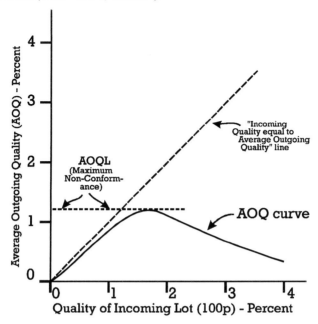

Figure 14.15 illustrates two properties of average outgoing quality. First, the broken line in the Figure at 45° between the two axes of the graph denotes where the average outgoing quality on the vertical axis equals the quality of incoming lots on the horizontal axis. Now, and as only to be expected, the average outgoing quality is seen always to be better than (or equal to) the quality of incoming material (i.e. the AOQ fraction non-conforming is always less than or equal to the fraction non-conforming of the incoming material, p). Thus we see in the Figure that the AOQ curve is entirely below the 45° broken line. Secondly, as the incoming quality initially falls (here, from $100p = 0$ per cent to about $100p = 1.3$ per cent), the outgoing quality similarly falls (from 0 per cent to about 1 per cent). Eventually, however, as incoming quality falls yet further (in Figure 14.15 from about $100p = 2.0$ per cent onwards), the outgoing quality begins to improve (as read on the vertical scale of the graph). This comes about because an ever-increasing number of incoming lots are rejected by the plan, and are consequently 100 per cent inspected and corrected. Between the fall in outgoing

quality and its eventual improvement, there is a turning point where the outgoing quality reaches the limit of its fall. Speaking now in terms of the percentage of non-conformances, rather than "quality", we might say that as the incoming percentage of non-conformances (100p) rises, there is a turning point where the percentage of outgoing non-conformances reaches a maximum and begins to fall. The turning point level in Figure 14.15 is denoted by the small dashed line at about 1.2 per cent on the vertical axis. The level of quality at the turning point (i.e. the 1.2 per cent in the Figure) is referred to as the *average outgoing quality limit (AOQL)*, the term *limit* referring to the worst level of outgoing quality possible with this sample plan. As incoming quality progressively deteriorates and all lots are being rejected by the plan, the AOQ value becomes zero — i.e. outgoing quality is 100 per cent conforming, due to the failure, inspection and then correction of *all* incoming lots. Note that a number of the Dodge-Romig sampling tables are indexed on the AOQL. That is, it is possible to specify a required AOQL and find from the corresponding table the sampling plan that will yield this AOQL value. (Sampling tables are introduced in sub-section 14.4.4.)

The AOQ and AOQL concepts and AOQL sampling tables are popular in manufacturing industry since the average outgoing quality limit is a safeguard. Thus when quality and the operation of the sample plan are going well, it is true that the average outgoing quality will be only slightly better than incoming quality. If incoming quality were suddenly and unexpectedly to deteriorate, however, the AOQ and AOQL tell the ultimate user what level of quality he could then expect. (Protection is the user's immediate concern, though following close behind are concerns that the reason for loss of control should be determined and that the producer should permanently eliminate the cause of the deterioration.)

14.4.3 The Operating Characteristic of a Sample Plan

The assurance of the AOQL is obtained at the risk of incurring the cost of inspecting and correcting failed lots. The cost of inspecting and correcting failed lots for a given level of incoming quality p, employing a sample plan of incoming lot size N, sample size n and acceptance criterion c, is clearly a function of the probability of acceptance of the lots themselves, P_a. The probabilities of accep-

Statistical Quality Control (SQC)

tance of lots over various levels of incoming quality through a sample plan are referred to as its *operating characteristic*. And just as we are able to represent and observe a property of a sample plan over a continuous range of incoming quality levels in Figure 14.15 (i.e. the AOQ), in such a way that it can be absorbed in a single glance, so are we able to represent and observe the operating characteristic of a plan over a range of incoming quality levels through the *operating characteristic curve* (the *OC curve*).[31]

An OC curve can be drawn for any sample plan — i.e. for any set of values of N, n and c. If the lot size N is reasonably large (i.e. several hundred), it is usually sufficiently accurate for practical purposes to base the calculations on the binomial theorem, as if $N = \infty$.[32] The statistical theory which allows us to calculate the probability of finding a specified number of non-conforming items in a sample of size n, for a given fraction p of non-conformancies in the population, and application of the binomial equation, have already been described in sub-section 14.3.1 in connection with the p and np attribute control charts (see Equation 14.43). Equation 14.44 in that sub-section is but a single example of the very many calculations that would be needed in order to construct the OC curve of a sample plan if the task were to be undertaken manually.

A critically important feature of an operating characteristic curve, literally illustrative of the power of the corresponding sample plan and its ability to do the job required of it, is its shape. Thus Figure 14.16 shows an OC curve for a sample plan $N = 2000$, $n = 150$, $c = 2$. Suppose that this plan were to be used to sample incoming items with a required and anticipated percentage non-

---

[31] In the early days of product and raw material sampling at Bell Telephone in the 1920s, OC curves were referred to simply as "probability of acceptance" curves. They were first termed operating characteristic curves in 1940 by Colonel H.H. Zornig, director of a weapons testing facility in Maryland, USA. The usage was subsequently popularised by Major (later General) Leslie Simon in his publications on quality. See Grant and Leavenworth (1996), op. cit.

[32] When lots are small or when the sample size n is 10 per cent or more of the incoming lot size N, it is advisable to use the hypergeometric distribution rather than the binomial. The hypergeometric distribution takes account of the interdependence of the sample (and any non-conformances therein) and the lot remaining after the sample has been taken (and the non-conformances then remaining).

conforming level of 1.5 per cent. Point A on the curve in the Figure and Point A' on the vertical axis of the graph show the probability of acceptance of lots with 100p = 1.5 per cent to be 0.76. If, however, incoming quality were to be lower than expectation, at 2.0 per cent, Points B and B' indicate that the probability of acceptance of lots with the plan remains high at 0.56. Just as seriously, if quality were better than anticipated, at 100p = 1.0 per cent, the probability of acceptance of such lots is only 0.90 — that is, the probability of rejection of these good lots is 0.10 (Points C and C' in the Figure).

Figure 14.16: The Operating Characteristic Curve (OC Curve) for a weak Sample Plan N = 2000, n = 150, c = 2

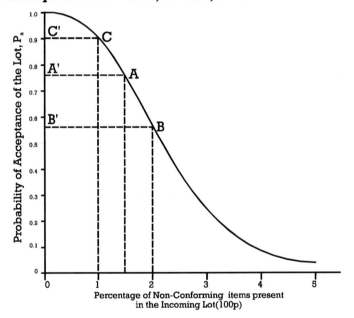

The OC curve and Points A, B and C in Figure 14.16 show this sample plan to be weak. It offers very poor protection if the expected incoming quality is 1.5 per cent, either in rejecting lots worse than the 1.5 per cent target or accepting lots better than this. So although the property of a sample plan may be expressed as its probability of acceptance of lots of a specified incoming quality level, the *power* of the plan may be better seen in its ability to accept lots better than this value and its ability to reject lots worse than this. The power of a plan is clearly manifest in the steepness of slope of its OC curve.

In turn, the key to the steepness of slope of the OC curve and thus the key to the power of a sample plan, is the absolute size of the sample, the value of n.

Figure 14.17 shows the OC curve for a sample plan for $N = 2000$, $n = 500$, $c = 4$. The probability of acceptance of incoming lots with $100p = 1.5$ per cent is 0.75 (Points A and A'). As a measure of this plan's power in relation to the OC curve in Figure 14.16, however, the probability of acceptance of lots in Figure 14.17 with $100p = 2.0$ per cent (Points B and B') is only 0.17 and the probability of acceptance of lots with $100p = 1.0$ per cent is 0.98 (Points C and C').

Figure 14.17: The Operating Characteristic Curve of a Powerful Sample Plan (N = 2000, n = 500, c = 4)

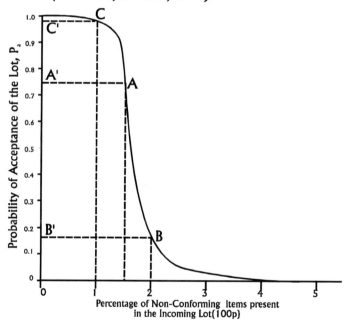

The acceptance number c also has an influence on the OC curve of a sample plan. Thus between one sample plan and another, if c is increased but *n* and N remain the same, the effect is to "stretch" the OC curve horizontally and uniformly to the right. Put in other words, the form and curvature remain the same on increasing the value of c, but the OC curve is elongated to the right such that the scale of the horizontal axis is increased.

Note that the minimum value of c for satisfactory single sampling is desirably 1. The OC curves of single sample plans with c = 0 are poor, even when n is large. Insistence that a sample should have zero non-conformances is a mistake associated with the unreliable and facile quality placebo of informal "spot checking".

A more common mistake in sampling affording equally small excuse to those who make it is to select a sample size n based on its being some arbitrary proportion of the size of the incoming lot N (for example, to select a "5 per cent sample" or "a 10 per cent sample"). Surely, information about the incoming lot can come only from examination of the sample n. It is true that the bigger the sample n in absolute terms, the more information it will yield. But its size relative to N must be largely irrelevant in the assessment of the incoming lot's quality.

14.4.4 Sampling Tables

The procedure for determining a sample plan is described in this sub-section as if printed sampling tables were to be used. In practice, nowadays, sampling plans are selected through one of several comprehensive computer software systems, OC curves being drawn in the twinkling of an eye in Technicolor on the VDU. Although the systems available have saved considerable time and improved the process of plan selection by users, the principles on which they are based remain largely as they were laid down by the pioneers of acceptance sampling from 1930 to 1980.[33]

A great many volumes of sampling tables have been published, each one aimed at a different aspect of acceptance sampling — sequential sampling, chain sampling, skip lot sampling, continuous sampling, and so forth. Three representative examples are described here. These are:

---

[33] The best known of the pioneers, regarded as the father of acceptance sampling, is undoubtedly Harold Dodge, another of Ma Bell's gifted children. On his retirement from Bell, Dodge was appointed Professor of Applied Mathematical Statistics at Rutgers University, New Jersey. Harold Dodge's name will be forever linked to that of Harry Romig, his colleague at Bell Laboratories at Murray Hill, NJ, and another distinguished member of the American quality fraternity. (Bell Laboratories is now known as AT&T Labs Research. Visit http://www. research.att.com/history/)

1. Set I of the Dodge-Romig volume of tables, the tables in the set being especially suited to the LQL and the manufacturer's interest;

2. The tables geared to the AQL and the supplier's interest, variously known as BS6001 Part 1, ISO/DIS 2859-1 and, in the United States, as ANSI/ASQC Z1.4 or, most popularly, as MIL-STD-105E, used extensively throughout the world and all henceforward referred to here as the *military tables*;[34] and

3. Set IV of the Dodge-Romig tables, being double sampling tables indexed on the AOQL and so most pertinent to the interests of the ultimate consumer.[35]

1. LQL Tables and the Manufacturer

It will be recalled from previous comment on the manufacturing manager's viewpoint that he will wish to designate a "limiting quality level" (an LQL) and subsequently employ a sampling plan that will give him best possible assurance of rejecting all lots in which actual quality is at the LQL value or worse. Set I of the Dodge-Romig volume of tables provides plans offering protection in these terms. Originally published in 1959, the volume itself is divided into four sets. Set I comprises what are described as "single sampling lot tolerance" tables. *Single sampling* means that the decision on whether to accept or reject an incoming lot is to be made on the basis of inspection of one sample only. *Lot tolerance* is synonymous with LQL — i.e. the level at or below which incoming

---

[34] The genealogy of the military tables can be related as follows: Bell Telephone (1928); the Ordnance Department of the US Army (1942); JAN-STD-105 (Joint Army Navy Standard 105)(1949); MIL-STD-105A (1950); 105B (1958); 105C (1961); the ABC (America, Britain, Canada) Working Group of defence personnel (1960–1962), whence the present military tables including 105D (1963), ISO2859 (1974), Z1.4 (1981) and MIL-STD-105E (1989).

[35] For Dodge-Romig, see H.F. Dodge and H.G. Romig (1959), *Sampling Inspection Tables*, Second edition, John Wiley & Sons; for BS6001, order through the BSI web site (http://www.bsi-global.com); for ISO 2859, order through the ISO web site at http://www.iso.ch; for Z1.4 see American National Standards Institute, New York; for MIL-STD-105D see US Government Printing Office, Washington DC, 23 April 1963. See also *Sampling Inspection*, jointly edited by members of the Statistical Research Group of Columbia University: H.A. Freeman, M. Friedman, F. Mosteller and W.A. Wallis, McGraw-Hill, 1948.

quality is not tolerable — beyond the maximum degree of acceptability of non-conformances. The sample plan must have a very high chance of rejecting any such lot. (Note that *lot tolerance percent defective* (*LTPD*) is simply the limiting lot tolerance in percentage terms.)

The user "enters" (i.e. looks up) Dodge-Romig Set I by the following three step process in order to determine a sample plan which meets his objective.

1. **Step 1:** by first deciding on and specifying the lot tolerance percent defective. There are eight tables in the Set, each separate table corresponding to the following LTPD values: 0.5 per cent, 1.0 per cent, 2.0 per cent, 3.0 per cent. 4.0 per cent, 5.0 per cent, 7.0 per cent and 10.0 per cent. Note that the probability of acceptance of a lot, P_a, at the LTPD specified, is 0.10 in all eight tables.

2. **Step 2:** by next determining and specifying the fraction of non-conformances p expected in the incoming material. This fraction is termed the "process average"; if it is not known beforehand, a reasonable upper estimate must be made, and an average determined as soon as possible when experience has been gained.

3. **Step 3:** by finally specifying the size N of the incoming lot.

Figure 14.18 is a fragment of Table 6 from Set I of the Dodge-Romig volume. Table 6 corresponds to an LTPD of 5.0 per cent, the probability of acceptance of a lot with this level of quality being the standard value of 0.10. If the incoming quality (process average) expected is (say) 1.80 per cent and the incoming lot size N = 2,500 units, the sample plan to be used and indicated in the Table is sample size n = 280 and acceptance criterion c = 9. This has been circled in the Figure.

Statistical Quality Control (SQC)

Figure 14.18: A Fragment of Table 6 of Set I of the Dodge-Romig Sampling Tables (LTPD = 5.0%, Probability of Acceptance 0.10) Highlighting the Plan and AOQL for Incoming Quality p = 1.51 to 2.00%, Lot Size N = 2001 to 3000

Partial View of
Dodge-Romig Set I Table 6
(LTPD 5.0%, P_a 0.10)

Lot Size	Process Average 1.01 to 1.50%			Process Average 1.51 to 2.00%			Process Average 2.01 to 2.50%			
	n	c	AOQL	n	c	AOQL	n	c	AOQL	....
1001 to 2000	180	5	1.6	230	7	1.7	280	9	1.8	....
2001 to 3000	210	6	1.7	280	9	1.9	370	13	2.1	....
3001 to 4000	210	6	1.7	305	10	2.0	420	15	2.2	....
⋮										

Sample Plan in Text

As a bonus, it can be seen that the Table also gives the AOQL if lots rejected by the plan indicated are then 100 per cent inspected. A further characteristic of the Dodge-Romig sampling plans is that if actual incoming quality is equal to or better than the process average specified (in the example given, 1.80 per cent), the plan gives a very high probability that the lot will be accepted. This advantage must be added to the 90 per cent protection given against the acceptance of any incoming lot with quality poorer than the LTPD chosen by the user (i.e. here 5.0 per cent). There is also an important cost implication, discussed below under 2. It should be remembered, of course, that although good protection is offered by the plan, there remains the consumer's risk, as defined in subsection 14.4.2. In this case, this is a probability of 0.10 that if a lot is received with quality equal to or worse than 5.0 per cent, it will in fact be accepted.

Figure 14.19 shows the OC curves for a number of sample plans from Dodge-Romig Set I, Table 5 (LTPD = 4.0 per cent). Regardless of the process average specified, the OC curve of every plan shows a probability of acceptance that an incoming lot with actual quality of 4.00 per cent or worse (i.e. the LTPD provided for by the plans in the Table) has only a 0.10 probability of acceptance (i.e. $P_a = 0.10$). That is, all OC curves go through a single point, as shown.

Figure 14.19: OC Curves for Four Plans from Table 5 of Set I of the Dodge-Romig Tables (LTPD 4.0%)

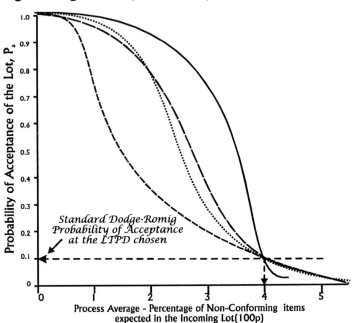

2. AQL Tables and The Supplier

With the LTPD, we have focused on the low end of the OC curve and a low probability (0.10) of acceptance of lots that are undesirable. A more obvious and fruitful area of interest would seem to be the high end of the curve and a high probability of accepting lots that are desirable. (The relationship between producer and consumer is, after all, predicated on the despatch and acceptance of good material, not the despatch and avoidance of bad.) The high probability of acceptance of satisfactory material that is usually aimed for is 0.95.[36] Now, to give effect to a sample plan (including N, n and c) and a probability of acceptance ($P_a = 0.95$), it is neces-

---

[36] The original military tables gave rise to probabilities of acceptance between 0.90 and 0.99. Simplification by standardising on 0.95 was suggested by Harold Dodge in an influential paper on the AQL in 1959, and taken account of by the ABC Working Group (H.F. Dodge (1959), *A General Procedure for Sampling Inspection by Attributes — Based on the AQL Concept*, Technical Report No. 10, The Statistics Center, Rutgers University, New Jersey, 15 December). Other tables based on $P_a = 0.95$ are those from Columbia University, NY (1948) and the Swedish Military Standard (1959).

sary to specify some particular, though discretionary, value of incoming quality (p), referred to as the acceptable quality level, or AQL. (Mathematically, it is not possible to leave p undefined, or to define it as 0.0.) When this has been done, sampling statistics may then be applied so as to formulate a sample plan that will indeed yield a 0.95 probability that lots with this level of quality will be accepted. Put another way, if incoming quality is at the nominated AQL value, it will have a 95 per cent chance of acceptance under the plan and a 5 per cent chance of rejection. As stated previously, the probability that material at the AQL or better will be rejected is referred to as "the producer's risk".

Definitions and explanations of the AQL in the various military volumes go to a great deal of trouble to make clear that *acceptable quality level* does not imply the commendation of this percentage of non-conformances. Sampling implies probability and the possibility that quality may be less than 100 per cent conforming. This being so, the AQL is a yardstick: if incoming quality is at the AQL or better, lots have a very high chance of acceptance. Nothing more.

Yet, as an aside, it is easy to see how matters might deteriorate if the central quality precepts of improvement and customer commitment were to become forgotten in the bustle of sampling. A supplier, with care, may be capable of sustaining long-term process quality between 1.6 per cent and 2.0 per cent, so that, after due consideration of the BEP (see below), an AQL of 2.0 per cent is agreed for sampling acceptance purposes. After a while, it may be found that 2.0 per cent has become the norm. Attention is now directed not to improving upon 1.6 per cent but to trapping lots worse than 2.0 per cent. Deming in particular has spoken out very strongly against the notion of the AQL in the military tables, and against acceptance sampling as a cure-all. He issues a general warning:

> "Most applications of the Dodge-Romig plans of acceptance and of Military Standard 105D are, I fear, pro forma, merely conforming to the requirements of a contract, drawn up by people without qualifications for drawing up a plan, and carried out by another group of people

equally qualified. Everybody does it, so we do too. The result is increase in cost.[37]

It is at least an advantage of the Dodge-Romig tables not shared by the military tables that the sample plan for a given process average p and incoming lot size N aims to minimise average total inspection. Average total inspection (ATI) comprises two parts, as shown in Equation 14.61 — i.e. the required inspection of the sample and the required inspection of lots that have in fact been rejected even though their quality was at the process average.

$$ATI = n + (N-n)(1 - P_a) \qquad \text{Equation 14.61}$$

A statistic more helpful than the ATI is the average *fraction* inspected, AFI, given in Equation 14.62.

$$AFI = \frac{ATI}{N} \qquad \text{Equation 14.62}$$

The Dodge-Romig sample plans are based on obtaining a minimum value of AFI for the process average specified.

It will be appreciated that a minimum AFI is obtained through a trade-off between the two elements of Equation 14.61, sampling and the inspection of rejected lots. Note, therefore, that if a supplier has agreed to bear the cost of inspecting rejected lots, he should beware his customer's suggestion that the sample size n might be reduced. A glance at Equation 14.61 will show that his own costs would be certain to increase, if not proportionately. A more rewarding topic of discussion for the two parties with regard to shared cost would be the AFI.

Before returning to the main theme of the text, a final cost argument must be stated, namely that the threat of or actuality of returning rejected lots for 100 per cent inspection is a spur to process improvement by the producer. It is summarised in Harold Dodge's own words:

> "One trouble with 100 per cent inspection, where it is practicable, is that the inspector merely cleans up the faults of others, sorting the good from the bad, and the

---

[37] W. Edwards Deming (1986), *Out of the Crisis*, MIT Center for Advanced Engineering Studies, Cambridge, MA, Chapter 15.

Statistical Quality Control (SQC)

production man takes it as a matter of course if just individual articles are returned to him for repair. But if a whole lot is returned to him, as when lot sampling is used, and he is required to undertake the entire corrective action, the steady outward flow of product is interrupted. If there are many lot rejections, he must get busy to find the cause and eliminate it in order to avoid further lot rejections. This is an indirect power of sampling — it forces correction of the process, where the fault lies."[38]

Whether Dodge's observation quite fits in with the notion of the modern supplier relationship is a question deferred until Chapter 16.

Like all collections of sampling tables, the military tables are far more than the numeric data themselves. They include operating procedures, advice and general information and together constitute a fully integrated sampling inspection system. Their popularity worldwide is in part also explained by their ease of use. The six steps required to develop a plan are outlined as follows:

i. The user must decide whether he is to sample for non-conformances or non-conforming items;

ii. The value of the AQL must be nominated (for non-conforming items, the range catered for in the tables is from 0.015 per cent to 10.0 per cent. For non-conformances, it is up to 1,000 in number);

iii. An internal table must next be referenced to determine the sample size to be used. (Seven alternative inspection levels are allowed for, denoted by I, II and III, and the specialist categories S-1, S-2, S-3 and S-4. Level II ("normal") is by far the most popular.);

iv. The choice must be made between single sampling, double sampling and multiple sampling;

v. The incoming lot size N is noted;

---

[38] H.F. Dodge (1948), "Administration of a Sampling Inspection Plan", *Industrial Quality Control*, Vol. 5, No. 3, pp. 12–19, November, reprinted in *The Journal of Quality Technology*, Vol. 9, No. 3, July 1977 (both US magazines). See also Grant and Leavenworth (1996), op. cit., Chapter 13.

vi. The appropriate table in the set is entered based on the accumulation of data from Steps (i) to (v), to determine therefrom: (a) for single sampling, the specification of the sample plan, i.e. the sample size n and the acceptance criterion c; and (b) for double sampling, n_1, n_2, c_1 and c_2 (see below).

Figure 14.20 illustrates three OC curves of single sampling plans based on a user-determined AQL of 2.0 per cent and a standard table probability of acceptance of 0.95. As in Figure 14.19, all curves pass through a single point.

Figure 14.20: The OC Curves of Three Single Sample Plans based on an AQL of 2.0 per cent and a Probability of Acceptance of 95 per cent

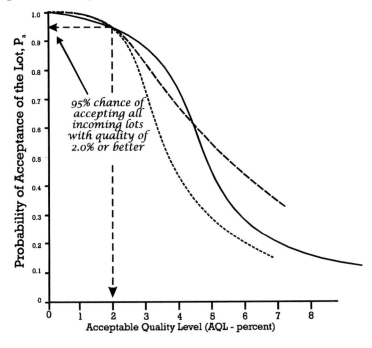

While a basic sample plan from the military tables protects the supplier reasonably against the rejection of too many lots which are at the AQL or better, there is no equivalent protection of the consumer against the acceptance of lots which are significantly less than the AQL. We can see at a glance in Figure 14.20 that incoming lots with 4.0 per cent non-conforming, twice the AQL, have variously high probabilities of acceptance.

It is consequently necessary to supplement the AQL tables and sampling system with a safeguard for the consumer if things begin to go wrong in the form of *tightened inspection*. Tightened inspection is the instigation under certain defined circumstances of an alternative sample plan, taking the place of *normal inspection*, the alternative having more stringent acceptance criteria, and so providing more certain determination of the incoming quality. More stringent acceptance criteria simply mean a smaller acceptance criterion and, perhaps, a larger sample size. A tightened sample plan corresponding to each normal plan is given in the military tables. The so-called *switching rules*, or *transition rules*, for moving from normal to tightened sampling and back again from tightened to normal are common throughout the tables. The rules are (1) institute tightened inspection when two out of five consecutive lots have been rejected under normal sampling; (2) switch back to normal inspection from tightened when five consecutive lots have been accepted; and (3) terminate acceptance sampling and commence 100 per cent inspection after ten lots have been inspected under tightened (after five lots, under MIL-STD-105E).[39] It goes without saying that any necessity to switch to tightened sampling is likely to entail communication and discussion with the supplier.

Eugene Grant and Richard Leavenworth consider the switching rules and the potential imposition of tightened inspection to be utterly essential to the operation of the military tables ("at the heart of all acceptance sampling systems based on the AQL"[40]). If so, it follows, then, that the military tables and the sampling systems based on them are not suitable for the sampling of isolated lots or the sampling of very short series of incoming production lots, where the switching rules cannot be applied.

---

[39] Simpler, less stringent switching rules have been suggested by Dodge in his 1959 paper (op. cit.). Dodge considered change necessary because of evidence that practitioners were misapplying existing procedures since they seemed to them to be uncompromising and excessively severe, especially the rules for switching from tightened back to normal sampling. Dodge's intercession again reminds all quality personnel of the importance of taking into account shop floor practicalities and the human factor.

[40] Grant and Leavenworth (1996), op. cit., Section 12.3.

The decision to employ sampling at all in the assessment of manufactured and raw material quality will be taken after due consideration of the cost of inspection, k_1, and the cost of admitting non-conforming items into production, k_2 — i.e. the BEP factors incorporated in Equation 14.58. The BEP is compared to the standard fraction of non-conforming parts, p_0, as explained in sub-section 14.4.1. In concluding that sampling is the correct course of action, the next central decision to be made if the military tables are to be used in formulating the sample plan is in regard to the nomination of the AQL.

The AQL is agreed by the producer and consumer with the evidence of the process average before them and experience, if any, of the current operation of the system. There may be an element of negotiation in the discussion, especially if the consumer wishes to encourage the producer to make process improvements (see the reference above to an AQL of 2.0 per cent). Alternatively, the AQL may be set by application of a formula.

The most popular way of setting an AQL by formula is to make it equal to the BEP. Thus if the breakeven point is 0.025, then the AQL is set at 2.5 per cent. The rationale in so doing is based on two arguments. First, if actual incoming quality is, in the event, equal to or better than the AQL, incoming lots will be accepted. And since incoming quality is equal to or better than the BEP, it is more economic that non-conforming items should be received into production for later correction. Secondly, if incoming quality is worse than the AQL, it is hoped that lots will be rejected and will then be 100 per cent inspected. And now, since incoming quality is worse than the BEP, it is more economic that 100 per cent inspection should indeed take place.

Unfortunately, this rule of thumb seems to suggest that a no-lose situation exists and that the BEP considerations in sub-section 14.4.1 need not be taken into account. Producer and consumer then find themselves either (1) sampling and accepting everything ($AQL > p$) or (2) sampling and rejecting everything ($AQL < p$). In either case, sampling is an unnecessary additional expense and its establishment and continuation a substantiation of Deming's remarks previously quoted.

A major problem with the AQL = BEP rule, other than the propensity of practitioners to misuse it, is that lots which are worse than the AQL may nevertheless be accepted for the reason previously discussed, thus upsetting the BEP cost equilibrium. The recommended BEP/AQL rules therefore make the AQL a little more severe than the strict breakeven point value. The rules are incorporated in the military tables, and are given in Table 14.11.

Table 14.11: Recommended Breakeven Point /AQL Equivalents from the Military Tables[41]

Breakeven Point Range	AQL	Breakeven Point Range	AQL
0.005–0.010	0.0025	0.040–0.060	0.040
0.010–0.0175	0.0065	0.060–0.105	0.065
0.0175–0.030	0.010	0.105–0.170	0.100
0.030–0.040	0.025		

3. AOQL Tables and the Ultimate Consumer

Set IV is the most popular of the four sets in the Dodge-Romig volume. The tables are indexed on the AOQL (see Figure 14.15) and provide for double sampling.

Double sampling (which is also catered for as an option in the military tables) means inspecting a first sample of size n_1, and then taking one of three courses of action:

1. To accept the incoming lot at once, without further investigation, if the number of non-conforming items in this first sample is equal to or less than an acceptance plan number c_1, where c_1 is the *first acceptance criterion*;

2. To reject the incoming lot at once, without further investigation, if the number of non-conforming items in this first sample is greater than an acceptance plan number c_2, where c_2 is the *second acceptance criterion*;

3. If there has been neither acceptance nor rejection, to take a second additional sample of size n_2, and to make a final decision to accept the lot if the total number of non-conforming

---

[41] See A.V. Feigenbaum (1983), op. cit., Section 15.18.

items in the two samples combined is less than or equal to c_2, or to reject the lot if the combined number is greater than c_2.

Double sampling is more popular than single sampling for two reasons.[42] First, it is significantly cheaper to conduct. This comes about because the first sample in double sampling is always smaller than the sample taken in single sampling, an advantage only partly offset in double sampling by the need on occasions to take the second sample. Depending on circumstances, double sampling entails from 10 per cent to 50 per cent less sampling inspection than single sampling. The second reason for its popularity is because it seems to give the incoming lot "a second chance" before staff must undertake the weary arrangements needed to return it to the producer or commence in-house 100 per cent inspection (albeit at the producer's expense) — see the remarks on practicality and the human factor in footnote 39.

Set IV of Dodge-Romig is entered by the following three-step process in order to determine a sample plan.

1. **Step 1:** by first deciding and specifying the AOQL desired. There are 13 tables in the set corresponding to the following AOQL values: 0.10 per cent, 0.25 per cent, 0.50 per cent, 0.75 per cent, 1.0 per cent, 1.5 per cent, 2.0 per cent, 2.5 per cent, 3.0 per cent, 4.0 per cent, 5.0 per cent, 7.0 per cent and 10.0 per cent.
2. **Step 2:** by next specifying the fraction of non-conforming items p expected in the incoming material.
3. **Step 3:** by finally specifying the size N of the incoming lot.

Figure 14.21 is a fragment from Table 7 of Set IV of the Dodge-Romig volume, corresponding to an AOQL of 2.0 per cent.

---

[42] Multiple sampling is an ingenious extension of double sampling. The decision to accept or reject may be deferred until many samples have been taken of size n_1, n_2, n_3 ... , each having an acceptance criterion c_1, c_2, c_3 ... . Multiple sampling is not, surprisingly, especially more effective than double sampling, and calls for the most careful organisation in its conduct in the typical shop floor environment.

Statistical Quality Control (SQC)

Figure 14.21: A Fragment from Table 7 of Set IV of the Dodge-Romig Sampling Tables, highlighting the plan and LTPD for Incoming Quality p = 1.60 per cent to 2.00 per cent, Lot Size N = 2,001 to 3,000

Partial View of
Dodge-Romig Set IV Table 7
(Double Sampling ; AOQL 2.0%)

Lot Size	Process Average									
	1.21% - 1.60%					1.60% - 2.00%				
	Trial 1		Trial 2		LTPD (0.10)	Trial 1		Trial 2		LTPD (0.10)
	n_1	c_1	n_2	$n_1 + n_2$	c_2	n_1	c_1	n_2	$n_1 + n_2$	c_2
1001 - 2000	80	1	160	240	8	5.8	110	2	205	315	11	5.5
2001 - 3000	115	2	195	310	10	5.3	160	3	310	470	15	4.7
3001 - 4000	120	2	255	375	12	5.0	235	5	415	650	20	4.3

Double Sample Plan in Text

If in some particular instance the incoming process average expected is (say) 1.8 per cent and the incoming lot size N = 2,500 units, the sample plan to be used may be summarised as :

$n_1 = 160$ units, $c_1 = 3$, $n_2 = 310$ units and $c_2 = 15$

The plan is circled in the Figure. The LTPD protection offered by this plan is also given in the Table and is 4.7 per cent (0.10 probability).

14.4.5 Sampling by Variables

The rightmost block of Figure 14.1 and not yet touched upon is *Sampling by Variables*. It is true that the great weight of attention and historical endeavour in the raw material and product control branch of SQC has been applied to sampling by attributes. The increasingly wide availability of easy-to-use measuring equipment and, especially, of SQC software systems may see the balance redressed in the years to come, however. A major problem in sampling by variables for the consumer is verifying the statistical distribution of the quality variable chosen for sampling. If manufactured batches that have been received have been made at different times, or have been made from material from different sources or have been partly inspected, the distribution of the variable may be skewed or bi-modal or anything but normal. Where a close relationship exists between supplier and customer in matters of quality, as it will do in so-called "partnership" arrangements, information on such matters can be provided as a matter of course. If it is, sampling by variables may be a particularly useful and inexpensive alternative to sampling by attributes. For example, a satisfactory frequency distribution can be plotted under so-called *known sigma*, or *variability known*, conditions with as few as 50 units in the sample, to yield far richer information for the consumer — positive information, for example, on key quality factors rather than a mere deduction relating to a fraction of non-conformances. See again Figures 14.11(a) to (d). Sampling plans and sampling tables that have been provided to permit sampling by variables for incoming lots, where lots are either known sigma (variability known) or *unknown sigma (variability unknown)* include BS 6002, ISO 3951 and (in the US) MIL-STD-414.

Chapter 15

Just-in-Time

15.1 Two Definitions

Though it has been imitated and adapted throughout Japan and the rest of the world, Just-in-Time remains synonymous with manufacture in all its aspects as it is practised by the Toyota Motor Company. The father of the system is widely acknowledged to be a former executive vice president of Toyota, Taiichi Ohno.[1] The term *Just-in-Time* and the original vision of the system in operation, however, are the legacy of Kiichiro Toyoda, the Company's founding president.[2]

The guiding star of Just-in-Time is the requirement to examine every facet of manufacturing activity and subsequently eliminate

---

[1] Taiichi Ohno (1912–1990) began his working life in 1932 at the Toyoda Spinning and Weaving Company, makers of semiautomatic looms, a company owned by Sakichi Toyoda, an inventor and founder of the Toyota manufacturing dynasty. He was transferred to the fledgling Toyota Motor Company in 1943. Ohno was appointed manager of the machine shop at Toyota's Koromo plant (the main site) in 1949 and promoted to the Board in 1954. He was made MD in 1964. Taiichi Ohno retired from Toyota in 1978, his perseverance in establishing Just-in-Time having by then succeeded to spectacular effect.

[2] Taiichi Ohno (1988), *Toyota Production System — Beyond Large-Scale Production*, English translation through Productivity Press. There may be an air of deference in Taiichi Ohno's contention that the JIT idea was first formulated by Kiichiro Toyoda rather than by himself. (The West is greatly indebted to The Productivity Press and its editor Norman Bodek for bringing translations of this and over 25 other important Japanese books on manufacturing to its libraries' shelves. A publication list can be obtained from Productivity Press's UK subsidiary American Technical Publishers Ltd., Hitchin, Hertfordshire.)

absolutely anything that does not contribute directly to the creation of the product itself or to the customer's enjoyment of it. The pages of The Manufacturing Manager's Handbook must be turned and Occam's Razor applied to each and every one. The total elimination of what is not necessary is often termed simply *the elimination of waste*. Waste is categorised under seven headings: overproduction; time (waiting); transportation; processing time itself; movement; production of non-conforming product; and stock.

Of the seven, it is the elimination of stock that has particularly caught the public's attention. The reason has been not the literal reductions in stockholding achieved and the financial savings that have resulted, considerable as they are, but the impact of the changes to operations that have been made to bring them about. The changed environment needed to operate with almost no stock, ideally zero stock, is a different world from the conventional one described in many Chapters of this book.

The new way of manufacturing — brought about only after a great deal of perseverance and hard work, especially by the engineering manager — is what many people would define as JIT, rather than the more fundamental "elimination of waste". The new way is to manufacture goods at a pace synchronised with the demand for them in the market. Thus if customers are buying 12 units a day of Product X, then the company will manufacture 12 units a day of Product X in response, and, furthermore, require the whole of the manufacturing and supply chain, internal and external, also to be synchronised with this rate of output — the cycle time of final assembly being *the drumbeat of fabrication*, as Robert Hall has put it, the drumbeat of fabrication being then the drumbeat of raw material supply.[3] If all this can be done, finished goods stock, work-in-progress, raw material stock, people and other resources, most definitely and legitimately needed to support the previous order of things, are no longer present because they are no longer relevant. Since they are no longer present, we can say that they constituted latent waste and have been eliminated. A massive reduction in costs is achieved.

The new order brings the company a further advantage parallel to what would be achieved through conventional manufacture con-

---

[3] Robert Hall (1983), *Zero Inventories*, Business One Irwin.

trolled by a perfectly managed master scheduling system coupled to an instantly responsive APS capability. Thus if the JIT manufacture of goods is synchronised with the demand of the market, manufacture is able immediately to respond when demand changes — the company being then able to ride through downturns as economically as it is possible to do so and able to capitalise on upturns to maximum possible profit, the time lags, difficulties and stock fluctuations illustrated in Figures 4.5 and 4.6, to give an example, being simply non-existent and of no concern.

The direction the company is to take — to Just-in-Time or to conventional master plan management and scheduling — will be decided only after great debate by the Board of Directors. Two considerations will be uppermost in the Board's mind:

First, whether Just-in-Time manufacture is compatible with the marketing and manufacturing environments in which the company must operate. Situations not conducive to JIT are:

- Those in which product must necessarily be manufactured in discrete lots, such as apply (say) to certain cooked foods, dyestuffs and other batch chemicals;

- Where the requirement for very many components is sporadic or very low in volume;

- Those where products are engineered-to-order and necessarily made-to-order, and where the re-engineering techniques outlined in Section 8.2 cannot be applied.

The engineering director and others must beware before dismissing Just-in-Time on these or other grounds of a failure of imagination. It is continually pointed out that progress in JIT calls for great creativity of mind and a willingness to think beyond the conventional.[4]

The second, as ever, is risk versus reward. A small company with repetitive manufacture and relatively simple plant, engaged,

---

[4] Taiichi Ohno ((1988), op. cit.) reminds us of Sakichi Toyoda's *Five Why's*. A person puts a question (the first *Why?*) asking why change needed to eliminate waste cannot be made in an existing situation, and receives an explanation. He challenges the explanation with a second question — the second *Why?*, and so on, eventually coming to the fifth question, a challenge which gets to the very heart of the matter and to which his respondent cedes.

say, in light assembly or machining, may see Just-in-Time as a far more promising alternative than the undertaking needed to develop formal master plan management and a shop scheduling capability. A large company with resources to match and expertise in the development of sophisticated, computer-centred systems, faced with the need to redevelop its entire manufacturing and purchasing operation for Just-in-Time, may regretfully conclude it is not the Toyota Motor Company. It is an irony here, may one say, that the company which does not hesitate to attempt the implementation of a very expensive, highly complex MRPII/ERP system, quails yet at the thought of embarking on the Just-in-Time journey, despite the fact that the building blocks of JIT can be put in place for very little cost and, with careful planning, with little risk. If its senior executives have something of Taiichi Ohno's vision and some measure of his tenacity, it is likely they will succeed, or largely so. The lengthy catalogue of disappointments and even outright failures with MRPII, on the contrary, needs no reciting.

The building blocks of Just-in-Time are outlined in Sections 15.2 to 15.7. The place of each one of them in the overall scheme of things is made clear, as is its contribution to the achievement of JIT's objective, whether that is defined purely as the elimination of waste, patent and latent, or whether it is defined as achieving responsiveness to the market.

15.2 ESTABLISHING PRODUCTION RATES

Although it is true that little progress can be made in actually achieving an even manufacturing flow as set out in this Section until the techniques and improvements described in later Sections have been applied, the calculations to determine these rates of production are dealt with first so that the objectives of the later techniques can be more clearly seen when their turns come. It is not uncommon for manufacturing personnel to embark on such activities as, say, the achievement of fast machine changeovers, without a clear understanding of why they are needed and how they are intended to contribute to the JIT system overall, and then to allow the old ways to reassert themselves because the rewards they expected did not materialise.

15.2.1 The Pattern of Final Assembly

The assumption is first made that predicted demand in the market over the master schedule month will be smooth. The task of determining the ideal pattern of final assembly is then to calculate a manufacturing rate that is similarly smooth, or, at least, is as smooth and level as possible.

Suppose three products, A, B and C, are manufactured in final assembly, and that the master schedule requirements for them over a given month are as shown in column 2 of Table 15.1. If there are 20 days in the month, the smoothed daily requirements for the three are as shown in column 3 of the table.

Table 15.1: Master Scheduled Requirements for Three Products in Final Assembly

Product Name	Monthly MPS Requirements	Daily MPS Requirements
Product A	2,560 units	128 units
Product B	8,960 units	448 units
Product C	1,280 units	64 units
Total	12,800 units	640 units

It is next necessary to determine the production run times required to make the various daily quantities of A, B and C. The production times per unit of A, B and C are given in Column 3 of Table 15.2, and the total times required for the daily requirements in Column 4. It can be seen that the total production time needed is 787.2 minutes.

Let us now suppose that 14 hours per day (840.0 minutes) manufacturing time is available. If so, then 52.8 minutes per day (840.0–787.2) remains of this time after taking account of actual production.

Table 15.2: Calculation of the Production Times Needed to Manufacture One Day's Requirements of A, B and C

	Set-up Time in minutes	Production Time for One Unit	Total Daily Production Time
Product A	2.0	1.6 minutes	204.8 minutes
Product B	5.0	0.9 minutes	403.2 minutes
Product C	6.0	2.8 minutes	179.2 minutes
Totals	13.0		787.2 minutes

The set-up times for Product A, Product B and Product C are given in Column 2 of Table 15.2. One set of set-ups for all three products takes 13.0 minutes, so that four set-ups per day are possible for the three products (i.e. 4 x 13 minutes < 52.8 minutes). Consequently, the smoothest pattern of manufacture of A, B and C possible in final assembly is:

> 32 units of Product A, followed by
> 112 units of Product B, followed by
> 16 units of Product C ...

... this cycle of manufacture being repeated four times per day.

Note in passing that if the set-up times for A, B and C in Table 15.2 were to be halved, the pattern of production of the three products would then become (16A, 56B and 8C) × 8. Ideally, if set-up times were negligible, the flow of production would take the form (B B B A B B C B B A) × 64. The purpose of striving for this ideal is not because of its potential value upstream in sales and distribution, but because of its levelling effect downstream in manufacture and supply, including the manufacture of component parts.

Since an objective of JIT is to manufacture in synchronisation with market demand, the actual manufacture on a particular day will depend on the previous day's sales. Suppose that the company's sales office reports sales of A, B and C as shown in Table 15.3, column 2. The differences between sales and the standard daily requirements are given in column 3 of the table.

Table 15.3: Adjustments to the Standard Daily Production Quantities to take account of Previous Day's Sales

Product	Actual Sales on the Previous Day	Actual Sales Less Standard Quantity
Product A	108 units	– 20 units
Product B	508 units	+60 units
Product C	76 units	+ 12 units
Net Sales	692 units	+ 52 units

The actual pattern of manufacture on this particular day is consequently adjusted to take account of the extra units. Thus, it is now:

27 units of Product A, followed by
127 units of Product B, followed by
19 units of Product C . . .

. . . this cycle of manufacture again being repeated four times in the day.

The additional time required to make the extra 52 units can be worked out by making the calculations in Table 15.2 with the new quantities of production (+55.6 minutes). More normally, for more complex and realistic situations on busy factory floors, the additional or less time required is calculated from the standard *cycle time* of final assembly.[5] Cycle time is the total number of minutes of manufacturing time available divided by the total number of units made in all. Here, it is 840.0 minutes ÷ 640 units, or 1.312 minutes per unit. Consequently, as a quick approximation, the additional time to make the extra units is 52 × 1.312 minutes, or 1 hour 8 minutes. (The final assembly cell leader will correct this time when an opportunity to do so presents itself during the day.)

Any additional manufacturing time necessary will normally be made available on the factory floor by overtime. Working patterns in JIT factories are typically two shifts, not three, with sufficient time following each shift for extra production, as discussed here,

---

[5] Cycle time is as simple a concept as the text says, and gives a good feel for the intensity of production. It is not to be confused with the time actually needed to manufacture. *A bus goes into town every hour, but it doesn't take the bus one hour to make the journey.*

and for the routine preventive maintenance of machinery as part of a TPM programme (see sub-section 15.6.2).

15.2.2 The Pattern of Fabrication

The flow of fabricated parts — sub-assemblies, components and so forth — needed to support the manufacture of final products is determined by the inescapable logic of materials planning as described in Chapter 9.

However, as the capability of the company to manufacture in small, frequent quantities improves (as the company learns to fabricate to Hall's drumbeat), the lot sizing calculations described in Section 9.6 become increasingly inappropriate. Instead, the supporting fabricated material requirements are likely to be more suitably planned through rate-based material rules such as those listed in Section 9.5.

Although discussion of plant organisation is deferred until Section 15.4, one may anticipate more severe problems in physically arranging production flow in fabrication areas than in arranging flow in final assembly. Heavy manufacture may require to be isolated because of dirt and noise; expensive, large capacity plant cannot immediately be replaced by small-scale units more suited to flow manufacture. In addition, the creation of an accurate, uninterrupted flow of materials into final assembly is likely to prove difficult to co-ordinate closely, because of the many diverse materials involved.

It may take many years of development and involve countless small reorganisations before materials are flowing satisfactorily through fabrication areas, at an even pace and in unison with final assembly.

15.2.3 The Pattern of Raw Material Supply

As the materials at the lowest levels of the bill come to be made in small lots and at frequent intervals, it is entirely natural that raw materials supplies required for their manufacture should be made to follow suit.

The facts of transport and materials handling naturally place at least some constraints on the smallness and frequency of the deliveries that can economically be made, although much ingenuity has been exercised to overcome these obstacles. Suppliers may pool transport and share costs. Trailers with one week's supply may be parked in secure areas, and daily or twice daily local deliveries made therefrom to the JIT customer. Most dramatic of all, for major contracts, is the establishment by the supplier of a new manufacturing facility, very close to the customer, for final stage manufacture and frequent inward delivery, perhaps many times daily.[6]

Practical issues that must be resolved with JIT raw material supplies are the streamlining of documentation; the likely demand for more frequent payment of invoices; and the need to redesign packages for increased clarity of identification and ease of handling. Some redesign of the company's receiving docks may also be necessary, with greater emphasis placed on traffic management (sub-section 18.1.2). Indeed, as mentioned in sub-section 18.1.1, it may be preferable for incoming goods to be delivered direct to their points of use throughout the factory, data relating to the receipts being communicated to a central stores point. (Communication from customer to supplier of changing daily delivery requirements is usually very simple — say, a kanban or kanban modification for the following day handed over when a day's supply is collected (see sub-section 15.5.1).)

Whether supplies are delivered directly to their points of use or not, if they are received daily, there is no question of their storage as stock. For this reason, and for many others, including the elimination of waste and the smooth operation of the kanban system, especially with regard to Kanban Rule 6, it is essential that their quality should be 100 per cent conforming (see sub-section 15.5.1, but also Section 18.1).

15.3 SMED AND FAST CHANGEOVERS

Changeover time is the time a machine must remain non-operational while a number of activities are performed in readiness for the start of the production run of the next product, activities which include changing tools and bits, parts set-up and,

---

[6] For all the prominence in the text given to very frequent supplies, it should be noted that the very many raw material supplies not used in mainstream production, or not used frequently, are likely to be delivered weekly rather than daily.

perhaps, verifying the first production piece(s) actually produced.[7] At a basic level in Just-in-Time, changeover time is self-evidently waste, since it adds nothing directly to the value of the product, and a programme to reduce it is justified for that reason.

In practice, what compels the initiation of a long-term programme to reduce changeover times and sustains it over the many years needed to make continual, incremental and often painstaking improvements is the prospect of two concomitant advantages that success confers. These are the ability, with very short changeovers, to reduce manufacturing lot sizes without affecting productivity or efficiency, and the ability to respond quickly to change in the manufacturing programme prompted by changing market demand.

The effects of short changeover times on stock levels and market responsiveness for three products A, B and C manufactured in final assembly have been demonstrated in sub-section 15.2.1. The lower the times become, the more the shop floor planner can level the manufacturing flow and the easier it is to adjust output to market demand. In sub-section 15.2.2 (fabrication and the manufacture of sub-assemblies), the targets that would now be selected for the application of changeover reduction techniques would be identified by following the process flow backwards, ultimately to the processing of raw materials, focusing on those processes with times currently least well-matched to final assembly and giving rise to the most stock.

The tools and techniques brought to bear to reduce changeover times are to be found in conventional work study and industrial engineering. Permanent study teams are typically formed comprising engineers and shop floor personnel familiar with the machines and processes involved, the teams meeting for a short time each week.

In common with so much else on the Just-in-Time journey, there are no hard and fast procedures for undertaking a study. However, a great many practitioners turn to the guidelines issued by Shigeo

---

[7] It is pointed out by UK SMED/JIT expert Alex Simpson that the term *changeover* is far to be preferred to *set-up*, since set-up is only one of the activities involved. Alex Simpson at *The Change Works Ltd*, Princes Risborough, Buckinghamshire, holds a number of training courses on Just-in-Time and Changeover time reduction.

Shingo in his *SMED* system. Shigeo Shingo is acknowledged as one of the most distinguished manufacturing engineers of the last century.[8] He was engaged by the Toyota Motor Company in 1969 and 1970 as a consultant to introduce and further develop the SMED methodology that he had been formulating over some 20 years for changeover time reduction, and to instruct local factory teams in applying these ideas in connection with the Toyota JIT programme. SMED stands for *Single-Minute Exchange of Die* — it was Shigeo's contention that the great majority of changeovers could be accomplished in less than ten minutes.

The three stages of SMED are described in sub-section 15.3.1 to 15.3.3 below. Before then, a word should be said about what some might wrongly regard as a rather mundane topic.

This is the need for meticulous, "positive" housekeeping within the factory — not only *a place for everything and everything in its place*, but a member of staff put in charge of it. Clutter will defeat quick changeovers just as dirt is liable to defeat quality. The term *positive* housekeeping is used to emphasise that everyone, including the manufacturing manager, is responsible for the good organisation, neatness and cleanliness of his area. Positive housekeeping contributes not only to SMED, but also to speedy and accurate movement of materials, the good management of tools, workplace vigilance and a sense of quality and discipline.

---

[8] Shigeo Shingo (1909–1990) was born in Saga City, Japan and graduated in mechanical engineering from Yamanashi Technical College. His first post (13 years) was as an engineer with the Taipei Railway Factory. In 1945, Shingo turned to management consultancy, first under the auspices of the Japan Management Association, and later (1959) through his own company. Shigeo Shingo advised many hundreds of companies throughout Japan, the USA and continental Europe, in all industrial groups, often being asked to conduct massive internal training programmes on their behalf. From the period 1961–1965, he was closely involved in the development of the "mistake proofing" technique of *poka-yoke* as a means of attaining 100 per cent quality. During his career, Dr Shingo made numerous important contributions to manufacturing science and literature, especially in the field of quality, and, from the mid-1970s, conducted many oversees tours. The annual Shingo Prize for *Excellence in Manufacture* was established in 1988 and is administered by the University of Utah.

15.3.1 SMED Stage I: Separating Internal and External Changeover Activities

A central distinction is made in SMED between two kinds of changeover operations. These are:

1. Internal operations, referred to by Shigeo Shingo as *IED* (*inside exchange of die*), necessarily performed when the machine under set-up is stopped; and

2. External operations, or *OED* (*outside exchange of die*), being activities which can be performed when the machine is still running on the previous job.

The *single minute* in SMED refers only to internal changeover time, or IED time.

Stage I begins with the careful documentation of both external and internal changeover activities and requirements, so that a methodical, detailed study can be made of them. In particular, if it is discovered that activities are being carried out when the machine is stopped which could or should be performed beforehand, in external time, procedures are amended and instructions given to correct the matter.

The facts to be documented may be gathered by old-fashioned methods (careful observation and the use of a stop watch) or by videotaping the operation. Documentation itself may comprise work study flowcharts or simple checklists detailing the various required procedures and such vital data as the numbers of dies and blades involved, pressure and temperature settings, etc.

Although Stage I is intended to comprise documentation only, nothing is sacrosanct in JIT; the opportunity might be taken at this point to introduce, say, the colour coding of tools and the use of tool tables. (Tool tables are, literally, tables with the outlines of tools marked out so that it can seen at a glance if any are missing.)

15.3.2 SMED Stage II: Converting IED Changeover Activity to OED Activity

The key to success in SMED is the conversion of internal changeover activities to external activities, or rather, the carrying out of external activities that permit certain internal ones to be eliminated.[9] The two categories of action taken encompass the preparation of conditions in advance, and function standardisation.

Preparation

Anticipating what needs to be done is an obvious measure that can substantially reduce the time spent in internal changeover. A very common instance given in SMED is the pre-heating of a die before IED commences, with the necessity then, of course, of manoeuvring a hot die onto the machine when IED activity finally begins.

Standardisation

The method of standardisation favoured is *function standardisation*. This is the standardisation of just those parts of the machine that are directly and specifically concerned with its changeover from one product to the next. In order to carry out function standardisation, the purpose, means and action of each of the individual machine operations must be analysed one by one. An example is given in Figure 15.1 of the standardisation of the heights of two dies P (310 mm) and Q (260 mm) in order to simplify the adjustment of the shut height in setting up a press. Shims, or blocks, of 50mm, as indicated in the Figure, are placed under Die Q, raising its height to that of the larger die, P. Further, shims of 50 mm are welded to the attachment edges of Die P so that the same clamping bolts can be used for both changeovers.

---

[9] Shigeo Shingo reports that it was his realisation at Toyota in 1969, when attempting, with the company's general manager, to reduce the four-hour changeover time of a 1,000-ton press, that IED could always be replaced by OED, that gave rise to SMED in its eventual form. After a period of six months, changeover of the press had been reduced to only 1½ hours. In the next three months, converting IED to OED, the time was reduced to three minutes. See Shigeo Shingo (1985), *A Revolution in Manufacturing: The SMED System*, English translation through The Productivity Press. This book is in two parts: Part 1 — Theory & Practice (130 pages), and Part 2 — Twelve Case Studies (230 pages). Of particular interest to the engineer, the book includes 235 technical sketches and 45 small plates. See also Taiichi Ohno (1988), op. cit.

Figure 15.1: Function Standardisation applied to Die Height

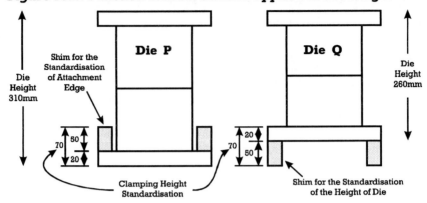

15.3.3 SMED Stage III: Streamlining IED and OED Operations

A great many techniques and tricks are available to the SMED team in this multi-step stage. Successive achieved reductions in time may naturally become progressively smaller as work proceeds. In particular, patience is called for when an improvement made turns out to be a dead-end and the team is forced to return to some previous position and start again.

Step 1: External Operations

Although the streamlining of external changeover activity does not directly contribute to achievement of the SMED goal, it should be performed nevertheless to eliminate the possibility of mistakes in the job overall. Examples of what might be done are the initiation of improvements in the storage and transportation of parts and tools, and the installation of carousels.

Step 2: Parallel Operations

Parallel operation means the employment of two or more operators on a changeover rather than one. This is liable to be especially effective where the changeover involves work at both the front and back of a machine or where the machine is large — the elimination of walking time invariably results in a substantial time reduction. The procedures to be followed in a parallel operation must be devised with great care. After they have been checked and agreed, they should be formally summarised in writing, perhaps in chart form but otherwise as standard shop floor worksheets. Other points of concern are: the need to avoid the unnecessary waiting of one operator on another; the crucial matters of safety and the avoidance of confusion; the establishment of communications between operators (buzzers and whistles are commonly used); and the acceptability of employing personnel from other work centres to assist in operations, usually justified since the time they are needed on secondment is so short.

Step 3: Functional Clamps

Two definitions are first necessary. A *clamp* is defined here as any device for attaching dies, fixtures and so forth to a machine. In SMED, it is said to be *functional* if the action needed to operate it is totally economic with regard to time, effort and power. An example of a functional clamp, or *one-turn attachment*, is illustrated in Figure 15.2 involving pear-shaped holes. Pear-shaped holes are commonly employed in SMED to eliminate the need to fasten large numbers of bolts. Thus instead of inserting and bolting down, say, 16 bolts, a lid is fitted with pear-shaped clamping holes. It is then lowered onto 16 bolt heads via the wide ends of the holes and turned so the bolts fasten within the narrow ends. The bolts themselves may in the event be turned once for additional security.

Figure 15.2: An Example of a Functional Clamp

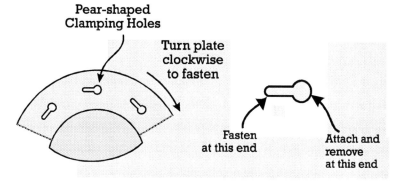

Step 4: The Elimination of Adjustments

Adjustments and subsequent test runs can account for 50 per cent of IED time. In SMED, the changeover team seeks not so much as to reduce this time, but to eliminate it. This is done by attempting to make sure that the initial setting of the machine (i.e. before the adjustments that might otherwise be found necessary) is in fact done correctly and precisely, first time. There are three principal approaches that the SMED engineer might try. Thus:

- **The Introduction of Calibration.** Intuition and "feel" as a method of setting machines must be comprehensively abandoned. Significant initial improvements, if not a complete dispensation of adjustments, will come about by the introduction of graduated scales. Visual adjustments should then be good to 0.5mm and to 0.1mm when using a dial gauge.

- **The Creation of Real Centre Lines and Real Reference Planes.** Before SMED, set-ups may need to be performed by trial-and-error because of the requirement to imagine centre lines and planes of reference. The following methods are available to eliminate this need: *the installation of reference scales within the machine; the installation of gauges; by making standard calibration marks; by the attachment of blocks and runners to help position tools;* and *by cutting grooves and slots for bedding down.*

- **The Combination of Different Set-up Functions in One Machine.** When a changeover to a different product is effected, the machine may need to be set up with the assistance of new tooling or fixtures. Thus, product X may require Fitting A to be installed in the machine for the set-up, product Y may require B to be installed and product Z may require Fitting C. In this third approach, all of the required fittings A, B and C are installed in the machine together. Other basic settings of the machine can consequently be left undisturbed as the operator changes over between A and B, B and C, or C and A when manufacture is switched between the three products X, Y and Z. The SMED slogan is *change only functions, leave mechanisms as they are*.

A further example is illustrated in Figure 15.3 involving the installation of V-blocks. Thus the changeover of a milling machine requires the cutter to be aligned with the centre of the workpiece. Two V-shaped blocks are now affixed to the cutting table and two further V-shaped blocks to the machine body. Cylindrical centring blocks then allow the machine cutter to be aligned immediately.

Just-in-Time 597

Figure 15.3: An Example of the Elimination of Set-up Adjustments

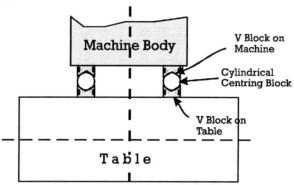

Step 5: Mechanisation

Mechanisation should normally be considered only when all other avenues of reduction have been explored; otherwise the team may find itself merely increasing the efficiency of an activity that, with deeper thought, could in fact be done away with altogether. An example of the too hasty initiation of mechanisation is the introduction of an air-driven nut runner to tighten nuts, instead of the installation of functional clamps to eliminate the necessity for extensive tightening. Further examples given by Shigeo Shingo in his text include: the use of revolving die holders; the mechanisation of die tightening and loosening; and rubber and air cushions for supporting dies.[10]

Application of SMED by changeover reduction teams has been astonishingly successful; the roll of honour, of western companies as well as Japanese, is a lengthy one. It is commonplace for a company after a short number of years of diligent effort to report reductions of times to 1/40th (2½ per cent) of their beginning durations.[11] (The jargon now is *OTED* — *one touch exchange of die* — changeovers in less than 100 seconds.)

---

[10] See Shigeo Shingo (1985), op. cit.

[11] In a postscript in his book (1985, op. cit.), Shigeo Shingo recounts with amusement the incredulity of an industrial journalist that the changeover time of a six-axis boring machine at Mitsubishi Heavy Industries had been reduced from 24 hours to 2 minutes 40 seconds. "I personally timed it with a stopwatch, so there is no mistake!" he replies.

Even with the admittedly simplistic examples in this Section, it can be seen that the subject matter is an intensely technical one, such that the engineering manager or shop floor operator might easily become captivated by it for its own sake. It is essential therefore that the manufacturing manager should continually direct the application of effort and should be continually at the forefront in applying the results. *Applying the results* means utilising the reducing times to enhance the company's responsiveness of manufacture, whether through the continued development of fully-fledged Just-in-Time as described in this chapter, or even simply through more effective operation of the conventional methods described elsewhere in the Book. This applies especially to Chapter 12 (APS), given the ability described there to reschedule work plans quickly and accurately online through the system. It would surely be the height of absurdity to reduce changeovers to three minutes while maintaining a three-week production freeze period.

15.4 PLANT ORGANISATION

15.4.1 Functionally Organised Plant

The organisation of equipment in the great majority of factories is according to its function, and it may truthfully be stated that so long as this state persists, the company seeking to implement Just-in-Time will not achieve its aims.

The *functional orientation of plant* will have arisen as the company grew and its product range expanded. In these circumstances, assigning a new machine to a location containing others of similar functionality will have seemed entirely rational — the new lathe to the lathe department (and lathe operators), the new drill to the drill department — unfortunately, after a time, the hidden cost and inefficiency incurred in supporting the arrangement becomes immense. Production jobs must travel long distances by roundabout routes in the process of their manufacture, giving rise to the waste of delay and the waste of substantial quantities of work-in-progress. The difficulty of scheduling the jobs, perhaps aggravated by poor shop floor control, gives rise to queues and yet further waste.

The functional orientation of equipment is illustrated in Figure 15.4 using four different geometrical shapes to denote four types

Just-in-Time

of equipment, each located in its own "department". Two imaginary product routes have been drawn to denote the paths of two particular jobs to manufacture products P10 and P11. On the left of the Figure, the potential of the plant to manufacture a further ten products is denoted by their product codes P12 to P21.

Figure 15.4: Functional Plant Layout and the Circuitous Routes of Two Jobs

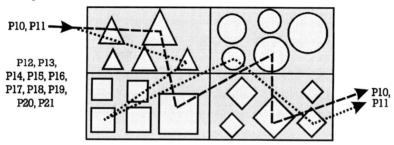

In order to eliminate the wastes of delay and work-in-progress and at the same time move towards a manufacturing environment capable of response to the pull of the market, the functionally oriented manufacturing plant must be radically reorganised. Reorganisation of manufacturing plant so as to create short routes and potentially permit the smooth flow of products all the way from the processing of raw materials to the final assembly of finished goods is the fateful step on the road to Just-in-Time, being at once the riskiest, the most costly and the most consequential in terms of enabling further progress to be made. If the company manufactures a relatively limited range of products, with shallow bills of material, a revised layout on "product flow" principles may not of itself be difficult to plan, although the planning of the individual activities that will bring the plan to fruition and the carrying out of the equipment moves and rebuilding work necessary are different matters. If the range of products made is broad and there are deep bills of materials, the reorganisation necessary is enormously more complex. It is normally accomplished by the creation of *manufacturing cells,* using the technique of *group technology.*

15.4.2 Group Technology: Introduction

In a nutshell, group technology comprises two steps carried out in parallel, or at least, carried out iteratively, as follows:

1. The assignment of manufactured products to families, or groups, the family members of a group having some commonality of manufacturing requirement (for example, having similar processing routes, being of similar size, shape, material — see 15.4.3);

2. The physical rearrangement of the plant so as to create a set of "mini processing lines", or *manufacturing cells*, each line being suitable for one, or perhaps two, family groups from Step 1.

The concept of group technology is illustrated very simply in Figure 15.5. In Figure 15.5, it is supposed that the twelve products P10 to P21 in Figure 15.4 have now been assigned to five family groups G1 to G5, as shown. (That is, G1 = P10, P12 and P16, and so on.) Further, it is supposed that the 20 units of plant in the four departments in Figure 15.4 have been rearranged physically to create the five mini-flowlines, or five cells, shown in Figure 15.5. In the new figure, each of the five families is seen to have been assigned to one or other of the five mini-flowlines, as indicated. All of the products in a family can be manufactured on the flowline to which it has been assigned.

Figure 15.5: Group-oriented Plant Layout (Family Groups and Flowlines Derived from Figure 15.4)

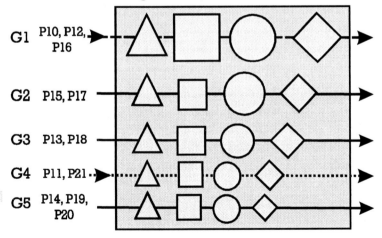

It can be seen with the new organisation that much of the waste associated with functionally oriented manufacture has potentially been eliminated. For example, products now travel short distances in their manufacture and their scheduling is perfectly straightforward. Delays, queues and work-in-progress will be very substantially reduced. Above all, so far as Just-in-Time is concerned, when the new arrangement is accompanied by short changeovers, the way is open to establish final assembly and fabrication patterns of production synchronised with market demand as described in sub-sections 15.2.1 and 15.2.2.

The layout of plant in the form of Figure 15.5 is said to be *group-oriented*. Group-oriented plant layout has at least in some measure the production advantages obtained when the plant has been built specifically for one particular product. The layout of plant built to accommodate a specific product is referred to in manufacturing as *product-oriented*. Examples of product-oriented plant are car assembly lines, petrol refineries and large-scale process plant scheduled by continuous simulation, such as for Ben's Home Brew described in Section 12.3. The efficiency of product-oriented manufacture, however, is obtained only with very large volumes of output. Group-oriented manufacture and manufacturing cells, by contrast, achieve somewhat comparable efficiency with small volumes. This is a major attraction of cell manufacture to the manufacturing manager, quite regardless of any Just-in-Time programme in hand.

15.4.3 Group Technology: Family and Cells

The creation of manufacturing cells on a limited basis to obtain the benefits of flow manufacture for products which are members of well-known and familiar product families has been a practice in engineering industry for many years. (Examples might have been a company's range of gearbox casings or range of grinding wheels.) What is different about group technology, however, apart from the underlying Just-in-Time objective, is the scale of application, and the requirement to form manufacturing families of products which are not obviously related and which indeed may be outwardly quite dissimilar. In group technology, two types of product family are recognised, Type A and Type B.

A *Family Type A* consists of products and components that are similar in shape, each member having all or most manufacturing operations in common. (The well-known and familiar product families in past years referred to above will all be Type A, of course, but there will be other Type A families not so well-known.) A *Family Type B* consists of products and components which are dissimilar in shape, but which nevertheless have one or more manufacturing operations in common.

The two most popular methods for determining manufacturing cell families and identifying their memberships are through a classification scheme and by material flow analysis.

The use of classification requires that each of the company's products should have been coded according to a scheme reflecting its design. *The Brisch System*, previously touched on in Section 3.5, is particularly well-suited to identifying families in group technology. The primary code, or monocode, permits the identification of products of similar shape (i.e. possible Type A family members), while the system's secondary codes, or polycodes, can be used to confirm Type A applicability and also identify potential members of the more numerous Type B families. Secondary code classifications are for distinguishing manufacturing commonality and include product length; diameter; L/D ratio; the grade and form of raw materials (e.g. bar, casting, forging, etc.); weight; the need for any special manufacturing service; and others.[12] Analysis of the codes by computer identifies potential families and their memberships, preparatory to final scrutiny by plant engineers and others thoroughly familiar with the products' manufacturing characteristics and local operating conditions.

Knowledge of local circumstances is even more important in the application of *material flow analysis*, the alternative method if products have not been coded in a way useful for group technology. One way of making a start is simply to sort through routing sheets, collating those indicating the same routes. This method is mentioned by the American Just-in-Time guru Richard Schonberger in his popular book.[13] Indeed, Richard Schonberger criticises

---

[12] Besides those in the text, a factor to be taken into account in formulating families and cells is the dependency of machine changeover times on the mix of products in the family. SMED and optimised sequencing (see Figure 12.8) will be less effective if family members have no commonality of set-up. This point applies equally, of course, to families identified through material flow analysis.

[13] Richard J. Schonberger (1986), *World Class Manufacturing*, The Free Press. For a text on Group Technology, see J.L. Burbridge (1975), *The Introduction of Group Technology*, Heinemann.

the classification/computer approach, and any consequent delay as products are coded, as an obstacle to JIT's development (*good intentions — but it set back progress several years*). A more comprehensive and more widely practised method of applying material flow analysis is to construct a product/machine matrix on the computer, and then constantly to reorder the matrix rows and columns until exclusive product clusters emerge. The products in each cluster are potentially likely to be assigned to the same cell.

Before confirming the identities of the machines that are to constitute each manufacturing cell, it is necessary to evaluate the workloads on the potential cell's capacity in manufacturing the output of each of the families to be made on it. If SMED has been accomplished and the company is poised to begin manufacture in response to the daily demands of the market, as described in Section 15.2, the load in minutes per day can readily be calculated as illustrated in Tables 15.2 and 15.3. If not, the production control manager and master production scheduler must determine workloads in the conventional way.

Figure 15.6(a) illustrates a possible manufacturing cell C1 comprising five machines M2, M3, M4, M5 and M7. The vertical dark bars in the Figure indicate the estimated potential loading on each machine to manufacture a Type A family group G10 that is to be assigned to the cell. (In practice, the position in Figure 15.6(a) might be reached by assigning several Type A families to C1, and evaluating the total load per machine required for all of them.) It can be seen from the Figure that the loads on M4 and M7 are uneconomic. One way of dealing with this problem is to remove from the family group G10 those products requiring the use of M4 and M7, and redefine the manufacturing cell as M2, M3 and M5.

However, Figure 15.6(b) illustrates a second possible manufacturing cell C2, comprising five machines M1, M3, M4, M6 and M7, and the loads on each machine to manufacture a Type B family G20 (denoted by the lightly shaded horizontal bars). Here, the utilisation of M3 and M7 is uneconomic. At first glance, it seems that the products in G20 requiring M3 and M7 will have to be eliminated from it to make cell C2 viable.

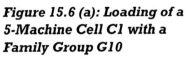

Figure 15.6 (a): Loading of a 5-Machine Cell C1 with a Family Group G10

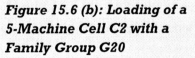

Figure 15.6 (b): Loading of a 5-Machine Cell C2 with a Family Group G20

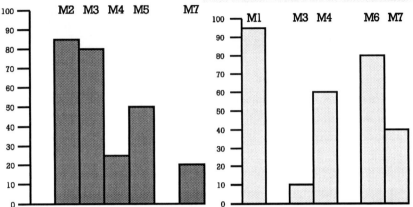

However, by combining C1 and C2 to form a potential new cell C3 with seven machines, M1 to M7, and evaluating the load of both family groups G10 and G20, the load is seen to be reasonably satisfactory, as illustrated in Figure 15.7 (the average occupation per machine is 78 per cent). Two of the machines, M5 and M7, in the proposed new cell are still under-occupied, however, so the planner will wish to examine remaining Type B families not yet assigned to cells to see which could be manufactured on one or other of them (or, with luck, both).

Figure 15.7: Loading of a New 7-Machine Cell C3 with Family Groups G10 and G20

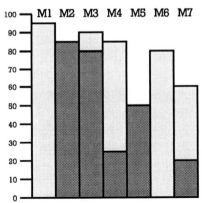

The juggling of products within families and families within manufacturing cells to formulate satisfactory, economical potential cell arrangements are clearly more complex activities than the simplified examples in Figures 15.6 and 15.7 show. The creation of cells containing 20 machines is not uncommon and cells of 30 are not unknown. Load balancing and the pursuit of efficiency, however, must be carefully watched to ensure that the cellular manufacturing goals of flow and simplicity are not compromised. Warning signs of a reversion to the inefficiency of functional layout are the emergence of products routes which are cell to cell, rather than entirely within a single cell.

One matter that is of the essence in the formulation of families and the creation of manufacturing cells is acceptance by the manufacturing manager of constant change. Neither of the methods for formulating families is perfect, and misjudgements are inevitable as well in the juggling process just described. In addition, calculations of loads will become out of date as sales patterns alter or changeover times continue to be reduced. The *status quo* must be constantly challenged; there must be a constant willingness to re-plan and rearrange.

A stumbling block frequently encountered by companies starting out on the group technology path is the presence on the shop floor of large items of exceptional equipment, the use of which is required by almost all products, or the presence of work areas which must be visited by almost all products but which simply cannot be differently set out, perhaps because of size or for environmental reasons (e.g. fumes).

The first point to be made may not be considered helpful by those already in this predicament, which is that the criteria for deciding on the purchase of equipment in the first place under Just-in-Time should include not only, as ever, cost and output quality, but also relative ease of use (required because of its need to be operated by multi-skilled workers in JIT U-shaped lines, as discussed in the next sub-section) and how well it fits into the cellular environment.[14] If it is a technically possible option, simple, single-

---

[14] The employment of cheaper, single-purpose machines mentioned in the text is also likely to fit in better with cellular duties undertaken by operators, especially as regards TPM (see sub-section 15.6.2).

purpose machines are to be preferred to a multi-purpose, sophisticated one. Financial calculations of the lower costs of a good cell arrangement, especially when taking account of the reductions in work-in-progress achieved and the revenue obtainable from the sale of the existing machine, may reveal that benefits more than outweigh the cost of changing to the simpler machines. However, if nothing can be done about the problem, it will be necessary to hold stock as illustrated in Figure 15.8, and make the best of a bad job by slick scheduling, perhaps through a kanban system (Section 15.5). Finally, it should also be remembered that if an item of equipment is dedicated to a cell, it is not available for the manufacture of products made elsewhere, outside the cell. The possibility of machine shortages arising in this way as machines are withdrawn from general use and incorporated within cells should be borne in mind in planning the implementation of the group technology programme.

Figure 15.8: The Need for Stock to support Exceptional Equipment in Cellular Manufacture

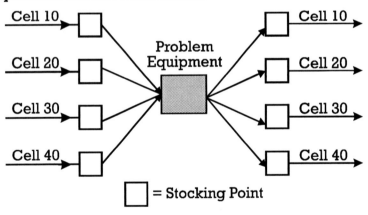

15.4.4 Group Technology: U-Shaped Lines

In the final step, changes are made that enable the company to realise the full potential of the new manufacturing environment. The changes constitute a major breakthrough in the pursuit of the twin objectives of Just-in-Time.

Quite simply, the machines in the new manufacturing cells are located close to each other, and they are arranged in U-shaped formation, as shown for M1 to M12 in Figure 15.9.

Just-in-Time 607

Figure 15.9: The JIT Manufacturing Cell, Showing the Proximity of Machines and Communication within the U

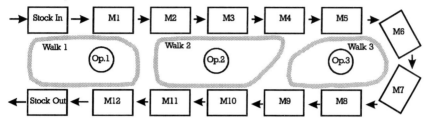

The proximity of the equipment at a stroke eliminates the need for containers, storage racks, fork lift trucks and other manifestations of latent waste, and the U-shaped lines permit the co-ordinated operation of machines in the cell by the shop floor workers assigned to it. In Figure 15.9, it is supposed that three operators have charge of the 12 machines and two stocking points. The area of responsibility of each operator (Op. 1, Op. 2 and Op. 3) is indicated by the thick grey lines marked Walk 1, Walk 2 and Walk 3. It can be seen that interaction and communication between the workers within the U could not be easier. Operators walk whichever routes are designated for the product being made, moving one piece at a time between tightly coupled work stations. Production appears to flow, with little stock in the U. The contrast with the scheduling of batches of work-in-progress from work centre to work centre inherent in functional organisation and described in Chapter 11 could hardly be more stark.[15]

As an aide to management and to effect good operator communications, use may be made of a so-called "andon board", a large electronic display panel suspended in the work area, updated on a continual basis with production progress in terms of parts produced and shift targets. Through a coloured light system, the andon is also

---

[15] To get over to shop floor staff the effect of reduced stock and tightly coupled machines, the image is sometimes employed of a convoy of lorries, each one separated by a distance of 500 yards, the lead vehicle travelling at 50 mph. The distances of 500 yards will not remain fixed; there will be constant telescoping. The 500 yards represents inventory, and if this distance is now reduced to 100 feet (still at 50mph), every driver must be on high alert. There will be a demand that all vehicles are in top condition (especially with regard to brakes and brake lights). There will also be pressure to develop signalling systems to communicate intended changes in speed or direction by the lead lorry. The use of homely analogies such as this is extensive in Just-in-Time, but some caution is necessary in translating Japanese lessons into western terms.

used to warn of impending problems, especially those relating to non-conforming quality and unevenness in production flows.

A further feature of the U-shaped manufacturing cell is the creation thereby of a "responsibility centre" of personnel. Cross training and the total absence of skill demarcation are prerequisites, of course. The cell leader and cell operators must work as a team, not only literally to achieve co-ordination of activity, but with regard to quality and continuous improvement as well. (Meetings may take place around a flipchart stand at the end of each shift – the "storyboard".) Richard Schonberger maintains that these aspects of cell manufacture are the most important prize of all. See Section 19.3.1.

15.5 KANBAN

A *kanban* is a card, or ticket, holding operational information.[16] The system of control based on kanban (plural) is a fundamental component of Just-in-Time and has two purposes. First, kanban govern the level of production at the JIT workstations, and the flow of materials between workstations in the U-shaped lines (and from suppliers). Secondly, the system is the means by which stock, little by little, is reduced within the whole manufacturing environment, thereby revealing instances of waste and presenting opportunities for its removal.

15.5.1 The Mechanics of Kanban

The mechanics of kanban are described using the terminology and symbols in Figure 15.10, which shows two machines, or workstations, in a manufacturing cell. The first (M1 — the *supplying*

---

[16] Billboards and banners, sandwich-boards and signs — all of these in Japanese are referred to as *kanban* (singular and plural), but the word was commandeered in 1953 by Toyota, in a mild attempt to cover up what they were doing, to mean what is described in Section 15.5. Toyota's kanban are, physically, cards about 3" × 5", contained in vinyl pouches, conveying brief operational information within the Company's manufacturing environment. The word has entered the English language with a somewhat broader sense — *a card or signal conveying information and indicating the need to take action within a Just-in-Time manufacturing system*. To avoid confusion and misunderstanding, the manager would surely be right to challenge the use of, or rather misuse of, the word in situations which are clearly nothing whatsoever to do with Just-in-Time manufacturing and which may even be diametrically contrary to JIT principles. There are a number of instructive kanban role playing games and models on the market. As might be expected, there are also sites on the Internet (www.promodel.com/aspire/kanban.html). The Japanese pronunciation of kanban is "con-bon".

workstation) manufactures pencil sharpener units, and the second (M2 — the *using* workstation) manufactures electric pencil sharpeners from the sharpener units. Also displayed in the Figure are symbols representing a completed sharpener unit, a cart for carrying either a part or a standard container of parts, a production kanban, a withdrawal kanban and a box for collecting kanban in the operation of the system. The scheme of manufacturing and the symbols in Figure 15.10 are carried forward to Figures 15.11 to 15.13 referred to later.

Figure 15.10: The Flow of Manufacture between Two Workstations, and Various Symbols Used in Figures 15.11 to 15.13

In its full implementation, there are in fact two types of kanban in the system, used for different purposes and holding different information: *production* kanban; and *withdrawal* (or conveyance, or transportation) kanban. Thus:

The Production Kanban

Production kanban are employed only at the supplying work centre. Each one specifies the serial number of the particular kanban concerned, and other identical data as follows:

- The number of production kanban issued to the workstation;
- The ID of the workstation;
- The name and code of the part or product made at the workstation;
- The number of parts in a standard container (if standard containers of parts are involved);
- The components involved in manufacture; and
- The location of the supplying workstation's outbound stocking point. (As the name says, the outbound stocking point is the place where finished parts, or standard containers of finished parts, are placed after manufacture.)

There is a simple but inviolable rule governing the production of a part, or of a standard container of parts, by the operator at the supplying workstation: *the work to manufacture a specific part or standard container of parts must be authorised by an associated production kanban (usually taken from the workstation's kanban box).* When the part or container has been made, it is placed at the workstation's outbound stocking point, and the kanban that was used to authorise production is attached to it.

Only a very small number of production kanban are held at the supplying workstation, and they are used and reused over and over again. Originally, say, at the beginning of a shift, the production kanban are introduced to the workstation by the production controller (he may deposit them in the kanban box for collection by the operator — see Figure 15.11). Thereafter, when the materials handler is withdrawing a part or standard container of parts from the outbound stocking point for transportation to the using workstation, in accordance with the procedure described below, he removes the production kanban attached to it and deposits it in the supplying workstation's kanban box for collection and reuse in due course. The operator at the supplying work centre then collects the kanban from his box, each one of which is authorisation to make another part or standard container. So in this way, the production kanban circulate within the work station, and manufacture there proceeds, synchronised with the steady withdrawal of parts as they are removed from its outbound stocking point.

Figure 15.11: The Use of Production Kanban to Control Production Flow at a Supplying Workstation

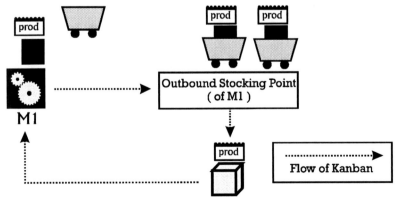

Just-in-Time

The operation of the system with respect to production at the supplying workstation and the circulation of the production kanban are illustrated by the schema in Figure 15.11, in which four kanban have been allocated to the workstation. The Figure shows one kanban at M1 (this being authorisation of the work shown as being in progress); one kanban with each of two finished parts, waiting in carrying carts at the outbound stocking point; and one kanban in the collection box.

The Withdrawal (or Conveyance) Kanban

The withdrawal kanban circulate between the supplying workstation and the using workstation. Each one specifies the serial number of that particular withdrawal kanban, and identical data, typically as follows:

- The number of withdrawal kanban issued to the supplying/ using workstation pair;

- The name and part number of the part supplied by the supplying workstation to the using workstation;

- The number of parts in a standard container (if one is used);

- The ID of the supplying workstation and the location of its outbound stocking point;

- The ID of the using workstation and the location of its inbound stocking point. (The inbound stocking point, as the name says, is the place where parts or standard containers of parts are placed when they are brought to the using work centre.)

The withdrawal kanban gives effect to the supreme rule of the kanban system: parts are never, never moved unilaterally from the supplying workstation to the using workstation. Instead, *a withdrawal kanban must be made available by the using workstation, and possession of this, and this alone, authorises the materials handler to collect a part or standard container of parts from the outbound stocking point of the supplying workstation and transport it to the inbound stocking point of the using workstation.*

It will be recalled that when the materials handler picks up a part from the outbound stocking point, he detaches its production kanban and leaves it behind in the supplying workstation's collection box. As he makes the part withdrawal, he has a second small but equally important system task to perform. He must now attach the withdrawal kanban in his possession to the part or standard container he is withdrawing, so that, as it is being transported, and when it is placed in the using workstation's inbound stocking point, it has attached to it the withdrawal kanban that was used as authorisation.

Only a very small number of withdrawal kanban are used in the system between a given using workstation and its supplying workstation, and they are used and reused over and over again. Originally, say at the beginning of a shift, the withdrawal kanban are introduced to the using workstation by the production controller (he may deposit them in the withdrawal kanban collection box located at the using workstation — see Figure 15.12). Thereafter, when the machine operator at the using workstation removes a part or standard container of parts from the inbound stocking point for use in actual manufacture there, he removes the withdrawal kanban attached to it and deposits it in the inbound kanban collection box. In due course, the kanban in this box are collected by the materials handler, and each constitutes authority to pick up another part/container from the outbound stocking point of the supplying workstation.

Figure 15.12: The Circulation and Role of the Withdrawal (or Conveyance) Kanban between the Supplying Workstation and the Using Workstation

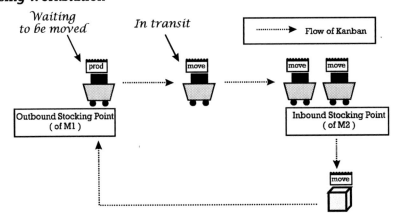

Just-in-Time

In this way, the withdrawal kanban circulate between the inbound stocking point of the using workstation and the outbound stocking point of the supplying workstation, and in this way also does the kanban system ensure that the flow of material into the workstation is evenly matched with that workstation's real requirements. (Taiichi Ohno observes that *Just-in-Time* is not the best expression — *Exactly-on-Time* would be more precise.)[17] Figure 15.12 illustrates the procedure described and the role of the withdrawal kanban. There are four kanban in the pictograph: one of them has been attached to a part now in transit and halfway from the outbound stocking point of M1 to the inbound stocking point of M2; there is one kanban with each of two sharpener units, waiting in carts in the inbound stocking point; and one in the kanban box ready for collection. (Note that the part waiting in the outbound stocking point of M1 has a production kanban attached to it, not a withdrawal kanban, since the materials handler has not yet come to remove it — compare Figure 15.11.)

It would be quite possible to join Figure 15.11 to Figure 15.12 and show the complete picture; indeed, with a very large illustration, it would be possible to sketch the many paths of all inter- and intra-workstation kanban links in a multi-step manufacturing cell.[18]

Two variations of the standard kanban control system are widely implemented for operational convenience.

The first is to drop the use of the production kanban if the quantity produced at the supplying workstation can be limited by the simple expedient of stacking completed parts in an area of controlled size. For example, instead of employing a production kanban in Figure 15.11, the operator at M1 pushes completed carrying carts into the outbound stocking point. The outbound stocking point has a maximum holding capacity of three carts: when it is

---

[17] Taiichi Ohno with Setsuo Mito (1988), *Just-in-Time for Today and Tomorrow* (English translation by Joseph Schmelzeis), Productivity Press.

[18] While the routes of kanban and parts can be illustrated and studied on the pages of a book, what is more difficult to appreciate are the literal dynamics of the system in action. The large number of related kanban throughout the manufacturing chain, controlling every work start, every material transfer and every supply delivery, are being attached, detached, deposited and picked up, all at an astonishing, dizzying pace and all in perfect synchronisation — *the invisible conveyor.*

full, he must refrain from further production; if there is space in the outbound stocking point, he may make a part; when the stocking point is empty or has in it only one cart, he knows further production is urgent. This simple system is referred to as *one-card kanban* and is illustrated in Figure 15.13. The Figure has been adapted from Figure 15.11 and shows that when the production in progress has been completed and the finished part has been transferred to the outbound stocking point, no further work can be done until a cart is removed to the using workstation by the materials controller. In a sense, an empty space at the outbound stocking point is itself the (purely visual) production kanban.

Figure 15.13: Substituting a Visual Signal for the Production Kanban (the One-Card Kanban System)

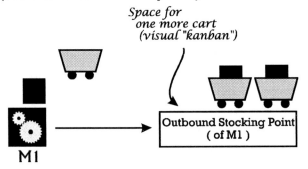

The second variation relates to external suppliers. When the external supplier delivers raw material stock to the inbound stocking point of the using company, he will, of course, have in his possession a withdrawal kanban (*withdrawal*, that is, from his company's outbound stocking point).[19] Strictly speaking, this withdrawal kanban should not be made available for re-use until the stock the supplier has delivered is removed from the inbound stocking point in the course of actual manufacture. It is an obvious convenience, however, of no threat to the integrity of the system, to remove and re-use the withdrawal kanban immediately the raw

---

[19] It may be clearer to refer to suppliers' kanban as *transportation* or simply *supplier* kanban rather than withdrawal kanban. Howsoever they are referred to, the important point is that a delivery is instigated by the conscious summons of the JIT-using company, responding to its own immediate needs, and is not "pushed on" by the supplier in accordance with a preformulated delivery schedule.

Just-in-Time

material stock is delivered to the inbound stocking point. The convenience is that the supplier's driver can take the re-issued authorising withdrawal/conveyance kanban back with him to his company as permission to make the next delivery.[20]

Other variations may be devised by a company to suit its special circumstances (Toyota have ten different types of kanban in all). But it is worth taking note of Ohno's warning: *Introducing kanban without actually practising the rules will bring neither the control expected of kanban nor the cost reduction. Thus a half-hearted introduction of kanban brings a hundred harms and not a single gain. Anyone who recognises the effectiveness of kanban as a production management tool for reducing costs must be determined to observe the rules and overcome all obstacles.*[21]

The rules Ohno refers to are the seven rules of the kanban system, and any implementation or variation should be most carefully assessed against each one. The rules are:

1. The using workstation retrieves from the supplying workstation the number of parts indicated on a withdrawal/conveyance kanban;

2. The supplying workstation manufactures parts in the quantity and sequence indicated by the authorising withdrawal kanban;

3. No parts are made or transported without a kanban;

4. Any container used must be standard for the part in question, always holding a standard number of them; non-standard containers must never be used;

5. A kanban must always be attached to the parts;

6. Parts which are non-conforming with regard to quality must be removed from the system at once; they must never be made available to a later process;

7. Reducing the number of kanban increases the sensitivity of the whole system.

---

[20] Richard T. Lubben (1988), *Just-in-Time Manufacturing*, McGraw-Hill. Part 3 of this book concerns JIT and Purchasing.

[21] Taiichi Ohno (1988), op. cit., p. 41. The somewhat dramatic statement quoted in the text is questioned by Setsuo Mito (1988), op. cit., p. 19.

At this point, it is impossible to continue to ignore the fact that purchasing managers throughout the Western world have instituted, in conjunction with their suppliers, stock replenishment methods which they insist on calling kanban systems. In brief, a company supplying a number of raw material items will call round at the purchasing company's premises (say, once per week) and check the stock levels of the supplied materials. A replenishment lot will be left behind of any material with stock lower than a certain "danger" level. The system is, of course, none other than the familiar *two-bin replenishment method*, used in his kitchen by every householder to control the supply of instant coffee. (When the jar becomes empty, the householder opens the spare, full jar of coffee standing in readiness and writes the item on his shopping list).

The purchasing manager's two-bin system of raw material replenishment is likely to be used to control the replenishment only of *Class C* items (i.e. the many items with a low annual value, as defined by Pareto analysis — see Figures 18.6(a) and 18.6(b).) His claim is that avoidance of the need to support a conventional information and ordering system for these products more than compensates for the raw material stockholding incurred, and presumably he has shown this to be true by detailed calculations involving the use of a stockholding cost as discussed in subsection 9.6.1. But it is not kanban. First, there is no means of reducing the level of stock in the system, the most important function of kanban, as we shall see below, not least because stock levels are simply not recorded or known in a two-bin system. Secondly, the golden rule of kanban is ignored. This is that it is the using workstation alone that *pulls* stock into itself, based on immediate need, and that the supplying workstation never unilaterally *pushes* it on. Two-bin replenishment may well be an economic procedure, but, by calling it kanban, the company may deceive itself. It may never discover how effective true kanban really can be if it is implemented according to the seven rules.

15.5.2 The Number of Kanban in the System

The second purpose of kanban is to enable stock to be reduced within the manufacturing environment in order to reveal instances of waste and opportunities for its removal. Stock is reduced by decreasing the number of kanban cards used within the system. As we shall see below, the number of kanban govern a trade-off between the level of stock and the level of production. Broadly speaking, when kanban are withdrawn, stock reduces, but so does the production rate; when cards are added, stock and the production rate increase.

To see the reason for this phenomenon, consider first a supplying/using workstation pair with only one kanban set (i.e. with only one production card and one withdrawal card). In such a case, the rate of delivery of parts to the inbound stocking point of the using workstation is constrained by the lowest of three rates. The first is the rate of manufacture of parts by the supplying workstation. Clearly, parts cannot be delivered any faster than they can be made. The second is the rate of use of parts by the using workstation. Withdrawal kanban cannot be released back into the system to begin a new cycle any faster than the parts are used. But the third is the rate of transportation of parts from the outbound stocking point to the inbound stocking point. This is so because, by the rules of kanban, a supplying workstation must wait until a withdrawal kanban is received back from the using workstation before the production kanban waiting at the outbound stocking point can be released, and this waiting time must include the transit time to the using workstation.

Consider next four situations:

- *Situation 1.* A supplying workstation with a rate of production of one part per hour; a using workstation with a rate of use of one part per hour; and a one-hour transportation time to the using workstation. One kanban set is all that is needed to maintain the *status quo*. That is, the availability of the withdrawal kanban is once per hour, since a part is needed by the using workstation once per hour immediately following its delivery to the inbound stocking point. When the part is withdrawn for use from the inbound stocking point, the withdrawal kanban that was attached to it is returned immediately to the outbound stocking point, releasing a further production kanban there.[22]

---

[22] If new production is initiated by a kanban at 10.00 am, the actual production that has just been completed was initiated by the kanban that had been returned at 9.00 am.

- *Situation 2.* Leading from Situation 1, there is a requirement to increase the production rate at the supplying workstation from one part per hour to four parts per hour (the workstation having this capability), matched by a requirement to use the parts at the rate of four per hour. However, the transportation time to the using workstation is one hour, and there is only one kanban set in the system. Now, although the production capability and the required rate of use are each four per hour, the actual rates are constrained to one per hour because the delivery of parts to the inbound stocking point is only once per hour, and withdrawal kanban are thus made available at the rate of only once per hour also.

- *Situation 3.* Leading from Situation 2, there is now a requirement to increase the production rate at the supplying workstation from one part per hour to four parts per hour (the workstation having this capability); and a requirement to use the parts at the rate of four per hour, both as in Situation 2. Again, the transportation time to the using workstation is one hour. However, we now introduce four withdrawal kanban into the system. Now, when a new part is produced by the supplying workstation (potentially every 15 minutes), instead of having to wait for one hour for the completion of the transportation of the part just made and the return of its card, up to three spare kanban are available and to hand in the kanban box, and one of them can be taken in order to authorise the newly produced part's immediate transportation and so initiate further production. That is, the four kanban in the system are each available at 15-minute intervals. Since the parts are used at the rate of four per hour, releasing the withdrawal kanban, the four kanban circulate over a one-hour cycle. However, although the production rate, the delivery rate of parts to the using work station's inbound stocking point and the rate of use of parts there are now all at four per hour, there is a constant procession of three parts at various stages *en route* to the work station, as well as the part just arrived there. Compared to Situation 2, therefore, the three parts in transit constitute an extra three units of stock.

- *Situation 4.* There is now a requirement that a supplying workstation should produce 120 parts per hour (the workstation having this capability), a requirement for use of the parts at 120 parts per hour and a lead time of transportation to the using workstation of 20 minutes. Again, if only one kanban set were available in the system, production and availability for use would be constrained to three parts per hour (one part per 20 minutes). However, since the desired rate of production is 1 part per 0.5 minutes, in order to keep the outbound workstation fed with withdrawal kanban at this rate, and so enable the system to achieve the desired rates of production, delivery and use, 20/0.5 withdrawal cards, or 40 cards, must be provided.

A general expression in words for the number of (withdrawal) kanban needed to enable the supplying workstation and using workstation to achieve their potential despite a lengthier transportation time is simply:

The number of kanban = the number of production units to be made during the transportation lead time.

From the Just-in-Time goal of achieving production synchronised with the pull of the market, the production rate at the supplying work station should be equal to the market demand rate. In calculating the number of kanban, therefore, the demand rate should be set either to a rate calculated as for Products A, B and C in subsection 15.2.1, or to a target rate reflecting the pattern of fabrication (15.2.2). Whatever rate is decided by the planner, it can be expressed as an hourly rate, say, $\bar{d}$ units per hour.[23] If the lead time is L hours, the number of kanban needed is $\bar{d} \times L$. However, it is common in calculating at least the initial number of kanban to add an additional fraction of $\bar{d}L$ as a buffer, here termed β, against short term variations in demand (i.e. increases), irregularities of supply receipts and the time required to respond to such deviations. Toyota suggest the maximum value of β should be 0.1. Taking account of this buffer, the number of kanban is now $\bar{d}L(1+\beta)$. Finally, parts in the system may be placed in carts, or containers. (A newly produced part consequently does not need an individual

---

[23] Ultimately, $\bar{d}$ is governed by the rate of removal of finished goods from the production cell literally in response to external demand, each end product that is thereby removed then releasing a kanban.

kanban provided there is space remaining in the container for it.) When containers are used, kanban cards relate to, and are attached to, containers, not individual parts. The final equation ("The Toyota Equation") is consequently given by Equation 15.1, where c is the capacity of the container for the parts in question.

$$\text{Number of kanban} = \frac{\bar{d} L (1+\beta)}{c} \qquad \text{Equation 15.1}$$

Thus if the demand rate is 160 parts/hour, with a lead time of 10 minutes and a 10 per cent buffer specified, the number of kanban required is given by Equation 15.2, assuming a container capacity of four and rounding up the result.

$$\text{Number of kanban} = \frac{160 \times \frac{10}{60} (1+0.1)}{4} = 8 \text{ kanban (rounded)}$$

$$\text{Equation 15.2}$$

But 8 kanban are merely the starting point, since they result in 32 units of stock in the system (i.e. 8 containers of 4 parts each). Over time, kanban are removed and the operational difficulties of working with the reduced stock and at the reduced production rate carefully observed. Action may be taken (say) to shorten the transportation time (i.e. to reduce L); to eliminate causes of variance in the demand rate $\bar{d}$; to permit a greater production time without the need for overtime by rescheduling plant maintenance; to increase available manufacturing time by further reducing changeover time; and to eliminate the receipt or production of non-conforming items. On this last point, it goes without saying that SPC should be practised in the manufacturing cell and by the external supplier because of Kanban Rule (6). Because of this rule, and Rule (3), if a non-conforming part is encountered, the whole of the manufacturing cell will come to a halt. In order to ensure the quality rule is followed, it is necessary that an effective means be provided to detect and remove at once any non-conformances that do arise or that do enter the system.

15.6 EQUIPMENT MAINTENANCE

A threat greater than non-conforming parts to the finely balanced flow of production through the Just-in-Time manufacturing system is the breakdown or malfunction of a machine. Action to prevent, or, at least, to minimise, equipment failure is long-established practice in traditional manufacturing, especially through the adoption of preventive maintenance. But the action taken in Just-in-Time is characteristically different. It includes the elimination of causes and the fostering of a team approach — in short, the adoption of *total productive maintenance, TPM*. Sub-section 15.6.1 outlines classic maintenance. Sub-section 15.6.2 describes TPM. The contrast in approach should be noted.

15.6.1 Classic Equipment Maintenance[24]

It would be absurd as well as unjust for the JIT protagonist to say that traditional manufacture is unconcerned with such aspects of equipment maintenance as the impact of the equipment's design on its maintainability or, say, with the installation of sensor equipment to detect impending machine failure.[25] Even so, the basis of the traditional approach is simply to determine, for a given piece of equipment, which of two policies, A or B, is to be adopted. *Policy A* is to undertake a programme of preventive maintenance to prevent breakdowns. (And since that programme could never be wholly

---

[24] The theory of maintenance management and repair has been developed over many years — for an introductory treatment, see Lawrence Mann (1983), *Maintenance Management*, The Free Press. An excellent short description is also given by Ray Wild (1980), *Production and Operations Management*, Holt, Rinehart and Winston, Chapter 20.

[25] A DTI Report issued as long ago as 1970 pointed out the cost to UK industry of ill thought-out equipment maintenance and the need for a comprehensive approach to the subject involving many disciplines — design, finance, the shop floor and so on. (Department of Industry (1970), *Report on Maintenance Engineering*, issued by HMSO, London. Also see Department of Industry (1975), *Terotechnology — An Introduction to the Management of Physical Resources*, HMSO.) The writers of the report coined the novel term *terotechnology* (from the Greek: *the art and science of caring for things*). Although the DTI's message to industry seemed to become lost, at least the word terotechnology did not, and lived on with the broad meaning now of the study and economic management of an asset's total life costs, including investment return, reliability, final disposal and so on, as well as best practice in maintenance such as through the five elements of TPM described in sub-section 15.6.2.

effective, to supplement it with a repair service.) *Policy B* is to undertake maintenance only as a result of a need to make a repair — i.e. on the occasion of a breakdown. If Policy A is decided on, a vital subsidiary task is to determine the most economic frequency of preventive maintenance to be performed. At each step in the decision-making process, the criterion used is strictly that of cost.

The notion of a trade-off between the cost of preventive maintenance and the cost of responding to breakdowns is often illustrated graphically. Thus Figure 15.14 shows the two costs and shows them to be "in opposition". That is, as the time between the carrying out of preventive maintenance rises (so that the overall cost of doing so falls), the incidence of breakdowns increases (so that the cost overall of response to breakdowns rises). The sum of the two is represented in the Figure by a third curve. Point P on this curve is the point of lowest total cost. That is, Point P defines the lowest combined cost of preventive maintenance and breakdowns (i.e. c on the vertical axis of the graph) and the time between performances of preventive maintenance needed to achieve it (t on the horizontal axis).

Figure 15.14: The Exchange of Costs of Preventive Maintenance and Responding to Breakdowns, and the Least Total Cost ("P")

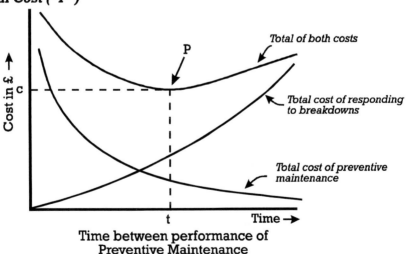

Figure 15.14 is similar to Figures 20.4 and 20.9 in so far that all of them are purely aids to conceptualisation. The curves drawn are

not derived from formulae, and the optimal points (here P) are not calculable. In this respect, they differ from the exchange curves and the EOQ in Figure 9.15, since these have been obtained from precise, readily stated mathematical relationships (Equations 9.2 and 9.4).

The key to choice between Policy A and Policy B is the predictability of breakdown in the machine in question. If the moment breakdown is to occur can be predicted with reasonable accuracy, preventive maintenance can be scheduled just before that time, so that Policy A is likely to be shown to be superior.[26] The propensity of a machine to break down must be ascertained from the diligent recording of historical data and their analysis. The pattern of breakdown may then be represented by a *breakdown time distribution graph*. Figure 15.15 illustrates two very different breakdown distribution curves, P and Q. Curves similar to Curve P apply if the length of time to breakdown — i.e. the machine's operating life — is normally distributed about a mean, so having the usual 3σ limits on either side of it. In the figure, the mean is at time p (100 hours) and the 3σ limits are at p_1 and p_2. The distribution comes about from the combination of very many components within the machine, each one (independently) having a random chance of failure. Curves similar to Curve Q by contrast indicate a high probability of breakdown immediately after maintenance or repair, the probability then constantly reducing. It can be shown that the distribution of this probability is exponential (see sub-section 3.4.2 and Figure 3.7). The pattern arises when the reliability of the machine depends on meticulous prior set-up of a number of closely interrelated components, so that the smallest error in one causes a chain reaction and consequent failure.

---

[26] The conclusion as to the superiority of Policy A in the text under the condition stated assumes that the cost to undertake preventive maintenance is less than the cost to effect a repair. If the cost to perform preventive maintenance is greater, clearly Policy B must be superior, even if the impending occurrence of a breakdown can be predicted exactly. As we see, such an argument is *purely* one of cost, as defined by manpower and time. What are more problematical in adopting Policy B are the effect of disruption to the manufacturing programme caused by the breakdowns and the possibility of deterioration in quality because of inadequate maintenance.

It should be noted at this point that in all these considerations, the assumption is made that a service or overhaul (i.e. the act of preventive maintenance) and a repair (due to a breakdown) have an equal effect on the resulting subsequent operating life of the machine. This assumption has an important practical consequence: it is valid only provided that, during the course of a repair due to a breakdown or similar incident, the engineer effecting it also carries out the activities associated with the machine's standard preventive maintenance, such as sharpening, cleaning, replacing or tightening.

Figure 15.15: Breakdown Time Graph Showing a Normal Breakdown Distribution (Curve P) and an Exponential Breakdown Distribution (Curve Q)

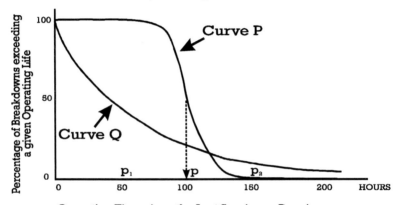

If the moment of breakdown is to be *predicted with reasonable accuracy*, the variability of the machine's operating life about the mean must be small (i.e. the time interval from p_1 to p_2 in Figure 15.15 must be small in relation to the mean of 100 hours). P.H. Morse[27] has shown that the more unpredictable the operating life of the machine — i.e. the larger the variance of its distribution — the more likely it is that Policy B will be superior. In addition, in a shop floor environment where very many machines may require repair at the same time, yet a further complication is likely to exist, namely that outstanding repair jobs will have to compete for the lim-

---

[27] P.H. Morse (1958), *Queues, Inventories and Maintenance*, John Wiley.

ited availability of maintenance engineering resources. Queuing theory must consequently be applied to find a best solution to the problem, and practical results for everyday use are likely to require the setting up of a simulation model and experimentation with: alternative values for the average cost and time to effect a repair; the costs and times set for carrying out preventive maintenance; the size of the maintenance crew; the number and percentage loading of machines; and the frequency of changeovers.

However, for the uncomplicated "single machine" case, credible results may be obtained merely from the use of a spreadsheet, allowing a choice to be made between Policy A and Policy B and giving a satisfactory value for the most economic duration of preventive maintenance for Policy A. The method requires that the costs of alternative courses of action should be iteratively compared, taking into account: (1) the probabilities of breakdown after various periods of operation; (2) the cost of carrying out preventive maintenance; and (3) the cost of carrying out a repair. The probabilities of breakdown are obtained directly from the collected historical data spoken of earlier; the use of mathematical formulae is therefore not required.

To illustrate the method, consider the normally distributed breakdown pattern represented in Figure 15.15 by Curve P. An alternative though less precise way of representing this pattern is by a histogram. The histogram corresponding to Curve P is given in Figure 15.16, with class intervals of 10 hours.

Figure 15.16: Histogram Corresponding to Curve P (Figure 15.15), Showing the Probabilities of a Breakdown after Time

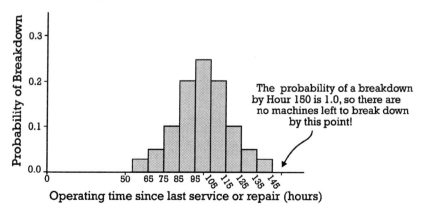

The probabilities relating to Figure 15.16 are given in Table 15.4 for the nine values of breakdown time (i.e. operating life). Note that the cumulative probabilities of breakdowns have also been given. Further note that the average time to breakdown in this case, or the *mean time to failure* (MTTF — see Equation 3.5), is obtained from the sum of the following values: the mid-point of each (ten-hour) class of "time to breakdown" multiplied by its probability. That is, (60.0 hrs x 0.025) + (70.0 hrs x 0.05) + (80.0 hrs x 0.10) + ... + (140.0 hrs x 0.0.025) = 100.0 hrs.

Table 15.4: Operating Life of a Machine (from Figure 15.16), and the Probability of Breakdown

Time (hours)	60	70	80	90	100	110	120	130	140
Probability	0.025	0.050	0.100	0.200	0.250	0.200	0.100	0.050	0.025
Cumulative Probability	0.025	0.075	0.175	0.375	0.625	0.825	0.925	0.975	1.00

Let us now suppose that the machine is working 250 days per year, 20 hours per day — that is, 5,000 hours per year. Let us further suppose that the cost of effecting a repair in the event of a breakdown is £210, and the cost of performing preventive maintenance is £70. Given the mean time to breakdown of 100 hours, the annual cost of Policy B (no maintenance) is consequently:

5,000/100 breakdowns per year × £210 = £10,500

We now evaluate the annual costs of adopting Policy A with nine alternative options of preventive maintenance frequency (i.e. 60 hrs, 70 hrs, etc.). An example calculation is given here for the maintenance interval of 90 hours:

Number of preventive maintenance visits p.a.	= 5,000/90
	= 55.5
Cost of preventive maintenance (55.5 × £70)	= £3,885
Probability of breakdown before next maintenance visit	= 0.375
Number of breakdown repairs per year	= 55.5 × 0.375
	= 20.8
Cost of repairs per year (20.8 × £210)	= £4,368
Total Cost of Policy A	= £8,253

Just-in-Time 627

The cost of Policy B and the nine options for Policy A are given in Table 15.5. (Also given is the cost of undertaking preventive maintenance at intervals of 50 hours — i.e. before there is any probability as indicated by the statistics that a breakdown will occur.) We see from the table that the best course of action is to adopt Policy A with preventive maintenance intervals of 70 hours.

Table 15.5: A Comparison of the Annual Costs of Alternative Machine Maintenance Strategies Relating to Figure 15.16

Policy	Preventive Maintenance Interval — hours	Total Annual Cost £
B	n/a	10,500
A	50	7,000
A	60	6,270
A	70	6,127
A	80	6,672
A	90	8,253
A	100	10,062
A	110	10,426
A	120	11,056
A	130	10,567
A	140	9,999

15.6.2 Total Productive Maintenance

It would be equally unjust for the JIT sceptic to claim that TPM comprises merely the traditional maintenance activities repackaged in a bright new form. To be sure, a bare recitation of the *technical* subject matter of both traditional plant maintenance and total productive maintenance shows almost complete commonality, and it would be surprising if it did not. But what marks out TPM is the requirement that machine maintenance should be elevated to high status within the company, that all those with responsibility for any facet of it should regard themselves as members of a team and that team members and senior management should have the highest commitment to achieving the very best results. Total productive maintenance presents a convenient and comprehensive vehicle whereby achievement of the high standards of machine reliability and product quality demanded by Just-in-Time and kanban can be attained. Training must inevitably lead the way if team working and co-operation are to become a reality and commitment is to be gained. The training given must be off-the-job, properly structured and professionally delivered, and should be given to engineers and production management, not simply to shop floor personnel. That said, it is widely agreed that the success or failure of a corporate TPM initiative will depend largely on its acceptance by shop floor workers, and the bulk of the training effort is likely to be in that direction. It must be explained to the operator who has hitherto believed maintenance to be the responsibility of the engineer that he himself must accept his share of it, so that, besides the desirability that he should regard the subject with positive enthusiasm rather than as a tiresome necessity, he will need to acquire many new technical skills. TPM involves a significant shift of work to the shop floor from maintenance engineering; it is said that 75 per cent of maintenance problems can be obviated or solved by shop floor personnel at a cost of some 3 per cent of their time.[28]

Changes in attitude towards maintenance and understanding of the reason for the team approach and the need for interdepartmental co-operation will come about only when all staff involved appreciate how the components of the subject fit together and appreciate also the contribution they themselves can make to it. To assist in the learning process — and the change process — it is normal to divide total productive maintenance into five categories, drawing attention to the links and relationships between them. The five are given as follows, along with comments of varying lengths.

---

[28] These and other figures relating to TPM financial savings are quoted with attributions by the Steinbachers in their book (Herbert R. Steinbacher and Norma L. Steinbacher (1993), *TPM for America: What it is and why you need it*, Productivity Press, p. 42). Note that the standard introductory work on TPM, translated from the Japanese, is by Seiichi Nakajima (1988), *Introduction to TPM: Total Productive Maintenance*, Productivity Press. There are now many titles available in TPM: see, for example, the many books on the subject by Terry Wireman.

Maintenance Prevention

Maintenance prevention is that aspect of TPM related to how easily the design of the equipment lends itself to maintenance — in a word, the machine's maintainability. If the machine is to be built to the company's own design, the engineer must listen carefully to operators and maintenance engineering staff before his work begins. If, more normally, it is to be purchased by an engineering team, a representative of operations and a representative of maintenance engineering section must give their verdicts on ease of maintenance and on the clarity of instructions and drawings before the decision to buy. A mistake at this stage is permanent.

Predictive Maintenance

The principal means of obtaining warning of possible impending machine failure is through SPC. For example, Figure 14.9 shows how tool wear can be tracked via a variables control chart. The theory of runs and the use of 2σ control limits described in sub-section 14.2.2 may also alert the operator to possible trouble ahead and warn him of the need to take action. Breakdown time distribution data, referred to in sub-section 15.6.1, can contribute by identifying the danger time and so the time for maximum vigilance. As well, data may be collected over a long period of time relating, say, to the numbers and types of machine adjustments made and machine parts replaced. Maintenance software systems are available to organise and analyse such data to help detect trends and predict potential problems. (Maintenance software systems are also useful in other areas of TPM — for example, in preventive maintenance (what parts are to be serviced) and in corrective maintenance.)

Predictive maintenance also includes the use of technical devices for monitoring machine condition as manufacture proceeds. Although there are a great many ways of carrying this out, common methods are through the following:

- *Vibration analysis*: the detection of wear on shafts and bearings, etc;
- *Lubrication analysis*: the analysis by spectrography and microscopy of the machine's lubricant during production,

keeping watch for signs of oxidation or contamination by metal, these indicating hot spots or partial component failure and the need to stop and take action;

- *Temperature measurement*: a commonly used method to warn of overloads, to identify the location of possible trouble and to determine the need for replacements;

- *Other technical methods:* surface texture and form measurement; tension and clamping force testing; eddy current testing; tachometry and stroboscopy; stress analysis; and many more. Although a simple start can be made in applying technical predictive maintenance, perhaps with a single machine, success will rapidly demand greater capability and sophistication, and commensurate operator training.[29]

Corrective Maintenance

Not every problem can be anticipated or forestalled by maintenance prevention or predictive maintenance. Corrective maintenance is concerned with carrying out investigations into past trouble and malfunctions with a view to changing procedures in operation or making equipment modifications. Methods for identifying and eliminating "special causes", described in sub-section 13.2.4, include the use of the Ishikawa diagram, the circle of continuous improvement (PDCA) and the setting up of Quality Improvement teams. The carrying out or not of corrective maintenance is a test of the company's commitment to TPM: to undertake it conscientiously and with perseverance requires true commitment to the ideals of the new regime.

One might also add to corrective maintenance as defined above the need for actual repairs to get machines back and running after a breakdown, often referred to as *breakdown maintenance*. To assist in repairs, diagnostic machinery may be installed to determine the

---

[29] Despite the association of the predictive methods given in the text with engineering, TPM is quite applicable to the process industries. Indeed, given the nature of process industry manufacture and the issues there of safety and stability, many would assert that the case for its adoption is even more compelling. See Tokutaro Suzuki (1994), *TPM in Process Industries*, Gulf Publishing Company.

seat of the trouble. The potential need to carry out repairs should be taken into account in shop floor layout and in the stocking of replacement parts in the engineering store (see sub-section 3.4.3).

Preventive Maintenance

Preventive maintenance is accepted intuitively as an obvious and inexpensive way of maintaining a machine in good condition. Thus in his private life, every citizen sees to it that his car is regularly subject to: (1) service — oil top-ups, tyre pressure adjustment and the cleaning of ignition plugs; and (2) inspection, with a view to replacement — tyre tread, battery condition and the wear on brake linings.

The centrality of preventive maintenance in total productive maintenance is similarly intuitive, the determination of what is to be serviced and inspected, and the periodicity of doing so, being made as part of predictive maintenance. Two problems in its conduct in a non-TPM environment may be a lackadaisical attitude in carrying it out by those responsible, whether engineer or operator, and a considerable reluctance of production staff to surrender the machine so that the work can be performed. The challenge to the champion of the TPM project is to change any such negative attitudes to positive ones — to keenness of performance and to co-operation in planning the necessary time slots. His triumph and the triumph of TPM is to succeed in doing so.

Autonomous Maintenance

In those companies that have embraced TPM, autonomous maintenance — maintenance by operating staff themselves — is held to be the mainstay of the subject. Shop floor workers have a unique knowledge of their machines and are the vanguard in the drive to achieve the system's aims. To make it reality, managers must be willing to give operators the freedom to make their own decisions about machine performance and adjustments, and must provide the training necessary to enable them to do so. On the opposite side, operators must be willing to accept the responsibility offered and to take on the challenges it brings. In the Just-in-Time environment, the responsibility of the shop floor operator with regard to autonomous maintenance ranks equally with his responsibility in kanban to stop production within the manufacturing cell because of non-conformance in product quality, and his responsibility to effect fast machine changeovers under SMED.

Even without its requirement as support for Just-in-Time, a very substantial cost case can be made to senior management justifying the adoption of TPM in its own right. And it is only senior management, again, by its attitude as much as by its provision of resources, that can bring about the transformation in company culture needed to make it successful.

It is, finally, misleading to say the implementation of total productive maintenance will take, say, three years, or indeed any number of years. The culture of TPM is one of continuous improvement — "implementation" is never finished.

15.7 WORKPLACE MANAGEMENT

Besides the responsibilities for autonomous maintenance, kanban and SMED above, there are many other activities in Just-in-Time requiring immediacy of action and which must be placed entirely in the hands of machine operators and supervisors. Three further examples previously described in the chapter are: the calculation of production rates and cycle times, and their amendment to take account of latest sales; the need to complete variables and attribute control charts as part of SPC; and the co-ordination of operations within manufacturing cells. All of these lend further weight to the need to give operators and supervisors freedom and responsibility and to provide them with training.

The smooth, correct carrying out of the activities in Just-in-Time, or rather, the very damaging consequences to the operation of the system of disruption and mistakes, go to show just how finely balanced its mechanisms are. The price of JIT is constant vigilance, so that while it is true that the manufacturing manager cannot take the hour-to-hour decisions mentioned, neither can he relinquish responsibility for their good management. Thus, when shop operators and supervisors take the action they do, in the course of so doing they complete charts and forms which are then available for ready reference at their work stations, along with standard worksheets and other data. In the manager's management of the workplace, these charts, forms and worksheets provide instant, visual evidence of the state of production and may provide clues leading to improvements that might be made to the system.

There are other matters of workplace management as well, mentioned in this chapter, which require the manager's thought and attention, these being beyond the remit of shop floor staff. Consideration must be given to revisions of plant layout; to the potential withdrawal of further cards from the kanban system and the seizing of other opportunities to eliminate waste; and to the possibility (perhaps suggested by the observed operation of the U-shaped lines) of acquiring new machines or installing automation.

The company could not get very far down the Just-in-Time path unless manufacturing management had an intense interest in the workplace. There is too much production novelty and too much emphasis on shop floor activity in JIT to make a strong commitment to the production workplace anything other than a natural and essential requirement. Management of the workplace through the inspection of visual controls and by keen personal observation has been termed *management by wandering around* (MBWA). It must be conducted purposefully — the shop floor is a rich source of ideas — there are always problems to be solved and initiatives that might be taken. The implementation of Just-in-Time is never finished.

Taiichi Ohno makes it very clear that commitment to workplace management from the very top of the company downwards has been a quite essential element in Toyota's success.[30] But he goes on to ask *what is the workplace?* Perhaps the manufacturing manager has other, subsidiary workplaces he would do well to visit — the sales office, his customers' factories and those of his major suppliers. Tom Peters and Nancy Austin, in their well-known management book *A Passion for Excellence*, remark on the number of "obvious" opportunities for immediate improvements that can be spotted when the manufacturer wanders around, especially in the marketplace. But they surmise that since so few of them are ever grasped, perhaps the obvious is not so obvious after all.[31]

---

[30] Taiichi Ohno with Setsuo Mito (1988), *Just-in-Time for Today and Tomorrow* (op. cit.), Chapter 3.

[31] Tom Peters and Nancy Austin (1985), *A Passion for Excellence*, HarperCollins. Available in paperback and a million-copy bestseller.

Chapter 16

Purchasing

The first tasks of purchasing in the manufacturing concern are to identify and select suppliers in the supply marketplace and secure their commitment to provide goods and services in accordance with the company's needs. (The company's needs in the immediate term are the materials required in first-stage manufacture ultimately to fulfil its master plan.) Next, there is a requirement to collaborate from time to time with technical budget holders in jointly identifying suppliers, the purchasing department then assuming final responsibility for the drawing up of contractual agreements in accordance with company policy. In all cases, purchasing must set up and operate channels of communication with nominated suppliers for the placement of orders. Subsidiary tasks include the encouraging of supplier development, especially in the areas of product quality and value analysis (sub-section 16.1.3); keeping watch on the supply marketplace for new opportunities or threats to existing supplies; and providing advice on the supply marketplace to others in the firm seeking to improve existing products or develop new ones. Lastly, purchasing must bring to bear considerable commercial judgement in the negotiation of agreements and in committing the company to legal and financial obligations.

16.1 SUPPLIERS

16.1.1 Sourcing

Sourcing is the term used to denote the process of finding suppliers of goods and services specifically required by the company.

As part of purchasing research, it can also mean finding suppliers of goods and services which may one day be useful or which may point the way to new avenues of product development.

If it is appropriate that the purchasing department is to have sole responsibility for identifying and selecting the supplier of a product or service required by the company, as normally it will be, sources available for investigation include the following:

a. *The Internet.* Use of the Internet in national and global searching and sourcing via standard search engines, as opposed to its use in order placement and e-commerce;

b. *Catalogues, including those by merchant distributors.* Note that most catalogues — and all directories, as below — are available on CD, making cross-indexed searches easier and faster;

c. *Trade journals and magazines;*

d. *Trade directories.* An example is *Kompass*,[1] a two-volume, 4,000-page book with a product classification system, a list of suppliers by classification and a compendium of corresponding suppliers. Also available are Dun and Bradstreet's *Key British Enterprises*; Kelly's; Rylands; and *The Buyer's Guide*;

e. *Yellow Pages and Industrial Yellow Pages.* These references, like many others, are available on the Internet;

f. *Sales representatives.* It will be recalled from Table 2.4, subsection 2.3.1, that personal selling is the most prevalent means by which industrial goods are sold;

g. *Exhibitions*;

h. *Foreign sources.* Apart once more from the ubiquitous Internet, there are a number of popular English-language directories of foreign sources, including, again, Kompass (1.25 million companies in 60 countries); Jaeger and Waldman; and *Wer Liefert Was?* (English edition). Other foreign sources include the

---

[1] *Kompass*, published by Reed Business Information at www.reedbusiness.com. Besides the two basic volumes mentioned in the text, there are three further volumes of company financial data, subsidiary companies and industrial trade names. All five volumes are available on one CD. There are 60 foreign versions of *Kompass*. *Kompass* is available on the Internet at www.kompass.com.

commercial attachés of foreign embassies; the London Chamber of Commerce; and the UK Trade and Navigation Accounts of UK imports.

If the material to be sourced has significant or special technical characteristics, sourcing may be carried out by the user, probably confining himself to sources (a), (c), (f) and (g). It is normally laid down, however, that a user is not to open direct technical discussions with a potential supplier without first informing the purchasing department, so that what is then embarked upon amounts to a joint purchasing venture. It is an inviolable rule, never challenged, that purchasing have sole authority for the placing of orders and the signing of contracts. Consequently, even though the user's discussions are "technical", the greatest circumspection must be exercised by him to avoid compromising the company's position in final negotiation.

In advising the technical user, or before beginning the sourcing investigation on his own account, the purchasing manager must thoroughly appraise the strategic position of the product to be bought; any special demands relating to quality; and its prominence of place in the manufacturing programme from the logistics viewpoint. For example, materials obtainable from only a small number of sources and of such central importance to production that an interruption to supply after deliveries commence would threaten the very survival of the firm will be classed as "strategic" — perhaps metals and ores; crops; and technically complex assemblies. The reliability of the supplier and the near certainty of continuity of supply will be uppermost in mind in the sourcing and selection processes, and in negotiation. Again, if very high levels of quality conformance are required, the purchaser may wish to investigate only those potential suppliers with well-established SPC programmes. And if the material to be bought is widely used in a possibly volatile manufacturing schedule, the initial scrutiny of potential sources may concentrate on those within a few hours' drive of the company and exclude those overseas.

The consideration of potential sources may be further constrained by the adoption by the company (or by the purchasing manager) of one or more so-called *source policies*, rules of good practice held by the company to be universally relevant to its purchasing operation. For example, a company manufacturing technologically advanced products may wish always to purchase components from large suppliers with substantial research and development programmes, so as to obtain the benefit of a stream of improvements.[2]

The dominant policy issue, however, is whether the company is to buy a particular mainstream raw material from one supplier only or from two (or more) alternative suppliers — i.e. the issue of sole supply or dual/multiple supply.

The arguments in favour of sole supply embrace price, quality and logistics. They include price because, by placing all business with one supplier, it is anticipated that he will accept a lower price for the goods in exchange for the higher volume sold. There are very strong arguments for a single supplier from the quality viewpoint. With a single supplier, the inspection/correction breakeven point of the incoming material (the BEP, Equation 14.58) can readily be established and monitored, whereas with two suppliers, at least if materials are mixed, the fraction of parts non-conforming will appear erratic, casting doubt on the validity of standard acceptance procedures. It is pointed out by W. Edwards Deming that the quality arguments in favour of a single supplier apply even if the alternative is two suppliers both capable of sending conforming material (*both good, but unequal*).[3] Finally, the logistical argument in favour of sole supply turns on the desirability and possibility with computer-generated raw materials plans to communicate new requirements to suppliers' factories electronically, directly through the planning system. The time required to implement and refine the necessary technical arrangements is consid-

---

[2] A source policy that may be forced on the purchasing manager in a company within a large conglomerate is that of *reciprocity* — a directive that he must buy materials where possible from other companies within the overall corporate group, regardless of his own preference, perhaps buying at a price determined by business and cost accountants at corporate headquarters. It is a policy that generally leads to inefficiency in the companies that are thus sustained by their captive customers.

[3] See Mary Walton (1986), *The Deming Management Method*, Mercury Books and Management Books 2000 Ltd. The advantage of a single supplier from the quality viewpoint applies only if goods are manufactured at, and despatched from, a single point. One company sending in goods made in two locations is very little better than two separate suppliers.

erable, and, given a preference, effort and expense seem best channelled in one direction, not two.

The topics of quality and logistics re-emerge in sub-section 16.1.3 under *supplier partnerships*, but the arguments are not all one way. The overriding merit of having two or more alternative suppliers is that of insurance. If an industrial or natural calamity strikes one, the company has an alternative to fall back on. And two suppliers keep the marketplace competitive, even if all that means is that one can be played against the other in angling for advantage in contract negotiation.

16.1.2 Supplier Appraisal and Selection

Time and common sense dictate that a full appraisal of a potential supplier should be made only where important services and materials are concerned. That is, the 80:20 rule must be applied. The appraisal process itself comprises two-stages: desk research and field research.

To conduct desk research, the supplier under investigation must be contacted and requests made of him for literature and company details, including his profit-and-loss account and balance sheet. Twenty minutes' scrutiny of these two documents by the purchaser's colleague in the accounts department will reveal a great deal more about the company than simply the bare financial facts (not that these are unimportant). Various ratios and trends in the figures can reveal something of how well the company is managed: inventory control, investment, operating costs, etc. All suppliers will make promises; a company that is not well managed may be one that cannot keep them.

Field research means making at least one visit to the supplier's place of manufacture, the purchasing manager accompanied as necessary by colleagues representing the production, quality and perhaps engineering functions. The fact-finding targets must be discussed beforehand: the supplier's plant and machines; his planning and control systems; TQC and SQC; technical expertise; shop floor practice and conditions; service and support. Following the visit, facts and opinions must be carefully recorded, perhaps on a standard visit form.

If one supplier only is to be selected from a qualifying shortlist of several, a formal means may be adopted in order to make the choice. One such, mentioned as a possible method in choosing a conceptual design (sub-section 3.2.2), is the *weights and marks* method. In the context of supplier selection, the various attributes and characteristics of an ideal supplier of the particular product to be purchased are set down as a list and a weighting from 1 (very unimportant) to 10 (supremely important) is assigned to each one. The weightings to be applied are voted on by the selection team. Each contending supplier is then marked out of 10 by the team from the viewpoint of how well he measures up as regards each individual attribute. Weights are multiplied by marks and the results totalled to obtain a score for each company.[4]

When the selection has been made, in a number of cases it will be sufficient to inform the supplier by letter and place orders in the conventional way as described in Section 16.2. In the more important instances, or if there are outstanding points to be resolved, or if the likely expenditure on the material to be bought is considerable, the supplier will be approached so as to arrive at a tailor-made agreement as to terms of supply and price. A discussion between supplier and purchaser for this purpose, and over which each has the power of veto, is, of course, a traditional *negotiation*. Negotiation is a skill requiring, for success, training and thoroughness in preparation and cynicism and resolution in conduct.[5]

The outcome is an agreement covering all the issues of technical specification, product performance, price, service, support and the rest. If the agreement is sufficiently different from the purchasing company's standard terms and conditions, as normally it will be, it will be set out in a formal document to be signed by both parties. It should be noted in passing that such a document takes precedence over anything that was said at the negotiation meeting

---

[4] It is common practice in many purchasing departments to place suppliers after evaluation on an ABCD list (A = approved; B = second choice; C = emergency only; D = avoid). While it is prudent to retain the original evaluation paperwork, as a starting point for any later re-evaluation of the losers, such lists rapidly lose their currency.

[5] Gavin Kennedy (1997), *Everything is Negotiable*, Third edition, Arrow Business Books. The negotiation that precedes the formation of a supplier partnership deal is no less hard-fought than the normal variety. Partnership negotiations, however, are likely to be more concerned with the potential *modus agendi* of the partnership rather than with isolated issues. They are also typically more protracted — many days, spread over many weeks or months.

itself. If points agreed at the meeting are omitted in the written agreement, they are lost. If what is written is not what was said, or not quite what was said, it is the document that prevails.

16.1.3 Supplier Partnership Agreements

The notion that close supply partnership agreements should replace the so-called arm's length supplier–purchaser relationships said to be traditional in UK and western industry undoubtedly has as its background Just-in-Time. To use Taiichi Ohno's expression, the *co-operating companies* are required under JIT to deliver 100 per cent conforming material on a daily basis under the kanban system, and to aim constantly to improve products through value analysis. These then are the three elements of a partnership agreement, western-style: quality, logistics and improvement. In exchange for their adoption, the supplier will receive, typically, sole rights of supply and a long-term guarantee of business (say, two years, renewable).

Partnerships and Quality

The supplier must adopt SPC and show that his process is capable of meeting the purchaser's specification by the submission of variables data, as described in sub-section 14.2.3. A handy way of recording process capability is through the capability index, as given in Equation 14.40. As part of a partnership agreement, the purchaser may award what have been termed *supplier accreditation certificates* for each supplier-process/purchased-material pair, and will require the regular submission of data as verification that the process remains capable and under control.

Partnerships and Logistics

Five actions are involved, to be taken in the order given below. Note that the logistics requirement of a supply partnership does not mean simply that the supplier is to deliver on time, which is surely an achievement one might expect of any competent company, but that he is to deliver on time to a schedule liable to variation as the purchasing company's requirements change because of the recalculation of its plans. Consequently, until the first of the five actions has been accomplished, all others are fanciful.

- **Action 1: Own Production Control.** A formal planning system must be installed within the company, based on the creation and ongoing management of a master production schedule, and the system so installed must be operating satisfactorily. Included in it, of course, is the generation of raw material requirements, each requirement specified by quantity and date. Since the master schedule is liable to change, raw material plan changes are likely also, although the effect of them on suppliers may be minimised by the use of the period order quantity rule, as described in sub-section 9.6.2.

- **Action 2: Own Internal Communication.** A close working relationship must be established between purchasing, production control and manufacturing, typically overseen by the company's master production scheduler. To effect this step in many companies, a number of buyers have been transferred from the purchasing department to the production control department to manage the schedule of incoming raw materials.

- **Action 3: Supplier Base Reduction.** There are three reasons for reducing the number of suppliers with whom the company does business. The first is that it simply is not possible to sustain the workload of operating partnership arrangements with too many suppliers, especially in the quality improvement sphere. The second is to reduce the number of technical links that must be established in order to communicate raw material plan requirements and plan changes. The third is to secure lower prices in exchange for larger, consolidated orders. A number of schemes have been suggested for reducing the number of suppliers. One popular method is to set up an initially empty register, and transfer existing suppliers to it, but (1) weeding out those that are rarely used, and (2) consolidating further business with those companies able to satisfy a wider range of materials, at the expense of individual, small suppliers. (Larger companies, especially those with semi-autonomous operating divisions, have made very effective use of software to recognise supplier duplication, such as Aspect Development's *Component and Supplier Management* (CSM) system.) Note that a danger exists in reducing the number of suppliers that valuable refinements of choice made by discriminating buyers over many years will be swept away. Clearly, for frequently used production material, the issue of sole supply must be faced at this point.

- **Action 4: Supplier Scheduling**. As described in Chapter 9, raw material requirements are liable to change whenever the master schedule or shop schedule is changed. Although in Just-in-Time, immediate response is required of the supplier to an amendment to requirements, in scheduled materials planning, it is common to negotiate *zones of change* with suppliers, perhaps as follows: a *Freeze Period* (say, one week ahead) — this means what it says: the purchasing company will make no alteration to requirements of the supplier over the coming week; a *Semi-Freeze Period* (from the end of the freeze period to two weeks ahead) — changes may be required, but the purchaser will pay any extraordinary costs incurred in making them, such as the additional cost involved in the payment of overtime rates; an *Unfrozen Period* (week three through to the planning horizon) — all changes must be accepted by the supplier.[6]

- **Action 5: Technical Communication**. Ideally, the communication to be involved should be between the purchaser's materials planning system, creating and amending raw material requirements, and the supplier's distribution and production system, revising planned despatches to the purchaser. That is, communication should be system-to-system, the means of transferring the data being by EDI. EDI is *electronic data interchange*, and refers to data sent by transmitter or data cable via a *value-added network*, or VAN.[7] The VAN can be regarded as

---

[6] In some circumstances, it may be more appropriate for the purchaser to make a direct claim on the supplier's capacity and to signify amendments to the time required of it, such as in the purchase of assembly effort, time on foundries, or time on major extruders.

[7] "Common carriers" of telecommunications traffic in the UK are BT and Mercury, providing basic networks as public services. VAN operators by contrast offer additional facilities or information — such as EDI or messaging — on a private subscription basis. The exchange of data across the network is made possible at the deep technical level by the adoption of common messaging "protocols" such as EDIFACT, TRADACOM or ANSI X.12. Of greater immediate concern to companies is the establishment of common software program data formats — in this context, between the purchaser and many suppliers.

a network of computer "post offices". The network subscriber who wishes to send data dials into the system and transmits the data, including the (electronic) address of the intended recipient. The message or data is directed to a computer convenient to the recipient's address, the computer being accessed by him on a frequent basis.

In summary, communication between supplier and purchaser under a partnership agreement changes in the way shown in Figure 16.1. The left-hand sketch in the Figure is the "before"; the right-hand sketch the ideal world of the system-to-system partnership.

Figure 16.1: Supplier Communication Before and After a Partnership Agreement

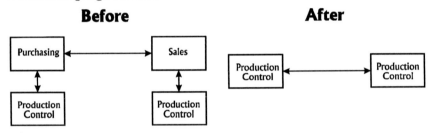

The obstacles to be overcome to achieve system-to-system integration are considerable. It is suspected that in very many cases where EDI is used, expensively transmitted messages are simply printed in clear English at the supplier's premises and used as if they had been received by fax. Indeed, many companies are finding that the comparative user simplicity and low cost of the Internet make it a far more attractive alternative than EDI.

Partnerships and Improvements

"Product improvement" by the supplier is achieved by the application of *value analysis* to the raw material components manufactured on the purchaser's behalf. In design and engineering, value analysis is a term used to denote the study of a product or material in terms of its constituent parts, its function and each part's production cost. (Value analysis refers to the study of materials that are already in production, while *value engineering* is reserved for the study of new products under design.) The objective is to eliminate all constituents that add cost but perform no useful function and to modify constituents that add cost disproportionate to the benefit contributed.

Value analysis is a team endeavour, typically carried out by the supplier's engineers and, perhaps, cost accountants, in rather the same way that quality improvement studies are conducted, such as those described in sub-section 13.2.4. Lines of investigation are to examine (1) whether the number of components can be reduced, (2) whether cheaper materials can be employed, and (3) whether the process of manufacture can be simplified. Value analysis studies by the supplier's team clearly require that it has a close knowledge of the function of the component supplied, the functions of its constituent parts, the physical stresses that will be applied in operation and the field conditions that will ultimately be encountered.

16.1.4 Supplier Performance

After the agreement to do business is finalised, there is much routine administration to perform. A supplier code is assigned and a computer record raised holding such details as the supplier's address, marketplace sector code, VAT number[8] and, if payments are to be made by BACS,[9] his bank details.

It is essential that the delivery performance and quality conformance of the supplier should be monitored from the very start of the operation of the agreement. Thus, when an order is placed, an *order number* is allocated to it, along with the material code, supplier code, quantity and due date. When delivery then takes place, the order number must be associated with the accompanying paperwork, enabling the computer to keep track of the quantity and

---

[8] VAT (value added tax) is the universal UK tax levied on all services and most goods (though not, notably, on food). VAT is added by the supplier to his invoice and is paid, along with the rest of the bill, by the purchaser. (The supplier's invoice (i.e. bill) must bear his official VAT registration number.) The VAT so paid is claimed back by the purchaser from HM Customs & Excise. However, VAT must be added to the purchaser's own invoices sent for payment to his customers. The amount charged, and collected, must then be paid direct to Customs & Excise promptly every three months.

[9] BACS (Banks' Automated Clearing System): payments made to suppliers in this way are effected by interbank transfers of funds, rather than by the raising and posting of cheques.

date of receipt (*v*. the quantity and date promised). The assessment of suppliers' quality performance requires separate action. Examples of what might be recorded and filed for analysis here are the fractions of parts non-conforming, "p" (sub section 14.4.2); sample rejections, if any; and process capability indexes.

The performance of suppliers may be set out, with analyses, on standard forms, perhaps with copies sent to the suppliers concerned for the addition and return of any free text comments of their own. Many companies have devised point-scoring systems so that poorly performing suppliers can be readily identified. If poor performances persist, the buyer should not procrastinate in re-sourcing the materials affected and purging the companies concerned from his list of approved companies.

16.2 ORDER PLACEMENT

Two ways in which a supplier's order may originate have already been described, the first being through the purchaser's materials planning system, the second directly from a negotiated agreement. In addition, in order to minimise administrative costs, small orders may be placed by phone or fax, perhaps with payment effected at once either by credit card or purchasing card.[10]

A prelude to order placement may be a *request for information* (RFI) — a form sent to a number of suppliers containing a brief questionnaire. Suppliers returning promising replies may then be sent a *request for a quotation* form (RFQ form). The RFQ may be straightforward or complex, depending on the item under consideration.

---

[10] The advantages of cards are their immediacy of use, so avoiding administrative delays and, especially, enabling *ad hoc* Internet purchases to be made easily. When a *credit* card is used for payment, the amount the purchaser is charged, and which he eventually pays to the credit card company, has VAT incorporated in it. Consequently, to claim this back from Customs & Excise, the purchaser must obtain a separate invoice from the supplier bearing his VAT registration number (a "VAT invoice"). When a *purchasing* card is used, the periodical bill presented by the purchasing card company, for payment by the purchaser, lists the items bought and shows, for each purchase, the VAT amount involved in the transaction. The purchasing card company's statement is accepted by HM Customs & Excise as evidence of VAT payment for repayment purposes. The purchaser's need for suppliers' VAT invoices is consequently eliminated. If subsequently an invoice is raised for other reasons, it should state prominently that it is not a VAT invoice.

16.2.1 Tenders

A special form of request, used by the manufacturing company on occasion but very commonly employed in government and government-controlled institutions, and having legal significance, is the *invitation to tender*. Invitations to tender by the buyer, are, in legal terms, *invitations to treat* (i.e. invitations to bargain, or negotiate). That is, the buyer's invitations to tender are not contractual offers. The suppliers' tenders, however, very definitely are contractual offers, so that acceptance of a supplier's tender by the buyer creates a legally enforceable contract, as described in subsection 16.2.3. The buyer is bound to consider all tenders that comply with the conditions laid down and are submitted by the date specified. He is not, however, obliged to accept the lowest bid, or accept any bid at all, unless there is a specific and unequivocal statement in the original invitation that he will indeed accept it — that is, where the invitation to tender amounts in reality to a contractual offer. The buyer would therefore be wise to phrase his invitation to tender cautiously, very much in the manner of an inquiry. (Note that the term *tendering* is used in everyday parlance to describe both the seeking of a tender from a supplier and the proffering of a tender by a supplier to a purchaser.)

There are three types of tendering: *competitive tendering*, *selective tendering* and *negotiated tendering*. All of them require painstaking preparation of specifications stating precisely what is required, including full technical detail, quality standards, quantities and dates.

Competitive Tendering

The purchasing manager may place an advertisement in a trade journal or similar publication inviting potential suppliers either to submit tenders as specified, or contact the manufacturing company for further details with a view later to tendering. The advertisement should be phrased with just as much care as any sales advertisement. As stated, the *tender document* (the technical and commercial requirements) should be prepared with even greater care, since it will form the basis of the contract, and will be referred to in the tender submitted by the successful supplier.

Selective Tendering

Invitations to tender are sent only to those suppliers with whom the purchaser wishes to do business.

Negotiated Tendering

Negotiated tendering refers to follow-up negotiation after tenders have been received in the course of competitive or selective tendering, before the acceptance of the successful bid, and is synonymous with *post tender negotiation* (PTN). PTN is undertaken perhaps to clarify certain points, including technical points, but most often to seek a reduction in the price. It has been said that negotiated tendering is not entirely fair, in so far that if Supplier A has been willing to change his tender later as a result of PTN, so would Supplier B have been had he been given the opportunity. But it is done and is said to be ethical by the curious argument that, since the supplier submits a tender at the highest price he thinks he can get away with, this not being considered unethical, the buyer is quite entitled to challenge it.[11]

As tenders are received, they should be date-stamped and locked away.[12] Only in rare circumstances should any tender be admitted after the closing date. The opening of tenders is a formal matter and should always be carried out by the purchaser in the presence of a witness. Subsequent tender analysis and selection may then be quite simple — a choice based merely on delivery undertaking and price. Alternatively, it may be a complex, lengthy

---

[11] See C.K. Lysons (1989), *Purchasing*, Second edition, Pitman Publishing, Chapter 7. There is now a fourth edition (1996).

[12] The theory of the sealed tender is based on the premise that suppliers will honestly compete with each other, all being governed by the competitive nature of the marketplace and each submitting its keenest offer. Reality is thought by many to be very different (notwithstanding the introduction in local government of compulsory competitive tendering in 1980, extended in 1988 and 1992, to eliminate price collusion among suppliers). There are some in manufacturing who regard tendering and the use of the sealed tender as *skill-less, bureaucratic and almost wholly clerical*, and contrary to the best interests of the company (David L. Sheridan (1991), *Negotiating Commercial Contracts*, McGraw-Hill). Others see the ability of the buyer to cast a very wide net through the advertisement of requirements initiating competitive tendering as a very positive advantage.

matter entailing technical assessment and the testing of samples submitted.

Note that the supplier's tender is a standing offer and, if not accepted by the purchaser, may be withdrawn by him, or may be deemed to have lapsed after a certain time, or may lapse because of a lapse date in its wording.

16.2.2 The Purchase Order

The majority of orders in the manufacturing concern are placed through the mechanism of the *purchase order*. The purchase order is a formal company document that conveys the instructions or detail of a required supply. The legal role of the purchase order will vary with circumstances. It might be an *offer* to form a contract to buy, in which case the supplier's acceptance of it seals the bargain. Alternatively, it might be an *acceptance* of an offer — say, an order placed immediately against a tender. Yet again, the purchase order might merely be an instruction — say, a "call-off" of material against a yearly contract already in existence. The function of the purchase order in such circumstances is to ensure good commercial housekeeping and orderliness. Its purposes may be summarised under four points:

1. To make clear what is being bought — the specific detail of the contract;

2. To impose on the contract certain express conditions required by the purchaser, such as the terms of payment which are to prevail — it is typical for these conditions to be printed on the reverse of the document;[13]

3. To act as formal control, so that the purchasing company can readily assess its supply position and its financial liability;

4. To act as a means of verifying that goods sent are as agreed, and that invoices presented for payment are valid debts for materials and services agreed to.

---

[13] The express conditions of the purchase order must not be onerous or objectionable to the supplier. If they are, he will demand that they be changed, nullifying the value of the purchase order as a convenient, standard document.

In the past, when the purchase order and its vital serial number were raised manually, copies would be sent to the supplier (two), accountancy department, the company's stores (goods-in section) and the functional department requiring the goods. Other traditional commercial documents linked to the purchase order via its serial number were (and often remain):

- *An advice note*: notification by the supplier of the imminent despatch of the goods, sent to the company's purchasing department;

- *A delivery note*: a statement of what is being delivered, accompanying the actual delivery;

- *A consignment note*: if the delivery has been consigned by the supplier to a third-party haulier for physical delivery, a note raised by the haulier verifying the identification of the goods and the name of the consignor (i.e. the supplier);

- *An unpacking note*: a separate list of items and quantities prepared if the contents of the shipment are numerous and complex.

Off-the-shelf application software has been available since the 1970s for dealing with the placement and progressing of supplier orders. All systems are centred around the purchase order number. That is, when the order is raised on the computer, a record is created with the order number as key, and with a great deal of space reserved on it for all the data which will eventually be collected. As each physical or clerical action takes place — acknowledgement, delivery, and so on — data are added to the record by the participants in the system. The order record is closed and filed when final payment has been made.

16.2.3 The Contract

The basis of commerce in the UK is the law of contract, the centre of this law being the contract itself.[14] The law of contract is not a

---

[14] Sir John Smith (1993), *The Law of Contract*, Second edition, Sweet & Maxwell. This is a short (260 pages) but highly authoritative and easy-to-read selection from a vast range of literature.

specific law contained in some particular statute passed by Act of Parliament.[15] Instead, it is derived from precedent — that is, it is derived by reference to court rulings in past cases, each such ruling itself taking cognisance of past decisions; the particular circumstances of the case to hand; and the principles that citizens of the realm are free to engage in lawful commerce among themselves, and are obliged to keep the promises they have made. The study of contract law, therefore, involves the study of past cases that have come before the courts and the principles that have been applied in deciding the outcomes of those cases.

A contract is a legally enforceable agreement between two or more parties. In the context of this Chapter, the agreement is likely to be for the supplier to provide materials or services under certain conditions and for the company to pay for them, with remedies in law provided, especially financial compensation, if the undertakings and promises agreed to are not complied with by one party or the other. For a contract to come into existence, two essential actions must take place.

First, there must be an offer to sell, such as a tender sent by a supplier, or else an offer to buy, such as a purchase order sent by the buyer without prior discussion. The offer must contain all the detail necessary for the subsequent agreement to be capable of being carried out in its entirety — for example, technical specifications must be set out, along with quantities, price, dates and the rest. (That is, there must be *certainty of terms* — no residual ambiguity.) An offer made by one party can be accepted or rejected by the other. A *counteroffer*, or alternative offer, by the other party is, in effect, a rejection of the original offer. An offer can also be revoked, provided this is done before its acceptance, and it can lapse "after a reasonable time". As explained in sub-section 16.2.1, an offer is to be distinguished from "an invitation to treat", which is an action by one party intended to initiate the bargaining

---

[15] There are, in fact, a small number of statutes passed by Parliament which modify the precedent set in the past by the courts — for example, *The Misrepresentation Act*, 1967, and *The Unfair Contract Terms Act*, 1977. See also footnote 18.

process. (Thus an RFQ is usually an invitation to the supplier to make an offer to supply.)[16]

The second essential action is that the buyer must accept the supplier's offer, and this must be done without further conditions, or, alternatively, that the supplier must accept the buyer's offer. Acceptance might be quite specific, such as by sending a letter of acceptance. In certain circumstances, the conduct of the other party might be deemed to constitute acceptance (for example, the despatching by the supplier of the actual goods, even though he has sent no formal acknowledgement, would be deemed acceptance). Doing nothing and saying nothing cannot be construed as acceptance.

There are also a number of conditions that must be true of the agreement if it is to constitute a legal contract. In the court, evidence that these conditions have been met will need to be produced if the case is to be heard.

The first condition is that there must be value to the contract. That is, there must be evidence that a bargain, or deal, has been struck. The most obvious indication that this is so is the stated promise to pay money in return for goods bought, but bargains might also take the form of the exchange of goods by bartering, or the payment for goods by the performance of some service. Value to the contract is referred to as *consideration*, being formally defined as *the thing given or done by the promisee in exchange for the promise.* Consideration may be *executed* or *executory*. Executed consideration refers to the requirement to pay in the case of a contract that is executed immediately on acceptance — say, a purchase by a company of a spare part for a machine repair, delivered for immediate cash settlement by a casual supplier without prior notice. Executory consideration is infinitely more likely to be the case in industry, however. This refers to the exchange of promises — the supplier promising to supply at a date in the future and the buyer promising to pay at a date in the future. Note that while consideration must be present, the law is totally

---

[16] Items in a shop window are *invitations to treat*, put out by the retailer and intended to induce the shopper to enter his premises and make an offer to buy the goods displayed.

disinterested as to whether the deal is adequate, fair or judicious. A bargain is a bargain, even if it is unwisely made.

The second condition is that there must be an intention to form legal relations. A social agreement such as a pledge by a parishioner to the vicar that he will provide a prize for the summer fête is not legally enforceable, but it is assumed in commercial agreements that the two parties intend to be contractually bound. If this is not the purchasing company's intention, because, say, the dialogue with the external company is purely exploratory, or is merely laying the ground for a further meeting, this should be made clear at the time.

Yet a third condition is that the two parties should each have the authority to contract. Even though the buyer may not have been granted such authority by the purchasing manager in a particular circumstance, perhaps because of the high value of the deal, if he acts in a manner that suggests he so has such authority, and does not state that his capacity to contract on behalf of the company is limited, and the supplier has no reason to believe it is limited, it is likely to be held that the agreement he reaches is legally enforceable. Similarly, agreements reached by users stemming from technical negotiations may also be held enforceable, so that the purchasing manager must make it clear to all potential suppliers that the commercial and legal sides of agreements are to be dealt with exclusively by him and his own staff, and never by others. *The principal* (i.e. the company) *is bound by the agent's actions.*

There are, in fact, a number of other conditions which must be true of a contract. For example, the contract must be within the law of the land — e.g. with regard to payment of taxes — and may not rest on such "unfair" conditions as the accidental death of a user of a machine, etc. (see footnote 15). (It should be noted in passing that the parties to a contract are said to be *privy* to it, and they can take action in law concerning it. We recall from sub-section 13.1.2 that Mrs Donovan, who was made ill by a snail in her ginger beer, could not take action against the café proprietor, because it was her friend, not she, who was privy to the contract to buy the drink from him. Mrs Donovan had to find another route to legal justice.)

Except in a small number of instances, such as in the sale of land, contracts are equally valid whether made orally or in writing. Oral (or parol) agreements, however, are clearly unsuitable for complex or lengthy agreements, or indeed for modern business generally. Offers, acceptances and the rest should therefore be made in writing, on official company forms, and all paperwork kept on file. There are well-known problems here in the use of computers. Thus while the courts will not accept any arbitrary *printed* output purporting to be "evidence", they will accept verified evidence relating to the contents of disks and tapes from which a printout might be obtained.

The *contractual terms*, or detail, of the contract are either *express* or *implied*. Before dealing with them, however, a distinction is made between contractual terms and *representations*. A representation is a statement made about the goods or service by the supplier intended to persuade the buyer to enter into the contract. The representation — *the car is reliable, economic to run, rustproofed, and has a mileage of only 10,000 miles* — is distinguished from a contractual term in so far as it is not eventually incorporated in the terms themselves. *Misrepresentation* can give rise to legal liability and even criminal prosecution, and is divided into three classes:

1. *Misrepresentation of fact*: the supplier has made an untrue statement about a factual matter. That is, the matter is specific and verifiable, rather than an advertising puff or a matter of opinion (rustproofed?);

2. *Material misrepresentation*: the fact which has been misrepresented is inherently important, and is not a triviality. The mileage of a second-hand car is important, whereas the condition of the exhaust pipe is not;

3. *The misrepresentation induced the contract*: the buyer of the second-hand car might justly claim that the apparently low mileage induced him to buy.

As an aside here, suppose a supplier intended to sell A, but by mistake put out a document that included both A and B, and, on the basis of the document, his offer was accepted by the buyer (who believed he was buying A and B). The contract now is for the supplier to sell A and B, not just A. He is not allowed in court to say (in legal terminology, he is "estopped" from saying) that he intended (in his mind) only to sell A. What must be relied on are objective tests — what is actually said, not what were subjective intentions. This precept is referred to in law as the doctrine of *estoppel*.

To continue, express contract terms are those which are put down in the agreement and which give it its unique meaning — that is, they are explicit, unmistakable and not simply implied. Examples are the identity of the materials to be delivered; the date of delivery; the quantity; price; the technical service to be provided; and so forth. (Whether the express contract terms are conditions or not is another matter — see below.)[17]

Express contract terms are to be distinguished from implied contract terms. Implied terms may relate either to fact or to law. Implied factual terms are those which both parties would have agreed to without hesitation, but overlooked or never bothered about. The court reads the implied terms into the contract, even though they were not expressly part of it. For example, *that the bags in which concrete will be delivered to the buyer's stockyard will be rainproof*. Implied terms relating to law are those implied by common law and commonsense — for example, *that the supplier's driver will exercise reasonable care when making the delivery and when unloading*.

Both express and implied contract terms are either *conditions* of the contract, *warranties* or *innominate* terms. The importance of these distinctions will be seen in sub-section 16.2.5, under breach of contract. A condition of a contract is a central element of the agreement, such that a failure to fulfil it will seriously detract from the contract's value to the party affected. Usually, the central elements of the agreement will be clearly seen as conditions from the sense and reading of the document. If it is the intention of the two parties that the performance of some action should be a condition, and there is thought to be an element of doubt on the matter in the wording of the draft, the text must be amended to make clear its desired status. This is no more true than where timeliness of deliv-

---

[17] The purchaser must be careful as to whose express terms are to prevail in a contract. If he makes an offer by sending in his purchase order (with its conditions), and the supplier acknowledges the order by returning his, the supplier's, conditions, the winner up to that point is the supplier. If the buyer is to regain the dominant position, he must now repudiate the supplier's conditions and reassert his own. This tussle between the two parties to secure the ascendancy of their respective terms has been referred to as *the battle of the forms*.

ery is concerned. If on-time delivery is vital and is to be regarded as a condition, attention must be drawn to it. The phrase often used to do so is that *time is of the essence*.

A warranty is a term that is not central to the contract, so that, if it is not fulfilled, the agreement nevertheless still retains most of the value anticipated, even though the warranted undertaking is not performed. Under normal circumstances, the date of delivery of a new machine tool to be installed on the manufacturing company's shop floor would be a warranty, not a condition. If the delivery were two weeks late, this might be annoying, but the detraction from the value of the contract overall would be small, given the machine's expected life, say, of ten years.

The last type of contract term is innominate. The word innominate means "having no name", and is used in law when a contractual obligation is either a condition or a warranty depending on the actual effect of an actual failure to fulfil the obligation, rather than on the inherent status of the obligation in the contract. For example, suppose that a contract stipulates that the supplier is to deliver 100 items, and in the event he delivers only 80. Two outcomes are possible: (1) for compelling technical reasons connected with the short delivery, the purchasing company finds it has to abandon its production programme and tear down its set-up — the delivery term of 100 units assumes the status of a condition; and (2) the purchasing company is able to proceed with its production programme, although it is forced to make a somewhat smaller batch — the term now has the status of a warranty.

16.2.4 Termination of the Contract

The normal termination of a contract arises, naturally, when both parties fulfil their obligations under it. The fulfilment by the supplier must be "substantial". If it is not substantial, payment by the buyer may be on a *quantum meruit* basis (= how much is taken). That is, the buyer may pay for only that portion of the work that has been completed. The performance of only a part of his obligation is often not acceptable to the supplier. The *quantum meruit* settlement will not be permitted if the contract stipulates that an entire undertaking is to be carried out, and that its fulfilment is a condition. In the catalogue of misfortune and exquisite justice which is the embodiment of contract law, we must turn to the leading case

Purchasing

on this matter, heard before the courts in 1795 and concerning Mrs Cutter. Mr Cutter, a seaman, was promised 30 guineas by Powell, the master of a vessel, to act as second mate on a voyage from Kingston, Jamaica to Liverpool, an undertaking of about two months, but he died three days before reaching port. Mrs Cutter sued Powell for that proportion of the money equal to the time her husband had served on board, but it was ruled that Cutter had failed to fulfil the undertaking he had given in entering into the contract, and so was owed nothing.[18]

The contract may also terminate when a date stipulated in the express conditions has been reached — say, 19 December 2009. Alternatively, it may be agreed by both parties that the contract should be brought to an end before the contractual obligations have been fulfilled. In such a case, the *agreement to terminate* is, itself, a separate contract, the consideration being the release of the two parties from having to complete their original obligations.

The contract may be terminated by *frustration*. This arises when conformance to its terms, or further performance of them, becomes impossible on either side due to some external factor. An example might be an agreement by a company to supply a number of items, this becoming impossible because of the destruction of its warehouse by fire before the despatch can take place. Likely reasons for potential frustration are often anticipated in contracts by the insertion of *force majeure* (= irresistible force) clauses, which stipulate specifically what is to happen if the circumstance should arise. Frustration cannot be claimed to end a contract if its performance, by chance, simply becomes very difficult. Nor can it be claimed if the cause of frustration (e.g. the fire) is brought about by the deliberate action of one of the parties; such action would be regarded as breach of the contract.

A contract may be brought to an end because of *mistake*. In this context, mistake — *operative mistake* — has a legal meaning, and is not to be confused with the everyday use of the term, as in "mis-

---

[18] *Cutter* v. *Powell*, 1795 6 Term.R 320 S&T. 433. Much sympathy is expressed for Mrs Cutter in this case, in legal textbooks, and it is good to see that Parliament rushed out legislation that would enable someone finding himself in similar circumstances to recover part of the fee, in the form of the Frustrated Contracts Act, enacted in 1943.

judgement". A *common mistake* means that both parties have made the same mistake about some central matter. The leading case is *Couturier* v. *Hastie*, in 1856, involving the sale of corn, which at the time of the contract formation was thought to be on board a ship at sea.[19] In fact, the corn in question had already been sold to a third party by the ship's captain because it was beginning to deteriorate. The contract was declared void due to common mistake. A *mutual mistake* arises when the two parties are at cross-purposes. Staying with our nautical Victorian theme, in 1864 two ships, each named *Peerless* and each carrying a cargo of cotton, managed to entangle two parties named Raffles and Wichelhaus. Raffles believed he was buying cotton on the first *Peerless*, and Wichelhaus thought he was selling cotton on the second *Peerless*.[20] A *unilateral mistake* arises when one party has made a mistake about a central part of the contract and the other party is aware of this mistake. The most usual instance of a unilateral mistake is one involving fraud, the perpetrator of the fraud being, of course, the second party. Cases of unilateral mistake are often centred round arguments about misrepresentation and the attempts by the victims of the fraud to protect their interests (for example, as to the ownership of goods they have paid money for).

The fifth and last reason for termination is through the failure of one party or the other to fulfil its principal obligations under the agreement: *breach of contractual conditions*. If it arises, such a breach is usually identified only when the contract has supposedly come to an end — a delivery that is made late, or goods that are delivered being found to be of non-conforming quality. Occasionally, an *anticipatory breach* may arise — say, an order cancellation issued by the buyer after the contract has been signed and before delivery is to take place. (In such an event, the supplier must take reasonable steps to mitigate his loss.)

Legal remedies for breach depend on whether the obligation that has not been performed is a condition or a warranty. If there has been a breach of a condition, the aggrieved party may terminate the contract and sue in the courts for damages, or may con-

---

[19] *Couturier* v. *Hastie* (1856), 5 HLC 673; (1852) 8 Exch.40.

[20] *Raffles* v. *Wichelhaus* (1864), 2 H & C 906.

tinue with the contract if he wishes. If there has been a breach of warranty, the wronged party may not terminate the contract. He can, however, sue in the courts for damages.

Damages are either *unliquidated* or *liquidated*. Unliquidated damages mean that the financial compensation which is to be awarded to the party suffering the breach, to be paid by the party which has failed to carry out its obligations, has not been calculated and expressed in financial terms beforehand, so that it is up to the court to decide the sum to be awarded, taking into account the evidence presented to it. The damages are arrived at on consideration of two factors. The first is the amount of money needed to compensate the innocent party for the *direct loss* he has sustained as a result of the breach — for example, the cost to put right a roof following faulty construction work. The second factor relates to the *indirect loss* suffered by the innocent party as a consequence of the breach. Indirect loss, however, is confined to loss stemming from circumstances known to both parties at the time the contract was signed. Rain through the leaky roof damaging the office furniture is one thing, but if the building had later been turned over to the storage of valuable *objets d'art*, that is another.

Liquidated damages, so called, are payments stated in the contract itself, and which fall due when various conditions and warranties which constitute the objectives of the agreement are not performed. An example is a condition that states that delivery shall be on 2 November 2006, and an accompanying liquidated damages clause that further states that the supplier *will pay liquidated damages to the buyer of £1,000 per day for every day the delivery is late*. The sums nominated in liquidated damages clauses must be arrived at by genuine calculation of the losses to the buyer if the various conditions and warranties are not performed by the supplier. No attempt should be made to turn them into penalties intended to punish or put pressure on the other party ("extravagant and unconscionable amounts"), and if they clearly are penalties, the supplier who does not achieve the performance required will, in the event, refuse to pay them, and will be supported in his refusal by the courts, regardless of the fact that he willingly signed the agreement in the first place. The claim that liquidated damages are penalties is a standard defence of suppliers resisting payment of them, so that the buyer would do well to follow the guidelines issued by the court. These are: (1) any sum stated in a clause should not be more than the maximum loss that could be suffered by the breach; (2) the sum should not be more than the consideration attaching to the contract itself; and (3) a single sum of money should not apply to every condition and warranty not performed. (If it did so, this would indicate that a serious attempt honestly to calculate the various potential losses had not, in fact, been made.)

On a practical front, it is important that the precise circumstance is defined, for each separate clause, under which the liquidated damages applying will be paid. (This is clearly likely to be difficult if it involves technical performance.) There is also the need to define the time they will be made should they become due, and the procedure for executing payment. When liquidated damages are payable, the amount concerned is strictly what has been defined. The buyer cannot ask the court to increase them because his loss has been greater than he calculated they would be. On the other hand, nor will he receive less if his real loss is less. Note that suppliers may attempt to insert *damage limitation* clauses into contracts during the course of negotiations, perhaps disguised as liquidated damages. Thus the supplier may propose compensation payments for, say, late delivery, which fall far short of the actual losses that would be suffered by the buyer. If manufacture subsequently goes badly, he may then refuse to put in the additional cost and effort that would enable the contract to be properly fulfilled, and take instead the easier option of paying the compensation. The buyer should be on his guard, therefore. It would, perhaps, be better that no mention of liquidated damages and damage limitation was made to tie his hands, and that matters, if necessary, were dealt with in court. Nevertheless, it is understandable that the courts should be a last resort. Apart from the law's delay, a case might take 50 hours of study and preparation, with additional time needed to attend court hearings, at a cost, perhaps, in excess of £200 per hour.

16.3 THE CARRIAGE AND RECEIPT OF GOODS

Two components constitute the subject matter of this Section, each of them having a significant bearing on the operational obligations and commercial position of the manufacturing company. The first

Purchasing 661

is the division of responsibility in a particular purchase between the company and its supplier for such matters as the carriage of the goods, their insurance and (if international transfer is involved) the payment of dock dues and duty. The second is the distinction between delivery of the goods and their legal acceptance, and the point at which *title*, or ownership, passes from one party to the other.

16.3.1 The Carriage of Goods

Although the purchasing manager and the supplier can make whatever joint arrangements they wish in allocating responsibility for, and carrying out, the many tasks necessary to effect the transfer of goods between their two factories, for the most part they are likely to be content to nominate one or other of the 13 standard terms drawn up by the International Chamber of Commerce, used worldwide and referred to as the *Incoterms*.[21]

(Note that while this topic has been dealt with from the viewpoints of the purchasing manager and the supplier, it might also have been considered in Chapter 2 from the viewpoints of the sales manager and customer. And if the manufacturing company were to operate a significant distribution chain, with say, regional warehouses or depots, the question of Incoterms would perhaps more appropriately appear as part of Chapter 20 as a topic under Distribution.)

The advantages to buyer and seller in choosing to nominate a standard Incoterm to govern the transfer of goods are that all the terms are well known through ICC booklets and guides, and that they are frequently and widely used throughout commerce. The

---

[21] Incoterms is an acronym of the International Chamber of Commerce Terms of Sale, the International Chamber of Commerce being an organisation based in Paris and dedicated to the promotion and facilitation of free international trade. The Incoterms were first formulated in 1936 and are revised from time to time, the last revision being in 1999, effective from 1 January 2000. See *Incoterms 2000 — ICC Official Rules*, 1999, published by The International Chamber of Commerce (ICC), Paris. Visit www.iccwbo.org for the ICC's web site. See also Prof. Jan Ramberg (1999), *Guide to Incoterms* (an official guide sponsored by the ICC). Also see other ICC Guides, including an Incoterms Flowchart. The ICC publication of terms is also available from the bookshop service of the Chartered Institute of Purchasing and Supply, Stamford, Lincs, as well as from Amazon.com.

principal publication, *Incoterms 2000 — ICC Official Rules*,[22] very helpfully makes clear, for each one, exactly what activities each party is responsible for. That is, following a 100-word explanation, the remaining text is divided into two clear sections headed "The Seller's Obligations — (then action points A1, A2, A3, etc.)" and "The Buyer's Obligations — (action points B1, B2, B3, etc.)". Naturally, a specific reference must be made in the contract between buyer and supplier as to which Incoterm (including its published source and year of publication) is to govern the agreement. However, in agreeing it, there is no reason at all why the provisions set out in the standard term should not be modified if some special condition is to prevail: Two examples are: "FOB Plymouth, SS Mayflower, Incoterms 2000, modified as follows . . ." and "DDU Springfield, Incoterms 2000, H. & B. Simpson Inc., Number 2 Warehouse, terms modified as follows . .".[23] In addition to modifications made by the two parties, it should be noted that Incoterms are silent on what remedies are to apply in case of breach of contract and on the passing of title to the goods from supplier to buyer.

The 13 Incoterms are set out in four groups, the groups named for the initial letter of the standard abbreviations of the terms included in them, as given below.

Incoterm Group E (Departure)

- **EXW (Ex-Works . . . — followed by a named place)**. The supplier fulfils his obligations to the buyer when he has made the goods available at his own premises. He is not responsible for loading them onto the buyer's vehicle or for preparing export documentation.[24] The buyer bears all costs and risks in

---

[22] See footnote 21.

[23] The two parties to an agreement must state clearly in the contract under which country's law a dispute is to be settled. If the buyer and supplier are UK companies, presumably they will specify the Law of England. However, the ICC has its own arbitration service and, if one party is not domiciled in the UK, this may be preferred. The cost of a hearing under French Law at the Parisian Court of Commerce can be substantial.

[24] The ICC comment on the EXW term specifically draws attention to the fact that the supplier has no duty to load the buyer's vehicle. If it is impractical for the buyer to load, the ICC recommends that the term FCA should be specified rather than EXW. In practice, the supplier often ends up loading the goods for

taking the completed load from the supplier's premises. Problems for the supplier with EXW are that the buyer may delay in making the collection, so affecting the supplier's storage costs and disrupting his everyday work (for example, the buyer's vehicle may arrive without prior warning, at a difficult time, causing disruption and congestion). *(Mode of transport: not applicable.)*

Incoterm Group F (Main Carriage Unpaid)

- **FCA (Free Carrier . . . — followed by a named place)**. The supplier fulfils his obligations when he has handed the goods over, cleared for export, into the custody of a carrier named by the buyer. The "place" may be a transport terminal. *(Applicable to all modes of transport.)*

- **FAS (Free Alongside Ship . . . — followed by a named *port of despatch*)**. The supplier delivers the goods alongside a vessel on the quay and must clear the goods for export. The buyer bears other risks and cost from this point. *(Waterways only.)*

- **FOB (Free on Board . . . — followed by a named port of despatch)**. Delivery and transit risks pass from the supplier to the buyer when the goods cross the ship's rail at the nominated port. The supplier must clear the goods for export. *(Waterways only.)*

Incoterm Group C (Main Carriage Paid)

- **CFR (Cost & Freight . . . — followed by a named destination port)**. The supplier must bear the cost of carriage, although other costs such as insurance remain the responsibility of the buyer. This is the first Incoterm of those so far that gives the supplier control over the movement of the goods, so providing him with an opportunity to manage distribution costs. *(Waterways only.)*

---

nothing, simply to clear his despatch dock; the canny supplier might offer to load the vehicle as a concession in negotiations, in exchange for a concession in his own favour. (If the contractual terms are to be as stated on the buyer's purchase order, however, the purchasing manager will usually stipulate "supplier to load" as a standing condition for Ex-Works purchases.)

- **CIF (Cost, Insurance and Freight . . . — followed by a named destination port)**. This differs from CFR only in that the supplier is now responsible for marine insurance as well. (Note that for all other Terms, the supplier must insure the goods until transit risks pass to the buyer). *(Waterways only.)*

- **CPT (Carriage Paid To. . . — followed by a named destination)**. The supplier clears the goods for export and bears all freight costs. However, liability for loss or damage passes to the carrier (and hence indirectly to the buyer) when the goods are delivered into the custody of the carrier at the port of destination. *(All modes of transport.)*

- **CIP (Carriage and Insurance Paid To . . . — followed by a named destination)**. As with CPT, except that the supplier must himself procure and pay for insurance for the cargo on board ship, although he is obliged to obtain only minimum cover. The supplier must clear the goods for export. *(All modes of transport.)*

Incoterm Group D (Arrival)

- **DAF (Delivered At Frontier . . . — followed by a named place at the frontier, before the customs barrier)**: Supplier clears for export, and fulfils his obligations when the goods have been made available at the named point (i.e. before customs clearance). It is vital for the two parties to specify the frontier place precisely — for example, is it to be the supplier's frontier or the buyer's? *(Any mode, but mainly rail and road.)*

- **DES (Delivered Ex Ship . . . — followed by a named port of destination)**. The supplier pays all costs and bears all risks in bringing the goods to the port of destination, and fulfils his obligations when the goods are made available to the buyer on board ship. Importation clearance and costs, and customs at the port, are the responsibility of the buyer. *(Waterways only.)*

- **DEQ (Delivered Ex Quay, Duty Paid . . . — followed by a named port of destination)**. The supplier makes the goods available on the quay at the destination port. The buyer must clear the goods for import, and bear all costs, duties, taxes and other charges. The term "Duty Paid" is added, but commonly the term is modified by the two parties to read "Duty Unpaid", the wording of the Term being correspondingly changed. It is also common for the two parties to make other modifications, such as by transferring responsibility for VAT to the buyer. *(Waterways only.)*

- **DDU (Delivered, Duty Unpaid . . . — followed by a named place (usually the buyer's factory) within the country of destination).** The supplier makes the goods available at the named place in the country of importation, and bears all risks and costs except duties and taxes. The buyer is responsible for customs clearance, including the cost of any delays. *(All modes of transport.)*

- **DDP (Delivered, Duty Paid . . . — followed by a named place (usually the buyer's factory) within the country of destination).** The maximum obligation of the supplier, and the complete opposite of EXW. The supplier is fully responsible for every cost and requirement in delivering the goods, including the payment of taxes, the obtaining of an import licence and the payment of import duty. On the other hand, the proficient supplier is able to affect service through the judicious choice of carriers and the correctness of his documentation, to the satisfaction of his customer. *(Mode of transport: not applicable.)*

16.3.2 The Receipt of Goods

Contract law as it applies to such matters as the delivery and supply of goods and the transfer of ownership in them, built up from cases over a great many years, was consolidated in formal legislation in the Sale of Goods Act, 1979, itself then modified by the Sale and Supply of Goods Act, 1994.[25]

In discussing the receipt of raw materials from the supplier, the first thing is to distinguish between *delivery* and *acceptance*.

Delivery can be defined merely as the voluntary transfer of physical possession from one party to another. Thus the signing of

---

[25] Margaret Griffiths (1996), *Law for Purchasing & Supply*, Second edition, Chapters 9 and 10.

a delivery note presented by the supplier or haulier simply acknowledges receipt of the goods. Section 34 of the 1979 Act specifically lays down that:

> "Where goods are delivered to the buyer and he has not previously examined them, he is not deemed to have accepted them until he has had a reasonable opportunity of examining them to ensure their compliance with the contract."

(The Act also states that the supplier must, on request, give the buyer reasonable time.)

Acceptance of the goods by the buyer in effect means the buyer's concurrence that the goods delivered comply with the contract's provisions in a number of vital regards — for example: delivery date; general material state, especially as regards design and quality; and quantity. From the legal viewpoint, since such compliance is likely to constitute fulfilment of the contract's central conditions, the most important effect of accepting the goods is that the buyer can no longer terminate the contract because of breach of condition relating to these matters (although he can still sue under the Sale of Goods Act for breach of warranty). Section 35 of the Act states:

> "The buyer is deemed to have accepted the goods when he intimates to the seller that he has accepted them, or when the goods have been delivered to him and he does any act in relation to them which is inconsistent with the ownership of the seller, or when, after the lapse of a reasonable time, he retains the goods without intimating to the seller that he has rejected them."

A court might well state that acceptance is implied when the buyer updates his stock records system with confirmatory details, and moves the goods out of Goods-In into the stores itself or onto the shop floor.

Just as delivery is not acceptance, so is acceptance not possession, in the sense of legal ownership.

Ownership of, or *title* to, the goods, is transferred to the buyer when the terms of the contract specify that it is to be transferred, having regard also to the conduct of the two parties and the circumstances applying.

A particularly important consequence of ownership arises if one party or the other goes into administration or receivership during the exchange of goods and money. For example, if the buying company were to go into administration before it had paid for the goods, and the supplier still retained legal title in them, the supplier could claim for their return by the appointed administrator. If it is the buyer who has title to them in these circumstances, however, the supplier must merely register his debt like any other creditor and is likely in due course to receive only a fraction of the price. The common practice, and advisability from the supplier's viewpoint, of retaining title to the goods until payment has been made is dealt with in due course.

While the standard Incoterms deal with the passing of risk and the incurrence of obligations to bear costs, they do not now stipulate the point at which title passes. (In the past, the transfer of title to the buyer was specified as taking place on collection in EXW, the point becoming progressively deferred as the terms moved to Delivered.)

If there is no explicit statement in the contract dealing with the transfer of title, transfer is governed by a number of rules laid down in Section 18 of the Sale of Goods Act. In briefly describing these rules, it is first necessary to distinguish between *specific goods* and *unascertained goods*.

Specific goods and *specific future goods* are goods identified and agreed at the time the contract comes into existence. Thus a machine tool distinguishable by its serial number is a specific good. A product being made to order is a specific future good.

Unascertained goods are likely to be associated with make-to-stock companies. An example of unascertained goods are 80 acrylic squares, to be selected from the company's stockholding of 350 squares, and being the subject of a customer's order. Unascertained goods are said to become *ascertained* when they are duly selected to fulfil the order — for example, when the 80 acrylic squares are picked and packed, ready for despatch.

The rules may be summarised as follows:

1. For specific goods which are in a deliverable state, and where everything has been done that needs to be done, title passes to the buyer immediately the contract is agreed, regardless of the fact that transfer to the buyer has not commenced and that payment has not been made; and

2. For specific future goods, and all unascertained goods, whether future or not, title passes to the buyer when the goods become in a deliverable state, and have been appropriated to the contract (i.e. when they have been selected from stock ready for packing), and when all other actions have been taken that are contracted to be taken.

The requirement that everything must be done that needs to be done must be looked at most carefully in the light of the Incoterm selected. Thus consider the case of *Carlos Federspiel & Co. (of Costa Rica) v. Charles Twigg & Co.*, heard in 1957.[26] The supplier, Twigg, contracted to manufacture a number of bicycles to be despatched under the Incoterm FOB, 1953 version. The bicycles were paid for and duly packed in crates bearing Federspiel's name and were awaiting loading on board ship, when Twigg went into receivership. From the description of FOB in that particular version of Incoterms, one more action needed to be taken by Twigg before his obligations were complete and ownership passed to Federspiel, namely the loading of the crates over the ship's rail. Consequently, it was held that title remained with Twigg (and indirectly with the receiver), and Federspiel lost its action for possession of the goods.

It is usual in the sale of goods for the supplier to insist on the inclusion in the contract of a clause stating that he retains title in them until payment has been made. Section 19 of the Sale of Goods Act specifically deals with retention of title by the seller for both specific and unappropriated material. If, then, goods are held by the buyer in their unaltered and original form, they may be reclaimed by the supplier in the event that the buyer goes into re-

---

[26] *Carlos Federspiel & Co. SA v. Charles Twigg & Co. Ltd.* (1957), 1 Lloyd's Rep 240.

ceivership or fails to make payment. However, if the goods have been processed, so that the original material has lost its identity, an action by the supplier to recover them will fail, since it is held that the material sold has become the buyer's property regardless of the supplier's retention clause to the contrary.[27] However, even though the original goods are lost to the supplier, if the buyer is in possession of other goods relating to a separate, second contract with the same supplier, albeit these being already paid for, title in these other goods can be claimed by the supplier against payment for the first contract. Among other things, this obviates the need for the supplier continually to identify and mark the materials sold to the buyer — for example, when materials are being supplied in a succession of repeat orders.

There are many instances in manufacturing where the company receiving goods never becomes the owner of them. For example, it may be sent components so that it can perform a specialised technical operation on them. When this has been done, they are to be returned or sent on to a third party.[28] Again, the company may receive free issue material from its customer for use in a job being undertaken on its behalf. Yet again, in a practice as wasteful to its supplier as to itself, it may enter into a so-called *consignment stock* arrangement, whereby it receives an excessive amount of material from its supplier, the supplier retaining title to it until portions are assigned by the buyer for use through a process of "call off".[29]

Transitory goods in these circumstances are referred to as *bailments*, the party supplying them being the *bailor* and the party

---

[27] It is possible for the supplier to protect himself indirectly against the processing of his goods by the buyer, by making a charge on the buyer's company, under Section 395 of the Companies Act, relating to the proceeds from the buyer's eventual sale of the processed material. Any such charge must be registered at the time of the contract.

[28] Manufacturing chains involving a succession of companies each performing a specialised operation are not uncommon in the chemical and pharmaceuticals industries, the arrangement being economic (when spare capacity is available) because of the size and cost of each specialist plant unit involved. The contracting out of manufacture in this way is referred to as *tolling* — see sub-section 9.4.2.

[29] The costs of holding stock — capital tied up; insurance; housing; quality; deterioration; management; and the rest — do not evaporate because the buyer has not yet paid for the material. So who does pay them?

receiving them the *bailee*. A formal definition of bailments is that they are "goods delivered in trust upon an expressed contract that the trust be faithfully executed on the part of the bailee". That is, the bailee must exercise due care in looking after the materials in his charge. A particular concern here is in accounting for the number of items constituting the bailment. Maintaining an accurate record of stock is notoriously difficult to achieve, as described in Section 18.3. Moreover, there are a wide variety of causes of inaccuracy, as seen in Table 18.2, and pinning down the reason or reasons for a discrepancy is virtually impossible. In the contract between the bailor and bailee, then, it would seem to be very difficult to phrase an exclusion clause protecting the bailee against loss of the material due to those causes in Table 18.2 which might be classed under the heading of negligence, but not against others in the Table which might be construed as inexcusable breach, if the causes of loss are unknown and unknowable. In *Levison* v. *The Patent Steam Carpet Cleaning Company* (1978)[30] the Carpet Cleaning Company lost Levison's carpet and did not know how. The Company's exclusion clause for negligence could not help it, because it could not show that the reason for the loss was indeed negligence. But nor could it show that the cause was not a "fundamental breach" of contract going far beyond mere negligence. In short, the onus of proof fell on the company to show the reason for loss, and, since it could not do so, it was held liable for it.

16.4 Price and the Marketplace

The price paid for material is a matter of high and continual importance to both purchaser and supplier and a critical factor in the profitability of both companies. The price settled on results from a fusion of three elements: competition within the marketplace, the cost of production incurred by the supplier and the value of the product in the eyes of the purchaser.

Competition, supply and demand are major topics in the study of economics. Economic theory talks of *the hand of the market* — the determination, as it were, by an invisible hand, of a balance of supply, demand and price. The price is the *equilibrium price*, the price

---

[30] *Levison* v. *The Patent Steam Carpet Cleaning Co. Ltd.* (1978), QB 69.

Purchasing

that brings about the balance of supply and demand in a free marketplace. An outline of this theory is sketched in sub-section 16.4.1.

For the manufacturing company, dramatic examples of the operation of the market economy and the interaction of supply, demand and price are often to be seen in its purchase of commodities — oranges, bauxite, boron, oil — with supplies and price subject to alarming fluctuations on a global scale. Commodities and purchasing are dealt with in sub-section 16.4.2.

16.4.1 Supply and Demand

The concept of an equilibrium price is illustrated in Figure 16.2. The curve on the graph labelled "supply" shows that when the price of a particular material is low, the willingness of the supplier to supply is low; when price is high, willingness to supply is similarly high. The curve labelled "demand" goes the opposite way. When price is high, the quantity demanded (i.e. sold) is low; as price falls, demand rises. The point where the supply and demand curves intercept is the equilibrium point and describes the balance of supply, demand and price.

Figure 16.2: The Economic "Demand and Supply Curves", and the Equilibrium Price

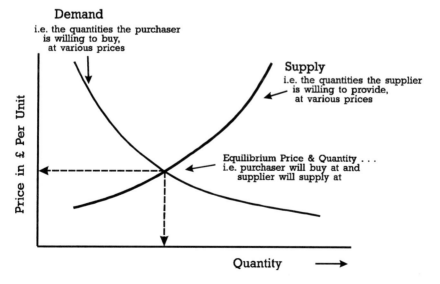

The concept of an equilibrium price applies under the theoretical conditions of perfect competition, perfect communication, perfect access to markets, and so on. Three possible factors among a multitude of them capable of creating imperfect conditions are:

- **A monopoly**: one supplier controlling the whole market;
- **An oligopoly**: a few suppliers only and no prospect of new ones;
- **A cartel**: suppliers that are party to a price-fixing agreement.

In the UK, any company controlling 25 per cent or more of the market as either buyer or seller can be referred to the Monopolies and Mergers Commission under the Fair Trading Act, 1973. Other pertinent legislation includes the Restrictive Trade Practices Act, 1976, and the Competition Act, 1980. The Director of Fair Trading, or the Restrictive Practices Court, can impose heavy financial penalties and order price cuts if it is found that prices have been rigged or that firms have acted in collusion in, say, submitting tenders.[31]

A moment's reflection is sufficient to convince any buyer (or salesman) that the effect of price on supply and demand is very different from one type of product to another. Intuitively, it seems that a change in the price of groceries, cigarettes or petrol will have a negligible effect on their overall sales, while a change in the price of cars, hi-fi or furniture will have a significant effect on them. The individual degree to which demand for a product is

---

[31] James Bates and J.R. Parkinson (1969), *Business Economics*, Second edition), Basil Blackwell. Legislation in the United States against unfair trade and monopolisation is far better developed than elsewhere in the world, and is referred to for an historical reason as *antitrust* law. It operates at both the federal and state levels. There are five major federal acts including The Interstate Commerce Act (1887) and, especially, The Sherman Antitrust Act (1890). Compliance is vigorously pursued by the Department of Justice in Washington, DC; by state bodies; and through civil actions brought by private citizens. Even the European Union (EU), an entity more noted for its distaste for the American commitment to competition and *le capitalisme sauvage* and for its leanings to protectionism and regulation, has issued diktats prohibiting restrictive practices and unfair pricing. Articles 85 and 86 of the Treaty of Rome and the Single European Act of 1986 all bear on this issue. For a brilliant survey of British industry from 1945 to 1999, demonstrating the consistently beneficial effect of competition and of a market free of government interference, in all sectors, see Sir Geoffrey Owen (1999), *From Empire to Europe*, Harper Collins.

changed by a change in its price is referred to as its *price elasticity of demand*.

In order to calculate the price elasticity of demand of a product, it is necessary to obtain two ratios. The first is the observed change in the quantity sold after a price change, divided by the quantity sold before the change, as follows:

$$\frac{\Delta Q}{Q}$$

The second is the change in price divided by the original price, as follows:

$$\frac{\Delta P}{P}$$

The price elasticity of demand e is then given by Equations 16.1 and 16.2.

$$e = \frac{\Delta Q}{Q} \div \frac{\Delta P}{P} \quad \text{Equation 16.1}$$

$$e = \frac{\Delta Q}{\Delta P} \times \frac{P}{Q} \quad \text{Equation 16.2}$$

For example, suppose that Material A has sales of 75 units/month at a price each of £100. When price is increased to £102, sales drop to 70. Material A's price elasticity of demand is thus given by Equation 16.3.

$$e = \frac{5}{2} \times \frac{100}{75} = 3.33 \quad \text{Equation 16.3}$$

We can now estimate the change in sales/month that would result if the price were to change from £100 to (say) £96, as given in Equation 16.4.

$$3.33 = \frac{-\Delta Q}{-4} \times \frac{100}{75} \quad \text{Equation 16.4}$$

whence $\Delta Q = 10$ units extra sold.

In economic parlance, products are said to have relatively elastic demand if $1 < e < \infty$. For such products, a small change in price will have a large effect on the quantity bought and sold. Products are said to have relatively inelastic demand if $0 < e < 1$. A change in price for products in this category will have a very small proportional effect on sales.

As only to be expected of any attempt to describe human behaviour by formulae, there are many caveats and exceptions to this simple notion. For example, any calculated elasticity e applies only at the particular price P used to calculate it; no account is taken of the ability of consumers to find substitute products when there is an increase in price of the product subjected to a price rise; and no account is taken of the relative change in income of the consumer group making the purchase. Nevertheless, price elasticities of demand, with all their imperfections, are useful shorthand indices by which products on a purchasing list or on a sales range can be considered and compared.

16.4.2 Commodities

In order to manufacture road-rail, tin trays, sandalwood furniture and party packs of sweet white wine, it is necessary to purchase *primary products*, or *commodities*, on world-wide markets.

The global nature of commodity markets means that the scale of supply is very large and that the sources of supply are subject to a wide range of disturbances. Equally to the point for the purchasing manager, they are characterised by very large fluctuations in price. If supply is curtailed, as ever it is price that regulates demand. Shortages occur due to the normal seasonal patterns of growth, crop failures, the raising of government barriers and the occurrence of geological mishaps. Excesses of supply and hence cheap availability occur due to harvest gluts, downturns in national economies and ill-judged excess production.

Instead of allowing the free play of price, supply and demand, other means of achieving equilibrium are for governments to attempt to regulate the market and for producers to make long-term changes to supply. Two instances of regulation are: (1) in Europe, the purchase and then destruction or storage of crops by the EU, and (2) the creation of consortia to maintain buffer stocks and buy and sell at regulated rates, as exemplified by the International Tin Council which collapsed so spectacularly in London in 1985. Two instances of response by the producer are: (1) to close down temporarily outlets of production, such as by mothballing mines; and (2) to embark on the long-term development of new sources of supply and the infrastructure to support them, such as by opening up new plantations.

Large swings in price are disliked by supplier and purchaser alike. For the manufacturing company incorporating commodities in its products, price changes, except in the long term, are difficult to pass on to customers. Considerable effort may consequently be made by the purchasing manager to stabilise price and ensure his own company's supply by entering into private agreements with suppliers, outside the maelstrom of world markets. For example, he may come to an agreement to take the whole of the output of a certain mine for a one-year period ahead at a fixed rate. A great deal of world trade in commodities is carried out in this way.

The prices agreed in private deals are reached by reference to those prevailing in the global, or free, market at the times the deals are struck, and it is to the global market the purchasing manager must turn if he has not secured such an agreement or if he wants additional material to supplement what he has already bought.

The global market finds its expression in major trading exchanges throughout the world, located in over 20 countries, where numerous specialist companies act as brokers by matching buyers and sellers of a vast array of products and produce. For convenience, the UK buyer will, of course, turn to a broker operating in one or other of the marketplaces, or exchanges, in the City of London, given in Table 16.1.[32]

If the purchasing manager requires either immediate delivery of a particular commodity, or delivery at a future date, a broker in the relevant City market will arrange the trade with a supplying

---

[32] The City of London is an area located within London itself, covering one square mile around, and just east of, St Paul's Cathedral on the site of the old medieval city. It has a workforce of some 500,000 people, of very many nationalities, employed entirely in banks*, brokerages and other financial companies and institutions. (*Astonishingly, there are 550 different banking organisations within the area.) The distinctive nature of the City's expertise, its economic structure and its trading links make it a world apart from the UK economy. In 1996, the City's contribution to GDP was $239 billion, 19 per cent of the UK total. (Report by Douglas McWilliams et al. (1997), issued by The Centre for Economics & Business Research (CEBR).)

company, shipment taking place direct from the supplier's country of origin to the purchaser's factory.

Table 16.1: The Principal Exchanges within the City of London

Marketplace Name	Principal Commodities Traded
London Futures and Options Exchange ("The London Fox")	Coffee, tea, cocoa, sugar
London Metal Exchange (LME)*	Non-ferrous metals
International Petroleum Exchange*	Oil
Grain & Feed Association	Agricultural produce
Baltic International Freight Futures Exchange	Shipping freight
London International Financial Futures Exchange ("LIFFE")	Bonds and currencies
London Stock Exchange	Company stocks and shares

* Daily trading by "open outcry" (2001).

Actual goods are known as "physicals", or "actuals". For most materials bought and sold, the authorities regulating the operation of a market specify certain standards that are to apply as to physical condition. Examples of specifications that might be laid down are: the lot sizes of supply, if any (for example, minimum weight); quality or purity; physical form; packaging; and delivery terms. If the exchange is to be effected immediately, the price paid is the *spot price* (or *cash price*). If, however, delivery is to take place at a future date, the broker or specialist buyer will seek to mitigate the effect of a rise in price over the interim period by *hedging* his exposure to risk through the purchase of *futures*.[33]

A future is a warrant, or "contract", either to buy or to sell a specified quantity of a commodity at a specified date in the future. Futures contracts (along with the obligations attached to them)

---

[33] A commodity future is one of a class of financial instruments referred to as *derivatives*. A derivative is a contract, or security, as opposed to an asset, the value of which is derived directly from a further, underlying index. For example, unit trusts, familiar to many citizens as a means of saving and investment, are very clearly derivatives, the value of the certificates issued by the managers of a scheme being based on the share valuations of a group of companies making up the trust fund.

may themselves be bought and sold on the exchange to which they relate in what is referred to as the *futures market*. The origin and primary purpose of the market are to enable the risks of adverse price changes to be insured against by both producer (i.e. supplier) and consumer (i.e. manufacturer).[34]

Traders in the futures market may be classed either as *hedgers* — individuals and companies principally interested in physical goods and seeking to eliminate the risk of price fluctuations; or *speculators* — individuals with no interest in the physical goods, courting risk and seeking to profit from short-term price changes. The supplier and manufacturer are, of course, very strictly, hedgers. Their activities and the mechanism of the market may best be illustrated by two examples. (The prices used in the first example are given in US dollars, the standard currency employed by the London Metal Exchange.)

First Example, Step 1

Suppose that an Australian mining and refining company has 1,000 tonnes of high grade zinc on 1 February, when the spot price of the metal is $900/tonne, and that it undertakes to sell to a stockist in the UK. The journey time to Southampton is three months, and the price that the stockist will pay is the spot price prevailing on the day of arrival in early May. To protect itself against a decline in price, the Australian company now *sells* forty 25-tonne lots of "Zinc July 1st" futures contracts on the London Metal Exchange at $937/tonne, 25 tonnes being the standard lot size and $937/tonne being the futures price for 1 July zinc prevailing on 1 February.[35]

---

[34] Although commodities futures have been traded in the City of London and on the Chicago Board of Trade since the middle of the nineteenth century, their first recorded use goes back to the seventeenth century and Japan. Rice stored in warehouses for future consumption was used as collateral to raise cash, the receipts issued being termed "rice tickets". Rice tickets were standardised according to the quantity, type and condition of the rice to which they referred, and eventually came to be traded as commercial currency in very much the way that commodity futures are today.

[35] In the jargon, the Australian company *short hedges* — i.e. it sells (goes "short") to protect itself against a potential reduction in price (hedges). It is the effect of the different objectives of the hedger (insurance against a fall in the spot price) and the speculator (reward for the risk of exposure) which generally leads to the futures price of a commodity being below its spot

That is, the company's broker offers 40 contracts on the market to sell 25 tonnes of zinc on 1 July, and these are bought by speculators at a price reflecting the market at the moment the deals are struck.

First Example, Step 2

On arrival of the load in Southampton on 5 May, some three months later, the spot price of zinc has fallen to $858/tonne. The price of Zinc July 1st futures has also fallen, by $45/tonne to $892/tonne. The company now *purchases* forty 25-tonne lots of Zinc July 1st futures contracts at the prevailing price of $892/tonne. It next *offsets* the forty contracts to sell Zinc July 1st with the forty contracts to buy Zinc July 1st, so ending its exposure in the futures market ("closing its position"). The financial outcome is as follows (though not taking into account the amounts that should be allowed for to cover the broker's commissions and the normal differences between buying and selling prices):

1. Income from the UK Stockist:
   1,000 tonnes × $858
   = $858,000 (this is a reduction of $42,000, or "loss", on the value of the metal as it was before leaving Australia).

2. Metal Exchange Account:
   Assets due to the sale of Zinc July 1st futures made on 1 February:
   40 × 25 × $937 = $937,000
   Liabilities arising from the purchase of Zinc July 1st futures on 5 May:
   40 × 25 × $892 = $892,000
   Gain on Metal Exchange dealings:
   $45,000

---

price, and for the gradual rise in the futures price as the contract's remaining life begins to shorten. The phenomenon is referred to as normal *backwardation*. In some circumstances, however, often when speculators are tending to dispose of futures, the futures' price declines, not rises, and the spot price is below the futures price. The market is then said to be *contango* — the zinc example in the text is a case in point. The interaction between hedgers and speculators is a vital feature of the market and enables it to remain active, liquid and competitive.

Purchasing 679

The company's net gain of the Metal Exchange account over the reduction in value of the cargo due to the fall in price in transit is thus $3,000 ($45,000 − $42,000).

Second Example

The second example is briefly given and involves a manufacturer of cereals. On 1 March, the manufacturer realises he will require one hundred tonnes of additional wheat in three months' time, and expects the price to have risen by then over the current spot price of £70/tonne. Accordingly, he buys one hundred tonnes of "Wheat June 1st" futures at the current forward price of £74/tonne. (He is now locked into this price. This is what he will pay and it is on this basis that he can now plan.) By the time 1 June is reached, however, the spot price has in fact declined to £65/tonne. (The price of Wheat June 1st futures is also, therefore, £65/tonne, since on the expiration date, the contract price and the spot price converge.) The manufacture now sells his futures (100 tonnes, June 1st) for £65/tonne, closing out his position in the market, and showing a futures loss of £900 (£7,400 − £6,500). He is now, however, able to buy one hundred tonnes of wheat at the spot price of £65/tonne, rather than £74/tonne, so his position overall is unchanged — in effect, he has paid £74/tonne, the lock-in price.

For the buyer who hedges, the purchase of futures fixes the price, protecting him against price rises but at the same time blocking him from taking advantage when price falls. The supplier who hedges is protected against price falls but blocked from price rises.

16.5 FOREIGN PURCHASES

The rate at which one foreign currency may be exchanged for another varies from minute to minute and, for a given currency in troubled times, may rise or fall by several percentage points in a week. In common with commodity prices, foreign exchange rates (*forex* rates) cannot be accurately forecast. It should be a central company policy on foreign purchases and sales, therefore, that the very substantial dangers in attempting to do so be forbidden and prevented. In this respect, taking no action at all with regard to a foreign purchase must count as forecasting, since the buyer who takes no action to protect himself against the volatility of the forex market immediately a foreign purchase is agreed is in effect leaving matters to chance. Chance is risk, and risk is speculation — will sterling have appreciated or depreciated against the currency in question when the time comes to pay? It is not acceptable to a company that its buyers of goods and services should be speculators, potentially at its own expense. Nor must the purchasing manager merely abrogate the paying of such purchases to the company's accounts department or to its bankers. He must understand the options available and instigate, or, at least, concur with, the operations taken to effect any such purchases. Sub-section 16.5.1 deals with foreign payments and the standard means for making provision for fluctuations in rates.

The second problem in effecting a foreign purchase is ensuring that its terms are actually carried out — that the goods really are despatched and really are what it was contracted to buy. The means of assurance for both buyer and seller in matters of delivery and payment is the *letter of credit*, described in sub-section 16.5.2.

16.5.1 Foreign Payments[36]

The existence of a rate of exchange of one currency for another comes about as the result of market demand, in just the same way that spot and future prices are determined for the sale and purchase of zinc and wheat.

Currencies and currency futures are traded in over a dozen major financial exchanges throughout the world, the market in the City being the London International Financial Futures Exchange (LIFFE, pronounced *life*). Although the procedure for obtaining

---

[36] Since 1979 in the UK, all government controls regulating foreign exchange have been removed, and forex has been available to buy and sell without restriction. A small number of other countries besides the UK also have no exchange controls — for example, the US, Canada and countries belonging to the European Monetary Union (EMU). Many other countries have exchange controls but are able to maintain a trade deficit if necessary, and so have little difficulty buying and selling abroad. Certain currencies, especially those relating to sub-Saharan African countries, are "non-convertible", meaning that they have no value outside their own countries. In order to obtain foreign goods, therefore, such countries must either barter their own produce in exchange (known as "countertrading" — see sub-section 16.5.3) or else must somehow obtain hard currency in the form of sterling or US dollars.

foreign currency preferred by the purchasing manager is likely to be through a commercial bank and the forward market, as described below, it will be appreciated that the banks themselves obtain their foreign currency by way of financial futures. The nominal value of contracts traded on LIFFE in January 2001 alone reached £8,000 billion.[37]

The financial futures market is certainly available to the purchasing manager requiring to obtain or hedge foreign currency if he wishes to use it. Its operation is as described for product and produce commodities in sub-section 16.4.2, the contracts traded being in lots of £25,000. LIFFE has also created a market in what it terms *traded options*. Traded options are a valuable alternative to the forward market for purchases involving relatively large sums (say, over £250,000). Like futures, traded options are also derivatives, being securities, or contracts, which have associated with them a range of five alternative exchange rates against the US dollar, all close to the spot rate. The purchaser must nominate a particular rate, termed his "exercise price", and, having done so, has a right to convert the security value to dollars at that rate, or do nothing, at any time until a specified date in the future. Two further means of obtaining foreign currencies, other than through financial futures and traded options, are by currency swaps and through currency pools. Currency swaps are associated with major purchases of very high value over long periods of time. A deal will be arranged by a specialist broker in the City, who will undertake to find a company in the foreign country concerned which requires the equivalent sum in sterling. Currency pools may be established by UK international businesses generating revenue overseas. A business is not required to repatriate its profits, so these can be used to make local payments to suppliers of goods that have been sent on to the UK.

The means by which the purchasing manager will most commonly obtain foreign exchange to pay for a purchase is through the *forward market*. (The forward market is similarly the most common way by which the sales manager will make provision for

---

[37] Quoted by John Foyle, LIFFE deputy chief executive, *The Daily Telegraph*, 5 February 2001, p. 23.

converting to sterling the future proceeds due from a foreign sale.)[38]

The forward rate of exchange of a currency quoted on the forward market depends on only the following factors:

1. The spot rate of exchange quoted by LIFFE and prevailing at the moment a particular deal is struck;

2. The relative rates of interest of the Bank of England and the national bank setting the interest rates to which the foreign currency relates;[39] and

3. The duration of the forward period involved.

The mechanism by which the market works is quite straightforward. When the purchaser states his requirement (the currency required and its date of delivery), the forex dealer, or the official in charge of foreign exchange at a specialist branch of the company's own bank, will buy the foreign currency at the spot rate, for deposit in the City of London at the national bank of the country in question (or at the Banque de France, Banco d'España — these institutions now having been reduced to the status of branches of the ECB — see footnote 39). The period the currency is to be on deposit is the duration of time until the requirement date specified by the buyer in the transaction. (Thus if the buyer requires the currency in 46 days' time, it will remain on deposit for 46 days.) When maturity is reached, the currency is then made available to the buyer, in effect at the exchange rate prevailing when the original purchase was made, but with one or other of two adjustments to it as follows.

---

[38] The procedures involved in sales are analogous to those illustrated for purchasing in the text, but additional figures are required relating to interest and exchange rates in the foreign currencies concerned (i.e. an alternative version of Figure 16.3 is needed). The sales manager contracts to buy sterling from the foreign bank, and pays for it in due course with the foreign currency when it becomes available from his customer.

[39] Since the surrender of their national sovereignties over interest rates by the 11 participants in European Monetary Union (EMU), the interest rate in euroland has been set by the European Central Bank (ECB), currently in Frankfurt. (It will be interesting to see whether one size can fit all.)

First, if the rate of interest offered by the foreign bank is lower than the rate of interest offered by the Bank of England, the purchaser's own bank will have lost money, since the deposit will have earned less interest. Accordingly, the buyer must pay his bank a *premium* (pm) over the spot rate of sterling that prevailed at the moment the transaction was entered into, to make good his bank's loss. In summary, the buyer will obtain the currency at the original exchange rate per £, less the premium.

Secondly, if the rate of interest offered by the foreign bank is higher than the rate of interest offered by the Bank of England, the buyer's bank will have gained money, since the amount concerned will have been on deposit at a higher rate for the period. Consequently, the buyer will obtain a *discount* (dis) from the spot rate of sterling at the time deal was struck, to make up the difference. In summary, the buyer will obtain the currency at the original spot rate per £, plus the discount.

Three examples are given below to illustrate the operation of the forward market, employing the rates of exchange given in Figure 16.3. Figure 16.3 is based on prices prevailing in January 1999; the prices are similar to those published in newspapers and on the Internet, although a number of simplifications have been made as follows: whereas official data published by LIFFE has such information as "mid-point spot price", "change on the day" and "bid/offer spread", the values in the Figure show only a single spot dealer selling price (offer price) and a single spot dealer buying price (bid price). The 1-month, 3-months and 12-months forward prices simply show a single price, and it is these prices that are used in the three examples.

Figure 16.3: A Simplified Table of Spot and Forward Prices for Five Foreign Currencies against the £ Sterling, from Rates Applying in January 1999

Country and Currency	Spot Price Dealer Selling (offer)	Spot Price Dealer Buying (bid)	1 Month	% p.a. (1 month)	3 Months	% p.a. (3 months)	1 Year	% p.a. (1 year)
euroland (Euro)	1.4068	1.4096	1.4030	3.3	1.3967	2.9	1.3747	2.3
Norway (N. Krone)	12.4534	12.4583	12.4754	−2.1	12.5093	−1.8	12.5760	−1.0
Japan (Yen)	186.980	187.771	185.965	6.5	184.290	5.8	177.700	5.0
USA (US Dollar)	1.6599	1.6658	1.6581	1.3	1.6557	1.0	1.6531	0.4
Australia (A. Dollar)	2.6823	2.6854	2.6784	1.7	2.6733	1.3	2.6623	0.7

The effect of the difference between a selling price and a buying price can be illustrated by reference to the US dollar in Figure 16.3. Thus: (a) from the figure, we see that the forex dealer sells $US at $1.6599 per £. A purchaser who wished to buy $1,000 would therefore pay £602.45 ($1,000/1.6599); (b) from the Figure, we see that the forex dealer will buy $US at $1.6658 per £. Thus a salesman wishing to sell $1,000 would obtain £600.31 ($1,000/1.6658). The difference of £2.14 is known as the dealer's *turn*.

Note that each rate of interest given in the figure is the rate of interest at the Bank of England minus the rate of interest of the foreign country, for the stated period ahead (banks offer different rates of interest depending on the durations of deposits). Also note that the rates for 1-month, 3-months and 12-months are published simply for guidance. A bank will quote a forward rate for any period ahead specified. The calculation of forward rates is a simple matter, being merely based on the difference in interest rates and the period ahead involved, for one unit of currency.

Example 1: The buyer wishes to obtain 50,000 euros in one month's time

From Figure 16.3, we see that the rate at which the dealer will sell euros for delivery in one month's time is 1.4030 euros per £. The working out which has been undertaken by the buyer's bank is as follows:

Spot rate for purchase of euros	1.4068 €/£
Premium for "one months" euros	0.0038 €/£
∴ Future rate (spot less premium)	1.4030 €/£
Cost of 50,000 euros in one month is	
£(50,000/1.4030)	= £35,638

The sterling cost of the protection offered by the forward market is thus £97. Note that when the transaction is agreed with the dealer or the bank, it cannot be revoked (although the currency can, of course, be retained, at interest, for use at a later time). Also note that the payment of the sterling by the buyer is not made until the date the forex is due to be made available. That is, the buyer's company has use of its money until that time. Commission to the bank is either not payable or is very small (say, 0.025 per cent).

Example 2. A UK company wishes to obtain 100,000 US dollars in 12 months' time to pay for capital equipment to be delivered then.

From Figure 16.3 for US dollars:

Spot rate for dealer selling US dollars	1.6599 $/£
Forward premium on 12-month US dollars	0.0068 $/£
∴ Future rate (spot less premium)	1.6531 $/£
Cost of 100,000 US dollars in 12 months is	
£ (100,000 / 1.6531)	= £60,492

The cost to the company from its use of the forward market is £247. Note that although it is protected from exchange rate fluctuations, the bank will make adjustments to the company's account in the likely event over the 12 months of interest rate changes.

Example 3. A buyer wishes to obtain 750,000 Norwegian Krone in three months' time to pay for forestry products from Norway to be delivered then.

From Figure 16.3:
Spot rate for dealer selling Norwegian Krone   12.4534 NKr/£
Forward discount on 3-month Norwegian Krone   0.0559 dis/£
∴ Future rate (spot plus discount)   12.5093 NKr/£
Cost of 750,000 N. Krone in 3 months is £ (750,000/12.5093)
= £59,955

In this example, because the rate of interest in Oslo is greater than that in London, there is a financial gain of £269 to the buyer from his use of the forward market.

16.5.2 Foreign Payments and Commercial Risk

Because of geographical distance, foreign language and differences in culture, law and time, as well as possibly complex customs and exchange regulations and the possibility of political unrest, the purchase of goods from overseas may carry many more commercial risks than from within the UK.

In order to minimise risk to both buyer and supplier, a very great deal of international trade is carried out via *letter of credit* (L/C), a means by which the buyer is assured of receiving the goods he contracts for and by which the supplier is assured of receiving the payment that is his due.

The procedures involved in the use of a letter of credit have been standardised by the International Chamber of Commerce (ICC). The version issued in 1993 is referred to as the Uniform Customs and Practice for Documentary Credits — UCP1993 for short.[40] Note that letters of credit are also referred to as "documentary credits", "letters of commercial credit" and "documentary letters of credit". Since the bank issuing a letter of credit commits itself to payment and takes on a number of risks not covered by

---

[40] UCP1993 is officially ICC Document Number 500. It contains 49 sections under seven headings, such as liabilities and responsibilities; transferable credit; documents; assignment of proceeds; and so on. It is as well for the buyer to refer specifically to UCP1993 in any contract with the supplier that is based on the use of a letter of credit.

insurance, letters of credit can be relatively expensive (perhaps £150 to £200 each). Consequently, if the buyer is absolutely sure of his source and all other matters, he is likely to avoid the expense of its use. On the other hand, if two parties within the UK are mutually distrustful, they may agree to the use of a letter of credit as a means of policing the agreement.

In paper form, the letter of credit is a standard document and contains the following information:

- *The name of the beneficiary*: i.e. the supplier's name and address;
- *The amount of the credit*: the amount can be qualified as *approximate* (e.g. 10 per cent difference) or *not exceeding — (some limit)*;
- *The dates when valid*: at least 10 days are needed, and preferably more, to give time for the preparation of shipment documentation;
- *The beneficiary's bank*: if this is omitted, the issuing bank is free to choose a branch of its own bank;
- *The style of payment*: "pay on sight", "pay within X days", and so on;
- *The documents required*: here the buyer specifies all documents which are to be presented with the goods — examples are bill of lading,[41] invoice, certificate of origin, quality analysis, technical inspection etc.;
- *Address of notification*: the name and address to be notified when the goods have arrived at the port of destination;
- *A description of the goods*: a concise but absolutely accurate description of the goods, and their quantity (quantity can be stated as approximate).

---

[41] Expressed in shipping terms, rather than in air or road freight terms, a bill of lading is a document issued by the master of a vessel, on behalf of the haulage company responsible for the shipment, that goods have been received in apparently good condition, and bearing other details such as the name of the consignor, the places of departure and destination, the price of the freight, and so on. The bill of lading is used as evidence of a contract to ship, and is assignable, any such assignee being then entitled to possession of the goods.

The detail specified by the buyer as being necessary for a particular purchase should be no more than is required for the purposes of confirmation and identification. Over-specification will meet with resistance by the supplier: the L/C is not intended to be a duplication of the original contract. Note, by the way, that although details may be broad, they must be quite correct, especially in regard to company and bank names. It is not unknown for customs' officials to hold up shipments on finding quite minor discrepancies in paper details.

Very commonly nowadays, letters of credit are presented in computer form. For example, the buyer's bank may send the buyer an e-mail, to include a copy of its software program. The details listed above for a paper document are input at the VDU, and the contents of the e-mail attachment downloaded to the bank's computer. The advantages in so doing are considerable — savings in time and the costs of a courier; the reduced chance of error because of software prompts when the data are originally input; and, above all, the elimination of transcription errors once the data are entered.

A letter of credit may be *irrevocable* or, less usually, *revocable*. An irrevocable L/C is one that obliges the issuing bank to make payment when all terms and conditions have been met. No term or condition can be altered without the express permission of the supplier. An irrevocable L/C may be either *irrevocable, confirmed* or *irrevocable, unconfirmed*. A revocable L/C is subject to possible recall by the buyer without the approval of the supplier.

The procedures followed in ensuring, for the purchaser, that the terms of an agreement are correctly complied with by the supplier and, for the supplier, that payment is made, are set out in ten steps below. In order to follow these more easily, Figure 16.4 shows the flow of the initial exchange of documents and the names of the four parties (i.e. supplier, buyer, issuing bank and advising bank).

Figure 16.4: The Initial Information Flow in Opening a Letter of Credit

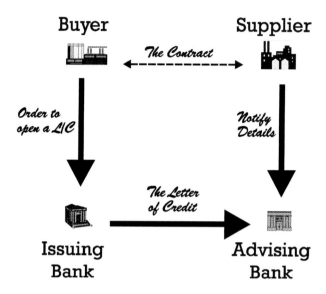

- **Step 1.** After the buyer and supplier are agreed on the terms of purchase, including the dates of payment and delivery, the buyer arranges for his bank to *open a letter of credit* on behalf of the supplier;

- **Step 2.** The buyer's bank (*the issuing bank*) prepares the letter of credit according to the buyer's instructions. The buyer's instructions specify what the supplier is to provide by way of documentation (see the earlier text);

- **Step 3.** The buyer's bank sends the letter of credit to *the advising bank* in the supplier's country This could be the supplier's own bank or it might be any other nominated bank;

- **Step 4.** The advising bank forwards the letter of credit to the supplier;

- **Step 5.** The supplier now studies all the conditions and detail in the letter of credit. Any errors and objections must be notified immediately;

- **Step 6.** The supplier makes the goods ready and despatches them with all documentation as required in the letter of credit;

- **Step 7.** The supplier presents the documents to the advising bank indicating full compliance with the terms of the letter of credit, and including any required evidence from third party inspectors;
- **Step 8.** The advising bank reviews the documents. If they are in order, they are forwarded to the issuing bank. If the letter of credit is irrevocable confirmed, the supplier is now guaranteed payment and may be paid at once by his bank;
- **Step 9.** Once the issuing bank receives the documents, it notifies the buyer, who then reviews them. If they are in order, the buyer effects payment to his bank and takes possession of the documents, which in turn enable him to take physical possession of the shipment;
- **Step 10.** The buyer's bank initiates payment to the advising bank, which pays the supplier if it has not already done so.

16.5.3 Countertrading

Countertrade is a general term for deals between companies in which payment for supplies is made, directly or indirectly, through the further exchange of goods or services, rather than by cash settlement. The Department of Trade and Industry believes that countertrading may account for some 10–15 per cent of world trade.[42]

Inevitably compared to straight cash settlement, countertrade increases the complexity and expense of doing business, but may be the only option where the country requiring goods has no convertible foreign currency. (The value of sterling or US dollars to a Third World supplier should be borne in mind by a UK buyer negotiating a deal.) Although countertrade is by its nature opportunistic, six alternative forms it might take are as follows:

1. *Barter.* Goods are exchanged for goods, although the DTI points out that, before the deal can be finalised, the purchaser's goods offered in barter must often first be made to

---

[42] Department of Trade (1998), *Countertrade and Offset: A Guide for Exporters*. Includes case histories and the names of specialist consultants. Phone 0870-1502-500 (DTI Publications) or visit http://www.tradepartners.gov.uk.

generate cash in the supplier's country after their receipt by him.

2. *Buyback.* The supplier of capital plant or capital equipment agrees to accept as payment part of the future output of the facility being provided.

3. *Counter purchase.* A supplier undertakes to purchase a specified amount of goods and services from the country being supplied, as a condition of securing the order. (As with many other forms of countertrade, such a counterpurchase deal is likely to involve government intervention and, often, very complex and intricate arrangements involving many parties.)

4. *Direct Offset.* The supplier agrees to incorporate materials and components, from the country of export, in the goods being supplied.

5. *Indirect Offset.* The purchasing country requires that the exporting country provide industrial co-operation and itself make purchases as a general *quid pro quo* for the business, these further deals not being directly connected with the export being supplied.

6. *Switch Trading.* When Country A has a large trade surplus with Country B, it may be possible for Country A to pay for goods from a third country, Country C, with goods from Country B. Switch trading is so called because it typically involves diverting cargoes on the high seas, in the foregoing instance, those destined from B to A, to Country C instead.

Chapter 17

Finance and Costing

The purposes of accounting are to control the company's financial affairs from day to day; to calculate and control the costs of manufacture of products and individual jobs; to summarise the company's financial standing from time to time, and so determine whether it is reaching its business goals; and to satisfy taxation and other regulatory bodies. The company's finance director, its accountancy manager (or *chief accountant*) and other accountants in the firm, including cost accountants, will have gained prestigious professional qualifications from one or other of a small number of accountancy bodies and so be licensed and qualified to manage the company's accounts to the standards required by the board of directors and by authority. Notwithstanding the specialisation of the subject, however, the manufacturing manager should be familiar with certain aspects of it, especially the structure of the company's principal financial accounts (to gain a deeper appreciation of corporate operations), the treatment of assets (both with regard to stock, fixed plant and proposals for capital expenditure) and product costing (as a means of measuring his own performance).

17.1 FINANCIAL ACCOUNTS

17.1.1 The Profit and Loss Account

The twin pillars of the company's financial accounts are the *profit and loss account* (P&L account), dealt with in this sub-section, and the *balance sheet* (sub-section 2).

For the company's financial year, the profit and loss account shows turnover, the cost of sales, gross profit, various categories of expense, corporation tax payable and dividend distributions. Various *schedules* are attached to these individual entries, as indicated below, a schedule in this sense being an explanation and breakdown of detail. Where the company is engaged in distinctly different types of business, or where its business is conducted in different major geographic zones, the individual turnover and profit before tax of each of them is also shown in supplementary notes. An illustration of a Profit and Loss statement is given in Figure 17.1. By accounting convention, brackets show that the figure concerned should be subtracted.

Figure 17.1: A Profit and Loss Account

Profit & Loss Account (all figures £)	
Turnover	800,000
Cost of Sales	(390,000)
Gross Profit	410,000
Distribution & Selling Costs	(110,000)
Administrative Costs	(50,000)
Profit	250,000
Other Operating Income	20,000
Operating Profit for the Year, before Taxation	270,000
Tax on Profit on Ordinary Activities	(50,000)
Profit on Ordinary Activities after Taxation	220,000
Dividends	(50,000)
Retained Profit this Year	170,000
Retained Profit brought forward	200,000
Retained Profit carried forward	370,000

Comments on the individual entries found in the P&L statement in Figure 17.1 are as follows:

Turnover

Turnover is made up of the total sales invoiced during the financial year, irrespective of whether or not "debtors" at the year end have in fact paid the company (*debtors* being customers with outstanding invoices). The turnover figure is exclusive of VAT.

Cost of Sales

The cost of sales is made up of: (1) raw material purchases for the financial year, after adjusting for opening and closing raw material stocks; (2) the costs of manufacture, again after adjusting stocks of work-in-progress; and (3) other expenses incurred in the buying and manufacturing processes. A separate explanatory schedule is attached to the financial accounts showing how the cost-of-sales figure for the financial year has been calculated, and giving a breakdown into the main headings.

Gross Profit

The gross profit is defined as turnover *less* the cost of sales, and is usually also expressed as a percentage of the turnover, so that ready comparison can be made with the gross profits of earlier years and the gross profits achieved by competitor companies. In Figure 17.1, it is 51.25 per cent (£410,000/£800,000).

Distribution, Selling and Administration Costs

Distribution and selling costs (usually the two are added together) and administrative costs are supplemented by separate schedules in the company's accounts. The schedules show all fixed and variable expenses incurred in operating the company's business during the financial year. Typical expense accounts are: wages; salaries; rent; rates; insurance; directors' remuneration; and depreciation.

Other Operating Income

Under this heading is included any income received by the company in connection with its normal trading activities, other than from sales. Examples might be as diverse as royalty receipts and rents received from letting properties.

Tax on Profit on Ordinary Activities

Corporate tax payable on Net Profits, as adjusted for tax purposes and after deducting standard depreciation allowances (termed *capital allowances*).

Dividends

Dividends declared by the board to the company's shareholders. These are paid to shareholders after prior deductions of income tax at the prevailing rate, the deductions being accounted for by the company direct to the Inland Revenue.

Retained Profits

Retained profits for the financial year are added to *retained profits brought forward* (i.e. from the previous year), the resulting figure being termed *retained profits carried forward*. Retained profits brought forward appear as revenue reserves in the company's balance sheet at the financial year-end.

17.1.2 The Balance Sheet

The balance sheet is a statement of the assets, liabilities and residual value of a company at a particular point in time — usually, at the end of the company's financial year. The balance sheet is arranged, or organised, to show fixed assets plus current assets less current liabilities. In turn, these are represented in total by issued share capital and revenue and (if applicable) capital reserves. An example of a balance sheet prepared on the above basis, in a vertical format, is given in Figure 17.2.

Figure 17.2: A Balance Sheet

Balance Sheet (Figures in £)	
Fixed Assets	500,000
Current Assets	200,000
Total Assets	700,000
less Current Liabilities	300,000
Net Assets	400,000
Represented By:	
Called up Share Capital	100,000
Balance Reserve — P&L Account	300,000
Shareholders' Funds	400,000

Finance and Costing

To illustrate how changes in assets affect the company's value, consider a company founded by a proprietor with £1,000 cash in the bank, who then takes two actions as follows: (1) he buys £400 of stock; and (2) he next buys a machine for £500 on a long-term loan. Presenting the Balance Sheet now in a lateral format, rather than vertically as before, the proprietor's start-up position is as shown in Figure 17.3.

Figure 17.3: A Proprietor's Start-Up Balance Sheet

Capital	£1,000	Assets: machine	£500
Liabilities		stock	£400
(i.e. loan)	£500	bank	£600
	£1,500		£1,500

Note that the proprietor's capital consists of the company's assets less its liabilities, namely £1,000 (£1,500 − £500). This does not mean the proprietor could wind up the company and obtain £1,000. If he wound it up, he might get only half for the machine and half for the stock, making total realised assets of only £1,050. A priority legal claimant on this is the company's only creditor, who is owed £500 with respect to the machine loan. So the proprietor would finish up with only £550. However, if the business is regarded as a "going concern", the proprietor's capital is indeed worth £1,000 — i.e. everything he originally put into the company, although now in different forms, not all simply cash at the bank.

Suppose the proprietor now sells £250 of his stock to a customer for £300, sending the customer an invoice, expected to be paid in the near future. The balance sheet is now as shown in Figure 17.4.

Figure 17.4: A Proprietor's Balance Sheet after a Business Transaction

Capital	£1,050	Assets: machine	£500
		stock	£150
Liabilities		debtor	£300
(i.e. loan)	£500	bank	£600
	£1,550		£1,550

Once more, the proprietor's capital is the company's assets less its liabilities, and this has very clearly reached £1,050 because of the £50 profit on the sale. The value of the proprietor's capital in this simple example might easily have been calculated also by tracking every transaction that occurred. In a realistic case of a limited company, however, this is not practical, and the company's value must be calculated somewhat obliquely using the assets-less-liabilities equation and profit from the P&L account. Note that if the proprietor were to make a "drawing" of £30 of his profits in cash for himself from the bank, the assets would reduce by £30 (£570 now at the bank) and the value of the business would thus be reduced to £1,020.

Differences between the simple example given and the balance sheet of a major limited company are:

1. The owners of the company are the shareholders, as explained in Chapter 1;

2. The company typically undertakes a far wider range of activities, implying a far greater variety of entries (though not necessarily of greater complexity); and

3. The existence of a legal requirement to provide certain details which do not appear in the example.

Information either pertinent to a limited company or required by law to be shown in the balance sheet includes the following:

a) A breakdown of the fixed assets, plus any information about their recent revaluation, and their original cost;

b) A breakdown of current assets, including loans to directors;

c) Investments held, especially large shareholdings in other companies;

d) Changes in reserves and provisions;

e) Guarantees and commitments;

f) Details on creditors where payment is due to them after one year (i.e. a class of long-term liability); and

g) Details of share and loan capital.

Finance and Costing 699

There is always something of a tussle with regard to disclosure, between the company, wishing to keep its affairs secret from competitors and City predators, and potential investors seeking maximum information.

17.1.3 The System of Accounts

The system of accounts to be described is a succinct means of controlling and analysing the receipts, expenditures and other financial activities of the company. The *accounts* referred to are numerous separate, logical groupings of transactions such as those relating to wages; VAT; raw material supplies; royalty receipts; fuel expenditure; and so on. (Note, therefore, that an account does not "balance" — see below.) Their detail and the number of them maintained by the company will depend on its activities and the finance director's views about control. The firm's complete collection of accounts is referred to as its "book of account", or *ledger*. The term "accounting" originally meant the management of these accounts.

Standing behind the ledger are what are known as *subsidiary books*, also variously termed books of prime entry, day books or nowadays very often *journals*. A journal is capable of holding (or directly referring to) not simply basic financial data, but supporting documentation such as legal agreements, invoices, technical specifications, letters and so on — information termed the "*narration*". It is a precept of accounting that, ultimately, all entries in the accounts relating to external receipts and payments should be traceable to original commercial documentation.

A fundamental convention of the ledger accounts is their format. They are divided into two parts, debits placed on the left hand side and credits on the right, often denoted by "Dr" (debit, or debtor) and "Cr" (credit, or creditor). The convention is summarised in Figure 17.5.

Figure 17.5: Debits and Credits

Debit (DR)	Credit (CR)
a benefit that is received by others	a benefit that is received by the company
(supply of value to others *by* this company)	(supply of value etc. *to* this company)

Use of the terms credit and debit in everyday English is often inexact. In accounting, however, the noun *credit* refers to a benefit *received by* the company *from* someone else (perhaps in the form of a supply of raw materials). Creditors, for example, are suppliers to whom the company owes money for the supply of goods and services (i.e. the suppliers are *in credit*). The verb *to credit* means to place on the credit side of the account, i.e. the right-hand side. The noun *debit* means the opposite — money or a good *received by* others *from* us (perhaps the supply of finished products to our customers or the payment of wages to our employees). Customers that owe the firm money are its debtors. The verb *to debit* means to place on the debit side of the account, i.e. on the left-hand side.

To illustrate an account and the notion of debits and credits, first consider a company's Temporary Wages Account for the recording and control of wages paid to temporary typists supplied by Tempo Secretarial Services. On 5 September and 18 September, we pay wages to Tempo typists of £90 and £100, and on 23 September receive a "credit note" for £50 from Tempo, relating to a previous mistaken overpayment to them by us. The Temporary Wage Account for September reads as shown in Figure 17.6.

Figure 17.6: Debiting and Crediting a Company Expense Account

| **Temporary Wages Account** ||
Dr	*Cr*
5 September Wages for X £90	23 September Rebate from Tempo £50
18 September Wages for Y £100	

We see from the Figure that the account was *debited with increases in the expense* (the benefit — or wages — received by typists X and Y), and was *credited with decreases in the expense* (the benefit received by the company — i.e. the repayment from Tempo). Put another way, having regard to the essential nature of this particular account, an increase in the activity that the account is recording (i.e. the paying of typists) gives rise to further debits — here the financial consequences of using Tempo's secretarial services.

The Temporary Wages Account is classed in accountancy as an *expense account*. Debits to an expense account increase the sum of

Finance and Costing

money paid out (i.e. wages) and credits decrease it (e.g. the Tempo rebate).

Consider next the company's Finished Goods Account, relating to the control of payments for finished goods, previously supplied by us to customers, also in September. On the 6th and the 19th we receive payments from Customer A and Customer B of £100 and £235, due to the deliveries of sales orders to them, and on 24 September we send a repayment of £50 to Customer C, due to a previous overpayment by C to us. The Finished Goods Account for September now reads as shown in Figure 17.7.

Figure 17.7: Debiting and Crediting a Company Revenue Account

Finished Goods Account	
Dr	Cr
24 September To Customer C £50	6 September From Customer A £100
	19 September From Customer B £235

We see here that the account was *credited with increases in the revenue* (the benefit received by us from Customers A and B), and was *debited with decreases in the revenue* (the repayment to Customer C on the 24th). That is, again having regard to the essential nature of this particular account, an increase in the activity that the account is recording gives rise to further credits — the financial rewards from our sales to customers.

The Finished Goods Account is classed in accountancy as a *revenue account*. Credits increase this type of account and debits (such as the repayment to Customer C) decrease it.

It is seen that the Temporary Wages expense account behaves oppositely to the Finished Goods revenue account. In the former, the activity being recorded creates debits — debits increase the account; in the second, the activity being recorded creates credits — credits increase the account. In financial accountancy there are three further types of account as follows:

1. *Asset Accounts:* Assets, like expenses, must be paid for — when we acquire an asset, we gain a benefit from it, but incur an obligation to pay for it. Consequently, debits to an asset account increase the account, and credits decrease it;

2. *Capital Accounts:* Capital accounts are analogous to revenue accounts — for example, if a proprietor supplies £1,000 of capital for the benefit of his business, the effect of so doing is similar to the effect of the receipt of £1,000 by way of revenue from a customer. Consequently, credits to a capital account increase the account, and debits decrease it;

3. *Liability Accounts:* Just as capital supplies value to the business, and gives rise to liability, so liabilities arise from previous supplies of value and the corresponding creation of claims on the business. Consequently, by analogy, credits to a liability account increase the account, and debits decrease it.

The five types of account and the effect on each of them of debits and credits are summarised in Figure 17.8.

Figure 17.8: Summary of Account Types in Financial Accounting

	Debits	**Credits**
Asset Accounts	Increase the account	Decrease the account
Expense Accounts	Increase the account	Decrease the account
Liability Accounts	Decrease the account	Increase the account
Capital Accounts	Decrease the account	Increase the account
Revenue Accounts	Decrease the account	Increase the account

With the meanings of debit and credit firmly in mind, and the distinction between the five types of accounts in Figure 17.8 also in mind, we turn to the basis of the system of accounts management used by the financial accountant. This is termed "duality", or, more popularly, *double entry bookkeeping*. Double entry bookkeeping is the cornerstone of financial control. As explanation, consider two rules developed in sub-sections 17.1.1 and 17.1.2. First, the Profit and Loss accounting rule may be succinctly stated as an equation, given by Equation 17.1.

$$\text{Revenue} - \text{Expenses} = \text{Profit} \qquad \textit{Equation 17.1}$$

Next, the Balance Sheet rule might be summarised as in Equation 17.2.

Finance and Costing 703

Assets − Liabilities = Capital + Profit Equation 17.2

Subtracting Equation 17.1 from Equation 17.2 gives Equation 17.3.

Assets − Liabilities − Revenue + Expenses = Capital
Equation 17.3

Rearranging terms in Equation 17.3 gives Equation 17.4.

Assets + Expenses = Capital + Liabilities + Revenue
Equation 17.4

Equation 17.4 is known as the "accounting equation". In examining it, we find that: (1) any increase in the value on the left-hand side must be balanced by an equal increase on the right, and (2) any decrease in the value on the left-hand side must be balanced by an equal decrease on the right. From these conclusions, we may derive the two fundamental principles of double entry bookkeeping, thus:

1. If there is any increase in the company's assets, or the incurrence of any expense (the left-hand side of the equation), then the increase must be balanced *either* by a corresponding increase in liabilities, or capital, or revenue (the right-hand side), *or else* by a decrease in some other asset or expense; and

2. If there is any increase in liabilities, capital or revenue (the right-hand side), this must be balanced *either* by an increase in the assets and/or expenses on the left, *or else* by a decrease in some other liability, capital or revenue account.

Remembering, now, that an increase in assets or expenses means a *debit* to these types of accounts, and an increase in liabilities, capital or revenue means a *credit* to those types of account, the balancing act implicit in the accounting equation can be summarised as follows:

1. **If there is an increase in an asset or expense account** — that is, if there is a ***debit*** to such an account — then this must be matched . . .

    either by an increase in a liability, capital or revenue account (i.e. a ***credit*** to such an account), *or* by a decrease in another asset or expense account (i.e. a **credit** to such another account).

2. **If there is an increase in a liability, capital or revenue account** — that is, a **credit** to such an account — then this must be matched...

   either by an increase in an asset or expense account (i.e. a **debit** to such an account),

   or by a decrease in another liability, capital or revenue account (i.e. a **debit** to such another account).

In other words, (1) every new debit to an account must result in an equivalent credit to some other account, and (2) every new credit to an account must result in a debit to some other account.

To illustrate double entry bookkeeping, consider Kevin Kilter, who starts up in business on 1 October, at the same time opening five accounts for the purpose of business control: a bank account; a capital account; an external supplies account; Brown & Co account; and a wages account. (1) On 2 October, Kevin Kilter pays in £1,000 to his company's bank account, on his own behalf, from private funds of no concern to the business. Kilter's next actions are (2) to purchase raw materials by cheque for £250 on 8 October; (3) to order equipment for £500 on 11 October from Brown & Co; (4) on 17 October, to pay £200 by cheque to Brown's towards the cost of the equipment previously ordered on the 11th; and (5) to pay £180 in wages on 23 October. At this point in time, Kevin Kilter's books (of account) are as given in Figure 17.9. The Figure distinguishes between asset and expense accounts (termed "Type 1") and liability, capital and revenue accounts ("Type 2"). We see from the example the control exercised by Kilter over ongoing financial transactions, over each account on an individual basis and over his financial position.

Figure 17.9: Kevin Kilter's Accounts after a Number of Financial Activities

Dr			Cr		
Bank Account (Asset, a Type 1 Account)					
2 October	Receipts	£1,000	8 October	Raw Materials	£250
			17 October	Equipment	£200
			23 October	Wages	£180
Kevin Kilter Capital Account (Capital, a Type 2 Account)					
			1 October		£1,000
External Supplies Account (Asset, a Type 1 Account)					
8 October	Raw Materials	£250			
11 October	Equipment	£500			
Brown & Co Account (Liability, a Type 2 Account)					
17 October	Cheque	£200	11 October	Equipment	£500
Wages Account (Expense, a Type 1 Account)					
23 October	Cash	£180			
(Trial Balance)		£2,130			£2,130

17.1.4 Other Financial Accounting Terms

Budgets

Budgets are used throughout the manufacturing concern to plan the activities of different departments of the company, to plan the achievement of financial results (e.g. profit) and to control the actions and performance of managers. The setting of production budgets and the tracking of variances therefrom are dealt with in sub-section 17.4.3. In the planning of financial results, assuming the company can manufacture everything that it is able to sell, the starting point is the sales budget — i.e. the sales forecast in financial terms (see Figure 2.7). Once the company has estimations of its projected sales and sales revenue, it can calculate consequent production needs, production and raw materials expenses and much else.

Cashbook

A separate account is kept in the cashbook of cash at the bank and cash on hand, the receipts and payments of money, and the present cash balance.

Cashflow

The basic concept of cashflow is that calculations and estimates of cash incomings (for example, from payments of invoices by creditors) and cash outgoings (payments to suppliers, payment of tax, etc.) should be set against each other at the financial year-end to determine the "liquidity" of the company (i.e. the amount of ready money available). A company's assets might be very substantial in terms of buildings, plant and stock, but it may nevertheless have insufficient cash to make timely payment of its short-term debts. Companies will normally prepare five cash flow statements covering each of the following: operating activities (i.e. cash flow from trading, including VAT); returns on investments; taxation; assets; and share dealings. Cash flow statements may also be prepared on a month-by-month basis to estimate ongoing monthly requirements for, or surpluses of, cash at the bank.

Directors' Report

This report must accompany the annual accounts and include a "fair" appraisal of the business (i.e. as to its past performance and its prospects); details of the directors' financial interests in the company; and certain social requirements that have been fulfilled, such as arrangements made to consult employees.

Ledger and Ledger Types

Ledgers were defined in sub-section 17.1.3. Note the distinction in accountancy between different ledger types: *personal ledgers* — the accounts of suppliers and customers; *private ledgers* — those relating to the company itself, such as factory fixtures and fittings; and *nominal ledgers (or impersonal ledgers)* — neither personal nor private, but of a general nature, such as wages or rent.

Ledger Records

Ledger records are the various records of sales, debts, receipts, encashments, purchases, invoice payments and so on, which em-

Finance and Costing

body and permit the summarisation and transfer of the corresponding accounts, so that, ultimately, they can be incorporated in the Profit and Loss Account. The ledger records — the firm's books — allow an auditor to trace all receipts and expenditures ultimately to their original sources. This requirement is one reason why all receipts for expenditure and all other evidence of the underlying validity of the entries in the accounts must be kept until the accounts are audited.

Profit (Types)

Gross profit is sales revenue less the cost of sales; *operating profit* is gross profit less distribution and administration expenses; *net profit* is operating profit less other expenses.

Stockturn

Stockturn is defined as "sales revenue / average stock", and is used as a financial yardstick of efficiency with regard to inventory control.

Trial Balance

The system of double entry bookkeeping described in sub-section 17.1.3 ensures that total debits (e.g. purchases, wages, expenses, etc.) equal total credits (capital, sales, receipts etc.). Each month, the accounts are checked to ensure that debits and credits do indeed balance. The check is referred to as the "trial balance". If the debits and credits do not balance, then there is an error. Note, however, that if they *do* balance, this does not necessarily mean that the accounts are correct. Two ways in which a balance might be achieved with incorrect accounts are; (1) because of a compensating error on both sides — say, a credit and a debit being both missing; and (2) because of an error of recording — for example, a payment to purchase a fixed asset being inadvertently debited to the wages account. Figure 17.9 is an example of a trial balance.

17.2 ASSETS

An asset is a property, or right, acquired by the company in the course of its business, and which can either be converted to cash, or else used for its future benefit. Examples of the company's assets are cash at the bank and its own machinery. (Rented offices and leased vehicles do not belong to the company and so are not assets.)

For accounting purposes, the two main categories of assets are *fixed assets* and *current assets*. Fixed assets, such as buildings, land and equipment, have a continuing use in the business — they are likely to be employed over several years. They are usually grouped under a small number of major headings and shown in the balance sheet in descending order of permanence (i.e. first land and buildings; then plant and machinery; then fixtures and fittings). Current assets are assets that are expected to be turned into cash in due course, or else consumed in the very short term in the course of normal operations. They are shown in the balance sheet in increasing order of liquidity (i.e. first stocks, then debtors, then cash itself).

The accountant also speaks of *monetary* and *non-monetary* assets. Monetary assets have a value which can be categorically stated in financial terms, such as cash at the bank and debts that it is confidently expected will be paid. The value of non-monetary assets is less certain, because they remain to be processed through the company's operations. Raw materials are examples of non-monetary assets.

17.2.1 Current Assets

Two of the principal sub-divisions of current assets are cash and debtors. Monies owed by debtors (i.e. customers who have purchased goods from the company but who have not yet paid their invoices) will normally count as monetary assets. (If any debts are bad or doubtful, however, or if the company normally finds a certain percentage of debts turn out to be bad, these should be excluded, and accounted for in a separate expense account called, say, "Doubtful Debts Reserve" in the Profit and Loss Account.)

A topic of obvious interest to the manufacturing manager (and the stores manager) is the valuation of stock. Valuation must pay regard, as ever, to the accounting principles of consistency and prudence, and for stock these may be summarised by the rule that value should be based on the lower of a material's manufacturing cost (or purchase cost) and its net realisable value.

Thus for raw materials, any spoiled or obsolete material should be valued at its scrap or sale value. That apart, if a bought-in part can be individually identified with the item as it was specifically delivered by the supplier, its valuation may be made by reference to the supplier's invoice. Even if it cannot be individually identified, but its purchase price is known not to vary, valuation can be made on this basis. For materials liable to variation in price and which cannot be individually ascertained, three principal possibilities exist: FIFO, LIFO and average price.[1] FIFO (First In, First Out) is a commonsense method and the one most usually used. Issues to the factory of raw material stocks are assumed to have a value corresponding to the earliest possible price paid for them, regardless of their physical identity. For example, suppose 200 items were bought in January at £1 each and 150 in February at £1.50 each, making a total stock of 350 units. In March, 250 units are issued to the factory. It is assumed that the value of the units issued is £275 (200 of the older units, at £1, plus 50 of the later ones, at £1.50). (The FIFO accounting rule produces the same effect as the FIFO stock rotation principle — see sub-section 18.1.1.) With LIFO (Last In, First Out), issues from stock are assumed to be at the latest price that was paid. In the case of the foregoing items, the value of the 250 units issued to the factory is £325 (150 of the newer units at £1.50 plus 100 of the earlier ones at £1). In the average price method, an average price is calculated by dividing the total amount paid by the total number of items bought. In the instance given, this is £1.21 (£425/350) and the value of the units issued is £302.50.

Finished goods are valued at their production cost (i.e. based on their direct cost and production overheads — see Section 17.4). It is wrong to value a finished good at its fully absorbed cost, let alone its selling price, since in the first case the full cost incorporates period costs not necessarily incurred in the period of actual manufacture, and in the second case, even if a sale seems certain,

---

[1] Two other systems of raw material valuation are NIFO (Next In, First Out), and HIFO (Highest In, First Out). NIFO is a variation of LIFO that prevents stock balances of negative value arising (see A.J. Tubb (1977), *Cost Accounting*, Hodder & Stoughton, pp. 48–50). HIFO presumes that the most expensive stock is issued first (*ibid.* pp. 50–52).

the selling price clearly incorporates value from an activity that has not in fact taken place. Two fundamental principles of accounting are: (1) that stock should be regarded as an asset until a sale has been made; and (2) that costs incurred in manufacture may only be classed as expenses in the profit and loss account when they relate to material that has actually been sold. If the costs incurred relate to stock, they must be incorporated in asset value. The costs of manufacture migrate in the accounts from being assets (having potential value) to being expenses (something used up and of no value) when, and only when, the sale is made and the asset's ownership is transferred to someone else.[2]

Work-in-progress items *within stores*, such as components and sub-assemblies, are also valued at production cost, since work on them has been completed up to that point in the bill of materials chain they have now reached. Work-in-progress *on the shop floor* is at an indeterminate stage in the bill of materials, however. It is therefore necessary to estimate its value based on: (1) the starting value of units, at their production cost, before the commencement of processing; (2) an estimate of the amount of cost so far expended — for practical purposes, the accountant may assume that 50 per cent of manufacturing in fact is complete; and (3) their completed value, again based at production cost. Thus if Sub-component A (£5 production cost) is being converted to Component B (£8 production cost), then if there are 100 units of A in progress on the shop floor, their value is deemed to be £650 ((100 × £5) + (50% × 100 × £3)).

17.2.2 Fixed Assets

Expenditure on fixed assets is usually termed *fixed expenditure*, as opposed to expenditure on services and wages, and on other

---

[2] Instructions on stock valuation were issued by the Accounting Standards Committee in a *Statement on Standard Accounting Practice on Stocks and Work in Progress* in 1975 and revised in 1988 ("SSAP9"). An interesting if incidental point is that although stock at a distribution warehouse or retail outlet should also be valued at the price originally paid to the supplier for it, or at its disposal value, this may be difficult to do if a large range of goods is sold and items in the range are constantly changing. In such a case, stock may be valued at the selling price less the gross margin normally added for profit.

Finance and Costing

types of assets, this being referred to as *current expenditure*.[3] (Note that many small items such as desk printers and office fittings are treated simply as expenses, even though they might be expected to last for some time.) The key to the treatment in accountancy of fixed assets is the notion of *depreciation*.

Year by year, a fixed asset is likely to deteriorate physically or to become increasingly outmoded. In other words, each year a part of the asset's value is "used up", until, eventually, its only remaining value is as scrap. In accountancy terms, one might say the portion of an asset's value that has been used up has the character of an expense. Normally, an expense is the cost of a resource that is consumed over a short time. Wages and advertising costs are expenses. For the fixed asset, the aggregate expense of keeping the asset over its life is its original cost less its disposal price (or at least, an estimate of what this latter will be). The expense arising from the decline in a fixed asset's value is termed a *depreciation expense*. The accounting procedure whereby the asset's notional value is reduced each year to take account of its incurrence is termed *depreciation*.

To see how the treatment of depreciation might be gone about, consider a machine that costs £12,000 when acquired, is expected to last for ten years, and which it is estimated will eventually have a scrap value of £2,000. Three common procedures for depreciating the machine's value over the ten years follow.

First, and simplest, we could decide to depreciate its value evenly over the ten years, i.e. at £1,000 per annum, so that, say, after three years the company is said to have incurred £3,000 depreciation expense and the machine to have a *depreciated value* of £9,000. Note that if this were to be done, it does not at all imply that the machine could be sold for £9,000 after three years. Indeed, the calculation is justified only on the assumptions that we are going to continue to use it and that the business remains a going concern. The £9,000 means, quite simply, that the company has used up £3,000 of its original value of £12,000.

---

[3] The older terms for fixed and current expenditure are *capital* and *revenue* expenditure, and seem to make the distinction between the two types more clear.

A second way of reducing the asset's value is to do so year on year by the same percentage. If the asset is bought at value V_1 and is to be disposed of at value V_2, and is to be depreciated over n years, the percentage to be applied is p, given by Equation 17.5.

$$p = \left(1 - \sqrt[n]{\frac{V_2}{V_1}}\right) \times 100\% \qquad \text{Equation 17.5}$$

Substituting the values in the example for the variables in Equation 17.5 gives Equation 17.6.

$$p = \left(1 - \sqrt[10]{\frac{£2,000}{£12,000}}\right) \times 100\% \qquad \text{Equation 17.6}$$

whence $p = 16.4\%$

The third alternative is to disregard the question of time, and depreciate the machine in accordance with its physical use. For example, its expectancy of use might be 10,000 hours. If in the first year it is used for 1,800 hours, it is depreciated by 18 per cent. This method is commonly applied to vehicles, based on their annual and expected lifetime mileages.

It is unlikely that the actual life of an asset and its actual residual value will be exactly what has been estimated. If its life and value are less, the value will have to be "written down" in the final year, although if there is prior warning of the misestimation, a correction should be made as soon as it is received. In the opposite direction, a fixed asset may keep going for years after it has been "written off", valued in the books each year at its scrap value.

One benefit of depreciating fixed assets is that the accounts present a clearer and fairer picture of the assets at the company's disposal. If depreciation were not done, it would appear that the value and state of the fixed assets were forever new, whereas at any one time their condition is a spectrum from new to old.

From the viewpoint of financial accounting, an equally important matter is the treatment in the accounts of the assets' value which has been said to have been used up — i.e. the treatment in the accounts of the depreciation expense. Because depreciation is an expense, it is duly entered in the profit and loss account, the effect of so doing being to reduce the company's net profit. This is shown in the simple example in Figure 17.10.

Finance and Costing

Figure 17.10: Depreciation entered as an Expense in the Accounts

Gross Profit	£5,000
Expenses	
Wages	£1,000
Rent	£500
Fuel & Oil	£1,000
Depreciation	£1,000
Net Profit	£1,500

In Figure 17.10, if a depreciation expense had not been charged to the accounts, net profit would have been £2,500, all of which could have been removed from the company for the benefit of the shareholders (and all of which would have been liable to tax — the Inland Revenue has a considerable interest in depreciation). As it is, net profit is reduced by the amount of the depreciation expense, so that only £1,500 can be removed.

Clearly, while the accountant has charged the depreciation amount of the fixed capital to expenses, a normal type of expense has not been incurred. Nothing has had literally to be paid for. The company has not had to make a payment, as it has had to do for wages or to its advertising agency. By making the allowance, all that has been done is to have "left the amount in the business". The amount involved has been retained in the company as a current asset. As a current asset, it would have been quite in order to have held it in a bank account earmarked for the eventual purchase of new assets when the time comes. The situation might be as shown as in Figure 17.11.

Figure 17.11: Depreciation isolated in a Reserved Bank Account

Net Current Assets	
Stock	£1,000
Debtors	£1,000
New Equipment Account (Bank)	£1,000
Cash at Bank	£500
	£3,500

Not only is it possible to reserve the amount in a separate bank account, it might be very sensible to do so. The account earns interest and the asset being depreciated will presumably in time need to be replaced. Alternatively, the decision might be taken by the directors to divert the additional assets, say, to stocking a wider range of products or to extending customers' credit periods. If both these actions were indeed taken, the net current assets in 17.11 might appear as shown in Figure 17.12 instead.

Figure 17.12: Increases in Stock and Debtors due to the Accounting Treatment of the Depreciation Expense

Net Current Assets	
Stock	£1,500
Debtors	£1,250
Cash at Bank	£750
	£3,500

In summary then, at each year-end, the amount by which the fixed assets are being depreciated for the year is debited from the fixed assets account and credited to the current assets account. At the same time, the fixed assets' value shown in the balance sheet is reduced by the depreciation amount, and the amount transferred to the profit and loss account as a depreciation expense.

Although different types of fixed assets are distinguished by companies in their accounts, such as land, buildings and vehicles, individual items are not listed as such. It is therefore necessary to maintain an *asset register* showing the individual entities of which they are comprised; the dates of their acquisition; their original costs; the original suppliers; the methods of depreciation; and the year-by-year "book values". The summary figures tally with the figures in the balance sheet and those in the profit and loss account.

17.3 THE EVALUATION AND ACQUISITION OF ASSETS

It is widely accepted that when a capital purchase is being proposed, the formal financial evaluation of its merits that the company requires to be undertaken should be prepared jointly by the

Finance and Costing

accountancy function and the department proposing the expenditure (accountancy to perform the calculations, the proposing department to supply the figures). Because of likely complex implications with regard to tax and investment allowances, accountancy are also usually best placed to decide on, or, at least, to advise on, how the asset is to be paid for — for example, whether by outright purchase, through leasing or by some other method.

17.3.1 Financial Evaluation

It is essential that the manufacturing company should have some scheme for evaluating the potential profitability of a capital investment proposal, say, for new plant or machinery, and so for comparing the merits of alternative proposals competing for resources.

The first step universal in all methods is to set out a stream of costs and benefits, in strictly financial terms, which will be associated with the asset's acquisition and deployment. Cost/benefit streams are the individual costs and individual benefits, in discrete periods, usually years, over the life of the asset. By "life" is meant the complete life while in the company's care, from the day of acquisition to the day of final disposal, perhaps as scrap. (We recall *terotechnology*, footnote 25, sub-section 15.6.1.) Figure 17.13 shows a cost/benefit stream over the life of an asset expected to last four years, with costs year by year, benefits year by year and costs *minus* benefits. Year 0 means the point of acquisition. The figures in other years relate to the total costs and total benefits occurring in those periods.

Figure 17.13: A Four-Year Cost/Benefit Stream (£)

Year	0	1	2	3	4
Cost £	1,000	300	0	0	0
Benefit £	0	800	600	500	300
(Cost − Benefit) £	+1,000	−500	−600	−500	−300

The most difficult task in asset evaluation is most definitely not the application of an arithmetical procedure to the costs and benefits, described in due course, but coming up with realistic values for them in the first place. Or rather, coming up with realistic values for the benefits. Costs require, for their calculation, analysis of the potential operation of the asset and a knowledge of product and expense costing (Section 17.4). Account must also be taken of the asset price, bank interest rate or company target investment rate, tax allowances and the running expenses of plant being currently operated. Benefits, on the other hand, require, certainly, current knowledge of profit margins, sales volumes and market share, but ingenuity and creative analysis as well. What must often be expressed in financial terms are the beneficial effects on revenue, say, of improved product quality, deeper market penetration, an extension of the company's selling range or the enhancement of its technical capability. However difficult benefits may be to estimate and quantify, it is quite wrong to omit them, although, equally, it is wrong to throw dice until the numbers look big enough to convince the MD of the proposal's worth.[4]

Evaluation of the proposal to acquire the asset based on the assembled stream of costs and benefits is made by taking into account the time value of money — that is, by acknowledging that to have a certain amount of cash now is more valuable than to have possession of it later. The analysis of costs, benefits and time is referred to as the *discounted cash flow* of the proposal. The two principal DCF methods used are *net present value* (NPV) and *internal rate of return* (IRR, also known simply as the DCF rate of return).[5]

---

[4] The difficulties of estimating the benefits of large projects are well known, especially in the public sector of the economy. Cost/benefit analysis has its origins in *program budgeting and systems analysis*, developed at RAND Corporation from the early 1940s to the mid-1960s. It is associated with US Defense Secretary, the late Robert McNamara, the nuclear arms race and "a bigger bang for a buck". See David Novick (1967), *Program Budgeting*, by Rand Corporation. The adoption of program budgeting as a means of associating government expenditure with basic public objectives became something of a priority at US state and county levels. See also Baruch Fischhoff (1977), "Cost Benefit Analysis and the Art of Motorcycle Maintenance", *Policy Sciences* (US magazine), No. 8.

[5] An alternative to NPV and IRR, which ignores the question of time, is use of the *payback* method. If a machine costs £15,000 to buy and will then yield benefits of £6,000 per annum, payback will be achieved half way through Year 3. Crude though it is, payback is still occasionally used in business. Alan Shea, presently of Anglesey and a one-time senior distribution manager with ICI, observes that payback is used when the company is under financial pressure and is open only to expenditure proposals that will self-evidently give a rapid return.

Finance and Costing

Application of net present value first requires senior management to state a rate of return, as a percentage per annum, that it considers to be a business target for returns on capital investment. (The target will typically be a good deal higher than bank interest rates.) A member of the accountancy department will also examine the costs and benefits submitted by the line manager supporting the proposal in order to allow for assumed rates of inflation; standard rates of capital depreciation and consequent tax allowances; and other essential factors of a purely financial nature.

Net present value can then be defined as *the total (=net) value now (=present value) of the cost and future benefits in acquiring the asset, applying a rate of interest equal to the business target rate.*

For example, consider the stream of benefits in Figure 17.13. If a (rather low) target rate of 10 per cent per annum were to be selected, the benefit of –£500 in Year 1, assuming the interest rate of 10 per cent, is –£500 multiplied by the fraction 0.91, or £455.[6] In other words, £455 invested for 1 year at 10 per cent per annum will yield £500. To find the net present value of all the future benefits, it is necessary to find the present value of each of the other benefits in Years 2 to 4 in the cost/benefit stream. The calculations of present values for all costs and benefits over the full life of the asset are displayed in Figure 17.14. The fractions applied to convert each future year's benefit to its present value are obtained by simple arithmetic, as explained in footnote 6.

---

[6] Working in positive values, rather than in benefits expressed as negative figures, in order to see how £455 is calculated, consider £1.00 in Year 0 at 10 per cent per annum. So £1.00 in Year 0 is worth £1.10 by Year 1, an increase by the fraction 1.1. To change the Year 1 figure from £1.10 to £1.00 (the actual benefit in Year 1), we merely divide it by 1.1. If we do so, then we must similarly divide the starting Year 0 figure by 1.1, obtaining £0.91 (1.00/1.10 = 0.91). That is, £0.91 in Year 0 is worth £1.00 in Year 1, at 10 per cent per annum. By analogy, £455 in Year 0 is worth £500 in Year 1 (£455/0.91 = £500).

Figure 17.14: Calculation of NPV (at 10% pa interest)

Cost/Benefit Stream at 10% pa

		Year 0	Year 1	Year 2	Year 3	Year 4
Cost less Benefit		+£1,000	-£500	-£600	-£500	-£300
Present value	Fraction applied	1.00	0.91	0.83	0.75	0.68
+£1,000						
-£455						
-£498						
-£375						
-£204						

-£532 = net present value

As we see from Figure 17.14, the net present value of the capital expenditure, at 10 per cent per annum, in this case shows a benefit of £532. The result allows the proposal to be compared with alternative expenditure proposals, at least in purely financial terms.

The Internal Rate of Return is the rate of interest, or rate of return on investment, whereby net present asset costs exactly equal net present asset benefits (i.e. the rate of interest that will yield an NPV of zero money). The concept of an IRR was developed in the early 1960s when its calculation became practicable through the use of the computer (the method employed is simply an iterative search). There are now many proprietary IRR software applications available. The internal rate of return of the cost/benefit stream in Figure 17.13 is 34.5 per cent per annum. The calculations are shown in Figure 17.15, in a display analogous to NPV in Figure 17.14. That is, at a rate of interest of 34.5 per cent per annum, the net present value of the benefits in Years 1 to 4 are exactly -£1,000.

Finance and Costing

Figure 17.15: Calculation of NPV at 34.5% pa Interest (the Internal Rate of Return)

Cost/Benefit Stream at 34.5% pa

	Year 0	Year 1	Year 2	Year 3	Year 4
Cost less Benefit	+£1000	-£500	-£600	-£500	-£300
Fraction applied	1.00	0.743	0.553	0.411	0.305

Present value:
- +£1,000
- -£371
- -£332
- -£205
- -£92

£0 = net present value

Not only does the IRR of 34.5 per cent allow the expenditure proposal to be compared with alternative proposals, but — a considerable advantage over NPV — it also allows it to be directly compared with company investment targets set by the board.

17.3.2 Financing Asset Acquisition

Commonly, if funds are available, a fixed asset will be bought by outright purchase. Outright purchase avoids involvement in the financial costs of borrowing, and permits the company to arrange the timing of the purchase and entry of the asset in its books so as to take maximum advantage of depreciation allowances and, if applicable, government grants. (It might also be added that purchase presents a stronger balance sheet to potential company investors.)

On the other hand, the accountant may turn to *leasing* as a means of payment. An advantage of leasing is that money that would otherwise be spent in purchase is available to be applied to something presenting almost equal opportunity. Again, lease payments are expenses in the profit and loss account, and have the effect, as shown in Figure 17.10 in relation to depreciation expenses, of reducing the company's liability to tax. Above all in a fast-moving technical environment, leasing has the immense advantage of allowing the company to keep fully up to date with the latest equipment, especially computers, by upgrading to new models when lease agreements expire.

There are two types of leases: *financial leases*, offered by some 200 merchant banks and finance houses in the UK, and *operating leases*, made available by a small number of capital equipment suppliers themselves.

The three parties to the formation of a financial lease agreement are: the equipment supplier; the finance house arranging the lease, known as the *lessor;* and the company wanting use of the equipment, the *lessee*. Formation proceeds through three steps (steps 1 and 2 being contiguous). Thus:

1. **Step 1:** the finance house buys the equipment at the price agreed between the supplier and the potential lessee;

2. **Step 2:** the lessee leases the equipment from the new owner (ie the finance house);

3. **Step 3:** the lessee takes physical possession of the equipment from the supplier, and has right of use.

The lessee now pays the lessor a monthly, quarterly or annual payment for the duration of the lease agreement, covering the cost of capital put up, at an agreed or implied rate of interest, administration and profit. By the terms of the lease agreement, the lessor will be obliged to maintain, service and insure the asset. On expiry of the agreement, when the capital outlay has been covered, the contract will usually provide either for continuation at a greatly reduced rate of payment, or for the asset to be purchased outright, at a nominal sum, or for the equipment to be surrendered.

Assessment by the accountant of the costs of a financial lease and his consideration of its advantages over, say, a straight bank loan or some other method of finance are carried out by his setting down the costs and allowances in the form of a cash flow, and evaluating its merits and the merits of the alternatives. Arithmetically, the calculations are straightforward. What the accountant brings to the process is a deep and up-to-date knowledge of the company's financial position, sources of available funds, taxation law and financial trends.

In an operating lease, it is the supplying company itself which leases the equipment, perhaps as an aid to marketing its products. (The supplier, the lessor in these circumstances, must find the capital to do so, of course.) Operating leases are especially associated with major suppliers of computers, which will typically undertake service and maintenance for a fee related to the equipment's capital cost. Because lease agreements are usually relatively short term — say, three or four years — there is likely to be a significant residual value in the asset at the end of the period. If this is expected, it should be reflected in lower rental costs demanded of the lessee.[7] In evaluating costs, therefore, the accountant must consider the decline in value over the agreement, rather than the asset's cost when new.

An alternative to leasing is *hire purchase*, or *lease purchase*. Hire purchase has very many similarities to leasing — the selection of the equipment by the intending user, a specific repayment period, an agreed or implied rate of interest on the capital, and so on. One difference is that the using company will normally take full possession of the equipment at the expiry of the term (making the method unsuitable as protection against technical obsolescence). A second difference, critical from the financial viewpoint, is that the company making use of the asset is deemed to be its owner for tax purposes from the moment it enters into the agreement. As a consequence, it is the using company which is permitted to depreciate its value as an asset in its own accounts, rather than the finance house or supplier. HP payments are typically greater than lease payments for equivalent purchases to compensate the finance house for this loss.

Hiring is distinguished from leasing and hire purchase in so far that the equipment which is hired is originally selected by the owner and held in a hire pool, rather than being directly selected from the supply marketplace by the company intending to make use of it. Consequently, the range of equipment is necessarily limited and is confined to popular brands of items in widespread use.

---

[7] If he is to take possession of the asset at the expiry of the lease, the lessor may be able to sell or re-lease the equipment as second-hand in a specialised market such as the Third World. In negotiating the lease agreement, the existence of any such market and its value to the supplier should be borne in mind by the purchaser. Also to be borne in mind is that the supplier is able to depreciate the equipment in his own books.

17.4 COST ACCOUNTING

It will be recalled from comments earlier that "stocks" — raw materials, components in store, work-in-progress and finished goods — constitute part of the current assets of the company. Consequently, all of the costs and expenditures involved in their acquisition and manufacture are, in a sense, investments. Only when a product is sold do the costs and expenditures involved in its manufacture assume the financial character of expenses. As expenses, they may be set against the revenue from the sale, so that the company can calculate profit (revenue less expenses).

There is consequently a need, in the manufacturing company, to keep track continuously of what costs and expenditures pertain to stock (and therefore to assets), and what pertain to goods that have actually been sold (and therefore to expenses). The easiest and most obvious way of doing this is to ascribe all of the costs and expenditures incurred in manufacturing to material itself. Having done so, all that need then be done is simply to track company activity — stock and product movements, and product sales — so that the costs and expenditures attributable to the two categories can be inferred.

Fulfilment of this need by the traditional means of allocating manufacturing costs and expenditures to products is the primary purpose of cost accounting, and is dealt with in sub-section 17.4.1.

It will be seen in the sub-section that the cost accountant must become deeply immersed in the detail of accounting for production. For example, topics which must be addressed include the financial treatment of scrap; the use of a common resource in the manufacture of several different products; the assignment of maintenance costs. . . . At the same time, there is a requirement, as ever, that all costs and expenditures should be accounted for in proper financial form and that standard books of account should be maintained through double entry bookkeeping. The maintenance of accounts capable of supporting the cost assignment scheme, yet also complying with financial accounting procedures, is accomplished through *integrated accounting*, a slight modification in presentation of standard financial accounting, and briefly described in sub-section 17.4.2.

Costs and cost accounts can also be used in conjunction with expected levels of production, derived from sales forecasts by materials explosion techniques described in Section 9.2, to permit budgets to be prepared at the *cost centre* level, a cost centre, or *cost pool*, being perhaps an area of plant or a manufacturing department. Budgets and their comparison with actual expenditure are means of monitoring the financial performance of cost centres and the managers responsible for them and highlighting possible points of concern.[8] The creation of budgets and standard costs and the analysis of variances therefrom are dealt with in sub-section 17.4.3.

A not unimportant topic finally is the use of product costs in decision taking, especially on matters of product profitability and product selling prices. Although there is no criticism in the cost accounting community of the conventional method of calculating product costs when they are used in their principal role of accounting for assets and expenses, and while the cost accountant repeatedly precautions against the use of these costs for decision taking, still conventionally calculated costs are widely used for this latter purpose.[9] So, although it is universally accepted that there is in reality no such thing as a "true cost", there are alternatives to the traditional method, such as variable costing and *activity-based costing* (ABC), which may be superior for the assessment of product profitability or for helping set product selling prices.

17.4.1 Product Costing

As stated, the purpose of product costing is to assign to the company's productive output all of the costs and expenditures incurred in its manufacture; in short, to assign costs to products. Two

---

[8] In a *cost centre*, the manager in charge has control of, and responsibility for, costs and expenditures incurred. In a *profit centre*, he has responsibility for costs and revenues. In an *investment centre*, such as a factory remote from corporate head office, he has responsibility for costs, revenues and capital investment.

[9] C. Drury, S. Braund, P. Osborne and M. Tayles (1993), *A Survey of Management Accounting Practices for UK Manufacturing Companies*, Research Paper, Chartered Association of Certified Accountants. In his *Costing: An Introduction*, Colin Drury cites this paper as revealing that "70 per cent of respondent companies use questionable information as a basis for decision-making".

stages are involved, given below. Note in the descriptions of the stages that a "production cost centre" is one where products are actually manufactured, as opposed to a "service cost centre", which provides a manufacturing service only (but the cost of which must nevertheless be accounted for). Thus:

1. *Stage I*: All manufacturing costs and expenditures are assigned to the production cost centres where they are incurred, in each case to give an accumulated cost;

2. *Stage II*: The cost in each production cost centre from Stage I is allocated to the products made there, allocations being made in some way reflective of the individual charge the production of each product makes on the total cost centre cost.

Stage I: Accumulating Costs

It is a useful and long-standing convention to regard a manufacturing cost or expenditure as belonging to one of three categories: materials, labour and expenses. (Use of the word *expense* may be correct but is less than felicitous. In the context of cost accountancy, it has the colloquial meaning merely of an incurred cost, other than for labour or materials, as opposed to the financial accountancy meaning of an item on the debit side of the profit and loss account.) Examples of expenditures from each of the three categories are: payments for raw materials purchased; the disbursement of machine operators' wages; and payment made for the consumption of electricity.

Although the purpose of Stage I is to enable the accumulated costs of the production cost centre to be allocated to products in Stage II, practical advantage is taken of the cost collection procedure and the detail of the final accumulation to extend their use to budgetary control. The individual costs which constitute the total are set down, categorised by type of material, labour and expense, to permit budgets for the various categories to be formulated and to permit actual performance then to be measured against budget.

In comparing performance against budget, account must be taken of whether a cost is variable or fixed. *Variable costs* are those which vary according to the volume of production in the cost centre. The more that is produced, the greater these costs will be. The cost of tools, power and, say, quality testing are examples. *Fixed costs* stay fixed over a wide range of output — say, the salary paid to the production supervisor. The budgets of costs which are variable will have been formulated based on an assumption of likely production output (the *production forecast*). Comparison of actual expenditure and budgeted expenditure must therefore take account of the difference between actual production and the production forecast, in the way described in sub-section 17.4.3.

Outside the sphere of local production cost centre budgetary control, if manufacturing costs are to be accounted for in Stage I so that they can be fully allocated in Stage II, consideration must also be given to costs incurred elsewhere as the result of each cost centre's manufacturing activity. Manufacturing activity, first, makes demands on general factory manufacturing overhead services, such as those performed by the wages office and the IT department. Secondly, it may make demands on one or several specialist factory service cost centres — say, the stores, the analytical laboratory or maintenance engineering. Based on the demands so made, some share of the costs of these services must therefore be calculated and levied on the production cost centre making them.

There is no exact or absolutely fair way of assigning factory and service costs to a particular manufacturing cost centre. The method decided on by the cost accountant will be one that seems reasonable to him, as being in accordance with the demands placed, and one that is relatively easy to account for and administer.

Common methods of assignment of general overheads are:

1. For factory rates and lighting costs — on the basis of the production cost centres' areas;

2. For administration and general management costs — on the basis of the number of employees in the cost centres; and

3. For engineering services — on the basis of capital employed.

Assignments of costs of specialist service cost centres are likely to involve ongoing record-keeping or the analysis of computer-held data, typical measures being: the number of materials requisitions (stores); the number of repair call-outs (maintenance engineering); and the number of scheduled production runs (production control).

One snag in the assignment of overheads and services to production cost centres is that the determination of charges to be made are unlikely in the event to be exactly correct, leading to an over- or under-recovery of the cost.

Under- or over-recovery is also relevant to Stage II. It comes about when the accountant estimates a total cost for a service for the coming year and charges the production cost centres in accordance with his assessment. For example, in order to simplify the charging of costs for heating fuel, a forecast of cost might be made for the budget year and then charged out in 12 equal monthly instalments. After a year that has included a severe winter, it will be found that actual factory expenditure on fuel has been higher than the total of the charges made to the cost centres. Rather than attempt to correct the past cost accounting by making detailed adjustments for the under-estimation, it is recommended that the shortfall in the cost recovery should simply be posted as an expense to the profit and loss account in the accounting period in which it is discovered. The financial accounts are thus maintained with total correctness, even though the product costs are not quite as representative as they might have been (SSAP9, see footnote 2).

Stage II: Allocating Costs

The purpose of this stage is to allocate in its entirety each production cost centre's cost to the products made there. In short, it is to find a cost for each product.

The first action that can be taken is to identify and set to one side *direct costs*, being those costs which are manifestly and unequivocally associated with the manufacture of each product made. The cost of a bought-in component incorporated in the item being manufactured, the wages of the machine operator performing the operation and the cost of special tools consumed during the manufacturing process are examples, respectively, of a *direct materials cost*, a *direct labour cost* and a *direct expense*. The direct cost of manufacture of a product is known as its *prime cost*.

The costs of the production cost centre which remain after the removal of all of the direct costs of the products made are known as *indirect costs*, being *indirect materials costs*, *indirect labour costs* and *indirect expenses*. Examples of them are expenditures on oil, solvents, the remuneration of the plant manager, water, steam, packaging and materials handling. The indirect costs of the cost centre, and any factory and service costs transferred in, as previously described, must be allocated in their entirety to the products made. The portion of the indirect costs attributed to any particular product is known as its *production overhead*. Summation of the prime cost and the production overhead gives the product's *production cost*, as illustrated in Figure 17.16. (The production cost is the value required finally for costing stock and accounting for its sale. It is not, however, a *fully absorbed cost*, which may be required for price setting or investment appraisal purposes — still to be incorporated are general company overheads not concerned with production, such as sales expenses, R&D, and central administration (see sub-section 17.4.4).)

Figure 17.16: The Cost Structure of the Production Cost

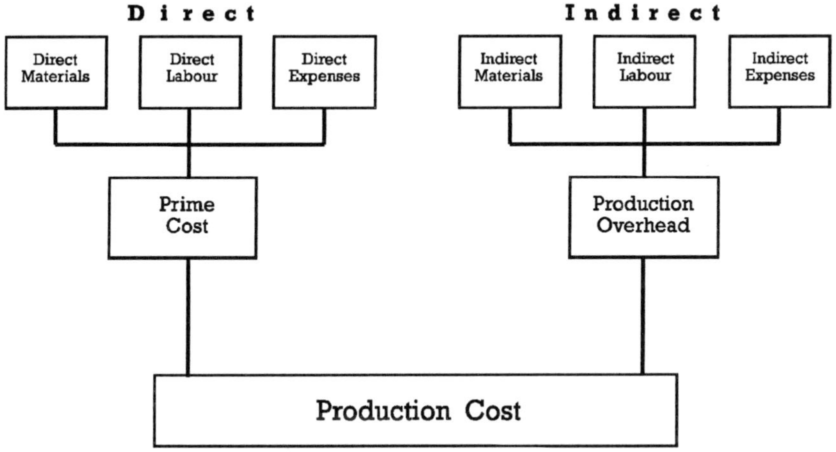

```
        Direct                              Indirect
┌──────────┬──────────┬──────────┐   ┌──────────┬──────────┬──────────┐
│ Direct   │ Direct   │ Direct   │   │ Indirect │ Indirect │ Indirect │
│ Materials│ Labour   │ Expenses │   │ Materials│ Labour   │ Expenses │
└──────────┴──────────┴──────────┘   └──────────┴──────────┴──────────┘
           │                                    │
      ┌─────────┐                          ┌────────────┐
      │  Prime  │                          │ Production │
      │  Cost   │                          │  Overhead  │
      └─────────┘                          └────────────┘
                    │                │
                ┌───────────────────────┐
                │    Production Cost    │
                └───────────────────────┘
```

If the cost centre is a sizeable factory department comprising a number of work centres, a valuable first step in product allocation is to apportion the cost centre costs to the individual work centres. Many of the costs may, in fact, be directly associable with them. For example, the cost centre's indirect labour costs may include the salaries of foremen permanently assigned to work centres. These salaries can therefore be immediately and directly attributed to them and removed from the indirect labour costs total. The method of apportionment of the individual costs not capable of direct allocation will be similar to the bases of apportionment of general and service overheads in Stage I; that is:

1. For building services — on the basis of the work centres' areas;

2. For administration and cost centre management costs — on the basis of the number of employees in the work centres; and

3. For engineering services — on the basis of capital employed.

As illustration, consider the allocation of managerial costs of £70,000 in a cost centre among three work centres A, B and C, on the basis of number of employees. This is shown in Figure 17.17, which is self-explanatory.

Figure 17.17: Allocation of Cost Centre Costs to Work Centres

Work Centre :	A	B	C	A+B+C
Number of Employees :	9	11	15	35
Allocation of £70,000 :	9/35 x £70,000	11/35 x £70,000	15/35 x £70,000	35/35 x £70,000
	£18,000	£22,000	£30,000	£70,000

The final level of allocation of the indirect costs — the goal of Stage II — is to the products themselves. (In the example immediately given, this is the allocation of the indirect costs now accumulated at work centres A, B and C to the products made at each work centre.)

The measure used to make the final allocation is referred to as the *allocation basis* or *cost driver*. Two common allocation bases are direct labour hours and machine hours. Labour hours are preferred for labour-intensive work centres (assembly areas, say); machine hours for highly mechanised work centres.

To illustrate allocation by direct labour hours, consider the allocation of the £18,000 indirect managerial costs of Work Centre A in Figure 17.17 among P1, P2, P3, P4 and P5, these being all of the products manufactured at WC A. Figure 17.18 shows the number of direct labour hours involved in the manufacture of each product. The total hours is 10,000, so that the rate to be applied per direct labour hour is £1.80/hour (£18,000/10,000). The volumes of production of the five products are also show in Figure 17.18, so that the number of direct labour hours per unit of production can be calculated. By multiplying direct labour hours per unit of production by the labour hour rate of £1.80, the indirect charge on each product is obtained as the result of this particular element of indirect cost (the overhead *burden*).

Figure 17.18: Allocation of Management Cost among Five Products on the Basis of Utilisation of Direct Labour Hours

Product :	P1	P2	P3	P4	P5	Total
Number of Direct Labour Hours :	2,500	1,500	2,000	3,000	1,000	10,000
Total Cost to be Allocated :	£4,500	£2,700	£3,600	£5,400	£1,800	£18,000
Number of Product Units Manufactured :	1,200	1,600	2,200	800	200	-
Direct Labour Hours per Unit of Product :	2.08	0.94	0.91	3.75	5.00	-
Cost per Unit of Product : (£1.80 x Number of Hours)	£3.74	£1.69	£1.64	£6.75	£9.00	-

Although the example deals only with a single indirect cost, namely managerial overheads, the remaining categories of cost must also be allocated. Bases other than direct hours may be chosen (for example, machine hours for electricity expenses). What is important from the viewpoint of accounting for stock as a current asset is that the allocation of manufacturing costs should be complete.

Nevertheless, there is disquiet among cost and management accountants that since the use of such a blunt instrument as direct labour or machine hours clearly yields dubious results, wrong decisions on, say, product profitability may be made by the manufacturing or sales manager because of it. An instance that is commonly cited is the product manufactured in small quantities on a frequent basis, with lengthy set-up times, intuitively believed by management to be costly to make, if only because of the disruption it causes, but which consumes only a small amount of direct labour or machine hours per batch and which attracts therefore only a small indirect cost burden.

Although its proponents maintain that Activity Based Costing answers these difficulties (see below), the cost accountant should first examine whether a little ingenuity might not be applied in the refinement of traditional cost accounting.

For example, a close technical assessment employing recording devices and work study methods may be made of the relative utilisation of various services in the course of manufacturing a standard lot of each of the various products made at a work centre. An example is given in Figure 17.19 of the relative utilisation of three expenses by products P1 to P5 at Work Centre A. Note the adjective *relative*. The values in Figure 17.19 may not represent exact, scientific measurements of expense utilisation (these may be unmeasurable), but merely oblique, approximate assessments. That is, on the basis that one lot quantity of P1 takes "100 units" of managerial effort, then one lot quantity of P2 takes 150 units of effort, one lot of P3 takes 80 units...

Figure 17.19: Relative Degrees of Consumption of Expenses Involved in the Manufacture of One Lot Quantity of Product

Expense/Service	P1	P2	P3	P4	P5
Managerial Effort	100	150	80	130	90
Analysis/QA	100	70	60	110	120
Materials Handling	100	170	230	220	160

The forecast number of production lots it is intended to manufacture can be derived from the production forecasts of the products and their manufacturing lot sizes. Making the assumption, purely for simplicity of illustration, that the manufacturing lot size of each product from P1 to P5 is 200 units, and using the production forecasts in Figure 17.18, the forecast number of production lots of the five products is as given in Figure 17.20.

Figure 17.20: Forecast Production Lots (derived from Figure 17.18 assuming product lot sizes of 200 units)

Forecast Production Lots (Production Forecasts /200)				
P1	P2	P3	P4	P5
6	8	11	4	1

Finance and Costing 731

Multiplication of the number of forecast production lots in Figure 17.20 by the relative utilisations of each expense in Figure 17.19 gives the relative consumptions of the expenses taken up in the manufacture of the five products. "Relative consumptions" might be renamed *relative units*. Figure 17.21 shows the calculations involved and the sum of the relative units of each of the five products for each of the three expenses.

Figure 17.21: Relative Units per Product, for each of Three Expenses

Expense	Relative Units					Total Relative Units
	P1	P2	P3	P4	P5	
Managerial Effort	6 x 100 = 600	8 x 150 = 1,200	11 x 80 = 880	4 x 130 = 520	1 x 90 = 90	3,290
Analysis / QA	6 x 100 = 600	8 x 70 = 560	11 x 60 = 660	4 x 110 = 440	1 x 120 = 120	2,380
Materials Handling	6 x 100 = 600	8 x 170 = 1,360	11 x 230 = 2,530	4 x 220 = 880	1 x 160 = 160	5,530

The next step in the allocation is to find the cost of the relative unit for each expense type by dividing the expense cost to be allocated by the total number of relative units for the expense. This is given in Figure 17.22 (introducing into the example now £6,200 expense costs for Analysis/QA and £24,000 for Materials Handling, to go alongside the £18,000 Managerial Costs calculated earlier).

Figure 17.22: Calculating the Cost per Relative Unit for each of Three Expenses

Expense	Cost	Number of Relative Units	Cost per Relative Unit
Managerial Effort	£18,000	3,290	£5.47
Analysis / QA	£6,200	2,380	£2.60
Materials Handling	£24,000	5,530	£4.34

The expense attributable to the manufacture of the total production forecast of each product is obtained from the number of relative units (Figure 17.21) and the cost per relative unit, and is given in Figure 17.23.

Figure 17.23: Costs per Expense to Manufacture the Production Forecasts of Five Products

Expense	Expense Cost for Total Production Forecast				
	P1	P2	P3	P4	P5
Managerial Effort	600 x £5.47 = £3,282.00	1,200 x £5.47 = £6,564.00	880 x £5.47 = £4,813.60	520 x £5.47 = £2,844.40	90 x £5.47 = £492.30
Analysis / QA	600 x £2.60 = £1,560.00	560 x £2.60 = £1,456.00	660 x £2.60 = £1,716.00	440 x £2.60 = £1,144.00	120 x £2.60 = £312.00
Materials Handling	600 x £4.34 = £2,604.00	1,360 x £4.34 = £5,902.40	2,530 x £4.34 = £10,980.20	880 x £4.34 = £3,819.20	160 x £4.34 = £694.40

Finally, the expense cost per unit of product attributable to each of the three expenses can be calculated by dividing the expense costs for the production forecasts (Figure 17.23) by the number of production units involved in the manufacture (which have been obtained from Figure 17.18). The results are given in Figure 17.24.

Figure 17.24: Indirect Expense Costs for Five Products

Expense	Unit Cost per Expense Category				
	P1	P2	P3	P4	P5
Managerial Effort	£3,282.00 / 1,200 = £2.73	£6,564.00 / 1,600 = £4.10	£4,813.60 / 2,200 = £2.19	£2,844.40 / 800 = £3.55	£492.30 / 200 = £2.46
Analysis / QA	£1,560.00 / 1,200 = £1.30	£1,456.00 / 1,600 = £0.91	£1,716.00 / 2,200 = £0.78	£1,144.00 / 800 = £1.43	£312.00 / 200 = £1.56
Materials Handling	£2,604.00 / 1,200 = £2.17	£5,902.40 / 1,600 = £3.69	£10,980.20 / 2,200 = £4.99	£3,819.20 / 800 = £4.77	£694.40 / 200 = £3.47

The sum of the unit costs per expense for every expense applicable to a product equals the product's production overhead. The production overhead plus the prime cost gives the product's production cost.

17.4.2 Integrated Cost and Financial Accounting

The notions and divertimentos of cost apportionment must now give way to the sterner matter of cost account management. There are two requirements.

The first requirement is to find a way of reflecting the dynamics of raw material receipt, production and sales in the accounting process itself — that is, to find a way of tracking the continually changing balance of capital and expense. As explained, stock, or material, is transformed, first, into work-in-progress, this being, financially speaking, a current asset, and then into achieved sales, the original investment so becoming an expense to be entered in the profit and loss account, its incorporation being necessary for the calculation of profit.

To track the movement of stock and determine its financial status at any time, the accountant employs a system of *control accounts*. A control account is a summary account, in which is summarised the individual transactions which constitute the recorded detail of the type of physical event with which the particular account is concerned. For example, when an item of raw material is received from a supplier and placed within the stores, a data transaction recording the receipt and placement is raised. At any point in time, the value of all of the raw material receipt transactions may be summarised to give the status of the Creditors control account and the debit side of the Stores Ledger control account. Similarly, data transactions relating to the issue from the stores of raw material to the shop floor and elsewhere in the factory are summarised to determine the status of the credit side of the Stores Ledger account. As many control account categories are raised as are needed to reflect the movement and changing status of stock and put into effect the chosen system of cost allocation. The control accounts maintained include ones summarising factory and work centre overheads and services needed for the purposes described in the previous sub-section.

The second requirement is to organise the various control and other accounts encompassing the manufacturing operation to create a unified system under the standard rules of accounts and double entry accounting described in sub-section 17.1.3. Because the system is in fact merely an expansion of standard financial accounting procedures, accommodating the additional detail of the control accounts, but otherwise fitting within the normal financial accounting framework, the process is referred to as *integrated accounting*.[10]

---

[10] A second method of dealing with cost accounts in manufacture is through *interlocked accounting*. This entails the maintenance of two separate principal ledgers, the financial ledger (for standard financial entries) and the cost ledger (for cost accounts), "interlocked" by a common ledger control account. Although this system may still be chosen for small manufacturing sites isolated from company headquarters, the need for duplicate entries and final

To illustrate the expansion of the financial accounts under integrated accounting, consider the following five activities of a manufacturing company (for brevity and extreme simplicity, all reference has been omitted to the payment of wages and to expenditures on manufacturing and non-manufacturing overheads). Thus:

1. In a particular period, the company purchases raw materials of £175,000 on credit;
2. Total stores requisitions of direct materials for the period in question amount to £160,000;
3. The cost of jobs completed and transferred to finished goods stock in the period is £250,000;
4. Sales for the period amount to £320,000;
5. The cost of goods withdrawn from stock and delivered to customers is £200,000.

The interest of financial accounting is with debtors and creditors, capital and liabilities, not, as such, with internal actions and operational control. Consequently, excluding the profit and loss account, only four accounts are necessary to describe Activities 1 to 5 in financial accounting terms. These are shown in Figure 17.25.

Figure 17.25: Standard Financial Accounts describing Five Activities

Dr	Cr
Purchases Account	
Purchase from Supplier £175,000	
Purchase Ledger Balances (Suppliers)	
	Goods Supplied £175,000
Sales Account	
	Debtors £320,000
Individual Sales Ledger Balances (Customers)	
Sales to A Customer £320,000	

reconciliation of the two sets of accounts weigh against it in an age when most accounting applications are computerised. For a worked example of interlocked accounting, see A.J. Tubb (1977), op. cit., pp. 250–265).

Finance and Costing

Under the system of integrated accounting, separate financial identities of the stores, shop floor and finished goods stocking points are acknowledged and accounted for. The financial description of Activities 1 to 5 then involves the use of seven accounts, plus the profit and loss account, as shown in Figure 17.26. (The number in brackets by each account name corresponds to the entry in Drury's Flowchart, Figure 17.27.)

Figure 17.26: Integrated Financial Accounts describing Five Activities

Dr		Cr	
Creditors Account (1)			
		Stores Ledger Control Account	£175,000
Stores Ledger Control Account (2)			
Creditors	£175,000	WIP Control Account	£160,000
Work-in-Progress Control Account (3)			
Stores Ledger Control A/C	£160,000	Finished Goods	£250,000
Finished Goods Stock Account (4)			
Work-in-Progress	£250,000	Cost of Sales Account	£200,000
Cost of Sales Account (7)			
Finished Goods Stock Account	£200,000	Transfer to the P&L Account	£200,000
Sales Account (11)			
Transfer to the P&L Account	£320,000	Debtors	£320,000
Debtors Account (12)			
Sales Account	£320,000		
Profit and Loss Account (9)			
Sales	£320,000		
Less Cost of Sales Account	£200,000		
Gross Profit	£120,000		

As with Figure 17.9, the purpose of Figure 17.26 is to show the operation of double entry accounting in the maintenance of control, here within the system of integrated accounting. Because of the omission of such vital elements as wages and overheads, however, it is difficult to see the full picture.

Instead, the full picture of integrated accounting is elegantly conveyed by Colin Drury's *Flowchart of Integrated Accounting*, given in Figure 17.27 and reproduced with permission from his *Costing: An Introduction*.[11] As stated, the accounts in Figure 17.26 correspond to the numbered accounts 1, 2, 3, 4, 7, 11, 12 and 9 in the flowchart.

Figure 17.27: Drury's Flowchart of Integrated Accounting

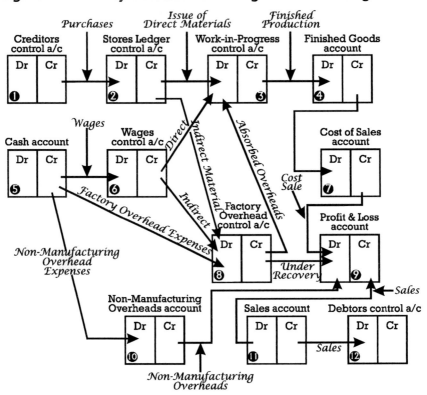

17.4.3 Budgets, Standards and Variances

Before describing one approach to the task of preparing budgets and standards, a distinction should be made between *job costing*, *batch costing*, *contract costing* and *process costing*. Although the accounting principles are, naturally, the same for all four, there are differences between them in practice and procedure.

---

[11] Colin Drury (1998), *Costing: An Introduction*, Fourth edition, International Thomson Business Press, Figure 5.1, p. 137.

Finance and Costing

As the name suggests, job costing is the identification and assignment of those costs incurred in completing a specific, individual job or works order on behalf of the customer commissioning it. Manufacture is usually though not necessarily of a single object. The job to be costed must be assigned a unique job identification number, to be recorded on all transactions relating to it, such as stores issues, labour hours expended, tools usage ... (A particular difficulty here is the seeming need to record such data as set-up and job duration, the incidence of scrap and the rest, through a complex shop floor data collection system, as described at length in Section 11.5.)[12] Standard values for indirect costs must be attached to the job cost, based on direct labour hours or machine hours, or, perhaps, on a system of relative units as described earlier.

Batch costing is similar to job costing except that the cost value arrived at is divided by the number of units in the batch to obtain a unit cost.

Contract costing is associated mainly with building and civil engineering works but also with the purchase of large, very long lead time structures in an engineer-to-order manufacturing environment. Contract costing is again similar to job costing, with incurred costs recorded on transactions along with a contract identification number. Differences from job costing are the vital need for close, ongoing communications between contractor and customer, the usual requirement for the customer to make stage payments as the work proceeds and the need to account for the cost of partly completed work (say, at a period end). Because the total number of outstanding contracts at any time is typically small, details of costs for each contract are usually maintained in a separate, dedicated contract ledger.

---

[12] The text says "*seeming* need to record . . .". Just because a job is uniquely associated with a customer does not mean necessarily that it should be individually costed. For a given product, even one that has a number of customer-specific refinements, if the materials, labour and expense expenditures are reasonably consistent in its manufacture from one job to the next, simplification might be achieved by adopting the conventions of process costing, based on the number of similar jobs manufactured in (say) a month. If consistency of expenditure is not present, the reason for variation should be investigated.

Process costing might be better termed period costing. Process costs are calculated from the units of product output achieved over a specified time period and the costs expended during that time to produce them. The period cost divided by the number of units produced gives the process cost per unit. Although process costing has been named as such because of its association with the process industries and continuous manufacture — paper, chemicals, packing lines — its use is equally valid in engineering batch manufacture when output volume is substantial. There are three principal differences from job costing:

1. Cost data collection is focused directly on the costs of operating the production process itself over the time period chosen;

2. There is a definite need to adopt a system of apportioning cost centre or work centre costs between products, as illustrated in Figure 17.17 *et seq.*; and

3. The cost accountant must become deeply involved in such particularities of production as scrap, component usages, rework and set-up.

The company adopting process costing is able to put in place perhaps the most powerful of all manufacturing cost control systems, one comprising three interlocking components: namely budgets, standards and variances. The rules and relationships of the components within the overall system are as follows:

1. *Budgets*: manufacturing budgets are prepared at the cost centre level, typically for the company's financial year, based principally on forecasts of production output, but also being guided by previous experience in manufacturing the products expected to be made and by variances found to exist between previously set standards and previous actual production;

2. *Standards*: notional, or *normal*, product costs are calculated based on the forecast production levels, forecast material usages and budgeted expenditure on raw materials, labour and expenses, the notional costs being then regarded for the budget period as "standards" against which actually achieved costs are to be compared for control purposes;

3. *Variances*: as actual production is achieved over the year and actual expenditures made, data are collected and regularly analysed to compare achieved costs against standards. A direct comparison, however, is not possible, since the circumstances prevailing during manufacture, especially production volumes and raw material and expense prices, are certain to be different from those assumed in the calculation of the standards. To make a valid comparison between performance and standard, therefore, in order to highlight true deviations in cost performance and enable any necessary corrective action to be taken, variance analysis must make allowance for the differences in circumstances.

The three components of the control system are now described in greater detail.

Budgets

A budget is a formal statement of expected revenue and proposed expenditure for a period of time, used for financial planning and familiar to everyone. In the manufacturing company, budgets are prepared and submitted before each coming financial year by all managers for their departments or areas of responsibility, the proposals submitted being then discussed and perhaps amended by the *budget committee*, a small high-level group of senior managers and senior accountants. After approval of his budget, a manager's performance in working within its limits is scrutinised continually by the accounting function. So although budget preparation takes place over just a few months, this being admittedly an intensely busy period, managerial concern with budgets is ongoing.

The crucial very first step in the budgetary process, before departmental budgets can be submitted, is the formulation, jointly by the sales and marketing department and corporate planners or by the board of directors, of sales forecasts for all products for the year, forecasts usually having been obtained by the consensus method, described in Section 2.5 and illustrated in Figure 2.7. Expectations of sales (and selling prices) naturally largely determine the company's planned revenue and, with it, the upper total of the company budget itself (*the master budget*). For the manufacturing manager, however, expectations of sales lead to the formulation of a one-year sales product production plan and its explosion through the bill of materials, to find the quantities of components and raw materials needed to support it. The mode of formulation of the plan will depend on the expected evenness of demand over the budget year, the availability or otherwise of capacity, inventory targets and management judgement. Alternative modes are: (1) to use the techniques of sales and operations planning, as described in Section 6.3, with the final requirement then to disaggregate group plans to the product level; (2) to create a master schedule in the conventional way, but with the requisite extended time horizon, perhaps using the device of pseudo forecasts, as described in subsection 6.5.2; and (3) to insert the forecasts directly, one-twelfth per month, plain and simple.

Each material to be manufactured in the budget year and the quantity of it required will be associated with a particular cost centre of manufacture. Consequently, each cost centre and the *production forecasts* of all the products to be made there can be considered one by one, and two actions taken. Firstly, direct labour costs likely to be incurred in the manufacture of each product can be allocated to it and recorded against the cost centre's budget. Secondly, a budget for each expense needed to achieve all required manufacture can be allocated to the cost centre, and the expenses apportioned between the products, perhaps by the relative units method, or through direct labour hours, or through machine hours. When completed, the *stage cost* of manufacturing the production forecast of each product can be arrived at, and with it each product's *stage price* (i.e. cost per unit).[13]

The calculation of stage costs and stage prices is an important milestone in the standard costing and budgeting process. Stage

---

[13] Some confusion may arise in standard costing terminology between a *cost* and a *price*. A cost, whether stage cost in the text or a standard cost, is a sum of money arrived at by multiplying a quantity (i.e. a number of units) by a price (a cost per unit). Confusion may be further confounded when considering the process of calculating costs, in which a cost may be found for the manufacture of one item of production, the cost (£) being then numerically identical to the item's price (£/unit). In short, a product's standard cost is the standard quantity expected to be made multiplied by the product's standard price. See A.J. Tubb's criticism of the definition of standard cost published by the Institute of Cost and Management Accountants, and its failure to make the foregoing distinction clear (Tubb (1977), op. cit., Chapter 13).

Finance and Costing

cost means the local cost of manufacture of material, and excludes factory overheads and any costs associated with prior stages of manufacture. Consequently, subject to variance analysis described below, the cost centre manager can be held entirely responsible for his expenditure of stage expenses and for stage costs achieved.

A full worked example of the procedure outlined is not given. Instead, possible final results that might have been obtained from such an example are illustrated in Figure 17.28. The Figure shows a bill of materials with a sales product S, four sub-assemblies SA1 to SA4, three lower level components C1 to C3, and five raw materials RM1 to RM5. (Note in the Figure that the usage of RM1 by SA1 is 2.0 to 1; that the usage of C1 by SA2 is 1.5 to 1; the usage of RM5 by SA4 is 0.5 to 1; and all other usages are 1.0 to 1.) The eight manufactured products are made in three cost centres CC100, CC200 and CC300. It is assumed that calculations involving direct labour hours and the many expenses in each work centre, as applied to the eight products, have resulted in the stage price of each product given in the Figure (for example, "stg £3/u" for SA1 (= stage price £3/unit)). Unit raw material prices are also given (for example "rm £2/u" for RM1 (= raw material price £2/unit)).

Figure 17.28: The Results of calculating Stage Costs and Stage Prices for All Products in each of three Work Centres

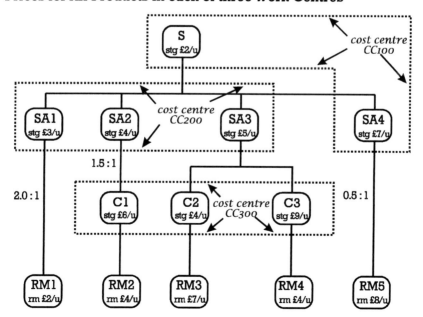

Standard Costs

Standard costs are obtained by, first, transferring into each cost centre as described above any manufacturing and factory overheads and allocating them to the products made there, as described in sub-section 17.4.1, and, secondly, performing what is popularly known as the cost *roll up*. The roll-up is the implosion of the bill of materials, starting with raw materials, and the accumulation of costs up the bill, level by level, until the sales products are reached at the top. Consider for example, sub-assembly SA3 in Figure 17.28 (excluding here any consideration of transferred overheads). The rolled-up price of the prior stage component C2 is £11/unit (£7/unit for RM3 + £4 stage cost) and the rolled up price of prior stage component C3 is £13/unit (£4/unit for RM4 + £9 stage cost). The standard cost of manufacture of one unit of SA3 is therefore £29 (1 unit of C2 at £11/unit + 1 unit of C3 at £13/unit + £5 stage cost). Figure 17.29 shows the flow of the roll-up/cost accumulation and the final standard costs per unit (again for clarity excluding manufacturing overheads). Since standard costs per unit are equivalent to standard prices, they are denoted by "Stand P.". Figure 17.30 shows how each standard price in Figure 17.29 was arrived at.

Figure 17.29: The Cost Roll-Up

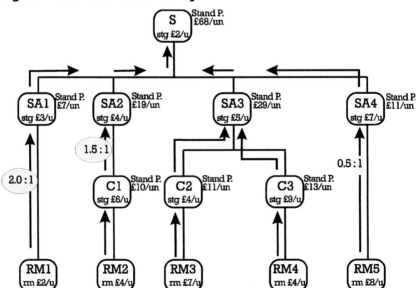

Finance and Costing

Figure 17.30: Calculation of Standard Prices from Stage Costs and Prior Stage Costs

Prod	Stage Cost	Prior Stage Costs	Stand. Cost/un	Prod	Stage Cost	Prior Stage Costs	Stand. Cost/un
C1	£6	£4	£10	SA2	£4	£10 x 1.5	£19
C2	£4	£7	£11	SA3	£5	£11 + £13	£29
C3	£9	£4	£13	SA4	£7	£8 x 0.5	£11
SA1	£3	£2 x 2.0	£7	S	£2	£7 + £19 + £29 + £11	£68

One is reminded that the various standard costs are used for valuing components, sub-assemblies and other work-in-progress from day to day in the maintenance of the company's system of accounts.

Variances

As production is achieved from month to month, a comparison between standard costs and actual costs is clearly not a straightforward matter. Standards are based on forecast levels of production and suppositions as to unit prices of raw materials, expenses and direct labour. Actual costs relate to the company's day-to-day response to customer demand and the payment of current prices.

In order to allow a meaningful comparison to be made, *variances* between the budgetary/standard assumptions and the conditions prevailing in practice must be taken into account. By isolating the effect of these differences, the cost accountant and the manufacturing manager are able to see what differences remain. If they are *adverse* — caused by higher usages of material or expenses, or by poor labour efficiency — corrective action can be taken. If they are *favourable*, the reasons for these too should be investigated.

Every element of cost, whether budgeted or actually incurred, is the product of two components: quantity (units produced, kilowatt hours burned, square feet used, labour hours expended, etc.) and unit price (£/unit). The fundamental division of variance analysis is consequently into *price variances* and *quantity variances*. The general expression for a price variance is as given by Equation 17.7; the general expression for a quantity variance is given by Equation 17.8. In both expressions, the term "quantity" may refer to units produced, kilowatt hours, square feet . . . whatever it is that has been the subject of the expenditure under analysis. Note also that if either variance is such that the company incurs a cost less than would be incurred under standard conditions, so that the variance is favourable, the letter "F" is written after the sum calculated; if the cost incurred is greater and is adverse, the letter "A" is written.

$$\text{Price Variance} = \text{Actual Quantity} \times \begin{pmatrix} \text{The difference between the} \\ \text{Standard Price per unit and} \\ \text{the Actual Price per unit} \end{pmatrix} \qquad \text{Equation 17.7}$$

$$\text{Quantity Variance} = \text{Standard Price per Unit} \times \begin{pmatrix} \text{The difference between the} \\ \text{Standard Quantity of units} \\ \text{budgeted to be used and the} \\ \text{Actual Quantity that were used} \end{pmatrix} \qquad \text{Equation 17.8}$$

In calculating and scrutinising any variance, a principle that must be followed before it can be attributed to the performance of a cost centre manager is that he must have complete control over the expenditure incurred. In the context of Figure 17.28, each cost centre manager's control is limited to the stage costs, and excludes prior stage costs and raw materials costs. (In the example illustrated by the Figure, it is also unlikely in practice that the manager will have a great deal of control, if any, over stage expense *prices*, so that his performance is likely to be judged entirely on quantity variances.)

Within the division of price variances, the basic categories are: (1) material price variance; (2) labour rate variance; and (3) overhead recovery rate variance. Within the division of quantity variances, they are: (1) material usage variance; (2) labour efficiency variance; and (3) overhead volume variance. The analyses of the three quantity variances are usually complicated by the need to isolate and display the individual effects of separate but concomitant causes of variation. Thus material usage, in the process industries at least, must be split between mix variance and yield variance. Labour efficiency variance in all industries may be split between "real" work hours, in which output is produced, and "idle" hours, being paid time comprised of waiting time, machine breakdown time and rest periods. Overhead volume variance may be split between capacity variance and operating efficiency variance.

The variances chosen for analysis by the cost accountant will be those within the company's control involving expenditures having the greatest effect on the overall cost of manufacture. A company carrying out, say, electrolysis will pay particular attention to price variance and quantity variance in the price and use of electricity. Another company will be similarly attentive to the material usage variance of sheet metal. Yet another will be attentive to labour efficiency variance in assembly output.

Adverse variances may merely be brought to the notice of the manager and require obvious local operational adjustment, but, where they are large or persistent, may demand full-scale technical/commercial investigation, perhaps along the lines described for quality in sub-sections 13.2.3 and 13.2.4. Simple examples frequently cited are a favourable material price variance (keen purchasing) being more than offset by an adverse material usage variance (poor quality in use); and an adverse labour rate variance (higher grade operators) being more than offset by a favourable labour efficiency variance (higher output).

The range of variance analysis calculations available in proprietary software application packages is large, so that the accountant must be judicious in choosing which ones to display and pursue. Two examples of calculations are given below based on Figure 17.29 (note as stated previously that F = favourable and A = adverse).[14]

Example 1: Raw Material Price Variance

The budgeted purchase of RM1 for the month of April is 2,000 units at £2/unit. Actual purchase is 1,930 units at £2.02/unit.

If   AQ = actual quantity;
      SP = standard price;
and   AP = actual price;

Then from Equation 17.7 we obtain Equation 17.9:

Price Variance = **AQ (SP − AP)**   *Equation 17.9*
                   = 1,930 × (£2.00 − £2.02)
                   = £38.60 A

---

[14] See Colin Drury (1998), op. cit., Chapter 15; and A.J. Tubb (1977), op. cit., Chapter 13, for many more examples.

Example 2: Material Usage Variance

> The budgeted manufacture of SA1 in April is 1,000 units, entailing a budgeted usage of 2,000 units of RM1. Actual manufacture of SA1 is 940 units, so that the *flexed* usage of RM1 is calculated to be 1,880 units.[15] Actual usage of RM1 is 1,800 units.
>
> If SP = standard price of RM1;[16]
> SQ = the (flexed) standard quantity of RM1;
> AQ = actual quantity of RM1.
>
> Then from Equation 17.8, we obtain Equation 17.10:
>
> **Quantity Variance** = **SP (SQ − AQ)**   *Equation 17.10*
> = £2.00 (1880 − 1800)
> = £160.00 F

17.4.4 Costs in Decision Taking

It is not possible in a short space to deal thoroughly with the presentation and manipulation of costs and costing information for "decision taking". Decisions concern commercial viability (product pricing, the launch of products and their removal from the selling range, etc.); the search for alternative means of manufacture (new production sites, contract manufacture, etc.); and technical investigation (plant improvements, product redesign, process research, etc.). It is a vast area with a literature to match, and includes not only conventional accounting and cost accounting, but some of the more recondite theories of optimisation and allocation championed by Eliyahu Goldratt and touched on in sub-sections 12.4.1 and 12.4.2. Costing "conclusions" and cost analyses are as likely to be illusions as insights. It is quite essential, therefore, that the manufacturing manager studying them should thoroughly appreciate the ultimate source and meaning of the data on which they

---

[15] *Flexible budgets* are those in which adjustments are made to allow for actual activity (v. the activity forecast at the time the budget was prepared). In the text, the standard usage of RM1, of 1,880 units, is said to have been *flexed* (OED = bent) from the budgeted usage of 2,000 units to allow for the different level of activity now prevailing.

[16] Use of the standard price of RM1 in accordance with Equation 17.10 allows the effect of the purchasing department's excess payment of £2.02 (from Example 1) to be isolated. The focus of interest in Example 2 is manufacturing's performance, not purchasing's.

Finance and Costing

are based, and the logic and assumptions of the calculations. Comments follow on Variable Costing, "CQP" analysis and Activity Based Costing.

Variable Costing

By universal convention in the UK and in accordance with the procedures laid down in SSAP9 (footnote 2), the company will prepare its accounts and value its stocks based on absorption costing as described in this Section. Furthermore, the notion of the absorbed cost, even of the fully absorbed cost incorporating a charge for non-manufacturing overheads, seems, somehow, *fair*. Manufacture could hardly continue without services and support. Nevertheless, as demonstrated in the last sub-section, the absorption of overheads to ascertain cost is based on a presumption of output, sales and stockholding that is unlikely in the event to prevail, perhaps leading to seemingly anomalous financial results.

Anomalies and misleading financial conclusions, especially as to profits, are especially liable to result when there is a major divergence between the master schedule and achieved sales, perhaps because of seasonality, capacity limitations and the need to build up stocks.

Consequently, for internal accounting, to obtain a more apposite picture of the company's position from the monthly profit statement and the profit and loss account, the company may turn to *variable costing* (also known as *marginal costing*, *contribution costing*, or *direct costing*).

In variable costing, the product cost is made up of only those costs which are directly attributable to it and which vary in proportion to the quantity of the product manufactured.[17]

Production overheads under accounting with variable costing are simply regarded as period expenses, and are posted to the profit and loss account in the period in which they are incurred.

---

[17] Variable costs are often identical to prime costs, but not necessarily so. A component of a prime cost may be directly associable with a product's manufacture, but may not vary in proportion to the volume of output. In costing generally, the proportionality of expense and overhead usage to output is a subject requiring separate attention, with usage/output relationships being expressed, perhaps, as formulae and recorded for reference in a "variability index".

A simple but telling illustration of the different operation of variable and absorption costing is shown in Figures 17.32 and 17.33, based on a product "P" having the cost, sales and production data shown in Figure 17.31.

Figure 17.31: Data relating to Product P (see text)

Product P	
Variable Cost	£7/unit
Fixed Overhead Cost	£400/month
Avg. Production Forecast	100 units/month
Absorbed Cost	£11/unit (£7/u + £4/u)
Selling Price	£15/unit

Over two consecutive months, the sales of Product P are 40 units and 160 units, but production is held steady at 100 units each month. The profits from sales calculated when absorption costing is used are £160 and £640. The analyses are given in Figure 17.32. The results using variable costing, however, indicate a loss in Month 1 of £80, and a profit in Month 2 of £880. The alternative calculations are given in Figure 17.33.

Figure 17.32: Uneven Sales/Production: Successive Profits under Absorption Costing

	Month 1	Month 2
Sales (units)	40 u	160 u
Production (units)	100 u	100 u
Opening Stock (£)	0	660
Production Cost (£)	1100 $^{100 \times 11}$	1100 $^{100 \times 11}$
Closing Stock (£)	(660) $^{60 \times 11}$	0
Cost of Sales (£)	440 $^{40 \times 11}$	1760 $^{160 \times 11}$
Total Costs (£)	440	1760
Sales (£)	600 $^{40 \times 15}$	2400 $^{160 \times 15}$
Net Profit (£)	160	640

Finance and Costing

Figure 17.33: Uneven Sales/Production: Successive Profits under Variable Costing

	Month 1	Month 2
Sales (units)	40 u	160 u
Production (units)	100 u	100 u
Opening Stock (£)	0	420
Production Cost (£)	700 $^{100 \times 7}$	700 $^{100 \times 7}$
Closing Stock (£)	(420) $^{60 \times 7}$	0
Cost of Sales (£)	280 $^{40 \times 7}$	1120 $^{160 \times 7}$
Fixed Costs (£)	400	400
Total Costs (£)	680	1520
Sales (£)	600 $^{40 \times 15}$	2400 $^{160 \times 15}$
Net Profit (£)	(80) ie Loss	880

In Month 1 under variable costing, all of the fixed costs of £400 contribute to the total costs. In Figure 17.32 under absorption costing, however, fixed costs are absorbed into the product cost, at the rate of £4/unit. In Month 1, therefore, with absorption costing, the element of fixed costs attributable to the 60 units of stock carried forward to Month 2 is excluded from the total costs. Consequently the profit is £240 lower than with absorption costing (60 × £4). In Month 2, when sales are greater than production, costs are higher under absorption costing, since fixed overheads are brought forward in the form of stock from the previous period.

In absorption costing, profit is proportional to both sales and production, and may appear erratic because of the effect of fluctuating stocks. In variable costing, profits are strictly proportional to sales, and stockholding has no effect on them.

Manufacturing companies with very seasonal demand opting for absorption costing in order to smooth out profit should beware of being left with unsold stock at the end of the season. Fixed expenses from prior periods have been capitalised, but if the stock proves unsaleable, its value will not be realised to pay for them.

Cost–Quantity–Price Analysis

The direct relationship between profit and sales under variable costing can be simply expressed as a formula. Thus if over a particular period:

Q = quantity sold in units;
s = selling price (£/unit);
v = variable cost price (£/unit);
F = total fixed costs for the period in £;
and P = net profit for the period in £,

then Equation 17.11 is clearly true:

$$Q(s-v) = F + P \qquad \textit{Equation 17.11}$$

Equation 17.11 may be used in endless ways to provide information for accountants, sales managers and corporate planners. Three examples are given using the data relating to Product P in Figure 17.31, over a particular month.

Example (i)

Find the sales breakeven point of Product P (i.e. find the number of units to be sold to achieve a profit of zero).

Let the breakeven point be Q units. Then from Equation 17.11, we have:

$$Q(15 - 7) = 100 + 0$$

Whence Q = 12.5 units (i.e. there is no solution if P is made in discrete units. Sales of 12 mean a loss, sales of 13 mean a profit.)

Example (ii)

Find the minimum number of units of Product P that must be sold to yield a profit of at least £2,000.

Let the number of units to be sold be Q. Then from Equation 17.11 we have:

$$Q(15 - 7) = 100 + 2,000$$

Whence Q = 263 units

Example (iii)

Find the selling price that must be charged for Product P to obtain a profit of £1,500 from sales of 1,000 units.

Let the selling price to be charged be s. Then from Equation 17.11, we have:

$$1,000(s - 7) = 100 + 1,500$$

Whence s = £23 / unit.

Finance and Costing

It is illuminating to express aspects of the CQP equation graphically. Perhaps the most useful display is the Profit-Quantity graph. Thus Equation 17.11 may be rearranged to give Equation 17.12. In the revised Equation, (s − v) has been replaced by the expression "c", meaning contribution, an important term used extensively in sub-section 12.4.2.

$$P = cQ - F \qquad \text{Equation 17.12}$$

The Profit-Quantity graph then is a simple plot of Equation 17.12, and is illustrated for Product P in Figure 17.34.

Figure 17.34: Profit-Quantity Graph for Product P (Figure 17.31)

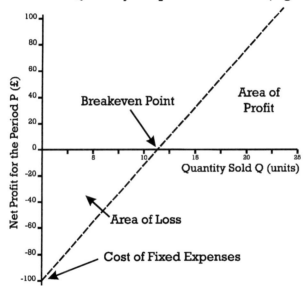

The likely validity in practice of CQP analysis and the PQ graph is challenged by two serious objections. First, the assumption is made that the results apply to a single product (or, at least, to sales within an unvarying product mix). This assumption is certain to be invalid, and any attempt to deal with the question of a changing mix leads us at once into Goldratt's morass. Secondly, it is supposed that the fixed costs are fixed for the whole of the period under analysis, regardless of the quantity sold. In practice, fixed costs will be reduced by drastic management action if sales slip below a certain level — the creation of redundancies, the factory-wide imposition of departmental budget cuts and the cancellation of the training budget are typical responses, not usually in that order.

Nevertheless, CQP analysis may have the same broad validity for the sales manager or corporate planner as, say, the notion of elasticity has for the economist (16.4.1) — a valuable tool of several available, though one to be used with caution.

Activity Based Costing

In sub-section 17.4.1, the traditional method of deriving product costs was described. Stage I consisted of the accumulation, for each production cost centre, of the expenses and other costs incurred in the course of production. In Stage II, it was described how these costs were then allocated to the products made at the cost centre, perhaps by a simple cost driver such as direct labour hours, or by a more elaborate technique such as that of relative units.

It is felt intuitively by all cost accountants that costs ascertained by the traditional method do not particularly well reflect the consumption of financial resources used in achieving production output. The example was touched on in 17.4.1 of a "disruptive" product with short production runs and lengthy machine set-up times, allocated a small cost because it involved a small number of labour hours. Other instances that might have been given are small costs allocated to products that make major demands on bill of material maintenance or on routing data maintenance, or to products that require extensive effort with regard to their quality management.

In 1988, Robert Kaplan and Robin Cooper proposed a radical amendment to traditional costing.[18] Instead of accumulating costs by geographically defined cost centres, under a single manager's control, and allocating them to products, costs were to be accumu-

---

[18] Kaplan and Cooper's original proposal was published in *Harvard Business Review*, September/October 1988, pp. 96–103. For the standard work, however, see R.S. Kaplan and R. Cooper (1997), *Cost and Effect: Using Integrated Cost Systems to drive Profitability and Performance,* Harvard Business School Press. Professor Kaplan is with the Harvard Business School, Cambridge, MA, and Professor Cooper with the Goizueta Business School, Emory University, Atlanta, GA.

lated by *activities* and then allocated. The new method was termed *Activity Based Costing* (ABC).[19]

The general procedure for ascertaining costs under ABC remains the same, but the previous geographic cost centres might be thought of as having been replaced by "activity cost centres". Stage I consists of the identification and accumulation of the expenses and other costs involved in each production activity (machine changeovers, engineering and product route data maintenance, QC and so on). Stage II consists of allocating these costs to the various products which are participants in each activity, employing a cost driver suitable to its nature.

The most critical and protracted step in the implementation of ABC is the identification of the activities that are to constitute the activity cost centres. Identification may take place through team discussion and interviewing, and should strike a balance between detail and generality. Too narrow a level of detail will make the task of identifying the costs and resources associated with activities too involved and time-consuming. Too broad a definition will make it difficult, if not impossible, to find a cost driver through which to allocate the costs to products in Stage II. It has been suggested that 20 to 30 activity cost centres are about right.

According to Kaplan and Cooper, all activity cost centres fall into one or other of four categories:

1. *Unit-level activity cost centres.* The activity associated with production takes place with every unit of product made. Examples are the performance of direct labour, the application of direct expenses such as the use of energy, and the incurrence of any expense associated with duration of machine utilisation, such as machine maintenance and plant depreciation.

---

[19] The new method of ABC caught on quickly in the manufacturing world, encouraged particularly by the *bien pensants* of management consultancy. A survey undertaken in 1994 reported that 20 per cent of UK firms had adopted ABC and a further 27 per cent were considering its adoption, very remarkable findings considering the thoroughgoing conservatism of the cost accountancy profession. (J. Innes and F. Mitchell (1995), "A Survey of Activity Based Costing in the UK's largest companies", *Management Accounting Research* magazine, June, pp. 137–154.)

2. *Batch-related activities.* The activity is associated with the commencement of manufacture of a batch of production, or with its termination, but not with the number of units actually made. Examples are machine set-ups, tear-downs, materials handling and raw material deliveries.
3. *Product-sustaining activities.* The activity is associated with the technical existence of each product on the sales and production range, rather than with actual physical output. Examples are the maintenance of the bill of materials and the entry of a product into the production schedule.
4. *Facility-sustaining activities.* The activity is necessary to the continuation of manufacture, but is not directly associable with any particular product. Examples are factory services such as heating and lighting. Because facility-sustaining activities cannot be directly allocated, and rejecting the overhead allocation schemes employed in traditional cost accounting, the costs of such activities are not assigned to products.

Stage II, leading to final cost ascertainment, entails the choice of a suitable cost driver to determine the allocation of each activity cost centre cost to the products participating in the activity. The most obvious characteristic of a cost driver is that it should truly reflect the product's participation. Thus *number of purchase orders placed* would seem to be a very suitable driver to use in order to allocate the costs of the activity *purchase order placement*, but not all are as obviously identified. Consider, for example, the number of machine set-ups. Transactions relating to the number of set-ups may be thought to be unreflective of the activity *machine set-up* if the times taken in setting up vary widely from product to product; if so, a more sophisticated driver must be arrived at to allocate the costs of this activity.

The arithmetical process of carrying out the apportionment of a cost centre cost when the data have been collected and the cost drivers decided upon is by the simple ratio method illustrated in Figures 17.18 to 17.24.

According to the survey mentioned in Footnote 19, the three most common uses of ABC by companies that have adopted it are:

Finance and Costing

(1) for cost reduction; (2) for performance measurement/improvement; and (3) for product/service pricing.

It is the use of ABC in cost reduction and in performance improvement which so disturbs Tony Rizzo.[20] Tony Rizzo of the Product Development Institute, Whippany, New Jersey, points out that in order to exert financial control and reduce costs under ABC, it is necessary to make changes of an essentially arbitrary nature (i.e. purely cost-driven changes) to the operation of activities. The action of so doing is as certain to bring about a deterioration in the performance of the activity, and have undesirable knock-on consequences elsewhere in the organisation, as tinkering with common causes in a stable system, described at length in sub-section 13.2.2. The cost drivers for allocating costs to products are no better than, and just as dangerous as, the facile measures frequently used in ISO 9000 to gauge "quality of service" (see Section 13.3).[21]

Not only is ABC flawed and dangerous in use, says Rizzo, it deceives the user into believing that the costs calculated thereby are true costs when none such exist or can exist. Before tumbling down Goldratt's rabbit hole, one should state that there is a rejoinder to Rizzo's argument posted on an Internet Bulletin Board (see footnote 20) by Jeff Blumberg, who also reminds the visitor that the alleged flaws of ABC were fully debated in the cost accounting community throughout the 1990s. No doubt the arguments for and against it will have been variously summarised in the proposals to adopt the system made to MDs in the companies in footnote 19.

---

[20] Tony Rizzo's article and the comments it gave rise to are most easily available through a link entitled "ABC (Activity Based Costing) — Fundamentally Flawed?" provided in a Theory of Constraints bulletin board hosted by APICS and maintained by John Caspari at http://members.home.net/casparija.

[21] One might imagine a manager criticised for the high cost of purchase order placement in respect of a product, promptly improving his cost performance by switching to one (very large) order per year. Tony Rizzo in his article (see footnote 20 above) gives two examples of cutting costs, one by removing spare capacity, the other by removing excess selling effort — thus destroying the business potential that these two conditions jointly create. (See also John Seddon, Section 13.3.)

Chapter 18

The Stores and Stock Records

On our journey through manufacturing, we now come to the Lost City. It is a curious fact that a facility providing service to so many big-name departments — purchasing, QA, manufacturing itself, engineering, sales — a facility directly affecting their operational effectiveness, should scarcely be spared a thought by those it serves.

It is in terms of service to others that the functions of the stores are best recited. For purchasing, the stores receives, counts and stores raw materials, and perhaps performs quality tests such as sampling or full inspection. When the goods have been put away, the database is updated via the purchase order number. For manufacturing, kits of parts are meticulously assembled for jobs to be started and conveyed to their points of use on the shop floor in timely fashion. Components and finished goods are stored after manufacture. And since no factory floor is without its crises, the stores' services to production are naturally made available at all times.[1] Engineering looks to the stores for the safe storage of spare parts needed for maintenance and repair, these also to be available at all times, and for the storage of tools, jigs, dies and so forth. The service provided on behalf of sales directly affects the service

---

[1] This means the stores must be manned at all times that production takes place — how else can service be provided? If it is not so manned, production floor workers requiring stock will obtain it, correctly completing the paperwork not always, reducing the level of records accuracy below what is required, removing accountability for such accuracy from stores staff themselves, and bringing down the consequences of records inaccuracy on the company's operations.

provided to the ultimate customer himself — accurately picked orders, carefully packed, correctly labelled.

And finally we notice the elephant standing by the racking, waiting for its name to be called — *the maintenance on behalf of the entire company of accurate stock records*. The stores manager and his staff are the front-line troops in a ceaseless battle to maintain the highest levels of accuracy through a system that is at once complex and vulnerable. Yet without such levels, every logistical system operated by the company loses its credibility and every delivery date promised to its customers is put in jeopardy.

18.1 STORES ORGANISATION

18.1.1 Physical Layout

A self-evident procedure in contemplating the layout of any building under design is first to list the various functions and operations that are to be accommodated. In the case of the stores, the list will contain goods-in and unpacking; a number of distinct storage points (say, heavy goods, slow-moving pallets, bin stores and racking); works order kitting stations; offices and amenity rooms; places for parking and charging forklift trucks; and outgoing goods packing and despatch areas.

Next, the designer will embark on the lengthy task of fact-finding so that the extent and placement of each area to be established can be determined — the number of raw material deliveries to be received each day, the minimum and maximum stockholding, the volumes of materials to be moved to and from the shop floor, the number of despatches per day expected to be made to customers.

It is at this point that the stores designer will become very conscious of the rapidity of change taking place in the tempo of modern manufacturing. Even without the extremes of Just-in-Time supplier receipts, kanban and Just-in-Time customer despatches, the quantities of stock ordered from suppliers, manufactured lot sizes and the delivery quantities demanded by customers are becoming progressively smaller and their frequency of movement correspondingly greater. The layout of the new facility must reflect this changing environment. While in the past the emphasis in design was on economy of storage density, and graphs were drawn to show how cost per cubic foot of storage space fell as the height of a stores or warehouse rose, today's emphasis is on velocity and flexibility. What occupies the mind of the designer now is the avoidance of potential traffic jams involving supplier vehicles; quick attention to incoming goods and shop floor receipts; perhaps the central control of multiple incoming delivery points throughout the factory; round-the-clock working; and the increasingly prevalent use in all stores operations of computer software.

The designer, of course, cannot provide for the future at the expense of the present. The stores must function smoothly from the start, but the certainty of change must be accepted and change anticipated so far as it is possible to do so. If the designer is an external architect, perhaps from a company specialising in storage and warehousing facilities, he must seek contributions to the design process not only, naturally, from the company's stores manager, but from the purchasing, manufacturing and sales managers as well.

The ability of a stores or warehouse to adapt to changing circumstances will be greatly helped by the adoption of a *variable location storage* system (always provided it is supported by well-conceived software). The traditional method of storage, the only one available before the days of computers, is the *fixed location system*. In the fixed system, every item to be stored is allotted a storage location (*a place for everything, and everything in its place*, as they say). In the variable system, all of the stores locations are maintained as a file by the computer system, and, for each one, the product and quantity currently stored there. When incoming stock is to be put away, the software determines the most suitable empty location for its storage, employing a computer algorithm as discussed below.[2] When stock is to be retrieved, its location is found by the system and picking information issued.[3]

The contribution made by a variable location storage system to adaptability and flexibility of operation rests in part on its inherent features and in part on the calibre of the software controlling its

---

[2] Programs that determine the location in which stock is to be placed in a variable storage system are referred to in the jargon as *put-away algorithms*.

[3] Notwithstanding the text, a fixed location system is nevertheless the better one for tools storage. When tools are kept in a variable location store, the set-up of the computer system can be such that each tool's location is unavailable to other items, and only that particular location is available to that tool (i.e. the system can be manipulated to mimic a fixed system, but only for tools). On a related matter, the storage, access and record-keeping procedures for tools should be as rigorously maintained by stores staff as they are for other items.

operation. Inherent advantages of a variable system include the following:

1. Far less space is needed than for a fixed location system. Stock occupying 100 units of space within a fixed system will require only 60 to 65 units when a variable location system is operated.[4] In design and layout, this means that, for a given storage budget, more generous provision can be made for later expansion under a variable system than under a fixed.

2. A changing mix of items over the years is catered for quite naturally.

3. The storage of seasonal goods is accommodated automatically without recourse, as in a fixed system, to overflow areas and other contingency measures. In a variable system, the seasonal stock simply occupies more locations.

4. It is easily possible to segregate incoming lots of material, assigning them exclusive locations, if this is desirable or necessary for technical or commercial reasons.

Before listing a number of software features that are likely to contribute to storage flexibility and effectiveness, two simple examples are given of data processing in (a) putting stock away in a variable system, and (b) retrieving stock. The examples relate to a product P50 in a storage facility in which locations are coded according to the following scheme: ARRSB, where A = aisle code, RR = rack number, S = shelf code, and B = bin number. (Thus Location C10B4 is aisle C, rack 10, shelf B, bin 4.)

Putting Away

On 12 Jul 2001, it is required to store 200 units of P50. The current stock position of P50 is as shown in Figure 18.1.

---

[4] See James Tompkins' contribution to James H. Greene (ed.) (1997), *Production and Inventory Control Handbook*, Third edition, page 25.8. Dr Tompkins' contribution (Chapter 25 — *Warehousing & Storage*) is thoroughly recommended as an excellent summary of the subject. Also see Roger B. Brooks and Larry W. Wilson (1995), *Inventory Record Accuracy*, John Wiley & Sons, Inc., p.65; the figure in the text has also been spoken of by attendees on GMCS's stores training course at www.gmcs.co.uk/stores.htm.

The Stores and Stock Records

Figure 18.1: Stock Position No. 1 of P50 (Variable Location Storage)

Location	Quantity (units)	Date Stored
A04F1	450	10 Jun 01
A06C3	500	30 Jun 01
A07A2	120	18 May 01
Total	1,070	

The computer scans the database for an empty location as near to existing stock of P50 as possible, and directs the storeman to put the stock in Location A08G4. After he has done so, and the storage transaction has been processed, the stock position of P50 is as shown in Figure 18.2.

Figure 18.2: Stock Position No. 2 of P50

Location	Quantity (units)	Date Stored
A04F1	450	10 Jun 01
A06C3	500	30 Jun 01
A07A2	120	18 May 01
A08G4	200	12 Jul 01
Total	1,270	

Retrieval

A few days after storage on 12 Jul 01, it is required to withdraw 150 units of stock of P50. Working on the basis of FIFO (see below), the computer determines that 120 units are to be retrieved from Location A07A2, and the balance of 30 units from Location A04F1. After the withdrawal has been made and the data transactions processed, the stock position of the product is as shown in Figure 18.3.

Figure 18.3: Stock Position No. 3 of P50

Location	Quantity (units)	Date Stored
A04F1	420	10 Jun 01
A06C3	500	30 Jun 01
A08G4	200	12 Jul 01
Total	1,120	

There is great scope in the design of the computer system governing variable location storage to contribute to stores flexibility and effectiveness. The following basic capabilities will be provided; many other refinements are likely to be incorporated in his system by the software vendor:

1. Ability to assign a category to each location relating to its convenience of access.

2. Ability to categorise products by frequency of movement, and, in conjunction with (1), to ensure that frequent movers are assigned to the handiest places and stock moving the least frequently is assigned to the less convenient places.

3. Where a choice of locations exists in storage, selection of the location nearest to existing stock of the product being stored.

4. In stock retrieval, adherence to the FIFO principle (first-in, first-out). Besides conforming to good storekeeping practice, this rule will also tend to lead to locations being emptied at the fastest possible rate, thus freeing space for further storage. (In Figure 18.2, the oldest stock is at A07A2, and withdrawal of 120 units leaves the location empty and available for further use. In Figure 18.3, the oldest stock is at A04F1, and this location will be continually selected for picking until it too is empty.)

5. The ability to override the system, both in putting stock away and withdrawing it. For example, if stock rotation and segregation are of low importance for a particular product, the storeman may wish to consolidate incoming material with stock already present, or may wish to withdraw stock from a partly filled location, out of turn, to release space sooner than it would be released by strict adherence to FIFO principles.

6. In order to assist variable location cycle count reconciliation, described in sub-section 18.4.2, allowing 24 hours (say) to elapse before selecting a location for re-stocking with the same material.

Other programs are required in support of the system besides those governing the placement and retrieval of stock. For example, reports may be generated on the percentage stores occupation; on locations that have not been used; on slow moving stock; and on material within so-many days of its expiry date.

A worry expressed by many stores managers considering switching from a fixed location system to a variable one is that stock may be placed in a particular location, but the location code then wrongly recorded, the stock thereby becoming "lost", since its actual location is no longer capable of discovery through the system. A number of safeguards are available here. First, if a storeman is directed by the system to place stock in a location recorded as being empty, and finds it occupied, he must abort the placement and report matters so that an audit of the location can be carried out. Secondly, periodically, all locations recorded as being empty on the system can be printed out, and a quick visual check made to verify that they are indeed empty. Finally, a powerful verification system based on secondary location codes can be instituted, as follows.

A unique, randomly generated secondary code is assigned to every stores location, and tagged to the end of the primary location code. For example, the secondary code 3729 may be generated and tagged to primary location code A08G4 to give a new code:

$$A08G4\text{-}3729$$

Full codes (i.e. primary codes and their tags) are held in only two places. First, they are displayed at the physical locations to which they correspond, but each inscribed in a size sufficiently small that it can be read only when a person is actually at the location. Secondly, they are held on the computer in a file available only for internal data processing (i.e. which cannot be accessed by the everyday user).

When the storeman puts stock away at a location, or retrieves it, he must record on the transaction the full code of the location, including the tag. The computer checks the validity of the code and rejects the transaction if the primary code and the tag do not match. For example, suppose the 200 units of P50 in Figure 18.2 had not been placed at Location A08G4, but had been wrongly placed in Location A08F4 instead, Location A08F4 having tag 6881. The storeman records on his transaction "A08G4-6881"*(he thinks he has placed it correctly at A08G4)*. The transaction is rejected because primary code A08G4 corresponds to tag 3729, not 6881. In order to help with the subsequent investigation and correction of the mistake, additional information is displayed with the error message that tag 6881 corresponds to Location A08F4.

In addition to well-conceived software, the variable location storage system also demands that stores staff should be given thoroughgoing training in the procedures needed to support it and thoroughgoing education so that they fully appreciate the ideas on which it is based. Training and education will also be needed if the variable location cycle counting system is to be implemented, described in sub-section 18.4.1. This relies on storemen reporting any stock withdrawal that results in a location becoming empty, and has the effect of obviating the need for cycle counting as a separate activity.

18.1.2 Fittings and Equipment

The commencement of design entails the consideration of very many more matters than layout (fixtures, fittings, materials handling equipment, systems) each one having a bearing on the services to be provided. The fine detail of the topics on which decisions must be made includes: pallet access; racking for bars and tubes (pigeon hole or antler?); open and closed shelving; clamps for fragile loads, soft loads and drums; the requirement or not for cranes; automation and automated guided vehicles (AGVs); and so on.

A very small number of topics have been selected as contributing to the manufacturing manager's appreciation of stores operations and concerns, and these are discussed below.

Receiving and Despatching Docks

As the tempo of manufacturing increases, the slick operation of goods receiving and despatching docks is of increasing importance. If these areas become bottlenecks, the synchronisation of material flow throughout the entire manufacturing chain is put at risk.

The first issue to settle is the number of docks that are to be provided.[5] As mentioned earlier, this requires, first, assumptions to be made on the likely number of vehicle arrivals and departures and typical unloading and loading durations. Based on these data, what must then be estimated are vehicle waiting and turnaround times and how these might be affected by the number of docks assumed to be provided. The principal tools for investigating questions such as these — queues and waiting times, the best number of "servers" and their percentage utilisations — are queuing theory and simulation (see sub-sections 11.2.4 and 12.2.1). By building a simulation model of the facility, many different scenarios can be tested and compared in order to see what number of docks would constitute the optimal solution. Simulation software incorporating queuing algorithms is available on the market specifically geared to stores and warehouse modelling; in many systems, completed models can be visually demonstrated on the VDU through animated graphics.[6]

The design of the dock itself must be such as to allow vehicles uncomplicated access (and access without obstructing the public highway for any length of time). In the UK, this will entail the clockwise circulation of traffic so that a vehicle can be easily reversed into a bay. To minimise the need for space still further, end access to the vehicle's load is normally catered for rather than side access. This imposes stricter, and consequently safer, procedures on the loading and unloading activities. It may be considered that the space savings achieved outweigh the disadvantage of more limited access to the stock.

Other matters which must be specified in dock/loading bay design are the width of berths and doors, the height of the loading bay platform, the provision of (permanent?) dock levellers — "where the factory meets the outside world" — and provision for the various kinds of mechanical handling equipment needed for the types of goods received and despatched.

---

[5] To avoid confusion and because of differences in the tasks performed and the apparatus needed, docks are usually dedicated either to the receipt or to the despatch of goods.

[6] For example, see Automod and Autostat from Autologic Systems, Stoke Poges, or visit http://www.autosim.com.

Materials Handling Equipment

The supply market for materials handling equipment available for use in the stores is almost as vigorous and extensive as the supply market for cars for use by the private motorist.[7] The procedures the stores manager and the private consumer follow in making a choice from the bewildering array of products available to them are also very similar.

For materials handling, the manager must specify with care the objectives that acquisition of the equipment is intended to achieve. James Tompkins, of Tompkins Associates, Raleigh, NC,[8] suggests that the investigator should address detailed questions under four general headings:

1. *The nature of incoming shipments* — vehicles to be serviced; unit loads to be handled, including their weights; the target unloading rate . . .

2. *The storage racks in which materials are to be placed* — aisle width and other working constraints; heights to be lifted . . .

3. *Stock retrieval* — weight and cube; the order picking system to be used; required manoeuvrability . . .

4. *Requirements in loading vehicles for despatch* — types of vehicles to be loaded; load weights and lifting heights; target loading rate . . .

---

[7] The history of modern mechanical handling equipment is as long and distinguished as the history of the motor car. The world's first electric automobile was demonstrated in Chicago in 1893, five years *before* the advent of the (far cheaper) petrol-driven vehicle. A prototype of the electric forklift truck was developed from the electric car in 1917 by Baker, Rauch & Lang of Cleveland, Ohio (now the Linde Lift Truck Corporation — visit their web page at http://www.awod.com/gallery/business/linde-baker/history.html), for stacking shells and bombs as part of the war effort, on the United States' entry into the Great War in that year. Commercial development of the electric FLT began immediately after the end of the war in 1918.

[8] James H. Greene (ed.) (1997), op. cit., Chapter 25, Table 25.2, has a checklist of 40 questions in all under the four headings given in the text.

The types of equipment available include simple hand pallet trucks, diesel and LP trucks, tow tractors, motorised pulley blocks, engine-powered side loaders and very many more.[9]

For all the variety, the four-door family saloon of the materials handling world is the electric forklift truck — simple and cheap to operate, quiet and free of fumes in indoor areas.[10]

It is perhaps better to categorise electric trucks into three groups: (1) counterbalanced forklift trucks; (2) reach trucks; and (3) pallet trucks. The fulcrum of the familiar counterbalanced forklift truck is the truck's front wheels, as illustrated in Figure 18.4(a). Reach trucks operate by having their forks within the wheel base of the truck when on the move — see Figure 18.4(b) and 18.4(c). By eliminating the need for such a heavy counterweight balance, the device is able to operate in considerably narrower aisles. Variations of the reach truck are the turret truck and the side loading truck. The electric pallet truck is intended to move palletised goods from place to place, not to stack them — the only lifting requirement is onto and off a low platform at the start and finish of the move.

Figure 18.4: (a) Counterbalanced FLT; (b) and (c) Reach Truck

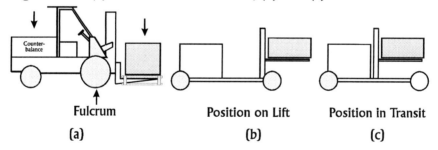

---

[9] See R.J. Carter (1985), *Stores Management and Related Operation*, Second edition, Longman Group UK Ltd. Also see David Jessop and Alex Morrison (1994), *Storage and Supply of Materials*, Sixth edition, Pitman Publishing.

[10] The economics of running an electric FLT are considerably affected by the flatness of the aisles and other working areas where they operate. Floor flatness also affects their safety of operation, since it has a bearing on the degrees of pitch and sway to which elevated loads will be subject. Machines employing laser measuring devices are able to determine the contours of a floor, and the levelling out of the surface can be achieved either by grinding or by laying a new floor as an apron on the old. The concrete used for flooring is specially treated for extra hardness and so as to inhibit dust.

Pallets and Packages

The ubiquitous wooden pallet (sometimes nowadays of plywood) is designed for use with the fork-lift truck, and comprises a top and bottom *board* separated and strengthened by *blocks, bearers* and *stringers*. A load is placed on the pallet's top board, known as its *load platform*, and the tines (or forks) of the lift truck are inserted within the pallet to begin the lift, movement and eventual storage of load and pallet together (see Figure 18.4(a)).

By the adoption throughout most of UK industry of a standard pallet load platform, 1,000mm × 1,200mm, the simplicity and effectiveness of the fork-lift truck and pallet are reinforced by the *de facto* near standardisation of the loads carried.[11] That is, what is likely to be carried on a pallet is a *unit load*, this being simply an individual loaded pallet, built up from separate packages in the form of a rectangular block, handled as a single lot and capable of being stacked onto other palletised unit loads. If a great many unit loads, then, are created on standard pallets, provision for their handling from one company to the next by standard equipment is more easily accommodated. The planning of unit load quantities and load dimensions at each link in the supply chain, taking into careful account handling operations and other factors, is referred to as *unitisation*, part of the fourth component of the "distribution mix" referred to in Section 20.1. Naturally, the sizes of packages in which goods are to be packed become progressively smaller from the factory gate to the ultimate consumer. In order to adhere to the rules of unitisation, it will frequently be necessary for the supply chain planner to override traditional packing quantities with regard to package design. Unitisation has been established by the diktat of the major supermarket chains in groceries distribution all the way from manufacturers' factories to the retailers' stock rooms.

At the bulk end of unitisation, a familiar unit load allowing packed goods to be transferred from one mode of transport to the next across great distances is one based on a standard ISO container, this being 8' wide × 8' high, and one of four standard lengths

---

[11] The dimensions and other characteristics of two-way and four-way pallets, box pallets, post pallets and other matters relating to unit loads, are the subject of BS2629, Part 1. A two-way pallet allows the tines of the FLT to be inserted from North and South; a four-way pallet allows insertion from North, South, East and West. Note that the dimensions of the US pallet are 48" × 40".

(10', 20', 30' and 40'). Container handling also entails standardised equipment — end loaders, side loaders, straddle carriers, gantry cranes, etc. — see Section 20.4 (*Transport of the Goods*).[12]

Although doubtless of small concern to the traditional stores, the study and development of packages are prominent activities in companies selling goods for widespread distribution into, say, the consumer market, the functions of the package being to protect the goods from the environment and in transit, especially from changes in temperature and humidity, and to allow their quick recognition. (Larger companies manufacturing consumer goods will employ a full-time packaging manager, or packaging engineer.)[13] Interest in packaging lies with the manufacturing manager (handling and filling); purchasing; distribution (storage, handling and transportation); and the sales manager (customer appeal through design, product enhancement, freshness on arrival and ease of use). Expectations of high standards in packaging now universal in the consumer market are becoming apparent in industry.

---

[12] Software is available to work out the most effective way to stack a pallet or pack a container to create an efficient unit load from many individual packages. The storeman/warehouseman defines to the system the dimensions and weights of the packages to be loaded, and the software employs simple trial-and-error algorithms to arrive at a best solution (in the time allowed it). The final stacking/packing scheme to be followed is illustrated in a 3D cutout diagram on the VDU. (Cape Pack 99 from Cape Systems, London, consists of three modules: *Pallet*, *Arrange* and *Design*. Visit http://www.capesystems.com/. Cape Systems have other products in this area.)

[13] In the past, the role of the packaging manager has been either to develop novel package designs for his company's products or to work with packaging companies in their development processes. More likely, nowadays, it is to ensure the company's compliance with the European Union's directive on packaging and packaging waste (as interpreted by the Environment Agency). This awesome monument to the Regulator's art speaks of *primary, secondary and tertiary* packaging; of *obligated manufacturers*; of *individual and collective compliance schemes*; and of *accredited reprocessors of waste*. In true EU fashion, the directive in fact has led to a considerable *decrease* in the amount of packaging waste recycled than under the previous free market system. (*Producer Responsibility Obligations (Packaging Waste) Regulations 1997 — User's Guide*, Department of the Environment.) The regulations were introduced for political rather than environmental reasons: see *The Sunday Telegraph*, 20 February 2000, p.19. Package recovery notes (known as "PRNs") are traded between companies for cash.

18.2 STORES OPERATIONS

18.2.1 The Receipt and Storage of Goods

It will be recalled from sub-section 16.2.2 ("The Purchase Order"), that when an order is placed with a supplier, it is assigned an order number, which is attached to all other data relating to it then raised in subsequent activities. Such activities and data are fundamental to commerce within the manufacturing company, and, of course, are of special importance to the goods-in section of the stores, though nowadays the medium of communication may have changed from typewritten notes to Electronic Data Interchange. It will be recalled, again from sub-section 16.2.2, that the paper trail that is laid consists of the following, in chronological order: *the purchase order itself* (to the supplier); *the advice note* (from the supplier); *the consignment note* (from the haulier); *the delivery note*; and *the unpacking note*.

Because data are accumulated at each point, the stores manager is able to access the database to see what deliveries are scheduled to arrive in the next few days, and so make due preparation to receive the various loads by ensuring labour and materials handling equipment will be available.[14]

If goods-in staff find that the goods are of the correct quantity and are of satisfactory quality, they will indicate their acceptance of them, acceptance being a step that is important legally as well as in practice, being discussed at length in sub-section 16.3.2. Alternatively, the goods may be liable to sampling, with the possibility then of their rejection (see sub-section 14.4.4). If they are accepted, they will be stored on, or in, whatever storage furniture is appropriate to the material, and which constitutes the fixtures and fittings provided for in stores design (18.1.2). Other examples of modes of storage than those previously mentioned include various configurations of pallet racking such as *individual access, drive-in (3-deep), drive-in (4-deep)*; cantilever and flow-through racking; drawers; and electromechanical carousels (horizontal and vertical).

---

[14] It is essential that the receiving company should be in a position to take charge of the goods on their arrival without delay where the delivery point is a railhead or port. If the carrier is forced to wait in railway sidings or at anchor awaiting the arrival of the company's transport, a hefty *demurrage* charge will be made by the railway or port authority, payable by the receiving company (demurrage = detention).

When the goods have been *located* (i.e. put away), the purchase order computer file and, of course, the stock records file are updated.

18.2.2 Stock Issue Procedures

The procedures followed literally for the issue of stock from the stores to those requiring its use are as one might expect: authorisation, scrutiny of documentation, the picking of material and the updating of the stock records. What is of special interest is the balance struck between control — the guardianship of the company's assets — and the wish to remove obstacles to the swift, smooth carrying out of manufacturing operations.

For this reason, there will usually be a spectrum of procedures: at one end, issues on verbal request for very low-value items; issues against a supervisor's signature for other items up to a certain value; the issue of certain tools only on presentation of a used-up old tool; loan issues against own signature; the release of material for scheduled production against a job number; capital issues only against a manager's signature.

The issue of goods for packing and external despatch in response to a customer's order follows a separate procedure related to the operation of the sales order processing system (see Section 2.4 and Figure 2.5). Because goods are to leave the company's premises, the safeguards laid down to ensure the validity of the addressee, the correctness of the package and overall authorisation must be strict.

18.2.3 Order Picking

Picking means the physical retrieval and marshalling of stock carried out so as to fulfil its issue either to the shop floor or to the external customer. Although picking efficiency, measured by the number of minutes to pick an item, rarely has a direct bearing on the service offered to the stores' customers, it has a major impact on overall stores or warehouse operating costs.[15] In a warehouse, some 55 per cent of labour costs are spent picking, and since 60 per cent of total costs are labour, picking accounts for 33 per cent of all direct costs.[16]

Because of this, picking demands close attention by the manager to see if reductions can be made in its cost.

Investigation of picking and consideration of possible improvements must start by the observation and recording of the distinct activities which make up the current picking operation, using the traditional skills of work study (often aided, these days, by the use of a camcorder). When complete, it will almost certainly be found that the activity consuming the greatest time is "travelling". As we see from the study quoted in footnote 15, travelling to the stock (to withdraw goods) and from the stock (to marshal them) is 60 per cent of the total time, implying that 20 per cent of all warehouse costs are spent in travelling to and from stock (33 per cent x 60 per cent). Travelling time is the Number 1 target.

Numerous schemes are possible for the deployment of stock to minimise the time spent travelling in the course of picking it and no particular one is superior in all circumstances. The application of simulation, referred to earlier, is especially valuable here for examining the effectiveness of alternative possible arrangements under different assumptions as to product variety, stock volume, distances and frequency of issue. Trial candidates are as follows:

- **One step picking:** This is the conventional arrangement whereby all stock is contained within a single facility, this being subject to a single picking operation (cf the double opera-

---

[15] In a warehouse, picking rate is measured by the quotient "total warehouse labour time (minutes)"/"number of orders lines picked". According to Dexion Ltd., 1.0 mins/line is excellent, 5.0 mins/line is average and 10.0 mins/line poor. In the same study, Dexion also report that 60 per cent of picking time is spent travelling, 20 per cent extracting stock, 10 per cent searching, and 10 per cent is split between documenting, reaching, sorting and counting. (*The Dexion Guide to Picking* (1993), published by Dexion Ltd., Hemel Hempstead. See also the Lansing Linde (footnote 7 above) *Order Picking* guide by Bruno Kulick and Robert Helbert. For more on picking, refer to *Towards More Efficient Order Picking* (1995), Second edition, The Institute of Logistics and Transport, Corby, Northants.)

[16] See The Institute of Materials Management *Monograph No. 1* (1988), and *Modern Materials Handling* magazine, Vol. 45, No. 12 (October 1990).

tion in two-step picking). The most frequently accessed products are located in the most convenient locations.

- **Zonal picking:** The single facility is divided into zones, or sections, each zone dedicated to the storage of various products of a specific type. When an order is to be picked, the computer assigns a marshalling location to it and generates a number of picking requirement notes, each one corresponding to a different zone. The storeman in charge of a zone picks his zone's products and marshals them in the location designated. (The alternative method of sending a single order note from zone to zone appears to demand considerably more organisation and to be less successful in smaller warehouses.)

- **Two-step picking.** Stock is kept in both a primary store (or bulk store) and a secondary store (or mini-store). The secondary store is positioned as close to the point of use of the material as possible and contains a full range of material, but travelling is greatly reduced because of its location and small size. There are two picking operations:

    1. From the primary store to the secondary store, to keep the mini-store topped up, the requisite picking operation being carried out infrequently, perhaps daily, based on summaries of indents against the secondary store; and

    2. From the secondary store in response to an issue request.

    Two-step picking is common in very large warehouses which respond to very small customer orders.[17]

---

[17] Notwithstanding footnote 1 and sub-section 18.3.3, paragraphs 1 and 2, two-step picking might be used to solve the stock records accuracy problem in a factory stores when access to stock is essential on occasions by shop floor staff. Shop floor access to the primary stores remains strictly prohibited and records of stock there are maintained at 100 per cent accuracy. The records of stock in the secondary store are "not accurate", but are frequently corrected by full stock counts, each such count accomplished in a short time. Even in a warehouse environment, the manager may question whether the maintenance of 100 per cent accuracy through a conventional, transaction-driven system in a secondary store is possible or, if it is, whether the effort is worthwhile. A more extreme example of record-keeping in an open environment is through *backflushing*. Suppose two units of Component C are used to make one unit of Product P; 900 units of C are originally issued to the shop floor, and 320 units of P are later manufactured. The presumed usage of C

- **Order bunching.** If many of the orders received contain items which are common or close together, they can be temporarily combined to enable multiple trips out to the same locations to be eliminated. The consolidation of Order 1 and Order 2 in Table 18.1 reduces the number of collection journeys to withdraw the four products from two to one. The two original orders are then separately built up from the marshalled, amalgamated stock. (As with all other methods of picking, the picking instructions generated by the computer should show the items to be picked in a convenient order based on their locations.)

Table 18.1: Order Bunching to Eliminate Picking Journeys

Order 1		Order 2		Amalgamated Order	
Product	No. of Units	Product	No. of Units	Product	No. of Units
A23	4	A23	4	A23	8
B21	6	B21	3	B21	9
C56	3	D55	2	C56	3
				D55	2

Picking methodology naturally cannot be divorced from the questions previously touched on of materials handling equipment. Equipment not previously mentioned that will be considered for the picking operation includes: ride-on picking vehicles, travelling along the aisles; automatic crane retrieval; conveyors and rollers; and RDTs (radio data terminals), allowing the ready communication of requirements from a central point to pickers already positioned close to the stock (see footnote 20, Section 11.5). In many large warehouses, ingenious bespoke picking and computer-controlled mechanical handling systems have been devised and built, at very considerable cost.

(640 units) is now deducted from (*backflushed against*) C's original stock balance, so that the stock of C calculated to remain is 260 units. In an open environment, subject to a multitude of activities, official and unofficial, there is no hope that the stock quantity remaining will tally with the backflushed record for long. The amount of stock originally issued should be as small as possible so that it can be quickly and easily counted and the record then corrected.

18.3 STOCK RECORDS ACCURACY

The maintenance of accurate records of what items are stored, their quantities and their locations is of prime importance to all stores, its accomplishment being fundamental to the basic functions of storing and retrieving stock. And as touched on a number of times earlier in the chapter, accuracy of stock records is a major requirement of planning systems, such systems being central to the company's operations.

18.3.1 The Stock Recording System

The maintenance on the computer of records of stores stocks is effected through the operation of a transaction-driven stock recording system. The architecture of the system is similar in a great many respects to the shop floor information system described in sub-section 11.5.1 and illustrated in Figure 11.10. A pictograph of the stock recording system is given in Figure 18.5.

Figure 18.5: The Stock Recording System

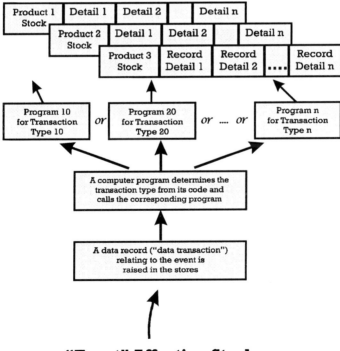

The "events affecting stock" in this case include receipts of raw materials from external suppliers; receipts of components from the shop floor; issues of material; the movements of stock in the stores from one location to another, etc. Each event when it occurs must be matched by the raising and processing of a corresponding data transaction. Examples of transactions are: *the receipt of p units of Raw Material R1 from Supplier S (stored in Location L1); the receipt of q units of Component C1 from B (stored in Location L2); the issue of r units of Component C2 to the shop floor with respect to Works Order W; the transfer of s units of finished product P1 from Location L3 to Location L4; a return from . . .; the scrap of . . . ; an external delivery to . . .*

The warnings given in sub-section 11.5.2 regarding the design and development of a shop floor information system and the possibility of its failure do not apply with quite such severity to the development of the data processing procedures within the overall stock recording system. Nevertheless, the fact remains that very many companies have poor records accuracy due to inadequate systems, and, if so, no amount of conscientiousness in their operation and no amount of personnel training will put matters right.[18] As in sub-section 11.5.2, it is essential that the potential system should be verified at the design stage by those who will use it — here the stores manager and his staff — perhaps through its presentation at a structured walkthrough (see 11.5.2 once more). One important check that must be made at a walkthrough is whether the transactions to be provided are comprehensive. If the procedures and technology existing in a particular stores affect stock balances in an unusual way, and this cannot be clearly represented and communicated because a corresponding transaction has not been provided, the records are certain to become inaccurate.[19]

---

[18] Anecdotal testimony from GMCS's *Stock Records Accuracy* training course over some fifteen years, up to 2001. Visit http://www.gmcs.co.uk/sra.htm.

[19] Software writers might also rethink their attitudes to transactions that create negative stock balances. For one thing, a negative balance may be due merely to the submission of transactions in a chronologically different sequence from the sequence of actual events when the stock level of the part happens to be low (i.e. *issue-receipt* instead of *receipt-issue*). For another, it is not for a computer programmer to dictate action in this (very obvious) circumstance: it is for the user to contemplate the situation and himself determine what is to be done, if anything. There should also be some evidence in the design of a stock recording system that those responsible for it have a

The Stores and Stock Records

If stock balances are to be read by a manufacturing planning system in order to calculate production requirements, they must clearly incorporate all stock, including stock on the shop floor (and elsewhere), as well as what is held in the stores. To do so, some systems, such as closed-loop MRP, may simply take note of stock due in from so-called *scheduled receipts* of components and raw materials held under their own control (see sub-section 10.2.1). Other systems may need to access two files, the first being the stores stock file, the second a file holding details of work-in-progress.

Because of the considerable difficulty in tracking work-in-progress and other shop floor data when the tempo, or pace, of manufacturing is rapid (see Figure 11.9 and supporting text), a modification may be made to the stores stock recording system by the addition of a data field entitled "WIP-stock-due-in". The field is maintained by the following three-step procedure:

1. When stock is issued to the shop floor, an identification number is assigned to it (associated usually with the works order number, this number being transferred to "production achieved" later);

2. At the same time as (1), the stores stock record of the issued material is immediately debited, regardless of the stock's temporary continued existence on the shop floor, and the WIP-stock-due-in field of the intended production material is credited with the corresponding amount expected to be manufactured;

3. When actual production has taken place, the newly manufactured material is received into stores and the normal stores stock field updated. The identification number of the received stock is matched with the ID number of the original issue and the WIP-stock-due-in quantity is set to zero.

The planning system now reads two fields to obtain the stock balance of a product: the normal stores stock and the WIP-stock-due-in. Because the recording of data relating to individual jobs on the

---

good knowledge of the problems encountered by stores staff from day to day. For example, two causes of inaccuracy (cited in Table 18.2) are *duplicate transactions* and *units of measure*. To warn of possible duplicates and to provide reasonableness checks on quantities are simple matters, but they are rarely provided for.

shop floor no longer takes place, shop floor accounting must be by process accounting techniques rather than by job or batch accounting (sub-section 17.4.3).

18.3.2 The Accuracy Goal

Inaccuracy in a stock record may lead to the creation of an invalid set of materials plans for a product's manufacture; if so, the invalid plans will in turn lead to the creation of invalid gross requirements for lower level components; and so on down the bill of materials to the plans for purchased products.

In the past, a 95.0 per cent level of accuracy (as defined in Equation 18.1 below) was declared to be the minimum level, below which system performance would substantially deteriorate.[20] More recently, training instructors and consultants have suggested 98.0 per cent. In practice, since records accuracy is the end result of a system subject to common causes of variation, as described in sub-section 13.2.2, the accuracy goal might be set at, say, 97.0 per cent ±1.0 per cent, a vitally important point about the recorded levels being that statistical analysis of them should show the system to be in a stable state.

The degree of accuracy of a group of stock records is arrived at by comparing the record of each product to the quantity of physical stock present and calculating the simple quotient given in Equation 18.1.

$$Stock\ Records\ Accuracy\ of\ the\ Group = \frac{Number\ of\ Records\ Correct}{Total\ Number\ of\ Stocked\ Items} \times 100\%$$

. . . Equation 18.1

Perhaps the most interesting question arising from the definition in Equation 18.1 is what it is that constitutes "correctness". That is, does the record have to match the physical count exactly to be correct, or is a degree of *tolerance* acceptable? One category of stock for which a difference between record and count must indeed be allowed comprises items that literally cannot be accurately measured. The volumes of liquids in bulk form are notoriously difficult to measure; the weights of paper and cloth,

---

[20] Roger B. Brooks and Larry W. Wilson (1995), *Inventory Record Accuracy*, John Wiley & Sons, Inc. To quote, and concur with, Professor Edward Davis of Darden Business School, University of Virginia: ". . . should be required reading for all manufacturing managers".

especially yarn, vary according to atmospheric humidity; items may be difficult to count or measure because of their physical form or style of packaging. A further category comprises items which could perhaps be accurately counted, but which would demand more time and attention to do so than seems worthwhile. Clues to the identities of items in this category are the methods used every day to handle and dispense them: small, inexpensive items are counted by weighing and applying a unit weight.

If an item is to bear a tolerance, two tolerance figures should be assigned. The first is a percentage and the second an absolute number.[21] The calculated tolerance figure then applied in deciding whether or not the item's record is to be deemed accurate should be whichever of the two is bigger at the time the count is made. Thus suppose that an item is assigned a percentage tolerance of ±5 per cent and an absolute figure of ±30 units. Two situations are examined:

1. At a particular time, the physical count of the item is 1,980 units. The tolerances are therefore ±99 units (±5 per cent of the count) and ±30 units.[22] The first figure, ± 99 units, is consequently selected and the record will be deemed correct if its value lies between 1,881 and 2,079 units.

2. At another time, the physical count of the item is 240 units. The tolerances are therefore ±12 units (±5 per cent of the count) and ±30 units. The second figure, ±30 units, is now selected, and the record will be deemed correct if its value lies between 210 and 270 units.

The complication of the absolute figure has been introduced to give credence to tolerances where items with generally large ini-

---

[21] As a rule of thumb, the absolute number might be the quantity arrived at by applying the tolerance percentage to 10 per cent of the delivery quantity or batch manufacturing quantity of the item. Thus, if the delivery quantity is 80,000 units and the percentage tolerance is ±5 per cent, the absolute figure is ±5 per cent × 80,000 × 10 per cent = ± 400 units.

[22] The percentage tolerance in the text is applied to the physical count quantity — that is, *given the actual count of 1,980 units, what is our tolerance with regard to the stock record figure?* (±99). This method is the opposite of that given in Brooks and Wilson (1995), op. cit., where the authors apply the assigned tolerance to the recorded figure, not to the count. There is a difference, though it is a small one.

tial replenishment quantities are selected for cycle counting when their stock quantities are very low, as described in sub-section 18.4.1. It is unrealistic to continue to apply percentage tolerances in these circumstances.

It is quite sufficient to confine all tolerances to a very small number of tolerance groupings based on percentages. Suggested figures are 0 per cent, ±1 per cent and ±5 per cent. If the number of products in the stores is small, the assignment then of each stocked product to one or other of the groups may be carried out on an individual basis by the stores manager and a representative of the accountancy department, employing the criteria of measurability and worth above. If there are a large number of products but they are conveniently categorised in groups, assignment might be by product group rather than individually. Other methods that have been used are assignment by the use of ABC analysis (see subsection 18.4.1) and according to each product's level in the bill of materials (the lower in the bill, it is said, the less critical the part). An argument against setting an item's tolerance based on these two methods, or on such similar methods as those involving, say, the item's financial value, is that if the stock is able to be counted or measured quite correctly and with perfect ease, the subsequent setting of a tolerance seems unnecessary and appears even to be an invitation to studied carelessness in the operation of the system.

Finally, in their lively and inspiring book *Inventory Records Accuracy*,[23] Roger Brooks and Larry Wilson repeatedly warn that tolerances are not the salvation of companies with poor records accuracy. Widening tolerances will not remedy a poor system or change attitudes or working practices, and will make very little difference to the accuracy percentage actually achieved.

It is to attitudes and working practices that we now turn.

18.3.3 Supporting the System

It is agreed by all stores managers and others familiar with the stock records problem that the stores must be strictly out-of-bounds to all staff except stores personnel having their place of work there. As stated in footnote 1, since this inviolable rule means shop floor operators cannot themselves access stock at any time, direct stores service must be available whenever it might be needed.

---

[23] Op. cit.

The stores is secured not simply by manning, padlocks and CCTV, necessary though they may be. It is secured also by the creation of a corporate attitude as to its integrity. This requires an explanation to the workforce of the reasons for the stores being off-limits and an explanation of the contribution of records accuracy to planning and customer service. Above all, the creation of a corporate attitude requires the active and unequivocal commitment of senior management. (Even the boldest shop supervisor requiring parts in a hurry one weekend is likely to respect the rule if he sees everyday that it is also respected, and vigorously prosecuted, by the managing director himself.)

The support of any system requires, first, that a comprehensive manual should be written and made available to those involved with it, to assist in training and later development and to act as a ready reference. Secondly, it requires that staff should undergo off-the-job training so that they thoroughly understand each transaction and the circumstances of its use. It is difficult to see how such training could be given without recourse to a training database. The training database allows each member of staff to work through case studies, his progress being later assessed by a trainer via a transaction trail. The database is returned to its original state at the end of each training session.

It may be suspected that the most prevalent causes of inaccuracy in the stock records are due not to poor understanding of the system but to mistakes inevitable in its operation — miscounting and misrecording, late and lost transactions, and so on. The problem with errors such as miscounting, and many others which cannot be detected by scrutiny of the transaction trail, is that they are quite untraceable after a few short weeks.[24] System improvements to remove these common causes of error cannot be effectively directed by management, because individual causes are largely unknown.

---

[24] One technique that has been used on an occasional basis for discerning the true causes of error is to institute a so-called *control group* of, say, 100 products. The physical stocks of all products in the group are counted every two or three days, and any discrepancies in the records followed up at once while events are still fresh in the minds of staff involved. The control group has proved useful as a means of monitoring the performance of a new system in its first few weeks.

Note that the view is taken, consistent with sub-section 13.2.3, that management must modify or improve the system, not bear down on those operating it. We recall Deming's special causes and common causes and the warning in 13.2.3 that "corrective action on a stable system ... will cause more trouble than it cures".

Although an error in a record can rarely be traced to a specific special or common cause (or to several, since the error may be the net accumulation of many small errors), it is of interest to see what practitioners perceive non-IT causes to be in the general case. Table 18.2 lists 20 common causes and two special causes (denoted by *s), and their believed prevalence, as reported over many years.[1]

Table 18.2 gives many clues as to how the procedures constituting the stock recording system might be refined or supported to eliminate or reduce common causes of error, defining *system*, now, in the wider, "outside in" sense illustrated by Figure 13.2. For example, one change, made in the light of two of the top three causes, and which account for 20.9 per cent of all errors made, previously suggested in sub-section 13.2.5, might be to require all applicants for jobs as storemen to pass clerical, eyesight and colour vision tests. Once the stores manager has identified and eliminated any special causes of error which may intrude into the operation of the system, so that a stable level is attained, the task must begin of refining and improving the system itself. One by one, then, the common causes of error, such as those in Table 18.2, are removed. Records accuracy begins a stepwise ascent from plateau to plateau, as illustrated in Figure 18.6, finally to stabilise between the high target limits mentioned earlier.

---

[1] Each attendee on GMCS's Stock Records Accuracy training course was asked to nominate the two most prevalent causes of error, not directly attributable to software, at his own place of work. Some 5,000 nominations collected over many years have been accumulated and normalised as given in Table 18.2.

Table 18.2: Top 20 Causes of Stock Record Errors due to Non-System Causes as Obtained from a Survey (see footnote 25)

Rank	Perceived Cause of Error	%
1	Incorrect counting	12.5
2	Missing transactions	8.6
3	Incorrect recording	8.4
4	Partially insecure stores	8.1
5	Stock placed in wrong location	6.8
6	Incorrect picking (i.e. picking wrong items)	6.5
7	BOM and/or backflushing errors	5.6
8	Slow reporting of transactions	5.2
9	Misidentification of parts	4.2
10	Errors introduced by actual stocktake (*s)	4.0
11	Working under too much pressure	3.9
12	Scrap or production missed	3.7
13	Use of the wrong transactions	3.6
14	Data keying errors	3.2
15=	Entry of the wrong units of measure	2.8
15=	Wilful lack of care	2.8
17	Duplicates — same transaction submitted twice	2.2
18	Misidentification of locations	2.2
19	Failure to count raw material receipts	1.9
20	Shrinkage (unreported deterioration/write-offs)	1.6
21	Issue of incorrect picking list	1.2
22	Theft (*s)	0.9
	Total	100

Figure 18.6: Stepwise Progression to High Records Accuracy

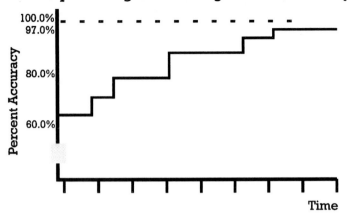

18.4 CYCLE COUNTING

Absolute assurance of a record's accuracy can be obtained, ultimately, only by counting the part's physical stock and comparing the two figures; if different, the certain recourse then to effect its correction is to amend the data directly. Counting and, if necessary, correction are governed by a system of *cycle counting*.

At its simplest, cycle counting means counting the physical stock of a few products each day, amending any records that are in error, so that over a certain period (the "cycle") all products have been counted. The process then starts all over again, giving rise to cycle counting's alternative name *perpetual inventory checking* (PI). Thus if there are 1,000 products to count and a 10-week cycle is chosen, 100 products will be counted each week, or 20 products a day, until that cycle is completed and the next one started.

Cycle counting is a commonsense method of verifying stock records, with none of the disadvantages such as disruptions to production or delays in customer despatch that accompany the annual stock count. Indeed, provided the stock records are known to be reasonably accurate, financial auditors will almost always agree to discontinue the year-end count and to accept the stock records figures in compiling the balance sheet, provided a cycle counting programme is also in operation as a fail-safe.[26]

---

[26] If the auditor for his own reasons insists on an annual stock count on top of cycle counting (and it is his right to do so), a separate data field should be provided on the product's record for the figure — see Error 10, Table 18.2.

The Stores and Stock Records 785

The subject is described here in two parts. The first — *Practice and Procedures* — deals with such issues as cycle length, the possibility of different lengths for different products and the selection of items to count from day to day. The second — *Reconciliation* — describes how a cycle count value is compared with a part's stock record, with a view, if they are different, to amending the record. Precautions must be taken in so doing because of the possibility of late or premature transactions in the system. A *late* transaction is one relating to an activity that took place before the cycle count, which should have been processed before reconciliation was attempted, but is received afterwards instead. A *premature* transaction is one relating to an activity — say, a receipt or issue — that may have taken place after the count and, again, is processed before reconciliation is made. Because the practice and procedures of cycle counting are affected by the reconciliation precautions applied, the two parts of the Section should be read in conjunction.

As well, it should be noted that there are very considerable differences in effectiveness and cost between the alternative methodologies, and that the simplest and most straightforward ones are unlikely to prove the best in most stores.

18.4.1 Cycle Counting Practice and Procedures

The Cycle Length

If all of the items in a fixed location stores are to be counted over the same cycle, a first task might be to explore what cycle periods would be obtained by the application of various alternative counting efforts. In performing the calculations, an assumption must be made as to the *counting rate* achievable by the cycle counter. Brooks and Wilson have given a figure of 25 parts per day, applying in certain circumstances.[27] This is used for now, but as we shall see in due course, counting productivity is very greatly affected by the method used to select the items to be counted and the procedures employed finally to reconcile the counts and the records.

---

[27] The figure of 25 parts/day pertains to the random selection of the parts in the group to be counted, and is given in Brooks and Wilson (1995), op. cit., p. 126, footnote 8. It represents the consensus of many hundreds of attendees on training courses given in the USA during the 1980s by the Oliver Wight Organisation.

If the number of cycle counters is C and the counting rate achievable is r items/day, and if the number of items in the stores is N, then the length of the cycle in days is given by Equation 18.2.

$$Cycle\ Period = \frac{N}{C \times r} \qquad Equation\ 18.2$$

Various alternative assumptions can now be made as to the counting effort actually to be applied and the cycle durations that would result. For example, if there were 3,000 items in the stores, then with one cycle counter and the counting rate of 25 items/day, the cycle length would be 3,000/(1 × 25) days, i.e. 120 working days, or 24 weeks. So, if cycle counting is regarded as a full-time job, is one person to be assigned, to obtain a 24-week cycle? Or are there to be six people for a cycle of four weeks? A very short cycle of only a few weeks seems excessive — why are records going wrong after such a short time? Is there a major system fault? Conversely, a very long period, certainly one longer than 52 weeks, may be unacceptable to the auditor. Management judgement must be brought to bear in deciding the best cycle length and the required, corresponding manpower needed to support it, weighing the factors of cost, possible difficulty in local circumstances and the records accuracy currently prevailing.

Rather than have a single cycle period applying to all products, if it is believed that parts can be classified in some way as meriting longer or shorter counting intervals, a popular notion is to assign the products to one or other of the classifications and apply a different cycle length to each one.

One simple classification scheme consistent with this purpose is in accordance with the number of transactions raised each year relating to each part. The greater the activity against the stock of a part, the greater the number of transactions and the greater the chance of error. Thus, parts subject to the most transactions are counted over a shorter cycle. A second more commonly met scheme is in accordance with *annual value*, this being defined for each part as "annual usage × unit cost". That is, if 900 units of part P are handled each year, and each unit has a cost of £2, the annual value is £1,800. The usage element of this expression also reflects activity, at least to a degree, and so also reflects risk to records accuracy, but the additional term brings in consideration of stockkeeping as guardianship of assets. The greater the annual value, the shorter the cycle.

Since the data obtainable from the records relating to both number of transactions and annual values are continua, it is necessary to devise a classification system so that a particular data value relating to a part enables that part to be assigned to one or other of the classes in the system. The scheme employed is one first suggested by H. Ford Dickie of General Electric Inc.,[28] and is based on *Pareto Analysis*[29] or *ABC Analysis*.

To carry out Pareto analysis on the products within a stores, it is clearly first necessary to determine the data values that will be used for classification. Suppose annual value is chosen, and that the values calculated for ten stocked parts P1 to P10 in the stores are as shown in Figure 18.7(a). The parts are next ranked, or sorted, in descending order of annual value. Thus the parts in 18.7(a) are displayed again in Figure 18.7(b), this time in the new order. The Pareto phenomenon now reveals that the top 20 per cent of the items in the sorted list account for approximately 80 per cent of the total value of all parts together. (The Pareto 80/20 division has been summarised as *the trivial many and the vital few*.) In Figure

---

[28] See H. Ford Dickie (1951), "ABC Inventory Analysis Shoots for Dollars, Not Pennies", *Factory Management and Maintenance* (US magazine), Vol. 5 — quoted by R.G. Brown in *Advanced Service Parts Inventory Control (ASPIC)* (1982) and James H.Greene (ed.) (1997), *Production & Inventory Control Handbook,* Third edition.

[29] Vilfredo Pareto (1848–1923) graduated in mathematics and physics from the University of Turin, initially pursuing a highly successful career within Italy in railway engineering and later steel. In 1893, at the age of 45, however, as the result of treatises he had published, he was offered, and accepted, the post of professor of political economy at Lausanne University, Switzerland. Throughout his academic career, Pareto appears to have been captivated by the notion of *the trivial many and the vital few*. Thus the three principal theories that he expounded relate to: what he held to be an historically consistent 80/20 distribution of wealth through all societies; the point at which the consumer's attitude to his purchases turns from satisfaction to indifference; and the "circulation of elites", this last concerned with the rise and fall of powerful groups within society (Professor Pareto's ideas on elite groups were believed at the time to be supportive of Fascism). His theory of indifference and the drawing of indifference curves continue to be taught in the economics of welfare; the theory of indifference relates to the willingness of consumers to rank the few products they really care about (the A products) and their indifference as to the ranking the remainder (the many B products). The theory was set out in *Manuale d'economia politica*, Vilfredo Pareto, 1906.

18.7(b), Parts P8 and P5 account for 73.4 per cent of the total annual value of all ten products. These two might be classed as "Group A" products. Parts P7, P10 and P4, the next 30 per cent of the products, account for 20.5 per cent of the total and might be classed as Group B. The remaining five products, 50 per cent of the total number, account for only 6.1 per cent of total annual value, and may be assigned to Group C. (With a realistically large number of products, an alternative method of classification is to define Group A products as those products accounting for 80 per cent of the total annual value, Group B as those accounting for the next 15 per cent and Group C as those products accounting for the last 5 per cent.). The divisions and classifications are quite arbitrary. The manager may choose as many groups as he wishes, although more than four may prove difficult to administer, and he may divide the list into any proportions he wishes.[30]

Figure 18.7(a): Annual Values of Ten Products

Part	Annual Quantity	Unit Value	Annual Value	Cumulative Annual Value as %	Rank
P1	10	£2	£20	x	10
P2	40	£1	£40	x	8
P3	15	£10	£150	x	6
P4	50	£4	£200	x	5
P5	115	£12	£1,380	x	2
P6	5	£5	£25	x	9
P7	30	£15	£450	x	3
P8	275	£8	£2,200	x	1
P9	15	£4	£60	x	7
P10	50	£7	£350	x	4
Total			£4,875		

---

[30] Since the Group A products are to be counted more often than the Group Bs and Cs, the stores manager may wish to promote a number of B or C Group items to special Group A status in order to keep a closer eye on them. For example, so-called *line stoppers* — cheap items bought in small quantities, and clearly destined for Group C, may be notoriously difficult to replenish if they run out, but may cause a production shut down if they do so. Many other troublesome or risky parts, or parts which seem continually difficult to get right, might similarly be individually identified and placed in Group A.

Figure 18.7(b): Ten Products after Pareto Analysis

Part	Annual Quantity	Unit Value	Annual Value	Cum. Annual Value as %	Rank	
P8	275	£8	£2,200	45.1	1	A
P5	115	£12	£1,380	73.4	2	A
P7	30	£15	£450	82.7	3	B
P10	50	£7	£350	89.9	4	B
P4	50	£4	£200	93.9	5	B
P3	15	£10	£150	97.0	6	C
P9	15	£4	£60	98.2	7	C
P2	40	£1	£40	99.1	8	C
P6	5	£5	£25	99.6	9	C
P1	10	£2	£20	100.0	10	C
Total			£4,875			

Calculation of the cycle length and the effort to be applied to the counting of any particular group is performed in the way described previously, the term N in Equation 18.2 this time denoting the number of products in the group rather than the number in the stores. However, the manager must now reckon with the resources and cycle periods as they are assigned to several groups at once, at the same time keeping track of total required manpower.

An obvious way to do so, and also to be able easily to look at various alternatives and their consequences, is to institute a "cycle counting spreadsheet". Figure 18.8 shows a snapshot of a simple spreadsheet set up to deal with the A, B and C cycles of a stores with 3,000 products, in which the possibility of cycles of 14 weeks, 20 weeks and 40 weeks is being examined and considered. As before, it is assumed that one person can count 25 parts per day. The calculations are self-evident. As previously discussed, the decisions finally reached on periods and the resources to be allocated are matters of judgement.

Figure 18.8: Calculations of Cycle Periods and Effort through the "Cycle Counting Spreadsheet"

Group	Group % of Total	Number of Parts in Group (% × 3,000)	Cycle Period (weeks)	Counts per Week	Counts per Day	Count Effort (counts/25)
A	20	600	14	42.8	8.5	0.34
B	30	900	20	45.0	9.0	0.36
C	50	1,500	40	37.5	7.5	0.30
Total		3,000		125.3	25.0	1.00

The procedures described so far in this sub-section are aimed at a fixed location stores. Although it is not impossible to apply them to a variable location stores, to do so would be cumbersome in the extreme: in order to verify the stock of a given part, it would be necessary for the cycle counter to visit every location where units of that part were currently stored, very considerably slowing down the counting rate. The preferred means of cycle counting stock in a variable stores is given in due course, but if the manager wished to persevere with the procedures above, the stock of a given product at a particular location should be treated as a *stockkeeping unit (SKU)*, i.e. as an entity uniquely defined by its product identity and place of storage in combination (the notion of an SKU is widely used in distribution, for obvious reasons — see throughout Chapter 20). Cycle counting as described above may then be based on verifying the stock of each SKU, not product, and reconciling the SKU count with the product record as it relates to the SKU location only. When the reconciliation has taken place, it must be possible to indicate on the record the fact that the stock at that particular location has been counted. The SKUs can then simply be treated from the viewpoints of cycle length and day-to-day selection for counting in just the same way as single, fixed location products.

Selecting the Parts to Count

If 1,000 parts are required to be counted over a 10-week cycle, every day a new batch of 20 must be identified. When the count has taken place, the 20 are placed on an "already counted" list and are not considered for counting again until the next cycle.[31] At the end of the cycle, every part in the population of 1,000 will have been counted once.

There are a number of ways in which the parts to be counted each day may be identified. Random selection, for example, incorporates elements of surprise and audit referred to in footnote 31. An order of selection based on parts' locations has the advantages in a fixed location stores of consistency of counting interval for each part from cycle to cycle, and of minimum travelling time for the cycle counter from one part's location to the next.

The method overwhelmingly superior to any, however, is identification based on low stock. The principal advantage by far in choosing parts to count at the times that their stocks are relatively low is that counting effort will be thereby greatly reduced (and cycle counting effectiveness thereby commensurately increased). In addition, a product with relatively low stock is *ipso facto* certain to have been subject to a number of withdrawals since its last replenishment, and, if, as a consequence, its record is in error, correction of it at this point is at a judicious time, being before a further withdrawal causes perhaps an unexpected stockout. Three low stock methods are described below, the third confined to a variable location stores. Note that in all three of them, the creation of Pareto ABC groupings loses its relevance and these are abandoned.[32] In the second and third methods, the notion of a target cycle period also becomes irrelevant.

1. Identification of low stock items by computer. The relative stockholding of a part is defined by the simple expression in Equation 18.3.

---

[31] If stock counting is regarded as continual spot auditing for the purposes only of reporting accuracy and checking the work of staff, rather than as a means of verifying the accuracy of the records and correcting any in error, then the decision may be taken that parts selected on one day should continue to be candidates for selection the next. If parts are to be returned to the pool, the notion of a cycle count is invalidated, since over any "cycle", some parts would never be counted and others would be counted many times.

[32] So much for Pareto Analysis. One is reminded of Dr Johnson's advice on a cucumber: *"A cucumber should be well sliced, and dressed with pepper and vinegar, and then thrown out as good for nothing"* (Samuel Johnson, 1709–1784, from *The Life of Johnson (Tour of the Hebrides, October 5th)* by James Boswell).

$$\text{Relative stockholding} = \frac{\text{Current stock level}}{\text{Maximum stock level}} \qquad \text{Equation 18.3}$$

The maximum stock level of each part is held as a separate field on the stock record and might be set initially, say, at 105 per cent of the part's replenishment quantity. The value is not critical; all that is required is that there should be reasonable consistency in the method of its derivation from one part to another. (It should be noted, that an item may not qualify for counting, even though its actual stock is low, if its record is in error and falsely indicates high stock. However, the requirement to count all items will ensure it is eventually counted.)

Before the cycle count each day, the required number of parts to be counted in the group are selected simply by identifying those with the lowest relative stockholdings among the parts which have not yet been counted in the particular cycle. The required number of parts to be counted is established though Equation 18.2, employing, however, a value for r far in excess of 25 parts/day (see below). As ever, the counting list is sorted in location order. Note that the parts selected for counting each day are recorded on an *ad hoc* file. Because all parts must be accounted for, any in the group not counted towards the end of the cycle must finally be selected for counting regardless of their relative stockholdings.

2. **Brooks-Wilson identification.** The cycle counter deals with a defined area of the stores each day, and is given a list of all parts and quantities in the area. He counts and records only those parts which he observes, literally, are easy to count, i.e. those seen to have very low stock or seen to consist of a very small number of distinct packages. (However, if he spots that the stock quantity of a part is different from the recorded quantity on his list by an order of magnitude, so that the record is obviously in error, that part is also included in his daily count.)

A careful note is kept of all the areas dealt with from day to day to ensure complete coverage of the stores in a reasonable time. An area may be visited several times in a month, at each successive visit different parts having reached low stock levels and having become candidates for easy counting.

The cycle counter submits transactions each day relating only to the low stock counts he has made and the parts counted because the records were suspected of being in error. The computer system records all parts counted and submitted over a period (say, six months). A report is produced listing any parts in the stores that have been missed, usually because their stocks were never low but perhaps for some other reason. These parts are separately and specially audited.

Roger Brooks and Larry Wilson report spectacular increases in cycle counting effectiveness through this method, and suggest that a counting rate of over 300 parts per day per person is readily attainable.[33]

3. Zero stock identification (variable location stores only). A characteristic of a variable location stores or warehouse not shared by one with fixed locations is that individual locations are continually falling empty. When a particular location does so become empty, it can be allocated by the system for re-use, as described in sub-section 18.1.1.

When the storeman withdraws stock from a location and thereby leaves it empty, he is required to notify the system that this has occurred. A special field for the purpose is provided on the withdrawal transaction. The foregoing, in two sentences, is variable location cycle counting — the raising of a constant stream of transactions carrying confirmatory data that locations have become empty. The data processing activity carried out by the system to effect stock reconciliation on receipt of information that a location is empty is described in sub-section 18.4.2 (end) and is illustrated by Figures 18.11(a) to 18.11(d).

We saw above with both the computer and Brooks-Wilson identification methods that periodic checks are instituted to ensure that any parts not counted after a certain time are audited. Periodic checks are similarly required with zero stock identification, but for locations. That is, the possibility exists that some locations in the stores will never be emptied, perhaps containing slow-moving stock and therefore remaining occupied quite legitimately, or perhaps instead because of an error in the records. Consequently, whenever a location is reported as empty to the system, its code must be written to a file. Every six months, the empty location file is compared to a complete file of stores locations, and every location that has not been reported as empty over the period must then be subjected to

---

[33] See Brooks and Wilson (1995), op. cit., p. 126.

an individual audit. Note also the safeguards against misplaced stock described at the end of sub-section 18.1.1.

The reported increases in counting rate, or counting effectiveness, through zero stock identification are parallel with those achieved through Brooks-Wilson, namely to a rate over ten times greater than with standard counting with random product selection to fulfil an ABC rota.[34]

18.4.2 Cycle Counting Reconciliation

In the introduction to this Section, it was remarked that in comparing a part's cycle count value to its stock record, precautions were necessary because of the possibility of late or premature transactions in the recording system. The circumstances of these two problems are described as follows.

Late Transactions

Suppose that a number of events occur relating to a part P from time t minutes to time (t + 20) minutes. Figure 18.9(a) represents the physical stock quantities involved, in particular the changes in stock level following a receipt and an issue. It can be seen that the third event to occur is the carrying out of a cycle count at time (t + 15) minutes, which duly records a stock quantity of 1,200 units.

---

[34] Roger Brooks and Larry Wilson cite the experience of Hyster Inc. and that company's attainment of very fast counting rates — see Brooks and Wilson (1995), op. cit., p. 129, footnote 9. From the 1970s to the 1980s, ICI Organics division operated the then largest warehouse in Europe at its site in Heywood, Lancashire, originally anticipating the need for eight cycle counters to count over a 12-month cycle. Alan Shea (see Chapter 17, footnote 5) states that by employing zero stock identification, effort was reduced to just two auditors.

The Stores and Stock Records

Figure 18.9(a): Three Events Occurring to Part P from Time t to Time (t + 15)

Physical Stock			
Time (mins)	Description of the Event	Event Quantity (units)	Physical Stock in Store
t	(Starting stock quantity)		1,000
t + 5	Receipt from supplier	500	1,500
t + 10	Issue to the shop	300	1,200
t + 15	Carrying out of cycle count	1,200	1,200

Figure 18.9(b) shows the stock record of Part P and the data transactions raised and submitted in response to the events depicted in 18.9(a). It is assumed that the stock record is correct at time t. The cycle count value is submitted as a transaction at time (t + 17) minutes. For the sake of illustration, the cycle count transaction is not allowed here to alter the stock record. At the time this transaction is received, however, the *Issue to the Shop* transaction of 300 units has not yet been submitted to the system. It is late. It can be seen that it is not finally submitted until time (t + 20) minutes.

Figure 18.9(b): Data Transactions Relating to Figure 18.8(a)

Stock Record and Data Transactions			
Time (mins)	Description of the Data Transaction	Transaction Value	Stock Record
t	(Starting stock record)		1,000
t + 6	Receipt from supplier	500	1,500
t + 17	Submission of cycle count	1,200	1,500*
t + 20	Issue to the shop	300	1,200

* Does not change the record in this example.

Because of the lateness of the submission and processing of the *Issue to the Shop* transaction of 300 units, if a comparison is made at time (t + 17) between the cycle count value of 1,200 units and the stock record of 1,500 units, it will appear that the record is in error by a 300 units excess. If the cycle count transaction were to have been allowed to change the stock record to 1,200 units at time (t + 17), the late transaction, when it arrived, would have then further changed the record to 900 units.

Premature Transactions

An alternative scenario is presented relating to Part P, this time from time t to time (t + 30) minutes. Figure 18.10(a) represents the physical stock quantities involved and, again, the changes in stock level. A cycle count is carried out at time (t + 20) minutes, and the value of 600 units is recorded.

Figure 18.10(a): Three Events occurring to Part P from Time t to Time (t + 20)

	Physical Stock		
Time (mins)	Description of the Event	Event Quantity (units)	Physical Stock in Store
t	(Starting stock quantity)		1,000
t + 5	Issue to the shop	400	600
t + 20	Carrying out of cycle count	600	600
t + 25	Receipt from supplier	700	1,300

Figure 18.10(b) shows the stock record of Part P and the data transactions raised and submitted in response to the events depicted in 18.10(a). (Again, it is assumed that the stock record is correct at time t.) Note, however, that the *Receipt from Supplier* transaction of 700 units is submitted at time (t + 27) minutes, before the submission of the cycle count transaction. The cycle count transaction, which relates to the stock level at time (t + 20) minutes, is not submitted until time (t + 30) minutes

Figure 18.10(b): Data Transactions Relating to Figure 18.10(a)

	Stock Record and Data Transactions		
Time (mins)	Description of the Data Transaction	Transaction Value	Stock Record
t	(Starting stock record)		1,000
t + 7	Issue to the shop	400	600
t + 27	Receipt from supplier	700	1,300
t + 30	Submission of cycle count	600	1,300*

* Does not change the record in this example.

Because of the earliness[35] of the *Receipt from Supplier* transaction — i.e. its submission before the submission of the cycle count transaction — if a comparison were to have been made between the cycle count value of 600 units and the stock record of 1,300 at time (t + 30), it would have appeared, wrongly, that the record was in error by an excess of 700 units.

It does not seem possible to identify a transaction as being late by the use of software unless further information pertaining to the sequence of physical events is added to the recorded data attached to each one. A scheme for doing so is briefly discussed at the end of this sub-section.

Failing help from software, the only solution to late transactions is to eliminate the possibility of their submission by closing off the location of each part which is to be cycle counted at some interval before the count takes place. The point chosen to do so must give sufficient time for all transactions relating to it and still remaining in the system to be submitted and processed before counting and reconciliation are undertaken. The close-off duration required can clearly be reduced by the prompt submission of transactions by storemen and by the provision of adequate technology for conveying transaction data through the system. In encouraging the first, the role of transactions must be explained to storemen, perhaps through a diagram such as Figure 18.5. As for the second, an online IT system is very obviously desirable, perhaps one making use of radio data terminals.

It is common practice to "close off" a stock location temporarily from picking and further receipt simply by suspending a coloured rope or ribbon across it.

Fortunately, it is not necessary to deal with premature transactions in an analogous fashion by keeping the stock closed off until reconciliation following the count. A simple software solution is available and is widely implemented in proprietary systems. This is described as follows in four steps:

---

[35] One might more correctly say that it is the cycle count transaction which is late, rather than the receipt transaction which is premature or early. The important point is that the reconciliation problem is confined entirely to the two general circumstances described in the text.

I. The stock of each part to be counted is closed off as described above, to enable late transactions to be flushed through the system.

II. Before the commencement of actual cycle counting, and when it is judged that all transactions from before the stock close-off have very definitely been processed, a computer "indicator" is set by the cycle counter on the stock record of each part he intends to count. Once the indicator has been set for a particular part, all transactions, including the cycle count, relating to the part are collected in a small, dedicated computer storage area to await the action of the reconciliation program in Step IV.

III. The stock of each part is kept closed off only until the cycle count has taken place. Immediately the part has been counted, but not a moment before, the location is released for stock picking and receipt in the normal way. However, the data transactions now raised relating to the released part, as well as being processed through the system in the standard way, are collected in the part's computer storage area referred to in Step II. The cycle count transaction itself may be submitted at any time prior to Step IV. When it is so submitted, it is entered in the storage area; it does not affect the stock record.

IV. At any convenient time later, the reconciliation program is run. The program accesses the dedicated computer transaction storage area of each part, and simply calculates the net stock balance (i.e. cycle count *plus* receipts *less* issues). If the net balance is different from the stock record at the time of calculation, the record is changed to the net value. The indicator setting is removed.

The four-step procedure is illustrated for Part P in Figure 18.11(a) and 18.11(b), these being derived from Figures 18.10(a) and 18.10(b).

Figure 18.11(a) represents activities relating to physical stock, the stock's location and the computer system, all initiated by the cycle counter in accordance with Step II above. (It is assumed that all transactions already in the system are duly processed by time $(t + 15)$.)

The Stores and Stock Records

Figure 18.11(a): Steps I and II of the Procedure to Deal with Premature Transaction (from 18.10(a))

Physical Stock			
Time (mins)	Description of the Event	Event Quantity (units)	Physical Stock in Store
t	(Starting stock quantity)		1,000
t + 5	Issue to the shop	400	600
t + 10	Close off stock location		600
t + 15	Set record indicator		600
t + 20	Carry out of cycle count	600	600
t + 21	Release stock location		600
t + 25	Receipt from supplier	700	1,300

Figure 18.11(b) shows the transactions and computer processing carried out in response to the events in 18.11(a). When compared to Figure 18.10(b), it can be seen that an additional column has been introduced, entitled "Special Storage Area". All transactions from time (t + 15) minutes are collected in this area after normal processing.

Figure 18.11(b): Step III of the Procedure to Deal with Premature Transactions (based on Figure 18.11(a)

Time (mins)	Description of the Data Transaction	Transaction Value	Stock Record	Special Storage Area
t	(Starting stock record)		1,000	
t + 7	Issue to the shop	400	600	
t + 10	(Location is closed off)		600	
t + 15	Record indicator is set		600	
t+ 21	(Location is released)		600	
t + 27	Receipt from supplier	700	1,300	700
t + 30	Submission of cycle count	600	1,300	600
t + 35	Run reconciliation program		1,300	1,300*

* Net value

When the reconciliation program is run at time (t + 35) minutes, the net sum of the transaction values in the special storage area is calculated. This is (600 + 700) units = 1,300 units. Since the stock record is also 1,300 units, it is left unchanged by the program.[36]

The combination of initial stock location close-off and the four-step procedure above can be used to effect the reconciliation of any part pre-selected as described in sub-section 18.4.1. It is also ideally suited for use with Brooks-Wilson identification of low stock parts, since this method is based on daily patrols of pre-selected areas of the stores — an area to be patrolled is closed off in good time to ensure late transactions are flushed through the system.

With a variable stock location system and employing zero stock identification, the two safeguards of prompt notification of the zero stock and the application of Rule 6 governing the operation of the put-away software, set down in sub-section 18.1.1, will virtually eliminate all possibility of reconciliation errors. Since both the putting away and retrieval of stock in a variable location environment are entirely under software control, the few unusual circumstances that can arise and lead to error can readily be trapped by the program. Examples of reconciliation and zero stock identification are given in the four sketches making up Figure 18.12. Figure 18.12(a) shows a starting stock record balance relating to part P50 and the stock quantities of the part in two locations. The storeman wishes to withdraw 150 units of material, 120 units from Location A07A2 and the balance of 30 units from Location A04F1. Figures 18.12(b), (c) and (d) show three alternative versions of the record after withdrawing the 150 units. In Figure 18.12(b), the stock record at Location A07A2 is correct; in sketch (c), there prove to be 12 units more stock actually at A07A2 than indicated on the record; and in sketch (d), there is a 15-unit shortage at A07A2.

---

[36] In many software applications providing cycle count reconciliation as described in the text, the optional facility is provided to edit the special storage area before initiating the reconciliation. The purpose is to allow the cycle counter to scan the transactions on the VDU and delete any which he detects from personal knowledge are late transactions that entered the system after the computer indicator was set. Invocation of the editing step option is sometimes referred to as *two-step reconciliation*.

Figure 18.12: Reconciliation and Zero Stock Identification

18.12(a)		18.12(b)		18.12(c)		18.12(d)	
Location	Quantity	Location	Quantity	Location	Quantity	Location	Quantity
A04F1	450	A04F1	420	A04F1	432	A04F1	405
A07A2	120	A07A2	0*	A07A2	0*	A07A2	0*
Starting stock record		* Location now empty. Stock record correct. 120 − 120 = 0		* Location now empty. Stock gain of 12. 120 − 132 = −12		* Location now empty. Stock deficit of 15. 120 − 105 = +15	

Transaction Sequencing and Automatic Reconciliation

If the actual time can be recorded at which each activity took place in receiving, moving, counting and issuing stock in the stores, then both late and premature transactions can be recognised as such and dealt with by software without any requirement to close off stock locations. The software compares the date/time of all transactions, *including those already processed*, to the date/time of the cycle count. To accomplish the reconciliation, the late transactions, which as stated can now, of course be recognised as such, are skipped, or ignored, and the premature ones, again recognisable, similarly correctly treated.

Although they would only be required to do so in relation to products which were to be cycle counted, it might be thought an unacceptable imposition, or at least a risk from the system viewpoint, to require storemen to record the time of each actual event on every transaction. However, the self-same logic can be applied simply from an indication as to the sequence of the physical events involved, recorded on each transaction. What then matters is whether a transaction relating to a specified part has a sequence number lower or higher than the sequence number of the part's cycle count transaction. With a real-time system based on RDTs, every transaction required by the user can be generated as he needs it, online, and a sequence number duly attached to it by software. A proviso here is that transactions are generated promptly when physical actions have taken place.

Chapter 19

Human Resources

Consistency is achieved in formulating human resource policy in each of the areas dealt with in this chapter by constant reference in so doing to dictates from two sources. First, there are the ethical principles held by senior management in its conduct of the business: the values of the company's founders; the upholding of racial and sexual equality; support for health and safety in working practices; and regard for the spirit and letter of the law. Secondly, there are the challenges confronting the company which must be dealt with and which directly involve HR: the demand, in staff dealings with customers, for flexibility and enterprise; the pursuit of ever-higher standards of commercial and technical achievement; the constant need for manpower cost savings; and the need to comply with the increasing burden on industry of government and EU regulations as they affect personnel.[1]

The application of policy through action from day-to-day and week-to-week as it concerns real people in such matters as communication, work direction, career appraisal and the enforcement of discipline, clearly falls to middle management, including the manufacturing manager.

---

[1] There has been much debate in academic circles regarding the distinction to be made (if any) between the terms *Human Resource Management* and *Personnel Management*. *HR* has been chosen here since it seems more definitely to encompass personal commitment, motivation, empowerment and so forth. *Personnel* perhaps suggests that the subject is confined to such matters as wage rates, company rules and legal obligations (i.e. that it is "workforce centred" — see Derek Torrington and Laura Hall (1991), *Personnel Management — A New Approach*, Second edition, Prentice Hall, p. 15).

To assist managers in the performance of this aspect of their jobs, the human resources manager will prepare guidelines and make periodic group presentations on topical issues. A number of activities which might be performed in some companies by middle management within line and staff departments may in others be performed entirely by HR — three examples are the preparation of training programmes for young managers; staff selection; and the provision of safety training.[2] In almost all companies, the HR manager will have exclusive responsibility for making offers of employment after the selection of preferred candidates from those applying for jobs, for negotiation with trade union representatives and for the final dismissal of employees. Besides its role as a service to middle managers, the human resources department will also act on behalf of senior management in ensuring that managers adhere to the personnel rules which have been laid down. Finally, for the HR manager, a particularly onerous part of the job, and one growing more onerous by the year, is interpreting and helping prepare for compliance with the legislation and regulations referred to earlier.

19.1 THE ORGANISATION

19.1.1 The Corporate Hierarchy

> O, when degree is shaked,
> Which is the ladder to all high designs,
> The enterprise is sick! How could communities,
> Degrees in schools and brotherhoods in cities,
> Peaceful commerce from dividable shores,
> The primogenity and due of birth,
> Prerogative of age, crowns, sceptres, laurels,
> But by degree stand in authentic place?
> Take but degree away, untune that string,
> And, hark, what discord follows!
> — *Troilus and Cressida*[3]

---

[2] The term *line department* is usually applied to company departments which directly generate revenue, or which distribute or manufacture material (purchasing, sales, etc.). A *staff department* by contrast is one providing an ancillary or support service (accountancy, research, and so on).

[3] From the oration by Ulysses extolling the virtues of accredited authority and a clear chain of command (Shakespeare, *Troilus and Cressida*, Act I, Scene III).

The style of company organisation adopted throughout industry is the *hierarchy*: traditional, intuitive and readily understood by all those required to work within it. A small part of a hierarchical organisation in manufacturing is illustrated in Figure 19.1, derived from Figure 2.2 but with a further layer of detail added. The description of company sections and departments in sub-section 1.2.2 also implies the existence of a hierarchical structure for the manufacturing company. A realistic organisation chart representing the corporate hierarchy may show five or six or more layers of control, depending on the size of the company and the complexity of its operations,[4] with, perhaps, "dotted line" relationships, such as those illustrated in the original Figure 2.2 to indicate the Marketing department's control of factors relating to the marketing concept. There are also likely to be occasional annotations denoting non-standard circumstances.

Figure 19.1: A small section of a Hierarchical Organisation Chart

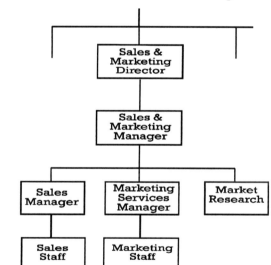

---

[4] The depth of the hierarchy is a function of the need for organisational control. Complex manufacturing operations involving many different specialisations of staff will require deeper hierarchies than even quite large-scale assembly plants. Deeper hierarchies are also necessary where the company is split into many different geographically separate divisions. The young manufacturing manager, of course, may speak ruefully of the height of a hierarchy, not of its depth. Nevertheless, unlike the flat organisation, the hierarchy does at least constitute a ladder for his ambition.

A hierarchical organisation is referred to in the jargon as being *mechanistic*. Yet although there may be no practical alternative to the acceptance of this structure, the HR expert contends that it has two disadvantages. First, he says, the rigidity of the hierarchy inhibits the company's ability to seize commercial and technical opportunities, since staff in a given place in the organisation obtain only half the facts pertaining to many situations and, in any case, are frequently unable to take necessary action because decision-making powers in the area concerned reside elsewhere in the hierarchy. The second disadvantage put forward is that the very nature of a hierarchy seems at first glance to be inimical to such present-day notions as empowerment and team working.

To avert the first danger, every organisation makes provision for permanent and temporary cross-functional, non-hierarchical groupings to facilitate the workings of its organisation. It could be argued that the board itself is such a group. Others encountered in this book relate to new product development (2.2.1 and 3.1), engineering change (3.5), master plan formulation (Chapter 6), total quality management (13.2.3) and the acquisition of capital assets (17.3). In reality, a particular company will have recourse to many more besides these, their identities dependent on the nature of its business. As well, temporary project teams will be set up from time to time by senior management to deal with *ad hoc* problems, and many departmental meetings, especially those involving such technical disciplines as manufacturing itself, engineering and quality assurance, will have present at them contributors invited to attend from other departments.

The expert's second contention, that the hierarchy, by being "undemocratic", is discouraging of the exercise of initiative and the taking of responsibility by staff, especially those at the bottom of the ladder, is far more dubious.[5] In sub-section 19.3.1, which is all about initiative and responsibility, it will be seen that the key

---

[5] The sham of Christian-name democracy in the large company was neatly summarised by the title and substance of her article in *Management Today* (August 1998) by Fiona Jebb: "Don't call me Sir — everyone knows I'm the boss!". Jebb's article includes interviews with Archie Norman (*the ever open cubicle*), at the time, chief executive of ASDA, and Sir Clive Thompson, of Rentokil Initial, a vigorous opponent of informality.

factors in these matters are *leadership, motivation, training* and *trust*, not the existence or otherwise of a hierarchy of command.

An advantage of hierarchical organisation is that the hierarchy is easily formed — and reformed — so as to give the optimal degree of managerial, administrative and technical control. Managerial control ensures that subordinates are subject to the right level of supervision, and that each one has a mentor to advise him and listen to his concerns. Administrative and technical control ensure that specialisations within the company can be accommodated and that managers have sufficient time to devote to vital tasks ancillary to general management, such as strategic planning and innovation.

Nevertheless, it is well known that for many years in the recent past, there has been a considerable "delayering" of hierarchies in the UK (accompanied by great savings in costs), as well as a move to the "broad banding" of salary rates. Doubtless many companies will find they have taken the delayering process, at least, too far, and that control and expertise now lost will require to be restored. There has also been talk in HR circles of *organic* organisations rather than mechanistic ones, these being companies with no formal command structure at all.

19.1.2 Human Resource Planning

Human resource planning can be considered over a number of alternative horizons. In the very short term (up to the master schedule horizon), the manufacturing manager must review the strength and composition of his workforce in the light of the manufacturing programme to be fulfilled, so that, if necessary, additional labour can be taken on in good time. The difficulty or otherwise of recruiting labour with the right experience and skills must clearly be taken into account, as must the time needed for recruits to reach full effectiveness in their new environment. The limited, purely numerical basis of planning at this level suggests *manpower planning* to be a more appropriate title than HR planning. It is of interest that a number of software companies involved in APS solutions offer manpower scheduling systems as well (for example, ILOG[6]). Manpower scheduling application areas include

---

[6] See Chapter 12, Footnote 5.

staff scheduling for air traffic operations and the control of maintenance and repair personnel in service industries.

More usually, HR planning means estimating the number of staff required in the one-to-five-year horizon, by skill, age and experience, and laying down plans to ensure the estimated numbers and types will duly be represented in the company when the time comes. The basis for doing so is simply through consideration of the balance of demand and supply.

Estimation of personnel demands in the one-to-five-year term for line departments begins with a review of likely future manufacturing volumes. That is, it begins with a review of medium-term sales forecasts. (A common means of obtaining such forecasts is through the Delphi method, described in Section 2.5.) It may not be correct, however, to calculate the number of staff required to support these levels of production by extrapolating current manning levels if it is intended in the future to introduce automated equipment or more effective working practices.

The starting point in any consideration of supply is clearly the company's existing staff complement, categorised by skill, age and experience. The breakdown of existing numbers can readily be obtained by analysis of personnel records.[7] What is more difficult is to judge how the current staff profile will change over the years. To do so in relatively straightforward circumstances, it may be sufficient simply to apply labour turnover and labour stability averages or trends through the medium of a spreadsheet, averages and trends being compiled over the years for each department and skill.

The expression for labour turnover for a single year is given in Equation 19.1. One of several alternative measures of labour stability is given in Equation 19.2.

---

[7] In the UK, the holding of personnel records on computer is subject to the Data Protection Act, 1984, and the company has a statutory duty to ensure that they are accurate. (The question of accuracy, however, applies only to matters of fact, not to matters of opinion.) An employee has a right of access to his own personnel record on giving written notice of his wish to see it. From 2007, regulations involving computer-held data will be extended to cover manual records. The Data Protection Act of 1984 has been extended by the addition of further regulations contained within the EU Data Protection Directive of 1995. The UK has been granted a 12-year transition in its implementation.

$$\text{Labour turnover} = \frac{\text{Number who left employment during the year}}{\text{Average number employed during the year}} \times 100\%$$

Equation 19.1

$$\text{Labour stability} = \frac{\text{Number of employees exceeding one year's service}}{\text{Total number of employees employed one year ago}} \times 100\%$$

Equation 19.2

In a large company, HR planning is typically in the hands of a small group of operations research specialists, and the medium of investigation is a fully-fledged simulation model. Among the phenomena simulated besides labour turnover and stability are the "ageing" of staff from recruitment to retirement and the probabilities of their promotion from grade to grade. The techniques applied to the simulation model include the evaluation of transition probabilities making use of Markov chains.[8]

Beyond the five-year horizon, the same equilibrium of demand and supply is pursued, but uncertainty is more profound. Ascertainment of demand requires the prediction of likely future directions of new technologies and the infrastructures that will be needed to support them (*product/company fit* — sub-section 2.2.1). In the ascertainment of supply, judgement must be brought to bear on many issues outside industrial practice, such as likely demographic, social and educational trends. On this scale of time, the thought occurs that HR policy might shape corporate plans, rather than that HR plans must be shaped by corporate policy — "planning with people in mind", as it has been put.[9]

The figures and equations contributing to the HR planning model are also valuable in everyday HR management. What factors

---

[8] The essential characteristic of a Markov chain, or Markov process, is the existence of a one-period transition probability from one state to another, new, state. Besides their use in HR planning, where a transition might be a promotion from one job grade to the next, or an employee's resignation from the company, Markov chains are used in Sales and Marketing to simulate the gains and losses of market share over time due to year-on-year brand switching by consumers. See Harvey Wagner (1975), *Principles of Operations Research*, Second edition, Prentice Hall, Chapter 18.

[9] Ian Beardwell and Len Holden (1994), *Human Resource Management*, Pitman. See Chapter 4, "Towards Human Resource Planning?", by Damian O'Doherty. The authors and chapter contributors are with Leicester Business School, De Montfort University.

induce an employee to stay in his job? What factors induce him to seek work elsewhere? It is common practice for HR managers to interview leavers to attempt to elicit their reasons for leaving, but it is widely acknowledged that it is extremely difficult to get at the truth — it has been suggested that a more profitable approach might be to question those who stay.[10] For the manufacturing manager, an appreciation of reasons for leaving and staying might provide valuable clues as to how his management might be made more effective, clues pointing, say, to the advisability of delegating more, to the essentiality of improving his department's amenities or to the advisability of providing more training. At the very least, an analysis of turnover and stability statistics constitutes quantitative evidence that may encourage managers to give careful thought to the need to make changes to the ways they run their departments.

A statistic that might seem almost a direct challenge to the departmental manager is that relating to absenteeism. The normal measure of absenteeism is as given in Equation 19.3.

$$Absenteeism = \frac{Total\ number\ of\ days\ lost}{Total\ number\ of\ working\ days} \qquad Equation\ 19.3$$

Higher levels of absenteeism in the manufacturing environment than elsewhere in the company may be caused in some factories by particularly stressful work: work that is noisy or repetitious or devoid of any requirement for skill. Even more so than with labour turnover and labour stability, "real" reasons for absenteeism other than for medical reasons, duly certified, are difficult to determine, but employees will be less likely to absent themselves if they know management monitors each absence and takes a keen interest in the reason for it.

19.1.3 Recruitment and Selection

Recruitment is the process of making known a job vacancy and persuading qualified personnel to apply for it. *Selection* is the choosing of a candidate from among those applying.

Recruitment is exclusively an activity undertaken by the HR manager and will typically account for a substantial proportion of

---

[10] Alan Cowling and Philip James (1994), *The Essence of Personnel Management and Industrial Relations*, Prentice Hall.

his time. From his everyday knowledge and perusal of statistics and news, the HR manager is familiar with the ever-changing state of the external labour market — the ease or difficulty of attracting external applicants for the various vacancies arising within the company. He is also familiar with the costs and relative effectiveness of alternative means of publicising vacancies and persuading potential recruits to apply. Popular media for attracting shop floor staff are regional and local newspapers; government job centres; and employment agencies. (Shop floor applicants are usually unwilling to move from their present places of residence to take up new employment.) Popular media for attracting management staff are the national press, the Internet[11] and recruitment consultancies.

In order to begin the process of recruitment, the HR manager must clearly be fully aware of the particularities of the job to be filled, either by reference to a corresponding standard job description or through discussion with the departmental manager. The principal points relating to the job will be set out in the advertising "copy" (*copy* is the original form of the advertisement, before it is typeset or processed ready for printing).

One reason of many for the greatest circumspection in drawing up the advertisement is to ensure that it complies with the law with regard to race and sex. Two of the corporate principles mentioned in the introduction to this chapter imply that the company does not discriminate between its employees, and therefore between its prospective employees, on the grounds of their race or sex. Moral certainties are not enough, however. The law requires that freedom from discrimination should be apparent at every step of the recruitment and selection processes, including in the choice made of an advertising periodical in the first place and in the wording of the copy published.[12] Note that there is no statutory requirement to

---

[11] For example, visit http://www.monster.co.uk for job vacancies.

[12] The Sex Discrimination Act, 1975, and The Race Relations Act, 1976. Limiting advertisements to publications read exclusively by one racial group or by only one of the sexes is an example of *indirect* discrimination. Note that there are also laws covering discrimination against job applicants on the grounds that they are, or are not, members of a trade union and discrimination against disabled persons. The Disability Discrimination Act, however, is principally concerned with the making of reasonable "work adjustments" on behalf of

invent neutral job titles (*cowperson, tradesperson* etc.) or to pepper copy with *he/she:* if wording might be misconstrued, a clear statement in the advertisement affirming the company's position with regard to equality in these matters will suffice.

Recruitment is a facet of corporate public relations every bit as important as others, so that speed and courtesy are called for in the handling of applications. Two documents often sent to each person applying are a formal application form and a company employment brochure. Debate among HR practitioners regarding the purpose of the application form and the information to be captured through it is ongoing.[13] The form is now accepted as being a crucial instrument for use in the shortlisting and selection processes, a special version perhaps being printed through DTP (*desk top publishing*) software for each job type applied for. (The remark has been made that in the past, forms seemed little more than IT input sheets from which successful applicants' personnel records were to be prepared.) The recruitment brochure is very obviously a most important document from the viewpoint of the applicant. Its purpose is not to sell the company's products or to persuade a stock market investor to purchase its shares, but to describe to the prospective recruit what the company does and how it operates, and to present a true picture of working life in the firm, including its "difficulties and distastes". The brochure — its wording, not its glossiness — is reported as having the single greatest influence on new graduates making job applications. Securing the commitment and regard of blue-collar workers should also be in mind when it is being prepared.

The activities involved in selection, including shortlisting, are shared between the HR manager and the manager of the department concerned, the precise split of responsibilities varying from company to company and from job type to job type. (The HR manager is likely to do almost all of the work in selecting staff for purely routine positions.)

---

disabled persons already in employment, not with job applicants (The Employment Act, 1990, and The Disability Discrimination Act, 1995).

[13] See, for example, Torrington and Hall (1991), op. cit.; Beardwell and Holden (1994), op. cit.; and Cowling and James (1994), op. cit.

If the number of candidates returning application forms is so large as to preclude testing or interviewing each one, a shortlist will have to be drawn up based on the facts submitted so far, scrutinising each CV and application form and, perhaps, scoring them by a points system against the job position to be fulfilled, rather in the way that examination papers are marked.

The two stages to final selection are testing and interviewing.

Although there are opponents in HR to subjecting job candidates to formal tests, there are others who support testing on the grounds of its objectivity. The two most common tests administered to applicants are a test of job knowledge and a test of mental ability. "Job knowledge" for shop floor applicants might be better termed trade knowledge. Questions relating to practical work and machine operation will be devised by the shop floor supervisor or foreman. Job knowledge tests for managerial applicants in manufacturing will be devised by the manufacturing manager and might well be based on material in appropriate chapters of this book. If objectivity and comparability are to be maintained, the company might feel that no managerial applicant should be excused tests regardless of his job history or educational qualifications.[14] Other types of tests used frequently in selection that may be considered, depending on the job applied for and the time available to conduct them, relate to *aptitude* (inherent ability); *conceptual ability*; *numeracy*; *attainment*; *manual dexterity*; *interest* (has the candidate carefully read the brochure?); *learning capability*; and *personality*. The administration of tests, especially those relating to learning and personality, requires training and knowledge of procedure, and is carried out by the HR manager or his staff, not by the department manager.

The interview receives a bad press, with newspaper and magazine articles appearing regularly saying that a candidate is judged within the first five minutes of the proceedings (*He has an engaging*

---

[14] There may be some surprises. Also, although an applicant's knowledge of his subject will be guaranteed if he has gained an institutional qualification, such as those in purchasing, accounting and quality, there are many subject areas not formally tested (inventory control, APS and MRP, for example). A candidate's answers to test questions may provide good leads to interview questions later.

character; *I don't like that silly tie*; and so on) and that selection by interview is no better than selection by throwing dice.

Interview horror stories do not condemn interviewing as a means of selection. They serve as serious warnings that the process must be carried out expertly and with preparation and purpose if it is to be successful. Success is a two-way street. For the interviewer, it means enabling a judgement to be made of character and personality and being able to delve more deeply into the candidate's work experience and knowledge. For the candidate, it means being able to form a view on whether the working environment suits his own style and whether he would get on with the people he meets.

The first requirement is that the interview process should be well organised (by the HR department) purely from the viewpoint of logistics — greetings in Reception, interview durations, breaks for coffee, and so on. Shop floor applicants will usually separately meet a representative of HR and their potential direct manager. Applicants for managerial posts are likely to have three interviews: HR, the manager and one perhaps with a panel of several managers and technical staff.

In order to achieve its purpose in full, every interview must clearly be planned in advance. The WASP structure has been suggested, as follows:[15]

- **W: Welcome** — Putting the candidate at ease and explaining the interview purpose;
- **A: Acquiring** — Acquiring knowledge, perhaps by going through the candidate's work experience in (reverse?) chronological order;
- **S: Supplying** — Supplying information in answer to the candidate's questions;
- **P: Parting** — Explaining what happens next, and in what time scale.

It is observed that interviewers are often reticent about taking notes during interviews, perhaps seeing it as discomposing or

---

[15] From Elizabeth Sidney, Margaret Brown and Michael Argyle (1973), *Skills with People*, Century Hutchinson.

even amateurish. While note-taking should not be as it is during police interrogations, the making of shorthand jottings, perhaps on application forms, will be seen by interviewees as professional and perfectly acceptable.

All of the evidence gathered must now be weighed in order to select the best candidate for the position to be filled. The difficulty of doing so is well known to those who have been in this position. It is with relief, then, that we may turn to one or other of two popular assessment checklists, the first being a seven-point plan proposed by Alec Rodger, the second a five-point plan by Munro Fraser.[16] Nevertheless, every HR manager will agree that choices cannot be made by applying mathematical formulae. While it is necessary to clear the mind of the magnetism of his character or the silliness of his tie, there is at least a place in staff selection for intuition and inspired judgement. The two plans are shown side-by-side in Table 19.1.

Table 19.1: Alternative Bases of Assessment for Judging and Selecting Employment Candidates

Rodger's Seven-Point Plan		Fraser's Five-Point Plan	
1. Physical make-up	Fitness, bearing, appearance, speech	1. Impact on others	Appearance, speech, manners
2. Attainments	Education, training and experience	2. Qualifications and experience	Knowledge and skills from past work
3. General intelligence	Including common sense	3. Innate ability	Perspicacity and speed of mind
4. Special aptitudes	Dexterity and other talents	4. Motivation	Willingness to work hard
5. Interests	Intellectual, social, and physical	5. Emotional balance	Stress felt in living and working
6. Disposition	Self-reliance, dependability		
7. Circumstances	Domestic, familic[17]		

---

[16] A. Rodger (1970), *The Seven Point Plan*, Third edition, now available from the National Foundation for Educational Research; J.M. Fraser (1958), *A Handbook of Employment Interviewing*, Macdonald & Evans.

[17] Care must be taken here not to breach the Sex Discrimination Act, 1975, or The Race Relations Act, 1976.

The final act of this drama (for drama it seems to the anxious candidates) is to inform the selected applicant of his good fortune.[18] Note that the contract of employment begins when he accepts the company's offer, not when he starts actual work — "*a contract of service is but an example of contracts in general, so that the general law of contract will be applicable*".[19]

It is possible that appointment and acceptance might be made orally. If so, the employer has a statutory duty under the Employment Rights Act, 1996, to send the new employee a "written statement" within two months setting out such details of the employment as pay, hours of work, place of work, job title and so forth. It is wiser, however, in this litigious age, for the company to send the selected candidate a formal letter of appointment stating the key terms particular to him (i.e. wages etc); an addendum describing such other benefits as welfare and pension rights; and, perhaps, a booklet of company rules setting out the specific obligations required of all employees. The company should take particular care in framing conditions relating to place of work, hours and duties: these should be drawn up widely if it wishes to preserve flexibility in its deployment of labour. Again, it may be wise for the company to require the candidate's formal, signed acceptance of the offer and the foregoing express conditions attached to it. Also part of the contract, of course, are implied terms (see subsection 16.2.3). For the employer, they are the duty to act in good faith and others including those relating to health and safety; and for the employee, duties of fidelity, obedience and to act with reasonable care and skill.

---

[18] The job offer may be subject to the receipt by the employer of "satisfactory references". If so, the prospective employee should beware that satisfactoriness is entirely a matter subjective to the prospective employer (i.e. the objective test of "reasonableness" cannot be applied) (*Wishart* v. *National Association of Citizens' Advice Bureaux Ltd.* [1990] Industrial Relations Law Reports 393). A referee is under no obligation to provide a reference, but, if he does so, he owes a duty of care to both the requestor and the subject of the reference with regard to facts and figures. Telephone requests for references take up less time and may elicit more forthright opinions.

[19] Lord Evershed MR, *Laws* v. *London Chronicle* [1959] 1 Weekly Law Reports 698.

19.2 REWARD MANAGEMENT

19.2.1 The External Labour Market

After the unfortunate loss of his sheep described in Chapter 12, footnote 40, Gabriel Oak was forced to seek work at the annual hiring fair at Casterbridge, joining a throng of shepherds, thatchers, carters and the like — *"two or three hundred blithe and hearty labourers waiting upon Chance..."*

The traditional competitive market determining wages and salaries through supply and demand is a constant presence in reward management, and is referred to as the *external labour market*. There are some instances where the market is as directly assertive in manufacturing industry as at the Casterbridge Hiring Fair: company lawyers and doctors, for instance, will receive salaries very close indeed to the rates prevailing in external legal and medical practices. The wage and salary rates advertised by the company in the process of recruitment must also be set by assessing them against those offered by other companies for comparable positions, even though in doing so, the organisation may be compromising the grading system on which its pay structure is otherwise based.[20]

The external labour market is also referred to in establishing the company's own internal pay structures, described in subsection 19.2.2. Thus the pay rates to be ascribed to the most junior job in the lowest grade of a structure and to the most senior job in the highest grade will be decided after due consideration of the actual rates for those jobs in the external market.

Indeed, once the company's pay structures have been set up, external market rates may be used to allocate all of the company's jobs to grades within a structure. For example, if Grade 3 in an internal structure spans the pay range of £10,000 to £12,000 per annum, and the pay range of Job X is about the same in the external labour market, then if Job X is performed within the company, it can simply be assigned to Grade 3. This method of assignment is referred to as *market pricing*, and is one of the five job evaluation

---

[20] To attract the desired calibre of staff or obtain staff of sufficient experience, the company may need to offer the market rate, this perhaps being the rate of pay at the mid-point, or higher, of the standard company grade for the job in question, rather than offer the grade minimum it might ideally prefer.

techniques described in sub-section 19.2.3. A danger in the use of market pricing is that external jobs for which pay ranges are published may be sufficiently different in work content from seemingly similar company jobs, so that the company jobs may be wrongly graded as a consequence. Thus company Job X may in reality be far more demanding than a benchmark job in the external market with the same title, such that a full evaluation of it, employing one of the more rigorous alternative techniques in sub-section 19.2.3, would have caused it to be placed (say) in Grade 4 at a higher salary. (A typical example of false comparability in manufacturing industry is to be found in the job *master scheduler*: the duties and responsibilities attached to it vary very widely from company to company. See footnote 31, however.)

For the reasons above, and many others, especially geographic, the pay rate associated with a specific job in the external market is not a single figure, but varies from external company to external company across a range of rates. Consequently, whenever reference is made to the external market, the reference point might be anywhere on the external scale, not necessarily at the mid-point — i.e. it might be in the top, second, third or bottom quartile.

The point on the external pay scale selected by the company whenever use is made of it for reference purposes is referred to as its *pay posture*, or pay position, and very evidently should be consistent. Consistency apart, the pay posture selected is a matter for senior management. The decision is clearly a most important one; the debate taking place before it is made will doubtless be preceded by the presentation, by the HR manager, of the pros and cons of the alternative positions, and a statement of their likely costs. It may be thought that the decision on pay posture, because it will affect, to some extent at least, labour turnover and stability, and the effectiveness of recruitment, will have a consequent impact on the relative achievability of the company's objectives in such HR-dominated matters as empowerment, quality-mindedness, focus on customer satisfaction and the acquisition of work skills.

19.2.2 Pay Structures

The term "grade" used earlier applies to a range of pay rates to which certain categories of jobs or skills are assigned. For example, it was stated that a particular company's Grade 3 might cover the pay range £10,000 to £12,000 per annum. If a number of grades are interrelated in a single scheme, their mutual arrangement is referred to in HR as a *pay structure*. (Thus Pay Structure P might be comprised of ten grades related in the way described below, by the numerical values of their pay ranges: Grade 1, Grade 2 . . . Grade 10.) Notwithstanding the obvious administrative advantages that would follow if there were only one structure for the entire company, it is likely in fact to be necessary to set up and maintain several pay structures. For example, the actual levels of pay and perquisites of office applying to senior management in sub-section 1.2.1 are certain to make it extremely difficult to fit these senior grades into the same arrangement as that applying to management jobs in sub-section 1.2.2. Again, the peculiar circumstances applying to shop floor staff, perhaps involving one or other of many published bonus schemes based on production output, are likely to necessitate separate grades and a dedicated pay structure for these employees.[21]

Reasons for setting up alternative pay structures are as given. Nevertheless, the greatest care must be taken to ensure that a common method of job evaluation and a common means of employee assessment are applied across all of them. The anomaly of having the same job potentially rated differently, depending on which pay structure it is to be assigned to, is to be avoided. Consistency across pay structures has also now generally been extended, by a so-called process of *harmonisation*, to eligibility for such company-financed benefits as pension allowances, annual paid holiday allowance beyond the statutory entitlement of four weeks and the free provision of medical insurance. (In the UK, non-wage, non-

---

[21] Published bonus schemes based on shop floor output or output rates include such curiosities and old favourites as: Halsey-Weir Premium; Barth Variable Sharing; Bedaux Point; piece rate; Gantt Task & Bonus; Emerson Efficiency; Rowan Premium; and Taylor's Differentiated Rate — see R.H.S. Beacham (1979), *Pay Systems — Principles and Techniques*, Heinemann. Because of the comparatively wide variety of skills and responsibilities required and exhibited in the "single" job of shop floor working, the Shop Floor Pay Structure might have, say, three grades, A, B and C, with rules governing their relationship similar to those governing the relationships within other pay structures in the company. Individual pay structures may, of course, be created to accommodate any distinctional jobs, not just those relating to shop floor working.

salary benefits of this type amount to an additional 10 per cent to 14 per cent of the average employee's pay.)

Figure 19.2(a) shows a pay structure named "Technical and Professional" for a Company X consisting of 18 grades, from Grade 1 (range £7,500–£9,000pa) to Grade 18 (range £86,000–£103,000pa). The minimum and maximum pay rates for the grades increase as grade numbers increase, ascending in accordance with the salary scale on the left of the Figure. Figure 19.2(b) is derived from Figure 19.2(a), and shows in some detail the pay rates relating to two of the grades, Grade 3 and Grade 4. In particular, Figure 19.2(b) illustrates the further pay structure terms *differential*, *mid-point* and *overlap*.

Figures 19.2(a) and 19.2(b): The "Technical and Professional" Pay Structure of Company X

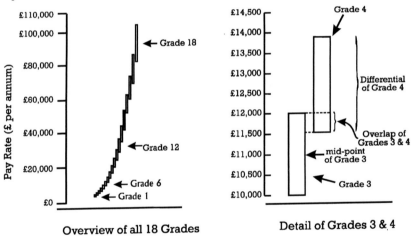

Overview of all 18 Grades   Detail of Grades 3 & 4

A differential, such as that indicated for Grade 4 in Figure 19.2(b), is formally expressed as a percentage, as set out in Equation 19.4.

$$Differential = \frac{(Maximum\ grade\ pay\ rate - minimum\ grade\ pay\ rate)}{Minimum\ grade\ pay\ rate} \times 100\%$$

Equation 19.4

The value 20 per cent has been chosen for all grades in this pay structure, so that, given the minimum salary for Grade 3 of £10,000, the maximum salary is £12,000. The mid-point is simply the arithmetical mean of a range's minimum and maximum, indicated in 19.2(b) for Grade 3 as £11,000. Finally, the existence of an overlap of pay rates between two adjacent grades recognises that an experienced employee at the top of one grade is likely to be of more value to the company than an inexperienced employee at the bottom of the next grade higher. Numerically, overlap is defined as the percentage of the higher grade that is covered by the lower one. Again in this pay structure, the value of 20 per cent has been chosen to govern all overlaps between grades. Now, had there been no overlap between Grades 3 and 4, Grade 4 would have ranged from £12,000 to £14,400, i.e. a difference of £2,400. With the chosen overlap of 20 per cent (£480), however, Grade 4 starts at £480 lower than £12,000, and so spans the range £11,520 to £13,920, these figures perhaps being published by HR department as £11,500 and £13,900.[22]

The number of grades in a pay structure is governed by five factors: (i) the minimum pay rate which is to be accommodated — i.e. the minimum of the lowest grade; (ii) the maximum rate — i.e. the top of the highest grade: (iii) the grade differentials to be applied; (iv) the grade overlaps; and (v) any requirement to introduce additional grades other than those determined by the arithmetic of factors (i) to (iv), in order to set apart particular levels in the management hierarchy. It has been assumed for "The Technical and Professional" pay structure in Figure 19.2(a) that the minimum pay rate to be catered for is £7,500 per annum, the maximum £100,000 per annum, that the differentials in all grades are to be 20 per cent and that all overlaps are to be 20 per cent. No additional grades have been inserted due to factor (v). On this basis then, it is a matter of simple arithmetic to find the required number of grades — 18 — and each of their ranges.

A particularly important element in the foregoing is clearly grade differential. The same differential is unlikely to be assigned to every grade throughout a pay structure, as effected in the exam-

---

[22] It is customary to round numbers — grade structuring is not an exact science. In addition, there are several possible arithmetical variants to the calculations in the text, the method chosen hardly being of great importance but such choice nevertheless better made by the HR manager than a programmer in the IT department. For example, having recalculated the minimum of Grade 4, it might have been more correct then to recalculate the grade maximum (obtaining £13,824), giving a new grade differential of £2,304, leading in turn to a new overlap of £461, leading in turn ...

ple. In practice, it has been the custom to set smaller differentials for lower grades (say, 15 per cent), medium differentials for middle grades (20–30 per cent) and larger ones for higher grades (perhaps 50 per cent). The smaller differentials at junior levels, it has been said, give encouragement to younger employees, since there is a greater likelihood that they will obtain promotion to higher grades if they are competent and industrious, while at senior levels, wider differentials allow greater recognition to be made by the company of differences in performance of these employees. In Figure 19.2(a), if differentials of 15 per cent had been assigned to Grades 1 to 4, 20 per cent to Grades 5 to 8 and 50 per cent to Grades 9 onwards, assuming a 20 per cent overlap between all of them,[23] pay rates from £7,500 to over £100,000 would be covered by 13 grades. In the recent past, a great many companies have broken with tradition and introduced grade differentials of 100 per cent or more, in what is termed *broad banding*. With differentials of 100 per cent and overlaps of 50 per cent, the required pay range in Figure 19.2(a) would be covered by 6 grades. Broad banding and the very important HR contribution it may make to such company objectives as mentioned earlier are vital, topical subjects in reward management, and are discussed separately in sub-section 19.2.4.

The procedure by which all jobs to be covered by a particular company pay structure are to be assigned grades can now be summarised in five steps.

1. The mid-point salary levels of the most junior and most senior jobs in the structure are obtained from the external labour market by market survey;

2. The number of grades and their ranges are obtained by calculation, as described above, paying particular attention to the various differential and overlap percentages to be applied;

3. All jobs are evaluated by one or other of the schemes described in sub-section 19.2.3.

---

[23] Overlap percentages between grades similarly need not be uniform across the pay structure. It is common to set overlaps at 40 per cent or more at higher grade levels in organisations where there is a great variety of jobs in the structure and additional payment flexibility is wanted.

4. Job evaluations and pay structure grades are verified for reasonableness and consistency by spot comparisons with market data;

5. All jobs are assigned to grades based on the outcome of the evaluations in Step 3. Any job that proves particularly difficult to assign, usually because it is a borderline case, is subjected to re-evaluation.

The carrying out of Step 3 imposes a considerable burden on the company in general and the HR department in particular, and is dealt with next.

19.2.3 Job Evaluation

Five alternative job evaluation schemes are described, the first two being so-called *quantitative* systems (*point-factor* and *factor comparison*) and the next three *qualitative* (*ranking, classification,* and *market pricing*). In a quantitative procedure, jobs are analysed so as to identify the distinct tasks, responsibilities and other requirements which constitute the duties of the job holder, each task and so on being then separately weighted against various criteria. The weights attaching to each job are added to obtain a *job size*, this being the job's numerical evaluation. In a qualitative procedure, jobs are considered in their entirety and evaluated by systematic comparison.

One of the most important considerations in selecting an evaluation scheme is that its results should seem fair to employees whose jobs have been subject to it. Fairness is not definable in absolute terms, of course, but staff will wish to see that the scheme used is rational, that the process of its use is thorough and that the outcome is reasonable and commonsensical. "Outcome" to an individual employee will ultimately mean the grade and pay scale to which his own job as a consequence is assigned, demonstrating the obvious high degree of connection between evaluation and the pay structure decisions on differentials and overlaps just discussed. (One of the undoubted advantages of broad banding is that, with far fewer grades, the specific grade assigned to a job is commensurately less sensitive to the preciseness of the evaluation technique and the strictness of the actual evaluation carried out.)

Point-Factor

Point-factor job evaluation plans are particularly appropriate for use in manufacturing, yielding consistent and comparable results across industry despite the diversity of work encountered within any particular organisation and from company to company. Their creation and use are described under five headings as follows.

1. Identification of factors. "Factors" are distinctive characteristics relating to the requirements of performance of a job or the circumstances in which it must be carried out, such as *problem-solving ability*; *willingness to assume responsibility*; *ability to plan and co-ordinate, and deal with complexity*; *management and other people-centred skills*; and *possession of manual dexterity*. In order to achieve across-company comparability, the factors chosen should be sufficiently comprehensive to cater for all company jobs in all intended pay structures. (The need for comparability is the reason job-specific skills such as *machining* or *cost accounting* cannot be used as job criteria in themselves; job skills must be contemplated in general terms.) It should also be felt, from a commonsense point of view, that the factors decided on are indeed reflective of perceived differences between jobs. Between six and a dozen factors may typically be identified for a company plan.

2. Weighting of factors. The relative importance of the intended plan factors must now be decided by assigning to each one a number of points, or "weight". The greater the factor weight, the bigger will be the "size" of any job to which that factor may in part apply. Because weighting is a critical step in setting up the plan and has a major influence on the job sizes finally calculated, the effect of the weights decided on must first be tested to ensure that their full-scale application will give acceptable, reasonable results.[24]

---

[24] Multiple regression may be used in the assignment. It is brought to mind that the purpose of regression is to employ independent variables (here, the weightings) to explain the behaviour of a dependent variable (i.e. the job size). See, for example, the use of dummy variables to determine sales forecasts in sub-section 4.5.4. It is a debatable point, however, whether the variables truly are independent in these circumstances.

3. The scaling of factor weights. The full measure of the weight that has been assigned to a factor will contribute to a job size only if that factor is present in the job to the absolute maximum extent possible. Otherwise, it is necessary to express the applicability of each factor in gradations — "hardly at all"; "applies somewhat"; "greatly applies"; "applies to maximum extent". Between four and a dozen degrees of application may typically be expressed for a given factor, in suitable phraseology, the weighting assigned to each degree ascending from a very small number of points (almost no applicability) to the full factor weight itself (maximum possible applicability). The manner of increase in points on the scale may be either by arithmetic or geometric progression, from the smallest to the maximum. Table 19.2 gives eight degrees of presence, or intensity, of the factor *thinking environment* (within the context of problem-solving), with a geometric progression of 125 per cent step increases from 21 points to the maximum weighting selected for this factor of 100 points.

Table 19.2: Eight Gradations of a Factor, with Brief Descriptions and Points

Description	Points
Strict routine	21
Routine	26
Semi-routine	33
Standardised	41
Clearly defined	51
Broadly defined	64
Generally defined	80
Abstractly defined	100

The number of gradations on the factor scale is dependent on the ability of a job evaluator to perceive or appreciate the differences that they imply. In turn, this will be dependent on the refinement of language by which these differences can be described. As an example, consider the full descriptions of the three entries *strict routine*, *routine* and *semi-routine* in Table 19.2:

- *Strict routine:* thinking within detailed rules and instructions, and/or under rigid supervision;

- *Routine:* thinking within standard instructions and/or continuous close supervision;

- *Semi-routine:* thinking within well-defined procedures and precedents, somewhat diversified and/or supervised.

Gradations of a factor that can be appreciated in the mind or observed directly even so can be troublesome to express in words. In application, the evaluator must have a thorough knowledge of the descriptions that finally evolve and their subtleties of distinction and, of course, a thorough knowledge of the requirement for the factor in a job under review. In practice, perhaps not surprisingly, evaluators who find many of the nuances somewhat difficult to distinguish in training are able to recognise them readily once confronted with an actual company job. Confidence and speed of evaluation grow quickly as more and more jobs are analysed.

4. The evaluation of benchmark jobs. A number of company jobs each regarded as representative of a particular area of endeavour are formally and carefully evaluated. These are the *benchmark jobs*, and their identification and selection will be made by the HR manager jointly with departmental managers. In order to conduct each evaluation, a *job description* (or *job profile*) must be prepared, with particular attention paid in doing so to the plan factors and factor scales and the job's implication in them. A job description must be a thoroughgoing statement agreed by those concerned as being accurate and fair. Those concerned will be not only the jobholder and his manager, but, perhaps, many others in the company if the job is representative of a large number of identical ones. Note that in preparation of the description, the job is visualised as being carried out normally and competently.

A job score or job size is the sum of the number of points allotted for each factor/factor gradation applying to the job. However, because of the seriousness of a possible mistake or misunderstanding by an evaluator at the benchmark phase, it is deemed essential that scores be verified for reasonableness before proceeding to the final step. The normal way of doing so is to review the result of ranking evaluated jobs by their job sizes, or point scores, and the result of assigning them grades and salaries within the pay structure on the basis of those scores as described in Steps 1 to 5 in sub-section 19.2.2.

Very clearly, benchmark evaluation must be carried out by a person trained to do so — perhaps by an external management consultant. Since there may be as many as 30 or 40 jobs to be scored, however, if an external consultant is initially engaged, the task is likely to be turned over after a short time to one or more cross-departmental committees for completion, the first few evaluations by the expert being made in parallel by future committee members as part of their training programmes.

5. Assign grades to all employees based on their jobs. If a jobholder's job is acknowledged to be identical to a benchmark job, then its size and grade are known immediately. If it is not so identical, or if the jobholder claims that it is not and should be allocated a higher score, then it must be separately evaluated just as the benchmark was. There are dangers here for the whole evaluation/grading process. Three of them are: (1) the allowance of appeals by staff against the job size or grade allocated them — if appeals can be made freely, they may be made by everyone to try his luck, and the evaluation process will become overloaded with work; (2) the misrepresentation of jobs through extravagant language in order to achieve a higher job score, including by managers attempting to secure larger salaries for their staff; and (3) the failure of self-depreciative staff to secure for their jobs the scores they merit. An interesting description of the problems that can confront an organisation attempting large-scale point-factor grading has been posted on the Internet by Brian Head and Anne Dunn of James Cook University, Queensland, Australia.[25]

Although a point-factor plan might be constructed in its entirety by a company, it is usual instead to turn to one of the many proprietary job evaluation schemes available from management consul-

---

[25] Visit http://www.jcu.edu.au/office/Executive/hay.html. There are a number of critical words at this site regarding the complexity of HRXpert, a software package that may be used to support the Hay Guide Charts.

tancies (securing at the same time, therefore, expert help in its application).[26] By far the best-known scheme, used by some 7,000 organisations in over 30 countries throughout the world, is that offered by the Hay Group through the *Hay Guide Chart and Profile Method*.[27]

The Hay Guide Chart and Profile Method[28]

Although Hay is a quite standard point-factor scheme, conforming to the rules just outlined, it employs very slightly different terminology. First, Hay is said to be based on three factors (Know-how, Problem-solving and Accountability), but, because these are defined at a relatively high level, they would be better thought of as "super factors". Each of these super factors is then broken down into elements which Hay calls *dimensions*. It is the Hay dimensions that correspond to the factors spoken of earlier in the text. For example, the Hay (super) factors do not have gradations of scale. Rather, it is the Hay dimensions at the lower level that have gradations of scale.

The Hay-defined factors and dimensions that make up the scheme are held by the Hay Group to be universal — characteristics relating to the consideration of all jobs regardless of organisation. In the scheme, the Hay factors have been allocated standard

---

[26] There are literally hundreds of schemes. In the UK, see *The Pay Points* and *DCM* methods from P-E International, *The Profile Method* from PriceWaterhouseCoopers and *EPFC* from Watson Wyatt.

[27] The Hay Group was founded in 1943, in Philadelphia, by Edward Ned Hay (1891-1958) and is dedicated to *an understanding of the world of work in the broadest management context*. Although point-factor evaluation itself was originally published in 1924 by Merrill Lott, the enormously successful Hay Guide Charts which employ the method were first devised by Hay co-managing partner Dale Purves in 1951. Visit the Hay Group website at http://www.haygroup.com. There are six Hay offices in the UK (under the name Hay-MSL) and 15 in the US, including the Group's world headquarters in Philadelphia, PA.

[28] The term *profile* in this title does not relate to job description, but to the balance of job points between the know-how, problem solving and accountability factors (see a little later in the text). The balance of points obtaining is an indication of the so-called "shape" of the job, and is a useful commonsense verification of an evaluation's correctness. For example, the job of Manufacturing Manager would be expected to be balanced reasonably evenly over all three factors.

Hay weights, and these in turn have been apportioned between the dimensions at the lower level of definition also in standard ways. Similarly, the dimension weights assigned to the dimension gradations have been apportioned in standard fashion throughout the scheme. (Geometric progression of 115 per cent has been used to apply them, rather than the 125 per cent in Table 19.2.) The Hay factor weights, dimension sub-weights and gradation weights have been refined and developed over many years by the Group, and are set out for users of the scheme in the form of ready reference tables, or *guide charts*. Thus in use, when a company job description is under consideration, the evaluator must simply carry out a three-part analysis:

1. Firstly, he must match a particular characteristic of the job under study with the correct Hay factor/dimension;

2. Secondly, he must match the degree of the characteristic present in the job with the gradation of dimension scale to which it corresponds; and

3. Finally, the evaluator must read the number of job points applying direct from the points set out on the Hay Guide Chart.

The universality of the Hay (super) factors is based on the self-evident truth that job content comprises three parts: (1) *Input* — know-how, and what is needed to carry out the job; (2) *Process* — problem solving and the application of know-how; and (3) *Output* — accountability for action and for the consequences of action. Very brief summaries of the Hay definitions of the three universal job factors and the eight job dimensions at the lower levels are as follows.

- **(Super) Factor 1: Know-how.** The sum of every kind of knowledge, skill and experience required to perform the job, including the requirement for knowledge in practical and interpersonal situations. There are three dimensions to Know-how:

    ♦ *Dimension 1: Depth and Range of Technical Know-how (8 gradations)*. Know-how in specialised fields, including technical and commercial expertise;

- *Dimension 2: Breadth of Management Know-how (5 gradations).* Skills brought to bear in planning, organising and controlling;
- *Dimension 3: Human Relation Skills (3 gradations)*: The practising of person-to-person skills (e.g. in advising, supervising or negotiating).

- **(Super) Factor 2: Problem-Solving.** The origination of thought required in the job, in evaluating, reasoning and drawing conclusions. Since problem-solving is necessarily based on know-how, the Hay points in the Problem-Solving chart are expressed as percentages of the know-how points. There are two dimensions:
  - *Dimension 1: Thinking Environment (8 gradations)*: The circumstances in which thinking takes place — the constraints or latitude in taking thought;
  - *Dimension 2: Thinking Challenge (5 gradations)*: The ease or difficulty of comprehending and resolving what it is that has to be thought about.

- **(Super) Factor 3: Accountability.** Accountability and answerability for the consequences of action, and the effect of the job on actual results subsequently affecting the company, directly or indirectly. There are three dimensions to the factor:
  - *Dimension 1: Freedom to Act (8 gradations)*: The existence or otherwise of guidance or supervision;
  - *Dimension 2: Job Impact on End Results (4 gradations)*: Whether the impact of what is done is incidental and indirect, or has a direct effect;
  - *Dimension 3: Magnitude of Area of Impact (4 gradations)*: The area of impact — a measure of the financial or physical importance of what it is that is impacted.

In using the scheme to carry out a job evaluation, there is an obvious need for an evaluator to obtain a close understanding of the full factor and dimension definitions and appreciate their shades of applicability according to the dimension gradations. As an example of the last, the following eight phrases summarise the definitions in the Hay literature used to describe the eight gradations of the dimension "Depth and Range of Technical Skills", the first of the three elements of the Know-how factor:

> Primary → Elementary Vocational → Vocational →
> Advanced Vocational → Basic Professional →
> Seasoned Professional → Professional Mastery →
> Unique Authority.

There are three Hay Guide Charts, one for each factor and each holding all of the factor dimensions and their gradations on the single chart. Because it needs to represent only two dimensions, the Problem-Solving Factor Chart is the most straightforward: the gradation descriptions of one dimension (8) are set out in the left hand edge of the chart and the descriptions of the second (5) across the top. A grid (8 × 5) is then drawn to allow the entry of the point scores (or rather, with this chart, the percentages).

The two remaining charts are rather more involved, since they must each accommodate three sets of dimension gradations. The chart designer has exercised not a little skill in arriving at elegant, easily read layouts. To illustrate the idea behind them, Figure 19.3 shows a fragment of Chart 1 (Know-how), and focuses on the points that might be applicable to an evaluation of the know-how content of the job *shop floor supervisor*. The job must be evaluated in three dimensions. In the first dimension, it has been assigned to Gradation 4 ("advanced vocational"). These descriptions are indicated down the left margin of the Chart (see Figure). Next, it has been assigned to Gradation 2 of the Management dimension, Dimension 2, drawn across the top. Finally, it has been assigned to Gradation 3 of HR Dimension 3, indicated in Figure 19.3 by the column "D3G3". In fact, it will be seen that there are three point values given here, ranging from 152 to 200. These are used, with guidance from a Hay expert, for fine-tuning the system. The middle point score of 175 has been chosen, circled in the Figure. To complete the evaluation of this job, it would, of course, be necessary to add the points obtained from the two other charts.

Figure 19.3: A Fragment from Hay Guide Chart 1 (Know-how), Showing the Points Applicable to a Shop Supervisor's Job

	← Dimen. 2 Grad. 1	Dimension 2 Gradation 2			Dimen. 2 Grad. 3 →	
	.... D3G3	D3G1	D3G2	D3G3	D3G1	....
Dimen. 1 Grad. 3						
Dimen. 1 Grad. 4 (Advanced Vocational)		115 132 152	132 152 175	152 (175) 200		*Shop Floor Supervisor* Advanced Vocational, Managerial Gradation 2 HR Skills Gradation 3 = 175 points for Factor 1 (at average level)
Dimen. 1 Grad. 5						

The need for guidance from a Hay expert is a reminder that any job evaluation scheme must be attuned to the particular circumstances and characteristics of the company using it. Despite the impression perhaps gained above — that the Hay point-factor scheme is a single formula applicable without modification to every organisation — in practice the Hay Group consultant is likely to tailor it for a better client fit. One way this is achieved is to modify the descriptions of the dimension gradations, changing their senses so as to correspond more closely with what the company sees as being important in the job rather than what is seen in it conventionally. By this means, the personnel and committees responsible for interpreting job descriptions in Hay terms during the carrying out of the evaluation programme can influence reward management in the direction which best supports the company's objectives.

The theme of reward management in support of corporate objectives is taken up in sub-section 19.2.4.

Factor Comparison

The use of factor comparison begins with the identification of some 20 to 30 key jobs in the general area of employment to be dealt with, and with the identification of a small number of *factors* which between them characterise those jobs. Identification of the key jobs must be made with care: it will be seen that these become the co-ordinates of the complete system. Agreed descriptions of them must be prepared with special attention paid in so doing to their involvement with the chosen factors (such involvement being reasonably representative). In addition, pay rates must be available for them, widely agreed as being "correct", whether obtained from the external labour market or internally. Of the factors, those used in the past, though purely for manual work, have been: *mental requirements*; *skill*; *physical requirements*; *responsibility*; and *working conditions*.

In the first step of the analysis, the key jobs are considered by the evaluator or by an evaluation committee, and ranked against each other in accordance with their degrees of involvement with each of the factors. For example, Figure 19.4 shows three key jobs — Job A, Job B and Job C — ranked according to four factors, F1 to F4. The figure shows that the order of "importance" of Factor 1 to the three jobs is A, B, C, and that the order of importance of Factor 2 is Job C, Job B, Job A, and so on.

Figure 19.4: Factor Comparison 1 — Job Rankings by Factor

	Factor F1	Factor F2	Factor F3	Factor F4
Job A	1	3	1	3
Job B	2	2	2	1
Job C	3	1	3	2

Next, each job in turn is examined by the evaluator or committee and the job "content", or job size, is apportioned between the factors. This is clearly a problematical and subjective task that will require a good deal of debate and crosschecking by those carrying it out. Figure 19.5 shows an evaluator's view of the percentage split of each of the previous three jobs by the four factors F1 to F4.

Figure 19.5: Factor Comparison 2 — Factor Percentages in Each Job

	Factor F1	Factor F2	Factor F3	Factor F4	Total
Job A	50	10	30	10	100%
Job B	20	20	20	40	100%
Job C	15	40	10	35	100%

Interpreting Figure 19.5, the evaluator has determined that Job A consists of 50 per cent of Factor 1, 10 per cent of Factor 2, 30 per cent of Factor 3 and 10 per cent of Factor 4. A check should be made at this juncture for consistency between the rankings in Table 19.4 and the percentages in Table 19.5. For example, Job A is top for Factor 1 in Table 19.4 and so it would be expected to have a preponderance of Factor 1 attributed to it in Figure 19.5. Similarly, Job C is bottom of the league in Figure 19.4 for Factor 3, and we see indeed that only a small percentage of it has been attributed to Factor 3 in Figure 19.5. (If an inconsistency is found which cannot be resolved by re-evaluation, the job is probably not key, or is otherwise unrepresentative. In any event, it should be dropped from the analysis.)

Next, the pay rates to be used for the key jobs are applied to the factor percentages to find the proportional pay rates attributable to the factors themselves. Figure 19.6 shows pay rates of £10.00/hour, £8.00/hour and £6.00/hour applied to jobs A, B and C, and gives the split of these rates according to the factor percentages in Figure 19.5. For example, interpreting Figure 19.6, we see that the pay rate for Job B attributed to Factor F4 is £8.00 × 40 per cent = £3.20.

Figure 19.6: Factor Comparison 3 — Job Pay Rates allocated between Factors

	Pay Rate per Hour	Split of Pay Rate across Factors (£/Hour)			
		Factor F1	Factor F2	Factor F3	Factor F4
Job A	£10.00	5.00	1.00	3.00	1.00
Job B	£8.00	1.60	1.60	1.60	3.20
Job C	£6.00	0.90	2.40	0.60	2.10

Finally, the pay rates per factor from Figure 19.6 are arranged as scales, showing, for each factor, the monetary rates applying to it and the key jobs giving rise to each such rate. Figure 19.7 shows four factor scales derived from the F1, F2, F3 and F4 columns of Figure 19.6.

Figure 19.7: Factor Comparison 4 — Four Key Job Factor Scales

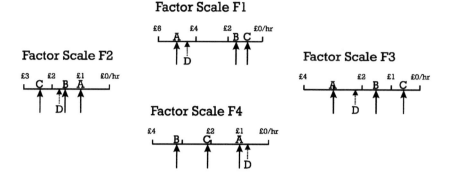

In reality, of course, there will be 20 or 30 key job graduations on each scale, not a mere three. Nowadays, also, it is usual to express the dimensions of scales in units rather than money, but with unit/money conversion factors.

Persevering with our example, suppose now that a rate of pay must be assigned to a new, non-key job, Job D. First, the job's description and contents are discussed, especially from the viewpoints of the four factors. Then, for each factor in turn, the demands of the new job are judged in relation to the demands of the key jobs vis-à-vis the factor. In Job D's case, it is decided: (1) for F1, that it lies a little below Job A; (2) for F2, that it is just above Job B; (3) for F3, that it is half way between Job A and Job B; and (4) for F4, that it is somewhat less than Job A. These four points are denoted in Figure 19.7 by vertical dotted lines below the scales. The four rates read from the scales are £4.50/hour, £1.80/hour, £2.15/hour and £0.80/hour, so that the rate allocated to Job D is £9.25/hour.

Factor comparison was devised in 1926 by Ned Hay himself, with others, and was at one time relatively popular.[29] It has now lost favour.

---

[29] Thomas H. Patten Jr., *Pay: Employee Compensation and Incentive Plans*, pp. 217–220; Eugene J. Benge, Samuel L.H. Burk and Edward N. Hay (1941), *Manual of Job Evaluation*, Harper.

Ranking

Jobs are considered in their entirety and placed in rank order after their judicious consideration in relation to a number of criteria. Although it provides no information on job sizes and, in its simplest form at least, signally fails the important test declared earlier of seeming fair to employees, ranking most certainly is used in making redundancy decisions when jobs have to be cut.

Classification (Grading)

Classification, or grading, is a refinement of ranking and is widely used as being quick and inexpensive.[30] The first requirement for its use is the setting up of a pay structure based on a number of representative jobs, as described in sub-section 19.2.2. Job descriptions of the further jobs to be classified are then prepared and considered, and each one placed in the pay structure by comparing its demands and characteristics with those of jobs to which grades have already been assigned. Quick and inexpensive though it may be, classification is unsuitable for more senior positions, which cannot satisfactorily be gauged against simple grade definitions since they make sophisticated or subtle demands on job holders, or indeed for manufacturing industry generally where novel positions are likely continually to arise which in reality are not directly comparable to standard job classes.

Market Pricing

Market pricing has been described in sub-section 19.2.1. It should be added that data on market pay rates and pay trends are now systematically collected and analysed by a number of market research companies, professional associations and management consultancies, and are thus available to employers wishing to establish rates for their own use. Indeed, the ready availability of external data calls into question the need for company-wide, protracted point-factor evaluation exercises. Provided reliance

---

[30] Thomas Patten describes the use of classification by auditors of the US Civil Service Commission (Office of Management & Budget) to deal with many thousands of wondrously diverse Federal jobs involving over 2.5 million employees in the US Government "General Schedule" job category, Grades 1 to 18 (see Patten, op. cit.).

can be placed on external job descriptions, as remarked in 19.2.1, complex evaluation schemes might perhaps be confinable to only a minority of company jobs.[31]

19.2.4 Reward Management and Company Objectives

It may be considered that while pay structures and job evaluation have fulfilled one objective of reward management — the creation of a logical framework for effecting staff payment — they have done little in a positive way to support an HR environment which demands of its staff "flexibility and enterprise" in dealing with customers and "ever-higher standards of commercial and technical achievement". In this sub-section, three ideas are described which are very much intended to prosecute the company's aims in these matters. They have come to prominence in the past few years and have been implemented in many organisations.[32]

Broad Banding

The mechanism for creating "broad bands" through large pay grade differentials and overlaps was described in sub-section 19.2.2. The 18 grades in Figure 19.2(a) to cover pay rates from £7,500 per annum to £103,000 per annum were reduced to 6 when differentials of 100 per cent were applied.

The use of broad banding implies that large numbers of company jobs will be allocated to the same grade and that very many employees will spend their entire careers within the company in

---

[31] For the US, the Hay Group, the American Materials Management Association and many such organisations publish well-known annual surveys of pay rates in manufacturing industry. In particular, the MMA survey covers such key manufacturing jobs as master scheduling, shop supervision and stores management and, importantly, includes revised definitions of these positions if the Association finds that there have been changes in their general work content. Similar surveys are published in the UK.

[32] See Helen Murlis (ed.) (1996), *Pay at the Crossroads*, The Institute of Personnel and Development. See, in particular, Chapter 2 by Stephen Palmer on trends in reward management.

one or two grades only.[33] The principal means, then, by which broad banding supports company objectives is by facilitating the easy transfer of staff from one job to another. When the company wishes to appoint an employee to a newly created position or to redefine his current job, there is a very strong likelihood that no alteration in his grade will be involved. Further, the employee's interest in the change is entirely centred on the job, not on his promotion to a higher grade or on his demotion to a lower one, as would be likely under a traditional structure.

Again, because employees' salaries are not minutely prescribed through a grading system, where, in the past, rewarding a member of staff for special merit and endeavour would have required the system's manipulation through his otherwise unwarranted promotion to a higher grade, broad banding gives departmental managers freedom to make local staff salary decisions directly, within the limits of their departmental salary budgets (although in accordance with guidelines issued by the HR manager or after consultation with him).

As mentioned under market pricing, the adoption of broad banding may also relieve the company of the burden of having to evaluate a large number of jobs under a point-factor scheme. Although mindful of the warning relating to job definitions, simple market pricing or factor comparison may be quite sufficient to place the great majority of company jobs in the small number of grades within the new pay structure.

Variable Pay

Variable pay is the term given to pay awarded for measurable, achieved results, such as commission paid to salesmen on the basis of sales volume gained, bonuses paid to shop floor staff on the

---

[33] Management guru Tom Peters seems largely in agreement with Ulysses about the possible effect of broad bands and flatter hierarchies on motivation and ambition. *"There's not much of a pyramid to climb! So how will people get their kicks — their bucks — their psychic compensation?"* he asks (Tom Peters and Nancy Austin (1985), *A Passion for Excellence*, HarperCollins). The continuance of an employee on a single grade throughout his career requires that, in the absence of grade status, considerable attention should be paid to his personal development and career progress, to reassure him and help sustain his ongoing commitment.

basis of the number of units of product machined or a bonus paid to the staff of an assembly department for achieving the company's master schedule.[34] It is pay "at risk". A fundamental feature of it is that to be obtained a further time, it must be re-earned. Incentive payments and the profits distributed in a profit-sharing scheme constitute variable pay; overtime payments, shift allowances and perquisites do not.

Nor is traditional performance-related pay variable. As the name says, such pay is related to the jobholder's inherent performance — to the skill he exhibits in carrying out the work or to the knowledge he has gained to enable him to do so — not to the actual outcome of his endeavour and performance. Consequently, performance-related pay is usually consolidated with an employee's basic rate. It is paid in anticipation of satisfactory performance and does not pass either of the tests of being related to results or having to be re-earned.

Two ways in which it is claimed that variable pay schemes promote company objectives are that they increase staff effectiveness by encouraging employees' co-operation and that they accord with the devolution of managerial responsibility by encouraging enterprise and the seizing of opportunities. There is also the advantage of tighter financial control of payments than with performance-related pay. While performance-related pay becomes submerged in the basic salary budget, variable pay always stands apart. The total amount paid can be related to a specific, limited reserve (for example, in the way that shared profits are related to profits earned).

---

[34] We should not forget W. Edwards Deming's objections to merit pay and incentives, however. Point 10 of Deming's famous 14 points states *eliminate numerical goals — substitute leadership instead* (Mary Walton (1986), *The Deming Management Method*, Mercury Books and Management Books 2000 Ltd., p. 202), and again *piece work robs the employee of his right to do work that he can be proud of* (*ibid*, p. 398). Deming's Red Beads Skit at his four-day seminar mocked incentive schemes. See William J. Latzko and David M. Saunders (1995), *Four Days with Dr Deming*, Addison-Wesley Publishing Co., Chapter 5. This book is an account of the experience and substance of attendance at one of Deming's famous four-day seminars that brilliantly captures the occasion, the one described having been held in Philadelphia, February 1990.

Competency-based Pay

The idea of a competency-based pay scheme is that employees should be rewarded for acquiring and utilising knowledge and skills identified as being relevant to the fulfilment of their departments' objectives and the objectives of the company.

Acquiring knowledge and skills is not the same as receiving training. Training and education must precede the acquisition of knowledge and skills, certainly, but two purposes of the pay scheme are to encourage students' willingness of study and, more importantly, to reward those of ability and industriousness for success in its outcome.

Setting up the training programme required to support a competency-based pay scheme is a major undertaking but, again, doing so is not the objective. The more important HR activity is the evaluation of its results in the hope and expectation that knowledge will have been absorbed by the programme's participants and that skills will have been acquired by them. Expert judgement must be made of employees' newfound abilities in such areas of competence as the exercise of managerial skill; knowledge of inventory control; knowledge of quality; negotiation; the acquisition of machine operation skills; etc. (The judgement of examiners of the company's candidates for the certificates and diplomas of outside professional institutions will also constitute most valuable additional evidence of competence.)

The brief presentation of the three trends described above is a fitting valediction to reward management. The schemes are proposals put forward by the human resource manager to senior management as his particular contribution to the creation of the culture of enterprise, achievement and customer care that the company wishes to see established among its employees.

19.3 WORKING RELATIONSHIPS

19.3.1 Empowerment and Teams

Empowerment is the transference from middle management to shop floor staff of full responsibility for the organisation, control and completion of work at the shop level, accompanied by the granting by senior management of the authority needed to assume such responsibility and the provision by the company of all training and other support necessary to exercise it.[35]

Empowerment is closely associated with team working. It will be recalled from Section 8.7, for example, that empowered teams were regarded as essential to the carrying out of final assembly in Quick Response. The reasons for the empowered team in these circumstances are that work must be accomplished quickly and that each assembly is likely to give rise to problems unique to itself — a stream of appeals to management for advice and approval would hardly make for practicable operation. It must be said, however, that a number of practitioners in the HR field do not confine their advocacy of empowerment and team working to such highly defined manufacturing situations as QR. Empowerment (they say) should be universally implemented, and they put forward alarming sociological arguments to support their case.[36]

Whether the limited or the extreme view is taken, it is agreed that if empowerment in any form is to succeed, complete trust and confidence must be placed in those who are to be empowered by those from whom authority and responsibility are to be removed. If trust is less than full-hearted, the fact of it will be sensed and commitment by staff to the new order of things will be held back. It is also agreed that there must be thoroughgoing preparation before the final transfer of responsibility, not only in drawing up rules and making clear to those who are to take the fateful step what their accountability will be, but, of course, in the provision on their behalf of training and education.

Training and education are required in *soft* subjects. *Hard* subjects are those involving indisputable facts and figures, and include

---

[35] Middle managers are not always the "losers" when empowerment is introduced to the manufacturing concern. Free of administrative chores, technical managers at least can devote more time to technical issues. Kaoru Ishikawa has an interesting view of middle managers. They are, he says, traffic policemen, standing aside when things are going smoothly, intervening when problems arise (Kaoru Ishikawa (1985), *What is Total Quality Control (The Japanese Way)?*, Prentice-Hall, Chapter VII). Ishikawa's advice to the middle manager may seem contradictory, but is not: *"Strive to become a person who does not have to be always present at the company, but become a person who is indispensable to the company."*

[36] See Chapter 1 ("The End of the Old Order") in Rob Brown and Margaret Brown (1994), *Empowered!*, Nicholas Brealey Publishing.

many of the technical disciplines studied under competency-based pay schemes: quality; inventory control; engineering methods; TPM; and so on. Soft subjects by contrast, presented on courses that include role play, games and much discussion, include such subjects as motivation; running a meeting; team working; and dealing with conflict and stress.

By far the most common means of finally introducing empowerment is through teams, each team having a remit closely defined by management and a membership appointed by management and HR. Measures of performance whereby a team's success in achieving its objectives is to be gauged must also be discussed and agreed.

Membership of each team must be considered with the greatest care. One reason for team failure is attributed to a poor mix of member "types" — too many *organisers* and *enthusiasts*, not enough *concluders* and *conservatives*, to use the jargon. The crucial appointment, however, is that of team leader, once again made by management and being a position carrying a salary premium. What is required of the team leader is, quite simply, leadership ability, a quality difficult to define but instantly recognised. A second reason for failure has nothing to do with mix or leadership. This is the launch of teams by management as if of itself this is sufficient, the teams launched having insufficient training, few resources and no clear objectives or measures of performance. The result of doing so is endless unproductive meetings, deterioration in company work performance and eventual abandonment of the programme.

Facilitators and other practitioners in HR teach that team development passes through four stages, given amusing names: (1) *forming* (team members are wary); (2) *storming* (anxiety and outbursts of conflict); (3) *norming* (the establishment of standards of behaviour); and (4) *performing* (the team is mature and established).

The advantages claimed for giving those close to the work jurisdiction over the work they do are that company objectives will be better served through increased flexibility of response to customer needs and that staff, motivated, will expend "discretionary effort" that will result in their increased effectiveness. In particular, for the team, especially the multi-disciplinary team, benefits are claimed of eliciting from staff bright ideas leading to improvements in quality, the elimination of wasteful practices and the adoption of slicker ways of working.

The establishment of empowerment and team working is hardly possible without the most careful preparation and planning. A programme to do so will make the greatest demands on the company's HR manager and his staff.

19.3.2 Strife

The conflict inevitable in any human society has a vocabulary all its own in industrial human relations. The dissidence of the employee may be expressed as: a *complaint*, dissatisfaction with a matter made in a relatively informal way to his immediate supervisor; a *grievance*, being a complaint formally made to management and to which a reply, also formal, is expected; or as a *dispute*, a grievance expressed collectively with other employees, usually on his behalf by a union or staff representative. The most common causes of disputes are dissatisfaction with wage rates, bonuses and perquisites; redundancy; supervision; and working conditions. The employer speaks of *discipline*. For him, the most common causes of dissatisfaction (with the employee) are poor timekeeping, unauthorised absence and poor standards of work.

The formal procedures put in place within the organisation by the HR manager to respond to grievance and to exercise discipline, and the patience, tact and shrewdness of his administration of them, have a major bearing on the smooth running of the company. Besides monitoring their operation, the HR manager will also be involved in interviews and often intensive discussion that it is hoped will eventually yield solutions to issues satisfactory to all sides.

If a solution to a dispute cannot be found, or if a disciplinary matter cannot be resolved, the two sides may turn to *conciliation, mediation* or *arbitration* and the services of a third party to break the deadlock. In the UK, industrial experts ready to take on the task are to be found at the *Advisory, Conciliation and Arbitration Service* (ACAS), a government body with headquarters in London and offices throughout the country set up under the Employment Protection Act, 1975, for this and related purposes. The role of the third party in conciliation is simply that of facilitator. In mediation, he will put forward specific recommendations. If employer and employee have agreed to arbitration, the third party will prescribe a solution which the protagonists have agreed in advance they will accept.

In the event of a dispute, and failing negotiation conducted through standard procedures, the employee, in concert with others, may engage in *industrial action* to further his case. Examples of industrial action are go-slows, working to rule, overtime bans and strikes.

Any one of these actions, if taken, would constitute a breach of contract by the employee, the first three being failures in his contractual duty of fidelity, the last a fundamental breach of it.[37] Furthermore, either the employee, if the action is unofficial, or the union or staff association, if it is official, unless statutory immunity from legal action applies, as described below, would be liable to action in law for a claim in tort, the principle torts applying being those of *contract interference* and *inducing a breach of contract*. (It will be recalled that a tort is a civil wrong for which redress may be sought before the courts. Thus Stevenson was found to have committed the tort of *negligence* in the unpleasant business of the snail, recounted in sub-section 13.1.2.)

Though it will doubtless be reluctant to do so, employees who are on strike can be dismissed by the company without notice for breach of contract. (There is no law which "permits" a person to break a contract of employment.) If the strike is unofficial, the strikers are considered to be acting as individuals. They have no right of appeal for unfair dismissal to an Employment Appeal Tribunal, since a tribunal has no jurisdiction over matters of contract, and each individual dismissal is regarded, in isolation, as being due to a breach of his particular contract by the employee concerned. If the strike is official (i.e. if it is endorsed by a union or staff association), and all strikers are dismissed *en bloc*, they also have no right of appeal for the same reason of breach of contract. However, an appeal can be made if dismissals of official strikers are selective. Since the dismissed employees have been treated differently from those not dismissed, the grounds of the appeal would be that there has been unfairness — that is, that the em-

---

[37] See Paul Lewis (1998), *The Law of Employment — Practice and Analysis*, Kogan Page. See also Margaret Griffiths (1994), *Law for Purchasing and Supply*, Pitman, Chapter 22.

ployer must have had hidden motives for his action that related to them but did not relate to others.

Statutory immunity from liability for certain torts, including those relating to contract above, is given under the Trade Union and Labour Relations (Consolidation) Act, 1992. In order for the Act to apply, however, certain conditions must be met. First, the dispute must indeed be *in contemplation or furtherance of a trade dispute*. Secondly, there must be a yes/no ballot of union or staff association members for the action proposed, with a simple majority in favour. Thirdly, the industrial action must be confined to a dispute directly affecting the employees balloted, at their place of work. That is, those involved in *secondary action* in support of other employees involved in a dispute elsewhere are not immune from tortious liability; if such action is engaged in, the company adversely affected is likely at once to seek, and obtain, from the courts, an injunction to put an end to it and to claim compensation for financial loss.

On the other side of the fence, discipline may be reinforced by: a formal *caution*; a *warning* (or *final warning*); *demotion*; or *suspension* for a period from the company (with pay). However, the manufacturing manager whose member of staff is the subject of the disciplinary proceedings may believe it to be strongly in the interests of his department and the company that the employee be dismissed. If so, to realise his belief, he must work closely with the HR manager. For one thing, dismissal falls squarely within the ambit of corporate policy commented on at the beginning of this Chapter. For another, dismissal, other than for breach of contract dealt with above, is hemmed about by legal obligations and restrictions.

In examining them, it is necessary first to distinguish between *wrongful dismissal* and *unfair dismissal*. A wrongful dismissal is a dismissal by the employer which is in breach of the contract of employment. An employee wrongfully dismissed may take legal action without restriction. (Damages awarded are usually related to wages applying to the contractual notice period.)

As well as for reasons of ethics, there is a need for the company to avoid unfair dismissal because of the exigencies of the Employment Protection (Consolidation) Act, 1978. Indeed, the company's own policy guidelines on the matter may well be drawn up with the Act's provisions as a framework, though, if so, the provisions are very likely to be regarded as minimum obligations. Note that the Act defines *fairness*, rather than *unfairness*, so that in any case before a tribunal, there is a burden of proof on the employer to establish that there was a fair reason for the dismissal, as defined under one or other of the five headings set out below. It is also necessary at a tribunal to show that the dismissal was "reasonable". Facets of reasonableness are that the severity of the action taken was matched by the seriousness of the offence; that the action was consistent with action previously taken against other employees in similar circumstances; and, most importantly, that fair disciplinary procedures, such as the issuance of written warnings and the granting of opportunities for employees to state their cases, had been put in place and were scrupulously followed. (Failure by the employer to follow procedure in every particular is a major cause of tribunal findings of unfair dismissal.) The allowed reasons for dismissal under the Act are:

1. *Lack of capability or qualifications.* The principal two reasons in practice are inherent incompetence and ill-health necessitating long-term absence from work. (Ideally on ill-health, the contract of employment should contain express provision for the maximum absence to be allowed for this reason.) If action is taken on the grounds of ill-health, there should be full involvement of the employee in the necessary fact-finding and decision-making processes.

2. *Misconduct.* Examples of misconduct are disobedience; serious negligence; a wilful failure to take prescribed safety precautions; damage to the company's commercial interests; falsification of records; drunkenness; and violence. (The last three eventualities are examples of *gross misconduct*, a concept not in fact defined in law.) The tests applied at a tribunal for determining whether a dismissal for misconduct was fair are whether suspicion of the employee's responsibility for it was well-founded and whether a thorough investigation was carried out.

3. *Redundancy.* Dismissal attributable to actual or intended cessation of business or to an actual or expected reduction of the work carried out by the employee.

4. *Statutory disqualification.* The employee cannot perform his duties without contravening the law. Usually, this means a driver losing his licence and being unable to drive. While fair reason for dismissal clearly exists under such a circumstance, an Employment Appeal Tribunal will look to the matter of reasonableness: if the driver has long service with the company, could he not have been readily redeployed elsewhere within the factory?

5. *Some other substantial reason.* The principal application of "SOSR" arises when the employer is forced for valid business or financial reasons to reorganise the company's operations and, to do so, must unilaterally change the terms and conditions of contract of employees. Employees not agreeing to the revised conditions may be dismissed for SOSR, the employer's case at a tribunal being economic necessity. Dismissal for SOSR may also apply when there has been a reorganisation due to a *transfer of undertakings* (i.e. a takeover). The dismissal of employees arising from reorganisation simply to reduce staff numbers will be on the grounds of redundancy, not SOSR.

19.4 HEALTH AND SAFETY

The imperative to secure and maintain a safe and healthy working environment has its origin in the ethical principles held by senior management related at the beginning of this Chapter. Thus, while it is true that a case might be made for promoting health and safety purely on financial grounds, and while there are indeed strict legal and regulatory requirements, behind the money and the law there are ghosts that remind everyone in the enterprise of their duty in these matters and remind them also of the price of failure: young women, their faces destroyed by phossy jaw; men decapitated or with limbs torn from their sockets; coal workers dead at 45 years of black lung disease; and machine operators with sliced fingers or toes crushed to the bone.

19.4.1 Management

While the need for uncompromising support for health and safety by senior management can hardly be overemphasised, responsibility at the practical level must clearly lie with local management, especially, here, with the manufacturing manager. The role of the human resources manager is likely to be administrative, especially regarding formal compliance with regulations. As well, the HR department will provide the company's *safety officer* with a base of operations within the corporate management structure whereby he can exert his authority and influence his colleagues.

The relationship of the safety officer to safety is analogous to the relationship of the quality control manager to quality. The appointment is a technical one, perhaps of a production or plant engineer.[38] Depending on local circumstances, his job will be to organise systematic safety reviews in the various factory areas; to provide local managers and supervisors with the benefit of his expertise during the conduct of the reviews; and to monitor the implementation of agreed changes in procedure made for H&S reasons. The safety officer will also investigate most carefully all accidents and near-misses.

The reasons for accidents and near-misses are what W. Edwards Deming called special causes, and indeed the Deming approach to the understanding and control of a human-centred system is nowhere more powerful than it is here. The H&S system that gives rise to a particular, prevailing H&S environment can be analysed in just the same way as the Total Quality system considered in sub-section 13.2.1. An "outside-in" system flowchart for H&S, on the lines of the TQC system flowchart in Figure 13.2, will include such factors (say) as plant and machine design; operator education and training; factory layout; standards of supervision; the incorporation of H&S obligations in job descriptions; and, perhaps, H&S-related payments and bonus schemes. What The Master taught over all those years is a fact directly attested to by many of the experts,[39] namely that the stabilisation and then improvement of such a system as this are

---

[38] For an appreciation of the technical knowledge required, see Jeremy Stranks (1992), *A Manager's Guide to Health and Safety at Work*, Second edition, Kogan Page. This is a relatively short book on the subject (200 pages). A full, standard reference work used by a safety officer, however, might be Ian Fife and E.A. Machin (1997), *Redgrave's Health and Safety in Factories, 1997 Supplement*, Butterworths Law.

[39] See, for example, Torrington and Hall (1991), op. cit.; Cowling and James (1994), op. cit.; and Michael Armstrong (1991), *A Handbook of Personnel Management*, Fourth edition, Kogan Page.

tasks for management, and management alone. Application of the Deming principles also gives a clue as to how the safety officer might monitor statistics on accidents. Thus we may recall von Bortkiewicz's work analysing deaths in the Prussian cavalry from kicks by horses, and the use of the c and u charts, in sub-section 14.3.1. Assuming the Poisson distribution of the incidence of accidents in the factory, control limits will be set as ever at ±3 standard deviations, where the standard deviation of the Poisson distribution is the square root of the mean (see Figure 14.14 and Equation 14.53).

While a *safe environment* means a workplace with safe systems of work, the environment being "safe" because the possibility of sudden, dangerous incidents occurring has been minimised, a *healthy environment* relates to freedom from harm emanating from the workplace itself. Thus, an unhealthy environment is one by contrast where, say, a dangerous atmosphere is present, such as air containing asbestos dust, or one that is excessively noisy or hot or stressful in some other way, or an environment where staff are exposed to radiation. Phossy jaw is a degenerative bone disease contracted from working in the presence of fumes from white phosphorous, a substance used in the manufacture of household matches until 1910.

The technical knowledge needed to assess whether a workplace is healthy rather than merely safe is very likely to be different from the production engineer's, and include such disciplines as *preventive medicine* and *occupational hygiene*. If the company lacks such expertise itself, the safety officer may obtain advice on these matters from the Employment Medical Advisory Service, a government body connected to the Health and Safety Commission (see below).

19.4.2 The Involvement of the Law

The first part of this sub-section covers government legislation and regulations — that is, statutory requirements under the criminal law. The second part briefly discusses liability under common law. The existence of legislation and regulations has an important bearing on action under the common law: as we shall see, one of the two principal claims of plaintiffs under common law is for the tort of *breach of statutory duty*.

Legislation and Regulation

Eight major statutes relating to health and safety in employment were enacted between 1833 and 1963, the last four being *The Mines and Quarries Act, 1954*; *The Agriculture Safety Provisions Act, 1956*; *The Factories Act, 1961*; and *The Offices, Shops, Railways and Railway Premises Act, 1963*.[40]

Next, between 1970 and 1972, the government appointed a Commission to review "the provision made for the health and safety of persons in the course of their employment . . . and to consider whether any changes (were) needed", the Commission being headed by Lord Robens (the *ci-devant* Alf Robens, a one time middle-ranking Labour Government minister, and better known later as chairman of the National Coal Board). Robens' report, published in June 1972, made a number of criticisms of legislation up to that time and a number of recommendations for change, the principal ones being:

- That there was too much law, and that it was too complex;

- That the balance between "prescriptive" and "goal setting" legislation should be shifted towards the latter;

- That the form of future legislation should be (1) *"framework law"*, supported by (2) specific *regulations*, then (3) *codes of practice*, and finally (4) *guidance*. Codes of practice were not to constitute legal requirements as such, but failure to follow them was to be regarded as incriminatory evidence in prosecutions. Guidance notes were to be items of practical help only, a failure to follow them not to weigh as evidence in court;

- That the then current factory inspectorate should be reconstituted.

---

[40] The very first legislation in the UK in this area related to health and welfare, rather than health and safety, and was enacted in 1802, under the reign of George III, as the result of public outcry at the loss of life and the incurrence of disease, namely scrotal cancer, suffered by young boys employed to clean out chimneys in the Lancashire textile mills. The Act limited the boys' hours of work and stipulated certain provisions regarding working conditions. Inspectors were appointed by local magistrates from volunteers, and (like the magistrates) were unpaid.

In 1974, the government implemented Robens' recommendations in the form of *The Health and Safety at Work Act* (HSAWA). The Act lays down in general terms the duties of the employer with regard to the health, safety and welfare of his employees, one provision here being a requirement that the company should issue a written statement of its policy. It also lays down the duties of the employee regarding his own self-care and the requirement that he should cooperate with the employer in these matters. In addition, the Act provides for a *Health and Safety Commission* (HSC), a body corporate with a remit to prepare regulations and issue codes of practice and guidance, and a *Health and Safety Executive* (HSE). The HSE is empowered to appoint factory inspectors, who, with local authority inspectors, have the right among other things to enter premises without notice, take photographs, make measurements and interview staff. An inspector may issue an *improvement notice*, to take effect within 21 days, but which can be appealed against to an Employment Appeal Tribunal, or a *prohibition order*, to take immediate effect.

The HSAWA is referred to as an *enabling act*. That is, it provides for a legislative mechanism whereby procedures specified in the offices of the Health & Safety Commission can be translated into legally compelling regulations and the semi-legal codes of practice. Thus the four statutes from 1954 to 1963 were not replaced or superseded by the 1974 Act. They remain, but through the Act their provisions over the years have been or are being transferred and incorporated piece by piece into the form of HSAWA regulations. In summary, then, the HSAWA permits new regulations, changes to existing ones and new or changed codes of practice to be drawn up and directly issued by the HSC, albeit with a government minister's signature, so obviating the need each time for fresh legislation and also, let it be said, so avoiding the need for their prior scrutiny by parliament. (The HSC points out, however, that there are provisions for informal and formal consultation with representatives of industry during two of the four stages in the lengthy internal process of formulation.) A major instance of the culmination of this process was seen in 1988, when 19 regulations and four codes of practice relating to dangerous substances were issued under the HSAWA, publicised throughout industry as *The Control of Substances Hazardous to Health Regulations* (COSHH).

Leaving to one side the dubiousness of Robens' proposition, that, because of the pace of technological change, an enabling act is a necessity, rather than merely a convenience to government authority, it must always have been seen as dangerous to place in the hands of a body of civil servants virtually unbridled power to create regulation. The grim reality of the flood of regulations and — worse — codes of practice now swamping industry was reviewed on the 25th anniversary of the Robens Report by Tom Smith, an independent regulatory expert in the H&S field, specialising in explosives.[41] Smith pointed out what is surely apparent to all — that the national situation that Robens originally criticised is now far, far worse. What has become of prime importance to many practitioners is neither health nor safety but paperwork and paperwork. As Robens put it then in 1972:

> "Our present system encourages rather too much reliance on state regulation, and rather too little on personal responsibility and voluntary, self-generating effort. This imbalance must be redressed. A start should be made by reducing the sheer weight of the legislation."

Alas, the outcome of his report has been that this weight, far from being lifted, has been reinforced by a yet greater weight of regulation, codes of practice and guidance.

---

[41] Health and safety directives pouring in from the EU are more "prescriptive" than regulations generated within the UK — i.e. their requirements are specified in more exact terms, in a manner opposite to Robens' second recommendation quoted in the text that there should be a move away from prescription to "goal setting". But undesirable and unnecessary though EU regulation may be, the ability of the British Official to make matters worse stands pre-eminent, a phenomenon described by Christopher Booker and Richard North in their book *The Mad Officials* (1994), published by Hodder and Stoughton. Thus, for H&S, Tom Smith (see text) points out that ten-page European directives invariably become 100-page regulations when touched by the magic wand of the HSC.

Visit http://www.homepages.enterprise.net/saxtonsmith/robens.htm. The site is maintained by Tom Smith of Davas Ltd., Kimbolton, Huntingdon, Cambridgeshire, experts on H&S regulations in the area of explosives, including fireworks.

Civil Liability

Obligations in the matter of health and safety under the common law centre round the *duty of care* and *statutory duty*. The duty of care arises from the relationship between the employer as manager and the employee as subordinate, rather than from the contract of employment, and was eloquently defined by Lord Atkin, as quoted in sub-section 13.1.2. Statutory duty in H&S relates to the requirement to conform to laws and regulations such as those described in the previous sub-section. If the company fails in either of these duties, and an employee is thereby *injured* (i.e. some detriment thereby befalls him), that employee may take action in the courts for damages, alleging either the tort of negligence or the tort of breach of statutory duty. (Action for breach of statutory duty is, in fact, barred under certain sections of the HSAWA and a small number of EU regulations, but the injured party may then be able to fall back on the Acts from 1954 to 1963. As explained above, these remain in force.)

Assuming the action is between the employee as plaintiff and the employer as defendant, the employee must show three things to succeed in an action for negligence:

a) That the employer owed the employee a duty of care;

b) That the employer did not fulfil the duty of care;

c) That as a result of (b), the employee suffered injury.

If causation is not present — i.e. if there is no link between (b) and (c), the action will fail. Thus consider *McWilliams* v. *Arrol*.[42] McWilliams was not wearing a safety belt when he fell from a considerable height at his work, seriously injuring himself. Arrol had not provided safety belts, but was able to show in court that in the past, when he had done so, workers had refused to wear them. There was no link between his failure to provide the safety belts and the injury — the injury was caused by the intransigence of McWilliams and his colleagues in refusing to wear this equipment. McWilliams had not shown causation, and lost his case. It should be added, however, that in general employers are expected to

---

[42] *McWilliams* v. *Arrol*, 1962, All England Reports, 623.

take all reasonable steps, say, through safety awareness programmes and training, to induce compliance with procedures, and if necessary to take disciplinary action to force the matter.

The degree of care which must be exercised by the employer will depend on the likelihood of an injury occurring and the likely severity of the injury if it does so occur. In a judgment in 1949, Mr Justice Asquith expressed the principle thus:

> "A computation must be made in which the quantum of risk is placed on one scale, and the sacrifice involved in the measures necessary for averting the risk is placed on the other."[43]

A second way the principle might be expressed is as a relationship as follows:

Likelihood of an injury $\times$ *Likely severity of any injury*
$\propto$ *Effort to be expended* $\times$ *Cost to be incurred*

Bearing in mind always the proportionality of risk and care in the expression, the employer is likely to have taken "sufficient measures" if: (1) he has ensured that the employee is fully aware of the dangers of his work and knows what precautions must be taken; and (2) he has made precautions readily available, and ensured that the employer knows of their existence. That is, it is not the duty of an employer to eliminate every possible risk. There are limits, namely the boundaries of reasonableness. Consider *Latimer v. AEC*.[44] AEC's workshop became flooded one night due to torrential rain, which led to spillages of oil over the floors. The factory manager, a minor hero of manufacturing, but anonymous, set his staff to work to clean up and spread sawdust on the oil. The supply of sawdust, however, eventually ran out still leaving a number of oily patches present. Work was nevertheless commenced. Latimer slipped on a remaining oily patch and broke his leg. Although Latimer was able to show causation and that the accident that did happen was "foreseeable", AEC was held not liable because the company had done all it reasonably could, and the only further

---

[43] L.J. Asquith in *Edwards* v. *NCB*, 1949, 1KB704.
[44] *Latimer* v. *AEC*, 1963, AC643.

action available to it was to close the factory. The degree of care exercised — cost and effort — was deemed appropriate to the risk of an accident due to the remaining oil and the probable nature of such an accident. The next step, closing the factory for a period, would have been an unreasonable response to the risk as it was analysed at the time.

If an accident occurs because of the malfunction of a machine or the sudden failure of a supplier's component — for example, the splintering of a metal rod — statute law in the form of *The Employers' Liability (Defective Equipment) Act, 1969*, comes to the aid of an employee so injured. Under the Act, the employer is deemed to be entirely liable for an accident due to these reasons. Justice for the employer will be served when he himself takes direct action against the equipment or material manufacturer. In the case against the manufacturer or supplier, it is unlikely that the employer will attempt to show causation for the failure based on technical or statistical evidence. Instead, he will plead *res ipsa loquitur*, "the thing speaks for itself". (Latin tags are widely used as shorthand by lawyers in case law.) If equipment failure is involved, the manufacturer may well attempt to show *contributory negligence* if he believes the employer's machine maintenance programme was inadequate.

The word "foreseeable" used earlier relates to a foreseeable cause of an accident, not a foreseeable consequence of one.[45] For example, in *Doughty v. Turner Manufacturing*,[46] an asbestos cement cover fell into molten metal, causing an explosion. In court, Turner Manufacturing was able to show that no similar accident of this type was known, and that it was not known that an explosion would occur. Although Turner Manufacturing was directly responsible for the literal occurrence of the accident, it was not liable in law for negligence, because it could not be shown that it had lacked reasonable foresight. The case highlights the essential need for the

---

[45] For an instance of an *unforeseeable consequence*, consider *Smith v. Leech Braine* (1962, 1QB405). In this case, molten zinc spat out of a galvanising tank, burning Smith on the lip. The burn caused cancer, from which Smith died. Leech Braine was held responsible for the escape of the metal (i.e. the cause) and consequently for everything that sprang from it, including the surprising death of Smith. (Note, however, that for liability to be incurred, the links in a chain of consequences must be unbroken, and no link must be too "remote".)

[46] *Doughty v. Turner Manufacturing*, 1964, 1QB518.

company's safety officer to keep abreast of H&S knowledge from systematic and careful study of H&S magazines and HSC/HSE publications. The defence offered by Turner Manufacturing of not knowing an explosion would occur has not been available to any other company in the same circumstances from the moment the facts were publicised in H&S literature.

Finally, it should be noted that it is a rule of law that an employer is liable to persons injured by the wrongful acts of his employees if they are committed in the course of their employment. The term used is *vicarious liability*, where the dictionary defines "vicarious" as "substituted", or "delegated". That is, in suing the company for negligence, the injured party will sue the company *vicariously*.

To succeed in his case, the plaintiff must show that the employee was carrying out an authorised act, albeit, perhaps, in an unauthorised manner, and that it was being carried out in the course of his employment. That is, among other things, no vicarious liability of the employer arises in respect of actions by the employee which have been expressly forbidden. Thus consider two drivers X and Y. In *Central Insurance Company* v. *Northern Ireland Road Transport Board*,[47] Driver X caused an explosion by smoking while unloading petrol. Since unloading petrol was part of his job, Northern Ireland Road Transport Board was held to be vicariously liable. In *Conway* v. *Wimpey* (a civil engineering contractor),[48] Driver Y was employed to carry his employer's staff, and, in particular, was expressly forbidden from carrying the staff of other companies. However he did so, and whilst being carried, they were injured. Wimpey was held not liable for their injuries, since it was not the job of Driver Y to carry the staff of another company. Note that both Driver X and Driver Y could be sued for damages privately by the respective injured parties. If vicarious liability can be shown, however, the employer will always be the more tempting target, since he is required to have insurance against civil claims under the Employers' Liability (Compulsory Insurance) Act, 1969.

---

[47] *Century Insurance Co.* v. *Northern Ireland Road Transport Board*, 1942, AC 509.

[48] *Conway* v. *Wimpey*, 1951, 2 KB266.

Chapter 20

Distribution

We recall that "place" is the third component of the marketing mix (sub-section 2.1.2). For a large number of manufacturing companies, especially those selling within the industrial market itself, the place from which the product is distributed to the ultimate user is the company's own factory. For them, distribution is a straightforward matter consisting of local sales order processing (SOP, Section 2.4), packing, despatch and transportation either by the company's own vehicle or by a third party transport operator. For a large number of other companies, especially those manufacturing goods for sale in the consumer market, the factory sale is to an independent, intermediary distributor — for example, to a merchant, a wholesaler or a retailer — with established warehousing and sales points throughout the market, providing (for a price) the degree of sales order processing and local despatch or direct sales services thought by the manufacturing company's sales and marketing manager to be appropriate to the company's products.

However, for reasons connected with customer service or with the economics of transportation, the manufacturing company may itself decide to take on the specialist role of intermediary distributor. Customer service reasons may include dissatisfaction with established intermediaries. For example, their speed of response to customer orders may be considered to be too slow; or their cost, or, rather, their price mark-ups, may be thought excessively high for the service provided; or, say, they may refuse, or be unable, to stock the full range of the company's products. Or, quite simply, the reason may be that despite the special skills and know-how involved in distribution, the company believes it is able to perform a better job itself, more cheaply. Transportation reasons may be related to the large volume or heavy weight of manufactured product made and the desirability of dispersing it throughout the market in a next stage after manufacture, in an economical manner as bulk loads.

Whatever the reasons for a distribution network's establishment, this chapter is concerned with the control and management by a manufacturing company of its own distribution outlets only, rather than with the topic of distribution in general, as it might be regarded by an independent intermediary. In particular, the chapter deals with the occasional need for the company to review its network's structure and with the stock replenishment of the various outlets. The special relevance of the chapter to the manufacturing manager, besides that of general interest, is the direct, close relationship that will be seen to exist between network replenishment and the master production schedule, dealt with in Section 20.2.

20.1 THE DISTRIBUTION NETWORK

20.1.1 Network Structure

The distribution network is the logical and physical arrangement of the components of the *distribution mix* intended to convey from customers information relating to their orders, and to provide for the satisfaction of those orders by the physical outward movement of stock. In a wider context, nowadays meriting the term *logistics* network, a network might also take into account all points along the supply chain from suppliers of raw materials and basic goods, perhaps through many possible alternative manufacturing sites, finally to the means for placing orders in the hands of individual customers. The design and set-up of a logistics network in such a context might involve, say, the establishment of consolidation and "cross-docking" centres, for the economic handling of incoming supplies, and postponement and break-bulk centres for dealing with outgoing material. The components of the distribution mix are generally taken to be five in number: inventory, warehousing facilities, communications, packaging, and transport. Although exceptions can always be found, the general network arrangement is based on customer service and warehousing points, or "nodes", arranged in "layers", termed *echelons*, the points on the outer layers of the structure being logically subordinate to points on inner layers.[1] A network is illustrated in Figure 20.1 comprising a master scheduling source of material supply, two regional warehouses (R1 and R2) at the next higher echelon and five storage depots (D1 to D5) at the top echelon. Thus in the Figure, depot D1 is subordinate to regional warehouse R1, which is in turn subordinate to the source of supply, and so forth.

Figure 20.1: A Simple Multi-Echelon Distribution Network with a Source, Two Regional Warehouses and Five Depots

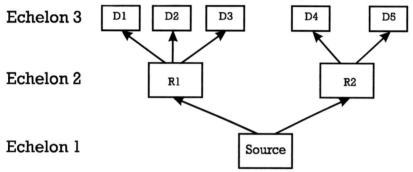

Again, now considering the left-hand half of Figure 20.1, the flow of information in the network is from D1 and D2 and D3, to R1, then from R1 to the Source, in the opposite direction of the arrows shown. The flow of physical goods is from the Source to R1, then from R1 to D1 and D2 and D3, in the direction of the arrows.

Although the inverse hierarchy illustrated in Figure 20.1 is overwhelmingly the most usual arrangement, depending on local circumstances, and bearing in mind the (necessary) existence of centralised data and network-wide communications, the structure may be the subject of many alternative variations. For example, after calculating how stock shortages and excesses among depots D1 to D3 might be eliminated by use of the transportation algorithm, described in Section 20.3, there would require to be direct physical links between depots at this logical level in order to put

---

[1] *Echelon* is derived from the French *échelle*, a ladder, and is military terminology for an arrangement of troops or equipment in parallel lines such that successive divisions are stepped somewhat out of alignment with each other (see inset — definition from *The Oxford Dictionary of Foreign Words and Phrases*, 1998, OUP).

into effect any solution arrived at. In terms of Figure 20.1, these links would be D1/D2, D2/D3 and D1/D3. Again based on Figure 20.1, links may be temporarily or even permanently established between all five depots; or directly between the regional warehouses R1 and R2; or between R1 and D4 and D5.[2]

The number and arrangement of echelons and nodes particular to a given company's distribution network will be decided by senior management, contributions to the debate being made by the distribution manager and the sales and marketing manager, all bearing in mind the geographic extent of the market for the company's products; the customer service it proposes to provide; and the finance needed to implement decisions. Establishment of a network involves considerable expense. To an even greater degree, however, it requires the accrual by staff of know-how and expertise in its operation. Usually, therefore, the physical infrastructure, systems and procedures must be put in place over many years as part of a long-term strategic marketing plan. (Hard lessons have been learned by companies attempting to set up networks quickly, the first being that the devil is in the detail.) Even as the plan is being developed, however, and certainly after it has been carried through, the facts on which it was originally based will have changed: the customer mix and the volumes of product sold; communications and transportation technologies; and the demographic and topographic characters of the areas served (topographic, for example, with regard to newly opened motorways, tunnels and bridges). Consequently, from time to time — perhaps every four or five years — the company's current distribution network should be reviewed to see how it might now be fine-tuned by the addition, removal or re-siting of a small number of the warehouses and depots that constitute it.

---

[2] Note that if a regional warehouse were to be set up adjacent to the factory, to serve the factory's geographic area, it must be described and treated as a distinct, logically separate facility in the distribution network, with the same formal procedures governing the flow of materials to it from the factory's stockroom as govern the flow of materials to other (remote) regional warehouses. Nodes can also be introduced into the network which are purely logical, and which fit into the overall system, but which have no physical existence. For example, major customers receiving full, direct loads may be entered at the highest echelon of the network as logical depots, so that they fit into the central replenishment system described in Section 20.2.

Factors to consider in reviewing the appropriateness of the network are: the mean elapsed time and variation in performance between the receipt of an order and the delivery of the goods (Figure 13.3); the percentage loss or gain in the recent past of market share (see Figure 2.4); the achievement or otherwise of customer service targets mentioned in Section 2.4 relating to the SOP system; and the cost required to support these operations. What changes are to be made to the network in the light of this evidence are matters of judgement very similar in nature to the judgement exercised in setting safety stock targets, described in sub-section 5.5.3.

A useful and systematic way of assisting the process, to generate ideas and, it may be hoped, to allow an initial proposal for change to be formulated, is to analyse the interplay of costs between the principal components of the distribution mix, in particular transportation, warehousing and inventory, as they are affected by the number of depots in the network.

20.1.2 Transport Costs

To see how such an analysis might proceed, first consider the trade-off between the number of depots distributing product, and so needing to be replenished, and transport costs. Transport costs can be classified under two headings. Firstly, there are the costs of *trunking* — i.e. the costs of operating large vehicles with full loads, travelling long distances to single destinations, usually on primary routes such as motorways. The greater the number of depots, the greater the trunking costs, although the rate at which the costs increase will get proportionally smaller as the number of depots rises, since the distances to be trunked will become rather less. Secondly, there are the costs of *local delivery* — i.e. the costs of delivering orders from a depot directly to many customers by relatively small vehicles, the distances involved being shorter but attention having to be paid to such customer-specific requirements as delivery timing. With only a few depots, local delivery costs will be very high, since the average distance to a customer from a stocking point will be large. As their numbers increase, so that each depot is located closer to the customers assigned to it, local delivery costs will fall in proportion.

The relations of trunking and local delivery costs to the number of depots in a network are illustrated respectively by Figures 20.2 and 20.3. The relation of composite transport costs — i.e. trunking plus local delivery — to the number of depots is illustrated by Figure 20.4.[3]

Figures 20.2, 20.3 and 20.4: Trunking, Local and Total Transport Costs in Relation to the Number of Depots

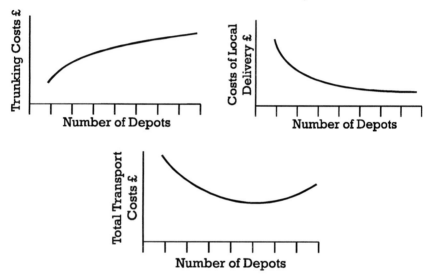

---

[3] The absence of numbered scales on any of the axes of the graphs in Figure 20.2 to Figure 20.9 may confirm the generality with which they are regarded by distribution experts, but may also cast doubt on the legitimacy of combining graphs with presumably different cost scales describing different phenomena (e.g. the summary graphs in Figures 20.8 and 20.9). Naturally, to carry out the analyses spoken of in the text, the company must obtain its own figures so that it can numerate the scales of its own graphs. However, some evidence at least of the equivalence, and therefore validity, of the graphed relationships in the text may be obtained from Martin Christopher et al. (1985), *Effective Distribution Management*, MCB University Press, Table 1. (Martin Christopher is Professor of Marketing and Logistics at The Cranfield School of Management, Bedfordshire, UK.) Christopher cites the breakdown of costs, as percentages of sales turnover, of "a large European grocery manufacturer" as follows: trunking 1.71 per cent; local delivery 2.09 per cent; SOP 0.89 per cent; warehousing (i.e. depot costs) 2.64 per cent; and protective packaging 2.00 per cent. (Inventory costs are omitted here.) The unnamed grocery manufacturer quotes a total distribution cost of 11.52 per cent of sales turnover. In industry generally, the figure is put at 10 per cent to 20 per cent.

20.1.3 Facilities Costs

The next trade-off considered is easily dealt with, namely the relationship between depot facilities costs and the number of depots. The facilities costs include: depot management and staff salaries; storage and equipment costs; and the costs of maintaining and operating the building itself. The approximation is made here that warehouse facilities costs rise linearly as the number of depots increases, as shown in Figure 20.5. Strictly, the rise in costs should be denoted by a series of small, equal vertical steps, one step for each extra depot.[4]

Figure 20.5: The Trade-off between the Cost of Warehousing Facilities and the Number of Depots in the Network

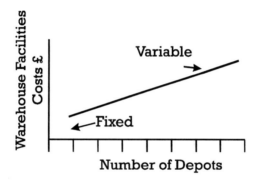

The third component of the distribution mix is inventory, or stock. However, in order to examine the trade-off between this and the number of depots, the elements that go to make up the total stock in the system must be considered separately, as below. The four terms used are those given by John Magee et al.[5]

20.1.4 Cycle stock (or working stock)

Cycle stock is defined here as the stock resulting from the lot sizes of manufacture of end products (or, if the company were to distribute bought-in items directly, purchasing lot sizes). The amount of cycle stock in the system is independent of the number of depots.

---

[4] Martin Christopher (1986), *The Strategy of Distribution Management*, Heinemann (see Figure 4.2 in the text).

[5] John F. Magee, William C. Copacino and Donald B. Rosenfield (1985), *Modern Logistics Management*, John Wiley & Sons, Chapter 4.

20.1.5 Smoothing stock (or stabilisation stock)

Smoothing stock is the stock manufactured before products are needed, in order to satisfy eventual actual demand, perhaps being manufactured in a pattern that will even out the use of capacity and achieve more economical plant operation, or to anticipate high seasonal sales (see "Manufacturing and Inventory Strategy", sub-section 6.1.1). As with cycle stock, the amount of smoothing stock in the network is also independent of the number of depots.

20.1.6 Transit stock (or pipeline stock)

The quantity of stock in transit, or "in the pipeline", is given by Equation 20.1, where time in transit includes not only all time spent en route, but time waiting to be despatched at one end of the journey and waiting to be unloaded at the other.

Transit Stock = Rate of Stock Movement × Time in Transit

Equation 20.1

Thus if the stock of a product is being withdrawn from a system at the rate of 1,000 units/week, and the transit time is 1½ weeks, the transit stock is 1,500 units. Within a geographically defined distribution network, the addition of a further depot will have virtually no effect on the total transit stock quantity, since the new depot merely diverts pipeline stock already present in the system, as illustrated in Figure 20.6. In the Figure, when there are two depots P and Q, transit stock to the two customers 1 and 2 is represented by (c + b + e). If Depot Q is removed, transit stock will be (a + d). The stock difference in reality as between these two scenarios is proportional to the small difference in distance in the Figure. Naturally, if the geographic area to be covered by the distribution network were to be expanded, say, by the introduction of a foreign country and the setting up of a depot there to service it, transit stock would increase according to Equation 20.1.

Figure 20.6: The Effect on Transit Stock of potentially removing a Depot from a Network

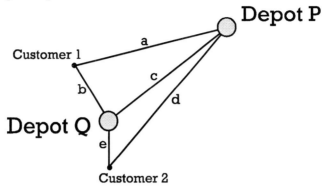

20.1.7 Safety stock

The first question to address in considering the effect of depot numbers on total safety stock is just where such safety stock is to be located. There are two options. The first is that all safety stocks — provided, we recall, to ensure product availability and so protect customer service — should be held at the depots where customer orders are received and dealt with. That is, referring again to the left-hand part of Figure 20.1, safety stocks should be calculated for the SKUs[6] located at Depot 1, Depot 2 and Depot 3, based on the variabilities of demand for them at each of these depots and duly held there in readiness. (The method chosen to calculate the amounts might perhaps be that described in sub-section 5.4.4.) The second option is that the safety stocks at one echelon should be amalgamated and held in readiness for despatch at the echelon one level immediately lower. Thus the safety stocks for customers at the three depots in Figure 20.3 might be aggregated and held at warehouse R1, one echelon removed from the final service point; that is, the combined safety stock is held as a buffer against variability in demand by the three depots on the regional warehouse. Under Option 2, some safety stock would also continue to be held at the depots, but in small quantities only, these being based on

---

[6] An SKU (pronounced as three separate letters) is a "stock keeping unit", this being a product of a particular identity (say, a Size 5 Hinge, code H500) qualified by its storage location (e.g. a Size 5 Hinge at the Lytham St Annes Depot, code H500/B/L or a Size 5 Hinge located at the source of manufacture in Blackpool, code H500/B/-).

the lead times of emergency replenishments from the regional warehouse and having an expectation of 100 per cent product availability there.

A good deal of intellectual effort continues to be expended to determine mathematically which of the two location options is correct.[7] Or rather, perhaps, the effort is expended simply to confirm what has already been demonstrated by a number of practitioners using linear programming trials and simulation. These have shown convincingly the correctness of Option 1. Thus R.G. Brown, whose distinguished name makes a welcome return to these pages, reports the use of linear programming by Kenneth F. Simpson, who has shown Option 1 to be superior in his paper "In-Process Inventories".[8] Again, Thomas Vollmann et al. cite the work of William Allen at Indiana University, employing simulation, and have reproduced a number of Allen's graphs of service level v. inventory, including a graph in which inventory was split 50:50 between the two echelons, showing the merits of Option 1 and the very poor performance of Option 2.[9] Vollmann states that in all of Allen's simulation runs, the results were the same, namely that carrying safety stock at the depot level was the most effective course of action. Vollmann et al. also cite results observed by Professor Karel van Donselaar regarding the distribution of TV service parts by Philips Consumer Electronics BV.[10]

---

[7] See, for example, Donald J. Bowersox, Michael Levy and Walter Zinn (1989), "The Effect of Inventory Centralization/Decentralization on Aggregate Safety Stock: the Square Root Law Revisited", *Journal of Business Logistics* (US), Vol. 10, No. 1, and other articles in this journal (e.g. Ronan, 1990). A general, popular *mise au point* of this subject by a logistics expert would be welcome.

[8] In *Materials Management Systems* (1977) and *Advanced Service Parts Inventory Control* (*ASPIC*) (1982), Brown cites Kenneth F. Simpson (1959), "In-Process Inventories", *Operations Research* (US magazine), Vol. 7, No. 6.

[9] Vollmann et al. (1988), op. cit., Figure 19.11. Vollmann et al. cite W.B. Allen (1983), "A Comparative Simulation of Central Inventory Policies for positioning Safety Stock in a Multi-Echelon Distribution System", PhD dissertation, Indiana University.

[10] Prof. K.H. van Donselaar's study cited by Vollmann was made at the University of Eindhoven, Holland. Eindhoven was for many years the location of the world headquarters of Philips Consumer Electronics BV (now Amsterdam). See also A.K. Chakravarty and A. Shtub (1986), "Simulated Safety Stock Allocation in a Two-Echelon Distribution System", *International Journal of Production Research* (UK magazine), Vol. 24, No. 5.

The argument supporting Option 1 is that the company's distribution and manufacturing performance, as the result of correctness in the operation of stock supply procedures and timeliness in effecting replenishments and material movements in the supply chain, at all levels *except* the final depot level, should be 100 per cent in accordance with plan. This should be provided for not by safety stocks and over-provision, but by high standards of internal performance, and, where emergencies arise, by the expediting of deliveries and similar supplementary action. With 100 per cent service at these lower echelons, the company is then free to concentrate its whole investment in safety stock — i.e. the discretionary stock it decides to provide to protect itself against uncertainty — at the one point in the supply chain where nothing can be done to remove such uncertainty — that is, at the depot level dealing directly with external customers. Option 1 is consequently able to provide the best possible customer service commensurate with the investment it is decided to make, in the way described in Chapter 5. Option 2 cannot be superior to Option 1. Indeed, given elements of genuine uncertainty at lower echelons, especially those arising from long replenishment lead times because of long transportation distances, by having diverted safety stock investment from the depots, customer service there is likely to be worse than it would otherwise have been.[11]

The second question to address is whether and by how much the safety stock in total for a given product, or rather, for its related SKUs held at all of the depots, would alter if a new depot were to be added to the system or an existing one removed from it. In answering it, we recall from Chapter 5 that the quantity of safety stock required to provide a chosen level of customer service, calculated by one or other of the methods described there, is directly connected with the variability of customer demand due to chance causes — i.e. it is closely connected with the standard deviation of the forecast errors. When a new depot is added to the distribution network, the demand for a given product at an exist-

---

[11] D. Rosenfield and M. Pendrock (1980), "The Effect of Warehouse Configuration Design on Inventory Levels and Holding Costs", *Sloan Management Review*, Vol. 21, No. 4. Also see John F. Magee, William C. Copacino and Donald B. Rosenfield (1985), *Modern Logistics Management*, John Wiley & Sons.

ing depot will be reduced, since a fraction of customer orders will be diverted from it to the new facility. When demand is so reduced, the element of variability connected with it will similarly be reduced, but not necessarily in direct proportion. That is, if demand for an SKU is reduced by 50 per cent, the amount of variability (and hence safety stock) connected with it will also decrease, but not necessarily by 50 per cent. When a depot is removed from the network, the demand for a given product at an existing depot will increase, since it will pick up part of the business from the depot removed. When demand is so increased, the element of variability will also increase, but again not necessarily in direct proportion. That is, if demand for an SKU is increased to 150 per cent of what it was, the amount of variability (and hence safety stock) will also increase, but not necessarily by 150 per cent.

The relationship between the degree of variability within sales demand (and hence the quantity of required safety stock) and the volume of demand that is subject to such variability varies according to an exponent α as follows:

$$\text{Variability} \propto \text{Demand}^{\alpha}$$

Suppose, then, that the total customer demand for a given product "i", stocked and sold by all the depots in a distribution network, is D_i. Then if there are n depots, on average the volume of demand for product i at each one is D_i/n.

The degree of variability applying to each depot is consequently $(D_i/n)^{\alpha}$. If the total safety stock in the network for product i is S_i, then S_i is made up of the individual safety stock amounts for i at each depot, as given by Equation 20.2. Equation 20.3 is derived from Equation 20.2.

$$S_i = n \times \left(\frac{D_i}{n}\right)^{\alpha} \qquad \text{Equation 20.2}$$

$$S_i = D_i^{\alpha} \, n^{1-\alpha} \qquad \text{Equation 20.3}$$

The value of α has been found empirically to vary from 0.6 to 0.9, and should be determined at the time by the planner for the products in question.[12] To illustrate the operation of Equation 20.3, the figures in Table 20.1 have been calculated assuming a value of $\alpha = 0.7$. It has been further assumed throughout the sequence of calculations that the total product demand D is constant. The first safety stock entry in the table when the number of depots is 1 has been arbitrarily chosen as 100 units. On this basis, by Equation 20.3, with the constancy of D, the subsequent safety stock entries as n increases from 2 to 8 are reflected by the progression of $n^{0.3}$ (i.e. $n^{(1-0.7)}$). For example, with n = 2, total safety stock is $100 \times 2^{0.3}$, and with n = 3, total safety stock is $100 \times 3^{0.3}$.

Table 20.1: Relative Amounts of Safety Stock Applying to "D" Units of Demand for an SKU as the Number of Depots in a Network Increases from 1 (base 100 units) to 8, Exponent $\alpha = 0.7$

No. of Depots	1	2	3	4	5	6	7	8
Total Safety Amount (units)	100	123.1	139.0	151.6	162.1	171.2	179.3	186.7
Safety per Depot (units)	100	61.6	46.3	37.9	32.4	28.5	25.6	23.3

Finally, a caveat should be entered regarding the setting of safety stocks as the number of depots grows larger. It was pointed out in Chapter 5, footnote 4, that safety stocks in retail outlets cannot be calculated by conventional means, and must be set in some other way, perhaps individually after investigation of the situation through simulation. In other words, it is suggested that there are limits to the applicability of Equation 20.2 and 20.3 as the number of depots n becomes large. The limits will depend on the sizes of the markets for the products concerned.

20.1.8 Total Network Costs

The four elements of the inventory component of the distribution mix — cycle stock, smoothing stock, transit stock and safety stock

---

[12] Magee et al. (1985), op. cit. The middle values of α (0.7 and 0.8) are often found to apply, although for faster moving products, the lower end of the scale is more likely. One instance where α in fact is greater than unity was given in Section 4.7, dealing with the recognition of lumpy products in a forecasting system by comparing the standard deviation of demand with the standard deviation of the forecast errors.

— can now be added together to examine the trade-off between the number of depots and the total cost of all inventory (valued as in sub-section 9.6.1). The relationship between the total of the four components and the number of depots is illustrated in Figure 20.7.

Figure 20.7: The Trade-off between the Combined Cost of Inventory and the Number of Depots in the Network

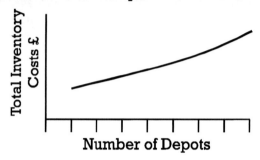

Note that an approximate relationship sometimes used by practitioners to obtain a quick estimate of the relative change in the total amount of inventory that would result from a change in the number of depots in a network is the rule of thumb represented by Equation 20.4, in which total inventory is held to be proportional to the square root of the number of depots:[13]

$$I_n = k\sqrt{n} \qquad \text{Equation 20.4}$$

where I_n = total inventory with n depots, k = constant and n = number of depots. Thus if a network with 9 depots (total inventory I_9) were to be reduced to 4 depots, then from Equation 20.4, the estimated reduced inventory holding would be:

$$I_9 \sqrt{4}/\sqrt{9}$$

— that is, inventory would fall by about 1/3 of the level of I_9.

---

[13] Safety stock is the predominant stock component of inventory, so that the closeness of the approximation in Equation 20.4 very much depends on the service level at which safety stock has been set. The approximation should not be used except for first-cut figures. For a complete, fully worked example of a stock calculation in a multi-depot environment, see Magee et al. (1985), op. cit., Chapter 11, Table 11.1.

The relation of the composite of warehousing facilities plus inventory to number of depots (i.e. Figure 20.5 plus Figure 20.7) is illustrated in Figure 20.8.

Figure 20.8: Warehousing Costs + Combined Inventory Costs in Relation to the Number of Depots in the Network

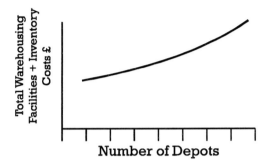

A final presentation of the interplay of costs between the principal components of the distribution mix is obtained by bringing together transportation, warehousing and inventory in a single figure through the combination of Figures 20.4 and 20.8. The results are shown in Figure 20.9.

Figure 20.9: Combined Transport, Warehousing and Inventory Costs against the Number of Depots in a Network

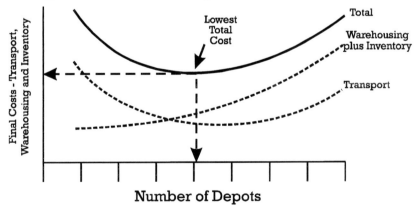

The usefulness of Figure 20.9 in the contemplation by the company of a revision of its distribution network is twofold. First, it reminds those considering it of the trade-offs involved in costs — for example, that eliminating a given depot may well cost more in extra trunking and local delivery costs to service the smaller network than it saves elsewhere. Secondly, the graph suggests that while there clearly is a minimum cost solution and a corresponding number of depots that would achieve it, because the "Total" curve is very shallow at the minimum cost point, then if a number is arrived at close to the optimal (either fewer of more), this will nevertheless yield a cost close to the true minimum. The sales and marketing department may believe that the presence in the field of a local depot is a great comfort to existing customers, and that in the selling effort its presence is taken as evidence by potential customers of the company's local commitment. Thus if it can be shown that, in purely operational terms, the addition of a further depot is more-or-less cost neutral from the viewpoint of expenditure overall, the argument may well be tipped in favour of its establishment because of the expectation that it will result in increased sales revenue.

20.1.9 The Siting of Network Outlets

If the analysis carried out in the preceding sub-sections lead to the decision that a new depot should be added to the network to cover a particular area where it is believed customer service is presently deficient, the final question remains as to where it should be sited in that area.

Formal procedures developed by distribution professionals to find an answer to the location question are invariably based on finding one that minimises cost. They are not and cannot be oriented to maximising potential new revenue or to pleasing existing customers, and this should be borne in mind by the sales and marketing manager in his scrutiny of the options and optimals that emanate purely from calculation.

Because of present-day network complexity and the sizes of geographic market areas, and the ready availability of powerful computing facilities that include graphics and online maps, by far the most common approach to finding a solution is through simulation.[14] A four-step procedure may be followed thus:

---

[14] The ILOG product *OPL Studio* may be used for this purpose.

Distribution

- **Step 1.** The lowest cost location is determined, low cost being defined as one having minimum total transport costs from the depot to customers. The method of doing so is likely to be by an iterative search procedure, perhaps in geographically large markets even employing the "great circle formula".[15] The assumptions in determining the location (which may be challenged in Step Four) are that transportation costs are linear with distance, and that the cost of building or renting a depot is uniform throughout the area under investigation. Although a minimum cost location is found, a number of practical alternatives with costs close to the minimum should also be determined for evaluation in Step Two.

- **Step 2.** Each potential location identified in Step One is evaluated to find the total cost to service customers therefrom. In particular, the effect on cost is simulated of potential changes to the existing network such as those previously mentioned — customer mix and volumes; demography and topography; etc. (Points in the area found to have equal costs can be joined on a map to form so-called *isocosts* — equal cost lines analogous to contours.)

- **Step 3.** The costs relating to transportation and inventory are fully and directly calculated.

- **Step 4.** The most promising models are investigated further through online simulation, the analyst imposing on them special, known practical conditions and constraints. These may include, say, the price of land; the close availability or otherwise of labour; the absence or existence of notorious local traffic problems; access to the motorway network; security considerations; and so on.[16]

---

[15] The *great circle formula* is a trigonometric relationship used in navigation to correct for the unsymmetrical curvature of the Earth in the calculation of geographic distances.

[16] The political and cost complexities involved in locating a foreign depot are very considerable: for example, cost issues include tax barriers and government grants. See N. Slack, S. Chambers, C. Harland, A. Harrison and R. Johnston (1995), *Operations Management*, Pitman Publishing, Chapter 6.

Where special constraints exist, especially those related to limited stockholding capacities at any of the network facilities, the use of simulation may be supplemented by the prior use of optimisation methods.

The creation of simulation models requires the painstaking collection of a great deal of data, the application of considerable expertise by the logistics manager, access to appropriate software and time. To obtain an approximate preliminary indication of a location quickly, therefore, especially when the area concerned is geographically small, it is often found useful to employ one or other of the simpler graphical and grid tools involving manual methods rather than a computer model.

One of the most elementary tools available to determine the *centroid* — the location that minimises the average distance from a depot to its various customer demand points — is a grid technique termed the "centre of gravity method".

In this method, the centre of gravity in the x and y co-ordinates of the area of concern are defined by Equations 20.5 and 20.6.

$$C_x = \frac{\sum d_{i_x} W_i}{\sum_i W_i} \qquad \text{Equation 20.5}$$

$$C_y = \frac{\sum d_{i_y} W_i}{\sum_i W_i} \qquad \text{Equation 20.6}$$

where C_x = x co-ordinate of the centre of gravity,
 C_y = y co-ordinate of the centre of gravity,
 D_{i_x} = x co-ordinate of the location of customer i;
 D_{i_y} = y co-ordinate of the location of customer i; and
 W_i = weight of goods moved from the depot to customer i.

(The geographic measurements and weightings do not need to be in any particular units: they must merely be self-consistent.) The centre of gravity derived from Equation 20.5 and 20.6 is often found to be close to the true centroid.[17]

---

[17] An indication that the centre of gravity determined by the method described in the text is not, in fact, identical to the least cost location is given by Alan Waller (Chapter 6 in John L. Gattorna (ed.) (1994), *Handbook of Logistics and Distribution Management*, Gower Publishing. A weight P (20 tons) is separated

Distribution

A homely extension of the centre of gravity method is the use of a mechanical analogue, known simply as the "weights-and-strings" method. A map corresponding to the area concerned is pasted onto a board, and weights in proportion to the transportation requirements of customers are suspended from the structure at the locations corresponding to those customers. The (literal) centre of gravity is found by balance as shown in Figure 20.10. Before one dismisses such a method compared to simulation or optimisation as artless or simplistic, he should remember that arriving at location decisions involves many other factors than the application of strict economics — business judgement, operational experience and local market knowledge, for example. The merit of the use of the weights-and-strings method in certain circumstances is that it promotes fruitful debate among those required to make the final decision.

Figure 20.10: Determination of a Depot Location by Centre of Gravity (Weights and Strings)

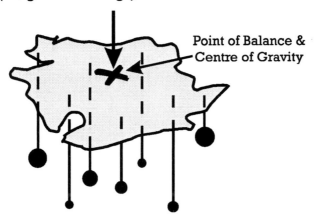

by a distance of 30 miles from a weight Q (10 tons). A depot located by the centre of gravity method would be at Place X in the sketch, 10 miles from P and 20 miles from Q, with total transportation requirements of 400 ton-miles. In fact, a more economical spot for the depot would be at the same location as P, incurring a cost of only 300 ton-miles.

20.2 THE REPLENISHMENT OF THE NETWORK

One means by which depots might acquire stock is through the individual placement of direct orders for SKUs on warehouses or on other points lower in the supply chain and the due fulfilment of those orders in the traditional way. If, however, satisfactory forecasts of demand for the SKUs at the depots can be formulated, the placement of orders and the requirement to anticipate and respond to them can be eliminated. Instead, the forecasts can be translated into depot replenishment requirements, together with replenishment requirements of prior stages of the supply chain and, ultimately, of the master schedule itself. The governing system of communication and stock supply necessary will heighten the responsiveness of the master schedule and the supply chain to customer demand at the depots. It will also reduce network stocks to the absolute minimum — i.e. to those needed to support the inter-site despatch lot quantities and the depot safety stocks.

Two alternative governing systems are described. The first, *distribution resource planning*, or DRP, is in almost every particular an image of closed-loop MRP described in Chapter 10. The second is a base stock method considered by many to be more practicable and more successful than DRP. It was devised by R.G. Brown and is termed here *fair shares*, for reasons that will become clear.

20.2.1 DRP

It is not the intention in this sub-section to go over again the procedures and logic of MRP or materials planning previously described in Chapters 9 and 10. Instead, the following DRP terms are presented to serve simultaneously as an introduction to the subject and as a reminder of the earlier Chapters: *scheduled receipts, planned orders* and *firm planned orders; the rescheduling assumption; partial and gross requirements;* and *the netting and exception logic.*

In the transformation of copies of their MRP software systems into DRP systems, software vendors are careful to substitute distribution terminology where it is more appropriate. Thus the manufacturing planning rules of MRP become "despatching rules", and MRP open orders become "orders in transit". Again, the levelling of the bill of materials carried out in materials planning and MRP has its counterpart in DRP. However, here, whereas the levelled materials bill descends from Level 0 (the MPS) to Level 99 (raw materials), the levelled distribution network descends from Level "–N" (the level number assigned to the highest echelon of the distribution network) to Level 0 (the MPS). The procedure in materials planning for the level-by-level computation of partial and gross requirements and the subsequent creation of plans, described in Section 9.3, similarly have their equivalents in DRP. That is, in DRP, the planning of replenishment quantities and despatch loads starts at the top of the network (i.e. at Level –N) and proceeds downwards, echelon by echelon, until the master schedule is reached at Level 0.

The DRP procedure and calculations will be illustrated for a simple two-echelon distribution network comprising two depots, A and B, and a master schedule source of supply as shown in Figure 20.11.

Figure 20.11: A Simple Two-Echelon Distribution Network

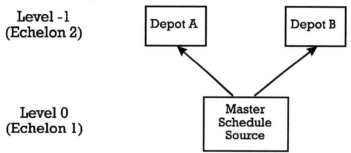

SKU 0122/A is stocked at Depot A and SKU 0122/B is stocked at Depot B, the on-hand quantities, despatch lot sizes and lead times of delivery being as given in Figures 20.12 and 20.13. In the figures, it is seen that the projected stock balances and the planned order requirements of each SKU have been calculated.

Figure 20.12: Requirements for SKU 0122/A at Depot A (DRP)

Transit Lead Time: 2
Safety Stock: 0
On-Hand (OH): 80 units
Past Due (PD): 0
Despatch Lots: 80 units

		Period										
		1	2	3	4	5	6	7	8	9	10	11	12
Sales Forecasts		10	10	15	15	17	17	20	20	30	20	20	20
In-Transit Orders	PD 0												
Projected Stock Balance	OH 80	70	60	45	30	13	76	56	36	6	66	46	26
Planned Order Despatch						80			80				

Figure 20.13: Requirements for SKU 0122/B at Depot B (DRP)

Transit Lead Time: 1
Safety Stock: 0
On-Hand (OH): 198 units
Past Due (PD): 0
Despatch Lots: 200 units

		1	2	3	4	5	6	7	8	9	10	11	12
Sales Forecasts		50	45	55	55	65	65	65	55	55	55	45	40
In-Transit Orders	PD 0												
Projected Stock Balance	OH 198	148	103	48	193	128	63	198	143	88	33	188	148
Planned Order Despatch				200			200				200		

Each planned order despatch in the two Figures gives rise to partial requirements for the parent product one echelon lower at the MPS source, taking account, of course, of the transit lead time of the product from the source to the particular depot. The lower level product's gross requirements are the sum of the partial requirements. These are set out in Figure 20.14. The master schedule to meet the gross requirements is calculated in the usual way through the mechanism of the projected stock balance. It is seen in the Figure that the MPS comprises two plans for 300 units each, needed in stock in Periods 4 and 8, manufacture to be started in Periods 3 and 7.

Figure 20.14: MPS Projected Stock Balance at Source

Lead Time of Supply: 1
Safety Stock: 0
On-Hand (OH): 255 units
Past Due (PD): 0
Planning Lots: 300 units

		1	2	3	4	5	6	7	8	9	10	11	12
Gross Requirements				200	80		200		80		200		
Scheduled Receipts	PD 0												
Projected Stock Balance	OH 255	255	255	55	275	275	75	75	295	295	95	95	95
Planned Orders				300				300					

Unfortunately, the practical problems to be overcome in operating DRP in a typical distribution environment are as severe as those encountered in operating closed-loop MRP in short lead time manufacturing. Perhaps the most intractable of them is that the DRP logic is essentially based on the scheduling of fixed despatch quantities for dates which are then liable to constant change, whereas distribution operations in reality often depend on arranging definite transport schedules and then synchronising materials movement with them. A number of ways of overcoming this apparent misfit have been suggested. One of them is to make extensive use of "period order despatch rules" — that is, make use of distribution versions of the POQ rule described in sub-section 9.6.2. A period order despatch rule will create a despatch plan for a specified date, the amount of material to be despatched being the requirements of the destination over a given period from the date of arrival of the replenishment to some later specified date.[18] When the requirements of the destination change, the despatch date stays the same, whereas the quantity to be despatched is varied.

Two further suggestions put forward by DRP expert André Martin are as follows:[19] (1) that the despatch dates arrived at by the DRP system should later be adjusted if necessary, directly at the VDU, to earlier times by the distribution planner; and (2) that ancillary software should be developed to move the DRP despatch dates to the scheduled transport dates. In either case, should the replenishment schedule be changed, the DRP system must be re-exploded through the levelled network to re-formulate and re-balance the lower-level gross requirements and plans.

Although stock shortages are not the rule with DRP, yet further troubles arise with the system should they occur. To deal with any such shortages without absorbing too much of the planner's time, Martin suggests rerunning the system perhaps two or three times, applying alternative despatching rules, each time involving increasingly small quantities. For example, a first run might re-

---

[18] To illustrate a "POD" rule referred to in the text: on 23 September, a despatch may be planned to take place on 30 October to a depot (destination) from a regional warehouse (source) to cover all calculated depot requirements for SKU X from 1 November to 14 November (say, 2,060 units). On 30 September, the recalculated depot requirements for X from 1 to 14 November are 1,280 units. The 30 October despatch date is maintained, but the despatch quantity is amended from 2,060 units to 1,280 units.

[19] André J. Martin (with Darryl V. Landvater) (1983), *DRP — Distribution Resource Planning*, Prentice-Hall. Also see A.J. Martin (1990), *Distribution Resource Planning: The Gateway to True Quick Response*, John Wiley.

create despatch quantities for only one week's supply, while a second might next eliminate the despatch of material intended to replenish safety stock.

Robert Brown's fair shares system avoids the problems inherent in matching specified replenishment lots to fixed transport schedules. With fair shares, replenishment lots are determined dynamically by the system from day to day, taking cognisance of stock available to be despatched, the transport arrangements given and the requirements of the network at the current time.

20.2.2 Fair Shares Replenishment ("DRPII")

The fair shares replenishment methodology, or DRPII, is more involved than DRP and will be described here in four stages, in all entailing eight figures. An example will be worked through based on the two-echelon distribution network in Figure 20.11 and the two depot SKUs, 0122/A and 0122/B. The same sales forecasts and starting stock balances for the SKUs apply as in Figures 20.12 and 20.13.

Stage 1: Communication of Net SKU Requirements to the MPS

Step 1. At a frequency corresponding to the time period on which the entire replenishment planning system is based (usually, therefore, each day or each week), the data records relating to all SKUs are scanned by the system to find the individual net replenishment needs of each one over the master schedule horizon. The net replenishment needs are the SKU quantities required to satisfy the SKUs' sales forecasts, taking account of stocks on hand. (That is, the net requirements for an SKU begin to arise when its projected stock balance falls to its safety stock level.) The net requirements for SKU 0122/A and SKU 0122/B are shown in Figures 20.15 and 20.16. Attention is drawn to the differences in these two Figures from the results applying to DRP in Figures 20.12 and 20.13. In the DRP example, the replenishment requirements calculated for the SKUs are based on the despatch lot sizes applying. In fair shares, the needs are simply net needs.

Figure 20.15: Requirements for SKU 0122/A at Depot A (Fair Shares)

Replenishments: net needs
Transit Lead Time: 2
Safety Stock: 0
On-Hand (OH): 80 units

	Period											
	1	2	3	4	5	6	7	8	9	10	11	12
Sales Forecasts	10	10	15	15	17	17	20	20	30	20	20	20
Projected Stock Balance OH 80	70	60	45	30	13	0	0	0	0	0	0	0
Net Requirements							4	20	20	30	20	20	20
Despatch of the Net Replenishments					4	20	20	30	20	20	20		

Figure 20.16: Requirements for SKU 0122/B at Depot B (Fair Shares)

Replenishments: net needs
Transit Lead Time: 1
Safety Stock: 0
On-Hand (OH): 198 units

	Period											
	1	2	3	4	5	6	7	8	9	10	11	12
Sales Forecasts	50	45	55	55	65	65	65	55	55	55	45	40
Projected Stock Balance OH 198	148	103	48	0	0	0	0	0	0	0	0	0
Net Requirements				7	65	65	65	55	55	55	45	40
Despatch of the Net Replenishments			7	65	65	65	55	55	55	45	40	

Step 2. In accordance with the usual principles, each SKU requirement at the depot level constitutes a partial requirement for the MPS product at the lower echelon, making due allowance for the lead time of delivery. In other words, the various sets of net requirements for the SKUs from Step 1 are combined and added to form the MPS gross requirements. After deducting the on-hand MPS stock, MPS plans to satisfy these requirements are formulated in the normal way by applying the product's planning rule.

The translation of the net requirements for SKUs 0122/A and 0122/B in Figures 20.15 and 20.16 to become the gross requirements of Product 0122 at the MPS level is shown in Figure 20.17. MPS plans of 300 units each are seen to be required in stock in Periods 7 and 11. It is noted that these dates are three periods later than the dates of the requirements illustrated previously in Figure 20.14

for DRP, reflecting the fact, previously stated, that fair shares is satisfying net requirements only rather than despatch lot quantities.

Figure 20.17: MPS Projected Stock Balance at Source

Lead Time of Supply: 1 Safety Stock: 0 On-Hand (OH): 255 units Past Due (PD): 0 Planning Lots: 300 units		Period										
		1	2	3	4	5	6	7	8	9	10	11	12
Gross Requirements		0	0	7	69	85	85	85	75	75	65	40	
Scheduled Receipts	PD 0												
Projected Stock Balance	OH 255	255	255	248	179	94	9	224	149	74	9	269	
Planned Orders							300				300		

Stage 2: Determination of the Products that are to be Assessed for Replenishment

The net requirements of all SKUs referred to in Step 1, Stage 1, are considered again to determine which of the SKUs, if any, will require replenishment over the next "X days". The value of X is set on a system-wide or individual basis and is chosen so as to trap a suitable number of qualifying candidates. If X is too small, there will be an insufficient choice of replenishment options for making up potential despatch loads at the later stages of the fair shares procedure. If X is too large, data will be processed unnecessarily.

The value of X in a typical system is likely to be set at about 14 days. In the example here, however, for illustration purposes, X is set at three periods. Figure 20.18 is derived from Figures 20.15 and 20.16. Looking ahead three periods in this new Figure, we see that SKU 0122/A is not trapped — the replenishment requirements over the next three periods are 0, 0 and 0. From the Figure, however, SKU 0122/B is trapped. Its replenishment requirements over the three periods are 0, 0 and 7 units.

Distribution

Figure 20.18: Trapping the SKUs which become critical "X" Periods Ahead (X = 3)

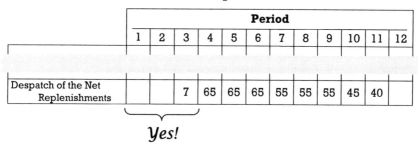

If any SKU is found to need replenishment over the chosen time period ahead, all of the SKUs relating to the corresponding parent product are considered together at the next stage of the fair shares procedure. In the example, because SKU 0122/B is trapped, both it and 0122/A are considered at Stage 3 (as well as the parent product itself).

Stage 3: The Calculation of the Fair Shares Replenishments

At this point, for each product identified in Stage 2, stock available at the lower echelon in the network is notionally allocated as replenishment for the higher echelon. That is, parent product replenishments from the first level are notionally allocated to fulfil the requirements of all their corresponding SKUs at the next level up. Note that the allocations at this stage are indeed strictly notional: the replenishment quantities determined are what might be sent. Decisions as to what actually will be sent are not made until Stage 4 when transportation options are considered.

The individual notional SKU allocations are built up in two steps. Step 1 applies only to SKUs with low stocks or where current stock shortages exist. For those in this position, the system calculates the minimum SKU replenishment quantities needed urgently and the latest dates by which they must be despatched, the total quantity of stock involved being then set aside from the starting stock amount. In Step 2, maximum potential distribution replenishments are calculated for these SKUs, and all others, based on what stock remains available. The allocations of this remaining stock made to the various SKUs are worked out on the principle of *fair shares for all*, a fair share being arrived at by taking into account individual net needs up to some specified time in the future.

Step 1: Calculating the Minimum Requirements. As stated, Step 1 of Stage 3 is concerned with the calculation and reservation of minimum stock requirements relating to just those SKUs with low stock. The stock of an SKU is deemed to be low if its balance is projected to fall below its safety stock level over the SKU's replenishment lead time. If an SKU is at risk in this way, a replenishment is notionally allocated to it from what is available to bring its stock up to the safety level. Because the relative stock levels of the various SKUs are likely to be different, so that there will consequently be different degrees of urgency for material, and since there may at times be insufficient stock available to satisfy all competing demands for it, allocation proceeds according to a *hierarchy of need*. Four gradations constituting the hierarchy are given below. These broadly correspond to rules suggested by Brown.[20] The rules, however, are pragmatic and therefore likely to differ at least in the detail from one software system to another according to the views of their programmers.

The Hierarchy of Need:

a) First allocate available stock to fill outstanding backorders for SKUs at any destination/depot. If there is insufficient master warehouse stock to do so, fill the backorders relating to the most important customers. Subtract any stock allocated from the stock quantity available.

---

[20] R.G. Brown (1982), *Advanced Service Parts Inventory Control (ASPIC)*, Second edition, Materials Management Systems Inc., Chapter 14.

b) Secondly, allocate stock so as to prevent the calculated projected stock balance of any SKU falling below zero over its replenishment lead time. If there is insufficient stock to do this, fill as many locations as completely as possible, holding back and earmarking the stock that remains at the source for contingency shipments later. Debit allocated stock from the stock available.

c) Thirdly, allocate stock so as to replenish the safety stocks of all SKUs. If there is insufficient stock fully to accomplish this, allocate what is available *pro rata*. Debit the allocated stock from the stock available. (Notice that this rule has the effect of equalising customer service across the network, at least as regards stock availability.)

d) Fourthly, keep back sufficient stock to make up any safety stock that might be deficient at the parent product/prior echelon stage.

In the example involving SKU 0122/A and 0122/B, and parent product 0122, the allocations under the four headings are as follows: (a) none — there are no backorders; (b) none — neither SKU requires an immediate despatch; (c) none — both of the depot safety stocks are zero; (d) none — the safety stock on 0122 at the lower echelon is zero.

Consequently, with regard to the 255 units of product 0122 available to be notionally allocated during this Step, none needs to be so allocated to fulfil minimum requirements and the example proceeds to Step 2.

Step 2: Calculating the Maximum Requirements. All stock remaining after Step 1 is now available to be notionally apportioned to each SKU by the fair shares method. Fair shares assigns a notional replenishment to each SKU covering its net requirements from the current period to a particular date in the future. (That is, the date in the future is the same one for all SKUs.) At this point, however, the date, or period ahead, is not known. The following simple three-part procedure may be used to determine it:

1. Examine the cumulative net replenishment requirements of all SKUs over the next one day, two days, three days, etc. (The individual total SKU requirements were calculated at Step 2, Stage 1, and are the same as the gross requirements at the prior echelon.)

2. Compare the cumulative net replenishment requirements in (1) to the total stock available to be allocated. Since the cumulative replenishments must be less than or equal to the total stock available to allocate, the period ahead can now be determined directly from (1).

3. Notionally allocate each individual SKU's replenishment based on its total net requirements from the current period to the period determined in (2).

Returning to the example with the two SKUs, the stock available to be allocated in Step 2 is 255 units, this being the on-hand quantity of 0122. Figure 20.19 is derived from Figure 20.17, and shows the gross requirements for product 0122 over the 12 periods. The gross requirements are synonymous with the total net SKU requirements. Figure 20.19 also shows the cumulative gross requirements from period to period. It is seen from these that the on-hand available stock will satisfy cumulative net SKU requirements for six periods ahead.

Figure 20.19: The Gross Requirements for Parent Product 0122 (i.e. the total requirements for the SKUs)

	Period											
	1	2	3	4	5	6	7	8	9	10	11	12
Gross Requirements	0	0	7	69	85	85	85	75	75	65	40	
Cumulative Requirements	0	0	7	76	161	246	331	406	481	546	586	

Just below 255 (pointing to 246)

It is next necessary to determine the total requirements for each of the SKUs for the six periods ahead. These values are obtained from Figure 20.20. Figure 20.20 is derived from Figure 20.18, but with the original period by period net requirements accumulated to give the cumulative net requirements for despatch. The Figure shows that

Distribution

the requirement for six periods ahead for SKU 0122/A is 44 units, and the requirement for six periods for SKU 0122/B is 202 units.

To summarise, what have been calculated by the end of Stage 3 for each SKU are the minimum quantity, if any, which must be despatched and the maximum quantity which could be despatched, together with a date when each potential replenishment is needed.

Figure 20.20: Despatch Requirements and Cumulative Requirements for the two SKUs

SKU 0122/A

	Period											
	1	2	3	4	5	6	7	8	9	10	11	12
Despatch of the Net Replenishments				4	20	20	30	20	20	20		
Cumulative Despatch Requirements				4	24	44	74	94	114	134		

SKU 0122/B

	Period											
	1	2	3	4	5	6	7	8	9	10	11	12
Despatch of the Net Replenishments				7	65	65	65	55	55	55	45	40
Cumulative Despatch Requirements				7	72	137	202	257	312	367	412	452

Stage 4: Deciding on the Physical Despatches

The first task at Stage 4 is to round each SKU's maximum replenishment to a practical shipment quantity as close as possible to the replenishment quantity, but not beyond it. (Algorithms to work out practical shipment quantities may not be applied to minimum replenishment quantities. Due to their urgency, they are likely to be sent in exactly the amounts recommended.) Note that a practical shipment quantity is not a standard planned lot size as it is in DRP. Practical quantities are calculated at the time within the fair shares system by the application of lot sizing rules attached to the SKUs, and such associated data as the capacities of over-packing boxes, minimum and maximum pallet loads, unit weights, dimensions and so on. When each SKU's practical shipment quantity has been arrived at, other data can also be associated with the potential despatch, such as how long the replenishment is calculated to last at its destination and its total weight and cube.

In the worked example, it is supposed that the nearest practical shipment quantity to 44 units of SKU 0122/A is 25 units, and that the nearest shipment to 202 units of 0122/B is 200 units. From Figure 20.20, it is seen that with a shipment of 25 units, stock of 0122/A at Depot A will then last for five periods (not the full six periods), while with 200 units of 0122/B, stock will last at Depot B for approximately six periods. The data and options are summarised in need date order in Figure 20.21. Other data such as weight, cube and the SKU stock currently at the destination that might typically be included in output have been fabricated and included in the figure.

Figure 20.21: Despatch Options in Need Date Order for SKUs 0122/A and 0122/B

Depot	Latest Ship Period	SKU	Min. Amount	Max. Amount	Practical Amount	Days	Weight	Cube	Depot Stock
B	3	0122	7	202	200	6	20	8	198
A	4	0122	4	44	25	5	3	1	80

Figure 20.22 is the last illustration relating to fair shares replenishment, and is intended to be a somewhat more realistic representation of final output than Figure 20.21. The replenishment quantities, latest despatch dates and other invented data relating to 18 different SKUs are shown, all involving despatches either to Depot A or Depot B.[21] The critical difference between DRP and fair shares can be seen in this final Figure. In fair shares, existing transport schedules to the depots are accepted without change: the system "loads" vehicles with the practical shipment quantities (column 6), in the sequence of their latest despatch dates, continuing to do so until each vehicle's capacity is reached. After the despatches have been authorised, the stock balances at the sending and receiving locations are adjusted. At the start of the next period, the whole process begins again from the beginning (i.e. no replenishment plans are carried forward).

---

[21] Note that SKU 1177/A appears in Figure 20.22 twice. Although its maximum fair share is 120 units, the practical shipment quantity is only 60 units, and depot stock will last only 2 periods. Consequently, 1177/A appears on the list two periods later for a second time with another recommended despatch of 60 units, making up the original 120 units.

Figure 20.22: Representation of Despatch Options to Two Depots for 18 SKUs

Depot	Latest Ship Period	SKU/ Product	Min. Amount	Max. Amount	Practical Ship Qty	Periods	Weight	Cube	Depot Stock
A	1	1206	38	38	38	4	55	3	0
A	1	1472	6	6	6	2	12	8	0
A	1	1691	40	40	40	9	30	12	10
B	1	1092	112	112	112	6	55	7	9
B	1	1727	14	188	188	9	44	5	27
A	2	1177	30	120	60	2	25	8	20
A	2	1401	28	125	125	17	30	4	30
A	2	1666	12	12	12	9	55	5	2
B	2	1179	52	164	150	12	100	4	30
A	3	0077	6	6	6	4	18	30	4
B	3	1810	14	57	50	9	14	5	12
B	3	0122	7	202	200	6	20	8	198
B	3	0790	18	32	32	4	8	5	12
B	3	1414	20	100	100	9	12	5	18
A	4	0122	4	44	25	5	3	1	80
A	4	1177	0	60	60	2	25	8	20
B	4	1200	22	114	100	5	25	7	18
B	5	1505	68	1032	200	10	44	102	100
B	5	1515	14	127	125	8	30	3	30

The benefits to the company of adopting either DRP or fair shares are greatly reduced inventory holding in the distribution network and far better operational decision-taking due to the obtaining of early notice of future shipment requirements. A benefit to the manufacturing manager is the greater confidence he is able to place in the appropriateness of the master schedule to the demands likely to be made on it by distribution.

Dominating the issue of choice between DRP and fair shares are the practical problems associated with DRP referred to earlier. Not surprisingly, successful DRP implementations seem to have been associated largely with low variety bulk distribution, while fair shares is associated with higher variety distribution in a more usual environment.[22]

20.3 NETWORK TRANSSHIPMENTS

Although imbalances of stock at nodes within the distribution network are hardly the rule when the company operates a centrally managed replenishment system such as DRP or fair shares, they may arise if replenishments are made through individual ordering in the traditional way. They may also arise when there have been failures in manufacturing supply or transport, or when similar logistical misfortunes have occurred.

One of the final lines of defence in replenishment is to transfer stock directly from locations with excesses to locations with shortages. Such stock transfers, or *transshipments* as they are usually called in distribution, may be between any two points in the network, although what is often in the distribution planner's mind when he speaks of transshipments are transfers between depots at the highest echelon.

Although there are practical limits to its use, the classic method for determining which excess stocks are to be sent to which shortage locations so as to effect transfer at least cost is through the *transportation algorithm*.[23] The transportation algorithm is a further

---

[22] An example of a successful DRP implementation has been given by Richard Watkins, relating to the distribution of active chemical ingredients by ICI Agrochemicals in Teesside to 40 National Companies within the UK. (Richard V. Watkins, "The Use of Distribution Requirements Planning in an International Business", *Proceedings of the BPICS Annual Conference*, December 1989, pp. 9–19. BPICS is now the Institute of Operations Management. ICI Agrochemicals is now Terra Nitrogen.) The DRP package used was from BT Smith Associates, modified and integrated with Cincom's MRPS MRP system. Users of fair shares (LOGOL) include General Motors, Eli Lilley and the US Navy (see footnote 18, Chapter 4).

[23] The transportation algorithm was first published in 1961 by A. Charnes and W.W. Cooper (*Management Models and Industrial Applications, Vols. I and II*, John Wiley). It has been employed with great success in determining optimum transshipments of relatively homogeneous, heavy products requiring prompt attention — two instances of its use relate to transshipping tomato ketchup and transshipping beer. It has apparently not been successful in the management of depot transfers of white and brown consumer goods. (Brown goods are toasters, irons and vacuum cleaners; white goods include fridges, freezers and washing machines.) Evidence of the circumstances of its success and failure

Distribution

example of combinatorial optimisation, illustrated in Figure 12.8 in connection with the travelling salesman problem and the minimisation of machine set-up times. The technique is a close relative of the mathematical programming models described at length in sub-section 12.4.2 in relation to bottleneck scheduling.

The operation of the transportation algorithm is described here by reference to a distribution network with three depots A, B and C with excess stocks and three depots P, Q and R with shortages. The depots with excesses are known as *sources* and the depots with shortages are known as *sinks*. It is assumed: (1) that the cost to transport one unit of product from any source to any sink is known; and (2) that the transport costs found are proportional to the number of units transferred (i.e. that the cost to transfer six units is 6 × the cost to transfer one). Initially, also, the assumption is made that the total amount of excess stock at the sources equals the total shortages at the sinks. This condition is imposed only for simplicity at the start. Towards the end of the explanation, a small modification to the procedure will be described to deal with the normal situation of excesses and shortages not being equal.

20.3.1 Excesses and Shortages Equal

The starting position is illustrated for the six depots by Figure 20.23. In the somewhat quaint language of the transportation algorithm, Figure 20.23 is referred to as the *initial tableau*. It will be seen that the three source rows in the diagram intersect the three sink columns, creating nine *squares*. A square is referenced here by its row and column, or source and sink — for example, AQ or BR. When given as such, the reference may have one of two meanings depending on context. First, it may literally mean the consideration of a stock transfer. That is, AQ could mean the

---

was related to the author by Mike Parsonage, a logistics expert formerly with Bass Brewers Ltd. and with Comet plc, Rickmansworth. The algorithm has also been used directly in optimised production scheduling. An example of such involving 41 machines and 100 parts at Ganton Technologies, USA, is given by Professor Jayavel Sounderpandian and Bala Balashanmugam (1991), "Multi-product, Multifacility Scheduling using the Transportation Model: A Case Study", *APICS Quarterly Journal*, Fourth Quarter, p. 69. The transportation algorithm software used was TSA88, one of a comprehensive range of optimisation products from Eastern Software Products, Alexandria, VA.

transportation of material from Depot A to Depot Q, and BR the transportation of material from Depot B to Depot R. (Where appropriate in these circumstances, the notation A→Q and B→R etc. has been used.) Alternatively, in the course of the explanation below, it may simply be a grid reference directing the reader's attention to a place within a tableau under study at the time (i.e. AQ = the intersecting square at A and Q).

It is observed that in each of the squares in the initial tableau, there is a small square in the upper right corner containing a number. The number is the cost in money to move 1 unit of product from the source to the sink. For example, the cost to move one unit of material from A to Q is £8 and the cost to move 1 unit of material from B to R is £14. It is also observed in the initial tableau that, as stated in the sub-section title above, the sum of the excess stocks at the three sources (62 at A, 90 at B and 88 at C = 240 units) is equal to the sum of the shortages at the sinks (75 at P, 108 at Q and 57 at R = 240).

Figure 20.23: The Initial Tableau

FROM \ TO	DEPOT P	DEPOT Q	DEPOT R	SENDING DEPOT EXCESSES ▼
DEPOT A	5	8	7	62
DEPOT B	15	25	14	90
DEPOT C	10	16	26	88
RECEIVING DEPOT SHORTAGES →	75	108	57	240 / 240

The Initial Solution

To find an initial transshipment plan regardless of cost, we begin the allocation of excess stocks to sink depots starting at the top left-hand intersection of the tableau, referred to as the *northwest corner* (i.e. square AP).

Distribution

In the northwest corner, as much stock as possible is allocated to the sink depot P by the source depot A. Since this exhausts the excess stock available at A, but still leaves P with 13 units of unsatisfied requirements, the allocation path is extended. Extensions are always *downwards or to the right*, allocating as much as possible at each point along the way until the receiving depots are satisfied.

The initial solution is shown in Figure 20.24. The source amounts allocated to the sinks are shown in circles in the various squares. The circles are referred to as *stepping stones*, and a square containing a stepping stone is known as a *stone square*. (It is seen that the stepping stones make a "path" from the top left of the tableau to the bottom right.) The cost of the first solution can also now be evaluated as shown in Table 20.2.

Figure 20.24: The Initial Solution (£4,408)

TO \ FROM	DEPOT P	DEPOT Q	DEPOT R	SENDING DEPOT EXCESSES ↓
DEPOT A	5 (62)	8	7	62
DEPOT B	15 (13) →	25 (77)	14	90
DEPOT C	10	16 ↓ (31) →	26 (57)	88
RECEIVING DEPOT SHORTAGES →	75	108	57	240 / 240

Table 20.2: Cost of the Initial Solution

Source/Sink	No. of Units	Cost per Unit of this Move	Total Cost
A→P	62	£5	£310
B→P	13	£15	£195
B→Q	77	£25	£1,925
C→Q	31	£16	£496
C→R	57	£26	£1,482
		Solution Total	£4,408

In order to find the least cost allocation plan, a series of successively better solutions is formulated through the *stepping stone procedure*. This consists of examining the effect on cost of redirecting, or reassigning, excess stock present at a stone square to an unused square in the tableau. If a reduction in cost is found to result, the alternative assignment is duly made and a new solution is thereby reached. When no improvement can be found, the solution already reached at that point is the optimum.

The First Improved Solution

Once more obeying the rule of top to bottom, left to right, and beginning the investigation in the northwest corner, examination of Figure 20.24 shows that there are four alternative ways stock might be reassigned from a stone square to an unused square. These are: from AP to AQ; from AP to AR; BQ to BR and BP to CP. It is next necessary to evaluate each of them in detail to find which would result in the greatest saving. When this has been done, the best alternative assignment is chosen to form the basis of the First Improved Solution. Note that to evaluate the relative merits of the alternatives, it is quite sufficient simply to consider the reassignments as they apply to a single unit of material.

- **AP to AQ.** Consider the reassignment of 1 unit of stock from the stone square AP to the unused square AQ. There is a saving in cost of £5 (A→P) and an incurrence of cost of £8 (A→Q). However, if 1 unit of stock is moved from AP to AQ, the balance of stock assigned to the sink depots would be disturbed. That is, Depot P would be receiving only 74 units and Depot Q would now be receiving 109 units. To compensate for this and restore the balance, a reverse move must be made from any stone square currently contributing to Depot Q to any square (stone or unused) that will contribute to Depot P. In this particular case, such a compensatory move would be of 1 unit of stock from stone square BQ to stone square BP. The cost effect of the reverse move would be a saving in cost of £25 (B→Q) and an incurrence of cost of £15 (B→P). The net cost of the first trial move and its twin compensatory move is consequently –£7 (–£5, +£8, –£25, +£15).

- **AP to AR.** The reassignment of 1 unit from stone square AP (−5) to unused square AR (+7) creates an imbalance at Depots P and R. This is corrected by the move of 1 unit from stone square CR (−26) to unused square CP (+10). The net effect is −£14 (−5 + 7 − 26 + 10).
- **BQ to BR.** Reassignment from stone square BQ (−25) to BR (+14) is compensated by a move from stone CR (−26) to stone CQ (+16). Net effect: −£21.
- **BP to CP.** Reassignment from BP (−15) to CP (+10) is compensated by the reverse move from CQ (−16) to BQ (+25), with net effect +£4.

The most effective reassignment is from BQ to BR. This is chosen and is now pursued. The others are abandoned.

We wish to reassign as many units as possible from stone square BQ to unused square BR. In the tableau of the Initial Solution (Figure 20.24) we see that there are 77 units at stone BQ. However, it is not possible to allocate all 77 units to BR, since the shortage at Depot R is confined to 57 units. Consequently, only 57 units are redirected, leaving 20 units behind at BQ. In the compensatory move, of course, all 57 units at CR are moved to CQ, giving a total in CQ of 88.

The tableau for the First Improved Solution can now be compiled and is shown in Figure 20.25. The cost of the solution is calculated in the same way as in Table 20.2 and is £3,211 (62 × £5 + 13 × £15 + 20 × £25 + 57 × £14 + 88 × £16).

Figure 20.25: The First Improved Solution (£3,211)

TO → ↓ FROM	DEPOT P	DEPOT Q	DEPOT R	SENDING DEPOT EXCESSES ↓
DEPOT A	5 (62)	8	7	62
DEPOT B	15 (13)	25 (20)	14 (57)	90
DEPOT C	10	16 (88)	26	88
RECEIVING DEPOT SHORTAGES →	75	108	57	240 / 240

The Second Improved Solution

Starting with the first improved Solution, there are four alternative reassignments that might be made, given below with their necessary compensatory balancing moves. (The reader must, of course, follow these moves diagrammatically through the new tableau in Figure 20.25, not the previous tableau in Figure 20.24.)

- **AP to AQ.** Stone AP to unused square AQ (– 5 + 8) compensated by stone BQ to stone BP (– 25 + 15). Net: –£7.
- **AP to AR.** Stone AP to unused square AR (–5 + 7) compensated by stone BR to stone BP (– 14 + 15). Net: +£3.
- **BP to CP.** Stone BP to unused square CP (–15 + 10), compensated by stone CQ to stone BQ (– 16 + 25). Net: +£4.
- **CQ to CR.** Stone CQ to unused square CR (–16 + 26) compensated by stone BR to stone BQ (– 14 + 25). Net: +£21.

The move AP to AQ is consequently selected (it is the only one that will effect an improvement on the First Solution). However, although there are 62 units at AP, only 20 of them can be moved, with 42 staying behind. The reason lies with the required compensatory move from BQ to BP: since there are only 20 units at stone BQ, only 20 units can take part in the reverse move. This consequently limits the AP move. The tableau for the Second Improved Solution is given by Figure 20.26. The cost of the solution is £3,071.

Figure 20.26: The Second Improved Solution (£3,071)

TO \ FROM	DEPOT P	DEPOT Q	DEPOT R	SENDING DEPOT EXCESSES ↓
DEPOT A	5 (42)	8 (20)	7	62
DEPOT B	15 (33)	25	14 (57)	90
DEPOT C	10	16 (88)	26	88
RECEIVING DEPOT SHORTAGES →	75	108	57	240 / 240

The Third Improved Solution

- **AQ to AR.** (– 8 + 7) compensated by BR to BQ (– 14 + 25); net effect: +10.

- **BP to BQ.** (– 15 + 25) compensated by CQ to CP (– 16 + 10); net effect: +4.

- **BP to CP.** (– 15 + 10) compensated by CQ to BQ (– 16 + 25); net effect: +4.

- **AP to CP.** (– 5 + 10) compensated by CQ to AQ (– 16 + 8); net effect: –3.

Thus the only reassignment which improves the Second Solution is from stone square AP to unused square CP, compensated by the reverse move from stone CQ to stone AQ. The move of 42 units from AP to CP can be made in full, this being compensated by 42 units from CQ to AQ.

The tableau for the Third Improved Solution is give by Figure 20.27. The cost of it is £2,945.

Figure 20.27: The Third Improved (Optimal) Solution (£2,945)

TO \ FROM	DEPOT P	DEPOT Q	DEPOT R	SENDING DEPOT EXCESSES ↓
DEPOT A	5	8 (62)	7	62
DEPOT B	15 (33)	25	14 (57)	90
DEPOT C	10 (42)	16 (46)	26	88
RECEIVING DEPOT SHORTAGES →	75	108	57	240 / 240

The Fourth Improved Solution

Four moves can be tried: AQ to AR; BP to BQ; CQ to CR; and CP to CR. It can be shown that each of them results in an overall positive cost. Consequently, the Third Solution represented by the tableau in Figure 20.27 is the optimal plan. (The optimal cost is some 67 per cent of the cost of the initial solution.)

20.3.2 Excesses and Shortages Not Equal

Very clearly, excess stocks at sources will rarely equal shortages at sinks. To deal with a case of inequality, a trick is employed common to the solutions of many types of combinatorial optimisation problems. Thus:

(a) Excesses > Shortages

When excesses are greater than shortages, a dummy sink location is introduced into the model having a shortage equal to the difference between them. The unit transportation cost to the dummy sink location from each source is set to zero. This will ensure that the excess stock is allocated to the dummy shortage location as part of the optimal solution. For example, if the excess at Depot B was 900 units rather than 90 units, and a dummy sink depot, "Depot S", were to be set up with a shortage of 810 units, the first 810 units of the excess stock at Depot B would be certain to be allocated to S and the final tableau would be as shown in Figure 20.28. The calculations would otherwise be as given previously.

Figure 20.28: Excesses Greater than Shortages

TO → FROM ↓	DEPOT P	DEPOT Q	DEPOT R	DUMMY DEPOT S	SENDING DEPOT EXCESSES ↓
DEPOT A	⌐5	⌐8 (62)	⌐7	⌐0	62
DEPOT B	⌐15 (33)	⌐25	⌐14 (57)	⌐0 (810)	900
DEPOT C	⌐10 (42)	⌐16 (46)	⌐26	⌐0	88
RECEIVING DEPOT SHORTAGES →	75	108	57	810	1050 / 240 + 810

(b) Shortages > Excesses

In a manner analogous to (a), when shortages are greater than excesses, the situation is resolved by the creation of a dummy source having excess stock equal to the difference and a unit transportation cost of zero. In the original example, if the shortage at Depot P was 750 units rather than 75 units, a dummy source location with excess stock of 675 units and zero cost is introduced, termed here Depot D. This will ensure that the first 675 units of Depot P's shortages are "satisfied" (at zero cost) by the excess stock at dummy Depot D as part of the optimal solution. The optimal solution is illustrated by the tableau in Figure 20.29.

Figure 20.29: Shortages Greater than Excesses

TO ╲ FROM	DEPOT P	DEPOT Q	DEPOT R	SENDING DEPOT EXCESSES ↓
DEPOT A	5	8 (62)	7	62
DEPOT B	15 (33)	25	14 (57)	90
DEPOT C	10 (42)	16 (46)	26	88
DUMMY DEPOT D	0 (675)	0	0	675
RECEIVING DEPOT SHORTAGES →	750	108	57	240 + 675 / 915

Note that the application of the transportation algorithm to an environment involving many different products is likely to be complicated beyond practicality by the existence of backhaul opportunities. For example, suppose at Depot B there is excess stock of SKU X and a shortage of SKU Y. Also suppose at Depot R there is a shortage of SKU X and excess stock of SKU Y. Then the overall assignment by an algorithm of excess stocks to sinks must clearly take account, in this instance, of the special excess/shortage relationship between B and R, and the opportunity to reduce cost by transporting X and backhauling Y. Although full linear programming might be used to resolve such complexities, the limitations of simplicity and homogeneity implied in footnote 23 are readily understandable.

20.4 TRANSPORT OF THE GOODS

It is recalled from the introductory remarks that this chapter is confined to the control and management by a manufacturing company of its own distribution outlets. So although transport is a speciality within industry of very considerable importance and scope, encompassing not only everyday means and modes of transporting manufactured product — say, road vehicles, freight trains and container vessels — but those which are less familiar, employed on unfamiliar routes, perhaps in foreign countries, consideration of the subject here is strictly limited.

Touching first on road transport, the self-evident advantage of this mode is that it offers a door-to-door service, with goods remaining on the vehicle. The company may own and operate its own fleet (known in distribution jargon as *own account*). Alternatively, a semi-permanent arrangement may be entered into with a haulage company, the haulier to carry out all distribution operations on the manufacturer's behalf, with dedicated vehicles, very probably bearing the manufacturer's insignia. Road transport services are also hired on an occasional basis, of course, from a national pool of many thousands of *common carriers*.

From the UK, the transport by road of goods into Europe is typically by trailer or in 12-metre containers (see sub-section 18.1.2). Although *part loads* can be despatched, either a haulage contractor or a *freight forwarding agent* (see below) may undertake to combine the company's own consignment with those of other customers in an arrangement referred to as *groupage*.[24] (The manufacturing company must ascertain whether despatches are made on fixed days or only when the haulier's container has been filled.) Full loads may then proceed to a roll-on, roll-off ("ro-ro") ferry, to a container port or to the Channel Tunnel container base.

As well, 1-day, 2-day and 3-day express services are available at a price throughout Europe and worldwide for small loads and parcels.

The distribution of goods by rail clearly requires either that the points of production and consumption be directly connected to the

---

[24] Backloads, or backhauls, are economic and always welcome in transport, and UK exporters frequently come to arrangements with European-based exporters to the UK. Note that the movement *A (UK) to B (France), then B (France) to C (UK)* is backhaul; whereas *A (UK) to B (France), then B (France) to D (France)* is termed *cabotage*. The letters "TIR" (French: *transport international routier* — international transport company) denote that a vehicle can be sealed for customs purposes. Thus if a vehicle from Country X must pass through Country Y en route to a destination in Country Z, the customs authorities of Country Y will seal the vehicle with tamper-proof seals at its border.

railway network or that supplementary road operations provide the links at extra cost. Although EWS and Freightliner trains carry a vast tonnage of container traffic, rail truly comes into its own for the transport of high density, low value goods: coal and coke; petroleum products; chemicals and aggregates; and iron and steel. "Company trains" comprising company-owned or leased wagons are those making direct deliveries between a manufacturer and a single customer.

Deep sea transportation is the term applied to ocean-going shipping to markets other than Europe. (A number of the Incoterms such as FOB and FAS described in sub-section 16.3.1 are terms of sale in practice very largely concerned with this mode of transport.) The vast proportion of manufactured goods to be conveyed by deep sea, other than bulk material, will be loaded in ISO containers on container vessels. The container operation begins when a gantry crane or straddle carrier loads an empty container onto a vehicle at a container base. This is then moved to the manufacturing company's premises, where it is loaded, sealed and returned to the base. From there, it is transported by vehicle or by container train to a container port, where a container crane lifts it into a specially built slot within the vessel. At the destination port, the process is reversed.

An important intermediary engaged by the industrial distributor is the *freight forwarding agent*. Forwarding agents may operate as individuals or on behalf of transport or shipping companies. Some deal with worldwide distribution; others specialise, say, in particular destinations or particular modes of transport. All offer expert, up-to-the-minute advice to clients on the mode of transport best selected for a particular despatch; they will arrange for the consolidation of loads and will book space with carriers. Freight forwarding agents will also advise on required documentation and can act as local intermediaries with customs officials. The costs of the freight forwarder's services are generally covered by commissions and margins obtained by him from the carrying companies he engages on behalf of his clients.

The various rates and costs of transportation charged by a carrier are laid out in his *tariff*. Tariffs are often complex and merit close scrutiny by the client company: quite small manipulations of an initial distribution plan taking account of tariff price breaks may result in significant cost savings. Deep sea tariffs may either be set by a *shipping conference* involved in the transportation, or may be "FAK" (see below). A shipping conference is a cartel of shipping companies operating between two specific ports (e.g. Southampton and Sydney; Dublin and New York). Conference operators control and regulate the frequency and cost of sailings between their two ports, fixing rates dependent on the value of the cargo, and being ones that "the traffic will bear". Conferences justify the operation of their cartels by pointing out that they guarantee firm sailing schedules and maintain consistent transit times. Other shipping companies attempting to offer services on a conference route, perhaps charging rates undercutting those of conference vessels, are discouraged from doing so. The conference will withdraw loyalty bonuses from those of its own customers placing business with the non-conference operator, and will engage in a temporary price war (setting a *"fighting rate"*). Persistence by the interloper may obtain its eventual reward in an invitation to join the conference. Notwithstanding the power of the shipping conferences, a number of well-capitalised international companies have made considerable inroads into conference business on the principal deep sea routes in past years, offering flat rate pricing for container carriage regardless of its value, termed *freight all kinds* (FAK).

FINIS

Selected Bibliography

*This bibliography includes major texts selected from those cited in footnotes throughout the book which the author believes the manufacturing manager should consider incorporating in his personal library if he wishes to take the subject matter referred to further. An asterisk * has been placed by publications that might take pride of place in that library.*

Chapter 1

Sir Geoffrey Owen (1999), *From Empire To Europe*, HarperCollins.

Chapter 2

Simon Cooper (1997), *Selling: Principles, Practice and Management*, Pitman Publishing.

Chapter 3

R.G. Day (1993), *Quality Function Deployment: Linking a Company with its Customer*, ASQC Quality Press, Milwaukee, WI.

Stuart Pugh (1991), *Total Design*, Addison-Wesley.

Chapter 4

S. Makridakis, S.C. Wheelwright and V.E. McGee (1983), *Forecasting: Methods and Applications*, Second Edition, John Wiley & Sons.

* Alfred P. Sloan (edited by John McDonald and Catherine Stevens) (1963), *My Years with General Motors*, Doubleday.

Chapter 5

R.G. Brown (1982), *Advanced Service Parts Inventory Control ("ASPIC")*, Second Edition, Materials Management Systems Inc. (This book is available through Mercia Software, Birmingham.)

C.D. Lewis (1975), *Demand Analysis and Inventory Control*, Saxon House. (See Chapter 12 for simulation of inventory problems.) See also Colin Lewis (1998), *Demand Forecasting and Inventory Control*.

John F. Magee, William C. Copacino and Donald B. Rosenfield (1985), *Modern Logistics Management*, John Wiley & Sons.

Chapter 6

* T.E. Vollmann, W.L. Berry and D.C. Whybark (1988), *Manufacturing Planning and Control Systems*, Second Edition, Dow Jones-Irwin.

Chapter 9

Ray Wild (1980), *Production and Operations Management*, Holt, Rinehart and Winston.

R.I. Levin, C.A. Kirkpatrick, D.S. Rubin (1982), *Quantitative Approaches to Management*, Fifth Edition, McGraw-Hill.

Chapter 10

* Oliver Wight (1981), *MRPII: Unlocking America's Productivity Potential*, Oliver Wight Publications Inc. (The late Oliver Wight is regarded as the father of MRPII (and therefore of ERP).)

Chapter 11

James R. Evans, David R. Anderson, Dennis J. Sweeney and Thomas A. Williams (1984), *Applied Production and Operations Management*, International Edition, West Publishing Company.

Chapter 12

* James H. Greene (ed.) (1997), *Production and Inventory Control Handbook*, Third Edition, McGraw-Hill. (This *vade mecum* comprises 37 chapters and some 1,150 pages, and is an indispensable reference in the manufacturing manager's library.)

Chapter 13

Walter A. Shewhart (1931), *The Economic Control of Quality of Manufactured Products*, First Edition, Van Nostrand. (Reprinted as a 50th anniversary commemorative reissue by The American Society for Quality Control, 1980, and again by CEEP Press, The George Washington University, 1986.)

John Seddon (1997), *The Case Against ISO 9000*, Second Edition, Oak Tree Press.

* W. Edwards Deming (1986), *Out of the Crisis*, MIT Center for Advanced Engineering Studies, Cambridge, MA.

A.V. Feigenbaum (1983), *Total Quality Control*, Third edition, McGraw-Hill.

* Kaoru Ishikawa (1985), *What is Total Quality Control (The Japanese Way)?*, translated by Prof. David J. Lu, Prentice-Hall. (This book is not a conventional text, but a stimulating and fascinating reminiscence of the author's life in Japanese quality. It was (understandably) a bestseller in Japan.)

Chapter 14

Eugene L. Grant and Richard S. Leavenworth (1996), *Statistical Quality Control*, Seventh Edition, McGraw-Hill.

Chapter 15

Lawrence Mann (1983), *Maintenance Management*, The Free Press.

Shigeo Shingo (1985), *A Revolution in Manufacturing: The SMED System*, English translation, The Productivity Press. (This book is in two parts: *Part 1 — Theory and Practice* (130 pages), and *Part 2 — Twelve Case Studies* (230 pages).)

* Taiichi Ohno (1988), *Toyota Production System: Beyond Large-Scale Production*, English translation, Productivity Press.

Richard J. Schonberger (1986), *World Class Manufacturing*, The Free Press.

Chapter 16

Margaret Griffiths (1994), *Law for Purchasing and Supply*, Pitman.

David L. Sheridan (1991), *Negotiating Commercial Contracts*, McGraw-Hill.

Chapter 17

Colin Drury (1998), *Costing: An Introduction*, Fourth Edition, International Thomson Business Press.

Fred Langley and Geoff Hardern (1994), *Introduction to Accounting for Business Studies*, Sixth Edition, Butterworth and Co.

Chapter 18

Roger B. Brooks and Larry W. Wilson (1995), *Inventory Record Accuracy*, John Wiley & Sons, Inc.

David Jessop and Alex Morrison (1994), *Storage and Supply of Materials*, Sixth Edition, Pitman Publishing.

Chapter 19

Alan Cowling and Philip James (1994), *The Essence of Personnel Management and Industrial Relations*, Prentice Hall.

Paul Lewis (1998), *The Law of Employment: Practice and Analysis*, Kogan Page.

Jeremy Stranks (1992), *A Manager's Guide to Health and Safety at Work*, Second Edition, Kogan Page.

This volume is supported by an online glossary located at http://www.glossaryofmanufacturing.com.

Index

α, 111-16, 118, 119, 135, 559, 868-9
β, 111, 114, 121, 137, 619-20
γ, 120-3
δ, 116, 119, 131
θ, 78, 99, 121-3
λ, 77-80, 144-5, 169-70, 172-3, 549
Λ, 81
μ, 134, 148-51, 516, 539, 543
π, 99, 100, 148, 159
σ, 134, 137, 148-51, 159, 165, 169-72, 174-5, 515-16, 520-9, 539, 540, 542-4, 548, 551, 623
Σ, 118, 134, 144, 168-9, 515, 521-2, 547, 874
φ, 100, 120-3
Φ, 159

80/20 division, 639, 780, **787-9**, 791, 794
A2 (sampling parameter), 529
A3 (sampling parameter), 531
ABC (activity based costing), 723, 730, 747, **752-5**
  activity cost centres, 753
  batch related activities, 754
  facility-sustaining activities, 754
  product-sustaining activities, 754
  unit-level cost centres, 753
  common uses, 754-5
  criticism of, 755
  stage I: identification and accumulation, 753-4
  stage II: allocation of costs, 753, 754
  cost drivers, 754, 755
ABC analysis (80/20), 780, **787-9**, 791, 794
ABCD checklist (in MRP), 351-2
ABCD list (supplier appraisal), 640n
absenteeism, 810
absorption costing, 747-9
ACAS (Advisory, Conciliation and Arbitration Service), 843
acceptable quality level (AQL), 558-9, 570-1, 574
acceptance criterion, 557, **577-8**
acceptance of goods, 666-7
accidents, reasons for, 848-9
accountability (Hay Chart), 830
accounting equation, 703
Accounting Standards Committee, 710n
accounts, financial, 9, 693 - 721
activity cost centres, 753
adaptive exponential smoothing, **115-17**, 130, 538n
advanced planning systems (APS) 16-7, 191n, 212-3, 287, 346, 353, 355, 356, 378, 393, 394, 399, 401-70, 583, 598, 807
  bottleneck systems, 336, 434, **447-70**
  continuous flow systems, 402-3, **430-47**

discrete event systems, 402-3, **409-30**
adverse variance, 743, 745
advertising research, 33
advice note, 650, 770
Advisory, Conciliation and Arbitration Service (ACAS), 843
AFI (average fraction inspected), 572
AGV (automated guided vehicle), 764
Akado, Yoji, 53
Allen, William, 866
allocated stock, 336
allocation basis (in costing), 727-8
alternative bills of materials (in planning), 309
American Society for Quality Control, 476n, 478, 517
Amsden, Robert T., 514n
annual stock check, 709, **784**, 784n
antitrust law (US), 672n
AOQ (average outgoing quality), 559
AOQL (average outgoing quality limit), **560-2**, 577-8
APICS (American Production and Inventory Control Society), 218n, 316n, 332n, 347n, 413n
appraisal of personnel, 803, **813**, 815, 816
appraisal of suppliers, 639-41
application form (recruitment), 812-813
AQL (acceptable quality level), 558-9, **570-1**, 574
arbitration, 843
ARIMA (autoregressive integrated moving averages (Box-Jenkins), 122-4
ARMA (autoregressive moving averages, 121
Armstong, Michael, 848n
Articles of Association, 2
ASPIC (book: *Advanced Service Parts Inventory Control*), 80n, 135n, 154n, 316n, 884n
Asquith, Lord Justice, 854
assemble-to-order ("quick response"), 9n, 12, 19, 87, 108, 228, 241, **247-86**
  definition, 247-8
  redesign for, 249-61
  common parts analysis, 248-61

final assembly schedule (FAS), 13, 19, 180, 247, 248, 255, 257, 261, 266, **267-74**
master scheduling of option variants, 269-74
modular bill of materials, the, 262-3
modular design, 255-261
option overplanning, 250, 276-8
order receipt and final assembly, 283-4
"quick response", 278-86
reducing costs (example), 278-83, **284-6**
super bill, the, 250n, 262-3, **265-7**, 269, 271-2, 275-7
assets, 2, 5, 14, **707-21**, 722
  account, 701-2
  current, 708-10
  definition, 707-8
  depreciation, 711-4, 721n
  evaluation, 715-9
  fixed, 708, 710-4
  register, 714
Atherton, E., 457
ATI (average total inspection), 572
Atkin, Lord, 473, 853
ATP, see available-to-promise
attribute control charts, 545-55
  count (c) chart, 546, 549-52, 554-5
  count per unit (u) chart, 546, 549-52
  data, 545-6
  demerit (D) chart, 555
  fraction/percentage rejected (p) chart, 546-9, 552-3
  number rejected (np) chart, 546-9
  quality score (Q) chart, 555n
attributes, of a product, 55-6, 58, 59-60
Austin, Nancy, 633
auto-correlation, 120, 121
automated guided vehicles (AGV), 764
autonomous maintenance (TPM), 631-2
autoregressive integrated moving averages (ARIMA) (Box-Jenkins), 122-4
autoregressive moving averages (ARMA), 121
available-to-promise (ATP), 199, **228-42**, 283, 366n
  calculation, 230-8

Index

capable-to-promise, 240
capacity available to promise, 238-41
  definition 229-30
  and make-to-order, 228-42
  use in make-to-stock, 235-6
average fraction inspection (AFI), 572
average outgoing quality (AOQ), 559
average outgoing quality limit (AOQL), **560-2**, 577-8
average total inspection (ATI), 572

B3 (sampling parameter), 531
B4 (sampling parameter), 531
backflushing, **773-4n**, 783
backloads (backhauls), 901n
backwardation, 678n
backwards scheduling, **413-5**, 434
BACS (Banks Automated Clearing System), 645
bailments, 669-70
balance sheet, 693, 696-721
Baltic Exchange, 676
bar coding, 367n, **383**
barter, 654, 680n, 690-1
Barth Variable Sharing, 819n
Barton, Graham, 192n
basis (in linear programming), 464-70
batch costing, 736, 737
batch net change (MRP), 350
batch (non-standard, in planning), 309
batch (process), 452
batch splitting, 381n
Bates, James, 461n, 672n
"battle of the forms", 655n
Bayes, Thomas, 124n
Bayesian forecasting, 120, **124-7**, 127n, 131
Beacham, RHS, 819n
Beardwell, Ian, 809n, 812n
Bedaux Point, 819n
Bell Telephones/Laboratories, 517, 563, 566n
benchmarking, 826-7
Bendell, Tony, 477n
Benge, Eugene J., 835n
Benoy, Mark, 405n, 415n, 430n
BEP (breakeven point), **555-7**, 576-7, 638
Berry, W. L., 227n, 254n, 318n, 321n

bill of configurations, 262n
bill of features and options, 262n
bill of lading, 687
bill of materials, 15, **81-6**, 180n, 262-3, 291, **293-8**, 310, 384, 393n, 454, 741, 780, 876-7
  engineering change, 85-6
  explosion, 208, 209, 252
  implosion, 742
  levels, 256, 292-3, **293-8**, 302, 316, 876-7
  loops in, 296-8
  management, 81-6
  structure, 82-3, 192n, 403-4
bill of resources, 393n
bimodal, 520n
binomial theorem, **547-9**, 549, 551, 563, 563n
Blackstone, J. H., 370n, 457n
Blumberg, Jeff, 755
Bodek, Norman, 581n
Bolander, Steven, 438n, 441
BOM, *see* bill of materials
bonus schemes, 379, 479, 819, **819n**, 838-9
Booker, Christopher, 852n
Boothroyd, G., 67n
bootstrapping (forecasting), 132
von Bortkiewicz, Ladislaus, 550, 849
bottleneck APS systems, 336, 434, 447-70
  allocating output, 452-70
  constraints, 448-9
  maximising output, 448-52
  scheduling of, 434, **448-452**
bottleneck scheduling, 434, **448-452**
Bowersox, Donald J., 866n
Box, George, 122
Box-Jenkins forecasting, 122-4
Bragg, D. J., 452n
branch and bound, **406-7**, 406n
breach of contract, 658-60, 844-5
breakdowns, 448, **621-7**
breakeven point analysis (BEP) (raw materials receipt), **555-7**, 576-7, 638
Brisch system, 82-3, 602
Britain, *see* United Kingdom
broad banding (HR), 19, 807, 822, 823, **837-8**
brochure (company), 812
Brooke Bond, 25

Brooks, Roger B., 760n, 778n, 779n, 780, 785n, 792-3, 794n, 908
"brown goods", 890n
Brown, Rob, 841n
Brown, Robert Goodell, 80-1, 112n, 133, 135, 136, 154, 157, 158n, 161n, 167, 168, 243, 316n 318n, 327n, 866, 876, 880, 884, 906
BS 5750, 504, 508
BSI (British Standards Institution), 477-8, 504, 509
bucket (in planning), 341
budget, 723, 724-5, 736, 738, **739-41**
  committee, 739
  in costing, 724-5
  flexible, 746n
  master, 739
  process, 739-41
buffer stock, see safety stock
Burbridge, J. L., 602n
burden of proof (health & safety), 853
business review (master planning), 189-93
buyback, 691
by-products (in planning), 304-5

c-chart (control chart), 546, **549-52, 554-5**
cabotage, 901n
CAD (computer aided design), 61
campaign (manufacturing), 435, 441
capable-to-promise, **234n,** 240
capacity available to promise, 238-41
capacity planning, 15, **187-8**, 192, 193-9, 238-41, 345, 353-4, 433-4, 450
  capacity requirements planning (CRP), 192, 208, **209-12**, 407-9, 453-4
  hierarchy of, 187-8
  resource planning (MPS), 193-9
  rough-cut capacity planning (RCCP), 188, **208-13**, 273, 353, 357, 370, 439
capital, 3-6, 410, 714; see also assets
capital account, 702, 704
capital expenditure, 711n
capitalisation issues, 5
CAPOSS-E, 416n
Carlos Federspiel & Co v. Charles Twigg & Co, 668

carriage of goods, 660-5
cartel, 672
Carter, R. J., 767n
cashbook, 706
cashflow, 706
catalogues, 636
causation (health & safety), 853
cause and effect diagram (Ishikawa diagram), 58, 496, 497-8
CBOT (Chicago Board of Trade), 677n
CCAS (Component Commonality Analysis System), 254n
cells, 601-6
cellular manufacture, 598-608
central limit theorem, 34, 145n, 514-7
centroid (distribution planning), 874
certainty of terms (legal), 651
CFR (cost and freight), 663-4
Chakravarty, A. K., 866n
Champernowne, David, 126
changeovers, 356, 437, 451-2, **589-98**, 601
changeovers, fast, 451-2, **589-98**, 632
Charnes, A., 890n
Chartered Institute of Marketing, 21
chartered secretary, 7n
chemical industry, 309, 403, 430
chemical industry planning, 300-2, 304-5, 305-7, 309-10, 310-1, 398, 460
chi-squared test, 144
Chicago Board of Trade (CBOT), 677n
chief accountant, 693
Christopher, Martin, 862n, 863n
Chrysler, 504n
CIF (cost, insurance and freight), 664
CIP (carriage and insurance paid to), 664
civil liability (for health & safety), 853-6
classification (of jobs), 823, **836**, 836n
"closing the loop" (in MRP), 16-7, **331-3**
closing off stores, 797-8
coding of products, **82-3**, 295-8, 393-9, 601-3, 602n, 760-2, 763-4
commercial risk, 686-90
commitment to the MPS, 179, **213-4**
commodities market (City of London), 674-9
  examples, 677-9
  futures, 676-7

Index

hedging, 676, 677, 678, 679
spot price, 676
commodity, 674
COMMODORE, 457n
common carriers, 901
common causes (of variation, in quality), 18, 119n, 142, 370, **489-90**, 514-5
common law, **473n**, 650-6, 853-6
common parts, 13, **250-5**, 257-61, 265, 267, 274, 283
  CCAS (Component Commonality Analysis System), 254n
  computer analysis, **253-5**, 254n
  general common parts, 250-2, 267, 274
  matrix analysis, **252-3**, 254n
  option common parts, 250-2
  super common part, 251
  see also assemble-to-order; modular design
communications, 642, **643-4**, 858
Companies Act 1985, 2, 669n
company, the
  brochure, 812
  company tasks, 14-9
  directors and managers, **6-9**, 841n
  foundation, **1-3**, 669n
  legal framework, 1-6
  methods of trading, 9-14
  organisation of, 804-7
  shares, 1, **2-6**
  total quality in, 486
competency-based pay, 840
Competition Act, 1980, 672
competitive tendering, 647
Component and Supplier Management System (CSM), 642
Component Commonality Analysis System (CCAS), 254n
components, **180**, 304
computer aided design (CAD) 61
computer analysis (common parts), **253-5**, 254n
computer system development, 383-91
  evolutionary development, 391
  inspection of design, 388-9
  open-ended architecture, 390
  requirements capture, 389n
  structured walkthrough, 388

consensus forecasting, 47-8
concept (marketing), 14, 21-2
conceptual design (of new product), **57-60**, 496
  controlled convergence, **59-60**, 496
  outcome, 60
  tools for creativity, 58
  weights and marks, 59-60
conciliation, 843
concurrent engineering, **69-70**, 488
conditions (contract), 655-6
conference (shipping), 903
conformance, **472n**, 475, 484, 493, 510, 542n, 545-6, 550-1
conformance to requirements
  in design, **57**, 484n
  product in actual use, 472
  quality of, 483-5, 484n
conjoint products, **305-7**, 433n, 460
consignment note, **650**, 770
consignment stock, **669**, 669n
constraints, 405, 407-9, 435-7; see also TOC
construction industry, 737
consumer
  legal protection, 473-5
  power, 471-2
  ultimate user, 473-4
Consumer Protection Act 1987, 474
contango, 678n
containers, **768-9**, 769n, 902
continuous flow scheduling, 402-3, **430-47**
  influence of the MPS, 431-2
  scheduling constraints, 435-7
  scheduling procedures, 432-4
  worked example, 438-47
  first trial schedule (packing), 440-4
  process flowchart, 438-9
  second trial schedule (distillation), 444-7
  third trial schedule (base liquor), 446-7
continuous improvement, **498-9**, 507, 630, 632, 644-5
continuous net change (MRP), 351
continuous probability function, 148-9
contract (job) costing, 736, **737**
contract (legal), 473n, **650-60**
  breach of, 658-60
  damages, 659-60

definition, 651
  of employment, 816
  pre-conditions, 651-3
  termination, 656-60
  terms, 654-6
  validity of, 653-4
contract termination, 656-60
  breach, **658-60**, 844-5
  by agreement, 657
  by frustration, 657
  operative mistake, 657-8
  quantum meruit, 656
  substantial fulfilment, 656
contractual damages, 659-60
  direct and indirect loss, 659
  limitation, 660
  liquidated and unliquidated, 659-70
contractual terms, 654-6
  certainty of, 651
  conditions, 655-6
  estoppel, doctrine of, 655
  express, 649n, 654-5
  implied, 654-5
  innominate, 655, **656**
  unfair, 653
contribution (costing), 455-8, **747**
contributory negligence, 855
control accounts, 733
control charts, 489-93, 496, **527-45**, 552-4
  attribute control charts, 545-55
  variable control charts, 489-93, 496, **527-8**, 532-45
control limits (UCL and LCL, on control charts), 491-2, 520n, **523-7**, 528-31, 533, 534n, 535-8, 540-4, 548-9, 551, 553, 554
Control of Substances Hazardous to Health Regulations (COSHH), 851
convertible currency, 680n
conveyance kanban, **611-6**, 617-9
Cooper, Robin, 752, 753
Cooper, W. W., 890n
co-operating companies, 641
COPICS, **382n**, 391n
co-products (in planning), **305-7**, 460
corrective maintenance (TPM), 630-1
correlation, **120**, 127-8
COSHH (Control of Substances Hazardous to Health) Regulations, 851

cost accounting, 18, 693, **722-55**;
  absorption costing, 747-9
  activity-based (ABC), 723, 730, 747, **752-5**
  batch costing, 736, **737**
  contract (job), 736, **737**
  contribution costing, 747
  marginal (direct) costing, 747
  process industry costing, 736, **738**
  stage I: accumulating costs, 724-6
  stage II: allocating costs, 726-32
  standard costs, 736, 737, 738, **742-3**
  uses of, including in decision taking, 722-3, 723n, **746-55**
  see also costs
cost/benefit evaluation, 715-9
cost centre, 723, **724-6**, 740, 744
cost centre budget, **724-5**, 740
cost drivers, **727-8**, 754, 755
cost pool, 723
cost-quantity-price (CQP) analysis, 747, **749-52**
cost roll-up, 742
cost structure, 727
costs, 63-7, 284-6, 389, 437, **722-32**
  direct production, 726
  distribution, 861-75
  of expenses, **724**, 726, 727
  fixed costs, **724-5**, 749, 750-1
  fully absorbed, 709, **727**
  indirect costs, 726-7
  of labour, **724**, 726, 727
  of materials, **724**, 726, 727
  overheads, **725-6**, 727, 729
  prime cost, **726-7**, 732, 747n
  production, **710**, 723-32
  of a project, 389-90
  of stock, *versus* sold goods, **710**, 722
  variable costs, 724-5, **747-50**
count (c) control chart, 546, **549-52**, **554-5**
count per unit (u) control chart, 546, **549-52**
counter purchase, 691
countertrading, 690-1
Cowling, Alan, 810n, 812n, 848n, 908
Cox, James, 457n
CPT (carriage paid to), 664
CQP (cost-quantity-price) analysis, 747, **749-52**
  profit-quantity (PQ) graph, 751

Index

Crabtree, D. M., 457n
credit card, 646n
credit (financial), 699-700
critical ratio rule, 374-6
Crosby, Philip B., 475, **478-9**, 488n
cross-functional teams, 806
Croston, John, 133, **134-5**
CRP, see capacity planning
CSM (Component and Supplier Management System), 642
currency conversion, 680n
currency market, 680-6
currency swop, 681
current expenditure, **711**, 711n
customs & excise, 645n, 646n, 901n, 902-3
customer, 11, 12, 18, **21**, 28, 51, 101, 247, 483-5
  demand, **101-7**, 868
  firm order, 337n
  internal (quality view), 484-5
  requirements, 21-2, 28, **51-3**, 247, 262, 264, 265, 283-4, 483-5, 507, 737
  see also customer service
customer service, 40-1, 139-41, 145n, 152-4, 166-70, 180, 200, 410, **471-2**, 857, 865
  defining, **156-7**, 158, 161, 166, 170
  and safety stock, **139-41**, 156-78
  targets, **141**, 156-7
CV (*curriculum vitae*), 813
cycle count reconciliation
  automatic, 801
  closing off stores, 797-8
  four-step procedure, 797-800
  late transactions, 785, **794-5**
  premature transactions, 785, **796-801**
  special storage area, 799-800
  transaction sequencing, 801
  two-step, 800n
  see also cycle counting
cycle counting, 764, **784-801**
  classification of parts, 780, **787-9**, 791, 794
  counting effort, 786, **789-90**
  counting rate, 785-6, 785n
  cycle length, 785-90
  defined, 784
  fixed location stores, **790**, 793

  practice and procedures, **785-94**, 798-800
  reconciliation of a count, 785, **794-801**
  selection of parts to count, 790-4
  variable location stores, **790**, 793, 800
  see also cycle count reconciliation
cycle stock, 155, **863**
cycle time, 587
cyclicality (in demand), **92**, 94

D-chart (control chart, demerit), 555
D3 (sampling parameter), 531
D4 (sampling parameter), 531
DAF (delivered at frontier), 664
Dale, Barrie, 35n, 53n, 477n, 496n
Data Protection Act, 1984, 808n
Data Protection Directive (EU) 1995, 808n
Davis, Edward, 778n
Day, R. G., 53n, 905
DCF (discounted cash flow), 716-9
DDP (delivered duty paid), 665
DDU (delivered duty unpaid), 665
debentures, 4-5
debit (financial), 699-700
decomposition, 93-9
deep sea, 902
defects, **472n**, 475, 484, 493, 510, 542n, 545-6, 550-1
delivery note, **650**, 770-1
delivery of goods, 650, **665-70**, 770-1
Delphi forecasting, 49
demand (sales), 87, 88, **101-8**, 439, 868
Deming, W. Edwards, 17, 35n, 119n, 476, **478-9**, 481, 488n, 495, 498n, 502-3, 509, 571-2, 638, 782, 839n, 848-9, 907
demonstrated capacity, 361
demurrage, 770n
density function (probability), 146-7
dependent demand (planning), 290-3
depots (in a distribution network), 865-75
  addition of, 867-9
  location of, 865-9, 872-5
  logical depots, 860n
  number of, 861-72

depreciation, **711-4**, 721n
  expense, 711, **712-3**
  importance of, 712
  methods of, 711-2
  treatment in accounts, 712-4
  value, 711-2
derivatives, **676n**, 681
DEQ (delivered ex quay, duty paid), 665
DES (delivered ex ship), 665
design (of a product), 14, **53-62**, 255-61, 488, 507, 542-3
  conceptual design, 57
  design brief, **51-3**, 484
  "design for"..., 62-73
  detailed design, 61
  modular design and assemble-to-order, 249, **255-61**, 285, 286
  product design specification (PDS), 54-7
  and quality, **70-3**, 541, 542, 543
"design for" some function ...
  assembly, 67-9
  ergonomics, 61
  low cost, 62-7
  manufacture, 62-73
  piece part producibility, 67
  production process, 69-70
  quality, **70-3**, 541, 542, 543
  worked example, 63-7
despatching docks, 764-6
despatching rules (DRP), 876-9
despatching rules (priority), *see* job despatching rules
detailed design, 61
Dexion Ltd, 772n
Dickie, H. Ford, 787
dimensions (Hay Guide Chart), 828, **829-31**
direct production costs, 726
Director of Fair Trading, 672
directors, 3, 6-8
  board of, 6-8
  company secretary, 7n
  finance, 6
  managing, 6,8
  production, 6
  report, 706
  sales and marketing, 6
  tasks of, 7

Disability Discrimination Act ,1995, 812n
discipline (industrial relations), 843, 845
discounted cash flow (DCF), 715-9
discounts, 328-30
discrete event APS systems, 402-3, **409-30**
  the scheduling engine, 415-20
  discrete event schedulers, 419-20
  Gantt charts, 429, 447
  heuristic schedulers, 415-8
  rule-based systems, 424-6
  scheduling rules, 420-30,
    examples, 422-3, **425-7**, 427-8
  see also bottleneck APS systems; continuous flow scheduling; discrete event scheduling tools
discrete event scheduling tools, 409-15
  forwards/backwards scheduling, 413-5
  horizontal loading, **413-5**, 418
  simulation, 409-13
discrete probability function, 146-7
discrimination, avoidance of, **811-2**, 812n, 815n
dismissal (of employees), 846-8
distribution
  costs of facilities, 863
  costs of stock, 863-9
  costs, total, 869-72
  costs of transport, 861
  lead time, 153, 154, 278, 283, **300-2**
  manufacturing involvement in, 857
  mix, **858-9**, 861
  network, 153, 448, **858-75**, 877
  transport, 900-3
  see also distribution network; distribution replenishment by DRP; distribution replenishment by "fair shares"; probability distributions
distribution network, 153, 448, **858-75**, 877
  reasons for establishing, 857-8
  replenishment by DRP, 876-80
  replenishment by "fair shares", 880-90
  structure of, 858-61
  transportation, 900-03

Index

transshipments, 890-900
distribution replenishment by DRP (distribution resource planning) 19, 302n, **876-80**
  benefits, 889
  depot requirements, 876, **877-8**
  despatch rules, 876-9
  firm planned orders, 876
  gross requirements, 876
  orders in transit, 876
  partial requirements, 876
  planned orders, 876
  replenishment lots, 880
  scheduled receipts (open orders), 876
  software, 876-7
distribution replenishment by "fair shares" (DRPII), 19, 153, 876, **880-90**
  benefits, 889
  cumulative requirements, 887
  gross requirements, 881, **886-7**
  rules, 884
  stage 1: communicating needs, 880-2
  stage 2: consideration of products, 882-3
  stage 3: calculation of replenishments, 883-7
  stage 4: physical despatches, 887-9
diversification, 25
dividend, **3-4**, 696
divisions (company structure), 7, 14-9
Dodge, Harold, 554, 566n, 567n, 570n, 572-3, 575
Dodge-Romig, 567n, **569-70**, 579
Donoghue v. Stevenson, 473
van Donselaar, Karel, 866
double entry bookkeeping, 702, **704-5**, 707, 722, 733, 735
double/linear smoothing, **111-5**, 123-4
double sampling, 578
Doyle, Peter, 24
DRP, 19, 302n, 876-80; see distribution replenishment by DRP
DRPII, 19, 153, 876, 880-90; see under distribution replenishment by "fair shares"
Drucker, Peter, 21, 27
Drury, Colin, 723n, 735, **736**, 745n, 908
duplicate transactions, 777n, 783

due dates (*v.* need dates), 332, 334, 335, 337, **340**, 342
dummy variables (in forecasting), 127
Dun and Bradstreet, 636
Dunlavy, Colleen, 2n
Dunn, Anne, 827
duty of care, **472-5**, 853, 854
dynamic despatching rules, 373-6; see *also* job despatching rules (prioritising)
dynamic programming, 326-7

"e" (mark on consumer packages), 475
E2 (sampling parameter), 539-40
"earnings per share", 5-6
Easter (in forecasting), 127
EBQ (economic batch quantity), 316n
echelon (distribution network), **858-60**, 859n, 865, 876-7, 883
economic manufacturing quantity (EMQ), 279, **316n**, 436
economic order quantity (EOQ), **316-20**, 327, 436, 588-9, 623
elasticity of demand, **673-4**, 752
Eli Lilly, 890n
elimination of adjustments (in, SMED), 595-7
elimination of waste (in JIT), **581-2**, 616-9
Emerson Efficiency, 819n
Employees, 9, **19**, 803n, 803-4, 837-40, 844-7 ; see *also* human resources; labour; reward management
Employers' Liability (Compulsory Insurance) Act, 1969, 856
Employers' Liability (Defective Equipment) Act, 1969, 855
employment, see human resources (employment)
Employment Act, 1990, 812n
Employment Appeal Tribunal, 844-7, 851
employment contract, 803-4, **816**, 844-5, 846-7, 853
Employment Protection Act, 1975, 843
Employment Protection (Consolidation) Act, 1978, 845
Employment Rights Act, 1996, 816

empowerment, 278, 284, 627-8, 803, **840-3**, 847-9
  advantages, 842-3
  definition, 840-1
  introduction in company, 841-2
EMQ (economic manufacturing quantity), 279, **316n**, 436
engine (scheduling), 415-20
engineer-to-order, 13-4
engineering, 9, 598, 757
  change, 82, **85-6**, 806
  concurrent/simultaneous, 69-70, 488
  design, 542-3
  tolerances, 540-4
England, Bank of, 166, 682-3, 684
England, Law of, **473n**, 662n
enterprise resource planning (ERP), **332n**, 351n; see also materials requirements planning; advanced planning systems
environment, safety of, 849
EOQ (economic order quantity), **316-20**, 327, 436, 588-9, 623
equality (racial and sexual), 803
equipment maintenance, 621-32
  breakdown time distribution, 623-4
  classic approach to determining policy, 621-7
  classic approach worked example, 626-7
  costs of breakdowns, 622-5, **626-7**
  mean time to failure (MTTF) (probability of breakdown), 625-7
  total productive maintenance (TPM) policy, 627-632
  five types of TPM maintenance, 629-632
equivalent products (in planning), 309-10
ergonomics, **56**, 61
ERP (enterprise resource planning), **332n**, 351; see also materials requirements planning; advanced planning systems
error addback, 227
estoppel, doctrine of (legal), 655
evolutionary development, 391
expectation, partial (statistical), 161-5
expectation (statistical), 163
expenses (in costing), **724**, 726, 727
external labour market, 817-8

EU (European Union), 672n, 674, 803
EU regulations, 803, **852n**, 853
euroland, 682n
European Central Bank (ECB), 682
European Monetary Union (EMU), **680n**, 682
European Union (EU), 672n, 674, 803
"evaporating cloud", 449n
Evans, James R, 373n, 461n, 906
exhibitions, 636
exercise price, 681
expenditure, **709-10**, 711n, 722
expense account, **695**, **700-4**
explosion of the BOM (fast), **191-2**, 192n, 193, 351n
explosion of the BOM in materials planning, 192, **290-5**
explosion of the BOM in MRP, 331-2, 349-50
explosion of the MPS, 184, 192, **200-3**, 208, 273-4, 414
exponential distribution, 363
express terms (contract), **654-5**, 655n
EXW (ex-works), **662-3**, 662n 667

factor comparison (jobs), 823, **832-5**
Fagan, Michael, 388n
Fair Trading Act 1973, 672,
FAK (freight all kinds), 903
FAS (final assembly schedule),
  definition and illustration, 13, 180, **247-8**
  lead time, 255-7
  relationship to master scheduling, 267-9
  and option variants, 270-3,
  order receipt, 283-4
  teams, 841
FAS (free alongside ship), **663**, 902
fast set-ups, 451-2, **589-98**, 632
"fair shares" replenishment, see distribution replenishment by "fair shares"
favourable variance, 743, 745
FCA (free carrier), 663
FCFS (first come, first served), 571n
feature redundancy (in design), 259-60
Feigenbaum, Armand, 76, 472n, 476, **480**, 503, 531n, 554, 577n, 907

Index

field reports (forecasting), 133
Fife, Ian, 848n
FIFO (first-in, first-out) (assets valuation), 709
FIFO (first-in, first out) (stock picking), 762
final assembly rate, JIT, 585-8
final assembly schedule, *see* FAS
financial futures market, 680-6
finance, **18**, 693-699, 707-11
finished goods, **722**, 735-6, 757
firm customer order, 337n
firm planned orders (DRP), 876
firm planned orders (MRP), **337-9**, 345, 346, 348-9
"five *why*'s", 449n
fixed costs, **724-5**, 749, 750-1
fixed expenditure, **710-11**, 711n, 749-51
fixed location storage system, **759**, 790
fixed planned orders (MRP), **337-9**, 345, 346, 348-9
flexibility of job holder, 803n
flow manufacturing, 402-3, **430-47**
FMECA (failure mode, effect and criticality analysis), **74-5**, 410
FOB (free on board), 663, 902
food industry, 309, 403, 430, 431
Food Safety Act 1990, 474
force majeure (legal), 657
Ford, 28, 504n
forecast (production, costing), **725**, 730
forecasting techniques,
  at the group level, 189-90
  causal techniques, 120-30
  dealing with errors, 130-2
  introduction, 87-9
  medium- and long-term, 44-5, **47-9**
  multi-period, 132
  naïve techniques, 108-20
  new products, **45-6**, 243-6
  neural networks, **128-30**, 130n
  software, **118-20**, 122-3, 125, 132, 135
  system, 87-9, 92, 108, 119, 122-3, 124, **130-2**, 133, 190n
  when demand is lumpy, 133-8, 869n

  see also sales demand data; sales forecasting (causal); sales forecasting (naïve)
foreign exchange ("forex"), 679-91
  commercial risk, 686-90;
  financial futures market, 680-6
  forward market, 681-6
  letter of credit, 680, **686-90**
  payment, 680-90
  rates, 680-1
  spot prices, 682-4
  traded options, 681
  worked examples, 685-6
foreseeability (accidents), 855-6
forex (foreign exchange), 681-6
forklift trucks, 766n, **767**
Forrester, J. W., **104-7**, 413n
forward market ("forex"), 681-6
forward scheduling, **413-5**, 434
foundation (of company), **1-3**, 669n
Fourier, Joseph, 99
Fourier analysis, 99-101
Fox, Mark, 433n
Fraser's five-point plan (interviewing), 815
freight forwarding agent, 901, **902**
frequency distribution, *see* probability distributions
frequency polygon, 371
frozen zone (MPS), 151-5, **203-6**, 216, 643
frozen zone (suppliers), 643
Frustrated Contracts Act 1943, 657n
fully absorbed costs, 727
functional clamps, 595
future, 676-9

---

gamma distribution, 144
Gane, Chris, 41n, **389n**
Gantt charts, **429**, 447
Gantt Task & Bonus, 819n
Gardener, John, 28
gateway work centre, **360**, 362, 458
Gattorna, John L., 156n, 874n
Gauss, Carl Friedrich, 145n
Gaussian (normal) distribution, 144, **145-9**, 158-60, 516, 517-9, 523-5, 539-41
Gaussian (normal) distribution, standardised, **149-50**, 163-4, 167

gearing ratio, 6
general common parts, **250-2**, 267, 274
General Electric, 480, 787
General Motors, **103**, 504n, 890n
Gerson, George, **158**, 167, 168
Gilb, Tom, 389n, 391n
global market, 675
glossary, 908
GMCS (UK training company), 316n, 760n, 776n, 782n
Goldratt, Eliyahu, 449n, **454**, 457n, 746, 751, 755
goods in, 649-50, 655-6, 658, 659, **666-7**, 758, 770-1
goods received note (GRN), 770-1
grade differentials (job), **820-1**, 821-2
grade harmonisation, **819**, 820
grades (job), **818-23**, 837-8
grades (of quality), 307-8
Grain and Feed Association, 676
Grant, Eugene L., 69n, 527n, 563n, 573n, **575**, 907
Gray, Chris, **179n**, 238, 300n, 307, 351n
"great circle formula", **873**, 873n
Greek letters, *see above*
Greene, James H., 438n, 449n, 450, 461n, 760n, 907
grievances, 843
Griffiths, Margaret, 473n, 665n, 844n, 908
GRN (goods received note), 770-1
gross profit, **695**, 707
gross requirements (DRP), **881**, 886-7
gross requirements (materials planning), **298-313**, 317, 325, 341, 342, 346
  calculation of, 298-300
  creating plans to meet them, 311-3
  minor change in, 347-8
  multi-site netting, **300-2**, 398
  partial requirements, 298-9
  total regeneration 349-51
group technology, 599-608
  concept, 600-1
  family and cells, 601-6
  classification of equipment (Brisch system), 602
  exceptional equipment, 605-6
  illustration, 603-4
  classification of equipment by material flow analysis, 602-3
  U-shaped lines, 606-8
groupage, 901

Hall, Robert, 582
Halsey-Weir Premium, 819n
Hardy, Thomas, 463n
harmonic analysis, 99-101
Harris, Ford W., 316n
Harrison, Jeff, 126
Hay, Edward Ned, **828n**, 835
Hay Group, **828-32**, 837
Hay Guide Chart, 827n, **828-32**
  accountability "dimension", 830
  example, 831-2
  gradations, 831
  guidance on, 831, **832**
  job content, 829
  know-how "dimension", 829-30
  problem-solving "dimension", 825, **830**
  profile, 828n
  "super factors", 828, **829-31**
  weights, 828-9
  see also point-factor job evaluation
Head, Brian, 827
Health and Safety At Work Act, 1974, 474, **851**, 853
Health and Safety Commission (HSC), 851
Health and Safety Executive (HSE), 851
health and safety (civil liability), 19, 472-4, 803, **847-9**, 853-6
  burden of proof, 853
  causation, 853
  common law, 853-6
  contributory negligence, 855
  duty of care, **472-5**, **853**, 854
  foreseeability, 855-6
  healthy environment, 849
  management responsibility, 847-9
  reasons for accidents, 848-9
  res ipsa loquitur, 855
  safe environment, 849
  safety officer, 848
  vicarious liability, 856
  see also health and safety (statutory liability)

Index

health and safety (statutory liability) 19, 803, **847-9**, 850-2
  Control of Substances Hazardous to Health Regulations (COSHH), 851
  early statutes, 850
  Employers' Liability (Compulsory Insurance) Act, 1969, 856
  Employers' Liability (Defective Equipment) Act, 1969, 855
  EU directives, **852n**, 853
  Health and Safety At Work Act, 1974, 474, **851**, 853
  Health and Safety Commission (HSC), 851
  Health and Safety Executive (HSE), 851
  healthy environment, 849
  improvement notice, 851
  legislation and regulations, 850-6
  management responsibility, 847-9
  prohibition order, 851
  reasons for accidents, 848-9
  Robens' Report, **850-1**, 852
  safe environment, 849
  safety officer, 848
  see also health and safety (civil liability)
healthy environment, 849
hedger, hedging, **677**, 667n, 678n
heuristics, 406n, **415n**, 415-6
heuristic schedulers, 415-8
Heywood, Tom, 457, **459**
"hidden factory, the", 475-6
hierarchy (corporate), 27, **804-7**
  delayering, 807
  depth, 805n
  disadvantages, 806-7
  organisation chart, 805
hierarchy (of capacity planning), 188
hierarchy (of need, in "fair shares"), 884-5
HIFO (highest-in, first-out), 709n
histogram, 146
Hopper, A. G., 514n
horizon (of MPS), 45, 87, 132, **182-4**, 209, 274, 278-83
horizontal loading (scheduling), **413-5**, 418
HSC (Health and Safety Commission), 851

HSE (Health and Safety Executive), 851
human resources (employment)
  absenteeism, 810
  appraisal, 803
  contract of employment, 816
  data protection, 808n
  training, **804**, 841-2
  training for Just-in-Time, 73n, **628**
  working conditions, 816
  working practices, 803
  equality, 803
  legal requirements, **803**, 804, 844-7
  see also industrial relations; human resources (organisational); human resources (policy & pay); recruitment
human resources (organisational)
  cross-functional teams, 806
  line and staff departments, 804n
  long-term manpower planning, 809
  medium-term manpower planning, 808-9
  organisational structure, 804-5
  short-term manpower planning, 807-8
  see also industrial relations; human resources (employment); human resources (policy & pay); recruitment
human resources (policy & pay), 19, 802-3, 803n, **804**, 847-9
  broad banding, 837
  competency-based pay, 840
  empowerment, 278, 284, 803, **840-3**, 847-9
  variable pay, 838
  see also industrial relations; human resources (employment); human resources (organisational); recruitment
Hyndman, R., 112n
hypergeometric distribution, 563n
Hyster Inc, 794n

IBM, 127n, 161n, 388n, 416n
ICI, 297n, 457n, 538n, 794n, 890
IED (inside exchange of die), 592-5; see also SMED

ILOG, **405n**, 407n, 807, 872n
Imai, Masaaki, 498n
implied terms (contract), 654-5
improvement notice (health & safety), 851
INCOTERMS, 283, **661-5**, 667, 902
  Group C (main carriage paid), 663-4
  Group D (Arrival), 664-5
  Group E (Departure), 662-3
  Group F (Main Carriage Unpaid), 663
indirect costs, 726-7
independent demand (planning), 290-3
industrial relations, 843-7
  arbitration, mediation and conciliation, 843
  complaint and grievances, 843
  discipline, 843, **845**
  dispute, 843
  grounds for fair dismissal, 846-8
  industrial action and strikes, 844-5
  unfair dismissal, **845**, 846
  wrongful dismissal, 845
  working relationships, 840-7
industrial surveys (of pay), 837n
inelastic (price), 673-4
infinite loading, **211**, 415
innovation of new products, 30-5, **51-86**
  failure and reliability, 74-80
  process, 31
  product brief, 51-3
  contents of brief, 52
  product design 14, **53-62**, 255-61, 488, 507, 542-3
input/output control, 357-8, **360-5**, 370, 375, 385, 394
inspection, 542, 542n, 559-61, 567n, 569, 570n, **572-3**, 575-6
Institute of Statisticians, 73
integer programming, 406, **461n**
integrated accounting, 722, **732-6**
  control accounts, 733
  example, 734
  flowchart, 736
  tracking stock movements, 732-3
  unified system, 733-6
interconnections (in design), 258-9
interest rates (in foreign exchange), **682-3**, 684

interest rates (to apply to stockholding), 155-6, 166, **319**
interlocked accounting, 733-4n
intermediate work centre, 362-6
intermittent demand, **133-8**, 222-3, 275, 869n
"internal customer", 484-5
internal rate of return (IRR), 715-9
International Chamber of Commerce, 661, **661n**, 686; see also INCOTERMS; letter of credit
International Financial Futures Exchange, 676
International Futures and Options Exchange, 676
International Petroleum Exchange, 676
International Standards Organisation (ISO), **478**, 503; see also ISO 9000: 2000
Internet, 636, 644
interoperation time compression, 382-3
interviewing job candidates, 803, 813, **814-6**
inventory
  planning and strategy, 15, **181**
  in distribution, 863-9
  determining levels of, 191-3
  records, 775-84
  see also stock
investment centre, 723n
invitation to treat, **647**, 652n
IRR (internal rate of return), 715-9
irrevocable letter of credit, 688
Ishikawa diagram, 58, 496, **497-8**
Ishikawa, Kaoru, 479n, **480**, 481, 497, 500, 841n, 907
ISO 9000 : 1994, **504-5**, 507
ISO 9000 : 2000, 478, **503-11**, 755
  assessors, 505, **509**, 510
  company QMS, the, 503-4
  criticism of, **510-11**, 511n
  documentation and records, 507-9
  history, 504-5
  ISO "family", the, 504-5
  reasons for accreditation, 509-10
  standard clauses (eight), 506-7
isocosts (in distribution planning), 873
issue (from stores), 771

Index

Jacobs, F. Robert, 452n
Jaeger and Waldman, 636
Japan, 18, 53, 476, 479n, 480, **481**, 498n, 608n, 677n
Japanese quality movement, 476, **479-81**, 500-1
Japanese Union of Scientists and Engineers (JUSE), 479n, **481**
Jenkins, Gwilym, 122
Jebb, Fiona, 806n
Jessop, David, 767n, 908
JICARS (Joint Industry Committee for National Reader Surveys), 33
JIT, *see* Just-in-Time
job costing, 736, **737**
job despatching rules (prioritising), **369-78**, 385, 451n
   assumptions, 372
   critical ratio, 374-6
   shortest processing time (SPT), 371n, **376-8**
   slack time, 373-4
   slack time per operation, **374**, 375
   static and dynamic, **372**, 385
job evaluation techniques, 818, **823-37**
   classification, 823, 836
   factor comparison, 823, **832-5**
   Hay Guide Charts, 827n, **828-32**
   market pricing, 817-18, **836-8**,
   point-factor, 823, **824-32**
   qualitative and quantitative schemes, 823
   ranking, 823, **836**
   surveys of industry, 837n
     weighting, 824
   see also reward management
job offer (recruitment), 816
job scheduling and despatch, *see* advanced planning systems; scheduling of work; shop floor control
job splitting, 381n
job status file, 391, **396-7**
Johnson, Samuel, 791n
joint products (in planning), **305-7**, 433n, 460
journal (financial), 699
Juran, Joseph M, 481
juridic personality (of company), 1
JUSE (Japanese Union of Scientists and Engineers), 479n, **481**

Just-in-Time ("Lean Manufacture") (JIT), 18, 315, 327, **581-633**, 641, 758
   applicability of, 583-4
   definitions, 581-4
   elimination of waste, 581-2
   establishing production rates, 584-9
   fast changeovers, 451-2, **589-98**, 632
   kanban, 18, 606, **608-20**
   plant organisation, 588, **598-608**
   redesign, 589
   responsiveness to market, 582-3
   training for, 73n, 628
   workplace management, 632-3

kaizen, 498n
Kalman filters, 124n
kanban, 18, 606, **608-20**, 641
   definition, 608n
   flow of manufacture, 609-16
   mechanics of, 608-16
   move kanban, **611-6**, 617-9
   number in system, 616-20
   one-card system, 613-4
   production kanban, 609-11
   seven rules of, 615
   "Toyota equation", 620
   two-bin replenishment system, 616
   variations, 613-5
Kane, Victor, 544n, 552n
Kaplan, Robert, **752**, 752n, 753
Kennedy, Gavin, 640n
Kirkpatrick, C. A., 316n, 461n
kitemark, **478n**, 510n
know-how (Hay Chart), 829-30
Kolmogorov, Andrei Nikolayevich, 516n
Kompass, 636
Kotler, Philip, 26
Kulick, Bruno, 772n

labour costs, 724, 726, 727, **728-9**, 744, 745
labour efficiency, 744
labour market, **808-9**, **817-9**
Landvater, Darryl, 179n, 238, 300n, 307, 351n, 879n
Lansing Linde, 772n
Laplace, Pierre-Simon, 516n

late deliveries, 12-13, 354n, **645-6**, 655-6, 659
late transactions, 781, 785, **794-5**
Latzko, William J., 479n, 839n
law
 common, 853-6
 company, 1-6
 contract, 650-60
 employment, 803-4, **816**, 844-5, 846-7, 853
 of England, 662n
 product liability, 473-5
LCL (lower control limit), 491-2, 520n, **523-7**, 528-31, 533, 534n, 535-8, 540-4, 548-9, 551, 553, 554
leadership, 807, 842
lead time and planning available-to-promise, 230
 FAS, 255-7, 278-83
 master scheduling, 182-4
 order point, 153n, **288-90**
 projected stock balance, 202
 safety stocks, 151-5
lead time and queue, **356-7, 359**, 360, 361, 362-6, 375, 376, 378, 451
 critical ratio rule, 374-6
 despatching rules and queue, 373-8
 input/output control, 360-2
 queues at intermediate work centres, 362-6
 vicious circle, the, 357-9
 virtuous circle, the, 360
lead time management, **378-83**, 452, 460
 batch splitting, 381n
 interoperation time compression, 382-3
 operation overlapping, **379-81**, 385
 operation splitting, **381-2**, 385
 window scheduling, 382n
lean DRP; see under distribution replenishment by "fair shares" (DRPII)
lean manufacturing, see Just-in-Time
learning curve, 62-7
"least unit cost", 328-30
Leavenworth, Richard S., 69n, 527n, 563n, 573, 575
ledger (financial), 699, 706-7, 733n
legal obligations (in HR), 803, 804, 816, **844-7**

letter of credit (L/C), 686-90
 flow of information, 688-90
 information in, 687-8
 revocable and irrevocable, 688
 UCP1993 (Uniform Customs and Practice for Documentary Credits), **686-7**, 686n
levels in the bill of materials, 293-6
Levin, R. I., 316n, 319n, 906
Levison v. The Patent Steam Carpet Cleaning Company Ltd., 670
Lewis, Colin, 144, 906
Lewis, Paul, 844n, 908
liabilities (financial), 696-9
liability account, 702
life cycle, **23-6**, 45-6
LIFFE (London International Financial Futures Exchange), 676, **680-1**, 683
LIFO (last-in, first-out), 709
limited company, 1-2
limited liability, 1-2
limiting quality level (LQL), 558
linear loss function, 161-5
linear programming, 406, 431, 458n, 460-2, **463-70**, 866
 basis (finding), 464-70
 definition, 461-2
 objective, 462
 slack variables, 470
 worked example, 463-701
line and staff departments, 804n
line stoppers, 788n
linear/double smoothing, **111-5**, 123-4
Ling, Richard, 218, 219n
liquidated damages, 659-70
locating stock, 759n, **771**
location of depots, 865-9, **872-5**
logical depot/node, 860n
logistics, **19**, 641-4, 866n, 867n, 874n
LOGOL, 135n, 890n
London, City of, **675-6**, 677n, 683
London Fox, 676
London Metal Exchange, **676**, 677
long-term forecasting, 44-5, **47-9**
lot size, **315-6**, 316-330, 452
Lott, Merrill, 828n
low-level coding, 250-1n, 293-6
lower control limit (LCL), 491-2, 520n, **523-7**, 528-31, 533, 534n, 535-8, 540-4, 548-9, 551, 553, 554

Index

LQL (limiting quality level), 558, **567-70**
LTPD (lot tolerance percent defective), **568-70**, 579
Lubben, Richard T., 615n
lubrication analysis, 629-30
lumpy demand, **133-8**, 222-3, 275, 869n
Lysons, C. K., 648n

machine capability, 538n
machine status, 391, **397**
machine utilisation, **363-5**, 370, 385, 450
Magee, John F., 156, 863, 867n, 869n, 906
maintenance prevention (TPM), 629
make-and-pack, **433**, 433n
make-to-order, **11-3**, 43, 87
  and available-to-promise, 228-38
  and consuming the forecast, 218-24
  demand forecasts, 12, 108
  late deliveries, 12-13, 645-6, **655-6**, 659
    master planning, **180**, 183, 186, 217, 256-7
  and projected stock, 202-3
  order book, 12, 43, **180**, 667
make-to-stock, **9-11**, 15
  consuming the forecast, 224-8
  demand forecasts, **107-8**, 200
    master planning, **180**, 182, 186, 200, **202**
  ownership, 667
Makridakis, S., 112n, 905
management
  in human resources, 803-4
  and quality, 495-6
  roles of, 8-9
  variables, **166-8**, 170, 173, 319, 682
  of workplace, 632-3
Mann, Lawrence, 621n, 907
manpower planning (long-term), 809
manpower planning (medium-term), 808-9
manpower planning (short-term), 807-8
manpower scheduling systems, 807-8
"manufacturer", duty of care, 473

manufacturing company, 1-6, **6-9**, 9-14, 486, 804-7, 841n; *see also* company, the
manufacturing resource planning (MRPII), 184n, **332-3**, 332n; *see also* MRP (closed loop)
manufacturing routings file, 393n
manufacturing schedule, **331-2**, 355
marginal costs, 747
market
  in the City of London, 676
  development, 25
  penetration, 25
  perfect, imperfect, 671-2
  research, 32-5
  saturation, 23, 24
  supply and demand, 671-4
market price, 670-1
market pricing (*of* jobs), **817-8**, 836-8
marketing, 9, 14, **21-35**
  concept, 14, **21-2**
  definition, 21
  department, 25, 27, 44-5, 51, 103, 141, 243, 245, **805**
  mix, 22-6
  strategy, **24-5**, 26, 27-9
  order processing (sales), 40-4; see also under sales
Markov chain, **809**, 809n
Martin, André, J, 879
mass customisation, *see* assemble-to-order
master plan (MPS), 12, **15**, 151-5, 179-246, 876, 881-2
  and company operations, 214
  in continuous flow manufacturing, **431-2**, 442-3
  definition, **179-80**, 179n
  feasibility of, 187
  overview, 184-8
  release, 214, 215; *see also* master plan formulation; master plan management
master plan formulation, 15, 151-5, 185-6, **189-214**, 276, 806, 878, 880
  arithmetical procedures, 200-03
  business review (S&OP-I), 189-93
  capacity requirements planning, 209-12
  capacity tests (S&OP-II), 193-9
  commitment to the MPS, 213

hierarchy of capacity planning, 188
illustration/overview, 214
product groups, 206-8
rough-cut capacity planning, 208
time fences, 203-06
see also master plan (MPS); master plan management
master plan management, 15, 184, 186-8, 204, **215-42**
  available-to-promise (ATP), 199, **228-42**, 283, 366n
  capable-to-promise, 234n, **240**
  consuming the forecast (make-to-order), **216-24**, 267, 271
  consuming the forecast (make-to-stock), 224-8
  customer service, 166-70
  overview, 186-8, **215-6**
  rescheduling the MPS, 166-70, 206, **216-7**, 287
  system messages, 151-2, **216-8**, 220, 221, 226-7, 322n
  see also master plan (MPS); master plan formulation
master production schedule (MPS); *see* master plan (MPS); master plan formulation; master plan management
master scheduler, the, 9, 27, 151-2, 186, 204, 215n, 220, **242**, 291, 818
master scheduler's remit, **242**, 818
material usage, **744**, 746
material variance, 744, 745
materials costs, 724, 726, 727
materials handling, 382-3, 588, **766-7**, 770
materials movement, 398
materials planning (calculations)
  dependent/independent demand, 290-3
  economic order quantity (EOQ), **316-20**, 327, 436, 623
  gross requirements, **298-313**, 317, 325, 341, 342, 346
  least unit cost, 328-30
  levels in the bill of materials, 293-96
  lot sizes, 315-6
  net requirements, **311**, 313
  part-period balancing, 322n, **323-6**, 327
  partial requirements, **298-9**, 311-3

pegging, 300
period order quantity (POQ), **320-3**, 322n, 327, 436
planning rules, 298, 312, **314-30**
rate-based planning, 313
Wagner-Whitin algorithm, 322n, **326-7**
see also materials planning (general); MRP (closed loop) process/chemical industry planning
materials planning (general), 15-6, 179-80, 215n, **287-330**, 378, 414, 433, 507, 646, 876
  closed-loop MRP, 331-52
  generating plans from net requirements, 311-3
  gross requirements, **298-313**, 317, 325, 341, 342, 346
  introduction to planning, 287-8
  levels in the bill of materials, 293-6
  order point (min-max), 153n, **288-90**
  planning rules, 314-30
  plans and manufacturing activity, 290-3
  process/chemical industry planning, 297, **300-11**
  see also materials planning (calculations); MRP (closed loop); process/chemical industry planning
materials requirements planning; *see* MRP (closed loop)
mathematical programming, 326n
Mather, Hal, 347n
matrix analysis (common parts), **252-3**, 254n
McWilliams, Douglas, 675n
media research, 33
mediation, 843
medium-term forecasting, 44-5, **47-9**
Melnyk, Steven, 371n, 377n, 378
Memorandum of Association, 2
merchandising, 25n
Mercia LINCS, **135n**, 313
metaheuristic, 406n
midpoint scheduling, 434
military tables (sampling), 567, 567n, 570n, **570-5**, 580
Milne, I. M., 297n
MIMI, 403n

Index

min-max system (order point), 153n, **288-90**
misconduct (of an employee), 846
miscounting (of stock), 781, 785
misrepresentation (legal), 654
  factual, 654,
  induced, 654,
  material, 654
mission statements, 502n
Mito, Setsuo, 613n, 615n, 633n
Mitsubishi, 597n
mix (distribution), **858-9**, 861
mix (marketing), 22-6
mixed integer programming, 461n
modular bill of materials, the, 262-3
modular design (for assemble-to-order), 249, **255-61**, 285, 286
  common parts, 13, **250-5**, 257-61, 265, 267, 274, 283
  desirable options as standard, 261
  extending FAS lead time, 255-7
  feature redundancy, 259-60
  interconnecting components, 258-9
  partially manufactured inventory, 257-8
  phantoms, 257n
  popular choices as stock, 260-1
  pseudo items, **251-2**, 263, 265
de Moivre, Abraham, 145n, 516n
Monopolies and Mergers Commission, 672
monopoly, 672
Morse, P.H., 624
motivation (of employee), 803n
move kanban, **611-6**, 617-9
moving averages, 94-9
MPS (master production schedule), see master plan; master plan formulation; master plan management
MRP (closed loop) 16, 17, 184n, 191n, 216, 287, 288, 300, 322n, **331-52**, 386, 414, 876, 878
  "closing the loop" - definition, 16-7, **331-3**
  due dates, 332, 334, 335, 337, **340**, 342
  firm planned orders, **337-9**, 345, 346, 348-9
  MRP messages, 345-7
  net change, 350-1

  planned orders, **336-7**, 341, 346
  rescheduling, 340-51
  rescheduling assumption, the, 341-5
  scheduled receipts (open orders), **334-6**, 341, 346, 777
  standard display, the, 340-1
  standard system, the, 300n
  three plan types in MRP, 333-9
MRPII (manufacturing resource planning, 184n, **332-3**, 332n; see also MRP (closed loop)
multi-period forecasting, 132
multi-site netting, **300-2**, 398
multiple regression, 824
multiple sampling, 578n
Murlis, Helen, 837n
Murphy, Nick, 382n

---

naïve forecasting, 108-120
Nakajima, Seiichi, 628n
narration (financial), 699
negative exponential distribution, 144
negligence, tort of, 473n
negotiated tendering, 647, **648-9**
negotiation, 635, 637, 639, **640**, 655n
"neighbour", legal definition of, 474
nervousness (in MRP), 348
net change (in MRP), 350-1
net present value (NPV), 715-9
net requirements (planning), **311**, 313
network (distribution), 153, 448, **858-75**, 877
  reasons for establishing, 857-8
  replenishment by DRP, 876-80
  replenishment by "fair shares", 880-90
  structure of, 858-61
  transportation, 900-3
  transshipments, 890-900
new product design, 14, **53-62**, 255-61, 488, 507, 542-3
new product innovation, 30-35, **51-86**
new product launch, 23-6, **243-6**
new product production, 243-6
Nielsen, A. C., 32-3
NIFO (next-in, first out), 709n
nodes (distribution network), **858**, 860, 860n, 890
non-conformance, **472n**, 475, 484, 493, 510, 542n, 545-6, 550-1

cost of, 475-7
extent of, 549, 554, 555, **555n**
non-conforming part/item, **546**, 546n, 549, 556-7, 557-60, 576, 637, 638, 641, 645-6, 658
  acceptance criterion, 557, **577-8**
  probability of acceptance, 563-5
  raw material, 556, **658**
non-convertible currency, 680n
non-standard batch sizes (planning), 309
normal (standard) costs, 736, 737, **738**, 742-3
Norman, Archie, 806n
normal (Gaussian) distribution, 144, **145-9**, 158-60, 516, 517-9, 523-5, 539-41
normal (Gaussian) distribution (standardised), 149-50, 163-4, 167
notional costs, 738
np-chart (number rejected), 546-9
NPV (net present value), 715-9
number of depots (in distribution), 861-72
Nyquist, Henry, 99

OC (operating characteristic), **562-6**, 563n, 569, 570, 574
OC (operating characteristic) curve, 569, 570, **574**
ocean-going (deep sea), 902
O'Doherty, Damian, 809n
OED (outside exchange of die), 592-6, see also SMED
offset, direct & indirect, 691
Ohno, Taiichi, **581**, 581n, 583n, 584, 613, 615, 633, 641, 908
oligopoly, 672
one-card kanban, 613-14
open-ended system architecture, 390-1
open orders (scheduled receipts) in DRP, 876
open orders (scheduled receipts) in MRP, **334-6**, 341, 346, 777
operating characteristic (OC), **562-6**, 563n, 569, 570, 574
operating characteristic curve (OC curve), 564-5, 569-70, **574**
operation overlapping, **379-81**, 385

operation splitting, **381-2**, 385
OPL Studio, 872
opportunity cost, 459
OPT (Optimised Production Technology), 449n, **452**, 454, 461n, 751
optimisation techniques, 326n, **461n**, 462
  branch and bound, **406-7**, 406n
  criticism of, **462-3**, 463n
  dynamic programming, 326-7
  integer programming, 406, **461n**
  linear programming, 406, 431, 458n, 460-2, **463-70**, 866
  mathematical programming, 326n
  mixed integer programming, 461n
  transportation algorithm, **890-1**, 900
  transshipments, 890-900
  travelling salesman problem, 428
  Wagner-Whitin algorithm, 326-7
option common parts, 250-2
option overplanning, 250, 276-8
order book, **12**, 43, 180, 667
order cancellations, 220n
order (firm customer), 337n
order lead time, 283
order picking, 759, 761, **771-4**
  equipment, **766-7**, 774
  FIFO (first-in, first out), 762
  one-step, 772
  order bunching, 774
  rate of, 772n
  two step, 773
  zonal, 773
order placement, 646-60
order point system (min-max), 153n, **288-90**
order processing, see sales order processing
orders in transit (DRP), 876
ordinary shares, 3-4
organisation chart, 805
organisation chart (marketing), **26-7**, 37-8
organisational structure, 804-5
Orlicky, Joseph, 332n
Osborne, A., 58n
outliers (in demand), **92**, 94, 126
overhead recovery, 744
overheads (in costing), **725-6**, 727, 729

Index

overhead recovery, 744
Owen, Sir Geoffrey, **384n**, 672n, 906
own account (transport), 901
ownership (title), 667-9
Oxford City Council, 510n

---

p-chart (fraction/percentage rejected), **546-9, 552-3**
pack-from-make, **433**, 433n
packages, **768-9**, 769n
packaging, 23, 25, 33, 35, 441-4, 474-5, 475n, **768-9**, 857, 858, 862n
packaging waste regulations, 769
pallets, 758, **768-9**, 768n, 770-1
pallet trucks, 767
Palmer, Stephen, 837n
paper, 403, 430
parallel operations (SMED), 594-5
Pareto analysis (in cycle counting), **787-9**, 791
Pareto, Vilfredo, 787n
Parsonage, Mike, 891n
part loads (transport), 901
part-period balancing, 322n, **323-6**, 327
partial manufacture (assemble-to-order), 257-8
partial requirements (DRP), 876
partial requirements (materials planning), **298-9**, 311-3
partnership, 1
partnership agreements, 639, 640, **641-5**
Patten, Thomas H., Jr., 835n, **836n**
pay, *see* job evaluation procedures; reward management
PDCA (plan, do, check, action) cycle, **498-9**, 498n, 507, 630, 632, 644-5
PDS (product design specification), 54-57
peg/pegging, 300
penetration of market, 25
percent annual demand, 161-6
percentage forecast errors, 158-61
performance-related pay, 829
period order despatch (POD), 879
period order quantity (POQ), **320-3**, 327, 436, 879

perpetual inventory checking (PI), 784; *but see* cycle counting; cycle count reconciliation
perquisites, **819**, 839, 843
personnel, 803n; *see* human resources
PERT (programme evaluation & review technique), 374n
Peters, Tom, 28n, 633, 838
petroleum, 403n, 430
phantoms (modular design), 257n
PI (perpetual inventory), 784; *but see* cycle counting; cycle count reconciliation
picking, *see* order picking
piece rate, 819n
pipeline stock, 864-5
plan, do, check, action (PDCA) cycle, **498-9**, 507, 630, 632, 644-5
plan types in MRP (three), 333-9
planned orders (in DRP), 876
planned orders (in MRP), **336-7**, 341, 346
planning rules, 298, 312, **313-30**
Plossl, George, 332n
POD (period order despatch), 879
Poisson distribution, **144-5**, 520, 550, 551, 849
point-factor (jobs), 823, 824-32; *see also* Hay Guide Chart
POQ (period order quantity), **320-3**, 327, 436
Poisson law, 549-50
Poisson, Simeon, 549n
policy stock, 139n
population, **515**, 516, 519, 520
post tender negotiation (PTN), 648
posture (pay), 818
PQ (profit-quantity), 751
predictive maintenance, 538, **629-30**
preference shares, 3
premature transactions, 796-801
preventive maintenance, 448, 621-3, **631**
price, 22, 24, 26, 62-7, **670-9**, 750, 755
and cost, 740n
elasticity, 673-4, 752
market price, 670-1
of new products, 62-67
spot, 676
standard price, 740n, 742-3
variance (costing), 743-6

price/earnings ratio, 6
price variance (costing), 743, **744-5**
primary data (market research), 32
primary product, 674
prime cost, **727**, 747n
priority rules, *see* job despatching rules
probability distributions
  exponential, 363
  gamma, 144
  hypergeometric, 563n
  introduction, 142-3
  negative exponential, 144
  normal (Gaussian), 144, **145-9**, 158-60, 516, 517-9, 523-5, 539-41
  Poisson, **144-5**, 520, 550, 551, 849
  standardised normal, **149-50**, 163-4, 167
  Weibull, 77n
  see also statistics (theory and terms)
probability of acceptance (quality), 563-5
problem-solving dimension (Hay Chart), 825, **830**
problem-solving techniques, 58
process batches, 452
process capability, 493-6, **538-45**
process capability indices, 543-4
process capability studies, 544-5
process control (statistical), 17-8, 69, 482, 513, **514-55**
process design, 69-70
process industry costing, 736, **738**
process monitoring, 535-8
process train, 432-4
process/chemical industry planning
  alternative bills of materials, 309
  by-products, 304-5
  co-products (joint products), **305-7**, 433n, 460
  equivalent products, 309-10
  industry definition, 413
  multi-site netting, **300-2**, 398
  non-standard batch sizes, 309
  quality grades, 307-8
  rate-based planning rules, 313
  recoveries, **303**, 460
  scrap and yield, 310-1
  usages, 309

see also materials planning (calculations); materials planning (general)
product, attributes of, 55-6, 58, 59-60
product code, 82-3, 295-8, 393-9
product costing, *see* cost accounting
product design, *see* design (of a product)
product design specification (PDS), 54-7
product development, 14, 25, **30-5**, 45-6
product diversification, 25
product group (MPS), 206-8
product life cycle, **23-6**, 45-6
product, primary, 674
product range, 25
production 9, 187, 188
production forecast (costing), 725, 730, 740
production forecast (MPS), 272-4
production kanban, 609-11
production management, 632-3
production overhead, 725-6, 747
production rates (JIT), 313, **584-9**
production strategy, 181, 437
"profile" (Hay terminology), 828n
profitability index, **455-6**, 457, 460
profit and loss account, 693-6
profit centre, 723n
profit-quantity (PQ) graph, 751
profit, 24, 695-6, **707**, 722, 749-52
program budgeting, 716n
prohibition order (H&S), 851
projected stock (make-to-order), 202-311
projected stock balance (MPS), 200-3
promotion, 23, **46-7**
protective capacity, 450
pseudo items (modular design), 261-2, 263, 265
PTN (post tender negotiation), 648
Pugh, Stuart, 59-60, 905
pull manufacture, 600-1, **608-16**
purchase order, **649-50**, 649n, 770
purchasing, 9, 16, 314, 328-330, 507, 555,558, 555-7, 572-3, **635-91**, 757
  card; 646n
  carriage of goods, 660-5
  contract to buy, 650-60
  commodity purchasing, 674-9

documentation and "notes", 646, **649-50**, 652, 770
foreign purchases, 679-91
order placement, 646-60
price, supply and demand, 670-3
purchase order, the, 649-50
quality of incoming goods, 555-7, 572-3, 638n
receipt of goods, 665-6
supplier partnerships, 641-6
suppliers (sourcing and selection), 635-41
tendering, 647-9, 651
Purves, Dale, 828n
put-away algorithm, 760-4
Putnam, Arnold, 369n, 373n
putting away (of stock), 759n, 771

Q chart (quality score), 555n
QA (quality assurance department), 757
QC circle, 480, 481, 500
QFD (quality, function, deployment), 52-3, 53n
QI teams (quality improvement), 493-4, **499-501**, 630
QMS (quality management system), 503-4
QRM (quick response manufacturing), see assemble-to-order
qualitative job evaluation, 823
qualitative research, 33
quality, see ISO 9000 2000; sampling of incoming parts; statistical process control; total quality control
quality characteristic, 477
quality circles, 480, 481, 500
quality, function, deployment), 52-3, 53n
quality grades (in planning), 307-8
quality improvement teams, 493-4, **499-501**, 630
quantitative job evaluation, 823
"quantity per" in planning, 309
quantity variance (costing), 743, 744-5
quantum meruit, 656
queues at gateway work centres, 356-60
queues at intermediate work centres, 362-6

queuing theory, 362-6, 765
quick response, see assemble-to-order

Race Relations Act, 1976, 811n, 815n
racks, 758, 764, 766
rail (transport), 901-2
random location storage, **759-60**, 764, 790
random variation in demand, 92, 94, 126, 142, 749
range (in SPC), 520, 521-2, **525**, 528, 531, 539
range (of products), 25
ranking (job evaluation), 823, 836
rate-based planning, 313
rational sub-groups, in sampling, 532-5
rates of production (JIT), 584-9
raw material sampling, 557-80
  by variables, 579-80
  double, 577-8
  multiple, 578n
  single, 567
  tables; see sampling tables
  supply pattern, 588-9
  see also purchasing; quality; sampling tables; suppliers
raw material supply in JIT, 588-9
raw material and product control, 513, 514, 548, 555-80
  acceptance, 555-80
  breakeven point (BEP) analysis, **555-7**, 576-7, 638
  consumer's risk, 556
  costs, see costs
  inspection, see quality
  producer's risk, 556
  sample plan, 557-66
  manufacturer's viewpoint, 558, 567-70
  operating characteristic (OC), 562-6, 569, 570, 574
  steps in development, 573-6
  supplier's viewpoint, 558-9, 570
  switching/transition rules, 575
  ultimate user's viewpoint, 559-62, 577-9
raw materials, 15-6, 179-80, 194, 292-3, 436, 453, 555-80, 641, 709, 758;

see also bills of materials; commodities; materials planning (general); materials requirements planning
raw material and product control, *see* stock
RCCP (rough-cut capacity planning), 193-9, **208**, 439
RDTs (radio data terminals), **383**, 774
reach trucks, 767
receipt of goods, **665-70, 770-1**
   acceptance, 666-7
   bailments, 669-70
   delivery, 666
   ownership (title), 667-9
   specific future goods, 667-8
   specific goods, 667-8
   unascertained goods, 667-8
receiving docks, 764-6
reciprocal agreements, 638n
recoveries (in planning), **303**, 460
recruitment, 804, 807, **810-2**
   advertising, 811
   application form, 812-3
   avoidance of discrimination 811-2
   bases for assessment, 815
   brochure, 812
   candidate testing/knowledge, 813
   curriculum vitae (CV), 813
   interviewing and scoring, 813-5
   job offer, 816
   policy, 804
   references, 816n
   shortlisting and selection, 810, 812-6
   see also industrial relations; human resources (employment); human resources (organisational); human resources (policy & pay)
recursion, 294-5; *see also* recursion
redundancy (employee), 846
redundancy (in design), 259-60
release of orders, 355, **356-68**
repair, 230n, 448, **621-7**
RFI (request for information), 646
RFQ (request for a quotation), **646**, 652
references (job application), 816n
regeneration of MRP, 349-50
relative units (in costing), 731-2
reliability, 75-80
   bath tub curve, 75-6
   definition and terms, 76-7

   measuring, 77-80
replenishment in distribution, 876-90
request for a quotation (RFQ) form, **646**, 652
request for information (RFI), 646
res ipsa loquitur, 855
rescheduling assumption, the, (MRP) 341-5
rescheduling material plans (MRP), 340-51
rescheduling messages (MPS), 206, **216-8**, 226-7, 322n
rescheduling messages (MRP), 345-7
rescheduling the MPS, 151-2, 166-70, 206, **216-17**, 287
research and development (R&D), *see* product development
resource requirements planning (RRP), 193-9
responsiveness to market, 582-3
Restrictive Practices Court, 672
Restrictive Trade Practices Act, 1976, 672
resumé (CV), 813
retail, **11**, 25n, 105-6, 154, 857, 869
retail audit, 32-3
revenue, **702-5**, 707, 722, 723n, 739
revenue account, 701-5
revenue expenditure, 711n
revenue reserves, 5
revocable letter of credit, 688
reward management
   assigning jobs to grades, 822-3
   bonus schemes, **819**, 819n
   "broad banding", 807, 822, 823, **837-8**
   competency-based pay, 840
   external labour market, 817-8
   grade differentials, 820-2
   harmonisation, 819
   harmonisation example, 820
   job grades, **818-23**, 837-8
   pay posture, 818
   pay structures, 818-23
   performance-related pay, 829
   variable pay, 838-9
   see also job evaluation procedures
rework, **335-6**, 335n, 475
Rice, W. B., 69
rights issues (shares), 4
Rizzo, Tony, 755

Index

road (transport), 901
Robens' Report (health & safety), 850-1, 852
Rodger's seven-point plan (interviewing), 815
roll-on, roll-off ("ro-ro") ferry, 901
roll-up (costing), 742
Romig, Harry, 566n, 567n
Rosenfield, D., 863n, 867n
rough-cut capacity planning (RCCP), 193-9, 208, 439
route card, 367
routings file, 355, 391-2, **393-4**, 420
Rowan Premium, 819n
RRP (resource requirements planning), 193-9
Rubin, D. S., 316n, 461n
rule-based schedulers, 424-6

safety officer, 848
safety stock, 81, 135-7, **139-78**, 225, 226, 865-9
  customer service targets, 156-78
  distribution networks, 865-9
  factors involved in, 141-56
  justification for, 139-41
  management variables, **166-7**, 168, **170**, 173, 175, 176
  master plan rescheduling, 166-70
  old method of calculation, 158-61
  option overplanning in assemble-to-order, 276-8
  policy stock, 139n
  setting levels, **156-74**, 867-9
  standard method of calculation, 161-6
  system, 174-8
  uniform service, 170-4
Sale of Goods Act, 1979, 474-5, **665-6**
Sale of Goods Act, 1994, **665-6**, 668
sales and operations planning (S&OP), 185, 187, 188, **189-99**, 432
  business review, 189-93
  future stock levels, 191-3
  group forecasting, 189-90
  MPS in financial terms, 190-1
  resource requirements planning, 193-9
  assessing feasibility, 194
  increasing capability, 193-4

load profile, 195-7
special bill of materials, 197-9
sales and selling, 9, 14, 24, **35-49**, 471-2, 749-52, 757
  analysis of results, 39-40
  forecasting; *see* sales forecasting
  foreign sales, 679-91
  goals and evaluation, 38-39
  management, 35, **37-40**
  manager of, 37
  and master scheduling, 228-30, 232-4, 242-5
  order processing, 39, **40-44**
  organisation and territories, 37-8; *see also* sales order processing
sales demand data, 87, 88, **101-8**, 439, 868
  cycles in demand, 92, 94
  in a distribution network, 868
  distortions due to time lags, 104-6
  informational obstacles, 102-3
  organisational obstacles, 103-4
  planning, use in, 107-8
  randomness in demand, 92, 94, 126, **141-2**, 749
  seasonality, **93-101**, 275, 749
  sporadic (lumpy) demand, **133-8**, 275, 869
  stationarity, 89-90
  step change, 90-2
  trading days adjustment, 106-7
  trend, 90-94
  see also forecasting techniques; sales forecasting (causal); sales forecasting (naïve); sales order processing
sales forecasting (causal), 120-7
  autoregressive moving averages (ARMA), 121
  autoregressive integrated moving averages (ARIMA) (Box-Jenkins), 122-4
  Bayesian forecasting, **124-7**, 127n
  introduction, 120
  see also forecasting techniques; sales forecasting (naïve); sales demand data
sales forecasting (naïve), 108-120
  adaptive exponential smoothing, **115-7**, 130, 538n

double/linear smoothing, **111-5**, 123-4
management, 130-3
naïve family, the, 108-20
"naïve one", 110n
single exponential smoothing, 110-1
single moving averages, 109-10
software in modern systems, 118-20
see also forecasting techniques; sales demand data; sales forecasting (causal)
sales order processing (SOP), 39, **40-4**, 102-3, 153, 220n, 228-30, 232-4, 243-5, 486, 487, 857, 861
flowchart, 42
leadtime, 283
management of, **40-1**, 228-9
and master scheduling, **228-30**, 232-4, 242-5
measures of service, 41
order cancellations, 220n
order placement, 646-60
promotions, 46-7
purchase order, 649-50, 770
role of department, **35-7**, 103, 243, 245
system, 41-4
uneven sales, 749-52
sample-mean, 515, **516**, 517, 538-41, 550
sampling (in market research), 34-5
sampling of incoming parts
acceptable quality level (AQL), 558-9, **570-1**, 574
argument for and against, **571-2, 572-3**
average outgoing quality (AOQ), 559, **560-2**, 574
cost of sampling, 572
Dodge-Romig tables, 567n, **569-70**, 579
double and multiple sampling, **578**, 578n
introduction, 557-60
lot tolerance percent defective (LTPD), **568-70**, 579
limiting quality level (LQL), 558, **567-70**, 570n, 573-5
operating characteristic (OC), **562-6**, 569-70, 574
sample plan 557

sampling by variables, 579-80
tightened sampling rules, 575
see also statistical process control; total quality control
Sarson, Trish, 41, 389n
scheduled receipts (open orders) (in DRP), 876
scheduled receipts (open orders) (in MRP), **334-6**, 341, 346, 777
scheduling of work, **353-6**, 368, 378, 391-9
and advanced planning systems, 407-9
backwards scheduling, **413-5**, 434
bottleneck scheduling, 434, **448-52**
data records, 391, **394-5**
finite loading of work, 211
forwards scheduling, **413-5**, 434
horizontal loading, **413-5**, 418
infinite loading, **211**, 415
kanban and manufacturing flow, 609-16
rules, 420-30
scheduling engine, 415-20
sequencing of work, **369**, 407-9
vertical loading, 209n, **413**
work centre capacity, 209-12, 331, 353, **361**, 417, 453-5, 458-9
work centre rules, 420-30
see also flow manufacture
Schonberger, Richard, **602**, 908
scrap, cost treatment of, 722
scrap, in planning, 310-1
seasonal factors, 93-7
seasonality, **93-101**, 127, 431, 749
secondary data (market research), 32
Seddon, John, **511**, 755n, 907
selective tendering, 647, **648**
semi-frozen zone (MPS), 151-5, **203-6**, 216, 643
semi-frozen zone (suppliers), 643
sequencing of work, **369**, 407-9
service parts, see spares
set-up, 356, 425, 427-8, 451-2, 586, **589-99**; see also changeovers; Just-in-Time
seven rules of kanban, 615
Sex Discrimination Act, 1975, **811n**, 815n
SFDC, see shop floor data collection
Shakespeare, William, 804n

Index

shareholders, **2-3**, 6, 698
shares, 1, **2-6**
  capitalisation issues, 5
  debentures, 4-5
  earnings per share, 5-6
  gearing ratio, 6
  ordinary, 3-4
  preference, 3
  price/earnings ratio, 6
  rights issues, 4
Shea, Alan, 717n, 794n
Sheridan, David L., 648n, 908
Shewhart control charts, *see* control charts
Shewhart's bowls, 517-20
Shewhart's chain reaction, 476-7
Shewhart Walter A., 476, 482, 498n, 499, 513, 514n, 517, 518, 527, 532, 907
Shingo, Shigeo, 590-2, **591n**, 593n, 597, 907
shop floor control, 9, 17, 287, **353-99**, 507, 590, 598, 757
  control of queues, 356-60
  final order release, 367-8
  information system, **383-99**, 777
  input/output control, 357-8, **360-5**, 370, 375, 385, 394
  lead time management, 378-83
  management, 632-3
  order identification, **367**, 367n
  performance of shop, 370-1
  release of orders, 355, **356-68**, 367
  route card, 367
  work scheduling; **353-6**, 368, 378, 391-9
  see also shop floor data collection
shop floor data collection (SFDC)
  control of materials movement, 398
  datafiles, 391-9
  design and development, 388-91
  job status file, 391, **396-7**
  machine status file, 391, **397**
  nature and scope, 384-8
  open-ended system architecture, 390-1
  routings file, 355, 391, **393-4**, 420
  transaction trail, 392
  transmission of data, 386-7
  work schedule file, 391, **394-5**
  see also shop floor control

short hedging, 677n
shortest processing time (SPT) rule, 371n, **376-8**
shortlisting (job candidates), 810, **812-6**
Sidney, Elizabeth, 814n
Simon, Major Leslie, 563n
Simpson, Alex, 590n
Simpson, Kenneth F., 866
simulation, *see* computer; discrete job systems; distribution; safety stocks; stock records
simultaneous engineering, **69-70**, 488
single exponential smoothing, 110-1
single moving averages, 109-10
single sampling, 567
sinks, 891
six sigma (process capability), 543
SKU, *see* stock keeping unit
Slack, N., 318n, 477n, 873n
slack time despatching rule, 373-4
slack time per operation rule, **374**, 375
slack variables (in linear programming), 470
Sloan, Alfred P., **103**, 905
slope (trend) in demand, 90, 94
SMED (Single Minute Exchange of Die) 451-2, **589-98**, 632
  converting internal changeover to external, 592-3
  preparation, 593
  separating internal and external activities, 592
  standardisation, 593-4
  streamlining, 594-8
  see also changeovers; Just-in-Time; set-up
Smith, Sir John, 650n
Smith, Tom, 852
smoothing, *see* sales forecasting (naïve)
smoothing stock, 864
social analysis (of the UK), 33
software, *see* advanced planning systems; computer system development; materials requirements planning, shop floor control; stock records
sole supplier, 638-9, 638n, **642**

SOP (sales order processing), 39, **40-4**, 102-3, 153, 220n, 228-30, 232-4, 486, 487, 857, 861
Sounderpandian, Jayavel, 891n
source policy, 637-9
sources (transshipments), 891
sourcing, **635-9**, 638n
spares, 80-1, 274
spares for discontinued machines, 80-1
SPC, see statistical process control
special causes (of variation, in quality), 370, 488, 489-90, 489n, **496-501**, 534, 544
specific future goods, 667-8
specific goods, 667-8
specification limits, 539, **542-4**
speculator, **677**, 678n, 680
sporadic demand, **133-8**, 222-3, 275, 869n
spot prices (forex), 682-4
SPT rule (shortest processing time), 371n, **376-8**
SQC (statistical quality control), see sampling of incoming parts; statistical process control
squares (transshipments), 891
SSAP9, **710n**, 726, 747
stabilisation stock, 864
staff departments, 804n
staff turnover, 808-9
stage cost (costing), 740-1, 740n, 742-3
stage price (costing), 740-1, 740n, 742-3
standard costs, 736, 737, 738, **742-3**
standard deviation, 148, 159, **522-3**, 526-7, 538-41, 551
standard display (in MRP), 340-1
standard features (assemble-to-order), 261
standard price (costing), 740n, **742-3**
standard system (MRP), 300n
standardisation (statistical), 149-50
static despatching rules, **372**, 385
stationarity (in demand), 89-90
statistical process control (SPC), 514-555
    attribute control charts theory, 545-52
    central limit theorem, 514-20
    count (c) chart, 554-5
    dispersion of sample means, 520-3
    fraction rejected (p) chart, 552-3
    introduction, 513-4
    monitoring the process, 523-7
    process capability, 538-45
    range, 520, 521-2, **525**, 528, 531, 539
    rational sub-group, 532-5
    sample-mean, 515, **516**, 517, 538-41, 550
    six sigma, 543
    variable control charts introduction, 527-32
    variable control in use, 532-8
    see ISO 9000 2000; sampling of incoming parts; statistical process control; total quality control
statistical quality control (SQC), 18, 502, **513-80**, 639; see also statistical process control; sampling of incoming parts
statistics (theory and terms),
    bimodal, 520n
    binomial theorem, **547-9**, 549, 551, 563, 563n
    central limit theorem, 34, 145n, **514-7**
    chi-squared test, 144
    classic v. Bayesian, 125-7
    continuous function, 148-9
    density function, 146-7
    discrete function, 146-7
    expectation, 163
    histogram, 146
    frequency polygon, 371
    partial expectation, 161-5
    Poisson law, 549-50
    population, 516, 519, 520
    probability density, 146-7
    standard deviation, 148, 159, **522-3**, 526-7, 538-41, 551
    standardisation, 149-50
    see also probability distributions
steel, 403, 430
Steinbacher, Herbert, 628n
step change (in demand data), **90-92**, 126
Stevens, Colin, 126
stock, 9-11, 104-6, 135-6, **191-3**, 298, 433, 436, 439, 590, 606, 616-9, 733
    allocated, 336

Index 937

available, 336
balance, projected, **200-3**, 273, 276, 277, 311, 315, 341, 343-4, 442-3, 878, 882
consignment, 669
cost of, 155-6, 319, 582, 710, 710n, **722**, 726, 747, 863-9
cycle (working), 155, **863**
distribution 866n, **870-1**
future levels, 191-3
imbalances, 890-900
issues (from stores), 771
MRP *and*, 332, 340
picking, *see* order picking
negative balance, 343-4, 709, **776n**
policy, 139n
records, *see* stock records
reduction and kanban, 616-9
replenishment, 153, 246, **288-90**, 616
safety, **139-141**, 177-8
smoothing (stabilisation), 864
transit (pipeline), 864-5
valuation, 192-3, 708-10;
see also inventory
stock exchange, **2**, 5-6, 676
stock keeping unit (SKU), 87, 119, **790**, 865, 868-9, 876-90
stock records, 311n, 332, 386-7, 757n, 758, **775-784**, 794-801
 accuracy, 762-4, 773n, **775-84**
 accuracy goal, 778-80
 errors, causes of, 367n, 777n, 782, **783**
 reconciliation of counts, 794-801
 software, 760, **762-4**
 system development, 776-8
 system flowchart, 775-6
 system support, 780-782
 transactions, **775-6**, 793-801
 tolerances, 778-780
 see also cycle count reconciliation; cycle counting
stocking points (in kanban), 608-13
stockturn, 707
stone squares, 893
storage bins and racks, **758**, 764,766
stores, 9, 722, **757-801**
 cycle counting, 784-801
 see also cycle counting
 fittings and equipment, 764-9

fixed location storage system, **759**, 790
functions, **757-8**, 757n
materials handling, 588, **766-7**, 770
picking, 759, 761, **771-4**; *see also* order picking
physical layout, 758-9
receipt and storage, 758, **770-1**
stock records, 775-784; *see also* stock records
variable location storage system, **759-60**, 764, 790
Stoves plc, 255n, 285
Stranks, Jeremy, 848n, 908
streamlining (in SMED), 594-8
strikes, 844-5
strategy, **24**, 27-29, 191-3, 476-7
structure of distribution network, 858-61
subsidiary books (accounts), 699
super bill, 250n, 262-3, **265-7**, 269, 271-2, 275-7
super common part, 251
super item, 251, 265-6, 270-1, 274, 276-8
super super bill, 266-7
super super item, 254n, **266-7**, 274
super-factors (Hay terminology), 828, **829-31**
suppliers, 510, 555, 573, **635-46**
 appraisal and selection, 639-41
 communication, 642, **643-4**
 Just-in-Time, 613-4, 614n
 partnership agreements, 322n, 639, 640, **641-5**
 performance, 645-6
 quality, 510, 555-7, **558-9**, 638, 641
 sole supplier, 638-9
 sourcing, 635-9
 see also sampling of incoming parts
supply and demand, 671-4
supply chain, 104-6, 191-2, 193, 279, 351n, 472-3, 484-5, 510, 669n, **858-60**
 dynamics, 279
 internal, 484-5, 484n
 simulators, **191-2**, 193, 351n
 time lags and, **104-6**, 279
Suzuki, Tokutaro, 630n
switch trading, 691
switching rules (sampling), 575
syndicated research, 33

system stability, **490-3**, 494-6

tableaux, 891
tariffs (transport), 902-3
Taguchi, Genichi, 71-3
Tallon, William, 254n
Taylor, Sam, 438n, 441
Taylor's Differentiated Rate, 819n
TBPM (time based process mapping), 279-83
teams, 19, 278, 284, 628-8, 645, 806, **840-3**
    development stages, 842
    empowerment and, 840-3
    Just-in-Time, **628**, 841
    membership of, 842
    quality improvement, 493-4, **499-501**
temperature analysis (TPM), 630
tenders, 647-9, 651
terotechnology, **621n**, 715
territory (sales), 37-8
theory of constraints (TOC), 403, 412n, **448-9**, 462, 755n
theory of runs (in SPC), 535-6
Thompson, Sir Clive, 806n
tightened sampling rules, 575
time bucket, **184-5**, 184n, 199, 209
time compression, 278-86
time fences, 182, **203-6**, 216
time lags, **104-6**, 109-17, 279, 283
time-phased order point (TPOP), 290
TIR, 901n
title in goods (ownership), 667-9
TNE (tolerable negative error), 475
TOC (theory of constraints), 403, 412n, **448-9**, 462
tolerance analysis, **67-9**, 539, 542-4, 567-70
tolerable negative error (TNE), 475
tolerances (stock records), 778-80
tolling, 669n
Tompkins, James, 760n, 766
tort, 473, 473n, **844-5**, 849, 853
Torrington, Derek, 803n, 812n
total productive maintenance (TPM), 370, 448, 621, **627-32**
    autonomous maintenance, 631-2
    corrective maintenance, 630-1
    maintenance prevention, 629

    predictive maintenance, 629-30
    preventive maintenance, 631
    team approach, 628
total quality control, 471-511
    cost of quality, 285, **475-7**, 476n
    definition and gurus, 477-83
    improving the system, 493-6
    introduction, **483-5**, 502
    Japanese example, 476, 479n, **481**, 500-1
    legal requirements, **471-5**, 487-8
    quality system, 71, **486-8**, 493, 501n
    special causes, 370, 488, 489-90, **496-501**, 534, 544
    stabilising the system, 371n, **489-93**
    definition, 483n
    strategy, 476, 498
    see also ISO 9000 2000; statistical process control; sampling of incoming parts; total quality management (TQM)
total regeneration (MRP), 349-50
total value, 471
Toyoda, Kiichiro, 581
Toyoda, Sakichi, 449n, **581n**, 583n
Toyota, 508n, **581**, 584, 608n, 633
"Toyota equation", 620
TPM (total productive maintenance), 370, 448, 621, **627-32**
TPOP (time-phased order point), 290
TQC, see total quality control
TQM, see total quality management
Trade Descriptions Act 1968, 474
trade union, 812n, **844-5**
Trade Union and Labour Relations (Consolidation) Act, 1992, 845
traded options, 681
trading days adjustment (of demand), 106-7
train (process), 432-4
training, **804**, 841-2; see also GMCS
training (quality), 73n, **501-3**
transit stock, 864-5
transaction sequencing (cycle counting), 801
transaction trail (SFDC), 392
transactions (late, cycle counting), 785, **794-5**
transactions (premature, cycle counting), 785, **796-801**

Index 939

transactions (stock records), **775-6**, 793-801
transfer batches, 452
transfer of undertakings, 847
transport in distribution, 900-3
transportation, 301-2, 857-8, 861-2, 900-3
  algorithm, 890-900, 890n
  bill of lading, 687
  costs (local delivery), 861-2
  costs (trunking), 861-2
  deep sea, 768-9, **902**
  despatch rules, 301-2, **876-80**, 887-9
  freight forwarding agent, **901**, 902
  rail, 901-2
  road, 901
  shipping conference, 903
  tariffs, 902-3
transshipments (in distribution), 890-900
  applicability, 890n
  excesses and shortages equal, 891-8
  excesses and shortages not equal, 898-900
  terms used, 891, 893
  transportation algorithm, **890-1**, 900
  worked example, 892-8
travelling salesman problem, 428
trend (in demand), **90**, 94
trial balance (accounts), 707
Trigg, Derek, **130**, 538n
Trigg's tracking signal (forecast errors), **130-1**, 538n
trunking, 861-2
Tubb, A. J., 709n, 734n, 740n, 745n
turnover (financial), 472, **694-5**
turnover (staff), 808-9
two-bin replenishment system, 616
two-level master scheduling, 247n

u-chart (control chart), 546, **549-52**
UCL (upper control limit), 491-2, 520n, **523-7**, 528-31, 533, 534n, 535-8, 540-4, 548-9, 551, 553, 554
UCP1993 (Uniform Customs and Practice for Documentary Credits 1993), **686-7**, 686n
UMASS system, 67
unascertained goods, 667-8
unfair dismissal, **845**, 846

unfrozen zone (MPS), **203-6**, 216, 643
unfrozen zone (suppliers), 643
Uniform Customs and Practice for Documentary Credits (UCP1993), **686-7**, 686n
unit loads, 768-9
United Kingdom (UK), 2, 33, 156n, 181, **384n**, 474, 509, 672, 680n, 687, 807, 808, 828, 843, 850
United States (US), 2, 156n, 185n, 332, 672n, 836n, 837n, 890n
unitisation, 768-9
units of measure, 777n, 785
unpacking note, **650**, 770
U-shaped lines, 606-8
upper control limit (UCL), 491-2, 520n, **523-7**, 528-31, 533, 534n, 535-8, 540-4, 548-9, 551, 553, 554
usages (costing), 744, 746
usages (in planning), 309
utilisation of machines, **363-5**, 370, 385, 450

value analysis, 644-5
value engineering, 644
variability index, 747n
variable control charts, 489-93, 496, **527-8**, 532-45
  loss of control of process dispersion, 537
  loss of process control, 537-8
  monitoring, 535-8
  process capability, 538-45
  six sigma, 543
variable costs, 724-5, **747-9**
variable costing, *see* costing
variable location storage, **759-60**, 764, 790
variable pay (HR), 19, **838-9**
variables sampling, 579-80
variance analysis, 739, **743-6**
  adverse, **743**, 745
  favourable, **743**, 745
  labour efficiency, 744
  labour rate, 744
  material, 744, 745
  material usage, 744, 746
  overhead recovery, 744
  overhead volume, 744
  price, 743, 744-5

quantity, 743-5, **746**
VAT (value added tax), 645, **645n**, 646n, 695
VATI analysis, 103-4
vertical loading, **209n**, 413
vibration analysis (TPM), 629
vicarious liability, 856
vicious circle, the, 357-9
virtuous circle, the, 360
Vollmann, T.E., 227, 254n, 318n, 321n, 327n, 416n, 452n, 866, 906

Wagner, Harvey, 326n, 406n, 461n, 470, 809n
Wagner-Whitin algorithm, 322n, **326-7**
Waller, Alan, 874n
Walton, Mary, 476n, 479n, 503n, 638n
warehousing, **858-61**, 863, 871
warehousing costs, **863**, 871
warranty (contract), **655**, 666
Warwick Manufacturing Group, 279n, 281n
"WASP" interview plan, 814
waste, eliminating, **581-2**, 599
waste regulations, 769
Watkins, Richard, 890n
Waugh, R. M., 457
webPLAN, 191n
Weibull distribution, 77n
weighting (job evaluation), 824
weights (Hay terminology), 828-9
"weights and marks" evaluation, **59-60**, 389-90, 640
Weights and Measures Act 1985, 474-5
Wer Liefert Was?, 636
Wheeler, Don, 536n
Wheelwright, S. C., 112n
"white goods", 890n
white noise, 92
Whitin, T. M., 326n
Whybark, D. C., 227n, 254n, 318n, 321n, 327n
Wight, Oliver, **332n**, 346n, 351, 358, 785n, 906
Wild, Ray, 318n, 373n, 406n, 461n, 621n, 906
Wilson, Larry, 760n, 778n, 779n, 780, 785n, 792-3, 794n

window scheduling, 382n
withdrawal kanban, **611-6**, 617-9
Woodhams, Jeff, 424n
work centres, allocation of costs to, 727-8
work centre capacity, 209-12, 331, 353, **361**, 417, 453-5, 458-9
   demonstrated, 361
   finite loading, 211
   gateway, **360**, 362, 458
   intermediate, 362-6
   machine status, 397
   operating value, 458-9
work schedule file, 391, **394-5**
working conditions, 816
working practices, 803
working stock (cycle), 155, **863**
work-in-progress, 278, 282, 298, **314-5**, 332, 340, 347, **360**, 366, 424, 450, 452, 599, **710**, 722, 733, 736, 777
workplace management, 632-3
works order identification, 367, 367n
workstation (supplying, in kanban), 608-11, **612**, 617-9
workstation (using, in JIT), **612-3**, 617-9
wrongful dismissal, 845

yield (in planning), 310-1
Yourdan, Ed, 389n

zero defects, **478-9**, 494
zonal picking, 773
Zornig, Colonel H. H., 563n